Handbook of Research on the Evolution of IT and the Rise of E-Society

Maki Habib
The American University in Cairo, Egypt

A volume in the Advances in IT Standards and
Standardization Research (AITSSR) Book Series

Published in the United States of America by
IGI Global
Information Science Reference (an imprint of IGI Global)
701 E. Chocolate Avenue
Hershey PA, USA 17033
Tel: 717-533-8845
Fax: 717-533-8661
E-mail: cust@igi-global.com
Web site: http://www.igi-global.com

Library of Congress Cataloging-in-Publication Data

Names: Habib, Maki K., 1955- editor.
Title: Handbook of research on the evolution of IT and the rise of E-society
   / Maki Habib, editor.
Other titles: Research on the evolution of IT and the rise of E-society
Description: Hershey, PA : Information Science Reference, [2019] | Includes
   bibliographical references.
Identifiers: LCCN 2018020673| ISBN 9781522572145 (hardcover) | ISBN
   9781522572152 (ebook)
Subjects: LCSH: Information technology--History. | Telecommunication--Social
   aspects. | Knowledge management.
Classification: LCC T58.5 .H35335 2019 | DDC 303.48/33--dc23 LC record available at https://lccn.loc.gov/2018020673

This book is published in the IGI Global book series Advances in IT Standards and Standardization Research (AITSSR)
(ISSN: 1935-3391; eISSN: 1935-3405)

British Cataloguing in Publication Data
A Cataloguing in Publication record for this book is available from the British Library.

The views expressed in this book are those of the authors, but not necessarily of the publisher.

For electronic access to this publication, please contact: eresources@igi-global.com.

Advances in IT Standards and Standardization Research (AITSSR) Book Series

Kai Jakobs
RWTH Aachen University, Germany

ISSN:1935-3391
EISSN:1935-3405

MISSION

IT standards and standardization are a necessary part of effectively delivering IT and IT services to organizations and individuals, as well as streamlining IT processes and minimizing organizational cost. In implementing IT standards, it is necessary to take into account not only the technical aspects, but also the characteristics of the specific environment where these standards will have to function.

The **Advances in IT Standards and Standardization Research (AITSSR) Book Series** seeks to advance the available literature on the use and value of IT standards and standardization. This research provides insight into the use of standards for the improvement of organizational processes and development in both private and public sectors.

COVERAGE

- Standards Research and Education Activities
- Descriptive Theory of Standardization
- Tools and Services Supporting Improved Standardization
- National, regional, international, and corporate standards strategies
- User-Related Issues
- Standardization for Organizational Development
- Emerging roles of formal standards Organizations and consortia
- Impacts of Market-Driven Standardization and Emerging Players
- Case Studies on Standardization
- Open source and standardization

IGI Global is currently accepting manuscripts for publication within this series. To submit a proposal for a volume in this series, please contact our Acquisition Editors at Acquisitions@igi-global.com or visit: http://www.igi-global.com/publish/.

Titles in this Series

For a list of additional titles in this series, please visit: www.igi-global.com/book-series

701 East Chocolate Avenue, Hershey, PA 17033, USA
Tel: 717-533-8845 x100 • Fax: 717-533-8661
E-Mail: cust@igi-global.com • www.igi-global.com

List of Contributors

Table of Contents

Detailed Table of Contents

Chapter 1

Jianping Peng, Sun Yat-sen University, China
Jing Quan, Salisbury University, USA
Guoying Zhang, Midwestern State University, USA
Alan J Dubinsky, Purdue University, USA

This chapter combines three less-studied factors on employee knowledge sharing, namely, social relationship, contextual performance, and IT competence. Using a survey study that was targeted to professional employees in a R&D department, we reveal that both social relationship—which incorporates degree of centrality of employee's social network and frequency of interpersonal interaction—and employee's contextual performance have significant positive impacts on knowledge sharing. This association, however, is found to be further positively moderated by employee's IT competence. Our work extends the literature pertaining to knowledge sharing by, not only providing an enhanced approach to measure social relationship, but also emphasizing that social relationship or contextual performance can magnify the impact on knowledge sharing through a high level of IT competence. The findings provide managerial and future research insights pertaining to promoting knowledge sharing by enhancing social relationship, rewarding contextual performance, and improving IT competence of employees.

Chapter 2

Rezvan Hosseingholizadeh, Ferdowsi University of Mashhad, Iran
Hadi El-Farr, Rutgers University, USA
Somayyeh Ebrahimi Koushk Mahdi, Ferdowsi University of Mashhad, Iran

Knowledge-work is a discretionary behavior, and knowledge-workers should be viewed as investors of their intellectual capital. That said, effective knowledge-work is mostly dependent on the performance of individual knowledge-workers who drive the success of knowledge-intensive organizations. Therefore, the study takes the perspective of personal knowledge management in enforcing the effectiveness of knowledge-work activities. This study empirically demonstrates that knowledge-workers' behaviors are dependent on their motivation, ability and opportunity to perform knowledge-work activities. This study provides insights and future directions for research on knowledge-work as a discretionary behavior in organization and the factors influencing it. Scholars can investigate the effect of empowerment of individuals on their tendency to knowledge-creation, knowledge-sharing and knowledge-application. Since personal-knowledge often raise the issue of knowledge ownership, further attention to ethical issues may bring valuable insights for KM in organizations.

International organizations and government agencies have developed and collected a wealth of knowledge resources relevant to poor communities; however, the people who need these resources most often do not know these materials exist or are unable to access or understand them. Electronic sources of knowledge materials and means of communication are rarely integrated with traditional methods of knowledge delivery. This chapter addresses the issue of knowledge sharing with poor communities and presents a software tool for developing multimedia knowledge materials suitable for people with little or no formal education. A multimedia editor uses a data structure composed of multimedia objects (texts, images, video and audio clips) to generate the knowledge browser. Local specialists with a basic knowledge of computing can modify and customize how the knowledge is presented by adding new materials relevant to the local environment.

E-communities (i.e., virtual communities that are established and interact primarily via the internet) are more significant than ever in today's modern workplace. Despite the potential advantages offered by e-communities, however, their formation and maintenance are often hindered by feelings of mistrust, unclear group processes, and limited technical expertise. This study analyzed nearly 2,500 survey responses from 600 students spanning 25 colleges/universities in order to develop practical implications for cultivating a sense of e-community among virtual work teams. Thematic results of our study revealed the significance of brand awareness, interpersonal facilitation, user-friendly design, fiscal barriers, and mobile accessibility. Based on these results, this study concludes with five corresponding implications for cultivating a sense of e-community in the modern workplace: increased integration, expanded physicality, supplemental training, financial entrée, and utilized flexibility.

Chapter 5

It is crucial for a company to maintain its image and reputation, and public relations (PR) plays a vital role in doing so. This study investigates strategies that help an organization rejuvenate its image after damage from ineffective PR. It is important to know which PR strategies engage stakeholders because it is critical for the survival of a company that it maintains healthy relationships with all entities. A case study was conducted to explore what ruins a company's image and what role a PR department plays in rejuvenating it. To gain valuable insights into this topic, interviews were conducted with fourteen PR professionals including people who are working in the mentioned case studies places and organizations that faced some crisis in this chapter. Results suggest PR plays a critical role during crisis management; through PR teams, organizations can turn adverse situations to their favor and reconstruct reputations that would otherwise be tarnished.

Chapter 6

Recently, enterprises have increased their competitiveness through supply chain collaboration to efficiently allocate resources using the internet. However, supply chain collaboration usually fails because information is usually confidential. Many studies have discussed strategies of supply chain collaboration via internet but only a few of the strategies can be implemented in practice. Therefore, this research builds an information exchange platform to share production and inventory information over internet to ensure on-time delivery. This platform is implemented in a panel manufacturing company and 10% on-time delivery increase with 2% quality improvement after adapting this system. This result demonstrates the usefulness of using online platform to immediately share information will improve one-time delivery and quality assurance.

Chapter 7

The MapReduce method is widely used for big data solutions. This method solves big data problems on distributed hardware platforms. However, MapReduce architectures are inefficient. Data locality, network congestion, and low hardware performance are the main issues. In this chapter, the authors introduce a method that solves these problems. Baran is a method that, if an algorithm can satisfy its conditions, can dramatically improve performance and solve the data locality problem and consequences such as network congestion and low hardware performance. The authors apply this method to previous works on data warehouse, graph, and data mining problems. The results show that applying Baran to an algorithm can solve it on the MapReduce architecture properly.

Chapter 8

With China becoming an economic powerhouse, there has been increasing need for more studies on issues related to information systems localization in China and ways to solve them. Most information systems adoption literatures have been conducted in the context of Western society, especially in America, and due to differences in the cultural, social, and legal environment, these theories and findings out of these studies need to be tested in the context of Chinese culture. This chapter adopts the technology, organization, and environment framework to explain why a Chinese apparel manufacturing company failed in its first enterprise resource planning (ERP) project, and how it achieved success in the second project with government's assistance and what they have learned from their first experience with ERP. This study provides insight on the characteristics of Chinese companies and the unique challenges they have encountered in the informatization process.

Chapter 9

Wesley A. Kukard, University of Otago, New Zealand
Lincoln C. Wood, University of Otago, New Zealand & Curtin University, Australia

This chapter reviews past radio frequency identification (RFID) literature within the fast-moving consumer goods (FMCG) industry and the impact of consumer benefits on the perceived risks of item-level RFID. Two new categories are used to measure this impact; the separation of consumers' interactions with the technology to in-store and after-sales allows the consumers expectation of privacy to changes depending on the surrounding environment. A quantitative survey on primary household grocery purchasers within the USA revealed that while consumers are aware of the associated privacy risks after sale, they would be willing to use the technology, given sufficient benefits. This important step in RFID literature changes the conversation from a privacy risk management focus to a balanced integration of the technology, focusing on consumer benefits to manage the roll-out within the FMCG industry.

Chapter 10

Alan D. Smith, Robert Morris University, USA

Although online trading with Amazon, eBay, and many others has its benefits, such as convenience and the ability to compare prices online, there are still many concerns about the integrity of the buyer, the seller, and/or the online action service provider (OASP). The empirical section investigated these relationships via multivariate statistical analysis of a stratified sample of working professionals resulting in 198 usable questionnaires from an initial sampling frame of over 550 professional personnel from five relatively large Pittsburgh, PA firms. It was found that buyers that felt feedback systems were viable were more willing to engage in online trading activities and more willing to pay a premium price for merchandise being sold by a seller with a better reputation, regardless of gender. Customers were especially concerned with the total price, including shipping cost, regardless of gender. In terms of the convenience of payment method, electronic forms were preferred in transacting online trading activities, regardless of age and gender.

Chapter 11

Leelien Ken Huang, Feng Chia University, Taiwan

The interaction between the cultural value of long-term orientation and internet banking technology acceptance is examined. A survey involving a total of 376 potential users was conducted in an internet banking setting in Taiwan. The results confirm previous TAM findings that both efficacy and belief variables have significantly positive direct and in-direct effects on the usage, but under the cultural influence of long-term orientation, users remain hesitant to accept internet banking technology because they are more concerned with face-to-face long-term bank relationships to ensure future gratification than with current social status influence to obtain immediate benefits (e.g., convenience). Practitioners may refer this cultural influence on users' behavior in Fin-tech development. The implications of the study are discussed.

Chapter 12

Nagayuki Saito, Keio University, Japan
Ema Tanaka, Waseda University, Japan
Eri Yatsuzuka, Mirai Factory, Japan
Madoka Aragaki, Business Breakthrough University, Japan

Seeking a safer internet environment for minors, the Japanese government enacted a new law in 2008 to promote both protective measures and empowerment activities. Under the law, many entities—including newly established non-profit organizations (NPOs)—are working to bring a safer internet environment to Japan. The Japan Internet Safety Promotion Association (JISPA), one such NPO established in February 2007, has been promoting a safer internet environment for minors by providing non-formal learning opportunities through educational materials and events. Efforts to improve children's online safety have evolved from offering e-learning content and guidelines to holding workshops in the real world. This chapter presents various measures taken by JISPA for the protection of children using the internet and verifies the effectiveness of these measures based on evidence. Measures to be verified are e-learning contents, workshop programs, and internet literacies among young people and parents.

Chapter 13

Insaf Khelladi, ICN Business School, France
Sylvaine Castellano, Paris School of Business, France

Some firms and industries were not willing to take full advantage of the internet and its endless opportunities, mainly because they rather focused on the inherent risks and challenges. However, when taking into consideration the specificities of the connected generation, the question is not anymore whether to go online or not, but rather to understand how, when, and where, especially in a luxury context. More specifically, the digital natives represent tomorrow's customers. This new market segment represents a main reason for luxury firms to adopt online strategies. Still, further analysis is needed to uncover the main objectives when firms decide to engage in digital activities. The authors herein investigate the concept of e-reputation. The authors expand on their initial study that focused on brand image and social media as determinants of online reputation. Recommendations and future research directions are suggested.

The purpose of this chapter is to examine and determine factors that lead to increased television ratings for soccer in the U.S. Undoubtedly, the topic of fantasy sports and the various roles it plays with types of fan involvement and their need for enhanced engagement with a complex social media landscape has intrigued scholars from a number of disciplines. How the various motivational factors, both intrinsically and extrinsically, impact the degree of fan involvement and loyalty have been investigated several times. The overall results have been mixed to say the least. The current chapter primarily focuses on fantasy soccer participation, involvement in soccer, presence of a local professional team, and social media interaction. After providing a brief history of soccer television ratings in the U.S., a conceptual model based on these factors is developed and explained. The factors of this conceptual model are tested through statistical analysis.

Chapter 15

A significant amount information can be relayed on Facebook, MySpace, and Twitter, but the question remains whether or not organizations are using this to their advantage, especially in the era of big data. The present study used a sample of working professionals that were knowledgeable in the various options of social networking to test these assumptions. The three hypotheses dealt with the interplay of online social networking, advertising effectiveness, gender and age trends, and remaining the interplay with positive comments of the use of the "like" function and its impacts on consumer behavior, as derived from the review of relevant operations literature and from applying the basic tenants of uses and gratification theory. All three specific research hypotheses were accepted in the null form.

Information technology (IT) is strategic for organization management, although many companies lack IT governance and planning, skilled people, defined and institutionalized methods and procedures, internal controls and indicators, and structures for agreement service levels and information security, legality, and economy. In this scenario, a minimum organization and control in the use of resources is needed to boost technical and administrative efficiency, with a focus on IT governance. An information technology strategic plan (ITSP) aims at discovering the resources and IT in an organization to direct the technological and information architecture to its strategic objectives. The Brazilian government issued a normative instruction (NI04) for public organizations to develop IT strategic plans so that they can purchase products and services. In order to help organizations develop, control, and manage their ITSPs, a model was created that defines a set of auxiliary steps in the construction of the ITSP.

Digital technology, artificial intelligence, the internet of things, and innovative technology applications are gradually transforming businesses and governments in emerging markets making them more competitive and offering opportunities for economic growth and prosperity. This chapter demonstrates Egypt's potential to enable a knowledge society through the deployment of emerging technology tools and applications across different sectors of the society. The chapter analyzes the critical success factors that are necessary for the realization of a digitally driven society where information is seamlessly exchanged for the optimal utilization of resources for decision-making purposes at the government, public, and private sector levels. The chapter highlights the need for the formulation of a nation-wide entrepreneurial ecosystem that promotes a tech-startup culture that can effectively contribute to transforming the society by enabling inclusion, universal access to the internet, more diversified educational opportunities and a comprehensive and conducive environment to development.

Chapter 18

For several decades the information systems field has studied the individual-level information technology (IT) adoption decision. With the mounting pressure to invest in updated technologies and governmental pressure to implement electronic medical records (EMR), the healthcare industry has searched for factors which influence the adoption decision. However, the adoption rate of ERM has been low due to resistance. In this study, the authors examine why traditional models of adoption which focus on the perceptions of the individual towards the innovation (or a micro-level of analysis) have been inadequate to explain ERM adoption issues. Thus, they examine the broader context within which the adoption/non-adoption decision takes place (or a macro-level of analysis), which incorporates the environmental pressures playing a role in the adoption decision. In this study, the authors adopt the technology-organization-environment framework to examine the context of a physician's decision about whether or not to adopt electronic medical record (or EMR) technology.

This chapter describes a user-driven innovation project in psychiatric services for children and adolescents in rural areas in Norway. The researcher applies a multilayer and dialectic perspective in the analysis of the user-driven innovation process that designed new ICT solution in compliance with a new decentralized treatment model with required treatment model. The researchers' findings suggest that contradiction appeared at material, cognitive, and organizational layers are crucial for path creation in such e-health projects. The contradiction in one layer leads to new contradictions in others, which together facilitate changes. Human actors, especially user groups in innovation processes, play an active role in leading the break from the existing path. Thus, this chapter contributes to the understanding of how user-driven innovation might help in deconstructing existing power structures across different layers in the change processes.

Cees Th. Smit Sibinga, IQM Consulting, The Netherlands
Maruff A. Oladejo, University of Lagos, Nigeria

Healthcare includes supportive services like blood transfusion. To manage blood supply and transfusion services, leadership development is paramount. E-learning has become a common global approach in teaching. However, there are limitations. Some are difficult to influence and eliminate. E-learning packages are promoted to effectively deliver education but are still not penetrated in clinical transfusion. Most clinicians have little knowledge of risks and benefits of hemotherapy. E-learning found its way into the field of blood transfusion. However, audits of clinical transfusion practice have demonstrated deficiencies in knowledge and practice that impact patient safety and in some cases result in death. WHO initiated a post-academic master course, "Management of Transfusion Medicine," focused on leadership in restricted economy countries. This chapter focuses on bridging the knowledge gap in management and operations of transfusion medicine.

Chapter 21

Silvia Cacho-Elizondo, IPADE Business School, Mexico
Niousha Shahidi, EDC Paris Business School, France
Vesselina Tossan, EDC Paris Business School, France

There is a growing tendency to use smartphones or other mobile devices for healthcare purposes, which offers a huge opportunity to improve public health worldwide and at the same time generates cost efficiencies and higher performance. In that vein, mobile devices make it easier to provide enhanced coaching and follow-up services through text or video messages and also through two-way interaction via social networks (e.g., Facebook) or virtual reality devices (e.g., Oculus). This delivery mode supports individuals or patients trying to break addictions, such as smoking or drinking. The authors propose and validate an explanatory model for the intention to adopt a mobile coaching service and applied it in the context of helping people in their smoking cessation efforts. This chapter uses the concepts of vicarious innovativeness, social influence, perceived monetary value, perceived enjoyment, and perceived irritation as key variables explaining the adoption patterns of this type of mobile coaching service.

Chapter 22

This chapter relates some social aspects, such as playfulness, customer service, and citizen safety with one of the simplest multicriteria techniques to implement, matrixes of weighing (MOW, matrices de ponderación [MDP]). Taking as starting point the work matrixes of weighing and catastrophes, a brief review is made of the MOW, highlighting new applications of the same, as well as new concepts that have emerged from its use. The objective of this work will be to present some applications of the matrixes of weighing, while explaining what they are and how they apply, the multilayer matrix of weighing with multiplicative factors (ML-MOWwMf). To achieve this general objective and secondary objectives, this chapter will make use of the integrated-adaptable methodology for the development of decision support system (IAMDSS [MIASAD])

This chapter expands research on low-carbon tourism by using the low-carbon travel scale (LCTS) to profile low-carbon tourists. The results demonstrate the LCTS's ability to effectively identify different levels of low-carbon tourists. A priori segmentation was conducted using the respondents' overall LCTS score as the segmenting criterion. The resulting four segments were labeled "not a low-carbon tourist," "minimal low-carbon tourists," "moderate low-carbon tourists," and "strong low-carbon tourists." This study (1) confirms the usefulness of the LCTS for identifying and segmenting travelers and (2) provides the sustainable tourism field with a more holistic tool for measuring sustainable travelers. Destination managers interested in marketing to low-carbon tourists can use this tool to identify how many low-carbon tourists come to their area, level of low-carbon tourists' tendencies, and what the destination can focus on to attract more of this travel segment.

Preface

The evolution of the information and communication technologies (ICTs) triggered the concept of e-society where e-technologies and services are fully integrated into all dimensions of the society. The rise of e-society introduces the ability to synergize people, technology, time and space. It is leading to revolutionize the way to conduct business, commerce, industry, government, healthcare, services, education, etc. and the way people daily lives, organizations and companies are interacting with new everyday IT-based applications. The power of the enabling technologies that support such revolution is reflected by the capability to deal with unlimited amounts of data facilitated by the digitalization of all forms of multimedia information and by the capability presented by the networking and web facilities reaching to any location in the word and in real-time beyond time and physical constraints.

The handbook aims to present and address the research development and evolution issues within the evolving Information Society due to changes and demands. It is important to understand such development, the challenges and the impact of information and communication technologies on the behaviors and processes of individuals, organizations and communities in the context of technological innovation and the evolution of e-Society. Broad areas of interest in the field of eSociety are: eBusiness, eFinance, eCommerce, eConsumer, eGovernment, eServices, eHealth, etc.

This handbook includes 23 chapters that contribute with the state-of-art and up-to-date knowledge on research advancement in the field IT evolution and development and he rise of e-Society. The chapters provide theoretical knowledge, practices, algorithms, technological evolution and new findings. Furthermore, the handbook helps to prepare engineers and scientists who are looking to develop innovative, challenging, intelligent, bioinspired systems and value added ideas for autonomous and smart interdisciplinary software, hardware and systems to meet today's and future most pressing challenges.

CHAPTER 1: KNOWLEDGE SHARING FROM EMPLOYEE'S PERSPECTIVE – SOCIAL RELATIONSHIP, CONTEXTUAL PERFORMANCE, AND IT COMPETENCE

This research combines three less studied factors on employee knowledge sharing, namely, social relationship, contextual performance, and IT competence. The research reveals that both social relationship—which incorporates degree of centrality of employee's social network and frequency of interpersonal interaction—and employee's contextual performance have significant positive impacts on knowledge sharing. Current work extends the literature pertaining to knowledge sharing by, not only providing an enhanced approach to measure social relationship, but also emphasizing that social relationship or contextual performance can magnify the impact on knowledge sharing through a high level of IT competence.

CHAPTER 2: OPTIMIZING KNOWLEDGE-WORK THROUGH PERSONAL KNOWLEDGE MANAGEMENT – THE ROLE OF INDIVIDUAL KNOWLEDGE-WORKERS' MOTIVATION, ABILITY, AND OPPORTUNITY

Knowledge-work is a discretionary behavior, and knowledge-workers should be viewed as investors of their intellectual capital. In addition, effective knowledge-work is mostly dependent on the performance of individual knowledge-workers who drive the success of knowledge-intensive organizations. This study empirically demonstrates that knowledge-workers' behaviors are dependent on their motivation, ability and opportunity to perform knowledge-work activities. This study provides insights and future directions for research on knowledge-work Since personal-knowledge often raise the issue of knowledge ownership, further attention to ethical issues may bring valuable insights for KM in organizations.

CHAPTER 3: A TOOL FOR CREATING COMMUNITY KNOWLEDGE OBJECTS

International organizations and government agencies have developed and collected a wealth of knowledge resources relevant to poor communities. However, electronic sources of knowledge materials and means of communication are rarely integrated with traditional methods of knowledge delivery. This chapter addresses the issue of knowledge sharing with poor communities and presents a software tool for developing multimedia knowledge materials suitable for people with little or no formal education. This is done by having a multimedia editor that uses a data structure composed of multimedia objects (texts, images, video and audio clips) to generate the knowledge browser. This approach enables local specialists with a basic knowledge of computing can modify and customize the presentation of the knowledge relevant to the local environment.

CHAPTER 4: A FAMILY OF INVISIBLE FRIENDS – CULTIVATING A SENSE OF E-COMMUNITY AMONG VIRTUAL WORK TEAMS

Despite the potential advantages offered by e-communities, their formation and maintenance are often hindered by feelings of mistrust, unclear group processes, and limited technical expertise. This study analyzed nearly 2,500 survey responses from 600 students spanning 25 colleges/universities in order to develop practical implications for cultivating a sense of e-community among virtual work teams. Thematic results of the study revealed the significance of brand awareness, interpersonal facilitation, user-friendly design, fiscal barriers, and mobile accessibility. Accordingly, the study concludes with five corresponding implications for cultivating a sense of e-community in the modern workplace: increased integration, expanded physicality, supplemental training, financial entrée, and utilized flexibility.

CHAPTER 5: BUILDING ORGANIZATION IMAGE – HOW TO CONTROL A PUBLIC RELATIONS CRISIS AND COMMUNICATION

This chapter investigates strategies that help an organization rejuvenate its image after damage from ineffective public relation (PR). It is important to know which PR strategies engage stakeholders because it is critical for the survival of company maintaining healthy relationships with all entities. A case study was conducted to explore what ruins a company's image and what role a PR department plays in rejuvenating it. To gain valuable insights into this topic, interviews were conducted with fourteen PR professionals including people who are working in the mentioned case studies places and organizations that faced some crisis. Results suggest that PR plays a critical role during crisis management while organizations can turn adverse situations to their favor and reconstruct reputations that would otherwise be tarnished.

CHAPTER 6: A WEB-BASED SYSTEM FOR SUPPLY CHAIN COLLABORATION TO ENHANCE AGILITY AND FLEXIBILITY

Recently, enterprises increase their competitiveness through supply chain collaboration to efficiently allocate resources using internet. However, supply chain collaboration usually fails because information is usually confidential. Many studies have discussed strategies of supply chain collaboration via internet but only a few of the strategies can be implemented in practice. Therefore, this research builds an information exchange platform to share production and inventory information over internet to ensure on-time delivery. This platform is implemented in a panel manufacturing company and 10% on-time delivery increase with 2% quality improvement after adapting this system. This result demonstrates the usefulness of using on-line platform to immediately share information will improve one-time delivery and quality assurance.

CHAPTER 7: BARAN – AN EFFECTIVE MAPREDUCE-BASED SOLUTION TO SOLVE BIG DATA PROBLEMS

The MapReduce method is widely used as a solution to solve big data problems on distributed hardware platforms. However, MapReduce architectures are inefficient in terms of data locality, network congestion, and low hardware performance. This chapter introduces Baran method that aims to solve these problems. Baran is a method that can dramatically improve performance and solve the data locality problem and consequences such as network congestion and low hardware performance. The Baran method was used for works on data warehouse, graph and data mining problems and the results were promising.

CHAPTER 8: A TALE OF TWO SYSTEMS – ERP IN CHINA: FAILURE AND SUCCESS

With China becoming an economic powerhouse, there has been increasing need for more studies on issues related to information systems localization. Most of the adopted information systems in the literatures have been conducted in the context of Western society, especially in America. Due to differences in the cultural, social, and legal environment, these theories and findings out of these studies need to be tested in the context of Chinese culture. This chapter adopts the technology, organization, and environment framework to explain why a Chinese apparel manufacturing companies failed in its first enterprise resource planning (ERP) project, and how it achieved success in the second project with government's assistance and what they have learned from their first experience with ERP. This study provides insight on the characteristics of Chinese companies, and the unique challenges they have encountered in the informatization process.

CHAPTER 9: CONSUMER VALUE TRUMPS PERCEIVED PRIVACY RISK – ITEM-LEVEL RFID IMPLEMENTATION IN THE FMCG INDUSTRY

This chapter reviews Radio Frequency Identification (RFID) literature within the Fast Moving Consumer Goods (FMCG) industry and the impact of consumer benefits on the perceived risks of item-level RFID. Two new categories are used to measure this impact; the separation of consumers' interactions with the technology to in-store and after-sales allows the consumers expectation of privacy to changes depending on the surrounding environment. A quantitative survey on primary household grocery purchasers within the USA revealed that while consumers are aware of the associated privacy risks after sale, they would be willing to use the technology, given sufficient benefits.

CHAPTER 10: CONSUMERS' CONCERNS FOR REPUTATION AND IDENTITY THEFT ONLINE TRADING

Although online trading with Amazon, eBay, and many others, has its benefits, such as convenience and the ability to compare prices online, there are still many concerns about the integrity of the buyer, the seller and/or the online action service provider (OASP). The empirical section investigated these relationships via multivariate statistical analysis of a stratified sample of working professionals resulting in 198 usable questionnaires from an initial sampling frame of over 550 professional personnel from five relatively large Pittsburgh, PA firms. It was found that buyers that felt feedback systems were viable were more willing to engage in online trading activities and more willing to pay a premium price for merchandise being sold by a seller with a better reputation, regardless of gender. Customers were especially concerned with the total price, including shipping cost, regardless of gender. In terms of the convenience of payment method, electronic forms were preferred in transacting online trading activities, regardless of age and gender.

CHAPTER 11: CULTURE AND INTERNET BANKING TECHNOLOGY – LONG-TERM ORIENTATION OVER THE ACCEPTANCE

The interaction between the cultural value of long-term orientation and internet banking technology acceptance is examined in this chapter. A survey involving a total of 376 potential users was conducted in an internet banking setting in Taiwan. The results confirms previous TAM findings that both efficacy and belief variables have significantly positive direct and in-direct effects on the usage, but under the cultural influence of long-term orientation, users remain hesitant to accept internet banking technology because they are more concerned with face-to-face long-term bank relationships to ensure future gratification than with current social status influence to obtain immediate benefits (e.g., convenience). Practitioners may refer this cultural influence on users' behavior in Fin-tech development. The implications of the study are discussed.

CHAPTER 12: COMPREHENSIVE INTERNET YOUTH PROTECTION POLICES BY PRIVATE ORGANIZATIONS AND EFFECTIVENESS VERIFICATION – INITIATIVES OF THE JAPAN INTERNET SAFETY PROMOTION ASSOCIATION AS A THEME

Seeking a safer Internet environment for minors, the Japanese government enacted a new law in 2008 to promote both protective measures and empowerment activities. Under the act, many entities, including newly established non-profit organizations (NPOs), are working to bring a safer Internet environment to Japan. The Japan Internet Safety Promotion Association (JISPA), one such NPO established in February 2007, has worked to promote a safer Internet environment for minors by providing non-formal learning opportunities through educational materials and events. Efforts to improve children's online safety have evolved from offering e-learning content and guidelines to holding workshops in the real world. This study reports various measures taken by JISPA for the protection of children using the Internet and verifies the effectiveness of the various measures based on evidence. Measures to be verified are e-learning contents, workshop programs and Internet literacies among young people and parents.

CHAPTER 13: PLAY IT LIKE BURBERRY! THE EFFECT OF REPUTATION, BRAND IMAGE, AND SOCIAL MEDIA ON E-REPUTATION – LUXURY BRANDS AND THEIR DIGITAL NATIVE FANS

Some firms and industries were not willing to take full advantage of the Internet and its endless opportunities, mainly because they rather focused on the inherent risks and challenges. However, when taking into consideration the specificities of the connected generation, the question is not anymore whether to go online or not, but rather to understand how, when, and where, especially in a luxury context. More specifically the digital natives represent tomorrow's customers. This new market segment represents a main reason for luxury firms to adopt online strategies. Still, further analysis is needed to uncover the main objectives when firms decide to engage in digital activities. The authors herein investigate the concept of e-reputation. The authors expand on their initial study that focused on brand image and social media as determinants of online reputation. Recommendations and future research directions are suggested.

CHAPTER 14: SOCIAL MEDIA AND MOTIVATIONAL COMPLEXITIES ASSOCIATED IN PROMOTING PROFESSIONAL SOCCER ENGAGEMENT

The purpose of this chapter examines and determines factors that lead to increase television ratings for soccer in the U.S. Undoubtedly, the topic of fantasy sports and the various roles it plays with types of fan involvement and their need for enhanced engagement with a complex social media landscape has intrigued scholars found a number of disciplines. How the various motivational factors, both intrinsically and extrinsically, impact the degree of fan involvement and loyalty have been investigated several times, the overall results have been mixed to say the least. The current chapter primarily focuses on fantasy soccer participation, involvement in soccer, presence of a local professional team, and social media interaction. After providing a brief history of soccer television ratings in the U.S., a conceptual model based on these factors is developed and explained. The factors of this conceptual model are tested through statistical analysis.

CHAPTER 15: ETHICAL DILEMMAS ASSOCIATED WITH SOCIAL NETWORK ADVERTISEMENTS

Significant amount information can be relayed on Facebook, MySpace and Twitter, but the question remains whether or not organizations are using this to their advantage, especially in the era of big data. The present study used a sample of working professionals that were knowledgeable in the various options of social networking to test these assumptions. The three hypotheses dealt with the interplay of online social networking, advertising effectiveness, gender and age trends, and remaining the interplay with positive comments of the use of the 'like' function and its impacts on consumer behavior, as derived from the review of relevant operations literature and from applying the basic tenants of Uses and Gratification Theory. All three specific research hypotheses were accepted in the null form.

CHAPTER 16: STRATEGIC PLANNING FOR INFORMATION TECHNOLOGY – A COLLABORATIVE MODEL OF INFORMATION TECHNOLOGY STRATEGIC PLAN FOR THE GOVERNMENT SECTOR

Information Technology (IT) is strategic for organization management (Stair, R.; Reynolds, G. 2005), although, many companies lack IT governance and planning, skilled people, defined and institutionalized methods and procedures, internal controls and indicators, and structures for agreement service levels and information security, legality, and economy. In this scenario, a minimum organization and control in the use of resources is needed to boost technical and administrative efficiency, with a focus on IT governance. An Information Technology Strategic Plan (ITSP) aims at discovering the resources and IT in an organization, to direct the technological and information architecture to its strategic objectives. The Brazilian Government issued a Normative Instruction (NI04) for public organizations to develop IT Strategic Plans so that they can purchase products and services. In order to help organizations develop, control and manage their ITSPs, a model was created that defines a set of auxiliary steps in the construction of the ITSP.

CHAPTER 17: THE ROLE OF INNOVATIVE AND DIGITAL TECHNOLOGIES IN TRANSFORMING EGYPT INTO A KNOWLEDGE-BASED ECONOMY

Digital technology, artificial intelligence, the Internet of Things and innovative technology applications are gradually transforming businesses and governments in emerging markets making them more competitive and offering opportunities for economic growth and prosperity. This chapter demonstrates Egypt's potential to enable a knowledge society through the deployment of emerging technology tools and applications across different sectors of the society. The chapter analyzes the critical success factors that are necessary for the realization of a digitally-driven society where information is seamlessly exchanged for the optimal utilization of resources for decision making purposes at the government, public and private sector levels. The chapter highlights the need for the formulation of a nation-wide entrepreneurial ecosystem that promotes a tech-startup culture that can effectively contribute to transforming the society by enabling inclusion, universal access to the Internet, more diversified educational opportunities and a comprehensive and conducive environment to development.

CHAPTER 18: UTILIZING THE TECHNOLOGY-ORGANIZATION-ENVIRONMENT FRAMEWORK TO EXAMINE THE ADOPTION DECISION IN A HEALTHCARE CONTEXT

With the mounting pressure to invest in updated technologies and governmental pressure to implement electronic medical records (EMR), the healthcare industry has searched for factors which influence the adoption decision. However, the adoption rate of ERM has been low, due to resistance. In this study, we examine why our traditional models of adoption which focus on the perceptions of the individual towards the innovation (or a micro-level of analysis) have been inadequate to explain ERM adoption issues. Thus, we examine the broader context within which the adoption/non-adoption decision takes place (or a macro-level of analysis), which incorporates the environmental pressures playing a role in the adoption decision. In this study, we adopt the Technology-Organization-Environment framework to examine the context of a physician's decision about whether or not to adopt Electronic Medical Record (or EMR) technology.

CHAPTER 19: USER-DRIVEN INNOVATION IN E-HEALTH CHANGE PROCESSES

This chapter describes a user-driven innovation project in psychiatric services for children and adolescents in rural areas in Norway. The researcher apply a multilayer and dialectic perspective in the analysis of the user-driven innovation process, that designed new ICT solution in compliance with a new decentralized treatment model with required treatment model. The researchers' findings suggest that contradiction appeared at material, cognitive and organizational layers are crucial force for path creation in such eHealth projects. The contradiction in one layer lead to new contradictions in other layers and this facilitate changes. Human actors, especially user groups in innovation processes, play an active role in leading the break from the existing path. Thus, this chapter contributes to the understanding of how user-driven innovation might help in deconstructing existing power structure across different layers in the change processes.

CHAPTER 20: MANAGEMENT AND OPERATIONS OF TRANSFUSION MEDICINE – IMPACT OF POLICY, PLANNING, AND LEADERSHIP ON BRIDGING THE KNOWLEDGE GAP

This chapter focuses on bridging the knowledge gap in management and operations of Transfusion Medicine. Healthcare includes supportive services like blood transfusion. To manage blood supply transfusion services, leadership development is paramount. E-learning has become a common global approach in teaching. However, there are limitations. Some are difficult to influence and eliminate. E-learning packages are promoted to effectively deliver education, but are still not penetrated in clinical transfusion. Most clinicians have little knowledge of risks and benefits of hemotherapy. E-learning found its way into the field of blood transfusion. However, audits of clinical transfusion practice have demonstrated deficiencies in knowledge and practice that impact patient safety and in some cases result in death. WHO initiated a post-academic Master course - Management of Transfusion Medicine, focused on leadership in restricted economy countries?

CHAPTER 21: WHAT WILL ENTAIL ADOPTION OF A MOBILE COACHING SERVICE? THE CASE OF SMOKING CESSATION SERVICES

Mobile devices facilitate easy way to provide enhanced coaching and follow-up services through text or video messages and also, through a two-way interaction via social networks (e.g. Facebook) or virtual reality devices (e.g. Oculus).This delivery mode supports individuals or patients trying to break addictions, such as smoking or drinking. This chapter proposes and validates an explanatory model for the intention to adopt a mobile coaching service and applied it in the context of helping people in their smoking cessation efforts. This chapter uses the concepts of vicarious innovativeness, social influence, perceived monetary value, perceived enjoyment, and perceived irritation as key variables explaining the adoption patterns of this type of mobile coaching service.

CHAPTER 22: NOVELTY ON THE MATRICES OF WEIGHING

This chapter relates some social aspects, such as playfulness, customer service and citizen safety, with one of the simplest multi-criteria techniques to implement, Matrixes Of Weighing (MOW, Matrices De Ponderación [MDP]). The objective of this work is to present applications of the Matrixes Of Weighing, while explain what they are and how they apply, the Multilayer Matrix Of Weighing with Multiplicative factors (ML-MOWwMf). To achieve this general objective and secondary objectives, the presented work is making the use of the Integrated-Adaptable Methodology for the development of Decision Support System (IAMDSS [MIASAD]).

CHAPTER 23: SEGMENTING LOW-CARBON TOURISTS BY LOW-CARBON TRAVEL SCALE

This study expands research on low-carbon tourism by using the Low-Carbon Travel Scale (LCTS) to profile low-carbon tourists. The results demonstrate the LCTS's ability to effectively identify different levels of low-carbon tourists. Destination managers interested in marketing to low-carbon tourists can use this tool to identify how many low-carbon tourists come to their area, their level of low-carbon tourists tendencies and what the destination can focus on to attract more of this travel segment.

Maki K. Habib
The American University in Cairo, Egypt

Chapter 1
Knowledge Sharing From Employee's Perspective:
Social Relationship, Contextual Performance, and IT Competence

Jianping Peng
Sun Yat-sen University, China

Jing Quan
Salisbury University, USA

Guoying Zhang
Midwestern State University, USA

Alan J Dubinsky
Purdue University, USA

ABSTRACT

This chapter combines three less-studied factors on employee knowledge sharing, namely, social relationship, contextual performance, and IT competence. Using a survey study that was targeted to professional employees in a R&D department, we reveal that both social relationship—which incorporates degree of centrality of employee's social network and frequency of interpersonal interaction—and employee's contextual performance have significant positive impacts on knowledge sharing. This association, however, is found to be further positively moderated by employee's IT competence. Our work extends the literature pertaining to knowledge sharing by, not only providing an enhanced approach to measure social relationship, but also emphasizing that social relationship or contextual performance can magnify the impact on knowledge sharing through a high level of IT competence. The findings provide managerial and future research insights pertaining to promoting knowledge sharing by enhancing social relationship, rewarding contextual performance, and improving IT competence of employees.

DOI: 10.4018/978-1-5225-7214-5.ch001

INTRODUCTION

An organization's core competitiveness often results from its ability to innovate (Higgins, 1995; Kandampully, 2002). Employee knowledge sharing plays an essential role in promoting sustained innovation (Spencer, 2003; Lin, 2007). It has been well documented in literature that knowledge sharing is critical to improve organizational problem-solving ability as well as generating creative responses (Carmeli et al., 2013). More recently, Dong et al. (2016) use a multi-level model to validate a positive effect from knowledge sharing to organizational creativity. Hence, it is important to encourage and foster knowledge sharing for organizations.

There are abundant research examining various enablers of and barriers to knowledge sharing in organizations, including organizational structure, technology adoption, culture, management style, synergy, employee's closeness to colleagues, business strategy, among others (e.g., Lilleoere & Hansen, 2011; Phang & Foong, 2006). On an operational level, several research projects study the technology platform hosting knowledge sharing activities. Majchrzak et al. (2000) investigate the effectiveness of how to share knowledge among different organizations using a virtual collaborative system.

Indeed, knowledge sharing is often regarded as a key aspect of human relationships (Chang & Liou, 2002) and a selective interpersonal process (Coming, 2004). Knowledge givers not only choose with whom to share their knowledge, but they decide what knowledge to share based on who the recipients are. Individual characteristics, such as five-factor model of personality, have great influence on knowledge sharing (Wang et al., 2011). Furthermore, interpersonal interactions are a necessary condition for knowledge sharing. Such interactions are based on a certain degree of interpersonal closeness (Connelly & Kelloway, 2004; Makela et al., 2007). In fact, Lilleoere et al. (2011) show that personal closeness to colleagues is a key enabler for knowledge sharing in organizations. Hau et al. (2013) also investigate the effects of personal motivation and social relationship on knowledge sharing. They use social ties, social trust, and social goals to model social capital construct, and find positive impact on knowledge sharing. Hence, personal relationships have a profound connection to knowledge sharing. In this study, we specifically capture the personal social relationship among employees using social network analysis (Wasko & Faraj, 2005).

Individuals tend to hoard knowledge (Bock & Kim, 2002; Bock et al., 2005). Accordingly, knowledge sharing is principally a voluntary act; virtually no one can make a person share knowledge. Knowledge sharing can be perceived as voluntary actions of individuals who are motivated by the returns—such as exchanges of favors, concessions, assistance, and courtesies—that they are expected to bring (Lee, 2001). Furthermore, knowledge transfer can demonstrate employees' image of competence and identity (Konstantinou & Fincham, 2010). Tagliaventi and Mattarelli (2006) view employee knowledge sharing as part of organizational citizenship. Hence, knowledge sharing can be considered a behavior that is *beyond* an employee's normal job requirements. Those individuals with high levels of job dedication and organizational commitment are those who are more likely to share their knowledge in order to help others. Such individuals are said to display elevated *contextual* performance. According to Borman and Motowidlo (1997), contextual performance can often be evaluated by "traits of persisting with enthusiasm, volunteering to help others, willingness to take additional duties," among others. Bozionelos and Singh (2017) even validate the nonlinear relationship of emotional intelligence with contextual performance. With all of these literature study, we believe it is important to include contextual performance as a study object in our research toward its impact on knowledge sharing.

Last but not the least, today's organization often operates with a heavy reliance on information technology applications. At same time, it is also noted that monitoring and manage knowledge are becoming increasingly difficult without any support of technology tools (Kalman et al., 2002). Information Technology (IT) does facilitate knowledge sharing by shrinking temporal and spatial barriers between knowledge workers, thereby creating easier access to information and knowledge (Hendriks, 1999). IT supports knowledge management by either organizing information systematically–codification –or enhancing personalization (Hansen, 1999; Hansen et al. 1999). More recently, Ale et al. (2014) propose a holistic architecture of knowledge management system as the platform to implement knowledge sharing while emphasizing the mapping with organizational structure.

With the realization of the important role that IT plays in knowledge sharing, it is natural to investigate employee's IT competency. At an individual capability level, study shows that employee's IT competence is significantly positive toward the attitude of knowledge management (Yun, 2013). Huysman (2006) finds that IT competence of employees is directly related to knowledge sharing motivation and behavior, and Phang et al. (2006) discern that information and communication technology plays a critical role in facilitating and supporting the process of knowledge sharing in organizations. Reflecting on our research interest in social relationship and contextual performance, we wonder whether IT competence is also moderating these two critical factors on their impacts toward knowledge sharing. In fact, there are some existing studies to determine IT competency's impact on contextual performance. Bassellier et al. (2001) outline the definition of IT competence of business managers, and specify that such IT competence is an enabler for business leadership. Youssef et al. (2014) investigate the relationship between IT and contextual performance in the European companies from 2005 to 2010. The study finds that internet use, as a part of IT competence of employees, is positively associated with contextual performance. The current study revisits the role of employee's IT competence by focusing on its moderating effect on employee social relationship and contextual performance vis-à-vis knowledge sharing behavior.

RESEARCH FRAMEWORK AND HYPOTHESES

With all the introduction information, we set up our formal research framework here and propose the research hypotheses built upon a thorough literature review.

Knowledge sharing is associated with an employee's willingness and capability to share. Since knowledge sharing is social process, social relationship at work are also likely to be critical in enabling sharing behavior. Extending the existing literature, we therefore examine individual employee knowledge sharing vis-à-vis impacts from both social relationship (via social network characteristics) and contextual performance (via willingness and capability of knowledge sharing). Furthermore, with organizational management mandates to use IT applications in various business operations, employees have to possess a certain level of IT competence to complete job tasks, establish workplace social relationship, go above and beyond to demonstrate the contextual performance, among others. Therefore, when analyzing the impact from social relationship and contextual performance on knowledge sharing, the moderating effect of employee's IT competence merits research attention and thus is included in the current work.

This study complements the research literature of knowledge sharing on social network analysis and contextual performance, thus it answers the research call from Wang and Noe (2010). Wang and Noe (2010) develop a framework for knowledge sharing and call for research in five emphasized areas. More specifically, one of these areas is social networks of interpersonal characteristics (i.e. social relationship in our study) and perceived benefits of motivation factors (i.e. contextual performance in our study).

Shown in Figure 1 is the hypothesized model. Study hypotheses portrayed in the figure are now developed and described below.

Knowledge Sharing

Knowledge sharing is the dissemination of knowledge within an organization. The purpose of knowledge sharing generally is to expand the value and use of knowledge through its exchange (Hendriks, 1999). For purposes of this study, knowledge sharing was defined as the degree to which an employee willingly and informally disseminates job-related information, irrespective of medium, from himself/herself to other organizational members.

Arguing that knowledge is a source of power, French (1968) concludes that a person equipped with knowledge possesses power and has easier access to resources as well as opportunities for advancement and bonuses. Rewards and evaluations can greatly influence employee behavior. Therefore, if that knowledge sharing behavior enables employees to achieve rewards or promotions, they are more willing to share knowledge with others. Furthermore, Stevenson (1997) believes that if managers show more trust in employees, the extent of knowledge sharing will be increased.

Knowledge sharing takes place between owners of knowledge and recipients of that knowledge, so that the emphasis is on the exchange and the relationship that exists during the process of knowledge sharing. A positive outcome of the knowledge sharing process is that new knowledge can be generated. Senge (1997) describes the knowledge sharing process from the point of view of *learning*, in which knowledge sharing includes a willingness to help the receiver understand, or learn, the meaning and connotation of the information. Davenport (1998) defines knowledge sharing as a voluntary act and differentiates it from a *report*. From his perspective, reports are information-exchange behaviors based on certain rules,

Figure 1. Hypothesized model

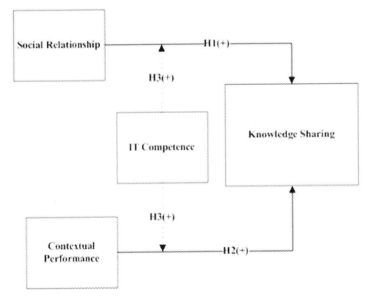

but knowledge sharing implies conscious exchange behavior not bound by rules. Hendriks (1999, p. 92) extends the notion of the importance of consciousness in the knowledge-exchange process by describing knowledge sharing as a process of communication, and by directly emphasizing the concept of a relationship: "Knowledge sharing presumes a relationship between at least two parties." The owner of the knowledge shares—through the process of externalization (i.e., expressing knowledge in comprehensible forms that can be understood by others)—and the recipient internalizes the knowledge. More recently, Dong et al. (2017) argues that team knowledge sharing can enhance employee creativity and Carmeli et al. (2013) illustrates the importance of knowledge sharing toward creative problem-solving, creative performance as well as leadership building.

Although research has fostered understanding of what knowledge sharing is, additional empirical work is needed to explain *motivational* factors for the transfer of knowledge between providers and recipients (Quigley, Tesluk, Locke, & Bartol, 2007). For instance, researchers interested in predicting knowledge sharing have applied concepts from social motivation theory (e.g., trust) to help explain knowledge transfer (e.g., Levin & Cross, 2004). Others have relied on reward and incentive theory (addressing, specifically, the impact of incentives on knowledge sharing) (e.g., Kalman et al., 2002). Kosonen et al. (2014) find that the key motivation of knowledge-sharing is from social benefits and learning benefits in an online idea crowdsourcing environment.

A more comprehensive literature review of knowledge sharing can be found in Wang and Noe (2010). The study develops a framework for knowledge sharing and call for research in five emphasized areas, "organizational context, interpersonal and team characteristics, cultural characteristics, individual characteristics, and motivational factors." Research in each of these areas are summarized and future research topics are outlined for knowledge sharing.

Social Relationship and Knowledge Sharing

Knowledge sharing is based on social relationship (Chang & Liou, 2002). Wasko and Faraj (2005) find that people share their knowledge when they are structurally embedded in a social network. Knowledge-sharing behavior is indeed a selective interpersonal process under specific circumstances (Coming, 2004). Knowledge givers not only choose with whom to share their knowledge, but they decide what knowledge to share. Scholars (e.g., Connelly & Kelloway, 2004; Makela et al., 2007) contend that interpersonal interaction is a necessary condition for knowledge sharing, and that such interactions are always based on a certain level of closeness in social relationship. Hollenbeck and Jamieson (2015) specifically point out that social network analysis has been underutilized and it is an important factor for strategic human resource management. Wang and Noe (2010) also review the literature and notice that social networks topic needs further research attention regarding individual's social network characteristics.

We formulate employee social relationship using social network analysis methodology. Social network analysis has recently made significant inroads as a useful mechanism in examining enterprise social relationship. Research shows that employee social networks have become increasingly valuable assets to organizations (Hemsley & Mason, 2012; Steinfield et al., 2009). However, extant work on knowledge sharing has paid little attention to employee social relationship based on social network characteristics. Wasko and Faraj (2005) argue that people contribute their knowledge both when they are structurally embedded in a network and when they perceive that doing so enhances their professional reputation. Their study utilizes a national legal professional association network and knowledge sharing occurs via the Message Boards on its website. Nonetheless, knowledge sharing must occur between at least two persons, which constitute a functional social network. The social relationship derived from employee social networks should, accordingly, influence knowledge sharing.

Prior research demonstrates that strong ties in social relationship are considered relatively more conducive than weak ties for sharing refined and deep levels of knowledge among the individuals (Kang et al., 2003). In general, a greater degree (or frequency) of social interaction provides participants with increased exposure to, and awareness of, unique knowledge. Accordingly, extensive network contacts can increase team members' understanding of their skills and knowledge and can help individuals find relevant experts when specific knowledge is needed (Ke et al., 2007). Hau et al. (2013) also investigate the effects of personal motivation and social relationship on knowledge sharing. They use social ties, social trust, and social goals to model social capital construct, and find positive impact on knowledge sharing. More recently, Sykes et al. (2017) collect data from employees and their supervisors to study how the social network ties (both positive and negative) interact with one another regarding job performance. In that study, the author(s) also provide a comprehensive listing of over 60 important social networks research literature from 2006-2010. Most of these literature focus on the two social network types in an organization: *Advice Network* and *Friendship Network*. Due to these two networks' popularity in literature, we continue to focus on these two types of networks in our social network analysis.

As per the social network characteristics, we continue to use a degree of centrality of members in a social network, and the frequency of their interactions between those members. The degree of centrality reflects individual's social network characteristics and represents the connections an employee has in a social network. This approach is consistent with the work of Granovetter (1973) and Luo (2010). Intuitively, then, a higher degree of centrality (as defined previously) of the social interaction network should lead to enhanced social relationship. Consequently, the enhanced social relationship should foster greater knowledge sharing. Based on the preceding discussion, the following hypothesis is posited:

H1: A higher level of employee social relationship positively impacts knowledge sharing.

Contextual Performance and Knowledge Sharing

Contextual performance refers to activities that contribute to the social and psychological core of the organization and that go beyond employees' required job mandates. They are activities conducive to achieving organizational goals, and include spontaneous behavior, organizational citizenship, pro-social behavior, dedication to organization, and voluntary completion of tasks outside formal job requirements (Borman & Motowidlo, 1997; Conway, 1999). Borman and Motowidlo (1997) is the seminal work to evaluate contextual performance by "traits of persisting with enthusiasm, volunteering to help others, willingness to take additional duties," among others.

As such, contextual performance in this study is defined as the degree to which an employee goes beyond the call of duty when performing his/her job. Thus, it essentially refers to proactive, non-mandated efforts that manifest one's affect.

Knowledge sharing is not an easy task, particularly because of individuals' reluctance to share what they know (Bock et al., 2005) and the voluntary nature of knowledge sharing. Therefore, fostering policies that encourage and promote knowledge sharing behaviors is a managerial challenge. Indeed, Wasko and Faraj (2005) find that people will share knowledge to enhance their professional reputation. Moreover, the gift-giving exchange theory developed by Mauss (2002) and suggestions from Konstantinou and Fincham (2010) imply that primary functional reasons for knowledge transfer are for supporting the team, avoiding "reinventing the wheel," and enabling others with different expertise to work on a problem. Also, Tagliaventi and Mattarelli (2006) examine individuals' knowledge sharing in a hospital unit and find that working in proximity with others and sharing common organizational values are important drivers for knowledge transfer. Because the transfer initiator exhibits a pattern of extra-role behavior, they conclude that knowledge transfer evokes new kinds of organizational citizenship behaviors.

Accordingly, knowledge sharing surpasses an employee's assigned job requirements. Employees who share their knowledge in order to help others enhance their performance must be willing to exceed required job mandates. This type of individual with a high level of contextual performance often shows more active tendency to conduct knowledge sharing. The foregoing discussion leads to the following hypothesis:

H2: A higher level of employee contextual performance positively impacts knowledge sharing.

Information Technology (IT) Competence

IT competence in this investigation was defined as the employee's perceived degree of familiarity of using enterprise IT applications as well as understanding of IT infrastructures in the organization.

Indeed, the relationship between IT competence and knowledge sharing at the organizational level has long been recognized. In an environment of increasing complexity of work, fast-changing organizational boundaries, and the growth of virtual communities and geographically-dispersed teams, it has become increasingly difficult to monitor and manage knowledge (Kalman et al., 2002). IT can enhance knowledge sharing by shrinking temporal and spatial barriers between knowledge workers and facilitating access to information about knowledge (Hendriks, 1999). IT can support two categories of knowledge management: codification and personalization (Hansen, 1999; Hansen et al., 1999). When explicit and structured knowledge is codified and stored in knowledge bases, IT can be used to help people share and reuse knowledge. In knowledge management organized around personalization, tacit and unstructured knowledge is shared largely through both direct personal communication and an IT platform. Majchrzak et al. (2000) further conduct a study to investigate the effectiveness of knowledge sharing beyond organizational boundaries using a virtual collaborative system. Ale et al. (2014) proposed a holistic architecture of knowledge management system to implement knowledge sharing with a focus of mapping with organizational structure.

IT competence may also be valuable in identifying appropriate IT applications with which to disseminate knowledge, thereby achieving complex knowledge transfer (Huysman, 2006), or at least have a positive attitude toward the concept of knowledge management (Yun, 2013). Phang et al. (2006) discern that information and communication technology plays a critical role in facilitating and supporting the process of knowledge sharing in organizations.

With regards to social relationship and contextual performance, IT competence is a critical factor influencing both of them. IT competence can influence an employee's social relationship and, consequently, affect knowledge sharing. Davison, Ou, & Martinsons (2012) demonstrate that interactive IT tools, particularly Instant Messenger (IM), can effectively support informal knowledge sharing in the Chinese context of guanxi (i.e., relationship building) by knowing "who knows what." Bassellier et al. (2001) outline the definition of IT competence of business managers, and specify that such IT competence is an enabler for business leadership. Youssef et al. (2014) investigate the relationship between IT and contextual performance in the European context from 2005 to 2010. The study finds that internet use, as a part of IT competence of employees, is positively associated with contextual performance.

In this milieu, an employee's competence to use various IT tools and applications is likely to moderate the impact of social relationship and contextual performance on knowledge sharing. The preceding discussion leads to the following hypothesis:

H3: A high level of employee IT competence has a positive moderating effect toward the impact of social relationship and contextual performance on knowledge sharing.

In summary of our research framework, we investigate the impact of social relationship of organizational employees and their contextual performance on knowledge sharing related with a specific business area. Moreover, we always want to include IT competence in the discussion because either social relationship or contextual performance has to be realized or demonstrated through the use of organizational IT applications. Thus, we argue that employee's IT competence moderates the impact of social relationship and contextual performance on knowledge sharing.

RESEARCH DESIGN

Knowledge-sharing behavior, employee social relationship, contextual performance, and IT competence are the key research objects in our study. To assess *knowledge sharing*, items from the work of Senge (1997) were employed. For *contextual performance*, a scale developed by Van Scotter and Motowidlo (1996) was employed. Wang, Guo, and Liu (2009) translated this well-established scale into Chinese and then back into English, and empirically tested it. For employee *IT competence*, a scale from Peng (2011) was used. Table 1 below lists all these measurement constructs for our research objects.

The above constructs are straightforward from literature, however, the employee social relationship construct is quite different from the previous survey scales. Granovetter (1973) suggests that social relationship reflect the exchange and the contact ties both in person-to-person and organization-to-organization contexts. Such relationships are different from the abstract relationships of traditional sociological analysis. Granovetter was the first to propose the concept of strong and weak ties, and he suggests that the frequency of interaction is one of the main dimensions to use in measuring the strength of ties. Another common approach in literature for measuring the strength of social relationship is to construct the social networks among the employees and calculate the degrees of centrality for each employee in his/her respective social networks (Luo, 2010).

Accordingly, both of the foregoing approaches to assessing an employee's social relationship were used in this research. First, employees were surveyed to capture the frequency of their social interactions. Second, social networks were constructed by the researchers to obtain the degree of centralities for each respondent. Network centralities reflect the strength of the individual's social relationship. Table 2 below lists the measurement constructs for employ social networks and frequency of social interaction, which are the two components for employee social relationship.

Our study adopts Luo's approach (2010) to construct several social networks for employees. Response to each question in his instrument depicts use of a social network. For example, one of the questions is, "With whom do you often discuss work-related issues?" The names provided by the respondent indicated social links between the respondent and the named colleagues. According to Ibarra and Andrews (1993),

Table 1. Measurement constructs for knowledge sharing, contextual performance, and IT competence

Knowledge Sharing	1 = strongly disagree, 2 = disagree, 3 = neutral, 4 = agree, 5 = strongly agree
KS1	I usually provide others with the locations of the knowledge they need. For example, when someone inquiries about certain knowledge, although I have no idea of it, I know the place where he/she can find it, such as the document that he/she needs is located in the file cabinet of one specific department, or the program needed is stored in some databases.
KS2	I usually provide others with the person who has the knowledge they need. For example, when someone inquiries about some certain knowledge, although I have no idea of it, I know who he/she can inquire about it, such as, who is the expert in CRM (customer relationship management), or who is strong in multimedia network technology, etc.
KS3	I usually provide others with specific knowledge and skills I have gained from the training courses held by the company and other advanced seminars, such as knowledge management and CRM symposiums.
KS4	I usually provide others with the regulations and the standard operational rules of working made by the company, such as employees' code of conduct, operating principles, and strategy of my enterprise.
KS5	I usually provide others with the internal materials of my organization, including documents, manuals, technical reports, methods, modes, patents, and so on.
KS6	I usually provide others with knowledge acquired from the mass media (such as website, news, magazines, and broadcasting).
Contextual Performance	1 = strongly disagree, 2 = disagree, 3 = neutral, 4 = agree, 5 = strongly agree
CP1	I am active and enthusiastic about completing difficult tasks.
CP2	I am insistent upon overcoming difficulties in completing tasks.
CP3	I am proactive about solving problems at work.
CP4	I am self-disciplined at work.
CP5	If something I do would affect my colleagues, I will inform them beforehand.
CP6	I give compliments to my colleagues when they succeed.
IT Competence	1=Very unfamiliar, 2=Not familiar, 3=Generally familiar, 4=familiar, 5=proficient
IT1	Your familiarity of using the operating system
IT2	Your familiarity in using office software
IT3	Your familiarity of computer hardware

Table 2. Items for constructing employee social networks and frequency of social interaction

Social Networks	Fill in not more than five employee IDs.
B1	With whom you usually participate in entertainment activities after work
B2	To whom you turn for help when having non-work-related hardships
B3	To whom you complain when facing setbacks at work or when blamed by supervisors
B4	To whom you turn for help when facing work-related problems
B5	With whom you consult before making important decisions at work
B6	With whom you often discuss work-related issues
B7	With whom do you often chat
B8	With whom you usually communicate and exchange work-related emails
Frequency of Interactions	1=strongly disagree, 2=disagree, 3=neutral, 4=agree, 5=strongly agree
FI1	I have frequent communications with my colleagues.
FI2	I keep constant contacts with my colleagues.
FI3	I have good relationships with my colleagues.

social networks can further be classified into an advice network and a friendship network. As such, networks derived from Luo's survey instrument can be consolidated into these two kinds of networks.

The advice network generally refers to a work-relationship network, and the friendship network can be perceived as an informal, personal relationship network. Constructing these networks allows calculation of the degree of centrality for each employee. Finally, both the frequency of social interaction and the network centrality of a specific employee can be combined to describe one's social relationship level.

Data Collection

The researchers visited the R&D department of a Chinese commercial elevator manufacturer that engages in design and development of commercial elevators. Data were collected over a one-month period. The R&D department often relies heavily on knowledge sharing, and this specific group has a manageable size of employees for use in constructing social networks for the purpose of obtaining social relationship information.

This R&D department has three offices, with a total of 80 employees. During the researchers' personal visits, 80 questionnaires were distributed, of which 76 were returned (an effective rate of 95%). Sample characteristics are shown in Table 3.

Data Preparation and Validation

Test results for reliability and validity of the Knowledge Sharing, Contextual Performance, and IT competence items are portrayed in Table 4. The reliability (Cronbach alpha) for these three constructs are all greater than 0.6. For validity, the Bartlett test of sphericity and the KMO test show that the measurement items are suitable for factor analysis, with the KMO values greater than the threshold of 0.5 (Humphrey, 1988), and the Bartlett test of sphericity is significant at the 0.001 level. These findings indicate that these constructs have good structural validity.

Furthermore, in order to construct data for employee social relationship, we have to first use the social network analysis approach. As noted earlier, previous studies demonstrate that the degree of centrality of a social network can reflect a person's importance in the network, as well as the strength of the social relationship with others. Several social networks were constructed for this particular R&D department.

In the study questionnaire, respondents were requested to record names of individuals predicated on each of the 8 questions in Table 2. After collecting the responses, it was apparent that for each of the above questions, responses could be represented with a social network: employee names as nodes and existing relationships (with regards to the particular question) as linkages among nodes.

UCINET software (Borgatti et al., 2002) was employed to generate all social networks based on survey responses. UCINET is a software package for the analysis of social network data. It comes with the NetDraw network visualization tool, as well as other tools for analyzing network characteristics—such as node centrality and degree. Therefore, given the eight social networks corresponding to the eight foregoing questions in the survey, UCINET calculated the degree of centrality for each employee in each of these networks.

We thus construct 8 social networks based on question B1-B8 from Table 2 and derive the centralities for each node in each of these social networks. Through factor analysis, centralities of each node were further consolidated into two variables: advice network centrality and friendship network centrality.

Table 3. Respondent demographics

		#	%
Gender	Male	60	79.0
	Female	16	21.0
Age	<30	48	63.2
	30-35	23	30.3
	36-40	3	3.9
	41-45	2	2.6
	>46	0	0.0
Company Tenure (years)	<5	65	85.5
	5-10	11	14.5
	11-20	0	0.0
	>20	0	0.0
Work Experience (years)	<5	43	56.6
	5-10	26	34.2
	11-20	7	9.2
	>20	0	0.0
Education	Lower than Professional School	2	2.6
	Professional School	6	7.9
	College	46	60.5
	MBA/MPM	22	29.0
Total		**76**	**100**

In additional, Frequency of interaction among employees was another factor obtained directly through the survey items (questions FI1-FI3 in Table 2). The consolidated result generated from factor analysis are presented in Table 5.

Please note that B7 is dropped after initial factor analysis due to a complicated factor structure. B7 has more than one loading factor greater than 0.4: 0.472 for the Advisory Network and 0.635 for the Friendship Network and the difference between them is less than 0.2. This may be attributed to the ambiguity of the question because it didn't specify clearly whether it was work or friendship related chat. Therefore, this item was dropped, and the factor analysis was rerun for the final results.

Correlation Analysis

Correlations between non-network related variables were computed, with gender, tenure, and education being control variables—per Wimbush et al. (1997). Conceivably, each employee's knowledge sharing should have inherent differences owing to these demographic control variables, even in the presence of the same social relationship, contextual performance, and IT competence. Shown in Table 6 are the correlation coefficients of knowledge sharing with social relationship and contextual performance. All are positive and significant, thus indicating that the stronger an employee's social relationship or the better his/her contextual performance, the greater the extent of knowledge sharing. In addition, knowl-

Table 4. Reliability and Validity tests for knowledge sharing (KS), contextual performance (CP), and IT competence (ITC)

		Construct		Reliability
	Item	Factor 1	Factor 2	α=.787
Knowledge Sharing	KS1	.824	--	.790
	KS2	.819	--	
	KS3	.792	--	
	KS4	--	.868	.658
	KS5	--	.741	
	KS6	--	.614	
	Eigenvalues after rotation	2.111	1.856	KMO=.742***
	Cumulative %	35.183	66.121	
Contextual Performance	Item	Factor 1	Factor 2	α=0.813
	CP1	0.816	--	0.781
	CP2	0.755	--	
	CP3	0.753	--	
	CP4	0.598	--	
	CP5	--	0.872	0.610
	CP6	--	0.725	
	Eigenvalues after rotation	2.327	1.613	KMO=0.845***
	Cumulative %	38.780	65.650	
IT Competence	Item	Factor 1		α=0.719
	IT1	0.887	--	0.719
	IT2	0.781	--	
	IT3	0.729	--	
	Eigenvalues after rotation	1.928	--	KMO=0.600**
	Cumulative %	64.260	--	

*** Significant at the 1% level. ** Significant at the 5% level.

edge sharing is weakly correlated with IT competence. These findings provide a preliminary analysis of individual knowledge sharing. The formal empirical model is presented in the next section.

The Model

We use Knowledge Sharing (KS) as the dependent variable and proposed the hypothesized model as follows:

$$KS = \beta_0 + \beta_1 SR + \beta_2 CP + \beta_3 ITC + \lambda_1 \left(SR * ITC \right) + \lambda_2 \left(CP * ITC \right) + \varepsilon$$

Table 5. Reliability and validity tests for social relationship (SR)

Degree of centrality of the Social Networks[1]	Friendship Network	Advice Network	Frequency of Interaction	Reliability
B1	0.892	--	--	
B2	0.876	--	--	$\alpha = 0.916$
B3	0.874	--	--	
B6	--	0.923	--	
B5	--	0.905	--	
B4	--	0.881	--	$\alpha = 0.922$
B8	--	0.774		
Frequency of Interaction				
FI1	--	--	0.880	
FI2	--	--	0.849	$\alpha = 0.820$
FI3	--	--	0.788	
Eigenvalues after rotation	3.239	2.647	2.292	KMO=0.822***
Cumulative %	32.392	58.862	81.786	

*** Significant at the 1% level.

Table 6. Correlation matrix

	Mean (Standard Deviation)	Knowledge Sharing (KS)	Contextual Performance (CP)	IT Competence (ITC)	Social Relationship (SR)
KS	3.20(.63)	1	.39***	.21	.45***
CP	4.25(.51)		1	-.184	.344***
ITC	3.73(.51)			1	.023
SR	3.68(.57)				1

*** Significant at the 1% level.

where KS represents Knowledge Sharing, SR represents Social Relationship, CP represents Contextual Performance, and ITC represents IT Competence. In order to test the moderating effect of ITC, two interaction terms of ITC with SR and ITC with CP are also included. SPSS is the analysis tool to estimate the model. We present our results in Table 7.

Results in Table 7 indicate that the model is significant, with an F-statistic of 9.841. Adjusted R-square is 0.409, indicating a relatively strong goodness of fit. The variance inflation factor (VIF) for each of the independent variables is below the threshold of 5.00, suggesting minimal evidence of multicollinearity. In addition, both the employee's social relationship and contextual performance have significant positive impacts on knowledge sharing. Specifically, for every unit increase in social relationship, there is a 0.485-unit increase in knowledge sharing. Similarly, for every unit increase in contextual performance, there is a 0.412 unit increase in knowledge sharing. Employee's IT competence is also positive and significant toward knowledge sharing. Every unit increase in IT competence is associated with a 0.343-unit increase in knowledge sharing.

Table 7. Regression results

Variable	Coefficient	VIF
Intercept	-0.021	
SR	0.485***	1.172
CP	0.412***	1.283
ITC	0.343***	1.147
ITC*SR	0.237**	1.084
ITC*CP	0.234**	1.124
Adj. R²	0.409	
F-statistic	9.841***	

***significant at the 1% level
**significant at the 5% level

As for the moderating effect of IT competence, support for this effect is observed. IT competence positively moderates the impact of social relationship on knowledge sharing with an interaction coefficient of 0.237. Similarly, it positively moderates the impact of contextual performance on knowledge sharing with an interaction coefficient of 0.234. Given the foregoing study results, all hypothesis, namely, H1, H2, and H3 are supported.

MANAGERIAL INSIGHTS

In this study, we formulate employee social relationship using social network analysis, collect information on employee contextual performance, and evaluate individual's IT competence, and conclude employee's knowledge sharing activities. According to Wang and Noe (2010)'s comprehensive framework for knowledge sharing and call for research, social networks in the area of interpersonal characteristics and perceived benefits in the area of motivation factors are our study's focus. We explore the impact of employee social relationship and contextual performance on knowledge sharing, and further incorporate employee's individual IT competence as a moderating factor.

Findings reveal that *both* social relationship and contextual performance have a significant positive effect on knowledge sharing. At the same time, it is interesting to note that employee's IT competence has a positive moderating effect on the influence of both of these variables vis-à-vis knowledge sharing.

This study extends the literature pertaining to knowledge sharing by, not only providing an enhanced approach to measuring social relationship (using social network analysis), but also by emphasizing that social relationship or contextual performance can magnify the impact on knowledge sharing through a high level of IT competence. Findings demonstrate that social relationship, contextual performance, and IT competence are important enablers for knowledge sharing. Social relationship emerge from frequency of interpersonal interactions, as well as from degree of centrality of consolidated social networks. Contextual performance is deemed as an organizational citizenship behavior, and motivates employees to work "above and beyond" than basic job requirement. Employee's high level of social relationship and contextual performance can often lead to more active knowledge sharing activities. IT competence also plays a critical role enabling a higher level of knowledge sharing through promoting social relationship build-up and improving contextual performance.

This study offers contributions to theory and research in the area of knowledge sharing from an individual employee's perspective. First, this investigation offers support regarding the facilitating efforts of social relationship on knowledge sharing. Using social network analysis, the findings indicate that the nature of social relationship (i.e., the degree of centrality of members in the social network and the frequency of their interactions) fosters knowledge sharing. Knowledge sharing has to occur among at least two employees, and an individual's existing social relationship can be the first platform to share knowledge. Stronger social relationship often leads to more intense knowledge sharing and dissemination. Organizations might want to identify employees with high level of social relationship as the "hub" of knowledge sharing activity. At the same time, providing certain human resource management programs to build up strong social relationship among employees can also lead to strong knowledge sharing culture overall.

Second, the research efforts find that contextual performance (i.e., extra-curricular efforts that contribute to organizational well-being) enhances knowledge sharing. Essentially, employees' engagement in non-mandated job performance can conduce to a salutary impact on knowledge sharing. This demonstrates that organizations require more than merely mandated efforts to induce knowledge sharing. Organizations might want to identify employees with high level of contextual performance and assign them with knowledge sharing initiatives. Based on our research, these employees would work hard to carry out the knowledge sharing activities beyond their own job routines.

Third, IT competence has a moderating effect on knowledge sharing vis-à-vis social relationship and contextual performance. Therefore, although prior work has found IT competence has a direct effect on knowledge sharing, it can also engender knowledge sharing through its auspicious association with social networks and non-mandated employee endeavors. Organizations might want to identify employees with savvy IT skills or high IT competence, and ask their suggestions on how to utilize IT applications to improve employee social relationship, such as adopting enterprise social media technology, implementing formal or informal collaboration or workflow tools, among others. These employees can also help to identify IT applications that can boost employee's contextual performance, for example, human resource management systems that capture employees' extra activity beyond job requirements.

With these results, we believe that knowledge sharing in organizations can be dramatically improved with stronger social relationship among employees, higher contextual performance from employees, and more versatile IT competence demonstrated by employees.

FUTURE WORK

There are several future directions to continue this work. First, results are based on data collected from a single firm. Multiple-firm data can help establish enhanced understanding of the associations between the strength of the relationships with knowledge sharing behavior.

Second, only R&D employees were considered in the present investigation. Conceivably, such employees may possess higher levels of IT competence compared with other organizational members. This may reduce the generalizability of the results of this study. Consequently, future investigations should include other types of personnel. Comparative studies of knowledge employees and other types of personnel could shed light on the interaction mechanisms of relationship strength and knowledge sharing.

Third, to enrich and expand the research on knowledge sharing behavior, other variables—such as corporate culture, industry type, and firm location—could be considered. Finally, the present investigation did not consider whether geographical distance in the social relationship and density in the social network have an impact on the facilitating effect of IT competence on knowledge sharing. Therefore, future empirical efforts should be directed at reconnoitering these potential phenomena.

REFERENCES

Ale, M. A., Toledo, C. M., Chiotti, O., & Galli, M. R. (2014). A conceptual model and technological support for organizational knowledge management. *Science of Computer Programming*, *95*(1), 73–92. doi:10.1016/j.scico.2013.12.012

Bassellier, G., Reich, B. H., & Benbasat, I. (2001). Information technology competence of business managers: A definition and research model. *Journal of Management Information Systems*, *17*(4), 159–182. doi:10.1080/07421222.2001.11045660

Bock, G. M., & Kim, Y. G. (2002). Breaking the Myths of Rewards: An Exploratory Study of Attitudes about Knowledge Sharing. *Information Resources Management Journal*, *15*(2), 14–21. doi:10.4018/irmj.2002040102

Bock, G. W., Zmud, R. W., Kim, Y. G., & Lee. (2005). Behavioral Intention Formation in Knowledge Sharing: Examining the Roles of Extrinsic Motivators, Social-Psychological Forces, and Organizational Climate. *Management Information Systems Quarterly*, *29*(10), 87–111. doi:10.2307/25148669

Borgatti, S. P., Everett, M. G., & Freeman, L. C. (2002). *Ucinet for Windows: Software for Social Network Analysis*. Harvard, MA: Analytic Technologies.

Borman, W. C., & Motowidlo, S. J. (1997). Task performance and contextual performance: The meaning for personnel selection research. *Human Performance*, *10*(2), 99–109. doi:10.120715327043hup1002_3

Carmeli, A., Gelbard, R., & Reiter-Palmon, R. (2013). Leadership, Creative Problem-Solving Capacity, and Creative Performance: The Importance of Knowledge Sharing. *Human Resource Management*, *52*(1), 95–121. doi:10.1002/hrm.21514

Chang, H.-T., & Liou, S.-N. (2002). Exploring Employee's Knowledge Sharing: The Social Network Approach. *Human Resource Management Review*, *2*(3), 101–113.

Comming, J. N. (2004). Work group structure diversity and knowledge sharing in a global organization. *Management Science*, *50*(3), 352–364. doi:10.1287/mnsc.1030.0134

Connelly, C., & Kelloway, E. (2004). Predictors of employees' perceptions of knowledge sharing cultures. *Leadership and Organization Development Journal*, *24*(5/6), 294–301.

Conway, J. M. (1999). Distinguishing contextual performance from task performance for managerial jobs. *The Journal of Applied Psychology, 84*(1), 3–13. doi:10.1037/0021-9010.84.1.3

Cross, R., & Cummings, J. N. (2004). Tie and Network Correlates of Individual Performance in Knowledge Intensive Work. *Academy of Management Journal, 47*(6), 928–937.

Davenport, T. H., & Prusak, L. (1998). *Working Knowledge: How Organizations Manage What They Know*. Boston: Harvard Business School Press.

Davison, R. M., Ou, C. X. J., & Martinsons, M. G. (2012). Information technology to support informal knowledge sharing. *Information Systems Journal, 23*(1), 89–109. doi:10.1111/j.1365-2575.2012.00400.x

Dong, Y., Bartol, K. M., Zhang, Z.-X., & Li, C. (2017). Enhancing employee creativity via individual skill development and team knowledge sharing: Influences of dual-focused transformational leadership. *Journal of Organizational Behavior, 38*(3), 439–458. doi:10.1002/job.2134

French, J. R. P. Jr., & Raven, B. (1968). The bases of social power. In D. Cartwright (Ed.), Studies in Social Power (pp. 150-167).

Granovetter, M. S. (1973). The Strength of Weak Ties. *American Journal of Sociology, 78*(6), 1360–1380. doi:10.1086/225469

Hansen, M. T. (1999). The search transfer Problem: The role of weak ties in sharing knowledge across organization subunits. *Administrative Science Quarterly, 44*(1), 82–112. doi:10.2307/2667032

Hansen, M. T., Nohria, N., & Tierney, T. (1999). What's Your Strategy for Managing Knowledge? *Harvard Business Review, 77*(2), 106–116. PMID:10387767

Hau, Y. S., Kim, B., Lee, H., & Kim, Y. (2013). The effects of individual motivations and social capital on employees' tacit and explicit knowledge sharing intentions. *International Journal of Information Management, 33*(2), 356–366. doi:10.1016/j.ijinfomgt.2012.10.009

Hemsley, J., & Mason, R. M. (2012, January). The Nature of Knowledge in the Social Media Age: Implications for Knowledge Management Models. In *2012 45th Hawaii International Conference on System Science (HICSS)* (pp. 3928-3937). IEEE.

Hendriks, P. (1999). Why share knowledge? The influence of ICT on the motivation for knowledge sharing. *Knowledge and Process Management, 6*(2), 91–100. doi:10.1002/(SICI)1099-1441(199906)6:2<91::AID-KPM54>3.0.CO;2-M

Higgins, J. M. (1995). Innovation: The core competence. *Strategy and Leadership, 23*(6), 32–36.

Hollenbeck, J. R., & Jamieson, B. B. (2015). Human Capital, Social Capital, and Social Network Analysis: Implications for Strategic Human Resource Management. *The Academy of Management Perspectives, 29*(3), 370–385. doi:10.5465/amp.2014.0140

Humphrey, W. S. (1988). Characterizing the software process: A maturity framework. *IEEE Software, 56*(2), 73–79. doi:10.1109/52.2014

Huysman, M., & Wulf, V. (2006). IT to support knowledge sharing in communities, towards a social capital analysis. *Journal of Information Technology, 21*(1), 40–51. doi:10.1057/palgrave.jit.2000053

Ibarra, H., & Andrews, S. B. (1993). Power, social influence, and sense making: Effects of network centrality and proximity on employee perceptions. *Administrative Science Quarterly, 38*(2), 277–303. doi:10.2307/2393414

Kalman, M. E., Monge, P., Fulk, J., & Heino, R. (2002). Motivations to resolve communication dilemmas in database-mediated collaboration. *Communication Research, 29*(2), 125–155. doi:10.1177/0093650202029002002

Kandampully, J. (2002). Innovation as the core competence of a service organisation: The role of technology, knowledge and networks. *European Journal of Innovation Management, 5*(1), 18–26. doi:10.1108/14601060210415144

Kang, S. C., Morris, S. S., & Snell, S. A. (2003). Extending the Human Resource Architecture: Relational Archetypes and Value Creation (working paper). CAHRS'.

Ke, J., Sun, J., Shi, J., & Gu, Q. (2007). The Empirical Research on the Relation between Social Capital and Team Performance in the R&D Department: The Mediating Role of Knowledge Sharing and Knowledge Integration. *Management World, 3*, 89–102.

Konstantinou, E., & Fincham, R. (2010). Not sharing but trading: Applying a Maussian exchange framework to knowledge management. *Human Relations, 64*(6), 823–842. doi:10.1177/0018726710388676

Kosonen, M., Gan, C., Vanhala, M., & Blomqvist, K. (2014). User Motivation and Knowledge sharing in Idea Crowdsource. *International Journal of Innovation Management, 18*.

Lee, J. N. (2001). The impact of knowledge sharing, organizational capability and partnership quality on IS outsourcing success. *Information & Management, 38*(5), 323–335. doi:10.1016/S0378-7206(00)00074-4

Levin, D. Z., & Cross, R. (2004). The Strength of Weak Ties You Can Trust: The Mediating Role of Trust in Effective Knowledge Transfer. *Management Science, 50*(11), 1477–1490. doi:10.1287/mnsc.1030.0136

Lilleoere, A. M., & Hansen, E. H. (2011). Knowledge sharing enablers and barriers in pharmaceutical research and development. *Journal of Knowledge Management, 15*(1), 53–70. doi:10.1108/13673271111108693

Lin, H. F. (2007). Knowledge sharing and firm innovation capability: An empirical study. *International Journal of Manpower, 28*(3/4), 315–332. doi:10.1108/01437720710755272

Luo, J. D. (2010). *Social Network Analysis*. Beijing, China: Society and Science Publication.

Majchrzak, A., Rice, R. E., King, N., Malhotra, A., & Ba, S. (2000). Computer-Mediated Inter-Organizational Knowledge-Sharing: Insights From a Virtual Team Innovating Using a Collaborative Tool. *Information Resources Management Journal, 13*(1), 44–53. doi:10.4018/irmj.2000010104

Makela, K., Kalla, H. K., & Piekkari, R. (2007). Interpersonal similarity as a driver of knowledge sharing with in multinational corporations. *International Business Review, 16*(1), 1–22. doi:10.1016/j.ibusrev.2006.11.002

Mauss, M. (2002). *The Gift: The Form and Reason for Exchange in Archaic Societies*. London: Routledge.

Motowidlo, S. J., & Van Scotter, J. R. (1994). Evidence that task performance should be distinguished from contextual performance. *The Journal of Applied Psychology, 79*(4), 475–480. doi:10.1037/0021-9010.79.4.475

Peng, J., Zhang, G., Chen, R., & Tan, Y. (2011). Impacts of Essential Elements of Management on IT Application Maturity—A Perspective from Firms in China. *Decision Support Systems, 51*(1), 88–98. doi:10.1016/j.dss.2010.11.031

Phang, M. S., & Foong, S. Y. (2006). Enhancing knowledge sharing with information and communication technology. In *Proceedings of 3rd International Business Research Conference 2006*, World Business Institute, Melbourne, Vic.

Quigley, N. R., Tesluk, P. E., Locke, E. A., & Bartol, K. M. (2007). A Multilevel Investigation of the Motivational Mechanisms Underlying Knowledge Sharing and Performance. *Organization Science, 18*(1), 71–88. doi:10.1287/orsc.1060.0223

Senge, P. (1997). Sharing knowledge. *Executive Excellence, 14*(11), 17–18.

Sobel, M. E. (1982). Asymptotic intervals for indirect effects in structural equations models. In S. Leinhart (Ed.), *Sociological methodology* (pp. 290–312). San Francisco: Jossey-Bass. doi:10.2307/270723

Spencer, J. W. (2003). Firms' knowledge-sharing strategies in the global innovation system: Empirical evidence from the flat panel display industry. *Strategic Management Journal, 24*(3), 217–233. doi:10.1002mj.290

Steinfield, C., DiMicco, J. M., Ellison, N. B., & Lampe, C. (2009, June). Bowling online: social networking and social capital within the organization. In *Proceedings of the fourth international conference on Communities and technologies* (pp. 245-254). ACM. 10.1145/1556460.1556496

Stevenson, M. A. (1997). The Antecedents and consequences of interpersonal trust in mixed-motive dyadic negotiation [Doctoral dissertation]. The Ohio State University.

Sykes, T. A., & Venkatesh, V. (2017). Explaining Post-Implementation Employee System Use and Job Performance: Impacts of the Content and Source of Social Network ties. *Management Information Systems Quarterly, 41*(3), 917–936. doi:10.25300/MISQ/2017/41.3.11

Tagliaventi, M. R., & Mattarelli, E. (2006). The role of networks of practice, value sharing and operational proximity in knowledge flows between professional groups. *Human Relations, 59*(3), 291–319. doi:10.1177/0018726706064175

Van Scotter, J. R., & Motowidlo, S. J. (1996). Interpersonal facilitation and job dedication as separate facets of contextual performance. *The Journal of Applied Psychology, 81*(5), 525–531. doi:10.1037/0021-9010.81.5.525

Wang, D., Guo, W., & Liu, X. (2009). Study on the Impact of Group Internal Social Network on Group Creativity. *Management Science*, (9): 25–28.

Wang, S., & Noe, R. A. (2010). Knowledge sharing: A review and directions for future research. *Human Resource Management Review, 20*(2), 115–131. doi:10.1016/j.hrmr.2009.10.001

Wang, S., Noe, R. A., & Wang, Z. M. (2011). Motivating Knowledge Sharing in Knowledge Management Systems. *Journal of Management, 40*(4), 978–1009. doi:10.1177/0149206311412192

Wasko, M. M., & Faraj, S. (2005). Why should I share? Examining social capital and knowledge contribution in electronic networks of practice. *Management Information Systems Quarterly, 29*(1), 35–57. doi:10.2307/25148667

Wimbush, J. C., Shepard, J. M., & Markham, S. E. (1997). An empirical examination of the relationship between ethical climate and ethical behavior from multiple levels of analysis. *Journal of Business Ethics, 16*(16), 1705–1716. doi:10.1023/A:1017952221572

Youssef, A. B., Martin, L., & Omrani, N. (2014). The complementarities between Information and Communication Technologies Use, New Organizational Practices and Employee's Contextual Performance: Evidence from Europe in 2005 and 2010. *Revue d Economie Politique Editions Dalloz, 124*(4), 493–504.

Yun, E. K. (2013). Predictors of attitude and intention to use knowledge management system among Korean nurses. *Nurse Education Today, 33*(12), 1477–1481. doi:10.1016/j.nedt.2013.05.018 PMID:23806194

Chapter 2
Optimizing Knowledge-Work Through Personal Knowledge Management:
The Role of Individual Knowledge-Workers' Motivation, Ability and Opportunity

Rezvan Hosseingholizadeh
Ferdowsi University of Mashhad, Iran

Hadi El-Farr
Rutgers University, USA

Somayyeh Ebrahimi Koushk Mahdi
Ferdowsi University of Mashhad, Iran

ABSTRACT

Knowledge-work is a discretionary behavior, and knowledge-workers should be viewed as investors of their intellectual capital. That said, effective knowledge-work is mostly dependent on the performance of individual knowledge-workers who drive the success of knowledge-intensive organizations. Therefore, the study takes the perspective of personal knowledge management in enforcing the effectiveness of knowledge-work activities. This study empirically demonstrates that knowledge-workers' behaviors are dependent on their motivation, ability and opportunity to perform knowledge-work activities. This study provides insights and future directions for research on knowledge-work as a discretionary behavior in organization and the factors influencing it. Scholars can investigate the effect of empowerment of individuals on their tendency to knowledge-creation, knowledge-sharing and knowledge-application. Since personal-knowledge often raise the issue of knowledge ownership, further attention to ethical issues may bring valuable insights for KM in organizations.

DOI: 10.4018/978-1-5225-7214-5.ch002

INTRODUCTION

Today's emerging age of knowledge economy has created a new class of employees, knowledge-workers (Packirisamy, Meenakshy, & Jagannathan, 2017), whose intellectual capital and whose tasks are widely unstructured and abstract (Shujahat, Sousa, Hussain, Nawaz, Wang, & Umer, 2017). As opposed to non-knowledge-work, the most important part of knowledge-work happens in the heads of employees even though the final result of their work has a manual character (Mládková, 2015). Most authors agree that there is a discernible trend in the workplace toward requiring employees to engage in some form of higher-level thinking, or cognitive processes, and to analyze information before undertaking actions (Jacobs, 2017). In these conditions, organizations are facing new challenges that will require the skills and creativity of knowledge-workers (Alexander, 2014). Research in knowledge management (KM) has acknowledged that individuals drive knowledge processes. The spotlight is on knowledge-workers, who are the true source of knowledge and are seen as the height of competitive advantage through continuous learning and innovation (Carleton, 2011). Nonetheless, there remains limited attention to the role of individuals in the discourse on KM (Rechberg & Syed, 2014; Carleton, 2011).

Extant literature has mostly focused on factors influencing KM effectiveness. The dominant literature in this field has viewed KM as an organizational initiative - highlighting the prominence of various organizational factors that impact KM effectiveness. Within this paradigm, KM is emphasized as a system that targets improving organizational effectiveness (Jennex, Smolnik, & Croasdell, 2009). Accordingly, KM success is a function of technological, organizational and environmental factors; including strategy, leadership/management support, knowledge content, processes, technology and structure (e.g. Yew Wong, 2005; Jennex & Olfman, 2005; Jennex et al., 2009; 2016; Basu & Sengupta, 2007; Lin, 2014; Sedighi, van Splunter, Zand, & Brazier, 2015). The literature lacks a framework for measuring KM effectiveness at the individual level, where individuals' participation will, directly or indirectly, affect organizational performance (Muhammed, Doll, & Deng, 2009; Hoq & Akter, 2012; Rechberg & Syed, 2014). Therefore, a new paradigm is needed that recognizes knowledge-workers as valued human assets; not as expendable cost centers (Serrat, 2017; Carleton, 2011; Turriago-Hoyos, Thoene, & Arjoon, 2016).

Historically KM was mostly concerned with explicit knowledge (knowledge-codification) and organizational knowledge. That said, the focus was less on the role of individual employees in the KM discourse (Muhammed et al., 2009; Hoq & Akter, 2012). Linking the individual-knowledge perspective to organizational success suggests a shift from traditional KM to personal KM (PKM) – focusing on individual and tacit knowledge (Cheong & Tsui, 2011; Muhammed et al., 2009). From the PKM perspective, knowledge is primarily created by individuals and then shared among a community of knowing (Ambulkar, Blackhurst, & Cantor, 2016; Muhammed et al., 2009). The value added of knowledge-workers is their tacit-knowledge and their capability to transmit it to actions (Davis, 2002). They capitalize on their personal and embedded-knowledge and depend less on codified and organizational-knowledge (El-Farr, 2009). Thus, knowledge-workers are the ones who are engaged in knowledge-work activities, and within them resides KM success (Hoq & Akter, 2012). From this perspective, knowledge-workers are seen as strategic-knowledge resources (Patalas-Maliszewska, 2013) and having significant value to organizations (Vaiman, 2010).

How to manage, improve and measure knowledge-work became central in the literature - arguing that effective knowledge-work activities such as knowledge creation, sharing and application are core goals for effective KM systems (Timonen & Paloheimo, 2011; Palvalin, Vuolle, Jääskeläinen, Laihonen,

& Lönnqvist, 2015). Therefore, the continuous improvement of knowledge-work performance is a key challenge for contemporary organizations – where their competitive advantage is derived from their ability to do so (Palvalin et al., 2015). That said, effective knowledge-work is mostly dependent on the performance of individual knowledge-workers who drive the success of knowledge-intensive organizations (Drucker, 1998; Palvalin et al., 2015) and it explores major challenges to human resource management (HRM) in managing knowledge-workers (Thite, 2004). As Jyoti and Rani (2017) noted, HR practices enhance the employees' knowledge, skills and abilities, increase their motivation and also empower them to use their knowledge, skill and abilities for organizational advantage. Therefore, effective HRM is one a major critical factor for attaining successful KM (Kuo, 2011).

A typology of knowledge-workers definitions, roles and knowledge-work actions could be deduced from the literature. Knowledge-work often is defined as a discretionary behavior and a system of activities that knowledge-workers opt to do. Thus, knowledge-workers are viewed as volunteers, investors, a valuable resource, self-directed learners and individual innovators and performers (Muhammed et al., 2009; Efimova, 2004; Kelloway & Barling, 2000; Drucker, 1998; Davenport, 2015; Ho, 2008; Mládková, 2015). Chadburn, Smith and Milan (2017) showed that Knowledge-workers prefer a flexible range of office settings that enable both a stimulating open and connected work environment, knowledge sharing, collaboration, as well as, quiet concentration locations, free of distractions and noise. The idea involves giving the knowledge-worker more responsibility for how work is done, thus, the knowledge-worker has more autonomy and flexibility to choose how, when and where the results are created (Palvalin, 2017). Therefore, managing knowledge-work should be mostly focusing on establishing conditions that increase the likelihood of knowledge-workers to make the "right" choices. Knowledge-workers make voluntary choices of when, how much and where to invest their knowledge and energy at work (Efimova, 2004). They are likely to engage in knowledge-work to the extent that they have the motivation, ability and opportunity to do so (Kelloway & Barling, 2000). In other words, an effective knowledge-worker needs to have clear goals (as a motivating factor) and the ability to perform the work flexibly in time and space (Van Iddekinge, Aguinis, Mackey, & DeOrtentiis, 2017; Palvalin, 2017; Shujahat et al., 2017). Moreover, knowledge-workers need to be engaged and have ownership of work, and their contributions need to be sustainable and are highly dependent on their ability and discretion (Kompaso & Sridevi, 2010). DW Rechberg and Syed (2014) highlighted the need for individuals' participation as a mandate for achieving a successful KM strategy. In fact, lack of individuals' participation in KM may not only hinder knowledge creation, but may also lead to a decline in organizational knowledge. Emphasizing the PKM perspective – Ambulkar et al. (2016) believe that the organizational ability to effectively manage knowledge is dependent on motivation, ability and opportunity. Motivated employees serve as important organizational assets and are the key to competitive advantage. To remain competitive, organizations must find effective ways to motivate knowledge-workers to generate and transfer knowledge and achieve higher levels of performance (Alexander, 2014).

More recently, researchers have drawn upon the MAO model of HRM and suggest that employee performance is a function of those three essential components (Hutchinson, 2013; Jiang, Lepak, Hu, & Baer, 2012; Okorogu, 2015). The MAO framework has successfully explained how and why motivation, ability and opportunity affect a wide range of organizational behaviors, among those are knowledge-work behaviors (Argote, McEvily, & Reagans, 2003). Therefore, focusing on PKM from an organizational behavior perspective and emphasizing the role of the individual in KM success has a lot of potential in the KM literature.

Moreover, Wright (2005) noted that individual workers apply knowledge processes to support their day-to-day work activities. Especially, as highest centers of learning, universities need to build information infrastructure and create a favorable atmosphere where teaching and non-teaching staff can take part in various KM activities. Most university employees could be considered as knowledge-workers; they are expected to have major roles in formulating the strategies and processes of modern universities. Moreover, university employees have an active role in changing universities' organizational cultures and individual behaviors relative to knowledge-work (Hoq & Akter, 2012). Therefore, the study context is university employees – a good representation of knowledge-workers.

Based on the preceding review, this study takes the perspective of PKM. It examines independent individual-level drivers (MOA) of knowledge-work. This perspective is based on the authors believe that Knowledge-workers are the ones responsible for creating, sharing and applying knowledge at work.

This chapter has three major objectives. The first is to understand the nature of knowledge-work and knowledge-workers. The second is to explain the impact of intrinsic and extrinsic motivation on knowledge-work, and the mediating role of ability and opportunity in this relationship. The third is to discuss the results and their impacts, emphasizing contributions to the improvement of knowledge-work as an organizational behavior.

THEORETICAL BACKGROUND AND HYPOTHESES

KM at the Individual Level

Success factors for effective KM systems are often confused or interchanged. Most of the literature focused on factors influencing the KM system – including information systems and their supporting formal and informal organizational mechanisms. For example, Jennex et al. (2009) highlighted that KM success is a multidimensional construct. Jennex and Olfman (2005) surveyed the literature on KM and identified twelve KM success factors. Later on, Jennex, et al. (2009; 2016) utilized a survey, based on an extensive literature review, to propose success factors, and validate them. Based on their findings, the definition and measure of KM success is a factor of various dimensions; business processes, impact on KM strategy, leadership/management support and knowledge content.

The exploratory study of Basu and Sengupta (2007) showed that integrated technical infrastructure, organizational culture, motivation and commitment of users and senior management support, all proved to contribute to the KM effectiveness. In addition, Lin (2014) showed that technological, organizational and environmental factors have different effects on KM adoption and implementation stages. Specifically, IT support has the strongest effect on the KM adoption stage, while a culture of knowledge-sharing has the strongest effect on the KM implementation stage.

The literature review shows that among all KM success factors, few studies have examined the role of the individual and accounted for the personal-knowledge perspective in KM success (Zhang, 2009). DW Rechberg and Syed (2014) showed an increased attention to the individual is essential to enhance the KM effectiveness in organizations. The review shows that existing KM practices may be improved through an increased focus on the role of individuals in designing and implementing KM in organizations. They proposed an individual-centric approach to KM that incorporates individuals' views in the design and implementation of KM practices. Without the participation of individuals, knowledge cannot be processed and KM may not be practiced. For KM to be effective, the focus has to be on individuals as their knowledge, skills, abilities, and other characteristics, and the way in which they create, share and put knowledge into action, will determine organizational performance. Accordingly, Reinhardt, Schmidt, Sloep and Drachsler (2011) presented a typology of 13 knowledge-work actions related to the roles of knowledge-workers. The knowledge-worker roles' typology includes the following: controller, helper, learner, linker, networker, organizer, retriever, sharer, solver, and tracker. Knowledge-work activities related to those roles include acquisition, analysis, authoring, co-authoring, disseminating, expert search, delivering feedback, information organization search, monitoring, learning and networking.

Therefore, some emerging literature highlights the importance of PKM in improving individual performance. Organizations should help individuals to be more effective at the personal level, organizational level and various social environments. Also, firms should assist in developing knowledge-workers' self-awareness of their abilities and limits (Cheong & Tsui, 2011). Thus, Knowledge-workers represent a new class of workers with different values, needs and motivation. Despite the critical role that knowledge-workers play in the creation and application of knowledge in the knowledge economy, the vast KM literature neglects the human element's role in knowledge-work at organizations and lacks clarity regarding what motivates knowledge-workers (Alexander, 2014). Consistent with this critique, Shujahat et al. (2017) results also signified the overarching role of the human and cultural approach to KM. Thus, this paper takes the PKM standpoint; focusing on the role of the individual, the knowledge-worker, in achieving effective KM activities.

Understanding Knowledge-Work and Knowledge-Worker

Knowledge-work and knowledge-worker are poorly defined in the literature with competing and ambiguous definitions related (Alexander, 2014). However, there have been numerous attempts to clearly define them, and they are often used interchangeably with other similar concepts such as professional work and creative work (Lone, 2016). The knowledge-worker terminology was introduced way back in the early 1960s. Machlup's (1962) work on production and distribution of knowledge development in the United States gave way to series of contributions and clarifications to the role of knowledge and terms such as knowledge-work, knowledge-worker, knowledge-organization, knowledge-economy and knowledge-society (Packirisamy et al., 2017).

Toffler (1970) foresaw the emergence of highly educated individuals who could be labeled as knowledge-workers. From Toffler's perspective, knowledge-workers were individuals who were primarily involved in research and development-related occupations, and who are responsible for creating, processing, and enhancing information as their primary work outcomes. Toffler's perspective on the exclusive nature of who uses knowledge in the workplace would have a lasting effect on how scholars define knowledge-work. Later, Drucker (1992) discussed the importance of knowledge as a contributor to the wealth of capitalist societies in which knowledge serves as a value-added component to work (As cited in Jacobs, 2017). Drucker (1969) and Bell (1968) were the main influencers when the concept emerged in the scientific discussion from 1974 to 1992. After this period, we can distinguish a slow diffusion period from 1993 to 2003, when the concept started to gain attention, and a fast diffusion period from 1999 to 2003, when the research proliferated. Based on the variety of existing definitions, many scholars claim that both concepts, knowledge-work and knowledge-workers, are still ambiguous (Timonen & Paloheimo, 2008). Todericiu, Serban and Dumitrascu (2013) noted that a wide range of definitions of knowledge-work from "those who create knowledge" to "those who use knowledge" are almost universally accepted. Despite the diversity of perspectives on how to conceptualize knowledge-work (Hislop, 2008), a clear definition has not yet been established. The problem with defining knowledge-work is the argument that knowledge is a mandate to achieve any work activity (Palvalin et al., 2015). There are four key types of knowledge-work based on various criteria (e.g. Reinhardt et al., 2011; Davis, 2002, Davenport, 2015). For example, Davenport (2015) focused on differentiating types of knowledge-workers by the level of integration and expertise, with different process-oriented interventions for each type knowledge creation, distribution and application. That said, classifications of knowledge-work could be deduced from the literature according to the following.

Knowledge-Work as a Profession

Knowledge-work is commonly defined as a profession or individual activities that involve information processing, creative problem solving, the production of knowledge, and/or varied and complex. Those activities require skills of highly qualified and educated professionals (Alexander, 2014). A profession is a specific kind of intellectual occupations (Jemielniak, 2012). This perspective is the dominant traditional perspective in the literature. By this definition, some professions under this classification are analysts, programmers, software engineers, designers, concept designers, managers, professors, scientists, medical doctors, and accountants (Vaiman, 2010; Olsen, 2016; Shujahat et al., 2017; Lone, 2016).. In this perspective, knowledge-work is identified by broad measures such as job titles or education levels (Mládková, 2015; Widmann, 2013). Knowledge-intensive work can either be based on scientific knowledge, such as in research and development occupations, high-technology engineering, or can be considered as professional work, such as lawyers and accountants (Widmann, 2013). It sounds that this approach is dependent on job content and industry-driven approaches, identifying knowledge-workers as employees within a specific set of occupations and those who work in particular organizations or in particular sectors or institutions (Mládková, 2015). This approach is rooted in the Tayloristic tradition of separating 'thinking' and 'doing' in organizations (Hislop, 2008; Bosch-Sijtsema, Fruchter, Vartiainen, & Ruohomäki, 2011). Knowledge in this context is the technical knowledge that has the power to improve the "can-do" attribute (Turriago-Hoyos et al., 2016).

This approach to knowledge-work has been criticized for being elitist and ignoring the fact that modern work often implies employee participation in planning, decision-making, and creative problem-solving across different occupations and organizational roles (Lone, 2016). Another critique is that Knowledge-work cannot be only deduced through looking at job titles or educational levels (Brinkley, Fauth, Mahdon, & Theodoropoulou, 2009; Lone, 2016). Thompson, et al. (2001) suggests that the emphasis on abstract theoretical knowledge leads to the neglect of other important types of knowledge required to accomplish tasks. An example is tacit-knowledge that does not necessarily reflect high levels of formal education or the occupation of knowledge-intensive professions (As cited in Hislop, 2008). In other words, the main weakness of this classification is that it focuses on past behavior (e.g. education, experience) rather than current behavior and contribution to the organization (Lone, 2016). Tacit knowledge is embedded in the behavior, attitude, perception, ideology and beliefs of individuals (Hoq & Akter, 2012). Knowledge-workers add value to organizations due their tacit-knowledge and their ability to transfer it into work activities (Davis, 2002).

Knowledge-Work as an Individual Characteristic

Based on this perspective, the creation of value or being innovative becomes the hallmark of knowledge-work rather than incumbency in a particular position (Tampoe, 1993; Wang & Ahmad, 2003; Hislop, 2008). According to Wang and Ahmad (2003) the nature of knowledge-work is complex, ill-defined, and requires a higher degree of creativity. Therefore, knowledge-workers are regarded as the new 'gold-collar workers' because they are educated, smart, creative and computer literate, as well as equipped with transferable skills. They are seen as innovative and energetic individuals with a high level of intelligence and self-discipline, and they are relentless in their pursuit of knowledge (Vaiman, 2010). This approach to knowledge-work emphasizes current behaviors. However, it could lead to a simplistic categorization of employees into two classes; those who are creative, and those who are not. Moreover, it is unclear whether knowledge-workers are inherently more creative or innovative, or whether their work settings provide more opportunities to express creativity (Lone, 2016).

Knowledge-Work as an Individual Activity

In this approach, knowledge-work is defined in terms of the balance of 'thinking' and 'doing' activities (Kelloway & Barling, 2000) and the term 'knowledge-worker' has evolved to include people who 'use their heads more than their hands' to produce value (Vaiman, 2010). The context of knowledge-work was introduced by Drucker (1959) when he used it as a term to separate knowledge-work from manual work. Drucker proposed that knowledge-workers are the ones who their work tasks primarily have to deal with information or knowledge-workers are the ones who develop and use knowledge in the workplace (Palvalin et al., 2015). Drucker (1998) defines knowledge-work as comprising those jobs in which incumbents work more with their heads rather than with their hands. In fairness Drucker does not specify the differences between knowledge and service workers, as service workers are not equivalent to knowledge-workers. However, critics have pointed out that if knowledge-work includes all work in which intellectual abilities are used, it could be stated that we all are doing some form of knowledge-work, and the concept would be not be very useful (Lone, 2016).

Knowledge-Work as a Dimension of Work

Finally, according to Kelloway and Barling (2000), building on criticisms of the former definitional strategies, scholars have suggested that categorical approaches to defining knowledge-work should be discarded, and that knowledge-work instead should be understood as a dimension of work that varies along a continuum (As cited in Lone, 2016).knowledge-work consists primarily of using employees' knowledge to meet organizational goals and objectives. Employees add value to knowledge-work through their ideas, intuition, analysis, judgment, synthesis and designs (Alexander, 2014). Knowledge-work is the sort of intellectual and cognitive work in which new knowledge is created and applied (Shujahat et al., 2017).

According to Kelloway and Barling (2000), knowledge-work is defined as a discretionary behavior focused on the knowledge usage. In this regard, Davenport (2015) takes a "process" perspective on knowledge-work. He suggests that the process orientation differs by whether workers create knowledge, share it, or apply it. According to Davenport's (2015), the primary purpose of knowledge-workers' contribution involves the creation, distribution, or application of knowledge. Based on Drucker's (1999) knowledge productivity theory, Knowledge-workers are said to be involved in defining the scope of their work, being self-managed, searching for new ways of doing things, continuously learning and teaching others, and emphasizing both the quality and quantity of the outcomes (Jacobs, 2017). Knowledge-work productivity depends on good self-management. For example, productive knowledge-workers should be able to self-manage productivity, self-motivate themselves and identify any need for attention (Davis, 2002). In other words, "managing oneself" and being autonomous are central features of work in the knowledge society insofar as a knowledge-worker needs to become aware of personal strengths via feedback analysis, self-examination, and building self-awareness (Drucker, 2005 cited in Turriago-Hoyos et al., 2016).

Turriago-Hoyos et al. (2016) addressed the role of knowledge-workers' virtues within the knowledge society according to the late Peter Drucker's management theory as synthesized by Maciariello (2009). They identified prudence, effectiveness, excellence, integrity, and truthfulness as the knowledge-worker's intellectual virtues, whereas practical wisdom, responsibility, cooperation, and courage are seen to constitute the knowledge-worker's moral character. Based on this perspective, all workers are knowledge-workers to a certain extent, depending on the nature and intensity of the possessed skills and working knowledge, rather than just claiming it as the possession of a minority group (Collins, 1997). In this view, knowledge-work is not a category and is not an occupation but is a dimension of work.

Knowledge-workers have value because of their knowledge and their abilities to apply it in work activities. They are expected to possess formal knowledge consisting of general principles, concepts, and procedures related to classes of problems and domains of work. They also have some procedural knowledge about typical procedures, forms, and rules governing a domain of work (Davis, 2002). According to Jacobs (2017) Knowledge-based tasks are the units of work that require individuals, in the presence of complex work situations, to call upon relevant sets of information, to decide which actions they should take based on the information, and to engage in those actions that will accomplish the unit of work. In this view, a more useful way to distinguish knowledge-based tasks is through the complexity of the work. That said, a knowledge-worker's organizational advantage is defined by tacit knowledge, effective information processing, superior soft skills, and creative problem-solving abilities (Carleton, 2011).

When we shift our attention from knowledge to knowledge-work, new dimensions emerge. If knowledge-workers give us the sustainable competitive advantage, we need to understand who they are and if and how they are different from the other so-called non-knowledge-workers (Thite, 2004). Thus, knowledge-work is defined as a set of employee activities. In this regard, Davenport (2015) takes a "process" perspective on knowledge-work. He suggests that the process orientation differs by whether workers create knowledge, share it, or apply it. According to Davenport's (2015) definition, knowledge-workers have high degrees of expertise, education, and experience. Moreover, the primary purpose of their jobs involves the creation, distribution, or application of knowledge.

To summarize, in this paper, we apply the term knowledge-workers within the broader category of highly skilled workers. Based on perceiving knowledge-work as an individual activity and as a dimension of work, knowledge-work is characterized by self-management (Davis, 2002) and knowledge-workers are best described as investors. As investors, employees choose the time and extent of investing their knowledge and often have the power to resist being told what to do (Davenport, 2015; Kelloway & Barling, 2000). Moreover, Davenport (2015) defined knowledge-work within three different activities: knowledge-creation, knowledge-sharing and knowledge-application. Each of these activities is seen as a discretionary behavior. Employees are likely to engage in knowledge work to the extent that they have the motivation, ability and opportunity to do so (Kelloway & Barling, 2000). Hence, the operational definition of knowledge-work is the process of knowledge creation, knowledge sharing, and knowledge utilization. The antecedents of these processes are the motivation, capability and opportunity (as cited in Shujahat et al., 2017). The implicit assumption of this study is that the success of knowledge-work depends on motivation, ability and opportunity of knowledge-workers to create, share and apply knowledge.

Motivation, Ability, and Opportunity to Knowledge-Work

The MAO framework is a well-established model for explaining work performance. Initially proposed by Bailey (1993) and developed by Appelbaum et al. (2000), MAO has become a commonly accepted framework to explain how human resource (HR) policies might influence employees' performance (cited in Hutchinson, 2013). This model suggests that a person's "capacity to work", "will to work" and "opportunity to perform" jointly determine the level of performance (Kelloway & Barling, 2000; Tuuli, 2012). The MAO framework also has been successfully employed to explain a wide array of behaviors such as consumer behavior, commercial information process and public relations (Hallahan, 2001), and firm-level decision-making and social capital activation (Binney, Oppenheim, & Hall, 2006). More recently, MAO has been used as a conceptual framework for explaining knowledge sharing behaviors (e.g., Chang, Gong & Peng, 2012; Siemsen, Roth, & Balasubramanian, 2008). Therefore, MAO might help in explaining how and why certain contextual individual properties affect KM outcomes.

Motivation to Knowledge-Work

Motivation is "an unobservable force that directs, energizes, and sustains behavior" most definitions refer to the idea that work motivation directly affects the direction, intensity, and duration or persistence of effort. Motivation is reflected in the choices workers make about whether to expend effort, the level of effort they expend, and how much they persist in that level of effort (Van Iddekinge et al., 2017). In the context of the MAO theory, motivation to knowledge-work refers to heightening arousal so that employees could be ready, willing, or interested in implementing knowledge-work (Hallahan, 2001; Leung & Bai, 2013). They cannot be enforced to share their knowledge but can be motivated to willingly do so. Therefore, motivated employees have the ability to positively impact organizational performance such as participating in knowledge-work activities (Alexander, 2014). KM initiatives' failure or success depends to a high extent on the knowledge-workers' willingness to adopt new practices and tools (Hussain, Ahmed & Si, 2010; Efimova, 2004). Ajmal, Helo and Kekäle (2010) revealed that the absence of incentives for employees who engage in KM initiatives was the most significant barrier to the success of KM initiatives in project-based firms. According to Yew Wong (2005) if individuals are not motivated to practice KM activities, then no amount of investment, infrastructure and technological intervention will make KM effective. Gumusluoglu and Karakitapoglu-Ayglin (2010) observed that knowledge-workers were generally attracted to careers that allowed them to develop their potential, stimulated their personal and intellectual capacity, and encouraged them to develop their career goals.

In examining motivation, Ryan and Deci (2000) distinguished between extrinsic motivation and intrinsic motivation. Research has emphasized the crucial role of intrinsic motivators in enforcing knowledge-work behaviors such as knowledge-sharing, transfer and contribution (e.g. Lin, 2007; Cruz, Pérez & Cantero, 2009; Huang, Chiu & Lu, 2013; Alexander, 2014). Incentives help to stimulate and reinforce positive employee behaviors and culture needed for effective KM (Yew Wong, 2005). Ajmal et al. (2010) revealed that the absence of incentives for employees who engage in KM initiatives was the most significant barrier to the success of KM initiatives in project-based firms. According to Yew Wong (2005) if individuals are not motivated to practice KM activities, then no amount of investment, infrastructure and technological intervention will make it effective. Hence, one of the important factors is to establish the right incentives, rewards or motivational aids to encourage individuals to share, create and apply knowledge. Liu (2012) showed that knowledge incentive mechanisms promote the psychological ownership by the knowledge owner, so that the employee actively carries out knowledge innovation. This implies that knowledge incentive mechanisms stress private proprietary characteristics of employees who possess real ownership when they innovate. This will deem such innovation as an extension of self; giving rise to a protective or defensive mindset, which then has an impact on individual knowledge creation behaviors because of the psychological ownership of knowledge. According to Jones and Chung (2006), knowledge-workers are more motivated with intrinsic motivators as compared to extrinsic motivators. They identified examples of intrinsic motivators, such as providing challenging work assignments, personal recognition, and realistic promotional opportunities. Farr and Brazil (2009 as cited in Widmann, 2013) provided some intrinsic motivators of engineers, including opportunities for self-actualization, learning, and continued professional development. Welschen, Todorova & Mills (2012) proposed a model that examines the role of intrinsic motivation in knowledge sharing. The results show self-efficacy, meaningfulness and impact are important motivators of attitude towards knowledge sharing, which in turn impacts intention to share knowledge. Accordingly, mixtures of rewards are needed to motivate knowledge-workers.

That said both intrinsic and extrinsic rewards are important to increase employees' willingness to share their knowledge, especially tacit knowledge (Huang et al., 2013). Thus, this study applies expected organizational rewards and reciprocal benefits as extrinsic salient determinants and self- efficacy and enjoyment in helping others as employees' intrinsic salient determinates to explain knowledge-work behavior. The theory of planned behavior posits an obvious argument: intention, which is assumed to capture intrinsic and extrinsic motivational factors determines behavior, hence action (Serrat, 2017). Intention refers to the individual's motivation and willingness to engage in a particular behavior as long as the behavior is under the control of the actor (Ajzen, 1991). The theory of planned behavior (TPB) as developed by Ajzen (1991) is one of the best social-psychological frameworks that explains and predicts human behavior

Hypothesis One: Intrinsic and Extrinsic motivation will be positively related to knowledge-work, such that employees performing knowledge-work are more motivated by intrinsic motivators than extrinsic motivators.

Ability to Knowledge-Work

Ability relates to performance primarily through job knowledge, such that high-ability workers tend to demonstrate higher performance because they are better able to acquire and use job-relevant knowledge, compared to those who possess lower levels of ability (Van Iddekinge et al., 2017). Ability refers to the extent to which individuals have the necessary resources (e.g. knowledge, intelligence, money) to make an outcome happen (Leung & Bai, 2013) and it is a strong predictor of organizational performance (Jyoti & Rani, 2017). It refers to individuals' skill or proficiency at solving problems or their knowledge of how to act (Binney et al., 2006). This view is based on the notion that people will not act if their actions do not serve relevant goals, and that when the ability to act is absent, the existence of a goal cannot lead to the intended result; and it suggests that the relationship between motivation and performance is stronger the higher the ability level.

Accomplishing knowledge-work is a result of personal capability, such as skills, experience, or intelligence. According to Argote et al. (2003) individual abilities are partially innate, but they are also enriched through training and experience; formal and informal mechanisms of accumulating personal human capital. Individuals' embedded ability to create the meaning of things, reflect and interpret situations has a crucial role in effective KM (DW Rechberg & Syed, 2014).

Several studies have also recognized the role of ability in knowledge sharing (Siemsen et al., 2008). Hussain et al. (2010) showed that individuals who possess more personal-knowledge capabilities are more effective in performing KM activities and ensuring KM success. Therefore, if knowledge-intensive organizations are the ones that attain their competitive advantages based on the uniqueness of embedded knowledge within their individual employees, then their knowledge-workers' abilities are the essential determinate for organizational success.

This study found that the ability is the dimension of high knowledge-work, e.g. the employees' ability to conduct knowledge-work refers to the extent of their embedded personal-knowledge and skills that enable them and are required to implement knowledge-work activities and tasks (Siemsen et al., 2008). According to Drucker (2006), the motivation of the knowledge-worker depends on him/her being effective and able to achieve. Productivity for the knowledge-worker, who produces knowledge, ideas, information, means the ability to get the right things done. Thus, highly able or knowledgeable individuals are presumably more capable of creating, sharing and applying knowledge than individuals with low-ability.

Hypothesis Two: Ability is positively related to knowledge-work such that this relationship will be stronger for employees of high-ability than those with low ability.

Since motivated employees make use of their cognitive, affective and conative abilities to achieve organizational goals (Kaur, 2015; Binney et al., 2006), thus it seems motivation has an impact on knowledge-work through ability as a mediator variable.

Hypothesis Three: ability has a mediator role in the relationship between motivation and knowledge-work.

Opportunity to Knowledge-Work

Opportunity in the MAO framework refers to the situational factors that can either enhance or impede information processing. MacInnis and Jaworski (1989) identified several situational factors such as time availability, attention paid, and distractions (cited in Leung & Bai, 2013). Chang et al. (2012) stated that knowledge does not easily transfer unless the knowledge-transfer agents have sufficient motivations and opportunities to transfer knowledge. In addition, Argote et al. (2003:578) argue that "ability and extra effort are even more valuable when coupled with opportunity". Siemsen et al. (2008) stated that one of the most important operational constraints among coworkers is time. Cleveland and Elli (2015) revealed that knowledge seeking behaviors depend to a large extent on the perceived time available to the knowledge seekers. In this study, we define time availability (TA) as the degree to which an employee has slack time available to participate in knowledge-work activities.

Hypothesis Four: Opportunity is positively related to knowledge-work such that this relationship will be stronger for employees of high- time availability than those low in time availability.

The precise inter-relationship among the MAO variables and how they interact to influence performance behaviors still remain largely unclear. Three competing models, a multiplicative, linear and constraining-factor model (CFM), reflect different levels of complementarity and interaction among motivation, ability and opportunity, and their impact on performance behaviors are specified (Tuuli, 2012). This multiplicative model predicts that when individuals possess little or no motivation, they will demonstrate similarly low levels of performance regardless of their ability level. Various theoretical backgrounds support the multiplicative model empirically, logically, and psychologically, it is convincing. (Van Iddekinge et al., 2017). Van Iddekinge et al. (2017) tested the interactive, additive, and relative effects of cognitive ability and motivation on Performance using a Meta-Analysis. A triangulation of evidence based on several types of analyses revealed that the effects of ability and motivation on performance are additive rather than multiplicative. Ability and motivation were similarly important to job performance.

Some studies have found support for the interaction, others have not and one study even found a negative interaction. The existing evidence for an interaction between motivation and ability in determining performance is extremely weak. For example, Campbell and Pritchard (1976) stated: "The attempts to account for additional variance in performance by some multiplicative combination of motivational and ability variables have been singularly unsuccessful" (p. 91). One reason for these inconsistent findings is the low statistical power in detecting interaction, which is associated primarily with the low reliability of the product term and with the small residual variance of this term when the main effects are controlled for (Ganzach, Saporta & Weber, 2000). Thus, Ganzach et al., (2000) showed that the interaction was positive when a logistic model was used and negative when a linear probability model was used. The reason for the difference in the results of the two models is examined, and the conditions under which this difference occurs are discussed.

While there is some theoretical evidence to suggest that MAO are complementary in driving behavior, existing empirical evidence from work-performance theories suggests that little explanatory power is gained by adding interaction terms (Siemsen et al., 2008). This paradox leads Siemsen, et al. (2008) to propose an alternative model referred to as CFM. The central notion of this model is that in the absence of any of the MAO variables, no action will take place, but it does not additionally impose a continuous change in the size of the effect. From this perspective, the multiplicative model does not exhibit a significantly improved fit over a linear model. Also, Minbaeva (2013) stated that none of the studies simultaneously considered the interaction effects among motivation, ability and opportunity. There is limited empirical evidence available about the joint effects and roles of motivation, ability and opportunity on knowledge-work activities.

Hypothesis Five: the multiplicative interaction among motivation, ability and opportunity will not explain significantly more variance than the linear model.

METHOD

Participants

The study utilized a survey for data collection. The survey was sent to 1,245 staff of the Ferdowsi University of Mashhad. The response rate was 28.11%., where 350 employees completed the survey. A total of 170 respondents were females (48.6%) and 180 respondents were males (51.4%). Most participants have a high-level education. The average work tenure was 14.75 years. Basic information of participants is illustrated in Table 1.

Table 1. Basic information of participants

Participants Characteristics	Frequency	Percent
Gender		
Male	180	51.4
Female	170	48.6
Education Level		
Diploma	47	13.4
B.A.	167	47.7
M.A.	118	33.7
Ph.D.	14	4
Years of tenure		
<5	43	12.3
5-10	71	20.3
10-15	56	16
15-20	48	13.7
20-25	83	23.7
>25	31	8.9
Occupation		
Administration	22	6.3
academic and graduate affairs	38	10.9
research and technology	45	12.9
cultural and student affairs	21	6
finance	51	14.6
planning and budgeting	59	16.9
faculty	99	28.3

Note: *n* = 350

Measures

Measurement items were developed on the basis of a comprehensive review of the literature and modified to suit the KM context. Knowledge-work was assessed with 11 items based on Chennamaneni et al. (2012), North and Gueldenberg (2011), and Siemsen et al. (2008). The items measured the extent to which employees create, share and apply knowledge during their day-to-day work activities. Motivation was measured by 22 items that are adapted from Lin (2007), Cruz et al. (2009), and Kankanhalli, Tan & Wei (2005). The items reflect the extent to which employees believe that they will receive extrinsic and intrinsic incentives through their knowledge activities. A total of 3 items measuring opportunity were adapted from Siemsen, et al. (2008), measuring the extent of time that employees spend to create, share and apply knowledge. Finally, the ability of employees to create, share and apply knowledge and experience was assessed by 4 item adapted from Siemsen et al. (2008) and Lee, Lee and Kang (2005).

Analytical Procedures

The data was analyzed based on structural equation modeling (SEM) techniques. The SEM process centers around two steps: validating the measurement model and fitting the structural model. The former is accomplished primarily through confirmatory factor analysis using LISREL, a software package based on SEM techniques. The latter is accomplished primarily through path analysis with latent variables analysis (Garson, 2008). We used partial least squares (PLS). PLS assesses the structural model - relationships among constructs. Moreover, the multiplicative interaction among MAO in hypotheses 4 was tested by using hierarchical linear modeling. Since the data was self-reported, all construct items were subjected to principal components factor analysis. The results indicated that multiple factors emerged to explain the data variance. Therefore, CMV does not appear to be a serious concern for this study.

RESULTS

Correlations and Statistics Information

The descriptive information of the variables is reported in Table 2. Correlations were computed among variables. The results suggest that correlations were statistically significant between all variables, with the exception of opportunity and Extrinsic Motivation, sharing knowledge. The correlations of KM with Intrinsic Motivation, Extrinsic Motivation, Ability and opportunity were statistically significant. Highest correlations are seen between the Intrinsic Motivation and KM, r = +.72, p < .01, two-tailed. Lowest correlations are seen between the opportunity and KM, r = +.19, p < .01, two-tailed.

Measurement Model

The measurement model is that part of a PLS model which deals with the latent variables and their indicators. The measurement model of all constructs was evaluated to demonstrate the quality of the measurement. In this study, the measurement model with all four constructs (knowledge-work, motivation, ability and opportunity) was assessed using confirmatory factor analysis. Table 3 shows loadings and the corresponding t-values of indicators in the measurement model. Overall, all loadings exceed

Table 2. Correlations and statistics table

SD	1M	1N	18	17	16	15	4	3	2	1	
0.48	2.25	350								1	1. Intrinsic Motivation
0.54	3.30	350							1	0.357**	2. Extrinsic Motivation
0.45	2.45	350						1	0.265**	0.690**	3. Ability
0.3	2.92	349					1	0.173**	0.073	0.250**	4. Opportunity
0.53	2.75	350				1	0.067	0.372**	0.542**	0.535**	5. Sharing
0.77	2.38	349			1	0.357**	0.157**	0.596**	0.316**	0.539**	6. Creation
0.57	2.4	350		1	0.623**	0.495**	0.270**	0.567**	0.373**	0.682**	7. Application
0.49	2.55	350	1	0.849**	0.765**	0.807**	0.194**	0.625**	0.518**	0.722**	8. K-Work

** Correlation is significant at the 0.01 level (2-tailed)

0.6 and each indicator is significant at 0.05 levels. Also, the reliability of the constructs (composite reliability), and the average variance extracted were used as the measures of convergent validity. The composite reliability should be greater than 0.5 and the average variance extracted should be at least 0.6., but we can accept 0.4. (Fornell & Larcker, 1981). Hence, the measurement model seems to possess adequate convergent validity.

The measurement model exhibited a good level of model fit. For knowledge-work construct, the chi-square/degrees of freedom ratio is 245.58/87. The GFI is 0.93, AGFI is 0.96, NFI is 0.93, CFI is 0.91, and RMSEA is 0.082. For motivation construct, the chi-square/degrees of freedom ratio is 4745.39/1793. The GFI is 0.93, AGFI is 0.95, NFI is 0.91, CFI is 0.92, and RMSEA is 0.078. For ability construct, the chi-square/degrees of freedom ratio is 5.29/2. The GFI is 0.97, AGFI is 0.91, NFI is 0.92, CFI is 0.94, and RMSEA is 0.082. For opportunity construct, the chi-square/degrees of freedom ratio is 29.19/9. The GFI is 0.93, AGFI is 0.90, NFI is 0.91, CFI is 0.89, and RMSEA is 0.077. Goodness of fit measures for the constructs of research model presented in Table 4.

Structural Model

The structural model analysis was conducted to examine the hypothesized relationships among constructs. The results from the structural model are shown in Table 4 and Figure 1. The results provided support for all the first four hypotheses. All of the path coefficients were statistically significant ($p < 0.05$) and greater than 0.30, which is considered meaningful. The relationship between motivation and knowledge-work is statistically significant; thus, intrinsic and extrinsic motivation will be positively related to knowledge-work. That said, intrinsic motivation has more influence on knowledge-work than extrinsic motivation. Linear regression results showed that Self-efficacy (b= 0.70, SE= 0.032, p<.05) and enjoyment in helping others (b= 0.46, SE= 0.029, p<.05) as intrinsic motivation indicators have a positive impact on knowledge-work more than organizational rewards and reciprocal benefits as extrinsic motivation indicators.

The R^2 indicates the amount of variance explained by the model. R^2 value determines the prediction power of the model. As showed in Table 5, approximately 72.5% of the changes in knowledge-work are

Table 3. The measurement model

constructs	Indicators	Items	Factor Loading	t-value	Std. Error	Composite Reliability	Average Variance Extracted (AVE)
Knowledge work	Knowledge creation	Q1	0.832	32.846	0.025	0.843	0.643
		Q2	0.768	27.826	0.028		
		Q3	0.765	18.646	0.041		
		Q4	0.691	13.322	0.052		
	Knowledge application	Q5	0.676	10.922	0.062		
		Q6	0.813	32.952	0.025		
		Q7	0.717	16.217	0.044		
		Q8	0.694	15.812	0.044		
	Knowledge sharing	Q9	0.642	4.510	0.142		
		Q10	0.741	7.307	0.101		
		Q11	0.752	13.060	0.058		
Motivation	organizational rewards	Q12	0.734	9.707	0.076	0.754	0.500
		Q13	0.804	26.550	0.030		
		Q14	0.722	15.320	0.047		
		Q15	0.889	51.624	0.017		
		Q16	0.747	12.069	0.062		
		Q17	0.834	26.923	0.031		
		Q18	0.698	7.810	0.089		
		Q19	0.729	9.661	0.075		
		Q20	0.632	6.479	0.098		
	reciprocal benefits	Q21	0.732	11.241	0.065		
		Q22	0.741	10.058	0.074		
		Q23	0.725	11.855	0.061		
	enjoyment in helping others	Q24	0.754	15.027	0.050		
		Q25	0.706	12.979	0.054		
		Q26	0.722	16.926	0.043		
		Q27	0.695	15.110	0.046		
		Q28	0.742	16.582	0.045		
	self- efficacy	Q29	0.657	12.820	0.051		
		Q30	0.671	10.873	0.062		
		Q31	0.737	17.948	0.041		
		Q32	0.671	12.064	0.056		
		Q33	0.763	26.424	0.029		
Opportunity		Q34	0.951	5.857	0.162	0.793	0.567
		Q35	0.725	3.529	0.206		
		Q36	0.422	2.682	0.251		
Ability		Q37	0.730	15.095	0.048	0.816	0.527
		Q38	0.798	25.228	0.032		
		Q39	0.710	14.078	0.050		
		Q40	0.658	12.092	0.054		

Table 4. Goodness of fit measures for the constructs of the research model

constructs	χ2/df	GFI	AGFI	NFI	CFI	RMSEA
Knowledge work	245.58/87	0.93	0.96	0.93	0.91	0.082
Motivation	4745.39/1793	0.93	0.95	0.91	0.92	0.078
Opportunity	29.19/9	0.93	0.90	0.91	0.89	0.077
Ability	5.29/2	0.97	0.91	0.92	0.94	0.082

Table 5. R² Value, Path Coefficients and Significance Levels of the model constructs

Constructs	R²	Path Coefficients	Std. Error	T Value	hypothesis
Motivation> KW		0.571	0.056	10.20	supported
Opportunity>KW	0.725	0.089	0.043	2.05	supported
Ability>KW		0.327	0.063	5.174	supported
Motivation>ability	0.443	0.665	0.038	17.308	supported

Figure 1. Path coefficients for MAO modeling to knowledge work
Note: The model shows path coefficients and corresponding t-value in parentheses.
*Significant at p < 0.0001

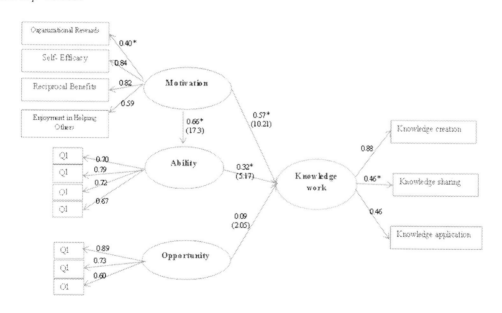

explained by motivation, ability and opportunity, and 44.3% of the changes of ability are explained by motivation.

We tested hypothesis 5 by using hierarchical linear modeling to examine the multiplicative interaction among MAO on knowledge-work. The multiplicative term between motivation and ability was computed and introduced in the regression equation as a predictor at level 3. Thus, in final model, their interaction effects (M×A: b= -0.245, SE= 0.075, p>.05; M×O: b= 0.627, SE= 0.089, p>.05; M×O×A: b= 0.356,

SE= 0.234, p> 05) were entered, implying that adding interaction terms could not significantly improve the predictive power of the model (ΔR^2= 0.005). To confirm the results, we used K-means clustering method, and the data was classified into three clusters including low-MAO, middle MAO and high-MAO. Cluster analysis is a statistical technique used to group cases into homogeneous subgroups based on responses to variables. The results revealed that the greatest extent of knowledge-work performance is related to the group that simultaneously has the high amount of motivation, ability and opportunity. Also, ANOVA showed that the difference between those three groups (low-MAO, mode MAO and high-MAO) was significant (F= 82.90, df = 2). Figure 2 gives a graphical representation of comparison groups.

DISCUSSION

We undertook this study based on the behavioral perspective of knowledge-work at the individual level. Without a doubt, KM has much to do with behavioral change. For that reason, high-performance organizations seek to minimize the drag of old mental models and help embed knowledge behaviors (Serrat, 2017). The individual's behavioral intention is believed to process his or her ability to share knowledge into actual knowledge-sharing (Mafabi, Nasiima, Muhimbise, Kaekende, & Nakiyonga, 2017).The results provide strong support to the proposed hypotheses. Findings confirm that knowledge-work is influenced by motivation, ability and opportunity. Our research model demonstrates good explanatory power for knowledge-work, with over 0.725 of the variance explained (R^2= 72.5%). The strongest di-

Figure 2. K-means cluster analysis of MAO effect on knowledge work
Note: Low-MAO (N=45): ability (M=12), motivation (M=58.18) and opportunity (M=10.38)
Mod-MAO (N=153): ability (M=14.67), motivation (M=76.99) and opportunity (M=11)
High-MAO (N=151): ability (M=17.83), motivation (M=93) and opportunity (M=11.61)

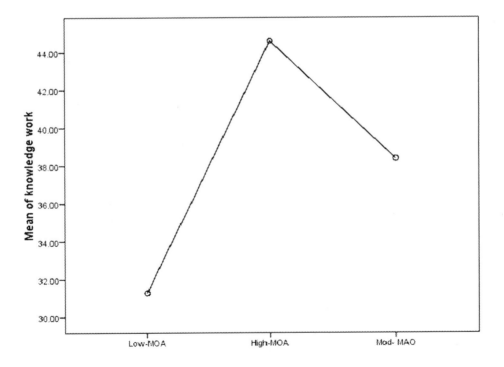

rect determinant of knowledge-work is motivation (.57 vs. .37 for ability and .09 for opportunity). The result also found that intrinsic motivators tend to be the most influential drivers in knowledge-work, as compared to extrinsic motivators. This is consistent with previous findings that highlighted the crucial role of motivation, especially intrinsic motivators, in improving KM activities (e.g. Cruz et al., 2009; Huang et al., 2013). Particularly, establishing the right incentive portfolio such as rewards and motivational aids to encourage people to share and apply knowledge is vital for knowledge-work effectiveness (Yew Wong, 2005). This is consistent with Argote et al. (2003) who argued that motivation is one of the causal mechanisms to participate in KM processes. Ajmal et al. (2010) also revealed that the absence of incentives for employees who engage in KM initiatives was the most significant barrier to the success KM initiatives.

According to Carleton (2011), some ways to motivate and retain knowledge-workers include: providing challenging and meaningful work, enabling learning and career development opportunities, ensuring adequate resources, recognizing contributions, and creating a supportive environment. Results also found that motivation has indirect effects on knowledge-work. As the model showed motivation explains 44 percent of the variance in ability. Hence, it seems ability plays the role of a mediator variable between motivation and knowledge-work. Approving with Kaur (2015), motivated employees make use of their cognitive, affective and conative abilities to achieve organizational goals.

Several studies (e.g. Siemsen et al., 2008; Binney et al., 2006; Jyoti & Rani, 2017) have also recognized the role of ability as a strong predictor of high KM performance. Furthermore, KM acts as a mediator between high-performance work system and organizational performance (Jyoti & Rani, 2017). This means, individuals who possess more personal-knowledge capabilities are more effective in performing KM activities and ensuring KM success (Hussain et al., 2010).

The result also found that the time availability as an opportunity to perform knowledge-work activities has a significant path in the model. In contrast with motivation and ability, this effect is weaker in influencing knowledge-work. Contrary to Siemsen et al., (2008), Hallahan (2001), and Cleveland and Elli (2015), time availability is not the most important operational constraints. Ability and motivation are relatively more important to performance in general, as well as in different contexts (Van Iddekinge et al., 2017). The present study also improves our understanding of the relative importance of ability and motivation. Considering the nature of knowledge-work, knowledge-workers are best described as investors. They choose whether or not to invest their skills in a given company. They often have the power to resist being told what to do. Therefore, they choose to engage in knowledge work to the extent that they have the motivation, ability and opportunity to do so (Davenport, 2015; Kelloway & Barling, 2000; Shujahat et al., 2017). Moreover, results revealed that the greatest extent of knowledge-work is related to the group that simultaneously has high motivation, ability and opportunity.

According to Wiig (1993) the organization's success is directly related to the quality and relevance of these activities; particularly knowledge-workers' expertise and their willingness to use that expertise to their employers' advantage. This argument implies that workers' behaviors are different depending upon their proficiency level (Yoon, 2012). Individual knowledge innovation and performance make organizations more productive (Muhammed et al., 2009). The performance of an individual knowledge-worker drives the success of knowledge-intensive organizations. Therefore, the improvement of knowledge-work performance is a key challenge of modern economy (Palvalin et al., 2015).

Knowledge-intensive firms need to leverage their individual knowledge assets via knowledge sharing to create collective knowledge resources. This process is, however, under the control of the knowledge-worker (Swart, Kinnie, Rossenberg & Yalabik, 2014).

However, successful KM is dependent on a well-functioning HRM and the employees' perceived behavior in knowledge creation, knowledge sharing and knowledge application (Lord & Farrington, 2006 cited in Kuo, 2011). Certainly, knowledge-workers require managers that act as facilitators, not controlling bosses. Knowledge-workers also need leaders who inspire and motivate knowledge-workers to perform based on agreed standards. Also, those new-era managers need to assess their workers' ability to perform. Since the process of influencing the performance of knowledge-workers is mainly developmental, they need also to hone skills in appraising, coaching, mentoring, and providing feedback. One measure of their effectiveness will be the quality of the relationships (internal and external) that they create (Serrat, 2017). Of course, not only managers of knowledge-workers can help stimulate their productivity (Carleton, 2011). A key implication of the behavioral perspective is that HR systems composed of different supportive HR practices are likely to foster the MAOs of different employees based on their role behaviors required for alternative organizational strategies (Collins & Kehoe, 2017). The HR function in organizations deals with individuals directly. It can therefore greatly impact the effectiveness of KM. According to Pauleen (2009), it is individuals who are meant to be responsible for their own knowledge development, and the HR ought to help them on this journey (Rechberg & Syed, 2014). In this regard, the most desirable forms of process improvement for knowledge-work can be participative, incremental, and continuous. Knowledge-workers are much more likely to agree with and adopt any process changes if they are involved in their design. However, most KM implementations within organizations do not employ a process-based approach (Davenport, 2015).

This study has some limitations that should be recognized to help produce higher quality research in this area. First, the research methodology is purely quantitative, thus this limits the depth of knowledge provided by qualitative methodologies. Second, opportunity measurement was limited to time availability, while there are other measurements of opportunity that future research can consider. Third, the sample is taken from one university in Iran; therefore, the context is geographically limited and industry-specific.

IMPLICATIONS

This paper presents an empirically validated MAO framework for improving knowledge-work. In this context, knowledge-workers must be treated as a valuable resource, which is a view consistent with Kelloway and Barling (2000), Drucker (1998), Mládková (2015) and Davenport (2015). Knowledge-work is a discretionary behavior, and knowledge-workers should be viewed as investors of their intellectual capital. They require less autocratic, more autonomous style of management than non-knowledge-workers. To be able to work independently and autonomously, knowledge-workers are required to self-manage, self-organize and self-control (Mládková, 2015). Their behavior is dependent on their motivation, ability and opportunity to perform knowledge-work activities.

"You can lead a horse to water, but you can't make it drink" is an adage of universal application. It signifies that you can give someone means and opportunity but cannot force that person to avail of them. The relationship between motive, means (or ability), and opportunity—and what happens when it is not close— explains much human behavior by dint of reasoned action (Serrat, 2017). However, it is very important for managers to measure how the changes in MOA can impact knowledge-work productivity. Because, the productivity of an individual knowledge-worker is the most important factor for good organizational performance (Palvalin, 2017).

The results also have implications for other human resources practices that attempt to affect, or are influenced by, ability and motivation, including training and incentive practices (Van Iddekinge at al., 2017). Results demonstrated the usefulness of the MAO model in explaining knowledge-work activities. Although, some researchers have focused on the role of motivation, our findings indicate that in addition to motivation, ability and opportunity have a significant influence on knowledge-work behaviors. In addition, ability plays the role of a mediator variable. As stated by Yew Wong (2005: 273), "employee development is seen as a way to improve and enhance the personal value of individuals. The skills and competencies of knowledge-workers need to be continuously developed in order for them to produce valuable contributions to a company. If not, as with other tangible assets, their value will depreciate".

The findings focused on the success of KM practices by individuals. An important implication of human resource practices is that they should aim to help individuals to be more effective at a personal-level by enhancing their ability and motivation. As stated by Jyoti and Rani (2017), a high-performance work system helps employees to create knowledge and motivate them with learning abilities in order to boost the productivity and efficiency of an organization. In this regard, organizations must work on these antecedents to ensure the knowledge creation, sharing and application (Shujahat et al., 2017) as well as managers should formulate an attractive incentive package to motivate employees to engage in KM initiatives. Such an incentive system should also encourage them to perform their activities to the best of their ability. Certainly, it is important to provide opportunities for employees especially time availability for engagement in knowledge-work activities.

FUTURE WORK

Future research could capitalize on the findings to attain a further understanding of the role of MAO on knowledge-work and subsequently organizational performance. The context of the study was limited to one higher-education organization and to one national-culture environment. Therefore, the same model could be tested at various organizations, national cultures, and industries, in order to generalize the results further. Particularly, the national and organizational cultures might have high impacts on individual constructs that affect knowledge-work activities.

Moreover, the research depended on quantitative data. It was insightful to know that there is a significant relationship between MOA and knowledge-work effectiveness. That said, adding qualitative input will provide richness to the findings and help scholars understand the complexity and depth of the relationship. This will also assist in triangulating the data and appreciate the personal constructs of knowledge-workers. For example, interviews with knowledge-workers can reveal many constructs that are embedded in the organizational and national cultures.

Furthermore, the opportunity construct depended on one variable, which was time availability. Although in the literature time availability is considered the most enabling factor to contribute to knowledge-work and – especially – when it comes to knowledge-sharing and knowledge-creation, future research can develop this construct through considering adding more variables (operational or situational) that enable (or even inhibit) action. Examples of those variables might include job design, information and communication technology, availability of meeting space etc.

Another major area of research is to deepen our understanding of how various HR practices influence MOA within various contexts, especially that the findings highlighted the importance of the individual in attaining effective KM activities. Motivation-enhancing, empowerment-focused and opportunity-enhancing HR practices for the knowledge-work process are obviously needed, so what are they and how they differ under various contexts. Lastly, since personal-knowledge often raise the issue of knowledge ownership, further attention to ethical issues may bring valuable insights for KM in organizations.

CONCLUSION

Although previous research has suggested the existence of significant organizational and technological factors for KM success, few studies have highlighted the role of the individual and its related constructs in KM success. This paper has highlighted the impact of motivation, ability and opportunity on knowledge-work. In contrast with traditional KM research, this study adopted the PKM perspective. In alignment, knowledge-work is defined as a discretionary behavior that is a function of motivation, ability and opportunity - independently.

The findings of this study supported the hypotheses that employee's motivation, ability and opportunity affect knowledge-work activities. In addition, when it comes to motivation, knowledge-workers are more intrinsically motivated than extrinsically when it comes to knowledge-work. Particularly, this is important as motivation has the highest impact on knowledge-work. Moreover, second in the ranking, ability has a high impact on knowledge-work. It is also recognized that motivation has a high correlation with ability, which indicates that motivation has also an indirect impact and ability seems to play the role of a mediator between motivation and knowledge-work. Opportunity is found to have a significant yet lesser impact on knowledge-work.

REFERENCES

Ajmal, M., Helo, P., & Kekäle, T. (2010). Critical factors for knowledge management in project business. *Journal of Knowledge Management, 14*(1), 156–168. doi:10.1108/13673271011015633

Ajzen, I. (1991). The theory of planned behavior. *Organizational Behavior and Human Decision Processes, 50*(2), 179–211. doi:10.1016/0749-5978(91)90020-T

Alexander, K. M. (2014). *Generation Y knowledge workers' experience of work motivation: A grounded theory study* [Doctoral dissertation]. Retrieved from https://pqdtopen.proquest.com/doc/1658144350. html?FMT=AI

Ambulkar, S., Blackhurst, J. V., & Cantor, D. E. (2016). Supply chain risk mitigation competency: An individual-level knowledge-based perspective. *International Journal of Production Research, 54*(5), 1398–1411. doi:10.1080/00207543.2015.1070972

Argote, L., McEvily, B., & Reagans, R. (2003). Managing Knowledge in Organizations: An Integrative Framework and Review of Emerging Themes. *Management Science, 49*(4), 571–582. doi:10.1287/mnsc.49.4.571.14424

Basu, B., & Sengupta, K. (2007). Assessing success factors of knowledge management initiatives of academic institutions–a case of an Indian business school. *Electronic Journal of Knowledge Management*, *5*(3), 273–282.

Binney, W., Oppenheim, P., & Hall, J. (2006). Towards the confirmation of the MOA model: an applied approach. In *Proceedings of the 2006 Australian and New Zealand Academy of Marketing conference*. Brisbane, AU: ANZMAC.

Bosch-Sijtsema, P. M., Fruchter, R., Vartiainen, M., & Ruohomäki, V. (2011). A framework to analyze knowledge work in distributed teams. *Group & Organization Management*, *36*(3), 275–307. doi:10.1177/1059601111403625

Brinkley, I., Fauth, R., Mahdon, M., & Theodoropoulou, S. (2009). *Knowledge Workers and Knowledge Work: A Knowledge Economy Programme Report*. London, UK: The Work Foundation.

Carleton, K. (2011). How to motivate and retain knowledge workers in organizations: A review of the literature. *International Journal of Management*, *28*(2), 459.

Chadburn, A., Smith, J., & Milan, J. (2017). Productivity drivers of knowledge workers in the central London office environment. *Journal of Corporate Real Estate*, *19*(2), 66–79. doi:10.1108/JCRE-12-2015-0047

Chang, Y. Y., Gong, Y., & Peng, M. W. (2012). Expatriate knowledge transfer, subsidiary absorptive capacity, and subsidiary performance. *Academy of Management Journal*, *55*(4), 927–948. doi:10.5465/amj.2010.0985

Chennamaneni, A., Teng, J. T., & Raja, M. K. (2012). A unified model of knowledge sharing behaviors: Theoretical development and empirical test. *Behaviour & Information Technology*, *31*(11), 1097–1115. doi:10.1080/0144929X.2011.624637

Cheong, R. K., & Tsui, E. (2011). From Skills and Competencies to Outcome-based Collaborative Work: Tracking a Decade's Development of Personal Knowledge Management (PKM) Models. *Knowledge and Process Management*, *18*(3), 175–193. doi:10.1002/kpm.380

Cleveland, S., & Ellis, T. J. (2015). Rethinking knowledge sharing barriers: A content analysis of 103 studies. *International Journal of Knowledge Management*, *11*(1), 28–51. doi:10.4018/IJKM.2015010102

Collins, C., & Kehoe, R. (2017). Examining strategic fit and misfit in the management of knowledge workers. *Industrial & Labor Relations Review*, *70*(2), 308–335. doi:10.1177/0019793916654481

Collins, D. (1997). Knowledge work or working knowledge? Ambiguity and confusion in the analysis of the "knowledge age". *Employee Relations*, *19*(1), 38–50. doi:10.1108/01425459710163570

Cruz, N. M., Pérez, V. M., & Cantero, C. T. (2009). The influence of employee motivation on knowledge transfer. *Journal of Knowledge Management*, *13*(6), 478–490. doi:10.1108/13673270910997132

Davenport, T. H. (2015). Process management for knowledge work. In J. vom Brocke & M. Rosemann (Eds.), *Handbook on Business Process Management 1* (2nd ed., pp. 17–35). New York, NY: Springer.

Davis, G. B. (2002). Anytime/anyplace computing and the future of knowledge work. *Communications of the ACM, 45*(12), 67–73. doi:10.1145/585597.585617

Drucker, P. F. (1998, Oct 5). Management's New Paradigms. *Forbes.* Retrieved from https://www.forbes.com/forbes/1998/1005/6207152a.html#5abe555931ee

Drucker, P. F. (2006). *The effective executive: The definitive guide to getting the right things done* (5th ed.). New York, NY: HarperCollins.

Efimova, L. (2004). Discovering the iceberg of knowledge work: A weblog case. *Paper presented at the Fifth European Conference on Organization, Knowledge, Learning and Capabilities,* Innsbruck, Austria. Retrieved from http://citeseerx.ist.psu.edu/viewdoc/summary?doi=10.1.1.128.9265

El-Farr, H. (2009). Knowledge work and workers: A critical literature review. *Leeds University Business School Working Paper Series, 1*(1).

Fornell, C., & Larcker, D. F. (1981). Evaluating structural equation models with unobservable variables and measurement error. *JMR, Journal of Marketing Research, 1*(1), 39–50. doi:10.2307/3151312

Ganzach, Y., Saporta, I., & Weber, Y. (2000). Interaction in linear versus logistic models: A substantive illustration using the relationship between motivation, ability, and performance. *Organizational Research Methods, 3*(3), 237–253. doi:10.1177/109442810033002

Garson, G. D. (2008). *Path analysis.* From Statnotes: topics in multivariate analysis. Retrieved from http://ondrej.vostal.net/pub/skola/statnote.htm

Gumusluoglu, L., & Karakitapoglu-Aygün, Z. (2010). Bilgi Çalisanlarinin Adalet ve Güçlendirme Algilarinin Örgüte, Lidere ve Ise Baglilik Üzerindeki Etkileri. *Türk Psikoloji Dergisi, 25*(66), 21–36.

Hallahan, K. (2001). Enhancing motivation, ability, and opportunity to process public relations messages. *Public Relations Review, 26*(4), 463–480. doi:10.1016/S0363-8111(00)00059-X

Hislop, D. (2008). Conceptualizing Knowledge Work Utilizing Skill and Knowledge-based Concepts the Case of Some Consultants and Service Engineers. *Management Learning, 35*(5), 579–596. doi:10.1177/1350507608098116

Hoq, K. M. G., & Akter, R. (2012). Knowledge management in universities: Role of knowledge workers. *Bangladesh Journal of Library and Information Science, 2*(1), 92–102. doi:10.3329/bjlis.v2i1.12925

Huang, M. C., Chiu, Y. P., & Lu, T. C. (2013). Knowledge governance mechanisms and repatriate's knowledge sharing: The mediating roles of motivation and opportunity. *Journal of Knowledge Management, 17*(5), 677–694. doi:10.1108/JKM-01-2013-0048

Hussain, I., Ahmed, S., & Si, S. (2010). Personal knowledge abilities and knowledge management success. *Journal of Information and Knowledge Management, 9*(4), 319–327. doi:10.1142/S021964921000270X

Hutchinson, S. (2013). *Performance management theory and practice.* London, UK: Chartered Institute of Personnel and Development.

Jacobs, R. L. (2017). Knowledge work and human resource development. *Human Resource Development Review, 16*(2), 176–202. doi:10.1177/1534484317704293

Jemielniak, D. (2012). *The new knowledge workers*. Cheltenham, UK: Edward Elgar Publishing. doi:10.4337/9780857933119

Jennex, M., & Olfman, L. (2005). Assessing knowledge management success. *International Journal of Knowledge Management, 1*(2), 33–49. doi:10.4018/jkm.2005040104

Jennex, M. E., Smolnik, S., & Croasdell, D. (2016). The search for knowledge management success. *Paper presented at the 49*[th] *Hawaii International Conference on System Sciences*, Koloa, HI. doi:10.1109/HICSS.2016.521

Jennex, M. E., Smolnik, S., & Croasdell, D. T. (2009). Towards a consensus knowledge management success definition. *Vine, 39*(2), 174–188. doi:10.1108/03055720910988878

Jiang, K., Lepak, D. P., Hu, J., & Baer, J. C. (2012). How does human resource management influence organizational outcomes? A meta-analytic investigation of mediating mechanisms. *Academy of Management Journal, 55*(6), 1264–1294. doi:10.5465/amj.2011.0088

Jones, E. C., & Chung, C. A. (2006). A methodology for measuring engineering knowledge worker productivity. *Engineering Management Journal, 18*(1), 32–38. doi:10.1080/10429247.2006.11431682

Jyoti, J., & Rani, A. (2017). High performance work system and organisational performance: Role of knowledge management. *Personnel Review, 46*(8), 1770–1795. doi:10.1108/PR-10-2015-0262

Kankanhalli, A., Tan, B. C., & Wei, K. K. (2005). Contributing knowledge to electronic knowledge repositories: An empirical investigation. *Management Information Systems Quarterly, 29*(1), 113–143. doi:10.2307/25148670

Kaur, K. (2015). Teacher motivation: A theoretical perspective. *Indian Streams Research Journal, 5*(2), 1–4.

Kelloway, E. K., & Barling, J. (2000). Knowledge work as organizational behavior. *International Journal of Management Reviews, 2*(3), 287–304. doi:10.1111/1468-2370.00042

Kompaso, S. M., & Sridevi, M. S. (2010). Employee engagement: The key to improving performance. *International Journal of Business and Management, 5*(12). doi:10.5539/ijbm.v5n12p89

Kuo, T. H. (2011). How to improve organizational performance through learning and knowledge? *International Journal of Manpower, 32*(5/6), 581–603. doi:10.1108/01437721111158215

Lee, K. C., Lee, S., & Kang, I. W. (2005). KMPI: Measuring knowledge management performance. *Information & Management, 42*(3), 469–482. doi:10.1016/j.im.2004.02.003

Leung, X. Y., & Bai, B. (2013). How motivation, opportunity, and ability impact travelers' social media involvement and revisit intention. *Journal of Travel & Tourism Marketing, 30*(1-2), 58–77. doi:10.1080/10548408.2013.751211

Lin, H. F. (2007). Effects of extrinsic and intrinsic motivation on employee knowledge sharing intentions. *Journal of Information Science, 33*(2), 135–149. doi:10.1177/0165551506068174145

Lin, H. F. (2014). Contextual factors affecting knowledge management diffusion in SMEs. *Industrial Management & Data Systems, 114*(9), 1415–1437. doi:10.1108/IMDS-08-2014-0232

Liu, M. S. (2012). Impact of knowledge incentive mechanisms on individual knowledge creation behavior – an empirical study for Taiwanese R&D professionals. *International Journal of Information Management*, *32*(5), 442–450. doi:10.1016/j.ijinfomgt.2012.02.002

Lone, J. A. (2016). Exploring knowledge work: Organizational practices and work characteristics in three knowledge work settings [Doctoral dissertation]. Retrieved from https://www.duo.uio.no/handle/10852/55141

Mafabi, S., Nasiima, S., Muhimbise, E. M., Kaekende, F., & Nakiyonga, C. (2017). The mediation role of intention in knowledge sharing behavior. *VINE Journal of Information and Knowledge Management Systems*, *47*(2), 172–193. doi:10.1108/VJIKMS-02-2016-0008

Minbaeva, D. B. (2013). Strategic HRM in building micro-foundations of organizational knowledge-based performance. *Human Resource Management Review*, *23*(4), 378–390. doi:10.1016/j.hrmr.2012.10.001

Mládková, L. (2015). Knowledge workers and the principle of 3S (self-management, self-organization, self-control). *Procedia: Social and Behavioral Sciences*, *181*, 178–184. doi:10.1016/j.sbspro.2015.04.879

Muhammed, S., Doll, W. J., & Deng, X. (2009). A model of interrelationships among individual level knowledge management success measures. *International Journal of Knowledge Management*, *5*(1), 1–16. doi:10.4018/jkm.2009010101

North, K., & Gueldenberg, S. (Eds.). (2011). *Effective knowledge work: answers to the management challenge of the 21st century*. Bingley, UK: Emerald.

Okorogu, C. I. (2015). *First generation meta-analytic review of the influence of human resource management single practices on organizational outcomes*: 1985-2015 [Doctoral dissertation]. Retrieved from http://aut.researchgateway.ac.nz/handle/10292/9829

Olsen, K. M. (2016). The power of workers: Knowledge work and the power balance in Scandinavian countries. *Employee Relations*, *38*(3), 390–405. doi:10.1108/ER-10-2014-0121

Packirisamy, P., Meenakshy, M., & Jagannathan, S. (2017). Burnout during early career: Lived experiences of the knowledge workers in India. *Journal of Enterprise Information Management*, *30*(1), 96–121. doi:10.1108/JEIM-01-2016-0041

Palvalin, M. (2017). How to measure impacts of work environment changes on knowledge work productivity –validation and improvement of the SmartWoW tool. *Measuring Business Excellence*, *21*(2), 175–190. doi:10.1108/MBE-05-2016-0025

Palvalin, M., Vuolle, M., Jääskeläinen, A., Laihonen, H., & Lönnqvist, A. (2015). SmartWoW–constructing a tool for knowledge work performance analysis. *International Journal of Productivity and Performance Management*, *64*(4), 479–498. doi:10.1108/IJPPM-06-2013-0122

Patalas-Maliszewska, J. (2013). *Managing knowledge workers: Value assessment, methods, and application tools*. New York, NY: Springer. doi:10.1007/978-3-642-36600-0

Rechberg, I. D. W., & Syed, J. (2014). Appropriation or participation of the individual in knowledge management. *Management Decision, 52*(3), 426–445. doi:10.1108/MD-04-2013-0223

Rechberg, I., & Syed, J. (2014). Knowledge management practices and the focus on the individual. *International Journal of Knowledge Management, 10*(1), 26–42. doi:10.4018/ijkm.2014010102

Reinhardt, W., Schmidt, B., Sloep, P., & Drachsler, H. (2011). Knowledge worker roles and actions—results of two empirical studies. *Knowledge and Process Management, 18*(3), 150–174. doi:10.1002/kpm.378

Ryan, R. M., & Deci, E. L. (2000). Intrinsic and extrinsic motivations: Classic definitions and new directions. *Contemporary Educational Psychology, 25*(1), 54–67. doi:10.1006/ceps.1999.1020 PubMed

Sedighi, M., van Splunter, S., Zand, F., & Brazier, F. (2015). Evaluating Critical Success Factors Model of Knowledge Management: An analytic hierarchy process (AHP) approach. *International Journal of Knowledge Management, 11*(3), 17–36. doi:10.4018/IJKM.2015070102

Serrat, O. (2017). *Knowledge solutions: Tools, methods, and approaches to drive organizational performance*. Springer Open. doi:10.1007/978-981-10-0983-9

Shujahat, M., Sousa, M. J., Hussain, S., Nawaz, F., Wang, M., & Umer, M. (2017). Translating the impact of knowledge management processes into knowledge-based innovation: The neglected and mediating role of knowledge-worker productivity. *Journal of Business Research*. doi:10.1016/j.jbusres.2017.11.001

Siemsen, E., Roth, A. V., & Balasubramanian, S. (2008). How motivation, opportunity, and ability drive knowledge sharing: The constraining-factor model. *Journal of Operations Management, 26*(3), 426–445. doi:10.1016/j.jom.2007.09.001

Swart, J., Kinnie, N., Rossenberg, Y., & Yalabik, Z. Y. (2014). Why should I share my knowledge? A multiple foci of commitment perspective. *Human Resource Management Journal, 24*(3), 269–289. doi:10.1111/1748-8583.12037

Thite, M. (2004). Strategic positioning of HRM in knowledge-based organizations. *The Learning Organization, 11*(1), 28–44. doi:10.1108/09696470410515715

Timonen, H., & Paloheimo, K. S. (2008). The emergence and diffusion of the concept of knowledge work. *Electronic Journal of Knowledge Management, 6*(2), 177–190.

Todericiu, R., Şerban, A., & Dumitraşcu, O. (2013). Particularities of knowledge worker's motivation strategies in Romanian organizations. *Procedia Economics and Finance, 6*, 405–413. doi:10.1016/S2212-5671(13)00155-X

Turriago-Hoyos, A., Thoene, U., & Arjoon, S. (2016). Knowledge workers and virtues in Peter Drucker's management theory. *SAGE Open, 6*(1). doi:10.1177/2158244016639631

Tuuli, M. M. (2012). Competing models of how motivation, opportunity and ability drive performance behaviors. In S. Laryea, S. A. Agyepong, R. Leiringer, & W. Hughes (Eds). In *Proceedings of the 4th West Africa Built Environment Research Conference*. Abuja, Nigeria: *WABER*.

Vaiman, V. (Ed.). (2010). *Talent management of knowledge workers: Embracing the non-traditional workforce.* New York, NY: Springer. doi:10.1057/9780230277526

Van Iddekinge, C. H., Aguinis, H., Mackey, J. D., & DeOrtentiis, P. S. (2017). A meta-analysis of the interactive, additive, and relative effects of cognitive ability and motivation on performance. *Journal of Management, 31*(1), 249–279.

Welschen, J., Todorova, N., & Mills, A. M. (2012). An investigation of the impact of intrinsic motivation on organizational knowledge sharing. *International Journal of Knowledge Management, 8*(2), 23–42. doi:10.4018/jkm.2012040102

Widmann, B. S. (2013). *Influence of leadership style on work engagement of knowledge workers in an engineering organization* [Doctoral dissertation]. Retrieved from https://pqdtopen.proquest.com/doc/1428738809.html?FMT=ABS

Wright, K. (2005). Personal knowledge management: Supporting individual knowledge worker performance. *Knowledge Management Research and Practice, 3*(3), 156–165. doi:10.1057/palgrave.kmrp.8500061

Yew Wong, K. (2005). Critical success factors for implementing knowledge management in small and medium enterprises. *Industrial Management & Data Systems, 105*(3), 261–279. doi:10.1108/02635570510590101

Yoon, K. S. (2012). Measuring the influence of expertise and epistemic engagement to the practice of knowledge management. *International Journal of Knowledge Management, 8*(1), 40–70. doi:10.4018/jkm.2012010103

Chapter 3
A Tool for Creating Community Knowledge Objects

Zbigniew Mikolajuk
Independent Researcher, Canada

ABSTRACT

International organizations and government agencies have developed and collected a wealth of knowledge resources relevant to poor communities; however, the people who need these resources most often do not know these materials exist or are unable to access or understand them. Electronic sources of knowledge materials and means of communication are rarely integrated with traditional methods of knowledge delivery. This chapter addresses the issue of knowledge sharing with poor communities and presents a software tool for developing multimedia knowledge materials suitable for people with little or no formal education. A multimedia editor uses a data structure composed of multimedia objects (texts, images, video and audio clips) to generate the knowledge browser. Local specialists with a basic knowledge of computing can modify and customize how the knowledge is presented by adding new materials relevant to the local environment.

INTRODUCTION

A body of knowledge built in a community over generations plays an important role in solving contemporary problems. However, this knowledge alone may not be sufficient to deal with the rapidly changing world within and around the community. New problems arising from changing market structures, the introduction of new methods in agriculture, health care problems, social changes, and the activities of government and global development programs require knowledge from external sources - the knowledge that will help the communities adapt to change. These external sources constitute an essential factor in empowering communities and disadvantaged social groups. The empowerment through knowledge is the most visible and meaningful at the community level.

DOI: 10.4018/978-1-5225-7214-5.ch003

Disadvantaged and poor communities must be made aware of availability of knowledge services and their rights to benefit from country and global knowledge resources. We need effective methods and tools for production of knowledge materials based on existing sources of knowledge such as printed publications and electronic materials made available on the Internet as well as on sources of indigenous knowledge.

The external materials must be transformed (translated, localized and contextualized) into knowledge presentations that are appropriate for diverse communities in developing countries. Most of the members of these communities have very little or no formal education or are illiterate and speak only their mother's tongues.

This chapter outlines problems of capturing and sharing knowledge at the community level. Figure 1 shows the scope of issues to be considered in the context of community knowledge management. Access to relevant knowledge or in many cases just knowing that needed knowledge is available is one of the critical issues for development initiatives. In order to reach remote and poor communities with large illiterate and semi-literate population we must design appropriate knowledge capturing and delivery methods, for example, the interactive theatre and visual presentations using traditional or electronic channels of communication. Knowledge materials must concern very specific local issues and be delivered in local languages.

A short story about a farmer in Mindanao, Philippines is an example of the importance of knowledge sharing in a community and the role of modern electronic means of communication. The farmer visited a village that had just established a telecentre. A group of people was looking at the computer screen. He joined them to watch a presentation in his language on how to raise ducklings. He liked the story and tried to apply the newly acquired knowledge. Now, he is one of the richest farmers in his village. (Mikolajuk, 2004).

Figure 1. Context of community knowledge management

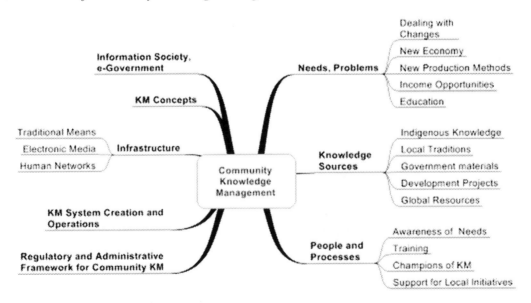

The story is not about the telecentre but about how important it is to access relevant knowledge in an appropriate format. A brochure, or radio broadcast or a lecture from an extension worker may not have had the effect of the telecentre. Most likely, if there were other duckling breeders around, the farmer would have learned from them instead. Nonetheless, new knowledge was delivered effectively. But this required that someone with the required knowledge packaged it in the appropriate format and reached the farmer.

The main purpose of this chapter is to review practical issues that have arisen through field experiences in sharing knowledge with the poorest communities and presentation of an experimental tool for development of multimedia knowledge objects at the community level. Knowledge services for development and rural communities are the subject of comprehensive reports published by development and research organisations, (The World Bank, 2011; Chaudhuri, 2015; Talyarkhana et al 2003). The assessment of impact of information technologies and knowledge sharing on the wellbeing of disadvantaged social groups is a research area providing directions of further development of knowledge services, (Geldof et al. 2011; Grunfeld, 2011; Helsper, 2008; Chaudhuri, 2015).

BACKGROUND

The knowledge needed by poor communities often already exists somewhere, but it is usually not available at the right time and the right place to those who need it most. To identify key factors to improving knowledge services, Practical Action (UK Charity), in collaboration with several universities, conducted analyses of knowledge gaps and of the demand for knowledge in rural communities in Bangladesh (Practical Action Dhaka, 2007) and Sudan (Abdelaziz, 2008; Practical Action, Khartoum, 2009).

Some of the main questions of community knowledge management are:

- What are the community knowledge assets and needs and how can they be recorded and preserved?
- What are the traditional means of knowledge sharing and is there a need for new methods or a convergence with electronic media?
- What are the domains where traditional knowledge needs to be supplemented by new sources of knowledge?
- How can communities be mobilized to develop and maintain their local knowledge repositories?
- What resources and external help are needed to develop a knowledge sharing system and provide the means to access external knowledge in the appropriate format and to contextualize knowledge to local needs?
- How can the sustainability of community knowledge management facilities be ensured?

A practical definition of knowledge is the ability to take effective action (Snowden, D., 2004). It means that when information is delivered it must also be internalized and its understanding demonstrated by its use. Knowledge may be delivered or shared in many forms. From the pragmatic point of view, we are interested in using available descriptions of knowledge and connecting people or institutions interested in knowledge sharing – suppliers and users (Mikolajuk, 2005; Gniazdowski & Chafetz, 2005).

Many organizations (e.g. FAO, CGIAR, IFAD, Global Forum on Agricultural Research, AGCO Advanced Technology Solutions) have created impressive on-line repositories of agricultural information materials (ODI, Overseas Development Institute, 2006). Yet, there is little evidence to show that these resources are used effectively by farmers (directly or through 'infomediaries') or that they have had a substantial impact in alleviating poverty. Some of the critical issues identified in FAO's report (Flor A. G., 2005), were:

- Appropriate content and context – how to ensure that the right information is produced and delivered in the right format to a wide range of stakeholders.
- Building on existing systems - how to capitalize on, rather than replace and lose the value of existing indigenous, and therefore highly trusted, information and information systems.
- Building capacity - how to strengthen the capacity of people involved in providing the right information in the right formats.
- Access, empowerment and democratization - how to ensure that relevant information actually reaches poor people, especially women, and empowers them to improve their livelihoods, instead of being captured by wealthier or more powerful sections of the community, or middlemen.
- Realistic approaches to technologies to support information and communication - how to build sustainable systems that extend and enhance existing systems and are further expandable and extendable.

In this chapter, we present a concept of a knowledge sharing network that includes community-based knowledge nodes (local knowledge nodes) that can provide direct access to knowledge resources for diverse groups of users and help identify the subjects most relevant to local demand for knowledge. We describe a prototype software tool for developing multimedia presentations (knowledge objects) tailored to needs and cognitive levels of members of poor communities. Development workers, local administrators, NGOs and community KM champions are the most likely target users for the methodology and software tool presented in this chapter.

Practical Answers of Practical Action is a current project that brings together partners in Asia, Africa, and Latin America to provide knowledge services to poor communities. (Mikolajuk, Cartridge & Noble, 2008). The project's overall objective is to demonstrate that access to appropriate knowledge is a vital factor in reducing poverty. It also stimulates a global network committed to producing and disseminating knowledge materials appropriate for all social groups of the society including illiterate people and disadvantaged communities.

MAIN FOCUS OF THE CHAPTER

Our vision is that all poor people will have access to appropriate knowledge they need to improve their livelihoods. Realizing this vision requires a network of knowledge sharing that pulls knowledge from around the world and local sources, and then packages it in the format and language appropriate for local context. By using the right language and context and the right media (text, images, animations, voice, and video) people with little education or people who are illiterate can access and share the knowledge they need. There are multimedia technologies that help produce these kinds of tailored knowledge materials.

To achieve our overall objective, we must aim to reach several specific goals:

- Build awareness of knowledge services, in particular among marginalized and disadvantaged social groups.
- Develop capacity at the country and community level to adapt knowledge materials available from global and country resources: this means producing knowledge objects that also include indigenous knowledge and address specific local problems and demand for knowledge.
- Help local, small ICT (Information and Communication Technologies) enterprises and organizations participate in producing multimedia knowledge materials.
- Achieve a "critical mass" of relevant knowledge products and dissemination channels via existing telecentre networks, mass media, and local knowledge nodes. These will help ensure the functional and financial sustainability of the knowledge sharing network.
- Stimulate the participation of SMEs (Small and Medium Enterprises) in developing the knowledge industry and help them contribute to building a knowledge society in their respective countries.
- Influence policy making to help supply knowledge services to poor people and respond to the need for appropriate technologies.
- Demonstrate the viability of participatory development of multimedia knowledge materials in communities and local enterprises, i.e. involvement of community members in developing and testing knowledge products.

From our experience, we know that the random dissemination of information does not constitute true knowledge sharing. Information needs to be contextualized, targeted and relevant to local circumstances, and it must be presented at the cognitive level of the intended audiences. Our current activities therefore also focus on several additional issues:

- 'Accompanying information': following up the dissemination of knowledge objects with a supportive phone call, for example).
- Gathering feedback through, for example, learning if the acquired knowledge has been used effectively.
- Localizing materials, e.g. through greater use of local languages and by putting people in touch with local suppliers and practitioners to gain first-hand experience (through Communities of Practice).

SOLUTIONS AND RECOMMENDATIONS

A proposed solution piloted by Practical Action in Bangladesh, Sri Lanka, Sudan, and Peru envisages the development of a network of local knowledge agents (local knowledge nodes). These agents serve diverse groups of knowledge seekers and provide access to knowledge materials ("knowledge objects") in electronic or traditional formats. A knowledge object, in this context, could be anything that contains or describes specific knowledge: e.g. a technical brief in print or electronic format, video clip, map, database, or traditional communication media such as puppet shows or street theatres, or a human expert.

The network will encompass small service nodes available directly to farmers and extension workers. If feasible, a local knowledge node can be connected via Internet to global knowledge nodes maintained by large organizations and government agencies. These organizations and agencies would share their knowledge resources in accordance with the protocol of the proposed network. By the end of 2009 Practical Action operated 4 large knowledge nodes in Bangladesh, 19 nodes in Sudan, and experimental facilities in Sri Lanka, Kenya, and Peru.

Community-based local nodes exist already in diverse forms and have the dissemination of knowledge within their missions. Being part of the proposed network will help them meet their own objectives and adapt knowledge from external sources to local needs, as well as contribute to global knowledge repositories and objectives. A potential beneficiary visiting the local node will be able to access both locally specific knowledge objects and globally available knowledge objects.

The following assumptions and principles should guide the design and operations of the network:

- The network must enable environments for knowledge sharing and team work among all stakeholders, including farmer-to-farmer communications.
- We must focus on the "first mile" of access to knowledge resources (multimedia, multilingual materials in electronic as well as non-electronic formats) as well as participatory design of knowledge objects.
- We must have a comprehensive system for collecting feedback from all stakeholders and users.
- The network must have technological and organizational flexibility within the overall framework of organic network development.
- The architecture of collaborating local and global nodes must provide unified access and search facilities.
- The network must pay attention to cultural environments, intellectual property rights, and quality of information materials.

The role of a local node is to develop and maintain knowledge objects tailored to the needs of local users, and if required, provide access to global resources. In the long-term the local nodes may become small enterprises that provide information services on a commercial basis and collect information about local suppliers; they thus play a constructive role in developing local communities of practice.

Global nodes should be synchronized to allow people to search and access all knowledge resources available in the system.

The following scenario of a farmer's enquiry about methods for sloping land cultivation illustrates the use of the system:

A farmer may contact the local node or ask the extension worker to obtain information about sloping land cultivation. A search in the local node repository may produce a list of relevant local knowledge objects. These local objects may include a report about local practices, information leaflet about equipment used by local farmers, and a short video produced by recent development project in the area. The local node may also have audio recordings or slide presentations about using new machines or traditional effective methods.

Further dialog with the computer-based system (browser) or knowledge node agent may narrow the search to knowledge objects that concern only the equipment used in sloping land cultivation and information about suppliers. An example in Figure 2 shows a browser about beekeeping.

A final list of knowledge objects can be reviewed by the user (farmer, extension worker or node operator) to determine the delivery method of selected knowledge objects. The farmer may view the collection of objects on the computer monitor (extension worker could demonstrate the objects on the laptop while visiting the enquirer), listen to audio clips (e.g. via mobile phone), or print relevant documents.

Local Knowledge Node

We use many terms in regard to knowledge sharing facilities. The following terms can be found in Practical Action's documents:

- Knowledge Dissemination Centre (Knowledge Centre, Information Resource Centre) - Sudan,
- Knowledge Centre (Rural Technology Centre) – Bangladesh,
- Digital Village, Community Resource Centre – Kenya,
- Resource Centre – general term used by Practical Action,
- Community Information Station – Sri Lanka,
- Telecentre – general term used by many organizations.

Figure 2. Knowledge objects in the format of Solanta multimedia presentation

We may use these terms interchangeably or agree on one term. In this chapter, we use the term "local knowledge node" to underline the network approach. The purpose of a knowledge node is to be a broker of knowledge relevant to needs of its community.

A local knowledge node is a small entity (enterprise, office, service unit, and centre) that offers to a local community the following:

- A collection of localized and contextualized knowledge materials (in electronic and traditional formats).
- Access to global knowledge resources, if connected to Internet or on CDROM's if not connected.
- Facilities to develop and adapt knowledge materials relevant to local needs, for example materials about cultivation of new varieties of vegetables or purification of water monitoring of local needs for knowledge materials.
- Assessment of usability and effectiveness of distributed knowledge materials (impact).
- Meeting and discussion place.

A local knowledge node is a function/facility that can be hosted by a telecentre or other establishment (e.g. school, VDC, community centre) that can provide basic infrastructure (an office, electricity, shared computer and communication equipment) for a fee or free of charge. A knowledge node contributes from its budget to the running costs and expenses of equipment and software. Diverse operational models of knowledge nodes can emerge in different countries and social environments.

Knowledge nodes can develop and expand depending on the demand for knowledge materials and the available resources. Stronger knowledge nodes can become important producers of knowledge materials to be shared throughout the network. In time, local knowledge nodes could become small enterprises and seeds of a new knowledge industry in a country.

The main impact of the network will be to contribute to poverty alleviation in areas covered by the knowledge services and to demonstrate viability and usefulness of knowledge services to the poorest people. Hands-on experience at the community level in adapting and producing knowledge products relevant to local demands and in harmony with local culture and methods of communication will provide critical inputs for planning long term solutions and their sustainability. Practical Action's project has already stimulated the incubation of small new enterprises and services, e.g. Rural Technology Centres in Bangladesh and the franchising of knowledge services in Peru and Bolivia.

Concept of Knowledge Object

We describe and present knowledge in forms ranging from documents, books and multimedia materials to oral stories, street theatres, and poetry recitation events. For these forms to have a real impact, both the knowledge object and the process of its uptake are important.

A Knowledge object is a presentation/description of a "chunk" of knowledge in a form that allows its audience to build the capacity to take effective action.

The process of development and delivery of knowledge objects encompasses:

- Defining the scope and objectives of knowledge object.
- Understanding the capabilities of target audiences to internalize information.
- Identifying existing sources of knowledge among target audiences.

- Exploring delivery formats (contextualization, localization, media options).
- Testing the target audiences' learning and knowledge sharing methods.
- Creating knowledge objects and facilitating their sharing.

The main purpose of knowledge objects is to enable people to gain knowledge - to know more or to know better. The capacity of the intended user/recipient of knowledge object to internalize new knowledge is one of the main attributes of the knowledge object and a guiding factor for the creator of knowledge objects.

For example, a knowledge object addressed to a literate farmer in Nepal that describes a bio-sand water filter could be a leaflet with a sequence of pictures and short texts in Nepali. The purpose of this object is to communicate knowledge of how to assemble the filter, where to find needed materials, and how to obtain financing (e.g. microcredit). Therefore, the attributes of the bio-sand water filter knowledge object (leaflet) must include the following:

- The problem addressed by the knowledge object (better drinking water),
- Intended users (characteristics of the users – literate nepali farmers),
- Language (nepali or perhaps one of many dialects),
- Geographic location for usage (mountain regions where water in rivers is muddy),
- Links to complementary knowledge objects (e.g. Concerning market and suppliers of filter components),
- Links to comments from other users of the knowledge object,
- Format of knowledge presentation (in this case – the leaflet).

In addition, the creator or distributor of this knowledge object should be able to check if the receiver of the knowledge object was actually able to use the acquired knowledge and assemble the filter. It means to provide a knowledge object appropriate for user's cognitive abilities.

Cognitive ability is the capacity to perform higher mental processes of reasoning, remembering, understanding, and problem solving, Bernstein et al. (2017).

A knowledge object is considered as a triad:

- Presentation entity (e.g. Book, multimedia material, oral story, live show),
- Context (collection of attributes mentioned above),
- Process (absorption and application of knowledge and its results).

The analysis of knowledge objects is a complex issue because it involves the consideration of:

- The actual knowledge represented by the object (validation and verification),
- The cognitive and learning abilities of users,
- The suitability of the presentation format,
- The process of applying the knowledge and its effects.

A picture below (Figure 3) shows a knowledge object – live demonstration of new varieties of grass to be used as a fodder for cattle. The receivers are illiterate farmers engaged in a government programme of re-cultivation of wastelands.

Figure 3. Knowledge object in the format of live demonstration (technical briefing for illiterate audience)

Context: Problem, Language, Local situation, Market, Regulations, Finances

A multimedia knowledge object could be a combination of video clips from the demonstration mentioned above and supplemented by recorded comments from farmers and additional explanations written or recorded in local language.

A multimedia knowledge object is a computer-based presentation that includes elements such as texts, photographs, video clips, audio clips, maps, animations, and graphics designed to share knowledge with intended audience.

A computer-based presentation of candle making is a knowledge object that can be delivered by village telecentres or development workers/project staff equipped with a laptop. For example, a PowerPoint presentation showing slides with pictures, voice explanations and short video clips can explain how the candle works, what materials are needed to make candles, how to prepare materials, how to make candles and package them for the market. A picture below (Figure 4) illustrates the concept of candle making knowledge object.

In the following sections, we describe the process of creating a multimedia knowledge object using the Solanta Editor, a software package developed by the Canadian company Solanta Technologies Inc. in collaboration with Practical Action.

Following the determination of the problem to be addressed by the knowledge object and intended audiences/recipients and their characteristics, and other attributes mentioned above, the process of development of the multimedia knowledge object includes:

1. Deciding which topics relevant to the problem must be included in multimedia presentation, for example, the knowledge object about candle may include topics such as materials for candle making, preparation of wax, candle moulding procedure, and packaging of candles;
2. Design of a logical structure of particular topics covering the problem area (browsing through the elements of the presentation);
3. Collecting of multimedia materials to be used for presentation of specific topics;
4. Selecting and formatting multimedia materials to be included in the presentation;
5. Selecting the software tool and compiling the multimedia presentation;

Figure 4. A knowledge object in the format of PowerPoint presentation

6. Testing the presentation and if possible obtaining some feedback/evaluation of the knowledge object from intended users;

7. Producing the multimedia presentation (knowledge object) in delivery format.

A multimedia knowledge object can be a relatively small structure addressing very specific problem, for example - the preparation of fruits for juice making or a complex multilevel structure, for example - the beekeeping manual.

SOLANTA MULTIMEDIA AUTHORING TOOL

This section is based on documents (Mikolajuk, 2005, 2006) and presents a prototype software tool developed by Solanta Technologies Inc. and its unpublished system documentation and User's Manual. The Solanta software package was designed as a tool for constructing and delivering multimedia presentations presenting knowledge to people with little or no formal education and no computer literacy. A data structure composed of multimedia files (texts, images, and video and audio clips) in a local language constitutes an input into a system (Editor) that generates the Knowledge Browser. People who do not know computer programming and possess only basic knowledge of applications such as MS Word Processor, Adobe Acrobat, PowerPoint, simple photo, audio and video can create multimedia presentations (Solanta Browser) using the Solanta Editor.

Preparation of Knowledge Presentation Structure (Input Data)

A creator of a knowledge presentation prepares a structure (a computer directory/folder) of knowledge objects. The example below shows the input data folder for presentation of hibiscus cultivation.

```
<DIR>          enHibiscus1
   <DIR>          enKnO-01-Land Preparation
   <DIR>          enKnO-02-Selecting Seeds
   <DIR>          enKnO-03-Planting
   <DIR>          enKnO-04-Weeding
   <DIR>          enKnO-05-Filling In
   <DIR>          enKnO-06-Flowering Time
   <DIR>          enKnO-07-Harvesting
   <DIR>          enKnO-08-Drying Hibiscus
```

The prefix 'enKnO-' is used by the Solanta system to indicate that a directory represents a knowledge objects in English. The prefix is optional but is recommended for documentation purposes. First 2 letters denote the language of the presentation. The prefix is helpful in maintaining multiple input directories and locating the knowledge object files in the structure. Each knowledge object of the logical structure of the presentation in Solanta system is presented in the Browser by icon (small picture), title (text caption), and voice recording (audio title). Local domain specialists with basic knowledge of computing can modify and customize the Input Data Structure of generated browser by adding new materials - knowledge objects. The Editor is available in English, Spanish, Arabic, Nepali, Bengali, Sinhala, and Tamil.

Figure 5. Attributes of knowledge objects in the input data structure and their visual effects.

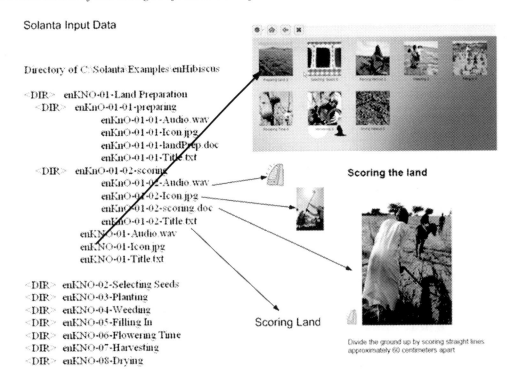

Solanta Browser

The Solanta Browser generated by the system from the input data allows for browsing through information materials by selecting icons that are accompanied by short descriptions (title) and voice explanations. The Solanta user environment allows for the user-computer interaction in which all user tasks (selection of an information material and executing an application) are performed in such a way that only correct actions are possible, i.e. the user cannot accidentally close or open a window, invoke multiple applications or destroy the information material. At any time, the user will deal with one window covering the whole screen (no close, move, resize functions in the menu bar). Direct operations at the operating system level are not available. The system can be set up in such a way that the browser opens automatically when the computer is powered on. A special code is needed to exit from the browser to the operating system. The EXIT button in the browser's menu shuts the computer down (power off).

Solanta Editor

Solanta Editor generates the XML coding for the browser determined by the input directory. The Editor is a tool for domain specialists who can, without training in XML coding, adapt information materials and customize the presentation of the domain knowledge. For example, general information on building bee hives can be supplemented with pictures of locally built bee hives and interviews with local beekeepers. Figure 6 shows the main dialog box (interface) of the Editor. The domain specialist can prepare an external directory (a structure of additional knowledge objects) and then "Import" the new objects into the existing structure. The elements in the existing structure can be modified, replaced or deleted. A "Preview" function allows for the examination of a modified structure before the delivery version is produced.

An Input Data Structure can be imported to the Editor and then, after entering the project (Browser) name, the browser is generated using the imported directory. Figure 7 shows the preview of generated Browser within the Editor interface.

Solanta system is an experimental software package developed in public private cooperation. Further work is needed to make it a more robust software product based on the concepts presented in this chapter. Practical Action's pilot projects using Solanta methodology and software are the first steps in field testing of the proposed solution for provision of knowledge services to disadvantage communities.

FUTURE WORK DIRECTIONS

The rise of e-society means that all members of the society (citizens of a country) benefit in all walks of life, to the extent possible, from advances of information technology. Access to relevant knowledge, in particular for people who live in poverty, harsh environments, regions lacking the basic infrastructure and income opportunities, is one of critical factors in building an e-society. There are many comprehensive publications concerning the diverse aspects and efforts of using information technologies in support of development projects and improving livelihoods of disadvantaged social groups, and community knowledge sharing. For example, valuable ideas and examples can be found in (SDC/Panos, 2005; Walsham, 2017; Figuères, 2011; The World Bank, 2011; Hearn et al., 2009; Helsper, 2008; Smuts et al., 2009).

Figure 6. Solanta editor interface

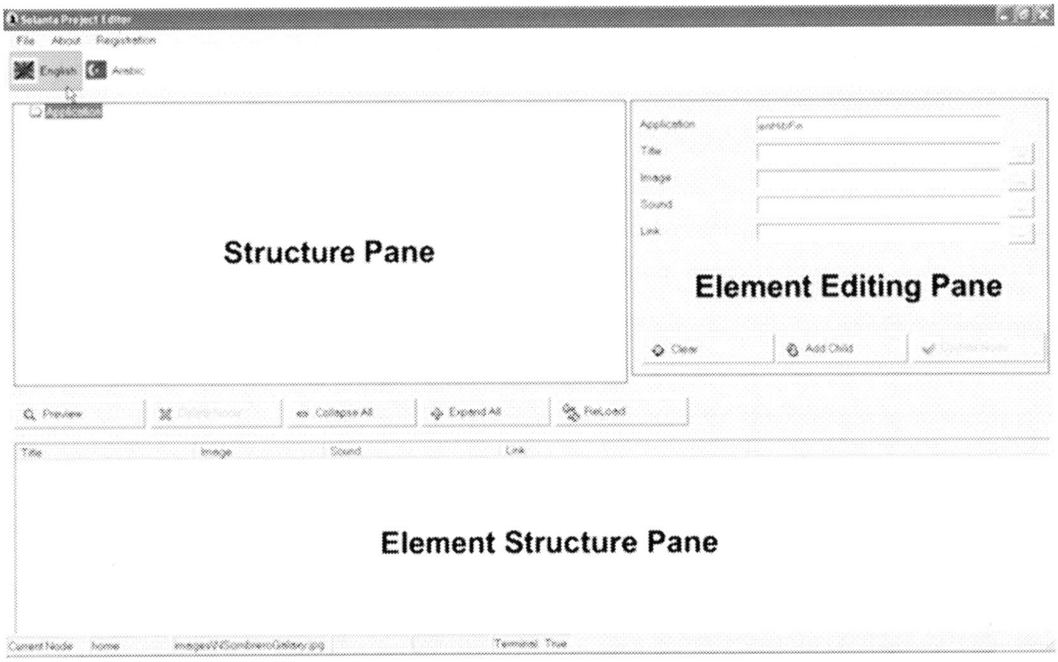

Figure 7. Preview operation of the editor

The main direction of future work is the integration of all elements of a system (see Figure 1) that will:

- Provide proper tools for knowledge capturing and sharing at the community level (language, spectrum of localized problems, submission and translation and exchange of knowledge objects)
- Have a context sensitive intelligent search engine (local and global) that will respond with the collection of knowledge objects relevant only to the problem described by the system user, ensure cognitive synergy between capabilities of the user and presentation of knowledge
- Develop the conceptualization and implementation of a structure of network of knowledge nodes at all levels of knowledge users and knowledge objects creators (community, region, global)
- Provide methodology and tools for the assessment of impact of knowledge services.

This chapter concerns the issue of proper software tools in some context of user requirements and current state-of-the-art of software technology. Further research and practical solutions are needed to deliver a tool for knowledge capturing and sharing that will provide adequate functionality for the integrated network of knowledge nodes mentioned above.

An example goal of the system could be helping a farmer who in given situation tries to get a better income from his farm or supporting a teacher in remote village who attempts to make better lessons plan and teaching materials.

CONCLUSION

Development organizations recognize the importance of knowledge management and sharing of knowledge as a vital factor in reducing poverty. In recent years, they have allocated substantial resources to implement knowledge management systems within their own structures. Yet local authorities and individuals still struggle to bring to their communities the knowledge they need to cope with overwhelming social and technological changes. Making the knowledge repositories of national or international institutions available at the community level would go a long way to bringing these efforts together. However, for local communities to truly benefit from global knowledge resources, the knowledge materials should be adapted and presented in appropriate language and format. A key research issue is the methodology for gaging the cognitive capability of intended user in relation to the complexity (cognitive level) of knowledge objects.

Effective knowledge sharing requires diverse means to produce and disseminate knowledge objects and appreciation of practical usage of knowledge objects (application of acquired knowledge). Using traditional and electronic methods together is particularly important for reaching remote and rural communities. For example, a puppet show can be recorded and shared on a DVD with sound tracts in different languages.

Easy-to-use tools are needed to develop capacity at the local level to produce and adapt knowledge materials in local languages and relevant to local problems. Locally developed knowledge materials should be a key part of any larger initiatives. Key issue is the networking of all institutions and individuals involved in preparation of knowledge materials.

In order to reach remote and poor communities with large illiterate and semi-literate population we must design appropriate knowledge sharing methods, including convergence of traditional means and electronic communication. Knowledge objects must concern very specific local issues and be delivered in local languages. A critical role in contextualization of knowledge objects and development of effective communication channels will play a feedback mechanism. We must learn about real demands for knowledge and understand the entire context and process of gaining and applying new knowledge.

We must foster creation and development of local knowledge industry by providing a platform (network) for sharing valuable knowledge objects. In time, local knowledge nodes could become small enterprises or franchised outlets.

REFERENCES

Abdelaziz, K. G. (2008). *Knowledge Gap Survey (internal report)*. Khartoum, Sudan: Practical Action.

Action, P. (2009). The Knowledge Gap Survey – Blue Nile State, Rosaris and Bau Localities (internal report).

Bernstein, D. A., Penner, L. A., Clarke-Stewart, A., & Roy, E. J. (2017). [*th ed.*). Cengage Inc. Retrieved from http://college.cengage.com/psychology/bernstein/psychology/6e/students/index.html]. *Psychology (Irvine, Calif.), 6*.

Bobrow, D. G., Cheslow, R., & Whalen, J. (2000). *Community Knowledge Sharing in Practice Systems and Practices Laboratory. Xerox Palo Alto Research Center*.

Chaudhuri, S. (2015). Urban poor, economic opportunities and sustainable development through traditional knowledge and practices. *Global Bioethics, 26*(2), 86–93. doi:10.1080/11287462.2015.1037141

Figuères, C. (2011). *Innovation and Technology for Poverty Eradication, report, International institute for Communication and Development*. IICD.

Flor, A. G. (2005). Participation and Partnerships in Rural Information Networks: Lessons Learned from five Asian Countries. In FAO Experts' Meeting on Rural Information Networks in Asia-Pacific: Innovative Practices and Future Directions, Bangkok, Thailand, December 14-16.

Geldof, M., Grimshaw, D.J., Kleine, D., & Unwin T. (2011). What are the key lessons of ICT4D partnerships for poverty reduction? policy brief. DFID.

Gniazdowski, A., & Chafetz, R. (2005). Knowledge Management for Mountain Development - Managing Knowledge with Context. *ICIMOD Newsletter, 47*(Winter), 15–18.

Grunfeld, H. (2011). The Contribution of Information and Communication Technologies for Development (ICT4D) Projects to Capabilities, Empowerment and Sustainability: A Case Study of iREACH in Cambodia [PhD Thesis]. Centre for Strategic Economic Studies, Faculty of Business and Law Victoria University, Melbourne, Australia

Hearn, S., & White, N. (2009). *Communities of practice: linking knowledge, policy and practice*. UK: Overseas Development Institute.

Helsper, E. J. (2008). *Digital Inclusion: An Analysis of Social Disadvantage and the Information Society.* Queen's Printer and Controller of Her Majesty's Stationery Office.

Mikolajuk, Z. (2004). Linking Knowledge Providers and Knowledge Users. In *Proceedings of the 21st Anniversary Symposium: "Securing Sustainable Livelihoods in the Hindu-Kush Himalayas: Directions for Future Research, Development and Cooperation", Working Session IV: ICIMOD*, Kathmandu, Nepal, December 5-6.

Mikolajuk, Z. (2005). Basics of Information and Knowledge Management. *ICIMOD Newsletter, 47*(Winter), 4–6.

Mikolajuk, Z. (2005). Information and Knowledge Management at ICIMOD – A Strategy Framework. *ICIMOD Newsletter, 47*(Winter), 7–10.

Mikolajuk, Z. (2005), Mountain Knowledge Partnership: A System for Knowledge Delivery in the Hindu Kush – Himalayan Region. In *Proceedings of the International Conference on Knowledge Management (ICKM)*, Malaysia, July 7-9.

Mikolajuk, Z. (2006), A Computer-based Knowledge Delivery System for Rural Communities – A Case Study using Beekeeping. In *Proceedings of the Knowledge Management International Conference and Exhibition, KMICE06*, Kuala Lumpur, Malaysia.

Mikolajuk, Z., Cartridge, R., & Noble, N. (2008), Practical Answers: A platform for knowledge sharing. *Waterlines- an International Journal of Water, Sanitation and Waste, 27*(2).

ODI, Overseas Development Institute, UK. (2006). R0093 Concept Note. Retrieved from http://www.odi.org.uk/RAPID/projects/R0093/Concept.html

Practical Action Dhaka. (2007). Knowledge Management of Rural Poor Communities - Bangladesh (final internal technical report).

RIN and JISC. (2009). Communicating knowledge: How and why UK researchers publish and disseminate their findings. A Research Information Network. Retrieved from www.rin.ac.uk/communicating-knowledge/JISC

Smuts, H., van der Merwe, A., & Loock, M. (2009). Key Characteristics in Selecting Software Tools for Knowledge Management, UNISA report, South Africa

Snowden, D. (2004). Notes from the workshop – Social network simulation: Creating knowledge flow, not knowledge content. In *Conference: Knowledge Management Asia 2004*, Suntec Singapore International Convention and Exhibition Centre, November 2-4.

Talyarkhana, S., Grimshaw, D. J., & Lowe, L. (2003). *Reaching the last mile: knowledge sharing for development. Knowledge and Information Services Unit, Intermediate Technology Development Group*, UK.

The World Bank. (2011). *The State of World Bank Knowledge Services - Knowledge for Development.* International Bank for Reconstruction and Development/The World Bank.

Walsham, G. (2017). ICT4D research: Reflections on history and future agenda. *Journal Information Technology for Development, 23*(1).

Warnock, K., & Wickremasinghe, R. (2005). *Information and Communication Technologies and large-scale poverty reduction Lessons from Asia, Africa, Latin America and the Caribbean* (K. Warnock & R. Wickremasinghe, Eds.). London, UK: Panos London.

KEY TERMS AND DEFINITIONS

Cognitive Capability: The mental capacity to understand and internalize information thus gain new knowledge or expand the remembered knowledge.

Knowledge Object: a presentation/description of a "chunk" of knowledge in a form that allows its audience to know more or to know better, and/or take effective action.

Knowledge Service: A service designed to deliver required knowledge objects in the appropriate format at the right place and time.

Local Knowledge Node: A facility (small enterprise) designed to develop, adapt and maintain knowledge objects tailored to the needs of local users and, if required, to provide access to global knowledge resources.

Multimedia Knowledge Object: A knowledge object in the form of computer-based presentation that includes elements such as texts, photographs, video clips, audio clips, maps, animations, and graphics.

Solanta System: A methodology and experimental software package that allow for constructing and delivering the multimedia knowledge objects by people with basic skills in computing (filing system, basics of MS Office).

Solanta Editor: A software application that generates the XML coding for the browser (Internet Explorer) based on the input directory containing multimedia files.

Chapter 4
A Family of Invisible Friends:
Cultivating a Sense of E-Community Among Virtual Work Teams

Ramon Visaiz
California State University Channel Islands, USA

Megan Jones
California State University Channel Islands, USA

Andrea M Skinner
California State University Channel Islands, USA

Ashley Van Ostrand
California State University Channel Islands, USA

Spencer Wolfe
California State University Channel Islands, USA

Antonio Arredondo
California State University Channel Islands, USA

J. Jacob Jenkins
California State University Channel Islands, USA

ABSTRACT

E-communities (i.e., virtual communities that are established and interact primarily via the internet) are more significant than ever in today's modern workplace. Despite the potential advantages offered by e-communities, however, their formation and maintenance are often hindered by feelings of mistrust, unclear group processes, and limited technical expertise. This study analyzed nearly 2,500 survey responses from 600 students spanning 25 colleges/universities in order to develop practical implications for cultivating a sense of e-community among virtual work teams. Thematic results of our study revealed the significance of brand awareness, interpersonal facilitation, user-friendly design, fiscal barriers, and mobile accessibility. Based on these results, this study concludes with five corresponding implications for cultivating a sense of e-community in the modern workplace: increased integration, expanded physicality, supplemental training, financial entrée, and utilized flexibility.

DOI: 10.4018/978-1-5225-7214-5.ch004

INTRODUCTION

Online communities (i.e., "e-communities") continue to gain in use and popularity. Characterized by Rheingold (2001) as a "family of invisible friends," e-communities offer a way for people to find connection in a world that often feels disconnected, and meaning in an seemingly meaningless society (see also Brown, 2002; Kim, 2000; Plant, 2004). Consequently, participation in online communities has risen exponentially in recent years, with 84% of internet users reporting they have personally reached out to an online group (Horrigan, 2001). Furthermore, approximately 80% of these users have chosen to remain in contact with at least one e-community on a regular basis, and nearly half (49%) say this process has enabled them to build a personal sense of community with others (Zhou, 2011).

E-communities show promise for the modern workplace as well. This is especially evident when it comes to virtual work teams. A sense of e-community has shown to positively correlate to job fulfillment and satisfaction, while increasing creativity and efficiency among employees (Garrett, Spreitzer, & Bacevice, 2017). Without the space-time restrictions of previous workplaces, e-communities also empower colleagues from around the globe to converge around professional expertise and result in increased cultural and technical diversity (Griffith & Neale, 2001). Such a reality saves employees on travel time and expense, while allowing them to collaborate asynchronously around the clock (Solomon, 2001; see also Kock, 2005).

Despite each of these potential advantages, however, a sense of e-community has proven especially difficult to cultivate in professional settings (Berry, 2006; Cohen & Gibson, 2003; Timmerman, 2000). This difficulty arises – in part – from a lack of nonverbal cues and interpersonal subtleties among virtual members, combined with technological demands and the ever-present potential for soft/hardware malfunctions: "The use of virtual teams adds complexity for management in many organizations because virtual teams are sociological and social systems just as is any team, but virtual teams also have their work processes intertwined with technological systems" (Berry, 2011, p. 192). This difficulty is especially significant because virtual teams that lack as sense of connectedness are also less likely to be satisfied with their work (Kirkham et al., 2002), less likely to prioritize online tasks (Klein & Barrett, 2001), and less willing to collaborate with one another during the *norming* phase of a work project (Hinds & Weisband, 2003).

The present study analyzed nearly 2,500 survey responses to develop practical implications for cultivating a sense of e-community among virtual team members. Through an expanded variation of Vorvoreanu's (2008) *Website Experience Analysis* (WEA), we engaged 600 undergraduate students at 25 universities throughout southern California to reveal their views toward seven of the most popular virtual collaboration programs in use today: Basecamp, Dropbox, Google Drive, iDoneThis, Join.me, Skitch, and Skype (Sharma, 2015; see also Hyatt, 2015). After offering a brief context for virtual collaboration and the role of e-communities, we discuss each of these seven groupwares in more detail. Next, we outline our study's methodology, and then reveal its five thematic results: (1) brand awareness, (2) interpersonal facilitation, (3) user-friendly design, (4) fiscal barriers, and (5) mobile accessibility. We conclude with five corresponding implications for how virtual users can increase a sense of e-community, and how software developers cano lead the way in this cutting-edge field of telecommunications.

E-COMMUNITY IN VIRTUAL COLLABORATION

Virtual collaboration (VC) traces back to the late 1970s, beginning with researchers' initial efforts with multiuser spaces and collaborative systems (Tate, Hansberger, Potter, & Wickler, 2014). The phrase co-operative learning emerged during the 1980s for pedagogical techniques allowing students to collaborate in groups over the Internet (Breen, 2013). *I-Rooms* subsequently became the way to define computer-mediated environments during the 1990s, and during the 2000s, terms like virtual worlds and virtual collaboration environments came into use as a way to "supplement the existing social web with virtual spaces that provide a means for the simultaneous presence of individuals" (Tate, Hansberger, Potter, & Wickler, 2014, pp. 2-3; Bosch-Sijtsema & Sivunen, 2013).

Today, VC occurs anytime employees or work teams in distinct geographic locations operate via telecommunication technology (see Konradt & Hoch, 2007; Peters & Manz, 2007). The specific term used to describe this process, however, is as expansive as ever (e.g., groupwares, digital work, learning networks, virtual teams, virtual employees, virtual organizations, virtual applications, online environments, and collaborative technology to name but a few). Such a diverse range of terms used to characterize VC also speaks to the wide variety of ways in which it is utilized today, as well as its range of potential advantages and disadvantages.

Advantages of VC for Virtual Teams

Virtual collaboration processes offer team members a myriad of potential advantages, and are most beneficial for work teams who rely heavily on group work, while being burdened with disparate time/spatial realities (Kock, 2000). Consequently, four of the most prominent advantages offered by VC include the ability for virtual teams to (a) transcend geography, (b) circumvent time, (c) reduce travel, and (d) increase diversity.

Transcending Geography

It has become increasingly difficult for traditional work teams to collaborate face-to-face (Hara, Solomon, Kim, & Sonnenwald, 2003). In contrast, however, virtual team members are freely able to "communicate, collaborate, and create outputs irrespective of time and space, because they are not bound by temporal constraints or geographical location as are most face-to-face teams" (Berry, 2011, p 188). This sensibility can be advantageous even when colleagues are located mere miles or meters away from one another, allowing them to avoid vehicular traffic or the time lost walking between buildings, offices, and conference rooms; valuable time that would have been spent commuting, can now be used for more efficient means.

Circumventing Time

In addition to the ability to transcend geography, VC processes also allow users to circumvent conventional time restrictions (see Hiltz & Wellman, 1997; Swan, 2000; Toomey & Adams, 2000). Rather than limiting work efforts to a nine-hour work day, virtual teams are able to work asynchronously: both around the clock and around the world. This advantage is especially significant in today's increasingly globalized society, with virtual teams working across multiple continents. The result is increased output and productivity for organizations, without a need to increase labor demands on the organization's workforce (e.g., Cogburn, & Levinson, 2003).

Reducing Travel

A third primary advantage of virtual processes is reduced travel expenses. American employees alone take more than 450 million business trips each year, equaling over $250 billion dollars in travel expenses (Certify, 2017). Through the use of VC, previously incurred travel expenses can subsequently be allocated toward other tools or resources, resulting in a society where "organizational boundaries become meaningless" (Dawson & Clements, 2004, p. 51).

Increasing Diversity

With obstacles related to time, location and travel expenses removed, virtual teams can increasingly be composed of diverse cultural members. As Karpova, Correia, and Baran (2008) write: "Another benefit of using virtual collaboration is the ability to bring together heterogeneous participants [from] a diversity of cultures, opinions, and communication styles" (p. 45). For each of these reasons, virtual processes have the ability to increase one's access to new ideas, perspectives, and approaches; and virtual users often gain enhanced argumentation, sensemaking, and group consensus skills.

Lack of E-Community in Virtual Teams

Despite each of the aforementioned advantages, VC's fundamental drawback is a weakened sense of e-community: communal bonds felt among virtual team members via telecommunication processes (see Cruz-Cunha, Miranda, & Goncalves, 2013). A sense of community among traditional colleagues has shown to positively correlate to a myriad of workplace benefits, including efficiency (Vaheen, 2015), productivity (Shuh, 2013), longevity (Goldsmith, 2009), and overall job satisfaction (Neuliep, 2003), to name but a few. Yet a comparable sense of e-community is difficult to create among virtual teams, due to three prominent shortcomings: (a) feelings of distrust, (b) unclear group processes, and (c) limited technical expertise.

Feelings of Distrust

Increased feelings of distrust, uncertainty, and even skepticism is common among virtual team members (see Brown & Poole, 2004; Hossain & Wellman, 1997). This reality can be especially detrimental on workplace effectiveness, due to the strong correlations that exist between trust and efficiency, as well as trust and deadline reliably (Iacono & Weisband, 1997). Feelings of trust – or the lack thereof – have also shown to correlate to virtual members' sense of security, confidence, and knowledge sharing (Jarvenpaa, Knoll, &, Leidner, 1998; Shu, & Chuang, 2011). VC teams often assemble and disassemble rapidly once their goals are reached, however, failing to provide ample opportunity for its members to build the level of trust necessary for a sense of e-community to take root (Munkvold & Zigurs, 2007). For each of these reasons, studies show the development of trusting relationships often stalls within VC contexts, resulting in a lack of e-community.

Unclear Group Processes

In addition to feelings of distrust, a shared sense of e-community is often hindered among VC teams because of unclear group processes (de Vreede & Briggs, 2005; Munkvold & Zigurs, 2007). VC teams often fail clarify a shared understanding of group procedures, which is particularly problematic since the nature of VC actually requires *more* defined procedures than face-to-face collaboration, not less (Dittman, Hawkes, Deokar, & Sarnikar, 2010; see also Breen, 2013). With unclear group processes, cultural differences can further detract from a virtual work team's functionality, resulting in feelings of confusion, disorientation, disengagement, and even anger. This reality not only creates increased challenges for virtual employees, but also for team leaders who attempt to cultivate a sense of e-community among those employees (Soetanto, Childs, Poh, Austin, & Hao, 2012).

Limited Technical Expertise

A final shortcoming of VC that hinders the creation of e-community is limited technical expertise. In order to explore the role of technology in VC, Butson and Thomson (2014) developed a prototype web-based networking environment to see what tools and features students preferred. This web-based virtual platform provided students the opportunity to interact using synchronous and asynchronous tools. Their results provided great insight into students' disinterest with e-collaboration software. Despite having all the tools to collaborate in both a synchronous and asynchronous manner, a majority of students still chose to work individually offline. Butson and Thomson's study illustrates how the VC learning curve can often lead to frustration. A lack of technical expertise can also cause certain team members to become disillusioned with an online platform, causing collaborators to disengage and potentially hindering the team's ability accomplish their set goals. The present study seeks to address each of these common shortcomings – feelings of distrust, unclear group processes, and limited technical expertise – by using Vorvoreanu's (2008) *Website Experience Analysis* (WEA) to explore seven of the most popular groupwares in use today.

GROUPWARES USED IN THIS STUDY

There are more VC technologies in existence today than ever before. In order to develop implications for contemporary users and developers, this particular study focused on seven of the most popular groupwares in existence: Basecamp, Dropbox, Google Drive, iDoneThis, Join.me, Skitch, Skype, (Sharma, 2015; see also Hyatt, 2015).

Basecamp

Basecamp is a project management and collaboration software used to help professional groups work together virtually. Basecamp was developed in 1997 by founders Carlos Segura, Ernest Kim and Jason Fried in order to help clients feel their businesses were being taken care of in the most organized and efficient manner possible (Fried, 2004). Founder Jason Fried believed that project management suffered when clients aren't involved in business processes, thus, the reason for developing Basecamp. Fried elaborates on this thought by stating: "You may think your collection of random emails, napkin scribbles,

IM chat transcripts, post-it notes, and handwritten notes are organized but what do your clients think?" (par. 7, emphasis original). Basecamp officially launched in 2004 and is headquartered in Chicago, IL. Features of Basecamp include file sharing, time tracking, instant messaging, milestone management, and collaborative document creation. Common users of Basecamp range from freelance individuals to mid-sized companies to multinational corporations (Basecamp, 2015).

Dropbox

Dropbox is an Internet hosting service headquartered in San Francisco, CA. Dropbox allows virtual users to share files with others who have a Dropbox account (e.g., documents, slides, videos, etc.) Dropbox was founded in 2007 by Drew Houston and Arash Ferdowski. Individuals who use Dropbox are able to create a free account where they are allotted a limited amount of storage. If/when users need more storage, they must subscribe (and pay) for additional space. Dropbox is currently competing against larger companies – such Google Drive – that have substantially larger user bases. For this reason, Dropbox has worked to increase its competitive edge by lowing prices and adding additional tools that make it easier for individuals to store files in the cloud. Newman (2014) comments on this reality: "For Dropbox, creating killer cloud-based applications will be the challenge. The company is going up against the likes of Microsoft and Google, who can tightly integrate cloud storage through their own operating systems and productivity suites." (p. 43, par. 2, 2014).

Google Drive

Similar to Dropbox in many ways, Google Drive is a cloud storage service that allows users to virtually store their photos, videos, documents, and more. Google Drive was launched in April of 2012; within six months, it had 240 million active monthly users (Protalinski, 2014). Two of Google Drive's primary features include Google Docs and Google Sheets. Each application can be used to create and edit various types of files. Google Docs has become a particularly popular service on college campuses and is used regularly by students and professors in higher education. According to the U.S. News and World Reports, Google Docs was one of the 5 must-download apps in 2014 (Sheehy, 2014).

iDoneThis

iDoneThis is an email-based productivity log that tracks and motivates productivity. The site achieves this goal by sending participants daily email reminders of what other group members have accomplished. Additional features include the creation of visual graphs, word clouds, and the ability to export data into text files and spreadsheets. In spite of these added features, iDoneThis is most commonly used for tracking employee or student productivity, rather than initiating collaborative efforts. iDoneThis was a Silicon Valley startup founded by Walter Chen and Rodrigo Guzman of AngelPad in 2011 (Tsotsis, 2011). For businesses, the cost of iDoneThis starts at $5 per group member, but is free for personal use.

Join.Me

Join.Me allows conference calls in over 45 countries at no cost. As many as 250 users can participate in a conference call at any one time. Join.Me is able to offer unlimited audio to its users via Voice Over

Internet Protocol technology (or, VoIP for short). Other features include recording, access to personal links, presenter swaps, and one-click scheduling that syncs Join.Me with Outlook and Google Calendar. As a part of LogMeIn, Inc.'s suite of products, Join.Me is designed with professional users in mind. It also offers the unique opportunity for businesses and companies to network with other business and companies (Perez, 2012).

Skitch

Skitch is a virtual tool that allows its users to collaborate in a creative manner. In the words of Yamshon (2014), "It's more than just a note-taking tool. You can markup a photo for fun, point things out on a map, markup a webpage, annotate a PDF, or use it as a blank canvas for a fresh idea, drawing it out from scratch" (par. 2). Skitch also offers an organizational component that can be used to compartmentalize documents. Originally developed by Plasq, a software company began in Melbourne, Australia, Skitch was acquired by Stepan Pachikov's Evernote Coporation in 2011. Skitch is presently offered as a free application for iOS, Android, and Windows (Mowshowitz, 1997).

Skype

Skype was released in 2003 as a video chat software. In more recent years, Skype has expanded it functionality to include file exchange, voice recording, and instant messaging, among other things. Skype was originally developed by entrepreneurs Janus Friis and Niklas Zennstrom in 2003. The technology was purchased by Ebay in 2005 for $2.6 billion, and again by Microsoft in 2011 for $8.5 billion (BBC News, 2011). Skype has since become one of the most popular applications for VC in the world, with over 50 million users worldwide. In the process, Skype has also helped to advance real time video streaming technologies. As Guha and Daswani (2005) predicted over a decade ago, "Voice over IP (VoIP) and instant messaging (IM) are fast supplementing email in both enterprise and home networks" (p. 1).

RESEARCH INSTRUMENTATION, PARTICIPANTS, AND PROCEDURE

Derived in part from Prominence-Interpretation Theory, *Website Experience Analysis* (WEA) measures a participant's experience in five distinct areas: trust, dialogue, openness, commitment, and involvement (Vorvoreanu, 2008). Each of these areas is assessed with a pair of quantitative and qualitative survey items. The quantitative item asks participants a Likert-type question, based on a scale from one to ten (1 = not at all; 10 = very much); the qualitative item asks each participant to explain the reason for their quantitative response in more detail.

For this study, we used an expanded variation of WEA that is better suited for the interactive nature of VC websites. Our research instrumentation still measured participants' experience across WEA's five distinct areas of trust, dialogue, openness, commitment and involvement; however, our questionnaire focused more on the software's perceived use and utility. (For a list of corresponding survey questions, please see Table 1).

Participants in this study included 600 undergraduate students enrolled in one of 25 universities spanning southern California. Participant ages ranged from 18 to 62 (N = 23.4). Three hundred and seventy-two of our participants self-identified as female and 224 identified as male. Four participants

Table 1. Survey questions, using an expanded variation of WEA

WEA Measure	Corresponding Survey Question
1. Trust	Would you trust using this website for an important project?
2. Dialogue	Do you feel this website does a good job of fostering dialogue and interaction among its users?
3. Openness	Do you feel this website does a good of allowing coworkers to share information?
4. Commitment	Do you anticipate using this website 5-10 years from now?
5. Involvement	Does this website help facilitate involvement from its users?

declined to specify gender. Students from all grade levels were surveyed, with the majority of participants identifying as seniors (N = 347). A variety of ethnic/racial backgrounds were also represented, including White (296), Hispanic/Latino (181), Asian (56), African American (50), and Middle Eastern/Persian (17). Participants hailed from 33 majors in total, namely Communication (144), Business (120), Psychology (77), Computer Science (56), Nursing (46), and Biology (46). GPAs ranged from 4.0 to 1.9 (N = 3.2).

After receiving IRB approval, we began by using convenience sampling to recruit potential participants; we later used snowball sampling via various social media platforms (i.e., Instagram, Facebook, and Snapchat). We began by explaining the study's scope and overview to each potential participant, and then offering them a physical copy of the study's questionnaire. Virtual participants were also explained the study's scope and overview. We then sent these potential participants an online survey, along with a hyperlink that directed them to a Google Form. All participants were given at least one week to complete the study's questionnaire.

Each participant completed 3.12 surveys on average, resulting in a total of 2,305 completed surveys. In effort to develop practical implications, we focused our analysis on the questionnaires' qualitative results. We began this analysis by coding each response in search of dominant themes. An intensive reading of our individual codings were then clumped and re-coded until more refined themes emerged from the data (Lindlof & Taylor, 2011). In effort to ensure the validity of our findings, each author also worked to make sense our preliminary data, and then to re-contextualize our results in effort to develop practical implications.

FIVE THEMATIC RESULTS

Due to e-community's significance among virtual team members, this study used an expanded variation of Vorvoreanu's (2008) *Website Experience Analysis* (WEA) to analyze 2,305 survey responses in the five distinct areas of trust, dialogue, openness, commitment, and involvement. The qualitative results of this study revealed five specific findings – one for each of WEA's five foci: (1) brand awareness, (2) interpersonal facilitation, (3) user-friendly design, (4) fiscal barriers, and (5) mobile accessibility. The present section discusses these five thematic results in more detail; the following section concludes by offering five corresponding implications. (Please see Table 2 for our corresponding measures, results, and implications).

Table 2. Corresponding Measures, Results, and Implications

WEA Measure	Thematic Result	Practical Implication
1. Trust	Brand Awareness	Increased Integration
2. Dialogue	Interpersonal Facilitation	Expanded Physicality
3. Openness	User-Friendly Design	Supplementary Training
4. Commitment	Fiscal Barriers	Financial Entrée
5. Involvement	Mobile Accessibility	Utilized Flexibility

Brand Awareness

Within the context of this study, organizational trust refers to the level of confidence users have in a website's ability to consistently perform at a high level (see Jenkins, 2012; McKnight & Chervany, 2000). To that end, we asked participants whether they trusted using each of the VC websites for completing an important project. The most common response to this question highlighted the value of brand awareness, with a large majority of participants (N = 412) referring to their familiarity – or unfamiliarity – with certain software programs.

Participants' awareness of a software program and/or its maker was shown to result in higher levels of trustworthiness and, therefore, a higher likelihood that they would feel comfortable using the website. The two specific programs with the highest levels of trust were Google Drive and Skype, with respective scores of 8.93 and 7.19 on a Likert-type scale from 1-10. While explaining her trust of Google Drive, one participant wrote, "I trust Google and know it well and have used it many times, so I'm comfortable with it" (white female). A second participant responded similarly by commenting, "I like Google and they have always made their products easy to use and get help with… I think it will be available for a long time since it's powered by Google" (white male). Participants responded likewise toward Skype by using the adjectives "familiar," "popular," "reputable," "well known," and "well established" to express the level of trust they felt toward the video conferencing software.

Conversely, several participants commented on their lack of familiarity with certain programs, resulting in lower levels of trust felt toward the VC software. When expressing her views of Join.Me, for instance, one participant reported, "I've never heard of this site before which makes me a little uncomfortable to use it" (Hispanic/Latina female). In response to Dropbox, another participant not only lamented that she had "never heard of it before," but also contrasted her inexperience with Dropbox to the aforementioned familiarity with Google: "I don't know why anyone would use [Dropbox] over Google Docs."

Despite the importance of brand recognition and its effect upon participants' levels of trust toward a particular program, iDoneThis was paradoxically disparaged for its apparent attempt to capitalize on Apple's use of a lowercase "i" (e.g., iPod, iTunes, iPhone). iDoneThis' use of an "i" at the beginning of its name was perceived by some participants as an attempt to fabricate familiarity among potential users, characterizing the attempt as "shallow" and even "dishonest." One respondent clearly commented, "The [iDoneThis] website seems sketchy because it tries to infer its associated with Apple in the name but I don't think it is" (white female). Consequently, the results of our analysis suggest that a software's brand recognition cannot be fabricated over night, but rather must originate through increased and repetitious integration into the users' day-to-day life – a distinction that is further developed within this study's first implication.

Interpersonal Facilitation

This study's second thematic result, interpersonal facilitation, referred to participants' desire for genuine dialogue and communal interaction, defined by Vorvoreanu (2008) as "the inverse flow of information… an indicator of two-way communication" (p. 238). In total, 388 of this study's 600 respondents referred to the benefit of face-to-face communication. In regard to how well it fostered dialogue and interaction among its users, Skype was again the quantitative outlier, scoring 8.80 on a scale from 1-10. The six remaining sites averaged 6.33 in this same category, with Skitch receiving the lowest overall average of 5.25.

One primary reason participants rated Skype so highly in the area of openness was because of its video-sharing platform. Participants reported enjoying the ability to see their virtual team members, even when they were unable to meet physically. Participants' qualitative responses also correlated this ability to see one another with higher levels of motivation, as well as lower levels of confusion and miscommunication. One participant specifically commented on the way Skype increased his motivation to participate in VC projects by writing, "I'm more likely to care and get things done when I can see who I'm working with, and they can actually see me" (white male). Meanwhile, more than two-dozen respondents referred to the way synchronous video helped to "clarify," "simplify," and "explain" communication processes among virtual group members.

The significance of interpersonal interaction supports previous research conducted by Berry (2006), Timmerman (2000), Kirkham et al. (2002), and Cohen and Gibson (2003), to name but a few. Each of these scholars cite a lack of physical presence as one of VC's primary shortcomings. Despite this importance, however, not all websites are able to integrate video sharing features into their design. For that reason, this study's discussion section further outlines alternative ways for users and developers to increase physicality among group members.

User-Friendly Design

In effort to measure participants' perceived levels of openness, we asked participants of this study whether the websites did a good job of allowing group members to share information. The most common response to this inquiry invoked a need for user-friendly design. Adjectives such as "easy," "simple," "efficient," "straightforward," and "user-friendly" were used by a slight majority of participants to commend specific websites. Altogether, 294 of the 600 participants referred to this reality by praising how easy it was to navigate Basecamp, Join.Me and Google Drive, while simultaneously criticizing Skitch, Skype and iDoneThis. One participant explicitly referred to the simplicity of Basecamp, and its ability to aid virtual group members: "It seems like it would be easy to write in and point to specific areas of a project, making it easy for other people to see what needs to be changed or stay the same" (Hispanic/Latina female). Another participant reported on his view of Join.Me by writing, "It's easy and reliable. [The] interface is user-friendly, and the software is compatible with almost all devices… it would be easy to share information with others" (white male). And yet another survey participant responded similarly about Google Drive: "I feel like the simplicity works in its favor to make it something easily adaptable for the work world" (white female).

An emphasis upon user-friendly design serves to highlight the need for VC software that clean, simple, uncluttered, and streamlined. In fact, participants of this study seemed more interested in understanding a software's purpose quickly, lest they become frustrated or lose interest, than they were in comprehending a software's full depth of options and functionality. This reality was especially evident when those options and functions were unclearly communicated to the user, as evidenced by one participant's critique of Skitch: "A lot of stuff going on here… confusing" (African American male). Similarly, a second participant disparaged Skype for being "too involved" (Hispanic/Latino male), and a third participant criticized iDoneThis for having "too many options to choose from" (white female).

Fiscal Barriers

Ledingham and Bruning (1998) characterize organizational commitment as the decision to maintain a relationship with the general public. Consequently, fiscal barriers emerged as the participants' primary consideration when anticipating whether they would still be using a website in 5-10 years. Nearly 1/3 of participants who did not foresee using a particular program in the future cited cost as their main determinant: "It costs money to join" (African American female, in response to Join.Me); "It cost money and not many people use it" (Hispanic/Latino male, in response to iDoneThis); and "I don't like paying for things that could be done for free" (white male, in response to Basecamp). In contrast, a substantial number of participants who predicted using Google Drive for years to come specifically referred to its complimentary access: "No cost" (white female), "It's free and easy to use" (white female), and "Google Drive doesn't cost anything… so I can see myself still using it in 10 years" (white male).

The impact of fiscal barriers upon whether or not students perceived themselves as longstanding customers highlights the tension between short-term and long-term considerations. Developers of VC software can seek immediate financial retribution from university-aged students, or they can seek to build the groundwork now for a professional relationship well beyond the university – a tension that is again explored within this study's subsequent implications section.

Mobile Accessibility

Finally, organizational involvement is indicated by an effort to facilitate relational ties (Ledingham & Bruning, 1998). In this regard, we asked participants whether the websites helped to facilitate involvement from/among their users. The fifth theme that subsequently emerged was mobile accessibility: downloadable applications or site optimization for cell phones. This proved to be the case for all seven websites examined in our study, as each site offered users an optimized version of itself on either IOS or Android platforms.

The two primary reasons respondents lauded mobile accessibility was for its ability to make communication easier and faster. According to one participant: "Being able to access [Basecamp] on any device makes it easy to stay in contact with others" (white female). A second participant responded similarly about Dropbox by writing, "The aspect of phone use plus laptop or desktop us makes it easy for users to interact" (Hispanic/Latina female), and a third participated added, "The fact that [Join.Me] can be used through an application on a phone will make it easier for anyone to use it and access it" (white male). Additional survey responses highlighted the ability for mobile accessibility to increase users' rate and speed of communication, making it more convenient for them to collaborate, problem solve, and finish tasks on time. To this end, participants described iDoneThis as "swift," "quick," and "rapid," while others described Google Drive as "fast," "speedy," and "efficient." One participant further elaborated on the speed and efficiency of Google Drive:

I am able to quickly respond to the users of this site through mobility use. That's what makes it so unique, because you can take out your cell phone and connect with users of this site. Mobility is the way to go... In today's world it is a must... to be fast and accessible [from] anywhere. (African American female)

FIVE CORRESPONDING IMPLICATIONS

We conclude this study by discussing five practical implications for users and developers of VC software: (1) increased integration, (2) expanded physicality, (3) supplementary training, (4) financial entrée, and (5) utilized flexibility. Each of these implications corresponds to this study's five thematic results outlined in the previous section, as well as the five specific areas outlined by Vorvoreanu's (2008) *Website Experience Analysis*: trust, dialogue, openness, commitment, and involvement. Each of these implications also address ways for VC users to create a healthy sense of e-community, as well as ways for VC developers who hope to lead the way in this cutting-edge field of telecommunications.

Increased Integration

The importance that participants of this study placed upon brand awareness reveals the need for increased integration by both users and developers of VC software. As one respondent succinctly put it, "iDoneThis? Never heard of it" (white male). This reality not only sheds light on how a program such as Google Drive was able to garner 240 million active users within six short months of its initial launch (Protalinski, 2014), but also reinforces the significance of *branding* – a contemporary buzzword in personal and organizational development (see Lair, Sullivan, & Cheney, 2005). Howard Schultz, the CEO of Starbucks, comments on the import of organizational branding by writing: "A great brand raises the bar... whether it's the challenge to do your best in sports and fitness, or the affirmation that the cup of coffee you're drinking really matters" (Daye, 2006, par. 1). Schultz's commentary not only highlights the value of a consumer's ability to recognize a brand under differing conditions, but also the value of attitudinal branding (i.e., brand ability to evoke a particular emotion or sentiment). His observations also stress the ubiquitous nature of branding in modern society, and its ability to influence everything from fitness to coffee.

As previously mentioned, however, iDoneThis was paradoxically disparaged by this study's participants for its semblant effort to coopt Apple's promotion of the lowercase "i" as a product prefix (e.g., iPod, iTunes, iPhone). Certain respondents perceived iDoneThis' similar use of a lowercase "i" as "shallow," "surface-level" and even "dishonest," with one participant noting: "The [iDoneThis] website seems sketchy because it tries to infer its associated with Apple in the name but I don't think it is" (white female). Responses such as this reveal that name recognition cannot result from superficial or one-dimensional attempts at (re)branding. Instead, genuine brand awareness must be developed over time through prolonged and sustained integration into users' daily lives.

Specific suggestions for increasing the brand awareness of VC software – and therefore increasing name recognition and feelings of trust among potential users – include formal agreements with colleges and universities, as well as partnerships with social media sites like Facebook, Twitter, and Instagram. Formal agreements with community colleges and four-year universities will allow software developers to get their products in front of more students, helping to familiarize those students with the product's name and functionality over time. By becoming a university-wide file sharing service, for example, a software program like Dropbox would be instantly integrated into the day-to-day of thousands of students' lives, increasing its capacity to compete with its more commonly recognized competitor: Good Drive.

An alternative way to improve brand awareness via increased integration is by partnering with social media sites like Facebook, Twitter, or Instagram. A staggering 96% of college students today report using Facebook (Martin, 2015). Meanwhile, 80% of college students use Twitter, 73% use Instagram, 48% use Pinterest, 40% use LinkedIn, 40% use Vine, 29% use Google+, and 29% use Tumblr, (Viner, 2014). Statistics such as these evidence students' awareness and familiarity toward these web applications, as well as their login procedures. Thus, integrating user profiles from existing social media into online VC programs can make the initial registration process quicker and more streamlined, while simultaneously utilizing the brand awareness associated with these social media websites in a way that makes new users feel reassured.

Expanded Physicality

A deluge of previous research has shown the primary drawback of VC to be its lack of physical interaction among members (e.g., Berry, 2006; Timmerman, 2000; Kirkham et al., 2002; Cohen & Gibson, 2003). As aforementioned, without being able to perceive the nonverbal communication that accompanies typical group work processes – body language, facial expressions, etc. – it is often difficult for trusting relationships to form among VC team members. Consistent with previous findings, this study revealed a lack of physical interaction to be a primary hindrance toward genuine dialogue and communal interaction (see Vorvoreanu, 2008).

Skype alleviated much of this concern through its video sharing platform; however, not all websites are able – or even advised – to infuse the use of video technology. Rather, users and developers of VC software should consider alternative ways to expand the physicality felt among virtual team members. Specific suggestions for doing so include the use and integration of avatars, virtual worlds, group bios, and third party social networks.

Recent studies have shown avatars to increase the level of personal responsibility virtual team members bring to their work, resulting in higher levels of work performance and greater levels of social bonding. This reality is especially evident when a person designs her/his own avatar: "Your identity mixes in with the identity of that avatar and, as a result, your visual perception of the virtual environment is colored by the physical resources of your avatar" (Swayne, 2013, par. 3). Taken one step further, avatars within the context of massively multiplayer online worlds (MMOWs) like *Second Life, The Sims, Minecraft*, or even *World of Warcraft* offer virtual team members an entire virtual world in which to interact. Kock (2008)

defines virtual worlds as "environments created by technology that incorporate virtual representations of various elements found in the real world" (p. 1). Kock goes on to discuss the unique opportunity virtual worlds offer their team members to establish shared patterns of behavior, which result in the potential for increased efficiency and productivity. To this end, the developers of *Second Life* claim more than 1,400 organizations currently use their virtual environment to hold meetings and training sessions (Tutton, 2009). Such an approach to virtual worlds offers a sense of place to dispersed users, as team members are able to gather together in a digital coffee shop, huddle around a digital fireplace, or walk through a digital park.

Our final two suggestions for increasing physicality are the creation of individual bios and the incorporation of social media networks. While these implications do not offer users a sense of physicality or place in the way avatars and virtual worlds do, they still increase *social ties* among virtual group members by sharing interests, hobbies, and background information with another (see Granovetter, 1973, 2004). Social ties are generally defined as information-carrying connections between people. Such ties can be characterized as "strong," "weak" or "absent," depending on the type and frequency of interpersonal interaction they entail. The development of strong social ties among VC users is important because they can counteract feelings of distrust (Iacono & Weisband, 1997). Strong social ties also correlate to higher levels of group efficiency, increased problem solving, and the ability for virtual teams to meet established deadlines. Conversely, weak ties correlate to a higher likelihood of frustration and misunderstanding (Breen, 2013).

In effort to strengthen the social ties among virtual team members, teams can create personal bios. These bios can be shared in a myriad of ways: during the group's initial meeting or on the organization's website. This information can also be collected and redistributed by the group's leader as a simple Word or PDF document. Meanwhile, the creation of a group page on social networking sites like Facebook or Google+ can instantaneously familiarize team members with one another through publicly shared photographs, status updates, etc. In this way, social networking sites serve as a way to capitalize on each of the aforementioned implications without having to create any new or additional material. In other words, team members can use their existing profile picture as a readymade avatar, their online profile as a readymade bio, and so on.

Supplemental Training

In response to a website's level of perceived openness, respondents rarely mentioned the need for increased transparency or additional opportunities to interact with the software developers. Rather, this study's most commonly cited need was that of user-friendly design. Said differently: participants rarely associated a website's perceived level of openness with *what* it said, but rather with its ability to visually communicate that information in a clear and concise manner. As a result, developers of VC software must recognize the importance of crisp, clean, and uncluttered design. Intricate and overly complex approaches to problem solving should also be avoided in favor of one-button solutions and easy to use applications.

Although users of VC software typically don't have the ability to directly affect its design, managers can still increase a program's user-friendly perception via supplement training (Warkentin & Beranek, 1999). Specific and easy-to-implement suggestions for supplemental training consist of tip sheets, online tutorials, in-person workshops, real-time help, designated personnel, and refresher courses. A simple one-page tip sheet can be created by the project's manager or an IT professional in order to offer others an overview of the VC software being used, to address commonly asked questions, and so on. Distributed in advance of the software's implementation, this would not only help to clarify and simplify its use, but would also serve as a reference later in the process. Similarly, online tutorials can easily be created by managers or IT professionals using a free program like Screencast-O-Matic to introduce a product to new group members, and/or to proactively address any anticipated questions. Online tutorials can also be disseminated using the precise software program in question as a way to introduce new users to the particular technology. In addition, each of these materials – tip sheets and online tutorials – can be used to formulate an in-person workshop. Workshops lack the ability to be used later as a reference point in the way tip sheets and online tutorials can. Their low-tech format can also serve to contradict the application and "spirit" of VC software. For these same reasons, however, in-person workshops can help to orientate and assimilate novice users who are aversive to a particular technology. The face-to-face nature of in-person workshops also allows opportunities for more organic and free flowing conversation, in which users' questions can be resolved directly.

The next two suggestions for supplemental training (real-time help and designated personnel) can also serve to persuade those who are reluctant to use a new or unfamiliar technology for collaborating online. Both of these suggestions can be accomplished virtually or face-to-face. Yet even when done virtually (by having an assigned person "on call"), they both offer a certain level of personal connection, as users are able to communicate with a physical person instead of referring to an aforementioned tip sheet or online tutorial.

Finally, refresher courses are yet another suggestion for supplemental training. As technology evolves, so does the need for continued learning. Meanwhile, users who have completed a workshop or other training session in the past are often reluctant to seek further help, or to admit they do not know certain information. In this way, refresher courses offer "reentry points" for both new and current users of VC software. By covering the software's basics, as well as any additional changes or developments, team members can help to proactively avoid much of the apprehension that accompanies virtual work.

Financial Entrée

It should be of little surprise that fiscal barriers emerged as this study's primary concern when anticipating whether or not college-aged participants will still be using certain software in 5-10 years. In fact, nearly 33% of respondents who did not foresee using a particular program in the future cited cost as their main determinant. Consequently, the need for developers to profit financially from their work creates an inherent tension with college students who cannot pay for their programs.

One potential solution to this quagmire is to consider avenues for financial entrée. In this way, developers of VC software can reach new clients now while they are still in college, in hopes of fostering long-term (i.e., paying) customers for their product in future years. Dropbox has sought to do this in recent years by lowing its prices and adding additional tools that make it easier for individuals to store files in the cloud (Newman, 2014). Although price reductions are a fine start, more subtle approaches to offering financial entrée include tiered pricing, free trial periods, and free access for current students.

Tiered pricing can be used to offer a lite version of VC software with limited functionality at a discounted rate. Meanwhile, free trial periods can offer either a lite or full version of the product at no cost for 4.5-9 months (a duration of time that aligns with most students' semester-based academic schedule). Finally, free access for current students can be confirmed through the use of a university email address, and can again offer either a lite or full version of the product for a predetermined trial period. Each of these suggestions take into account the students' concern over fiscal barriers by offering entry points that keep their long term earning potential in mind. Thus, by addressing the barrier of price now, developers of VC software can nurture dividends for years or even decades to come.

Utilized Flexibility

This study's final theme revealed the value of mobile accessibility. In response to whether a website helped to facilitate involvement from/among its users (i.e., organizational involvement), participants lauded mobile accessibility for its ability to make communication processes faster and easier. For this reason, we offer the suggestion for developers of VC software to prioritize their development and implementation of mobile apps. Rather than seeing a program's mobile iteration as a limited or secondary version of its full site, developers should seek to maximize their program's mobility, seeing it as an equal – if not leader – in the future life of their program.

Even more significant than our suggestion for developers to forefront mobile applications, however, is our suggestion for users to consider additional ways in which they may capitalize on the perceived benefit(s) that participants cited with mobile accessibility: namely, the freedom they felt to collaborate on the go, on their own terms, and on their own time schedules. Konradt and Hoch's (2007) analysis of leadership functions within virtual teams revealed the importance of flexibility-related work roles. Consequently, users of VC software must capitalize on the freedom and flexibility that e-collaboration inherently offers. Rather than supervising virtual team members in the same way one might supervise a physical work team. For example, users of online VC programs should avoid time stamping work and allow team members to work from a location of their choice. An additional way for managers to utilize the flexibility of VC software is to consider a Results Only Work Environment (ROWE).

The *Results Only Work Environment* (ROWE) is a human resource management theory that measures employee output, as opposed to correlating salary and compensation to the number of hours an employee works (Ressler & Thompson, 2010). By focusing solely upon whether or not an organization's well-defined goals have been met, ROWE allows leaders to overlook insignificant details related to employees' daily routines, while simultaneously affording higher levels of freedom and autonomy to those employees to accomplish their goals in a time and manner that they prefer. With ROWE, virtual team members need not "clock in" or "clock out" like traditional employees. Nor are they expected to work eight hours a day over the course of five consecutive workdays. Instead, during the course of a typical week virtual team members of ROWE should be expected to complete whatever tasks or duties are appropriate for that duration of time – nothing more, nothing less. They should subsequently be evaluated by their results, and left free to utilize VC software in order to accomplish those results in whatever time arrangement they deem fit.

CONCLUSION

Despite its potential limitations, the advantages of VC have spurred its adoption in the modern workplace by more organizations than ever before (Cassivi, Lefebvre, Lefebvre, & Leger, 2004; Maznevski & Chudoba, 2000). Yet popularity alone does ensure user success. Indeed, a sense of community has shown to positively correlate to employee efficiency, longevity, and quality of work; however, a weakened sense of e-community among virtual team members is one of the most prominent drawbacks of VC. Consequently, this study analyzed nearly 2,500 survey responses from 600 undergraduate students spanning 25 colleges/universities in order to develop practical implications for creating e-community among virtual work teams. Perceptions surrounding seven of the most popular groupwares in use today revealed the significance of brand awareness, interpersonal facilitation, user-friendly design, fiscal barriers, and mobile accessibility. Based upon these results, we concluded by outlining five corresponding implications: increased integration, expanded physicality, supplementary training, financial entrée, and utilized flexibility.

Future researchers might consider augmenting this study's qualitative approach with more quantitative analysis. Further research could seek to quantify the participants' desire for increased interpersonal interaction via path analysis and/or structural equation modeling (see Kock, 2010, 2013). Other potential avenues for quantitative researchers include a cost analysis for financial entrée, in addition to correlations between brand awareness and user satisfaction, mobile accessibility and user duration, etc. Each of these suggestions serve to complement our present study of e-community, while highlighting next steps for virtual team members and VC developers who hope to capitalize on the internet's potential for creating "a family of invisible friends."

REFERENCES

Basecamp. (2015). Basecamp is free for teachers! Retrieved from https://basecamp.com/teachers

BBC News. (2011). Microsoft confirms takeover of Skype. Retrieved from http://www.bbc.com/news/business-13343600

Berry, G. R. (2006). Can computer-mediated asynchronous communication improve team processes and decision-making?: Learning from the management literature. *Journal of Business Communication*, *43*(1), 344–366. doi:10.1177/0021943606292352

Berry, G. R. (2011). Enhancing effectiveness on virtual teams. *Journal of Business Communication*, *48*(2), 186–206. doi:10.1177/0021943610397270

Bosch-Sijtsema, P. M., & Sivunen, A. (2013). Professional virtual worlds supporting computer-mediated communication, collaboration, and learning in geographically distributed contexts. *IEEE Transactions on Professional Communication*, *56*(2), 1112–1124. doi:10.1109/TPC.2012.2237256

Breen, H. (2013). Virtual collaboration in the online educational setting. *Nursing Forum*, *48*(4), 284–299. doi:10.1111/nuf.12034 PMID:24188438

Brown, H. G., Poole, M. S., & Rodgers, T. L. (2004). Interpersonal traits, complementarity, and trust in virtual collaboration. *Journal of Management Information Systems*, *20*(4), 115–138. doi:10.1080/07421222.2004.11045785

Brown, N. R. (2002). "Community" metaphors online: A critical and rhetorical study concerning online groups. *Business Communication Quarterly*, *65*(2), 92–100. doi:10.1177/108056990206500210

Butson, R., & Thomson, C. (2014). Challenges of effective collaboration in a virtual learning environment among undergraduate students. *Creative Education*, *5*(1), 1449–1459. doi:10.4236/ce.2014.516162

Cassivi, L., Lefebvre, L., Lefebvre, L. A., & Leger, P. (2004). The impact of e-collaboration tools on firms' performance. *International Journal of e-Collaboration*, *15*(1), 91–110.

Certify. (2017). Understanding the average cost of business travel. Retrieved from https://www.certify.com/Infographic-TheAverageCostOfBusinessTravel.aspx

Cogburn, D. L., & Levinson, N. S. (2003). US–Africa virtual collaboration in globalization studies: Success factors for complex, cross-national learning teams. *International Studies Perspectives, 4*(1), 34–51. doi:10.1111/1528-3577.04103

Cohen, S. G., & Gibson, C. B. (2003). *In the beginning: Introduction and framework.*

Gibson, C. B., & Cohen, S. G. (Eds.), *Virtual teams that work: Creating conditions for virtual team effectiveness* (pp. 1–14). San Francisco, CA: Jossey-Bass.

Cruz-Cunha, M. M., Miranda, I. M., & Goncalves, P. (2013). *Handbook of research on ICTs for human-centered healthcare and social care services.* Hershey, PA: IGI Global. doi:10.4018/978-1-4666-3986-7

Dawson, R., & Clements, K. (2004). Virtual collaboration with clients. *Consulting to Management, 15*(4), 50–53.

Daye, D. (2006). Brand quote. *Branding Strategy Insider.* Retrieved September 6, 2015 from http://www.brandingstrategyinsider.com/2006/09

De Vreede, G.-J., & Briggs, R. O. (2005, January) Collaboration engineering: Designing repeatable processes for high-value collaborative tasks. *Paper presented at the annual Hawaii International Conference on Systems Science,* Maui, HI. 10.1109/HICSS.2005.144

Dittman, D. R., Hawkins, M., Deokar, A. V., & Sarnikar, S. (2010). Improving virtual collaboration outcomes through collaboration process structuring. *The Quarterly Review of Distance Education, 11*(4), 195–209.

Fink, L. (2007). Coordination, learning, and innovation: The organizational roles of e-collaboration and their impacts. *International Journal of e-Collaboration, 3*(3), 53–70. doi:10.4018/jec.2007070104

Fried, J. (2004). Basecamp launches. *Signal vs. Noise.* Retrieved from https://signalvnoise.com/archives/000542.php

Garrett, L. E., Spreitzer, G. M., & Bacevice, P. A. (2017). Co-constructing a sense of community at work: The emergence of community in coworking spaces. *Organization Studies, 38*(6), 821–842. doi:10.1177/0170840616685354

Gergle, D., Kraut, R. E., & Fussell, S. R. (2013). Using visual information for grounding and awareness in collaborative tasks. *Human-Computer Interaction, 28*(1), 1–39.

Granovetter, M. D. (1973). The strength of weak ties. *American Journal of Sociology, 78*(6), 1360–1380. doi:10.1086/225469

Granovetter, M. D. (2004). The impact of social structures on economic development. *The Journal of Economic Perspectives, 19*(1), 33–50. doi:10.1257/0895330053147958

Griffith, T. L., & Neale, M. A. (2001). Information processing in traditional, hybrid, and virtual teams: From nascent knowledge to transactive memory. *Research in Organizational Behavior, 23*(4), 379–421. doi:10.1016/S0191-3085(01)23009-3

Guha, S., & Daswani, N. (2005, December 16). An experimental study of the Skype Peer-to-Peer VoIP System. Retrieved from http://techreports.library.cornell.edu:8081/Dienst/UI/1.0/Display/cul.cis/ TR2005-2011

Hara, N., Solomon, P., Kim, S. L., & Sonnenwald, D. H. (2003). An emerging view of scientific collaboration: Scientists' perspectives on collaboration and factors that impact collaboration. *Journal of the Association for Information Science and Technology*, *54*(10), 952–965.

Hiltz, S. R., & Wellman, B. (1997). Asynchronous learning networks as a virtual classroom. *Communications of the ACM*, *40*(9), 44–49. doi:10.1145/260750.260764

Hinds, P. J., & Weisband, S. P. (2003). Knowledge sharing and shared understanding in virtual teams. In C. B. Gibson & S. G. Cohen (Eds.), *Virtual teams that work: Creating conditions for virtual team effectiveness* (pp. 21–36). San Francisco, CA: Jossey-Bass.

Hongwei, W., Yuan, M., & Wei, W. (2013). The role of perceived interactivity in virtual communities: Building trust and increasing stickiness. *Connection Science*, *25*(1), 55–73. doi:10.1080/09540091.20 13.824407

Horrigan, J. B. (2001). *Online communities: Networks that nurture long-distance relationships and local ties*. Pew Internet & American Life Project.

Hossain, L., & Wigand, R. T. (2004). ICT enabled virtual collaboration through trust. *Journal of Computer-Mediated Communication*, *10*(1).

Iacono, C. S., & Weisband, S. (1997, January). Developing trust in virtual teams. *Paper presented at the annual Hawaii International Conference on Systems Science*, Maui, HI.

Jarvenpaa, S. L., Knoll, K., & Leidner, D. E. (1998). Is anybody out there? Antecedents of trust in global virtual teams. *Journal of Management Information Systems*, *14*(4), 29–64. doi:10.1080/07421222.199 8.11518185

Jenkins, J. J. (2012). Engaging the internet generation: An experiential analysis of the world's wealthiest nonprofit organizations. *Florida Communication Journal*, *40*(1), 17–28.

Jenkins, J. J. (2014). The diversity paradox: Seeking community in an intercultural church. New York: Lexington.

Karpova, E., Correia, A., & Baran, E. (2008). Learn to use and use to learn: Technology in a virtual collaboration experience. *The Internet and Higher Education*, *12*(4), 45–52.

Kim, A. J. (2000). *Community building on the web: Secret strategies for successful online communities*. Berkeley, CA: Peachpit Press.

Kirkham, B. L., Rosen, B. M., Gibson, C. B., Tesluk, P. E., & McPherson, S. O. (2002). Five challenges to virtual team success: Lessons from Sabre Inc. *The Academy of Management Executive*, *16*(3), 67–79.

Klein, J., & Barrett, B. (2001). One foot in a global team, one foot at the local site: Making sense out of living in two worlds simultaneously. In M. Beyerlein (Ed.), *Advances in interdisciplinary studies of work teams: Virtual teams* (Vol. 8, pp. 107–125). Stamford, CT: JAI. doi:10.1016/S1572-0977(01)08021-9

Kock, N. (2000). Benefits for virtual organizations from distributed groups. *Communications of the ACM, 43*(11), 107–112. doi:10.1145/353360.353372

Kock, N. (2005). Using action research to study e-collaboration. *International Journal of e-Collaboration, 1*(4), i–vii.

Kock, N. (2008). E-collaboration and e-commerce in virtual worlds: The potential of Second Life and World of Warcraft. *International Journal of e-Collaboration, 4*(3), 1–13. doi:10.4018/jec.2008070101

Kock, N. (2010). Using WarpPLS in e-collaboration studies: An overview of five main analysis steps. *International Journal of e-Collaboration, 6*(4), 1–11. doi:10.4018/jec.2010100101

Kock, N. (2013). Using WarpPLS in e-collaboration studies: What if I have only one group and one condition? *International Journal of e-Collaboration, 9*(3), 1–12. doi:10.4018/jec.2013070101

Konradt, U., & Hoch, J. E. (2007). A work roles and leadership functions of managers in virtual teams. *International Journal of e-Collaboration, 3*(2), 16–35. doi:10.4018/jec.2007040102

Lair, D. J., Sullivan, K., & Cheney, G. (2005). Marketization and the recasting of the professional self: The rhetoric and ethics of personal branding. *Management Communication Quarterly, 18*(3), 307–343. doi:10.1177/0893318904270744

Ledinghan, J. A., & Bruning, S. D. (1998). Relationship management in public relations: Dimensions of an organization-public relationship. *Public Relations Review, 24*(1), 55–65. doi:10.1016/S0363-8111(98)80020-9

Lindlof, T. R., & Taylor, B. C. (2011). *Qualitative communication research methods*. Thousand Oaks, CA: Sage.

Lipnack, J. S., & Stamps, J. (2000). *Virtual teams: People working across boundaries with technology*. New York, NY: John Wiley.

Markus, M. L. (2005). Technology-shaping effects of e-collaboration technologies: Bugs and features. *International Journal of e-Collaboration, 1*(1), 1–23. doi:10.4018/jec.2005010101

Martin, C. (2015). Social networking usage and grades among college students: A study to determine the correlation of social media usage and grades. Retrieved August 4, 2016 from http://www.unh.edu/news/docs/UNHsocialmedia.pdf

Maznevski, M. L., & Chudoba, K. (2000). Building space over time: Global virtual team dynamics and effectiveness. *Organization Science, 11*(1), 473–492. doi:10.1287/orsc.11.5.473.15200

McKnight, D., & Chervany, N. (2000). *The meanings of trust*. Minneapolis, MN: Carlson School of Management.

Milner, H. (2010). *The internet generation*. Medford, MA: Tufts University Press.

Morse, J. M. (1994). "Emerging from the data": The cognitive processes of analysis in qualitative inquiry. In J. M. Morse (Ed.), *Critical issues in qualitative research methods* (pp. 23–43). Thousand Oaks, CA: Sage.

Mowshowitz, A. (1997). Virtual organization. *Communications of the ACM, 40*(9), 30–37. doi:10.1145/260750.260759

Munkvold, B. E., & Zigurs, I. (2007). Process and technology challenges in swift-starting virtual teams. *Information & Management, 44*(3), 287–299. doi:10.1016/j.im.2007.01.002

Nan, N., & Lu, Y. (2014). Harnessing the power of self-organization in an online community during organizational crisis. *Management Information Systems Quarterly, 38*(4), 1135–1158. doi:10.25300/MISQ/2014/38.4.09

Newman, J. (2014). Dropbox and you: A future where apps drive cloud storage. *PC World, 32*(7), 40–43.

Pallot, M., Martinez-Carreras, M. A., & Prinz, W. (2010). Collaborative Distance. *International Journal of e-Collaboration, 6*(2), 1–32. doi:10.4018/jec.2010040101

Perez, S. (2012, December). LogMeIn's Dropbox competitor Chubby reveals pricing. *Tech Crunch*. Retrieved from http://techcrunch.com/2012/12/17/logmeins-dropbox-competitor-cubby-reveals-pricing-stays-competitive-at-7-per-month-for-100-gb/

Peters, L. M., & Manz, C. C. (2007). Identifying antecedents of virtual team collaboration. *Team Performance Management: An International Journal, 13*(3), 1–14.

Plant, R. (2004). Online communities. *Technology in Society, 26*(1), 51–65. doi:10.1016/j.techsoc.2003.10.005

Protalinski, E. (2014). Google announces 10% prices cut for all compute engine instances. *TNW News*. Retrieved August 1, 2015 from http://thenextweb.com/google/2014/10/01/google-announces-10-price-cut-compute-engine-instances-google-drive-passed-240m-active-users/

Ressler, C., & Thompson, J. (2010). *Why work sucks and how to fix it: The results-only revolution*. New York, NY: Portfolio Publishing.

Rheingold, H. (2001). *The virtual community: Homestead on the electronic frontier*. New York: HarperPerennial.

Sheehy, K. (2014, August 24). 5 must-download apps for college students. *U.S. News & World Report*. Retrieved from http://www.usnews.com/education/best-colleges/articles/2014/08/21/5-must-download-apps-for-college-students

Shu, W., & Chuang, Y. (2011). Why people share knowledge in virtual communities. *Society for Personality Research, 39*(5), 671–690.

Soetanto, R., Childs, M., Poh, P., Austin, S., & Hao, J. (2012). Global multidisciplinary learning in construction education: Lessons from virtual collaboration of building design teams. *Civil Engineering Dimension, 14*(3), 173–181.

Solomon, C. M. (2001). Managing virtual teams. *Workforce, 80*(1), 60–64.

Swan, K. (2001). Virtual interaction: Design factors affecting student satisfaction and perceived learning in asynchronous online courses. *Distance Education, 22*(2), 306–331. doi:10.1080/0158791010220208

Swayne, M. (2013). Bonding with your virtual self may alter your actual perceptions. *Penn State News.* Retrieved September 1, 2015 from http://news.psu.edu/story/275626/2013/05/02/research/bonding-your-virtual-self-may-alter-your-actual-perceptions

Tate, A., Hansberger, J. T., Potter, S., & Wickler, G. (2014). Virtual collaboration spaces: Bringing presence to distributed collaboration. *Journal of Virtual Worlds Research, 7*(2), 111–122.

Timmerman, T. A. (2000). Racial diversity, age diversity, interdependence, and team performance. *Small Group Research, 31*(1), 592–606. doi:10.1177/104649640003100505

Toomey, L., & Adams, L. (2000). *U.S. Patent No. 6,119,147.* Washington, DC: U.S. Patent and Trademark Office.

Tsotsis, A. (2011, October 18). AngelPad's third demo day: Fifteen startups take flight. *TechCrunch.* Retrieved from http://techcrunch.com/2011/10/18/angelpads-third-demo-day-fifteen-startups-take-flight/

Tutton, M. (2009). Going to the virtual office in Second Life. *CNN News.* Retrieved September 10, 2015 from http://www.cnn.com/2009/BUSINESS/11/05/second.life.virtual.collaboration/

Viner, S. (2014). Social media statistics: How college students are using social networking. *Study Breaks Magazine.* Retrieved September 8, 2015 from http://studybreakscollegemedia.com/2014/social-media-statistics-how-college- students-are-using-social-networking/

Warkentin, M., & Beranek, P. M. (1999). Training to improve virtual team communication. *Information Systems, 9*(4), 271–289. doi:10.1046/j.1365-2575.1999.00065.x

Yamshon, L. (2014). Skitch is a multi-purpose editing tool for doodling on any document. *Tech Hive.* Retrieved from http://www.techhive.com/article/2450075/skitch-is-a-multi-purpose-editing-tool-for-doodling-on-any-document.html

Zhou, T. (2011). Understanding online community user participation: A social influence perspective. *Internet Research, 21*(1), 67–81. doi:10.1108/10662241111104884

Chapter 5
Building Organizations Image:
How to Control a Public Relations Crisis and Communication

Badreya Al-Jenaibi
United Arab Emirates University, UAE

ABSTRACT

It is crucial for a company to maintain its image and reputation, and public relations (PR) plays a vital role in doing so. This study investigates strategies that help an organization rejuvenate its image after damage from ineffective PR. It is important to know which PR strategies engage stakeholders because it is critical for the survival of a company that it maintains healthy relationships with all entities. A case study was conducted to explore what ruins a company's image and what role a PR department plays in rejuvenating it. To gain valuable insights into this topic, interviews were conducted with fourteen PR professionals including people who are working in the mentioned case studies places and organizations that faced some crisis in this chapter. Results suggest PR plays a critical role during crisis management; through PR teams, organizations can turn adverse situations to their favor and reconstruct reputations that would otherwise be tarnished.

INTRODUCTION

According to Al-Jenaibi (2015) a research conducted in crisis management, public relation plays a very crucial role. With help of different teams of PR and social media organizations can seizure opportunities to turn all possible circumstances in its favor and protect its reputation which could be destroyed or stained because of the current situation. During crisis the public relations team should make certain that what reason and parties were accountable and liable, and they should provide their aid to managers when compulsory. By seeing the impact of crisis abruptly, proficiently and expertly companies can mitigate the impact of crisis in eyes of stakeholders and during crisis media communication plays a crucial role in enhancing positive results of the company.

DOI: 10.4018/978-1-5225-7214-5.ch005

Kirat (2007) stated that reputation of a company is priceless for company at the same time it is also related to its stakeholders and customers. Customers only purchase products of the company that they think it have some kind of value, quality and honestly. So if the image is tarnished, it means the sales of company also decreases with the passage of time. A company gets increasing number of opportunities with good image and reputation but when this image is tarnish the whole business come to an end.

According to Al-Jenaibi (2014) a study in which 20 UAE organizations were test for using internet for PR it was investigated for both public and private organizations. She found that public relation members are fulfilling its role but when it comes to public relations through internet, PR staff is failing to fulfill their roles. The staff is not able to control the information that is transmitted to public through internet. It is a common perception that what is online indicates and what is going on traditional media about the organization.

To survive, people engage in many activities to satisfy both primary and secondary needs. During this satisfaction, crises arise whether among employees, employees and internal stakeholders, employees and external stakeholders, employees and managers, or managers and consumers. Organizations compete for higher profits and market shares, and that competition leads to crises. No day passes without interventions from religion or industry that arouses crises, and a proper set of activities is required to manage them. The role of PR is important during crisis. During crises, organizations must tell the truth, tell it all, and tell it fast (Briguglio, 2004). According to Shaw (2006), crisis management is:

...the coordination of efforts to control a crisis event consistent with strategic goals of an organization. Although generally associated with response, recovery and resumption operations during and following a crisis event, crisis management responsibilities extend to pre-event awareness, prevention and preparedness and post event restoration and transition. (p. 66)

When examining site of different UAE companies, a large number of sites indicated to have municipal welfare. For instance, a huge space in ADNOC'S website has been left to show its commitment to environmental protection so basically it is using internet and its site as a tool for public relations. In public sector Dubai municipality also indicates that it is applying good deal of environmental protection. These companies have also made use of some high quality educational items and pictures in order to attract viewers to make more visits. Some other services involve posting good quality picture, stories related to children reports that make people aware of different things, declaration related to public service, advantageous links of sites, manual regarding different training programs, and internet services (Al-Jenaibi, 2011).

Crises are negative events, not welcome by organizations worldwide. Some negative functions associated with crisis management include ushering many types of competition, both healthy and unhealthy. They destroy life and property, and they ruin images of organizations and countries since investors become skeptical easily regarding investments. The role of public relations (PR) is important when overcoming crises. If an organization or country wishes to prosper during or after a crisis, it must focus on the importance of PR during this critical time.

Importance and Significance of the Study

Different public relations used different strategies in order to communicate their concerns it organizations for example some of them used their websites in order to communicate changes in the organization due to implementation of different changes because of crisis or implementation of environmental changes in management.

Few extant studies examine PR and its significance to managing crises. This study is expected to help government officials, countries, and public and private organizations enhance their images. It elucidates the significance of PR to various stakeholders during crisis management, identifies the nature of crises, examines how companies have handled those situations, and explores frameworks and activities to overcome crises through effective PR. In the literature review, causes of crises in the UAE are highlighted, including methods used to overcome them. Successful and unsuccessful methods are highlighted explored, followed by proposals for effective PR solutions that can be used during future crises.

Methods used to answer this study's research questions include case studies and interviews, chosen because they provide valuable insights into these problems. The researcher was availed detailed answers to questions posed but faced several barriers while gathering data because content was limited and participants were reluctant to discuss crisis management strategies in interviews due to the fierce competitive markets in which they operate. Six UAE companies that have faced critical situations were selected for case studies, and fourteen PR professionals were selected for face-to-face interviews. These people were between 32 and 45 years old, and held either BS or BA degrees. The research questions and hypotheses addressed in this study were:

1. What tactical plans do PR offices use when dealing with crises in UAE firms?
   H1: PR firms offices with crises in UAE firms effectively.
2. What approaches and methods are most effective for restoring trust?
   H2: PR offices have developed plans to deal with crises in UAE firms effectively.

This paper defines crisis management from a UAE perspective. It highlights approaches media undertake to handle crises, the role PR departments play during crisis management, and the strategies PR departments use to rebuilt company image. The rewards companies can reap by building a positive image after facing a crisis, and various techniques to handle crises, are discussed in detail.

The paper aims to discover the role of the PR during crises. The main purpose of the PR practitioners can be split into five main objectives: protecting brand name or public image building, shedding the spotlight on the company and its activities, earning a place in the newsletter and the media coverage, getting the public and governmental attention through advertisements and grabbing the attention of the investors. However, when a crisis occurs especially if it will affect the name of the company, the earlier the PR Department notice the potential of crisis occurring, the better handling of the crisis and minimizing the damage.

LITERATURE REVIEW

Defining Crises Control

Crisis management is a term refers to a well-organized strategic execution of a plan that aims to lower and minimize the damage that can be dealt to the company's name, brand, public image and reputation through certain actions and tools (Bundy, et al., 2017). The purpose of crisis management is to protect the company reputation. Crisis management activities include researching the crisis thoroughly, preparing relevant press releases and press conferences and maintaining the team spirit through internal communication tools.

According to Nwosu (1996), a crisis is an event of extreme difficulty or danger. Crises can be emotional or unemotional, and every person likely faces a crisis during his/her life. Black (1989) defines crisis management as a process an organization adopts to handle unexpected events that are harmful to the image, reputation, or survival of an organization. Usually a company has no plan to tackle such events. If an organization's history is examined carefully, it is due to crises that the organization evolved. Crises change the face of an organization, the reason some UAE universities teach crisis management, but the ratio of those that do to those that do not is low (ey-Ling, 2011); of twenty-four UAE universities, only two offer crisis management courses.

Al-Jenaibi, (2015) stated that public relations have a main role during crises and is important during their effective management. She showed that there are various daily functions for public relations where such daily responsibilities identical during crisis. That is shown in their role in maintaining and even improving their organization's relationships by effectively communicating with the organization's target audience audiences. Their role is connected with creating a close connection between the company and even the other entities as a whole. In fact, communication is a great and important advantage of the public relations. By having good effective communication skills, there is a great support to PR position and even providing them with a method to convince others effectively.

Due to advancing technology, contemporary UAE companies handle news, information, and communication differently during a need for crisis management. According to Kirat (2012), major crisis management techniques in the UAE focus on effective management of news, managing media and people, and dealing with information technologies, and all media must be used effectively and efficiently during crises. PR is meant to do more than devise strategies (Ashcroft, 1997); it is a critical organizational function during a crisis. Effective crisis planning is important to all firms since a crisis can destroy an organization, affecting several stakeholders poorly. Past crises suggest PR practitioners are important during planning and restructuring of an organization's image. The first step is to identify critical steps (Coombs, 2007). Crisis management divides into three phases: a) planning before a crisis, b) response to a crisis, and c) measures taken after a crisis.

Main PR Roles Before the Crises

Public relations role is to protect the organization's image through showing the nature of their work. The PR practitioners always are trying to product organizations' services and activities and image from any negative issue that occur. In fact the main reason behind that is to protect its reputation to make its position in the eye of customers good, effective, unique and even in turn to attract other customers and suppliers to have or do business with the company (Rivero, 2014)

According to Barton (2011), the best practice an organization can adopt to reduce the threat of crises is to have a plan based on the experiences of other organizations in the industry, and that plan must be updated regularly. Second, a team should exist that is devoted to handling crises. Third, the team should occasionally practice crisis management so it knows what to do when a crisis occurs, much like an organization that practices evacuating a building in case of a fire. Finally, PR should have pre-drafted messages to deliver during a crisis, and the company's legal department should review those messages critically to reduce financial losses (Banks, 2001).

Influence of Economic Crises on UAE Companies' Reputations

There are more examples towards the economic issue. For example, according to a report written by Sara Townsend (2017) that showed a problem in the economy in the UAE where it stated that the UAE's public deficit widened significantly in 2016, this issue required a great intervention by the public relation sector. Those people who are concerned with the issue and improvements were supported and encouraged to manage the issue through more fundamental support via making but this sector handled investments in the country and increased it. In this case, the problem declined greatly. The tools used to solve the issue are how to convince investors to increase their investments in the country. Moreover, the UAE government need to extend more facilities provided to investors to remain and continue their investments (Al-Jenaibi, 2008). That matter was not discussed in the local media but only on the Arabian Business newspaper that showed under the title of "UAE economy on the up in 2017, but late payments still an issue". Then that was followed with events of how to overcome the issue and encourage more investment in turn, the black picture was changed and the stability of the country's political system encouraged other investors to invest their money in the UAE. Consequently, values occurred, and more areas were improved (Townsend, 2017)

According to Thafer (2013), much like other oil-rich states in the UAE, Dubai is not only an oil-rich entity; its growth depends on tourism and other industries. It is important that Dubai maintain its image to attract new businesses after suffering a financial crisis in 2008. If Dubai is unable to maintain its image and reputation as a hub that attracts investors worldwide, it might suffer great loses. The crisis caused a collapse in Dubai's real estate industry, and investors remain hesitant to invest in its infrastructure, especially regarding hotel construction. Dubai must manage its reputation to ensure that investors can profit though investment. Some negative effects of the crisis included: a) projects from India were delayed or abandoned, b) delayed and abandoned projects caused a surge in unemployment, and c) approximately seventy financial institutions lent money to Dubai to help manage the crisis (Jain, 2012). According to Bitar (2013), areas primarily affected by the economic crisis are the financial, real estate, and construction sectors. Both public and private sectors took preventative measures to reestablish their reputations and manage the crisis. Some private companies reduced activities or merged with other companies to remain solvent, and for some public companies, authorities passed laws to prevent excision of investor rights. After the crisis, companies are striving to regain their reputations, and along with transparency and good corporate governance, investors are enjoying more opportunities from relaxing of laws that allow entrance into new markets, diversifying risk.

Best Performs for Media Preparation During a Crisis

Before the crisis appears, PR must solve and pacify the communication between its clients and media stories before it get out of control or the media and the public gets a glimpse of crises. Lerbinger (1997) argues that when an organization faces a crisis, it should never convey the words "no comment" because it makes stakeholders think the organization is hiding something that if discovered would implicate the company or its managers. Whatever statement a PR department offers, it should be clear; statements given without clarity and that contain too many technical terms result in a confused public (Coombs, 2007). A spokesperson representing an organization during a crisis should not appear nervous; he/she should have controlled expressions, and should not be shown exhibiting nervous habits such as pacing. Statements should lack "uhms" and "ohs" that reflect unpreparedness (Council, 2003). Finally, PR and its spokesperson should have access to all points they need to convey to the public so a coherent message is delivered from the organization.

Selecting the Best Communication Networks During a Crisis

Regarding a company's virtual presence, a webpage should exist dedicated to handling the crisis (Downing, 2003). It is best to use intranets to target internal stakeholders, but the Internet should target external stakeholders. It is also best practice to use mass notification since it notifies all public actors simultaneously (Kent, 2007).

The Significance of PR During Crisis Management

When the crisis becomes well known in the public eyes, PR must try to handle the media and provide explanations through press conferences and press releases.

According to Coombs (2007), PR's role is important during crisis management because in an information age, news travels faster than everything else, and if a crisis is handled inefficiently, there is more at stake than what appears readily. A company should defend itself as soon as possible. The first hour after a crisis is usually the most critical, and it is during this hour that PR practitioners must justify the company. The future of a company depends wholly on PR professionals; they make or break the company at that moment. PR practitioners should use three steps to prevent damage from crises: a) they should avoid crises as much as they can, b) address them before they escalate, and c) PR should turn adverse situations to the company's favor. Conducting PR requires much planning, and if PR remains unplanned, the result is like running a business without a growth plan. Contemporary businesses are different from businesses of the past; they are highly exposed to the public, media, and other threats, and they constantly need to maintain their images. Consequently, they must involve PR in each business decision (Ebersole, 2013).

The Importance of Image-Building After a Crisis

The PR department must have ongoing communication with certain groups (media, other organizations, governments and the public masses) to inform and ensure them that organization took the necessary measure and to ensure that they will not face a similar incident again. This step must be done to prevent the name of the company of being stained with mud and losing its trust. If there is no action of PR employees done after the crises the company will lose public figure which was built over the years. Which may also lead to bankruptcy of the company.

A crisis can threaten a company's reputation or public safety. Many definitions of crises exist, the majority of which include tarnishing firm reputation and injuring both internal and external stakeholders. Commonly, the entire public suffers from crises organizations face (Kirat, 2012). Crises usually conclude with negative consequences, and PR practitioners are charged with improving the image or reputation of the company. Common threats crises cause loss of reputation, capital, and safety of associated public actors. Sometimes a crisis is so big it takes lives (e.g., Tylenol). Product harm and accidents are examples that take lives, and a company faces a smaller market share and lawsuits as a result (Dilenschneider, 2000). To repair a reputation after crisis management, public safety is the first threat a company needs to address. If public safety is not addressed properly, the crisis intensifies (Coombs, 2004). Financial losses and reputation-building/repairing are addressed in a later stage. The role of PR during crisis management is to protect the organization and its stakeholders, and to perceive and reduce threats caused by crisis management (Coombs, 2007).

Best Actions for Response to Initial Crisis

Jorden (1993) suggests that the most effective news travels quickly and accurately, so the first hour of crisis is critical, and PR must deliver crisis news to stakeholders during that hour. Care should be taken that all facts conveyed are accurate (Cohen, 1999), and all PR practitioners of the firm and the spokesperson should be aware of the facts to know what messages to convey to the public. When there are threats of both financial loss and public safety, public safety should be the primary concern. All communication channels should be employed to notify stakeholders. A spokesperson should appear sympathetic toward the situation, but remember that sympathetic does not mean nervous (Dean, 2004). Internal stakeholders are as important as external stakeholders, so all employees should be apprised to deliver a message coherently throughout. Employees and their families often experience post-traumatic stress after crises, so free consultation and training should be provided to avoid further negative outcomes (Hearit, 2006).

Bundy, Pfarrer, Short & Coombs (2017) stated that PR instruments are extremely financially savvy, and regularly give you a more noteworthy level of control than all the more comprehensively focused on promoting efforts. Consider utilizing these PR apparatuses to assemble your business' notoriety:

- **Web-Based Social Networking:** Web-based social networking gives you a chance to sidestep the media and go straight to your clients. Utilizing person to person communication locales, for example, Facebook and Twitter enable you to take after and be trailed by columnists, drive web activity, oversee issues by reacting rapidly to reactions or pessimistic observations, and increment introduction for your business image.
- **Business Occasions:** Occasions are open doors for businessmen to pick up a presentation for their organizations, advance new items or administrations and ensure exact data comes to focused clients.
- **Bulletins:** Print or messaged bulletins are a decent method to advance your business, speak with clients and keep them educated on new items and administrations.

- **Talking Engagements:** Talking at occasions where clients are probably going to go to help position you as a pioneer or trailblazer in your field. As an entrepreneur or pioneer, assembling your notoriety for being a specialist likewise manufactures the notoriety of your business - and draws new clients.
- **Group Relations:** Building great associations with individuals from the group where you work together help manufacture client steadfastness. Discover where the clients in your group live by gathering postcodes for the purpose of the offer.

In summary, the PR talk about the issue in the media as a nearby issue. At the point when the PR turn out to the media to clarify what happens, they need to give them an answers about the main subject and it kick the bucket line to the issue so they can keep their imager clean for their costumer.

SEVERAL PLANS TO REBUILD IMAGES

If there is no evidence of a crisis and someone is accusing the organization for no apparent reason, the best repair strategy is to attack the accuser with evidence (Kellerman, 2006). During less critical situations, a spokesperson denies the allegation by stating that the media has not portrayed any such situation. A scapegoat strategy is also possible, in which PR blames someone internal or external to the organization. Crisis managers and PR practitioners sometimes use excuses, and simply apologize for events that triggered a crisis (Lerbinger, 1997). Provocation is also used as a repair strategy, suggesting a crisis was inevitable and the organization had to take corrective measures in response to an unwanted event. Events are also sometimes called accidents, a situation that gets out of control no matter how well planned the crisis management. To save an organization's reputation, managers occasionally invent justifications for a crisis, suggesting losses were fewer than losses realized (Tyler, 1997). A sandwich strategy occurs when a manager tells stakeholders about the good the organization has done for them, and then discusses recent negative events before closing with promises of a better future. To minimize the effect of a crisis, victims are compensated for losses, and sometimes after admitting culpability, a PR spokesperson asks for forgiveness from the public, suggesting they are all in this together (Ulmer, 2006)

Methods

A case study is an appropriate method when a researcher requires in-depth investigation of an issue, which in this case is rebuilding reputations after UAE companies face crises (Feagin, Orum, & Sjoberg, 1991) According to Yin (1993), when multiple cases are studied, it is called a collective case study approach. When all researches in a field suggest the same findings, it is usually referred to as a case study, not a type of sampling research like a survey study. In this scenario, the researcher used six UAE companies to suggest hypotheses and discover what each company did to rebuild its reputation after facing a crisis. Benefits of case studies are that they are selective and focus on only one or two issues, which in this case is rebuilding images and reputations and helping to understand systems of crisis management. Analysis of published news in some local newspapers in the UAE were cited and analyzed such as the National, CBC, Gulf news and Emirates newspapers.

Research Design

Interviews with PR people in the same organizations and places that faced the crisis were collected in this paper. and the case study method were used in this study. The case study method was used because it helps organizations learn from the experiences of other organizations. It helps in devising crisis management plans before a crisis occurs. In-depth interview analysis was used to explore how organizations deal with crises. A blend of both approaches ensures findings are generalizable to a population.

Instrument

A structured interview guide was developed to interview PR professionals. All questions were open-ended, and probing was used to gain valuable insights from crisis-management managers and PR spokespersons. All content narrated in the guide was based on the role PR plays during crisis management. Various methods were used to conduct the interviews, including telephone interviews, face-to-face interviews, and e-mail conversations. The highest response rate and most valuable insights were gathered from e-mail conversations. Data were collected from seventeen venues, including hospitals, municipalities, and banks. The first interviews were with people who worked in the analyzed local case studies such as IKEA and Freij Entertainment and because of the sensitive topic, the were not cooperative the researcher and they hided many information but the researcher used many published articles in the local newspaper to analyze the case studies. Their comments were included in the case studies analysis parts. The second interviewers were with PR people in the local hospitals, municipalities, and banks including AlFardan exchange, Dubai Islamic Bank, Saderat Iran Bank, National Bank of Abudhabi, AlAin, AlNoor and Tawam hospitals, AlAin and AbuDhabi municipality. 28 interviewers were interviewed face to face and some of them prefer to reply through emails because they thought it is a sensitive topic. 16 females and 12 males whose ages are between 30 to 55. 20 interviewee holds a BA and BS degrees and others have a diploma. Their majors are Business, Communication, Engineering, Geography, Social science, public administration and IT.

Validity and Reliability of the Instrument

The interview guide was pilot tested on sample respondents to remove ambiguities present in both statements and questions, and probing questions were designed around yes/no answers to ensure instrument reliability. The interview guide was prepared by considering oral interviews since they offer in-depth insights. All statements were neutral so they would not lead respondents to an answer. The instrument was tested and retested on various samples until all respondents understood its content similarly.

Case Study Method

A case study is usually based on an example, understanding of an entire context, a context's complexity, and analysis of a problem, and solutions are sometimes proposed. Case study analysis is qualitative because the focus is on achieving thick descriptions (Stake, 2006). The cases in this study were selected not only to describe places and people, but also to analyze interpretations subjects hold concerning a complex context. Relativity was constructed between practitioners and cases, especially to answer "why" and "how" questions in a complex context. (Yin, 2005). Six cases were considered, chosen especially since they contained issues (e.g., crises) that aid in building theories as methodologies. All cases dealt with crises and an organization forced to cope with not only the crisis, but also rebuilding a reputation.

Emirates Airlines

Experts specializing in strategies and institutional communication have agreed that Emirates airlines has provided professional lessons in dealing with the aircraft combustion incident on August 26, 2016. There are five digital lessons provided by Emirates in a professional manner during that period when highways are in the time of news transmission in both cases. The PR employees used two main tools:

- 18 crew members uniting.
- Transparency, honesty and the speed of communication with the public through traditional and social media.

The Emirates Airlines discussed many issues in the local newspapers like Albayan newspaper. They mentioned that "There are five lessons or strategies we have learned from Emirates in the art of managing crises, especially in terms of reputation and brand protection":

1. Always be prepared.
2. Be transparent and reliable.
3. You have to be proactive.
4. Watch and answer the media.
5. Protect your company image.

You will never know when the crisis will occur and when you will call or speak to your brand. Of course, Emirates' marketing and public relations team had a "crisis management strategy" and a plan of implementation to meet the potential for future events. Therefore, the company has implemented this strategy to contain the situation calmly to reassure the public to protect the image of the brand (Al-Bayan, 2016).

So, Emirates Airline has provided lessons in resolving crises through transparency and the speed of communication with the public as it quickly put the information on the sites of communication so as not to be exposed to rumors and incorrect information was true.

IKEA

Ikea is a Swedish company founded by Ingvar Kamprad in 1926. It is known for producing high-quality products at low prices, and it operates in forty countries. The IKEA horsemeat scandal nearly ruined the company's reputation, but PR tactics saved the company. The Swedish meatball scandal began February 2013. Horse DNA was found in packets marked as pork and beef. The scandal originated from Sweden, and the meat was supplied to thirteen countries. As soon as the controversy began, the company pulled its stock from twenty-one countries to ensure public safety and company reputation (Masudi, 2013). IKEA believed meat supplied to the UAE was hilal, coming from Arabic origin instead of Sweden, so there was no threat of horsemeat contamination in the country. To satisfy its customers, IKEA sent the meat to laboratories in Abu Dhabi for further testing, proving the meat supplied to the UAE was free from the controversy that had arisen in Sweden (DuBois, 2013),

From this case, it is evident that not all publicity is positive. After the controversy, the company's popularity decreased, and the company now measures popularity figures daily. IKEA isolated the scandal to one area and mitigated its effects in other areas by sending products to local labs for testing, helping the company reduce the crisis (Kavoussi, 2013). IKEA markets itself as an economy seller, and some people believed it was trying to reduce costs by selling horsemeat. The company stated that the problem stemmed from lack of supervision at the supplier's end, and immediately cancelled orders of meatballs and sausages from the same supplier to demonstrate integrity to customers. Stock suspected of being infected was pulled from stores worldwide, and although the action resulted in short-term losses, it ultimately restored customer loyalty so consumers felt safe returning to IKEA. "We took this matter very seriously when the issue happened. A senior manager in the UAE indicated that " The meatballs recall in other IKEA store came from other supplier. The meatballs we serve here in IKEA are specially made for us. They all came from Saudi which is a different supplier who had the issue. To avoid loyal customers, we requested for certification from our supplier for the meat origin.Thus, it's ensured that it's of beef origin as expected" (Personal communication, January, 2014)

Public safety and sympathy for customers were more important than profit, proving it through strict measures (News, 2013). Public perception is important, and it was important that the company take responsibility and remedy the crisis. The scapegoat strategy places culpability where it belongs. It condoles the public and shifts negative perceptions to other entities. Responsibility should be taken and threats should be eliminated. Public safety should be given prime importance, and the person or company responsible should face the consequences for negligence. News and television are the most important media, and companies must hear concerns before communicating sympathy.

Freij Entertainment

The world's largest entertainment provider, Freij originated in Europe in 1987. It specializes in amusement rides, outdoor events, circuses, travel, and other forms of entertainment. The company diversified operations worldwide, and one of its hubs in the Middle East is in Dubai. It was the first entertainment company to provide mobile rides in the UAE, and its rides are renowned for reliability since the company upgrades and maintained them constantly. Freij entertainment offers something for everyone. The company owns a source of entertainment for ride lovers all over the world, the Dubai Sky Wheel, but Freij suffered a crisis in January 2013 when an iron rod fell from the Ferris wheel in Dubai Global Village. The event would not have been an issue, but the rod fell on the head of a person visiting the village and died instantly. This was a critical situation because it is the primary duty of every organization to ensure public safety in the environment in which they operate. As an immediate response, all rides owned by Freij entertainment were closed. Two men testified that they told the operator about the fault, but he did nothing to prevent the accident. The wheel continued to operate for thirty minutes after the incident, and it took approximately two hours to unload all of the riders (Subaihi, 2013). To manage the crisis, the people responsible for the event were arrested immediately, and all rides were closed. The company admitted its fault, apologized to the public, and participated in the investigation; it did not place blame elsewhere. New work-process and ride-maintenance policies were passed, and in the future, rides would be evaluated more frequently and complaints about rides from customers would be handled more efficiently (Emirates247, 2013). Media were not blamed for the problem. Instead, Freij helped the media know the facts, making media a friend with the company. The company apologized and asked for forgiveness because if it had not, people would have boycotted the product. It is always about safety of people, so financial losses should not be projected or discussed. The victim's family should be compensated and justice should be granted to earn respect from stakeholders. Companies should avoid media pollution and fill communication gaps where needed.

Damas

Damas is a leading jewelry brand in the Middle East (Damas, 2013). The company operates in more than six countries, with approximately two-hundred forty retail outlets. Other than jewelry, the company also deals in valuable watches. The group originated in Syria, and has been in business since 1900. The company bases its target audience according to demographics. Damas operated only in the UAE until it decided to go global with its brand name in 2000. Systems within the organization were dishonest and opaque; officials took money from the organization's accounts for personal use, and the takers promised to return the borrowed money, but never did. This sparked questions regarding the integrity of the company, and stakeholders began losing faith. Due to fraud, the share price of Damas decreased by 13.5% in the UAE. The organization shifted from private to public ownership, after which it was discovered that there was confusion about the theft of money regarding disclosure to stakeholders. To demonstrate good faith to stakeholders and that the business could operate normally after facing a financial crisis, the brothers who held the company were fined and banned by the government to exercise executive roles. (Complinet, 2010)

An external audit was conducted to remedy all financial flaws as soon as the theft was discovered. Officials who were indicted were replaced to restore the faith of stakeholders. Business was backed by heavy investments, and funds were returned to help normal operations. The company cooperated with officials to unveil the facts, and later communicated those facts to the public once authorities had confirmed them. People still trust the company and continue to buy Damas' products. The brothers were punished—a lesson for the entire business community—and they suffered this fate because they were unable to communicate at multiple levels effectively (Hope, 2009). Instead of communicating at one level, PR practitioners should communicate to all levels so everyone receives the same message. Building a positive image is advantageous, but PR must not confuse image and reality in the minds of consumers. A company should give consumers what it promises because false commitments tarnish an organization's reputation. Proactive approaches and planning are paramount, but they cannot prevent or save a company from crisis. Plan for the worst, cater to the genuine concerns of customers, do not leave loose ends, and demonstrate an organization's humane side to consumers.

In summary, addressing crises is related to the internal and external institutions, it is one of the main objectives of the public relations team. It plays an important role in the successful management of the crisis facing the institution before the crisis occurs through the preventive programs it plans, as well as during and after the crisis. Crisis management in UAE institutions is very strong. Most state institutions have excellent public relations teams and know how to handle and manage crises.

QUALITATIVE DATA ANALYSIS: INTERVIEWS ANALYSIS

Protecting Image is First

In a world where information represents knowledge and power, reputation is everything to an organization. A good reputation earns loyal customers and ushers huge investment opportunities for stakeholders, and a bad reputation can ruin an organization. A company's goodwill depends on reputation, which is paramount to being awarded contracts and negotiating mergers and acquisitions; a bad reputation means total loss. Public actors, stakeholders, employees, and investors benefit from the stability of a company. If a company is unstable, or if PR does not communicate stability, profiting and growth are impossible. PR communicates products to customers and creates a path to government and legislation. It enhances the image of a company and thus increases production by attracting opportunities, and they attract enterprise customers, reducing the effects of recession.

Public Relations Actions During a Crisis

During a crisis, PR practitioners must enhance corporate image and turn adverse situations to opportunities. They must also increase awareness of products and services, communicate flaws and achievements, and introduce gatekeepers to control the flow of information. The approach of every PR practitioner must be transparent and professional because PR is superior to marketing regarding branding an organization and its products. Organizations invest in a good PR team because they need to communicate internal happenings to stakeholders and develop two-way communication between managers and the public; PR bridges the gap between suppliers and buyers. News and information are communicated to external actors through a reliable PR team.

Rewards for Developing a Positive Organizational Image

When the PR practitioners were asked about the rewards they receive when they achieve their goals, most reported that they are rewarded with leaves, and in extreme cases, promotions with fringe benefits are promised. Both intrinsic and extrinsic reward systems are common in the organizations. Some organizations compensate better monetarily, and others focus on recognition and appreciation. For high-level PR practitioners, interactions between top managers and PR teams increase, and those working in PR are occasionally offered shares in the company.

Values to Measure Firm Reputation

Standards developed by PR practitioners to measure reputation (good or bad) of their organizations include whether stakeholders and the organization have low interactivity and feel distant, suggesting firm reputation is at-risk. If a firm's communication strategy is transparent, honest, and clear, and people enjoy socializing, the company can assume a good reputation both in and out of the firm. Some respondents believed market share and awareness of a firm are indicators. Cumulative indicators are used sometimes to measure awareness, customer satisfaction, and brand image. One respondent reported that if the majority—say eighty percent—of customers are satisfied, a company has a good reputation.

Crisis Cases Related to Company Image

Most respondents believed they have not faced crises due to rigid and regularly updated crisis management programs. One respondent from a municipality reported that sometimes a customer must visit a new building because the old building is having technological issues. Companies usually try to overcome small problems to enhance their image by addressing customer complaints and maintaining infrastructures.

Interviewees believed that Public Relations employees are the most important employees in the company who highlight and convey a positive image to the company. Public relations employees play a great role in protecting the image and reputation of the organization by writing positive articles about the company and publishing them in the local media, highlighting the company's offers and communicate with publics. So that the company will not lose its customers and it will improve its image and location in the community.

Tactical Planning During a Crisis

Some processes defined by respondents regarding strategic planning during a crisis include handling complaints effectively and efficiently, without delays. Pre-communication messages are drafted and approved by legal departments, systems are kept honest and transparent, and errors are admitted and rectified as soon as possible. Avoiding rumors and improving interactions among departments are some strategies respondents mentioned. Others were unaware of whether their organizations have a crisis management program.

All interviewees agreed that using transparency, honesty when dealing with the media is the best way to protect the company image during crises.

Implications to Theory

Karl Marx's structural conflict theory provides some insights into crisis management. The theory suggests the structure and organization of society leads to conflicts and crises, arising when organizations compete for scarce resources (Best, 2007). Sources of crises include poverty, oppression, injustices, shirking responsibilities, exploitation, and exclusion, and crises occur in society due to class oppression and unjust behaviors from entities. The theory implies that competing benefits and interests of multiple groups influence economic and social settings (Oyekola, 1995). The theory also proposes that economic and social-setting disruptions cause crises in both societies and organizations. Every organization competes for resources, and resources appear at the core of crises. While obtaining resources, crises are inevitable, but the fittest have learned and developed crisis-management strategies to survive adverse conditions. When equilibrium in society is not maintained, critical situations arise, especially when there is power and abundance on one end and adversity on the other end (Kothari, 1979). To develop crisis-management strategies, companies must understand both the nature of conflict and factors that contribute to crises. After identification of a crisis, results must be communicated to save the organization's reputation. Of all factors involved in a crisis, addressing public safety takes priority over financial losses and organizational assets. The structural theory of conflict defines and explains both a framework for crisis management and how PR practitioners can address conflicts and crises. The theory suggests that during a crisis, how stakeholders perceive a company's reputation and how PR manages the crisis determine whether a company saves its reputation.

DISCUSSION AND CONCLUSION

PR plays a critical role during crisis management. PR teams are able to turn adverse situations to their favor and build a company's reputation that would otherwise be tarnished. Different kind of tools were used for public relations for example good quality picture, stories related to children reports that make people aware of different things, declaration related to public service, advantageous links of sites, manual regarding different training programs, and internet services these are all tools that were used by public organizations.

As suggested by Karl Marx and his theory, if a crisis is handled improperly, a company's reputation can be lost, including the investment opportunities it had. Sources of crises include natural disasters, ineffective complaint handling, low-quality products, non-sympathetic behaviors toward stakeholders, lack of interaction, lack of resources, and increasing competition. PR practitioners can resolve crises, but they must be involved in the development other relevant information. PR should not delay acceptance of blame; they should correct a situation and help authorities investigate the matter. As Mausdi (2013) explains regarding the IKEA case, as soon as the controversy arose, the company pulled stock from twenty-one countries to ensure public safety and protect company reputation. This earned favorable attitudes from the public, which were beneficial to the firm in the long-run. PR should use television, social media, and news media to communicate transparently and immediately to build an organization's image. According to Bitar (2013), areas affected primarily by economic crises include finance, real estate, and construction. However, it is evident from the case studies and interview analysis that PR firms are dealing effectively with crises in UAE firms, and PR firms have developed effective strategies to deal with crises faced by firms such as IKEA, Freij, and Damas.

Each organization have PR individuals who contact outside organizations. Additionally, every organization have some terrible time and had a few emergencies administration that necessities to stay cover and nobody outside of the organization needs to think about it. There where they truly require the PR individuals to cover the issue and don't let anybody from outside critique it. Dealing with the media very fast and publishing transparency news is the best tactic to solve crises. However, if the PR secure the information about crises, the organization dint pulverized by another significance, the organization will close or the organization will not trusted by the client. By utilizing demonstrated advertising (PR) instruments and exercises, you can advance uplifting states of mind and practices towards your business that will help change over intrigued purchasers into clients.

SCOPE OF THE STUDY

Investigating crises is a sensitive issue in the academic papers. No organization intent to discuss the negative points about its role during crisis. The research covers more information about crises by using online sources and interviewing PR practitioners who refused to mention their names. The researcher faced difficulties to gather the sources and interview participants, she gets formal letters from her employer to collect interviews. This study determines the significance of PR during crisis management regarding various stakeholders, identification of the nature of a crisis, how companies handled crises in the past, and what frameworks and activities overcome crises through PR. In the literature review, previous causes of crises in the UAE are highlighted, including methods used during a crisis to overcome them. Successful and unsuccessful methods used to handle crises are also highlighted, followed by a proposal of effective PR solutions regarding crises. The researcher suggested many future researches such as crises after applying VAT in the Gulf region, Organizations and media relations during crises and why crises issue is a sensitive issue in organizations?

REFERENCES

Agnes, M. (2017). 3 Important Crisis Management Trend Projections For 2017. *Forbes*. Retrieved 4 25, 2018, from https://www.forbes.com

Al-Jenaibi, B. (2008). The effects of media campaigns on different cultures. *World Academy of Science. Engineering and Technology International Journal of Humanities and Social Sciences*, *2*(10), 1067–1070.

Al-Jenaibi, B. (2011). The Changing Representation of the Arab Woman in Middle East Advertising and Media, Global Media Journal--Arabian Edition, 1(2).

Al-Jenaibi, B. (2015). E-Collaboration, Public Relations and Crises Management in UAE Organizations. *International Journal of e-Collaboration*, *11*(3), 10–28. doi:10.4018/ijec.2015070102

AlBayan newspaper. (2016). Experts: Emirates has provided professional lessons in crisis management. Retrieved from https://www.albayan.ae/economy/local-market/2016-08-08-1.2692476

Ashcroft, L. S. (1997). Crisis management - public relations. *Journal of Managerial Psychology*, *12*(5), 325–332. doi:10.1108/02683949710183522

Banks, K. F. (2001). *Crisis communications: A casebook approach 2nd Edi*. Mahwah, NJ: Lawrence Erlbaum.

Barton, L. (2011). *Crisis in organizations II* (2nd ed.). Cincinnati, OH: College Divisions South-Western.

Best, S. G. (Ed.). (2006). *Introduction to peace and conflict studies in West Africa: A reader*. Spectrum Books.

Black, S. (1989). *Introduction to Public Relations*. West African Book Publishers Ltd.

Briguglio, P. (2004). Crisis Management: A White Paper. *MMI Public Relations*. Retrieved 8 31, 2013, from http://www.mmipublicrelations.com/white/paper/crisis-management-a-white-paper/

Bundy, J., Pfarrer, M. D., Short, C. E., & Coombs, W. T. (2017). Crises and crisis management: Integration, interpretation, and research development. *Journal of Management, 43*(6), 1661–1692. doi:10.1177/0149206316680030

Cohen, J. R. (1999). Advising clients to apologize. *California Law Review*, 72, 1009–1131.

Complinet. (2010). *DFSA Takes Action Over Damas Failures*. USA: Thomson Reuters.

Coombs, W. T. (2004). Structuring crisis discourse knowledge: The West Pharmaceutics case. *Public Relations Review*, 30(4), 467–473. doi:10.1016/j.pubrev.2004.08.007

Coombs, W. T. (2007). Protecting organization reputations during a crisis: The development and application of situational crisis communication theory. *Corporate Reputation Review*, 10(3), 163-176.

Coombs, W. T. (2007). *Crisis Management and Communications. UAE*: Institute of PR.

Coombs, W. T. (2007). *Ongoing Crisis Communication: Planning*, Managing, and Responding.

Council, C. L. (2003). *Crisis management strategies.*

Damas. (2013). *About Damas*. Retrieved 8 31, 2013, from http://www.damasjewel.com/articledisplay.aspx?mid=33&id=25

Dean, D. H. (2004). Consumer reaction to negative publicity: Effects of corporate reputation, response, and responsibility for a crisis event. *Journal of Business Communication, 41*(2), 192–211. doi:10.1177/0021943603261748

Dilenschneider, R. L. (2000). *The corporate communications bible: Everything you need to know to become a public relations expert*. Beverly Hills: New Millennium.

Downing, J. R. (2003). American Airlines' use of mediated employee channels after the 9/11 attacks. *Public Relations Review*, 30(1), 37–48.

DuBois, S. (2013). How IKEA can get back on the horse after a meat scandal. *CNN*. Retrieved 09 01, 2013, from http://management.fortune.cnn.com/2013/02/26/ikea-horsemeat/

Ebersole, G. (2013). The Importance of Public Relations and Crisis Management Planning To Your Business. *Crisistraining.net*. Retrieved 9 1, 2013 from http://www.crisistraining.net/crisis-media-training_workshops_The-Importance-of-Public-Relations-and-Crisis-Management-Planning-To-Your-Business.htm

Emirates247. (2013). Global Village rides closed after visitor's death; 3 arrestedError! Hyperlink reference not valid.. Retrieved 09 1, 2013 from http://www.emirates247.com/news/emirates/global-village-rides-closed-after-visitor-s-death-3-arrested-2013-01-26-1.492484

Ey-Ling, S. (2011). 2010 Practice Analysis: Professional competencies and work categories in public relations today. *Public Relations Review, 37(3),* 187–196.

Feagin, J., Orum, A., & Sjoberg, G. (Eds.). (1991). *A case for case study*. Chapel Hill, NC: University of North Carolina Press.

Hearit, K. M. (2006). *Crisis management by apology: Corporate response to allegations of wrongdoing*. New Jersey: Lawrence Erlbaum Associates.

Hope, T. G. (2009, December 16). Damas says it must restructure, delay debt payments to survive. *The National*. Retrieved from http://www.thenational.ae/business/banking/damas-says-it-must-restructure-delay-debt-payments-to-survive

Kavoussi, B. (2013). *Ikea Horse Meat Controversy Hurts Company's Reputation: Analysis. The Huffington Post*.

Kellerman, B. (2006). When should a leader apologize and when not? *Harvard Business Review*, 84(4), 73–81. PMID:16579415

Kent, M. T. (2007). Taxonomy of mediated crisis responses. *Public Relations Review*, 33(2), 140–146.

Kirat, M. (2007). Promoting Online Media Relations: Public Relations Departments' Use of Internet in the UAE. *Public Relations Review*, 33(2), 166–174. doi:10.1016/j.pubrev.2007.02.003

Kirat, M. (2012). *Crisis Management Strategies*. Sharjah: University of Sharjah.

Kirat, M. (2012). *Dubai Police PR Management: Strategy of Almabhouh Assassination Crisis*. University of Sharjah.

Kothari, R. (1979). *The North-South Issue*. Mazingria.

Lerbinger, O. (1997). *The crisis manager: Facing risk and responsibility*. New Jersey: Lawrence Erlbaum.

Masudi, F. (2013, 03 01). *Meatballs on menu are halal*. Retrieved 09 01, 2013, from Gulf News: http://gulfnews.com/news/gulf/uae/general/meatballs-on-menu-are-halal-ikea-says-1.1152651

News, C. (2013, 02 25). *Horsemeat found in Ikea meatballs in Europe*. Retrieved 09 1, 2013, from CBC NEWS World: http://www.cbc.ca/news/world/story/2013/02/25/horse-meat-ikea-meat-balls.html

Nwosu, I. E. (1996). *Mass Media and African War*. Star Printing and Publishing Corporation Limited.

Oyekola, O. (1995). *Foundations of public relations*. Western Africa: Ibadan Bombshell Publication.

Carney, A., & Jorden, A. (1993). Prepare for business-related crises. *The Public Relations Journal*, 49(8), 34–35.

Rivero, O. (2014). *Importance of Public Relations in Corporate Sustainability*. Retrieved from https://globaljournals.org/GJMBR_Volume14/4-The-Importance-of-Public-Relations.pdf

Shaw, G. L., & Harrald, J. (2006). The Core Competencies Required of Executive Level Business Crisis and Continuity Managers. In 11th Annual 2006/2007 Disaster Resource Guide (pp. 66-69).

Stake, R. E. (2006). *Multiple Case Study Analysis*. New York: Guilford Press.

Subaihi, T. A. (2013, 1 26). Operator warned before Global Village Ferris wheel death. *The National*. Retrieved 09 01, 2013, from http://www.thenational.ae/news/uae-news/operator-warned-before-global-village-ferris-wheel-death-says-family

Townsend, S. (2017). UAE economy on the up in 2017, but late payments still an issue. *Arabianbusiness.com*. Retrieved from http://www.arabianbusiness.com/uae-economy-on-up-in-2017-but-late-payments-still-issue-662176.html

Tyler, L. (1997). Liability means never being able to say you're sorry: Corporate guilt, legal constraints, and defensiveness in corporate communication. *Management Communication Quarterly*, *11*(1), 51–73. doi:10.1177/0893318997111003

Ulmer, R. R. T. L. (2006). Effective Crisis Communication: Moving from crisis to opportunity. Thousand Oaks, CA: Sage.

Yin, R. (1993). *Applications of case study research*. Newbury Park, CA: Sage Publishing.

Yin, R. K. (2005). Applied Social Research Methods Series (Vol. 5. *Case Study Research: Design & Methods, 3rd ed.*). Sage.

Chapter 6
A Web–Based System for Supply Chain Collaboration to Enhance Agility and Flexibility

Ping-Yu Chang
Ming Chi University of Technology, Taiwan

ABSTRACT

Recently, enterprises have increased their competitiveness through supply chain collaboration to efficiently allocate resources using the internet. However, supply chain collaboration usually fails because information is usually confidential. Many studies have discussed strategies of supply chain collaboration via internet but only a few of the strategies can be implemented in practice. Therefore, this research builds an information exchange platform to share production and inventory information over internet to ensure on-time delivery. This platform is implemented in a panel manufacturing company and 10% on-time delivery increase with 2% quality improvement after adapting this system. This result demonstrates the usefulness of using online platform to immediately share information will improve one-time delivery and quality assurance.

INTRODUCTION

With the rapid changes (high product variety, customization, and the bullwhip effect) in the manufacturing environment, supply chains have faced on-time delivery and material shortage uncertainties. These uncertainties result from poor management of information from suppliers, manufacturers, and customers. For instance, suppliers promise on-time delivery of components but usually fail to meet promised due dates because of uncertainties within their production line. A delay or materials shortage caused by suppliers will increase production lead times and the possibility of late delivery. To reduce uncertainties, supply chain collaboration becomes a pertinent strategy for enterprises to enhance their competitiveness. Furthermore, building a platform to integrate information from different echelons and accurately transfer information to accurate supply chain echelons will be an important step towards supply chain collaboration. Although the impact of using a web-based platform to share supply chain information

DOI: 10.4018/978-1-5225-7214-5.ch006

has been thoroughly discussed in the literature (Fedorowicz et al., 2008; Cassivi et al., 2008; Pick et al., 2009; Arinze, 2012), its effectiveness in a practical implementation has not yet been demonstrated.

Therefore, this study develops a web-based information platform based on the opinions of panel manufacturing industry supply chain management experts. In addition, this study analyzes the required information and parameters in constructing a web-based platform to improve on-time delivery and production scheduling. The platform is implemented in the same panel manufacturing company to understand its usefulness and the effect on the supply chain. This study is expected to achieve the following objectives.

1. Identify information required to improve supply chain collaboration.
2. Construct and implement a web-based platform to realize the usefulness of the developed hierarchy.

The reminder of this paper is presented as follows. In Literature Review Section, a review of literature pertinent to the problem under study is presented. Information Platform Structure Section discusses the platform structure in detail. Empirical Study Section presents the empirical study and the results obtained from the panel manufacturing company. In Implementation of the Concept Section, the implementation steps of the platform are presented. Finally, we present our conclusions in Conclusion Section.

LITERATURE REVIEW

Supply chain management (SCM) was first introduced by Oliver and Webber (1982). The purpose of SCM is to identify and integrate the resources and procedures of different companies in a supply chain. The integration enhances the efficiency of the supply chain that is achieved with information and profit sharing. SCM integration includes coordination and collaboration with partners, which can be suppliers, intermediaries, third party service providers, and customers.

Kalakota & Robinson (2001) defined electronic SCM as using information technology and the Internet to construct the information channels of SCM. Figure 1 describes the structure of electronic SCM. In Figure 1, suppliers and customers share their information with the enterprise using the Internet. Enterprise represents the company with the highest bargaining power in the supply chain. This can be a manufacturer, distributor, or retailer. To manage the shared information, enterprise can construct a platform for uploading and analyzing information so that the efficiency of the supply chain can be enhanced. The innovation of the Internet and the rapid growth of the world wide web have transformed traditional services such as purchase, order, product, sale, transport, and accounting over the Internet. This transformation has reduced order lead times and has resulted in the creation of a support infrastructure for B2B (Business to Business) relationships. Suppliers use the Internet for information sharing to maintain good relationships with manufacturers and retailers (Klein & Rai, 2009; Maloni & Benton, 1997; Simatupang & Sridharan, 2005; Madlberger, 2009; Hadaya & Pellerin, 2008). Furthermore, companies can use the B2B model for price comparison and for seeking business partners (Klein, 2005; Richard & Devinney, 2005; Soosay et al., 2008).

El-Gayar and Fritz (2010) proposed a web-based multi-perspective decision support system with a multi-criteria decision framework for information security planning and management. Their system is tested through scenarios and the results show that priorities become apparent, affecting the final decision outcome based on user preferences. Wu and Chuang (2010) use Innovation diffusion theory (IDT) with multi-stage analysis to identify key external antecedents that affect the rate of e-SCM diffusion.

Figure 1. Electronic SCM

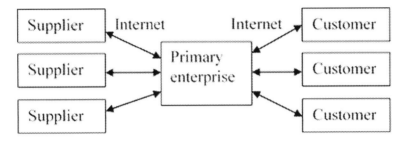

Their study considers both financial and non-financial performance in a complementary manner, and proposes a novel research model for the relationships among external antecedents, stage-based e-SCM diffusion, and firm performance. They use empirical findings to identify the relative effects of external antecedents on diffusion stages and, in turn, firm performance. Chan and Chan (2010) study how flexibility and adaptability in delivery quantity and due date can improve the performance in a network of two-level multi-product MTO supply chains. They use agent-based simulation to model the operations of supply chains with number of cost items and customer demand fill rate as performance measures. The simulation results indicate that the introduction of such flexibility and adaptability can improve the aforementioned performance, but that capacity utilization will have an impact on the coordination between adaptability and flexibility.

Rymaszewska et al. (2017) address how servitisation can utilize the third wave of Internet development, referred to as the Internet of Things (IoT), which may unlock the potential for innovative product-service systems on an unprecedented scale. They propose a framework that is aimed at proving a better understanding of how companies can create value, and add it to their servitisation processes with, the data obtained by the IoT based solutions. Han et al. (2017) use a partial least squares approach to structured equation modelling analysis on 162 questionaires from supply chain practitioners. They found that transactional IT flexibility significantly affects operational IT flexibility which significantly affects strategic IT flexibility. de Mattos and Laurindo (2017) analyse the relationship of assimilation of suppliers portal, integration of supply chain and performance. They survey 95 suppliers of a company in the automotive segment and the results indicate that the technological factor and environment had greater effects on assimilation of the collaborative platform.

Although supply chain integration is known to improve efficiency and profits, some uncertainties still needed to be resolved. Davis (1993) and Strader et al. (1999) pointed out that customers are the main uncertainty in the supply chain. They also concluded that demand uncertainty results from information delay and incorrect information sharing that can be improved using collaborative forecasting. Trkman et al. (2010) investigate the relationship between analytical capabilities in the plan, source, make, and delivery area of the supply chain and its performance using information system support and business process orientation as moderators. Their findings suggest the existence of a statistically significant relationship between analytical capabilities and performance. To react to the uncertainties, upstream suppliers will have high inventory levels to adjust to on-time delivery requirements for the downstream companies. Kristianto et al. (2012) improve the integration of a supply chain in all aspects of inventory allocation and manufacturing processes that incorporates manufacturing and product design into logistics design. An optimum supply chain network is developed within their study. They use a system dynamic-based computer simulation model to validate the operations of the supply chain; their results show that fewer stockholding points and a shorter review period of demand can improve performance of a supply chain.

Because real demand information is not known to suppliers, a bullwhip effect will easily occur for the upstream industries. Hence, strengthening the level of information sharing so that industries in the supply chain can have better forecasts, coordination, and cooperation becomes a key factor for SCM to be successful (Rodriguez et al., 2007; Wilson & Duffy, 2010). The objective of information sharing is to send the right information to the right companies at the right time so that inventory levels, distribution, and order fulfillment can be accomplished with better efficiency and lower cost. In addition, supply chain risk can be lowered with information sharing. Tan et al. (2012) propose a Multi-Criteria Decision Making (MCDM) technique to support decision making in context-aware B2B collaboration. They use empirical investigations to compare this proposed technique against other short-listed MCDM techniques. Their results show that the proposed technique with deviation measurement can provide the most stable and robust decision.

Lavastre et al. (2012) conduct an empirical study of 142 general managers and logistics and supply chain managers in 50 different French companies. The result demonstrates that Supply Chain Risk Management (SCRM) must be a management function for organizations to be effective. Effective SCRM is based on collaboration with industrial partners. Ueki (2016) investigates the effect of putting pressure of ISO 9000 or 14000 on downstream customers on customer-supplier collaborations. This study finds that ISO requirements improve the collaborative relationships and process control between focal firms and suppliers. Krolikowski and Yuan (2017) investigate the impact of customer-supplier relationships on firm innovation using empirical data of U.S. firms for the period from 1980 to 2005. Their find that a strong customer-supplier relationship will motivate suppliers to invest more in innovation. Wu et al. (2016) examine the effect of internet-based collaboration on product innovation performance of supplying firms. Original survey data is applied to test the performance of internet-based collaboration and the results show that high face-to-face interaction will improve the performance of the internet-based collaboration. Hu et al. (2016) study revenue sharing contracts in two different supply chain structures to understand the optimal configuration between focal firms and suppliers. They derive optimal production quantity, ordering, and price policies for revenue sharing contracts. Zhang & Cao (2018) explore the impact of collaborative culture and interorganizational systems use on supply chain collaboration by examining a moderated mediation model. Their results indicate that collaborative culture enhances supply chain collaboration directly as well as indirectly by facilitating interorganizational systems use.

Chen et al. (2017) review the literature to reveal what has been studied and what are the gaps in the current body of knowledge, and also to comment on what the future research agenda should include. Their results indicate that research about supply chain collaboration for the purpose of sustainability is gaining growing attention in the business field; however, environmental and economic considerations still dominate the research.

INFORMATION PLATFORM STRUCTURE

To increase supply chain visibility, this study develops and constructs a web-based production information exchange platform. This system can be defined as a communication interface between suppliers and manufacturers. Suppliers provide their production information to the platform for manufacturers to predict the arrival date of components to avoid any delay of scheduled activities. The constructed platform in this study is implemented in a panel manufacturing industry between suppliers and manufacturers. In the studied industry, information sharing is transformed from traditional phone and fax to web and email. Using only email to transfer information would consume time to receive and analyze data. A platform, however, will analyze the data automatically with the incorporated equations and knowledge.

The environment of the platform is shown in Figure 2. In Figure 2, the required production information is first collected in a supplier's database system and then is uploaded onto the platform for manufacturers. Using the environment in Figure 2, a main enterprise can optimize production scheduling with the shared information and also have better management of its suppliers. The structure of the platform is described in Figure 3 with two parts of an information flow. The first part is that manufacturers request that the production information of suppliers be uploaded to the platform before starting production scheduling. Suppliers then provide their production information to the platform. As soon as the required information is obtained, manufacturers will download the information (the second part of the information flow) from the platform so that scheduling can be optimized.

The platform is constructed based on the literature and experts' opinions. Experts' opinions are acquired using subjective interviews with experts in a panel manufacturing company. The experts' opinions are used to determine the specifications and required information of the platform. According to the experts' opinions, order information, material information, and production quality information are the most important functions for improving managerial efficiency and reducing cost.

Figure 4 describes the information flow of the platform. In Figure 4, suppliers will transfer their information to the web server that is located in the main enterprise of the supply chain. The server will analyze the provided information and send the required information to the manufacturing plants. The server will also analyze capacity utilization in each plant, material quality, and on-time delivery possibility for each order so that capacity can be better utilized and orders can be better fulfilled.

Figure 2. Environment of the platform

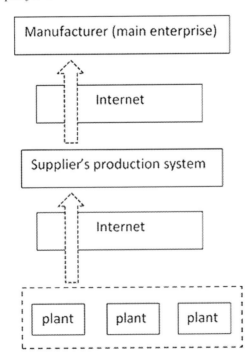

Figure 3. Production platform

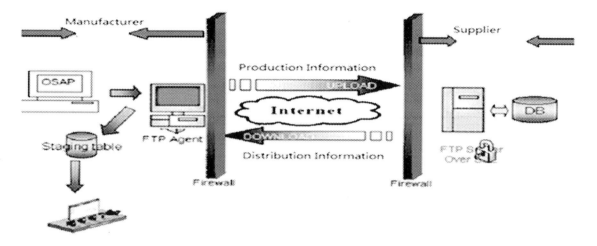

Figure 4. Information flow structure

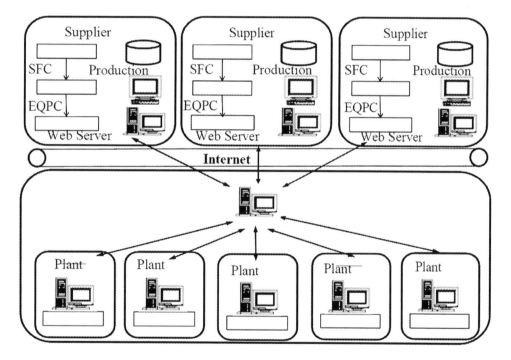

Figure 5 illustrates the steps and relationships in constructing the platform. In Figure 5, the idea of constructing the platform is initiated from the requirements of the enterprise and manufacturing plants. Data are collected to identify the scope of the platform; then the functions of the platform are determined. The enterprise and manufacturing plants provide their data and process requirements to confirm the specifications.

Figure 5. Steps and relationships of the platform

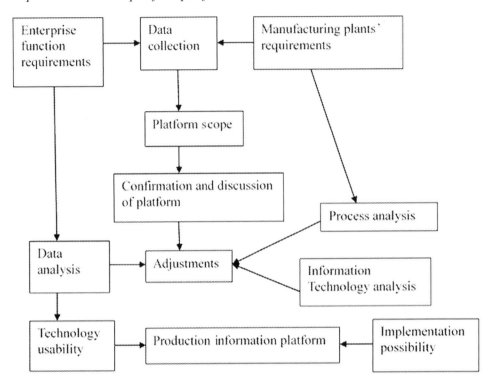

According to experts' opinions, quality and due date estimation are the two most important elements of production information. Hence, a quantitative estimation to quote the due date will assist the production line to understand the arrivals of components and raw materials from suppliers so that scheduling accuracy can be improved. Equation (1) represents the formula to quote the due date where the descriptions of the parameters are as follows (Hopp and Spearman, 2008).

μ : average production rate

σ : standard deviation of the production rate

m : product to be produced

s : expected service level

ℓ : due date quoting

In equation (1), the quoted due date can be categorized into two parts. The first part is the average time required to finish the order, while the second part is the safety lead time. Furthermore, m can be calculated by adding work-in-process, quantities to be produced before the order, and the quantities of the order. The role of safety lead time is to provide a buffer allowing reaction to the variance of production rate. If the standard deviation of the production rate is zero, then no safety lead time should be included because the production rate is consistent.

$$\ell = \frac{m}{\mu} + \mathrm{M} \frac{z_s^2 \sigma^2 \left(1 + \sqrt{\frac{4\mu m}{z_s^2 \sigma^2} + 1}\right)}{2\mu^2} \tag{1}$$

In this study, the production rate and standard deviation are calculated based on historical data. Because a seasonal effect always exists in the TFT industry, capacity utilization should also be considered to determine the safety lead time. Therefore, this study adjusts the safety lead time using a multiplier (*M*) that is determined based on capacity utilization.

EMPIRICAL STUDY

To test the usefulness of the platform, this study implements the platform in a panel manufacturing industry with due date quoting formula to measure the associated improvement of quality and on-time delivery. The required information from suppliers is WIP level, production rate and variance, and orders awaiting production. we analyze one year of data to determine the production rate for further calculation. Also, a seasonal effect is found in panel demand and incorporating capacity utilization into the due date quoting formula will improve the quality of the forecast. Table 1 demonstrates multipliers for four quarters to enlarge or shorten the safety lead time based on capacity utilization. The multipliers are based on interviews with experts in the panel manufacturing industry. One multiplier is assigned to each capacity utilization range for each of the four quarters.

If capacity utilization is less than 60% in the first quarter, no safety lead time should be included because it is low demand season and almost 50% of capacity is available for further usage. However, when capacity utilization is between 90% and 100% in the fourth quarter, the experts tune the multiplier up to 1.5 (more safety lead time) to ensure on-time delivery. To determine the effect of the multiplier, actual due date, due date quoting without multipliers, and due date quoting with multipliers of 20 orders are compared. These 20 orders are in the fourth quarter with 90% capacity utilization; the average production rate for one year is 4142.857 panels per day with a standard deviation of 1107.335 panels. This fourth quarter information and the 90% capacity utilization indicate that the value of the multiplier is 1.5. Figures 6 and 7 demonstrate comparisons of actual due date and quoted due dates (with and without multipliers) with service levels of 95% and 90%, respectively.

Table 1. Multipliers of safety lead time

Capacity utilization (*U*)/quarter	First	Second	Third	Fourth
$U < 60\%$	0	0	0.6	0.6
$60\% \leq U < 80\%$	0.6	0.6	0.8	1
$80\% \leq U < 90\%$	0.6	0.8	1	1.2
$90\% \leq U$	0.8	1	1.2	1.5

In Figures 6 and 7, QDD (Quoted Due Date without multipliers), QDD adjusted (Quoted Due Date with multipliers), and ADD (Actual Due Date) are presented for orders A to T. In Figure 6, twelve orders are delayed using QDD while only two orders are delayed using QDD adjusted with a 95% service level. Although two orders are still delayed using multipliers within the QDD formula, the longest delay time is 0.35 day (8.4 hours), still acceptable based on the experts' opinions. In Figure 7, fourteen orders are delayed using QDD while eight orders are delayed using QDD adjusted with a 90% service level. Clearly, Figures 6 and 7 show that using a higher service level will result in more accurate due date forecasting, but the accuracy improvement can be enhanced by using the multipliers.

Furthermore, the delayed orders are fourteen and twelve using QDD for service levels of 90% and 95%, respectively. The delayed orders are eight and two using QDD with multipliers for service levels of 90% and 95%, respectively. The results demonstrate a significant impact by using the capacity multipliers on the accuracy of due date quoting. This will improve the percentage of on-time delivery.

With the multipliers and due date quoting formula, the percentage of on-time delivery is increased after implementing the system in December. The on-time delivery percentages for one year are shown in Figure 8. In Figure 8, the on-time delivery percentages before implementing the platform are all below 90%. The on-time delivery percentages then increase from lower than 90% to more than 95% after implementing the platform. The results in Figure 8 indicate that using a web-based platform efficiently integrated supply chain information and improved on-time delivery.

IMPLEMENTATION OF THE CONCEPT

The concept of sharing supply chain information using a web-based platform is demonstrated in the previous section. To implement the concept, a company has to develop its own IT capabilities and its ability to control the supply chain. The reason is that the company needs the IT ability to construct the web-based platform and to coordinate its suppliers' systems' compatibility. Also, the company should have enough bargaining power to negotiate with the suppliers for ongoing uploading of their production information. To be more precise, the panel manufacturing company in this study takes the following steps to collaborate with the supplier.

Figure 6. Due date comparison with 95% service level

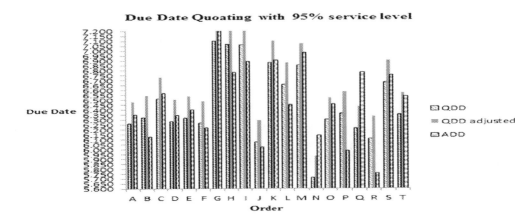

Figure 7. Due date comparison with 90% service level

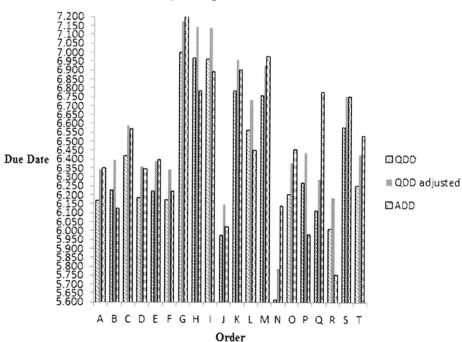

Figure 8. Due date improvement

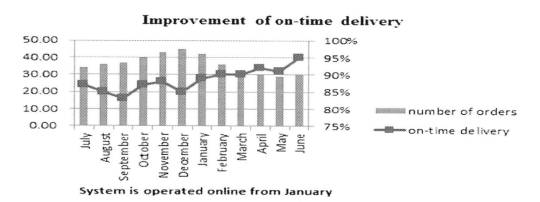

1. Constructing the server for the web-based platform including operating systems and database systems.
2. Constructing a production information framework to integrate the supplier's information with the panel manufacturing company. The production information includes order contents, material requirements, and production quality requirements.

3.   Improving the information system compatibility between the supplier and the panel manufacturing company to enhance the effectiveness of the supply chain collaboration. To improve compatibility, eight areas must be addressed: confirm suppliers' IT ability, product coding, information sharing agreement, information exchange office, timetable for implementation, hardware installation and software development, evaluating and adjusting the platform, and bringing the platform online. Figure 9 demonstrates the flow of the eight steps.

In the confirm the suppliers' IT ability step, platform specification including programming capability and information uploading features should be finalized. In the product coding step, product code between the two companies must be kept the same to maintain the consistency of the information. After leveraging the product code of both companies, an information sharing agreement with a confidential policy must be signed and an office to be in charge of information exchange should be formed in both companies. The information exchange offices are the communication windows that are responsible for developing the project time table, the specification for the platform, and addressing every delay in the project. Once the information exchange office is built, the panel manufacturing company develops the schedule for implementing the platform, including hardware and software installation and development. The hardware installation involves setting up the FTP (File Transfer Protocol) server for the supplier, while the software development includes setting up the supplier's IP (Internet Protocol) address and data uploading function, and the panel manufacturing company's IP address and firewall function. After the platform is ready, it will be evaluated and adjusted for online operations.

To better realize the implementation of the proposed method and model, a real system is constructed to demonstrate the idea of the platform and the data structure. Figures 10 and 11 show the platform entrance screen and the inventory summary data structure. In Figure 10, suppliers should log into the material surveillance management to update their inventory and work-in-process data. The updated data will be reviewed by the focal firm immediately for further decision making support.

Figure 11 shows the inventory data structure in the platform. The inventory data structure contains vendor's and supplier's names, part number, model number, in-process quantities, total quantities, and inventory quantities. With these information, supplier and vendor can exchange their production and inventory information to synchronize their production time and quantities. The information can also be used to monitor the product quality and trace the quality issues back to manufacturing process to improve the quality.

The introduction of this platform is not accepted by the panel manufacturing industry and its suppliers. Functions and effectiveness are doubted by both supply chain echelons. However, after numbers of discussions and meetings to all the departments and suppliers, the platform is finally accepted by the departments in the panel manufacturing industry and it suppliers. The reasons of this success are the support from the presidential office and the seeded teachers. The presidential office realizes the importance of the system and persuade all the departments in the company and suppliers to attend the meetings and use the system. To promote the system, one or two employees in each department are trained as seeded teachers and these seeded teachers will help other workers in operating the system and address to their questions.

Figure 9. Procedures for improving compatibility

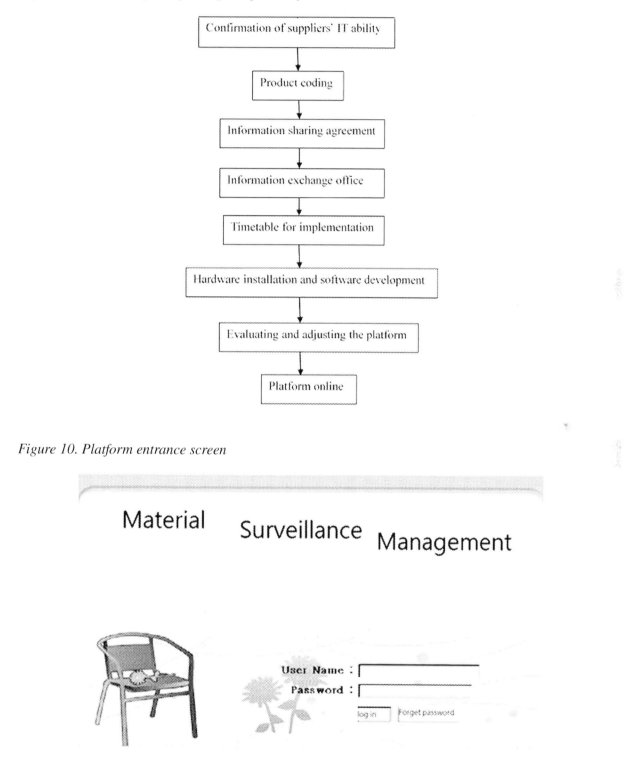

Figure 10. Platform entrance screen

Figure 11. Inventory data structure

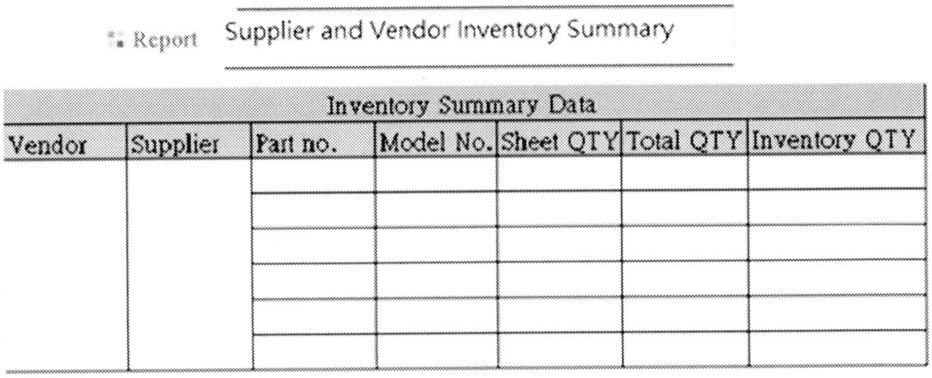

Report	Supplier and Vendor Inventory Summary

Inventory Summary Data						
Vendor	Supplier	Part no.	Model No.	Sheet QTY	Total QTY	Inventory QTY

CONCLUSION

This study constructs a platform to integrate suppliers' production information with manufacturer's scheduling to improve quality and on-time delivery. The specification of the web-based platform is determined by interviewing manufacturing industry experts. Also, a due date quoting equation with multipliers is applied to forecast possible due dates. The constructed platforms are applied in a panel manufacturing company. The results show significant improvements in due date and quality after implementing the platform.

The results demonstrate the usefulness of adopting the platform in supply chain collaboration, and provide indications for enhancing the competitiveness of the panel industry. To be more precise, only the panel manufacturing company and one of its upstream suppliers are integrated within the web-based platform. If all the companies within the panel supply chain can be involved in the platform, quality and due date can be ensured at every stage of panel manufacturing. Furthermore, sharing information across all of the supply chain companies within a platform will also enhance the visibility of the supply chain and reduce the unit cost of a panel. With lower unit cost and higher quality, many strategies can be applied to enhance the competitiveness of the panel supply chain. However, integrating a supply chain using such a platform will usually result in difficulties in information confidentiality that will result in the destruction of the supply chain collaboration. The success of the collaboration in this study is because the panel manufacturing company has higher bargaining power than its suppliers, forcing suppliers to overlook their confidentiality issues. Therefore, the success of supply chain collaboration can be maintained if the platform can be constructed and maintained by the company with the highest bargaining power, or a coordinating organization such as a governmental department or academic office.

FUTURE WORKS

Although this study improves on-time delivery percentage and quality with the constructed platform, some facets are yet to be considered and can be topics of future research. For example, the multipliers of this study are based on seasonal demand and capacity utilization. However, the effect of the product life cycle on the multipliers is not yet established. A multiplier that is determined based on more factors will refine the safety lead time to the point where it will optimize production scheduling. Also, the proposed due date quoting method is only considered demand forecasting and capacity utilization without incorporating suppliers' manufacturing process differences, components inventory levels and storage characteristics, and other forecasting methods. Suppliers usually offer different components and have different manufacturing process that will result in different lead time, WIP, and quality. Incorporating the characteristics of components and manufacturing process will improve the accuracy of the due date quoting method and on-time delivery.

REFERENCES

Arinze, B. (2012). E-research collaboration in academia and industry. *International Journal of e-Collaboration*, *8*(2), 1–13. doi:10.4018/jec.2012040101

Cassivi, L., Hadaya, P., Lefebvre, E., & Lefebvre, L. A. (2008). The role of collaboration on process, relational, and product innovations in a supply chain. *International Journal of e-Collaboration*, *4*(4), 11–32. doi:10.4018/jec.2008100102

Chan, H. K., & Chan, F. T. S. (2010). Comparative study of adaptability and flexibility in distributed manufacturing supply chains. *Decision Support Systems*, *48*(2), 331–341. doi:10.1016/j.dss.2009.09.001

Chen, L., Zhao, Z., Tang, O., Price, L., Zhang, S., & Zhu, W. (2017). Supply chain collaboration for sustainability: A Literature review and future research agenda. *International Journal of Production Economics*, *194*, 73–87. doi:10.1016/j.ijpe.2017.04.005

Davis, T. (1993). Effective supply chain management. *Sloan Management Review*, *35*(4), 35–16.

De Mattos, C. A., & Laurindo, F. J. B. (2017). Information technology adoption and assimilation: Focus on the suppliers portal. *Computers in Industry*, *85*, 48–57. doi:10.1016/j.compind.2016.12.009

El-Gayar, O. F., & Fritz, B. D. (2010). A web-based multi-perspective decision support system for information security planning. *Decision Support Systems*, *50*(1), 43–54. doi:10.1016/j.dss.2010.07.001

Fedorowicz, J., Laso-Ballesteros, I., & Padilla-Melendez, A. (2008). Creativity, innovation, and E-collaboration. *International Journal of e-Collaboration*, *4*(4), 1–10. doi:10.4018/jec.2008100101

Hadaya, P., & Pellerin, R. (2008). Determinants of manufacturing firms' intent to use web-based systems to share inventory information with their key suppliers. *International Journal of e-Collaboration*, *4*(2), 29–54. doi:10.4018/jec.2008040102

Han, J. H., Wang, Y., & Naim, M. (2017). Reconceptualization of information technology flexibility for supply chain management: An empirical study. *International Journal of Production Economics*, *187*, 196–215. doi:10.1016/j.ijpe.2017.02.018

Hopp, W. J., & Spearman, M. L. (2008). *Factory physics*. New York: McGraw Hill.

Hu, B., Meng, C., Xu, D., & Son, Y.-J. (2016). Three-echelon supply chain coordination with a loss-averse retailer and revenue sharing contracts. *International Journal of Production Economics*, *179*, 192–202. doi:10.1016/j.ijpe.2016.06.001

Kalakota, R., & Robinsion, M. (2001). e-Business: Road map for Success (2nd ed.). Boston: Addison Wesley.

Klein, R. (2005). Customization and real time information access in integrated eBusiness supply chain relationships. *Journal of Operations Management*, *25*(6), 1366–1381. doi:10.1016/j.jom.2007.03.001

Klein, R., & Rai, A. (2009). Inter-firm strategic information flows in logistics supply chain relationships. *Management Information Systems Quarterly*, *33*(4), 735–762. doi:10.2307/20650325

Kristianto, Y., Gunasekaran, A., Helo, P., & Sandhu, M. (2012). A decision support system for integrating manufacturing and product design into the reconfiguration of the supply chain networks. *Decision Support Systems*, *52*(4), 790–801. doi:10.1016/j.dss.2011.11.014

Krolikowski, M., & Yuan, X. (2017). Friend or foe: Customer-supplier relationships and innovation. *Journal of Business Research*, *78*, 53–68. doi:10.1016/j.jbusres.2017.04.023

Lavastre, O., Gunasekaran, A., & Spalanzani, A. (2012). Supply chain risk management in French companies. *Decision Support Systems*, *52*(4), 828–838. doi:10.1016/j.dss.2011.11.017

Madlberger, M. (2009). What drives firms to engage in interorganizational information sharing in supply chain management? *International Journal of e-Collaboration*, *5*(2), 18–42. doi:10.4018/jec.2009040102

Maloni, M. J., & Benton, W. C. (1997). Supply chain partnerships: Opportunities for operations research. *European Journal of Operational Research*, *101*(3), 419–429. doi:10.1016/S0377-2217(97)00118-5

Oliver, R. K., & Webber, M. D. (1982). Supply-chain management: logistics catches up with strategy. In M. G. Christopher (Ed.), *Logistics, The Strategic Issue*. London: Chapman & Hall.

Pick, B. J., Romano, N. C. Jr, & Roztocki, N. (2009). Synthesizing the research advances in electronic collaboration: Theoretical frameworks. *International Journal of e-Collaboration*, *5*(1), 1–12. doi:10.4018/jec.2009010101

Richard, P. J., & Devinney, T. M. (2005). Modular strategies: B2B technology and architectural knowledge. *California Management Review*, *47*(4), 86–113. doi:10.2307/41166318

Rodriguez, W., Zalewski, J., & Kirche, E. (2007). Beyond intelligent agents: E-sensors for supporting supply chain collaboration and preventing the bullwhip effect. *International Journal of e-Collaboration*, *3*(2), 1–15. doi:10.4018/jec.2007040101

Rymaszewska, A., Helo, P., & Gunasekaran, A. (2017). IoT powered servitization of manufacturing – an exploratory case study. *International Journal of Production Economics, 192*, 92–105. doi:10.1016/j.ijpe.2017.02.016

Simatupang, T., & Sridharan, R. (2005). An integrative framework for supply chain collaboration. *International Journal of Logistics Management, 16*(2), 257–274. doi:10.1108/09574090510634548

Soosay, C. A., Hyland, P. W., & Ferrer, M. (2008). Supply chain collaboration: Capabilities for continuous innovation. *Supply Chain Management, 13*(2), 160–169. doi:10.1108/13598540810860994

Strader, T. J., Lin, F. R., & Shaw, M. J. (1999). The impact of information sharing on order fulfillment in divergent differentiation supply chains. *Journal of Global Information Management, 7*(1), 16–25. doi:10.4018/jgim.1999010102

Tan, P. S., Lee, S. S. G., & Goh, A. E. S. (2012). Multi-criteria decision techniques for context-aware B2B collaboration in supply chains. *Decision Support Systems, 52*(4), 779–789. doi:10.1016/j.dss.2011.11.013

Trkman, P., McCormack, K., Valandares de Oliveria, M. P., & Ladeira, M. B. (2010). The impact of business analytics on supply chain performance. *Decision Support Systems, 49*(3), 318–327. doi:10.1016/j.dss.2010.03.007

Ueki, Y. (2016). Customer pressure, customer-manufacturer-supplier relationships, and quality control performance. *Journal of Business Research, 69*(6), 2233–2238. doi:10.1016/j.jbusres.2015.12.035

Wilson, W., & Duffy, K. P. (2010). Improved information connectivity and visibility throughout the global supply base. *International Journal of e-Collaboration, 6*(4), 54–68. doi:10.4018/jec.2010100104

Wu, I. L., & Chuang, C. H. (2010). Examining the diffusion of electronic supply chain management with external antecedents and firm performance: A multi-stage analysis. *Decision Support Systems, 50*(1), 103–115. doi:10.1016/j.dss.2010.07.006

Wu, J., Wu, Z., & Si, S. (2016). The influences of internet-based collaboration and intimate interactions in buyer-supplier relationship on product innovation. *Journal of Business Research, 69*(9), 3780–3787. doi:10.1016/j.jbusres.2015.12.070

Zhang, Q., & Cao, M. (2018). Exploring antecedents of supply chain collaboration: Effects of culture and interorganizational system appropriation. *International Journal of Production Economics, 195*, 146–157. doi:10.1016/j.ijpe.2017.10.014

Chapter 7

Baran:
An Effective MapReduce–Based Solution to Solve Big Data Problems

Mohammadhossein Barkhordari
Information and Communication Technology Research Center, Iran

Mahdi Niamanesh
Information and Communication Technology Research Center, Iran

Parastoo Bakhshmandi
Information and Communication Technology Research Center, Iran

ABSTRACT

The MapReduce method is widely used for big data solutions. This method solves big data problems on distributed hardware platforms. However, MapReduce architectures are inefficient. Data locality, network congestion, and low hardware performance are the main issues. In this chapter, the authors introduce a method that solves these problems. Baran is a method that, if an algorithm can satisfy its conditions, can dramatically improve performance and solve the data locality problem and consequences such as network congestion and low hardware performance. The authors apply this method to previous works on data warehouse, graph, and data mining problems. The results show that applying Baran to an algorithm can solve it on the MapReduce architecture properly.

1. INTRODUCTION

According to data volume growth in information systems, social networks and sensors, it is necessary to design and implement systems that can manage this huge amount of data and be capable to analyze them. Huge data may have other specification too. Velocity can be another property. If data do not process in a specific time, it will not have any value. For example, patient data that are generated by different devices must be processed in pre-determined time. The third property can be variety and it shows that data contain different types like multimedia, text, string, stream etc. The data processing system must be able to manage these types of data. If data has all or some of above features, it is called "Big data".

DOI: 10.4018/978-1-5225-7214-5.ch007

To solve big data problems, usually traditional algorithms cannot be used. Big data problems are usually solved on the distributed platforms. Distributed platforms have their own problems. One of the main problems is data locality problem. Data locality problem is not existence of the required data on the processor node. Data locality problem causes processor nodes use network to achieve the required data and using network causes following problems:

- Not proper use of node hardware because of node wait to receive data
- Network congestion
- Join received data from other nodes with node local data
- Save intermediate results for iterative problems.

One the most important methods that big data problems are solved by is MapReduce. MapReduce is a programming method that is executed on large hardware clusters (Dean et al., 2008). MapReduce also have above problems and so it is not appropriate for problems like data warehouse, graph and data mining.

In this chapter, some conditions are proposed that if it is possible to apply them on MapReduce problems they can be solved properly. These conditions are called Baran conditions. The proposed conditions are used for different types of problems and the results shows that the proposed conditions solve problems with lower execution time. The solved problems are in different fields like graph, data mining and data warehouse.

The structure of this chapter is as follows. In section 2, related works are discussed. In section 3, Baran conditions are illustrated. The proposed conditions are then evaluated in different fields in comparison with prevalent methods of each field. The final section is the conclusion.

2. RELATED WORKS

In this section related works bout MapReduce optimization, big data tools are investigated

2.1. MapReduce

The two main components of the MapReduce architecture are Mappers and Reducers. The data items in the MapReduce architecture are <Key, Value> pairs. All operations involve these pairs. Every algorithm can utilize this architecture. Each node of Mappers and Reducers takes part in solving a problem. Mappers execute an algorithm and generate intermediate results. These results may be aggregated or filtered according to keys. In the second phase, a Reducer generates the results by combining <Key,Value> pairs on their keys. Combiners are sometimes used to prevent network and process bottlenecks. Combiners act in a similar way to Reducers and improve their performance and speed.

Many attempts have been made to improve the MapReduce architecture. Figure 1 presents five approaches used in (Osman et al., 2013) to optimize the MapReduce architecture.

In Figure 1, the first step in MapReduce optimization tries to improve the job scheduling and the distribution of the tasks over the nodes. MapReduce++ (Zhang et al., 2012) estimates the execution time for each task. In each job, a task with a minimum execution time is then selected. This method improves the overall execution time. The same MapReduce++ method is used in (Polo et al., 2009), but the scheduling is performed by dynamic resource allocation using parameters specified by the user.

Figure 1. MapReduce optimization techniques

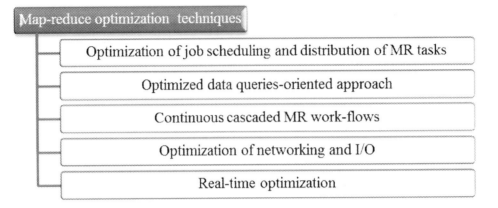

In StarFish (Polo et al., 2011), real-time resource allocation is used. In this method, user configuration is not necessary. StarFish creates a profile for each task of a job by task monitoring. StarFish also uses workflow aware scheduling. With this method, processes are transferred to nodes that contain related data, thereby decreasing network congestion. In EA2S2(Wang et al., 2017) a storage layer for heterogeneous systems is designed and by task categorization tries to improve data locality. SwiftAnalytics(Rupprecht et al., 2017) introduces a method to store objects. This method uses data locality aware writing method. By using this method additional I/O s are omitted.

In (Tang et al., 2016) an optimized MapReduce workflow for scheduling is used. Tasks are first divided to processing task or I/O tasks and then scheduling is done according to data locality. In (Yao et al., 2017) according to work load of finished tasks resources are allocated to the Mapper or Reducer. In (Wang, W et al., 2016) an architecture is used for queue and a scheduling algorithm with two policy is used. Schedule policy is based on the shortest queue and maximum weight and these two policy is used for data locality and data load balancing among nodes. Dawn In (Wang, W et al., 2017) an adaptive network scheduler is introduced that include an online plan and an adaptive scheduler for tasks. Online scheduler consider task dependencies and specifies appropriate nodes for task execution. AdPart (Harbi et al., 2016) proposes a distributed RDF that creates a primitive classification on data. Simultaneously a query optimizer replicates useful data segments among nodes.

In the second step in Figure 1, information is presumed to exist in a structured format. Therefore, structured query languages (SQL) can be used for data management. Some important work in the area of networking and I/O optimization are BigTable (Chang et al., 2008), Hive (Thusoo et al., 2010), Pig (Olston et al., 2008), Hbase (Khetrapal et al., 2006), Cassandra (Lakshman et al., 2009).

In the third step in Figure 1 (continuous cascaded MR workflows), iterations and loops are added to MapReduce. In some attempts to optimize the MapReduce architecture, such as those based on HaLoop (Bu et al., 2010) and Twister (Ekanayake et al., 2010), a loop is implemented as a task in a job with predetermined conditions or as a number of repeats. Intermediate results are kept in a distributed shared memory (DSM). Intermediate results are sometimes stored on a local hard disk because of performance issues. Nova (Olston et al., 2011) is a method that supports incremental/non incremental iterative algorithms. This method is implemented on Hadoop and Pig. In Nova, it is not necessary to process previous data before new data. Thus, new data items can be processed on arrival. Spark (Zaharia et al., 2012) uses resilient-distributed datasets (RDDs) rather than DSM, which is usually used in MapReduce methods. As a RDD is an in-memory method, I/O costs decreases dramatically. In this method, the data are fragmented into parts, and each part can be rebuilt if a fault occurs. Spark can be used by iterative algorithms. If the defined in-memory space is not sufficient for algorithm execution, the data are transferred to a hard disk according to user-defined configurations.

In the fifth step in Figure 1 (real time optimization), pure MapReduce is used for batch processing. However, this cannot solve real-time problems. Chukwa (Boulon et al., 2008) proposed a real-time log file processing method. In this method, each Mapper acts as a data producer, and each Reducer acts as a data collector. Two methods have been proposed to receive data from Mappers. With the first method, data are stored in a DSM, where as they are stored in local node memory with the second method. Although the second method is faster than the first, it is more risky because if local data is corrupted we cannot restore it. In some methods, such as Yahoo S4(Neumeyer et al., 2010) and Twitter Storm (Nathan et al., 2012),the MapReduce structure is changed, with processing nodes employed that can process data, create new data, or aggregate data.

Data mining algorithms can be used with some of the above methods. Mahout (Chu et al., 2007) implements some data mining algorithms on distributed nodes, but their implementation is based on batch processing and does not support iteration. Presto (Venkataraman et al., 2011) uses R language to deal with Mahout problems.

Based on the aforementioned problems, we conclude that pure MapReduce is not suitable for solving iterative problems. Many attempts have been made to manage the intermediate results generated in each iteration. We divided iteration management solutions into three groups:

- **DSM:** In DSM, the shared memory is used to store intermediate results. This method is not appropriate because it incurs many I/O costs. In addition, as the nodes have to access a DSM network, network congestion increases.
- **RDDs:** This method does not incur high I/O costs, but other problems, such as network congestion, remain. In addition, if the RDD is full, the data have to be flushed to a disk. Iterative big data problems, such as Apriori with an unknown number of iterations, will rapidly fill an RDD, and I/O costs will be incurred when the RDD is full.
- **Local Memory Usage:** In this approach to iteration management, each node stores its own intermediate results, and an iteration management algorithm tries to locate jobs on related nodes. I/O costs and network congestion are also encountered with this method because data locality problem. In addition, if disk failure occurs, the intermediate results will be lost. With above descriptions we can conclude that:
  - Adding loop structure to MapReduce architecture is not always equal to increasing performance and in special cases it can help us for better results management.
  - Job scheduling and MapReduce task distribution is completely depends on problem type and even in two problems with same type we may not use same solution and per problem and data job scheduling and task distribution have to be changed.
  - I/O and network optimization can help to optimize problem solution but it is not works always and for all types of problems.
  - Query oriented approach is only a facilitator for creating MapReduce jobs and it does not guarantee the best performance.
  - Real time approach needs a comprehensive recognition of problem and obviously for each problem and each execution environment it needs its pre requirements.

As it shows above none proposed techniques and methods are not general even for a type of problem. In this chapter we introduce a general method which by using that all MapReduce problems which can satisfy required conditions, can be solved properly without problems like data locality, network congestion, hardware inefficiency and etc.

2.2. Big Data Tools

According to (Zhang et al., 2015) problems in big data can be divided to three part as it is shown in Figure 2.

Iterative algorithms and machine learning algorithms are problems that require applying algorithm on the intermediate results several times to achieve the final results. Queries are another group of problems that extract the results of a search or calculation from various data sources. They usually do not have iteration. The third group are stream problems that require real time processing.

To solve three groups problem use four solutions that is depicted in Figure 3.

Figure 2. Big data problems categorization

Figure 3. Big data solutions

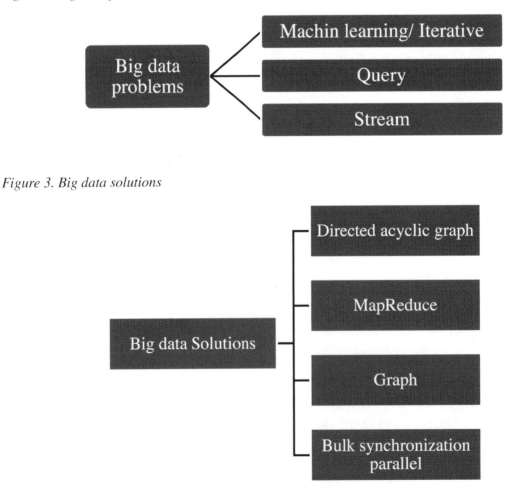

DAG (Directed acyclic graph) is a solution that uses acyclic graphs and graphs with no loop to solve problems. The next solution uses graph to solve problem. The last group is BSP (bulk synchronization parallel) that is a parallel method to solve problem. In this method algorithm is executed on different nodes and the results are exchanged among nodes. Collective models are the same as MapReduce but the nodes do not wait for other nodes results. According to above description and (Zhang, 2015) big data tools can be categorized as Figure 4.

As it is shows in Figure 4, Hadoop is used for many tools as infrastructure. Some of tools implement iteration in MapReduce because pure MapReduce do not support iteration. Haloop, Twister and Spark are the most prominent tools for iteration management.

Some other groups of tools do not use Hadoop as infrastructure. This type of tools are based on message. One the most important infrastructures that solves problems based on message is MPI (Message passing interface). According to high performance MPI is used in many tools. Graph problems are solved properly with MPI and MPI outperforms other methods like MapReduce or DAG. Because in MapReduce or DAG there are serious restrictions for iteration management, graph prominent tools usually do not use MapReduce. Some of important tools that solve graph problem are Giraph, Hama, GraphLab and GraphX. Some of tools like reef and Harp use various methods for iteration management.

A group of tools try to solve query problems. Some of them like Dryad-LINQ and Drill use DAG to solve query problems. They are not Hadoop-based. Because query problems do not require iteration management MapReduce tools are more successful in this area. These tools uses DAG and MapReduce. The most important tools in this field are Pig, Hive and Tez. Some of tools that mainly use for stream

Figure 4. Big data tools categorization

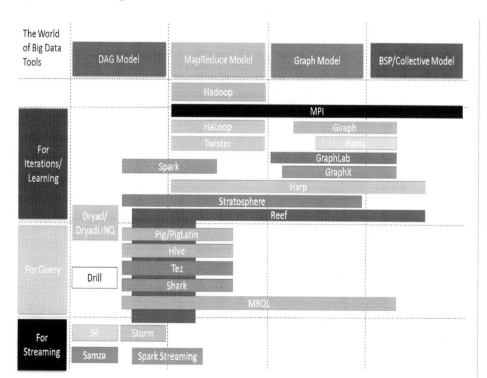

real time processing are based on DAG (S4 and Storm). Some other tools like Spark streaming are based on DAG and MapReduce.

The mentioned methods have their own problems that causes algorithm execution time increase, not proper use of hardware and network congestion.

3. BARAN

In this section, Baran method is introduced. To solve problems with the MapReduce architectures properly, each node has to do its related calculations locally. In this way, the network cost for the data exchange decreases to zero, and only the results have to be sent over the network.

In MapReduce problems, there are three main pillars: the hardware architecture, data, and algorithm. For each node in MapReduce, there are two main entities: the data and the algorithm. Therefore, to make each node independent, some changes must be done in the data and the algorithm. To solve data problems, it is necessary to localize the data. Baran unifies the data format to localize data.

In the algorithm section, the algorithm must be changed according to the simultaneous and independent execution of the algorithms on the nodes. An algorithm meet BARAN conditions if the algorithm can be divided over nodes, and each node can execute its algorithm division simultaneously and independently (without needing data from other nodes). To convert an algorithm to BARAN, a type of Mapper must be used in the MapReduce architecture. This type of Mapper is non-filtering. A non-filtering Mapper is a Mapper that does not apply any aggregating filter on any keys from the <Key, Value> pairs. In the Baran architecture, all filtering is done on the Reducer layer. In other words, to solve a MapReduce problem effectively on each node non-filtering Mappers must be used.

Furthermore, if the problem is iterative, it must be scaled down to Mappers. In this phase, a big iteration problem must be converted to smaller iteration problems and the global iteration nature of the problem is omitted. Figure 5 shows Baran conditions.

A MapReduce problem can be solved with higher algorithm execution speed if it has Baran conditions can be seen in Figure 5.

Data unification, using non-filtering Mappers, and scale down iterations (if they exist) to the Mappers.

3.1. Data Unification

In this part, data unification is explained by an example. If Table 1 is considered as input data items and Table 2 defines column IDs then Table 3 can be generated by Table1 and Table 2 data items.

Using this conversion, all input data items can be converted to the unified format. For each algorithm, unification must be performed according to the algorithm's requirements and this sample can be used for data warehouse problems.

3.2. Using Non-Filtering Mappers

Non-filtering Mappers are Mapper that do not apply aggregation filters on the Mapper results. In this section, an example of filtering Mappers and non-filtering Mappers for the "top two" problem is investigated. If filtering Mappers is used in the "top two" problem as shown in Figure 6, the result will be incorrect.

Figure 5. Baran conditions

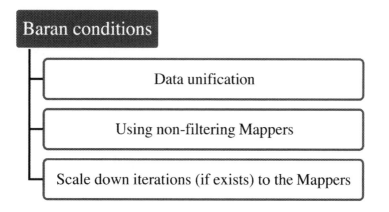

Table 1. Input data items

Symptom	Treatment	SSN	Age	Family	Name	ID
S1	T1	8838232	43	Mahdavi	Ali	1256
S8	T2	5524813	29	Alavi	Hossein	1257
…	…	…	…	…	…	…

Table 2. Column definitions

Column Name	Column ID
ID	1
Name	2
Family	3
Age	4
SSN	5
Treatment	6
Symptom	7

In the "top two" problem, non-filtering Mappers must be used because they do not omit any keys, and the results will be true. Figure 7 shows the correct results.

3.3. Scale Down Iterations (If Exists) to the Mappers

To solve problems like the graph all pairs shortest path (APSP) with MapReduce, It is required to scale down the iteration to the Mappers. To solve the APSP problem, the graph must be divided into smaller graphs, and the APSP algorithm and the iteration must be executed on subgraphs. With this method, a big iteration problem is converted into *n* smaller iterations. To solve the APSP problem, suppose a graph like Figure 8.

Table 3. Unified data format

Value	Row ID	Column ID
Ali	1256	1
Mahdavi	1256	2
43	1256	3
8838232	1256	4
T1	1256	5
S1	1256	6
S2	1256	7
…	…	…

Figure 6. Filtering Mappers

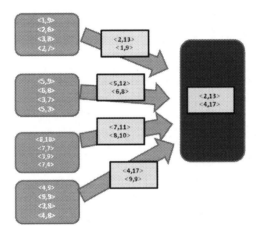

Figure 7. Non-filtering Mappers

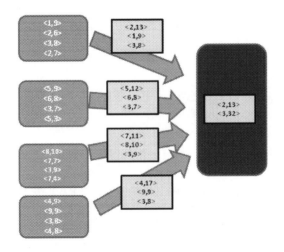

Figure 8. Input graph

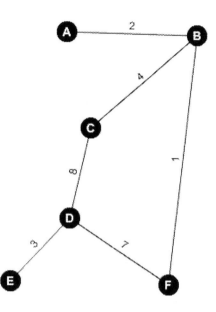

First, the graph is divided into two subgraphs. Figure 9 shows the subgraphs.

In this stage, each subgraph is located on a node. Each node executes APSP on its subgraph. The results are shown in Table 4.

In this section, the deleted edges are added to layer 2 Mappers, and new paths are created with Φ and Θ operators. Figure 10 shows this process.

The results are sent to the Reducer, and the Reducer results are shown in Table 7.

4. EVALUATION

To evaluate Baran method, it is used to solve different problems. Because Baran makes each node, independent and nodes do not need other nodes data to complete their process so algorithm execution time decreases. To evaluate Baran it is used for different fields.

4.1. Data Warehouse

To use Baran for data warehouse it is first required that Baran conditions are met. Because data warehouse problem is not iterative, first two conditions must be met. To achieve data unification, data format must be changed from Table 1 and Table 2 to Table 3. With this conversion data format will be unified over all nodes so each node can execute its query independently. To execute a query over nodes first input query in converted to comprehensible query for the nodes and then the query is executed simultaneously on the Mapper nodes. The results then gathered in the Reducer. In this step, no aggregation condition is applied on the Mapper results and aggregation condition is applied on the Reducer (non-filtering Mappers).

Figure 9. Subgraphs

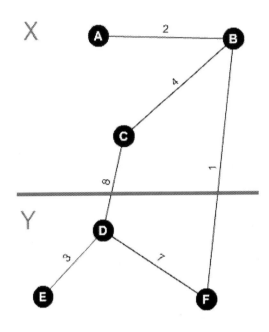

Table 4. The APSP execution results

Sub Graph	Key	Value
X	AB	2
	BC	4
	AC	6
Y	DE	3
	DF	7
	EF	10

Baran method is used to solve data warehouse problem in ScaDiPasi (Barkhordari et al., 2015). To decrease the required space for data storage Aras (Barkhordari et al., 2017) and Atrak (Barkhordari et al., 2017) are proposed. These methods also use RAM in addition to HDD to achieve higher query execution time.

The Mapper nodes architecture in Aras and Atrak is as Figure 11.

Baran also can be used to integrate multi-dimensional data sources over distributed platforms like Hadoop. Baran method is used in Arvand (Barkhordari et al., 2018) to integrate and transfer multi-dimensional data sources to scalable and distributable big data platforms. In this method, data with maximum granularity is stored on each node.

The proposed methods are compared with prominent data warehouse tools like Flink, HadoopDB and Spark. The results show that by applying Baran conditions the query execution time decreases.

Figure 10. The deleted edges addition

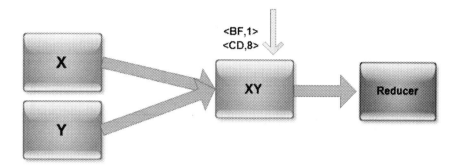

Table 5. The necessary operators for the Mapper results combination

Description	notation
Right/Left join	Φ (<xy>,<zx>)
Full join	Θ (<wx>,<xy>,<yz>)

Table 6. The results after application of the operators

Operator	Key	Value
-	AB	2
-	BC	4
-	AC	6
-	DE	3
-	DF	7
-	EF	10
Φ (<AB>,<BF>)	AF	3
Φ (<BC>,<CD>)	BD	12
Φ (<AC>,<CD>)	AD	14
Φ (<CD>,<DE>)	CE	11
Φ (<BF>,<DF>)	CF	8
Φ (<BF>,<EF>)	BE	11
Φ <DF>,<CD>)	CF	15
Θ (<AB>,<BF>,<DF>)	AD	10
Θ (<AB>,<BF>,<EF>)	AE	13
Θ (<BC>,<CD>,<DE>)	BE	15
Θ (<BC>,<CD>,<DF>)	BF	19
Θ (<AC>,<CD>,<DF>)	AF	21
Θ (<AC>,<CD>,<DE>)	AE	17
Θ (<BC>,<BF>,<DF>)	CD	12
Θ (<BC>,<BF>,<EF>)	CE	15
Θ (<CD>,<BC>,<BF>)	DF	13
Θ (<CD>,<DF>,<BF>)	BC	16

Table 7. The Reducer results

Key	Value
AB	2
AC	6
AD	10
AE	13
AF	3
BC	4
BD	12
BE	11
BF	19
CD	12
CE	11
CF	8
DE	3
DF	7
EF	10

Figure 11. Mapper architecture

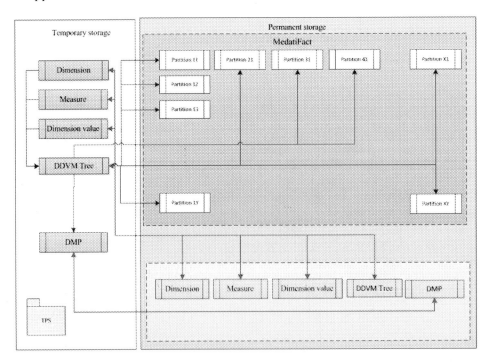

4.2. Graph

Baran can be applied to solve graph problems. The graph problems are iterative and all Baran conditions must be met. To evaluate Baran for graph problems, some of graph problems like APSP (All pairs shortest path), loop detection and pattern matching are solved by ScaDiGraph (Barkhordari et al., 2017). In ScaDiGraph all node have the same format, non-filtering Mappers are used and iteration are limited to the Mappers. In other words, main graph problem is divided to many (the number of the Mappers) subgraphs and the results are sent to the Reducer. In the Reducer by using In-Memory databases and normal DBMS (Database management systems) the final results are generated. The proposed method is compared with prominent tools like Pegasus, Pregel and PowerGraph. The results show that ScaDiGraph outperforms other methods.

4.3. Data Mining

Baran is useful for data mining problems. Data mining problems are iterative so to use Baran for data mining all three conditions must be met. To evaluate Baran for data mining, association rule mining algorithm is selected. ScaDiBino (Barkhordari et al., 2014) uses unified data format for each node and by changing data format iteration is omitted. The proposed method outperforms tools like Mahout and MLLib.

5. CASE STUDIES

5.1. Case Study for Graph Problems (Barkhordari et al., 2017)

"Because of the large amount of information that can be stored in a graph data structure and because of the importance of analysing graph information, it is essential to have a scalable and distributable framework for analysing the large amounts of information contained in a graph. Single-node solutions are not adequate for managing large graphs. ScaDiGraph omits iterations among hardware nodes by dividing a graph structure into smaller pieces. This type of division has two important merits. First, large graph iterative problems are divided into small, iterative problems, which can be solved by a hardware node. Second, many weak or medium hardware nodes can be used to solve large graph problems.

The proposed method divides the graph structure and solves problems on each hardware node separately. With the proposed architecture, all the results are gathered in the Reducer node. The hardware nodes act independently. In addition, graph data and states do not need to be exchanged, and the results of each hardware node are calculated separately. The following three steps describe the proposed method:

1. The main graph is divided into subgraphs; the number of subgraphs depends on the Mapper count. The same number of nodes can be used for each Mapper.
2. Each Mapper executes an algorithm on its subgraph.
3. The results of all Mappers plus the deleted edges are sent to the Reducer.

No paths are omitted in the second step, which means that the Mappers are non-filtering. Figure 12 illustrates the architecture of the proposed method.

Figure 12. Proposed method architecture

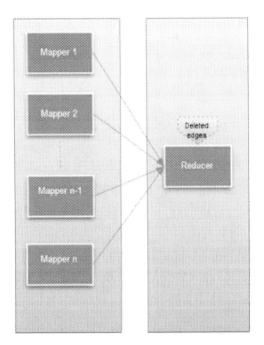

The operator for a combination of Mapper results is the following: Left or Right join. Table 1 shows the notations for this operator. In Table 8, <xy> is the edge added to the Mappers' results.

When the calculation is complete, each Mapper node sends the results to the Reducer node with the format that appears in Table 9.

The deleted edges are listed in the Reducer with the format shown in Table 10.

In the Reducer node, a database management system (DBMS) is used to achieve higher performance and a faster calculation speed in comparison with methods that do not use DBMSs. An in-memory database is used to decrease the I/O time on the hard disk drive (HDD). The table is partitioned to prevent a full scan of the table. In table design, partitioning is a method in which a table is partitioned by field

Table 8. Notation for operator on Mapper results

Description	Notation
Left or Right join	Φ (<xy>,<zx>)

Table 9. Mapper results format

Source
Destination
Value

Table 10. Deleted edges format

Source
Destination
Value
Visited

values. In the query execution time, when there is a condition on the field and field value, only the related part of the table is scanned. When the Mappers send the results with the Table 2 format, partitioning must be applied to the "Source" and "Destination" fields at the same time. Because this arrangement is not possible on the same table, the Mapper results are stored in two tables: partitioning is applied to the "Source" field in one table and the "Destination" field in the other.

In this paper, ScaDiGraph is used to solve several large graph problems. The proposed method is applied to the all-pairs shortest paths (APSP), loop-detection, and pattern-matching problems. APSP is an algorithm that computes the shortest paths between all pairs of vertices. Loop-detection is another graph problem that is very important in solving various real problems. In this algorithm, all the loops in a graph are extracted and reported. Finally, pattern matching is an algorithm that detects a sequence of vertices in a graph.

5.1.1. APSP

APSP is an algorithm with $O(n^3)$, where n is the number of vertices. Thus, with a large graph, it is impossible to solve a problem that contains many vertices in a timely manner. However, with ScaDiGraph, a large graph is divided into m (number of Mappers) small graphs. As a result, a large $O(n^3)$ is converted to $O((n/m)^3)$ smaller graphs, which enables the APSP algorithm to solve these graphical problems much faster. The following example illustrates the proposed method. In the case of the graph shown in Figure 13, the input graph is divided into two subgraphs.

There is no limitation on graph division. In this example, we use partitions that have an equal number of vertices. Figure 14 illustrates the division of the graph.

In this phase, each subgraph (X, Y) is assigned to a Mapper. Each Mapper calculates APSP for its subgraph. The results are shown in Table 11.

In this stage, which is illustrated in Figure 15, the deleted edges are added to the Mappers' results. New paths are calculated with a Φ operator.

The results from each node are sent to the Reducer. The results following the application of the join operators are shown in Table 12.

The final results are shown in Table 13.

The following APSP algorithm is executed on each Mapper for the subgraphs and on the Reducer for the deleted edges.

```
For k=1 to SubgraphNodesCount
    For j=1 to SubgraphNodesCount
        For i=1 to SubgraphNodesCount
            {
```

Figure 13. Input graph

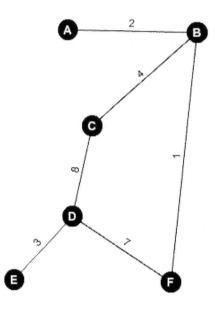

Figure 14. Divided subgraph

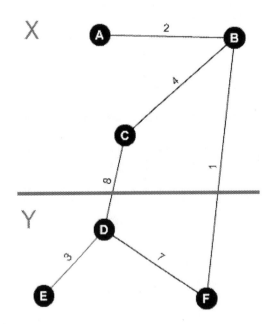

Table 11. Calculated APSP on each subgraph

Subgraph	Key	Value
X	AB	2
	BC	4
	AC	6
Y	DE	3
	DF	7
	EF	10

Figure 15. Adding deleted edges

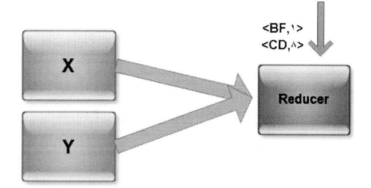

```
        If  (distance(node(k), node(i)) != infinity) &&
(distance(node(i), node(j)) != infinity)
            {
            distance(node(k), node(j))= distance(node(k), node(i)) +
distance(node(i), node(j));
            Insert into Mapper_Results(Source,Destination,Value)
                    Values(node(k).Name, node(j).Name,
distance(node(k), node(j)));
            }
        }
Send_Edges(Mapper_Results,Reducer. Mapper_Edges_SRC);
```

As shown in the above code, all the paths for the graph nodes on the Mapper are calculated, and the results are stored in the Mapper_Edges_SRC table. This code is also executed on the Reducer node for the nodes of the deleted edges, and the results are stored in the Deleted_Edges_SRC table.

The following code is executed on the Reducer node for the APSP algorithm.

Table 12. Mapper results

Operator and Key	Key	Value
-	AB	2
-	BC	4
-	AC	6
-	DE	3
-	DF	7
-	EF	10
Φ(<AB>,<BF>)	AF	3
Φ(<BC>,<CD>)	BD	12
Φ(<AC>,<CD>)	AD	14
Φ(<CD>,<DE>)	CE	11
Φ(<BF>,<DF>)	CF	8
Φ(<BF>,<EF>)	BE	11
Φ(<DF>,<CD>)	CF	15
Φ(<AF>,<DF>)	AD	10
Φ(<AF>,<EF>)	AE	13
Φ(<BD>,<DE>)	BE	15
Φ(<BD>,<DF>)	BF	19
Φ(<AD>,<DF>)	AF	21
Φ(<AD>,<DE>)	AE	17
Φ(<CF>,<DF>)	CD	12
Φ(<CF>,<EF>)	CE	15
Φ(<BD>,<BF>)	DF	13
Φ(<CD>,<BD>)	BC	16

Table 13. Reducer results

Key	Value
AB	2
AC	6
AD	10
AE	13
AF	3
BC	4
BD	12
BE	11
BF	19
CD	12
CE	11
CF	8
DE	3
DF	7
EF	10

```
Copy_Edges(Mapper_Edges_SRC, Mapper_Edges_DST);
Copy_Edges(Deleted_Edges_SRC, Deleted_Edges_DST);
Create local index on column "Destination" for each partition on table "Map-
per_Edges_SRC";
Create local index on column "Source" for each partition on table "Mapper_Edg-
es_DST";
While (Select exists (visited) from Deleted_Edges_SRC where visited=0)
{
For i= 1 to Deleted_Edges_SRC.PartitionCount
 {
Join(Mapper_Edges_SRC.partition(Deleted_Edges_SRC.Partition(i).PartitionName),
Deleted_Edges_SRC.partition (Deleted_Edges_SRC.Partition(i).PartitionName));
Deleted_Edges_SRC.Partition(i).visited=1;
Insert join results into Mapper_Edges_SRC;
Insert join results into Mapper_Edges_DST;
Insert new edges into Deleted_Edges_SRC;
Insert new edges into Deleted_Edges_DST;
Join(Mapper_Edges_DST.partition(Deleted_Edges_SRC.Partition(i).PartitionName),
Deleted_Edges_SRC.partition (Deleted_Edges_SRC.Partition(i).PartitionName));
Insert join results into Mapper_Edges_SRC;
Insert join results into Mapper_Edges_DST;
Insert new edges into Deleted_Edges_SRC;
Insert new edges into Deleted_Edges_DST;

Delete from Deleted_Edges_SRC where visited=1;
}
 For i= 1 to Deleted_Edges_DST.PartitionCount
 {
Join(Mapper_Edges_SRC.partition(Deleted_Edges_DST.Partition(i).PartitionName),
Deleted_Edges_DST.partition (Deleted_Edges_DST.Partition(i).PartitionName));
Deleted_Edges_DST.Partition(i).visited=1;
Insert join results into Mapper_Edges_SRC;
Insert join results into Mapper_Edges_DST;
Insert new edges into Deleted_Edges_SRC;
Insert new edges into Deleted_Edges_DST;
Join(Mapper_Edges_DST.partition(Deleted_Edges_DST.Partition(i).PartitionName),
Deleted_Edges_DST.partition (Deleted_Edges_DST.Partition(i).PartitionName));
Insert join results into Mapper_Edges_SRC;
Insert join results into Mapper_Edges_DST;
Insert new edges into Deleted_Edges_SRC;
Insert new edges into Deleted_Edges_DST;
Delete from Deleted_Edges_DST where visited=1;
}
}
```

```
Select Source, Destination, Min(Value) From Mapper_Edges_SRC group by Source,
Destination;
```

As shown in the above code, the following tasks are completed:

1. Mapper_Edges_SRC is copied to Mapper_Edges_DST to create partitions on the "Source" and "Destination" fields. Then, a local index is created on the partitions on the "Source" or "Destination" fields. If the partition is on the "Source" field, then the local index is created on the "Destination" field, and vice versa.
2. A while loop in the above code is repeated until there are unvisited rows in the Deleted_Edges_SRC table.
3. The "join" function is repeated up to the number of Deleted_Edges_SRC's partition count. The "join" function joins the related partitions of Mapper_Edges_SRC and Deleted_Edges_SRC and calculates the distances among the joined nodes.
4. After the "join" function, new edges that previously did not exist are added to Deleted_Edges_SRC to execute the related calculations for the new edges.
5. Steps 3 and 4 are repeated for Deleted_Edges_SRC and Mapper_Edges_DST. Finally, the visited rows from Deleted_Edges_SRC are deleted.
6. For the Deleted_Edges_DST table, steps 3, 4, and 5 are executed with Mapper_Edges_DST and Mapper_Edges_SRC.
7. Finally, the shortest paths for the "Source" and the "Destination" fields are selected.

5.1.2. Pattern Matching

To detect a pattern or a sequence of vertices, we use a modified version of the APSP algorithm. In pattern matching, the visited vertices rather than the path costs are extracted. For example, to find the "BCDF" sequence in the graph in Figure 6, the graph is first divided into two subgraphs, as shown in Figure 7. Each Mapper then retrieves the paths that have a maximum length of four edges (input string length). Table 14 shows the results achieved with the Mappers.

The deleted edges are then added to the graph, as depicted in Figure 8. New paths with a maximum length of four edges with the Φ operator are extracted. Table 15 shows the results. In Table 8, all the paths that have a length of more than four edges are discarded.

Table 16 shows the results after the Reducer phase.

Table 14. Extracted paths on each subgraph

Subgraph	Key	Value
X	AB	AB
	BC	BC
	AC	ABC
Y	DE	DE
	DF	DF
	EF	EDF

Table 15. Mapper results

Operator and Key	Key	Value
-	AB	AB
-	BC	BC
-	AC	ABC
-	DE	DE
-	DF	DF
-	EF	EDF
Φ (<AB>,<BF>)	AF	ABF
Φ (<BC>,<CD>)	BD	BCD
Φ (<AC>,<CD>)	AD	ABCD
Φ (<CD>,<DE>)	CE	CDE
Φ (<BF>,<DF>)	BD	BFD
Φ (<BF>,<EF>)	BE	BFDE
Φ (<DF>,<CD>)	CF	CDF
Φ (<AF>,<DF>)	AD	ABFD
Φ (<AF>,<EF>)	AE	-
Φ (<BC>,<CE>)	BE	BCDE
Φ (<BD>,<DF>)	BF	BCDF
Φ (<AD>,<DF>)	AF	-
Φ (<AD>,<DE>)	AE	-
Φ (<CF>,<DF>)	CD	CBFD
Φ (<CF>,<EF>)	CE	-
Φ (<DB>,<BF>)	DF	DCBF
Φ (<CF>,<BF>)	BC	CDFB

Table 16. Reducer results

Key	Value
BF	BCDF
CD	CBFD
DF	DCBF
BC	CDFB

The pattern-matching algorithm is executed on each Mapper for the subgraphs and on the Reducer for the deleted edges.

```
For k=1 to SubgraphNodesCount
    For j=1 to SubgraphNodesCount
        For i=1 to SubgraphNodesCount
```

```
        {
            If  (length(path(node(k), node(i))) <= length(InputPattern)) &&
(length(path(node(i), node(j))) <= length(InputPattern))
                {
                    path(node(k), node(j))= path(node(k), node(i)) +
path(node(i), node(j));
                    if (length(path(node(k), node(j)))<= length(InputPattern))
                    {
                        Insert into Mapper_Results(Source,Destination,Value)
                            Values(node(k).Name, node(j).Name, path(node(k),
node(j)));
                    }
                }
        }
Send_Edges(Mapper_Results,Reducer. Mapper_Edges_SRC);
```

The above code-execution process is the same as that for the APSP Mapper code, except that the code path among the graph nodes is calculated instead of the distance among the nodes. The maximum length of the path is equal to the length of the Input string for pattern matching.

The following code is executed on the Reducer for the pattern-matching algorithm.

```
Copy_Edges(Mapper_Edges_SRC, Mapper_Edges_DST);
Copy_Edges(Deleted_Edges_SRC, Deleted_Edges_DST);
Create local index on column "Destination" for each partition on table "Map-
per_Edges_SRC";
Create local index on column "Source" for each partition on table "Mapper_Edg-
es_DST";
While (Select exists(visited) from Deleted_Edges_SRC where visisted=0)
{
For i= 1 to Deleted_Edges_SRC.PartitionCount
 {
Join(Mapper_Edges_SRC.partition(Deleted_Edges_SRC.Partition(i).PartitionName),
Deleted_Edges_SRC.partition (Deleted_Edges_SRC.Partition(i).PartitionName)) ;
Deleted_Edges_SRC.Partition(i).visited=1;
Filter results where length(results.path) < length(InputPattern));
Insert join results into Mapper_Edges_SRC;
Insert join results into Mapper_Edges_DST;
Insert new edges into Deleted_Edges_SRC;
Insert new edges into Deleted_Edges_DST;
Join(Mapper_Edges_DST.partition(Deleted_Edges_SRC.Partition(i).PartitionName),
Deleted_Edges_SRC.partition (Deleted_Edges_SRC.Partition(i).PartitionName)) ;
Filter results where length(results.path) <length(InputPattern));
Insert join results into Mapper_Edges_SRC;
```

```
Insert join results into Mapper_Edges_DST;
Insert new edges into Deleted_Edges_SRC;
Insert new edges into Deleted_Edges_DST;
Delete from Deleted_Edges_SRC where visited=1;
}
 For i= 1 to Deleted_Edges_DST.PartitionCount
 {
Join(Mapper_Edges_SRC.partition(Deleted_Edges_DST.Partition(i).PartitionName),
Deleted_Edges_DST.partition (Deleted_Edges_DST.Partition(i).PartitionName)) ;
Deleted_Edges_DST.Partition(i).visited=1;
Filter results where length(results.path)<length(InputPattern));
Insert join results into Mapper_Edges_SRC;
Insert join results into Mapper_Edges_DST;
Insert new edges into Deleted_Edges_SRC;
Insert new edges into Deleted_Edges_DST;
Join(Mapper_Edges_DST.partition(Deleted_Edges_DST.Partition(i).PartitionName),
Deleted_Edges_DST.partition (Deleted_Edges_DST.Partition(i).PartitionName)) ;
Filter results where length(results.path)<length(InputPattern));
Insert join results into Mapper_Edges_SRC;
Insert join results into Mapper_Edges_DST;
Insert new edges into Deleted_Edges_SRC;
Insert new edges into Deleted_Edges_DST;
Delete from Deleted_Edges_DST where visited=1;
}
}
Select Source, Destination, Value From Mapper_Edges_SRC where Value= InputPat-
tern;
```

The above execution process is the same as that for the APSP code; however, the final step extracts the rows that have "Value" fields equal to the Input string's length.

5.1.3. Loop Detection

The proposed method can be used for loop detection in a graph; the pattern-matching solution can be used to detect a loop in a graph. If, in the Reducer phase, the *Key*s are repeated, then we have a loop in a graph. For loop extraction, we can detect duplicate *Key*s that do not have more than two common vertices in their paths. For example, to find the loops in the graph in Figure 6, the graph is first divided into two subgraphs, as shown in Figure 7. Each Mapper then extracts the paths. Table 17 presents the results of the Mappers.

The deleted edges are then added to the graph, as demonstrated in Figure 8. New paths with the Φ operator are extracted. Table 18 shows the results.

Table 17. Extracted paths on each subgraph

Subgraph	Key	Value
X	**AB**	**AB**
	BC	**BC**
	AC	**ABC**
Y	**DE**	**DE**
	DF	**DF**
	EF	**EDF**

Table 18. Mapper results

Operator and Key	Key	Value
-	AB	AB
-	BC	BC
-	AC	ABC
-	DE	DE
-	DF	DF
-	EF	EDF
Φ (<AB>,<BF>)	AF	ABF
Φ (<BC>,<CD>)	BD	BCD
Φ (<AC>,<CD>)	AD	ABCD
Φ (<CD>,<DE>)	CE	CDE
Φ (<BF>,<DF>)	CF	BFD
Φ (<BF>,<EF>)	BE	BFDE
Φ (<DF>,<CD>)	CF	CDF
Φ (<AF>,<DF>)	AD	ABFD
Φ (<AF>,<EF>)	AE	ABFDE
Φ (<BD>,<DE>)	BE	BCDE
Φ (<BD>,<DF>)	BF	BCDF
Φ (<AD>,<DF>)	AF	ABCDF
Φ (<AD>,<DE>)	AE	ABCDE
Φ (<CF>,<DF>)	CD	CBFD
Φ (<CF>,<EF>)	CE	CBFDE
Φ (<BD>,<BF>)	DF	DCBF
Φ (<CF>,<BF>)	BC	CDFB

Because we have duplicated *Key*s in Table 19, we could have loop(s) in the graph. For loop extraction, the duplicated *Key*s are first identified. Paths that have the same *Key*s and less than three common vertices are then extracted as loops.

Table 19. Reducer results

Key	Value
AD	ABCD
AD	ABFD
AE	ABCDE
AE	ABFDE
AF	ABCDF
AF	ABF
BC	BC
BC	CDFB
BE	BCDE
BE	BFDE
CE	CBFDE
CE	CDE
CF	BFD
CF	CDF
DF	DCBF
DF	DF

The loop-detection algorithm is executed on each Mapper for the subgraphs and on the Reducer for the deleted edges.

```
For k=1 to SubgraphNodesCount
   For j=1 to SubgraphNodesCount
      For i=1 to SubgraphNodesCount
         {
              If(length(path(node(k), node(i))) <= InputLength) &&
(length(path(node(i), node(j))) <= InputLength)
              {
                  path(node(k), node(j))= path(node(k), node(i)) +
path(node(i), node(j));
                  if (length(path(node(k), node(j))<= InputLength)
                  {
                      Insert into Mapper_Results(Source,Destination,Value)
                          Values(node(k).Name, node(j).Name, path(node(k),
node(j)));
                  }
              }
         }
Send_Edges(Mapper_Results,Reducer. Mapper_Edges_SRC);
```

The above code-execution process is the same as the pattern-matching process. The maximum length of the path is equal to the length of the input value for the loop detection.

The following code is executed on the Reducer for the loop-detection algorithm.

```
Copy_Edges(Mapper_Edges_SRC, Mapper_Edges_DST);
Copy_Edges(Deleted_Edges_SRC, Deleted_Edges_DST);
Create local index on column "Destination" for each partition on table "Map-
per_Edges_SRC";
Create local index on column "Source" for each partition on table "Mapper_Edg-
es_DST";

While (Select exists(visited) from Deleted_Edges_SRC where visisted=0)
{
For i= 1 to Deleted_Edges_SRC.PartitionCount
  {
Join(Mapper_Edges_SRC.partition(Deleted_Edges_SRC.Partition(i).PartitionName),
Deleted_Edges_SRC.partition (Deleted_Edges_SRC.Partition(i).PartitionName)) ;
Deleted_Edges_SRC.Partition(i).visited=1;
Filter results where length(results.path)<= InputLength;
Insert join results into Mapper_Edges_SRC;
Insert join results into Mapper_Edges_DST;
Insert new edges into Deleted_Edges_SRC;
Insert new edges into Deleted_Edges_DST;
Join(Mapper_Edges_DST.partition(Deleted_Edges_SRC.Partition(i).PartitionName),
Deleted_Edges_SRC.partition (Deleted_Edges_SRC.Partition(i).PartitionName)) ;
Filter results where length(results.path)<= InputLength;
Insert join results into Mapper_Edges_SRC;
Insert join results into Mapper_Edges_DST;
Insert new edges into Deleted_Edges_SRC;
Insert new edges into Deleted_Edges_DST;
Delete from Deleted_Edges_SRC where visited=1;
}
 For i= 1 to Deleted_Edges_DST.PartitionCount
  {
Join(Mapper_Edges_SRC.partition(Deleted_Edges_DST.Partition(i).PartitionName),
Deleted_Edges_DST.partition (Deleted_Edges_DST.Partition(i).PartitionName)) ;
Deleted_Edges_DST.Partition(i).visited=1;
Filter results where length(results.path)<= InputLength;
Insert join results into Mapper_Edges_SRC;
Insert join results into Mapper_Edges_DST;
Insert new edges into Deleted_Edges_SRC;
Insert new edges into Deleted_Edges_DST;
Join(Mapper_Edges_DST.partition(Deleted_Edges_DST.Partition(i).PartitionName),
Deleted_Edges_DST.partition (Deleted_Edges_DST.Partition(i).PartitionName)) ;
```

```
Filter results where length(results.path)<= InputLength;
Insert join results into Mapper_Edges_SRC;
Insert join results into Mapper_Edges_DST;
Insert new edges into Deleted_Edges_SRC;
Insert new edges into Deleted_Edges_DST;
Delete from Deleted_Edges_DST where visited=1;
}
}
 Duplicate_Set =(Select Source, Destination, Value From Mapper_Edges_SRC hav-
ing count(concat(Source, Destination))>1)
For each concat(Source, Destination) in Duplicate_Set
{
   For i= 1 to Count(Values)-1 //Number of paths
    For j= i+1 to Count(Values)
     {
        If (Intersect(Value(i),Value(j))==2)
             Insert into Results(Value(i),Value(j))
     }
}
```

The above code-execution process is similar to that for pattern matching; however, at the final step, paths that do not have more than two nodes in common are extracted."

5.2. Case Study for Data Warehouse Problem (Barkhordari et al., 2015)

"In this section, the proposed method for finding patient similarity (PaSi) is illustrated. ScaDiPaSi is a scalable and distributed method which is based on MapReduce. In this method, patients' input data is converted to a unified format as explained below. This conversion has two main benefits. First, changes in input data do not change the ScaDiPaSi format; therefore, we can accept any data format without any changes in our format. Second, this format is suitable for MapReduce architecture and helps us to distribute data over nodes. Moreover, each node can do its tasks without the need for other nodes' information. Because of these advantages, we can easily solve PaSi problems over distributed nodes. Patients' records in various formats can be stored, and efficiency can be achieved by independent calculations.

Table 20 shows ScaDiPasiDataSource structure. In this table, data source names and ID are stored.

Table 20. ScaDiPasiDataSource

Data source Name	Data source ID
Hospital 1	1
Hospital 2	2
Hospital 3	3
Lab 1	4
...	...

Suppose that we are working with the information in Table 21 from Hospital 1 data source.

If we define the columns as in Table 22 (ScaDiPasiColumn), the Table 21 data items can be converted into Table 23 (ScaDiPasiFact).

Table 4's data format has several advantages:

- Dynamic columns definition
- Completion of all fields is not necessary
- Unified data format
- Data storage size reduction

Table 21. Input data items

...	Symptom 3	Symptom 2	Symptom 1	Treatment	SSN	Age	Family	Name	ID
...	S3	S2	S1	T1	8838232	43	Mahdavi	Ali	1256
...	S6	-	S8	T2	5524813	29	Alavi	Hossein	1257
...	...	...	...	...	...	...	...	...	...

Table 22. ScaDiPasiColumn

Data Source ID	Column Name	Column ID
1	ID	1
1	Name	2
1	Family	3
1	Age	4
1	SSN	5
1	Treatment	6
1	Symptom 1	7
...	...	...

Table 23. ScaDiPasiFact

Value	Row ID	Column ID
Ali	1256	1
Mahdavi	1256	2
43	1256	3
8838232	1256	4
T1	1256	5
S1	1256	6
S2	1256	7
...	...	...

The proposed data format is appropriate for the MapReduce structure, and allows us to execute queries simultaneously on different nodes. There are several steps to using ScaDiPaSi:

- **ETL (Extract/Transform/Load):** First, information from different data sources is gathered, and the Meta data table (like Table 15) and data table (like Table 16) are created. Following pseudo code shows data conversion stage.

```
For (int i=0;i< InputRows[i].RowsCount; i++)
    Insert into ScaDiPaSiFact (ColumnID, RowID, Value)  values
        (GetColumnID(InputRows[i].DataSourceID, InputRows[i].ColumnName),
         InputRows[i].RowID, InputRows[i][ColumnName].Value)
```

GetColumnID function retrieves ColumnID of a specific field from ScaDiPasiColumn table. Input parameters are DataSourceID and ColumnName.

Also to identify equal fields on different data sources it is necessary to have ScaDiPasiEqual table. Table 24 shows ScaDiPasiEqual.

- **Data Allocation:** Because of the unified data format of ScaDiPaSi, data can be distributed over different nodes. Processing power and memory of each hardware node can be important factors to allocate data items to each node.
- **Query Execution:** To execute queries over MapReduce architecture, the queries first have to be converted to an appropriate format for ScaDiPaSi. Then each converted query is sent to the nodes separately for execution, and the RowIDs of the results are returned. Finally, the extracted RowIDs are sent to the Phase 2 Mappers, and patients' information is retrieved.

As it is shown in Figure 16, each *Phase 1 Mapper* sends its results as <RowID, 0, Score> triples. In the *Phase 1 Reducer*, aggregation is done on *Score* based on RowID, and the final *Score* per RowID is calculated. In the *Phase 2 Mapper,* other fields with corresponding RowIDs are extracted. The resulting formats of *Phase 2Mappers* are as <RowID, ColumnID, Value>. In *Phase 2 Reducer*, results of *Phase 2 Mappers* are aggregated. As well, *Phase 1 Reducer* results are sent directly to the *Similarity Ranker*, which sorts RowIDs according to their scores; then, when a RowID is selected by the user, other related information is extracted.

Table 24. ScaDiPasiEqual

DataSourceFieldName2	DataSourceID2	DataSourceFieldName1	DataSourceID1
ColumnName 4	14	ColumnName 1	1
ColumnName 14	5	ColumnName 7	2
ColumnName 41	6	ColumnName 11	9
ColumnName 22	7	ColumnName 31	4
…	…	…	…

Figure 16. ScaDiPaSi process to execute query

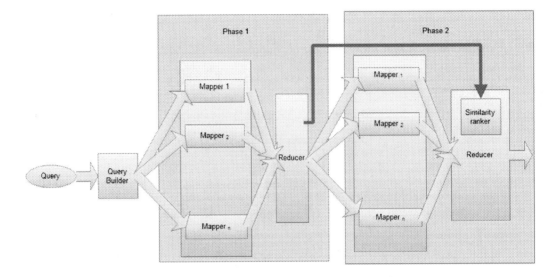

Here are pseudo code about "Query builder", "Phase 1 Mapper", "Phase 1 Reducer", "Phase 2 Mapper" and "Phase 2 Reducer". In "Query builder" function we have input parameters from query part. For example "where Field1=Value1 and Field2=Value2 and … ". First all ColumnIDs are extracted from ScaDiPasiColumn table. Then all rows that are equal to extracted ColumnIDs are retrieved from ScaDiPasiFact table.

```
Query_Builder (ColumnNames[],ColumnValues[])
{
//This part adds equal column names to input column names
      ColumnNames[]=ColumnNames[]+
        Execute_Query ((Select DataSourceFieldName1 from ScaDiPasiEqual
              where DataSourceFieldName2= ColumnNames[0] or
                    DataSourceFieldName2= ColumnNames[1] or …)
        Union
        (Select DataSourceFieldName2 from ScaDiPasiEqual
              where DataSourceFieldName1= ColumnNames[0] or
                    DataSourceFieldName1= ColumnNames[1] or …));
//This part retrieves column IDs
      ColumnIDs= Execute_Query("Select ColumnID from ScaDiPasiColumn
          where ColumnName=ColumnNames[0] or ColumnName= ColumnNames[0] or
…" );
//This part merge column names and column IDs in data set
      Return(Merge(ColumnNames[],ColumnValues[]),);
}
Phase_1_Mapper()
{
```

```
        Emit("Select RowID,0 as ColumnID, 2 as Score From ScaDiPasiFact
                where
            (ColumnID='columnID1' and Value='Value1') or
            (ColumnID='columnID2' and Value='Value2') or  …"
            ScaDiPasi_Mapper_P1_intermediate, Local);
        Emit("Select RowID,0 as ColumnID, 1 as Score From ScaDiPasiFact
                where
            (ColumnID='columnID1' and Value like '%Value1%') or "
            (ColumnID='columnID2' and Value like '%Value2%') or "
            (ColumnID='columnID3' and Value like '%Value3%') or ... ",
            ScaDiPasi_Mapper_P1_intermediate, Local);
        Emit("Select RowID,0 as ColumnID, Sum(Score) as Score From ScaDiPasi-
Fact
            Group by RowID", ScaDiPasi_Mapper_P1,ReducerP1);
}
Phase_1_Reducer()
{
      Emit("Select RowID,0,Sum(Score) as Score From ScaDiPasi_Mapper_P1
            Group by RowID"   , ScaDiPasi_Reducer_R1, ReducerP2);
}
Phase_2_Mapper()
{
      Emit("Select RowID,ColumnID, Value From ScaDiPasiFact
        Where RowID in
        (Select distinct RowID from ScaDiPasi_Reducer_P1)" ScaDiPasi_Mapper_
P2,ReducerP2);
}
Phase_2_Reducer()
{
     Emit("Select P1.RowID,P2.ColumnID, P2.Value from ScaDiPasi_Reducer_P1 P1,
          ScaDiPasi_Mapper_P2 P2 where P1.RowID=P2.RowID order
              by score descending", Final_Ranked_Result,ReducerP2)
}
```

Emit function execute queries and put results into the specified table on the specified server. If the specified table does not exist, it creates a table with the specified name.

For the *Score* calculation, many algorithms can be used. Here we use a simple algorithm, in which input patient data items are compared with the same data items of existing patients. If the data item value of the existing patient is exactly equal to the input patient data item value, then its *Score* is equal to two. Otherwise, if the patient data item value is partially similar to an existing patient data item value, then the *Score* is equal to one. If there is no similarity between the input data item value and the existing data item values then the *Score* is equal to zero.

In the data sources there are many misspellings, imprecise terms, colloquial terms, etc. To solve these problems we use Meta data to create associations between columns. In the *Query builder* phase, we can define column groups which contain the main term together with its colloquial terms, imprecise terms and prevalent misspellings. When an input column is used in a query, all other group members are considered and their related information is gathered. Table 25 shows ScaDiPasiMisspell table.

To add this part to Query_Builder() bold codes have to be added in pseudo code.

```
Query_Builder (ColumnNames[],ColumnValues[])
{
//This part adds equal column names to input column names
      ColumnNames[]=ColumnNames[]+
      Execute_Query ((Select DataSourceFieldName1 from ScaDiPasiEqual
                where DataSourceFieldName2= ColumnNames[0] or
                      DataSourceFieldName2= ColumnNames[1] or …)
      Union
      (Select DataSourceFieldName2 from ScaDiPasiEqual
                where DataSourceFieldName1= ColumnNames[0] or
                      DataSourceFieldName1= ColumnNames[1] or …)
      Union
      (Select OriginalExpression from ScaDiPasiMisspell
                where Misspell = ColumnNames[0] or
                      Misspell = ColumnNames[1] or …));

//This part retrieves column IDs
      ColumnIDs= Execute_Query("Select ColumnID from ScaDiPasiColumn
            where ColumnName=ColumnNames[0] or ColumnName= ColumnNames[0] or
…" );
//This part merge column names and column IDs in data set
      Return(Merge(ColumnNames[],ColumnValues[]),);
}
```

It is possible to change the ScaDiPaSi architecture to remove potential bottlenecks. If there is a bottleneck in the *Reducer* phase, we remove these via combiners. Figure 17 shows ScaDiPaSi architecture with combiners.

Table 25. ScaDiPasiMisspell

Misspell	OriginalExpression
Misspell 1	Expression 1
imprecise term 2	Expression 1
colloquial term 3	Expression 1
Misspell 6	Expression 1
…	…

Figure 17. ScaDiPaSi architecture with combiners

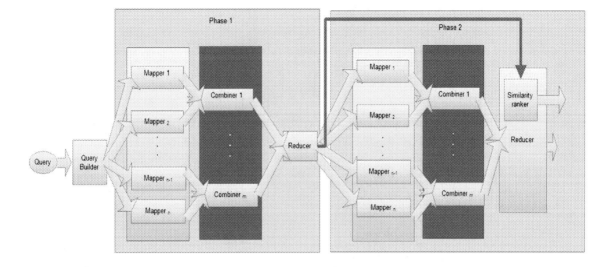

Following pseudo codes show combiner function."

```
Phase_1_Mapper()
{
        Emit("Select RowID,0 as ColumnID, 2 as Score From ScaDiPasiFact
                where
            (ColumnID='columnID1' and Value='Value1') or "
            (ColumnID='columnID2' and Value='Value2') or "
            (ColumnID='columnID3' and Value='Value3') or ... ",
ScaDiPasi_Mapper_P1_intermediate, Local);
        Emit("Select RowID,0 as ColumnID, 1 as Score From ScaDiPasiFact
                where
            (ColumnID='columnID1' and Value like '%Value1%') or "
            (ColumnID='columnID2' and Value like '%Value2%') or "
            (ColumnID='columnID3' and Value like '%Value3%') or ... ",
            ScaDiPasi_Mapper_P1_intermediate, Local);
        Emit("Select RowID,0 as ColumnID, Sum(Score) as Score From ScaDiPasi-
Fact
            Group by RowID", ScaDiPasi_Mapper_P1,CombinerP1);
}
Phase_1_Combiner()
{
      Emit("Select RowID,0,Sum(Score) as Score From ScaDiPasi_Mapper_P1
            Group by RowID"   , ScaDiPasi_Combiner_R1, ReducerP1);
}
Phase_1_Reducer()
{
```

```
        Emit("Select RowID,0,Sum(Score) as Score From ScaDiPasi_Combiner_P1
              Group by RowID"   , ScaDiPasi_Reducer_R1, ReducerP2);
}
Phase_2_Mapper()
{
        Emit("Select RowID,ColumnID, Value From ScaDiPasiFact
          Where RowID in
          (Select distinct RowID from ScaDiPasi_Reducer_P1)", ScaDiPasi_Mapper_
P2,CombinerP2);
}
Phase_2_Combiner()
{
        Emit("Select RowID,ColumnID, Value From ScaDiPasiFact
          Where RowID in
          (Select distinct RowID from ScaDiPasi_Reducer_P1)", ScaDiPasi_Combiner_
P2, ReducerP2);
}
Phase_2_Reducer()
{
    Emit("Select P1.RowID,P2.ColumnID, P2.Value from ScaDiPasi_Reducer_P1 P1,
            ScaDiPasi_Combiner_P2 P2 where P1.RowID=P2.RowID order
                by score descending", Final_Ranked_Result,ReducerP2)
}
```

6. CONCLUSION

MapReduce is used to solve many problems, but many issues decrease its performance. Nonexistent data items on local node, network traffic, hardware inefficiencies are the main issues. The three main components of the MapReduce architecture are the hardware architecture, data, and algorithm. Therefore, for node tuning and lower algorithm execution time, the data and algorithm must be changed. If each node can solve its problem separately without needing other nodes' data, then the best performance is achieved.

In this chapter, we introduced Baran, which easily solved different domain problems. Generally, each MapReduce problem can be solved effectively if it observes Baran conditions. If the data can be unified, non-filtering Mappers can be used in the Mappers, and the iteration nature of the problem (if exists) can be scaled down to the Mappers the problem will be solved properly by MapReduce method. Baran is evaluated in many fields like data warehouse, graph and data mining problems. The results show that using the proposed method decreases algorithm execution time.

For future work, answering the following questions is important: Which types of problems can observe Baran conditions? Is it possible to use this method for other types of problems like online data mining, stream processing, etc.?

REFERENCES

Dean, J., & Ghemawat, S. (2008). MapReduce: Simplified data processing on large clusters. *Communications of the ACM, 51*(1), 107–113. doi:10.1145/1327452.1327492

Harbi, R., Abdelaziz, I., Kalnis, P., Mamoulis, N., Ebrahim, Y., & Sahli, M. (2016). Accelerating SPARQL queries by exploiting hash-based locality and adaptive partitioning. *The VLDB Journal, 25*(3), 355–380. doi:10.100700778-016-0420-y

Herodotou, H., Dong, F., & Babu, S. (2011). Mapreduce programming and cost-based optimization? crossing this chasm with starfish. *Proceedings of the VLDB Endowment International Conference on Very Large Data Bases, 4*(12), 1446–1449.

Herodotou, H., Lim, H., Luo, G., Borisov, N., Dong, L., Cetin, F. B., & Babu, S. (2011, January). Starfish: A Self-tuning System for Big Data Analytics. CIDR, 11, 261-272.

Osman, A., El-Refaey, M., & Elnaggar, A. (2013, June). Towards real-time analytics in the cloud. In *Services (SERVICES), 203 IEEE Ninth World Congress on* (pp. 428-435). IEEE. 10.1109/SERVICES.2013.36

Polo, J., Carrera, D., Becerra, Y., Torres, J., Ayguadé, E., Steinder, M., & Whalley, I. (2009). *Performance management of mapreduce applications*. Academic Press.

Rupprecht, L., Zhang, R., Owen, B., Pietzuch, P., & Hildebrand, D. (2017, April). SwiftAnalytics: Optimizing Object Storage for Big Data Analytics. In *Cloud Engineering (IC2E), 2017 IEEE International Conference on* (pp. 245-251). IEEE.

Tang, Z., Liu, M., Ammar, A., Li, K., & Li, K. (2016). An optimized MapReduce workflow scheduling algorithm for heterogeneous computing. *The Journal of Supercomputing, 72*(6), 2059–2079. doi:10.100711227-014-1335-2

Thusoo, A., Sarma, J. S., Jain, N., Shao, Z., Chakka, P., Zhang, N., . . . Murthy, R. (2010, March). Hive-a petabyte scale data warehouse using hadoop. In *Data Engineering (ICDE), 2010 IEEE 26th International Conference on* (pp. 996-1005). IEEE. 10.1109/ICDE.2010.5447738

Wang, S., Zhou, X., Zhang, L., & Jiang, C. (2017, July). Network-Adaptive Scheduling of Data-Intensive Parallel Jobs with Dependencies in Clusters. In *Autonomic Computing (ICAC), 2017 IEEE International Conference on* (pp. 155-160). IEEE. 10.1109/ICAC.2017.13

Wang, T., Wang, J., Nguyen, S. N., Yang, Z., Mi, N., & Sheng, B. (2017, July). EA2S2: An Efficient Application-Aware Storage System for Big Data Processing in Heterogeneous Clusters. In *Computer Communication and Networks (ICCCN), 2017 26th International Conference on* (pp. 1-9). IEEE.

Wang, W., Zhu, K., Ying, L., Tan, J., & Zhang, L. (2016). Maptask scheduling in mapreduce with data locality: Throughput and heavy-traffic optimality. *IEEE/ACM Transactions on Networking, 24*(1), 190–203. doi:10.1109/TNET.2014.2362745

Yao, Y., Wang, J., Sheng, B., Tan, C. C., & Mi, N. (2017). Self-adjusting slot configurations for homogeneous and heterogeneous hadoop clusters. *IEEE Transactions on Cloud Computing, 5*(2), 344–357. doi:10.1109/TCC.2015.2415802

Zhang, G., Li, C., Zhang, Y., Xing, C., & Yang, J. (2012). Mapreduce++: Efficient processing of mapreduce jobs in the cloud. *Journal of Computer Information Systems*, 8(14), 5757–5764.

Olston, C., Reed, B., Srivastava, U., Kumar, R., & Tomkins, A. (2008, June). Pig latin: a not-so-foreign language for data processing. In *Proceedings of the 2008 ACM SIGMOD international conference on Management of data* (pp. 1099-1110). ACM.

Khetrapal, A., & Ganesh, V. (2006). *HBase and Hypertable for large scale distributed storage systems.* Dept. of Computer Science, Purdue University; doi:10.1145/1376616.1376726

Barkhordari, M., & Niamanesh, M. (2014, August). ScadiBino: An effective MapReduce-based association rule mining method. In *Proceedings of the Sixteenth International Conference on Electronic Commerce* (p. 1). ACM. 10.1145/2617848.2617853

Barkhordari, M., & Niamanesh, M. (2015). ScaDiPaSi: An effective scalable and distributable MapReduce-based method to find patient similarity on huge healthcare networks. *Big Data Research*, 2(1), 19–27. doi:10.1016/j.bdr.2015.02.004

Barkhordari, M., & Niamanesh, M. (2017). ScaDiGraph: A MapReduce-based Method for Solving Graph Problems. *Journal of Information Science and Engineering*, 33(1).

Barkhordari, M., & Niamanesh, M. (2017). Aras: A Method with Uniform Distributed Dataset to Solve Data Warehouse Problems for Big Data. *International Journal of Distributed Systems and Technologies*, 8(2), 47–60. doi:10.4018/IJDST.2017040104

Barkhordari, M., & Niamanesh, M. (2017). Atrak: A MapReduce based warehouse for big data. *The Journal of Supercomputing*, 73(10), 4596–4610. doi:10.100711227-017-2037-3

Barkhordari, M., & Niamanesh, M. (2018). Arvand: A Method to Integrate Multidimensional Data Sources Into Big Data Analytic Structures. *Journal of Information Science and Engineering*, 34(2), 505–518.

Boulon, J., Konwinski, A., Qi, R., Rabkin, A., Yang, E., & Yang, M. (2008, October). Chukwa, a large-scale monitoring system. *Proceedings of CCA*, 8, 1-5.

Bu, Y., Howe, B., Balazinska, M., & Ernst, M. D. (2010). HaLoop: Efficient iterative data processing on large clusters. *Proceedings of the VLDB Endowment International Conference on Very Large Data Bases*, 3(1-2), 285–296. doi:10.14778/1920841.1920881

Chang, F., Dean, J., Ghemawat, S., Hsieh, W. C., Wallach, D. A., Burrows, M., ... Gruber, R. E. (2008). Bigtable: A distributed storage system for structured data. *ACM Transactions on Computer Systems*, 26(2), 4. doi:10.1145/1365815.1365816

Chu, C. T., Kim, S. K., Lin, Y. A., Yu, Y., Bradski, G., Olukotun, K., & Ng, A. Y. (2007). Map-reduce for machine learning on multicore. In Advances in neural information processing systems (pp. 281-288). Academic Press.

Ekanayake, J., Li, H., Zhang, B., Gunarathne, T., Bae, S. H., Qiu, J., & Fox, G. (2010, June). Twister: a runtime for iterative mapreduce. In *Proceedings of the 19th ACM international symposium on high performance distributed computing* (pp. 810-818). ACM.

Lakshman, A., & Malik, P. (2009). Cassandra: A structured storage system ona p2p network. In *Proceedings of the twenty-first annual symposium onParallelism in algorithms and architectures* (pp. 47–47). ACM. 10.1145/1583991.1584009

Nathan, M., James, X., & Jason, J. (2012). *Storm: Distributed real-time computation system*. Academic Press.

Neumeyer, L., Robbins, B., Nair, A., & Kesari, A. (2010, December). S4: Distributed stream computing platform. In *Data Mining Workshops (ICDMW), 2010 IEEE International Conference on* (pp. 170-177). IEEE.

Olston, C., Chiou, G., Chitnis, L., Liu, F., Han, Y., Larsson, M., ... Tian, C. (2011, June). Nova: continuous pig/hadoop workflows. In *Proceedings of the 2011 ACM SIGMOD International Conference on Management of data* (pp. 1081-1090). ACM. 10.1145/1989323.1989439

Venkataraman, S., Roy, I., Schreiber, R. S., & AuYoung, A. (2011). *Presto: Complex and continuous analytics with distributed arrays*. Academic Press.

Zaharia, M., Chowdhury, M., Das, T., Dave, A., Ma, J., McCauley, M., ... Stoica, I. (2012, April). Resilient distributed datasets: A fault-tolerant abstraction for in-memory cluster computing. In *Proceedings of the 9th USENIX conference on Networked Systems Design and Implementation* (pp. 2-2). USENIX Association

Zhang, B. (2015). *A Brief Introduction of Existing Big Data Tools*. Retrieved from scholarwiki.indiana. edu/Z604/slides/big%20data%20tools%20v2.pdf

Chapter 8
A Tale of Two Systems:
ERP in China – Failure and Success

Wendy Wang
Trident University International, USA

Yun Wu
Salisbury University, USA

ABSTRACT

With China becoming an economic powerhouse, there has been increasing need for more studies on issues related to information systems localization in China and ways to solve them. Most information systems adoption literatures have been conducted in the context of Western society, especially in America, and due to differences in the cultural, social, and legal environment, these theories and findings out of these studies need to be tested in the context of Chinese culture. This chapter adopts the technology, organization, and environment framework to explain why a Chinese apparel manufacturing company failed in its first enterprise resource planning (ERP) project, and how it achieved success in the second project with government's assistance and what they have learned from their first experience with ERP. This study provides insight on the characteristics of Chinese companies and the unique challenges they have encountered in the informatization process.

INTRODUCTION

An enterprise resource planning system (ERP) is an information system that integrates business processes, its purpose is to make the right information available to the right people at the right time to make the right decision. A successful ERP system benefits organization by managing resources productively and proactively; it can help to improve business performance, support information sharing, ensure compliance, cut cost, and increase customer satisfaction (McGaughey & Gunasekaran, 2007; Ravasan & Rouhani, 2014). Organizations adopt ERP since it is considered a strategic tool to gain competitive advantages, and/or the competitors are doing it (Johansson & Newman, 2010; McGaughey & Gunasekaran, 2007; Ravasan & Rouhani, 2014). Millions of dollars are invested in acquiring and implementing ERP. According to paramount consulting, there has been an increase in ERP implementation costs. The average total

DOI: 10.4018/978-1-5225-7214-5.ch008

cost of ownership increased from $2.8M in 2014 year to $4.5M in 2015. Disney Corporation spent $400 million for a two-year project (Seddon, Calvert, & Yang, 2010). The Allied Market Research anticipated that by the year of 2020, the ERP market could reach $41.69 billion worldwide with a growth of 7.2 percent per year. Cloud-based ERP shows an even higher growth rate as a result of a steady increase of mobile devices and social media utilization in organizations. Such cloud-based ERP solution offers extra benefits such as low investment cost and flexible real-time data storage and access, it enables small and medium companies take the advantages of ERP systems. With the concerns over data loss and risk of security beach, such growth slows down somewhat in 2017.

Like most large IT projects, ERP systems are sophisticated software packages that require an alignment of organizational processes with the ERP processes. This causes considerable difficulties for firms to adopt and implement. According to Paramount consulting, over 75% of the ERP projects in 2017 went through moderate to major customization, very few organizations did not do any customization. Many ERP projects failed to realize the intended benefits. According to analyst firm Gartner, despite the industry's efforts on providing better customer service and advanced IT systems, approximately 75 percent of all ERP projects fail. Even large firms such as Hershey lost $150 million in revenue after spending $112 million for a system which caused logistics problems in the first year (Seddon et al., 2010). There are 30%-50% of the organizations that claimed project success, since there are different ways to define ERP success, when we add international dimension, the definition and measurement becomes more difficult and complicated (Agourram, Robson, & Amine, 2007), the actual success rate can be lower. Closer examination suggested that projects that claimed to be successful might not mean they had been on time or within the budget (Brown & He, 2007; Markus & Tanis, 2000). Paramount consulting reported 74% of respondents exceeded their original budget in 2017.

China is an emerging market for ERP. In 1980s, the investment in ERP is negligible, and during 1990s, it was less than 50 million per year. During 2000-2005, annual spending increases from $71 million to $380 million (Brown & He, 2007). According to PR newswire, ERP market is expected to grow 14.25% each year during the period of 2014-2019. All these investments make Chinese market a priority of international and domestic vendors. However, these expenses are not very effective, with low success rate and problems such as shortage of talents with ERP implementation experience, incompatibility of ERP logic with local culture, difference of tax structure and management style etc. (Malaurent & Avison, 2015).

Given the importance of ERP, the scale of investment, and the high failure rate, the quest to answer the question of why some projects are successful whereas most fail has generated a lot of research interests. Researchers and practitioners have identified many factors that can lead to the ERP failure in the context of the western world, e.g., system quality, information quality, service quality, user satisfaction, individual benefits, management support, strategic alignment, project management, and commitment to change etc. (Hsu, Yen, & Chung, 2015; Ravasan & Mansouri, 2014; Velcu, 2010; Lai, I. K.W., 2006). A few studies documented what companies have learned and their subsequent efforts. Malaurent and Avison (2015) reported a case that described a mostly unsuccessful implementation of a French multinational corporation's ERP project in its Chinese subsidiaries. The project failed since many ERP imposed features did not fit in the Chinese context. For example, the ERP system enforced less than 90 days payments once the products were delivered, however, the standard cycle in China was usually half a year; how the tax is calculated in China is different from the one prescribed in the ERP system. All these made the system impractical to use. To avoid the project being totally abandoned, the Chinese users got around these mismatches by coming up with unique solutions. These solutions made the system workable in China, yet also created data inconsistency and lack of data transparency issue for company headquarter. Finally, the French headquarter set up a project team to evaluate whether each workaround can be either formalized or corrected. The result proved to be a system acceptable to local Chinese users and management. The success of this project is attributed to the management attitude change, the practical approach taken to the workarounds, and the improved understanding between headquarter and Chinese local branches, users, and the management via good communication.

BACKGROUND

Information technology such as ERP systems has been considered as strategic tool to improve performance, manage firm risk and performance volatility. The emergence of cloud computing, social media, mobile devices, and enterprise systems has changed the way business operates while bringing advantages. Organizations must carefully select and adequately implement an IT solution to realize the intended benefits (Tian & Xu, 2015). Various theories have been applied to understand the IT adoption, e.g., technology acceptance model (Venkatesh, Morris, Davis, & Davis, 2003), diffusion of innovation (Wu, Cegielski, Hazen, & Hall, 2013), and information processing view (Cegielski, Allison Jones-Farmer, Wu, & Hazen, 2012). Researchers also investigate the IT implementation extensively to identify the best practices (Argyropoulou, Ioannou, Koufopoulos, & Motwani, 2009; Maldonado & Sierra, 2013).

Technology, Organization, and Environment Framework (TOE) and ERP

Most ERP literature focus on one or a few ERP success factors: the fit between business processes and the ERP system, software selection and support, executive commitment, training, user satisfaction, clear goals and objectives, support within the company, vendor knowledge, suitability of hardware/software, and data accuracy/integrity (Ebru, Duygu, & Ceren. 2015; Saade & Nijher, 2016; Maldonado & Sierra, 2013; Van Velsen., Huijs., & Van der Geest, 2008; Zhang, Lee, Huang, Zhang, & Huang, 2005; Muscatello & Chen, 2008). Because the impact of ERP is organization-wide, across different functional areas, it would be helpful to examine the whole process of system adoption from various perspectives with all stakeholders. Tornatzky and Fleischer (1990) proposed the technology, organization, and environment (TOE) framework to explain the process of innovation in the context of an enterprise. This framework covers a wide range of factors related to innovative technology adoptions of organizations, hence it is chosen as the research framework in this study.

According to the TOE framework, the technology context mainly refers to relevant technology available to the organization for possible adoption. Because IT department's understanding of various IT solutions is critical in selecting the proper one, in this research, we also include it as one of the technology factors. The organization context refers to the internal condition of the firm such as organizational structure, firm size, managerial structure, human resources, and the communication style. In this study, we choose financial resources, perceived direct and indirect ERP benefit as organization context indicators. The environment context comprises market competitiveness, competitors, the legal and regulatory environment (Oliveira, Thomas, & Espadanal, 2014). Government policy and regulations have been playing an essential role in innovation diffusion (Krishnan, Teo, & Lymm, 2017), to encourage and promote usage of information technology, many countries have initiated governmental interventions (Krishnan et. al., 2017). Chinese companies are even more heavily influenced by governmental policies and regulations.

Few studies have examined Chinese government's role in IT innovation adoption, we would like to include it with competitive pressure-both domestic and overseas to describe the environmental context.

In addtion to ERP, TOE has been widely used in other technology adoption research, e.g., open sources, EDI, and general information systems (Krishnan et. al., 2017; Jia, Guo, & Barnes, 2017; Oliveira et al., 2014; Zhu, Li, Wang, & Chen, 2010). Zhou et al. (2010) used TOE theory to systematically and quantitatively investigate the post-implementation success of ERP in Chinese retail industry. They use the ERP implementation quality (project management and system configuration) as the technological context, leadership involvement and organizational fit to represent the organizational context, and external organizations that have in-depth technology knowledge and know how that can help the assimilation of the system within the focal organization as the environmental aspect. After studying about 100 Chinese companies in retails that have had the ERP project for at least two years, the results show that ERP implementation quality and organizational readiness significantly affect *post*-implementation success, whereas external support does not.

System Success

As mentioned earlier, there have been various opinions and definitions for system success, among which system usage is an important one (Maldonado & Sierra, 2013). Since ERP system usage is usually mandatory in China, it would not be a suitable indicator for system success. In this study we use user satisfaction instead. In addition to user satisfaction, three more factors are selected to measure system success from previous literature (Delone & McLean, 1992; Zhang et al., 2005): individual impact, organizational impact, and business performance improvement. The individual impact refers to the impact of implementation and usage of ERP system on users; the organizational and business performance improvement is defined as the ERP project's impact on cutting costs, providing better information, and realizing ERP implementation goals.

In this study, we apply TOE framework to examine why a Chinese apparel company failed in its first ERP system and how it succeeded in its second project using knowledge gained from their failure. Factors discussed earlier are presented in Figure 1. Since we have no control over the ERP implementation project, a case study is a suitable method to examine the project in the natural setting (Yin, 1994). Using the proposed TOE framework, we can get a comprehensive view of factors that lead to the failure and success of ERP project.

A TALE OF TWO SYSTEMS

In this paper, we will discuss the ERP project in an apparel manufacturing and sales company, henceforth, PB. PB is located at Ningbo, a beautiful sub-provincial port city in the northeast Zhejiang province in China. According to the latest census data, the city has a population of 7.6 million in 2010. Ningbo has several clothing brands famous throughout the country, among which PB is one of them. With its more than 3,000 apparel manufacturers and over 12% of China's overall apparel production, Ningbo is certainly one of centers for fashion industry in China.

Figure 1. Technology, organization, and environment framework

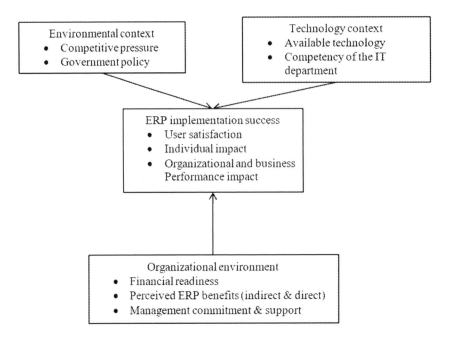

Thanks to Deng Xiaoping's "open door" policies announced in 1978, China opens itself up to the world, its economy started to flourish and grow. These policies encouraged the pioneering generation of entrepreneurs in 1980s. Undaunted by lack of resources and knowledge of modern management, these entrepreneurs were remarkably bold to start their own company, many were very successful, and some eventually became industry leaders (Tse, 2016). PB's two founders were among these pioneers. In 1990s, two brothers started PB with 7 sewing machines and $2,500. After nearly 30 years, PB established 4000 stores in 31 provinces in China, and accumulated over $1.2 billion sales in 2016. In addition to brick-and-mortar stores, the company also owns a mature online business and logistics network, which set a record of fulfilling $1 million sales in a single day in 2016. PB submitted the IPO application in 2014 and became the first domestic fashion brand listed on the A-share market in China in early 2017. In 2018, PB made its debut at New York Fashion Week as a model Chinese fashion brand. PB's commitment to adopt information systems contributes to its astonishing transformation from a mom and pop style business to a mature online business with global reach within a short period. The informationzation process of PB has not always been a smooth ride, there have been trials and failures, highs and lows. This paper examines why it failed in its first system and what PB had improved to achieve success in the second project. Insights gained from PB's ERP effort help understand the IT adoption in Chinese companies.

To establish the construct validity and reliability, this paper collects evidence from multiple sources: face-to-face interviews, direct observations, archival records and documents, and hands-on interaction with the system (Yin, 1994). When we first contacted PB's IT director for interview request in 2009, the company has successfully finished an ERP project implementation after a series of fiascos in 2002. Along with the request for an interview, we faxed the questions using TOE framework, and asked PB management to reflect on each of the following questions for their first and second ERP projects.

Technology Context

- What kind of ERP system has been considered? Please provide information on software, hardware, network, and system architect.
- Employees' experience with information system when the ERP was implemented.
- The number of IT personnel and their technical backgrounds, IT department's experience with complicated systems like ERP, and the role of IT personnel in the project.
- Vendor(s) selection process, and how vendor(s) coordinated with PB's IT department and other stake holders.
- The strength and challenges that PB has regarding informatization of the company.
- The vision of PB's informatization effort.

Organizational Context

- The percentage of PB's annual budget to information technology, and the determinant of budget allocation.
- The organizational strategies regarding manufacturing, customer service, and product developments. For manufacturing, the focus is on efficiency, reliable production, or supply chain; for customer service, the emphasis is on after sales service, or identifying the current trend; for product development, the focus is on unique product design, new product, or responsiveness to the latest trend etc.
- The perceived direct and indirect ERP benefits.
- The management style of the organization and the decision-making process: highly centralized or decentralized, rule-based or relationship based.
- The role of IT department in the organizational hierarchy.
- Management's involvement in the project.

Environmental Aspect

- The competitive environment for the apparel manufacturing and sales when the ERP project was considered.
- Government's role to the informatization of the organizations.
- Discuss government policies and regulations on information technologies adoption, specific actions the government has taken.

ERP Implementation Success

- Users' feedback on the ERP system regarding response time, data quality, user-friendliness, and impact on their productivity, etc.
- The impact of the ERP system on organizational and business performance improvement.

The IT director responded to our request and connected us with the top management team. Our request for an onsite visit was approved a few months later. The onsite visit lasted two days, including a three-hour interview with the vice general manager, a one-and-a-half hour with the IT director, meetings with five IT staffs who were involved in the project, and interactions with some of the end users. We were also granted access to PB's application document for Ningbo government ERP project fund. During the interviews, we carefully documented the whole visit. To get firsthand experience, we also asked IT director to log in to the system and show us how the system operated. Next, we will discuss our findings on factors that contributed to the failure of the first ERP project in 2002 and the success of the second project 7 years later. These factors are arranged using the TOE framework.

The Old ERP System

Environmental Context-Competitive Pressure

PB's earliest ERP effort was in 2002, it started with high hope, and ended in a fiasco. The city's apparel market was saturated with thousands of domestic apparel manufacturers, most had annual sales of over $1.5 million among which some targeted the domestic market, and others mainly catered to overseas demands. The global economic downturn weakened demand from the international markets and forced the export-oriented companies turn to domestic markets. The competition was further intensified by international clothing brands racing to the Chinese market.

Environmental Context-Government Policies

Chinese government has adopted a national strategy of applying science and technology to ensure modernization and sustainable economy. In 1980s, the government issued a series of policies and regulations to encourage software development. Starting from 2000, the central government has increasingly backed high technology industrialization, and demanded local officials to formulate policies and provide funding to support the innovative technology adoption. Since it took time for local government to respond, when PB implemented their first ERP project in 2002, no resources from Ningbo government were available yet.

Organizational Environment

The possibility of reaping great rewards motivated PB to pursue ERP. Confronted by the increasingly competitive apparel manufacturing market, PB perceived ERP system a strategic tool to help company stay competitive. The management believed that the system would bring many direct and indirect benefits, e.g., streamline the flow of information and data across business functions, and improving product quality and customer service etc. The high risk and low success rate of ERP projects made PB reluctant to invest more than necessary for fearing of loss. Only less than 1% of the company's budget was allocated to the first ERP project, and even smaller budget for user training.

Technology Context

The IT department in PB did not have much ERP experience in 2002, although the management considered the system strategic to the survival of the organization, they were not sure how to approach it, and eventually the vendor made all the major decisions related to the project. Since PB did not know the technology, and the vendor did not understand the business aspect of the project well, once the system was finished, it was found to have many issues, which will be discussed next.

Project Failure

ERP is not merely a system, it embodies the western philosophy and economic organization, it is built on the assumption that there is a set of rational and impersonal rules, and the company structure is relatively stable. However, both conditions did not exist. PB started as a family business, which personal connections often outweighed company rules and guidelines; the company has been in fast expansion mode, its structure changes frequently to accommodate such growth. Not meeting these two conditions brought a lot of problems, as soon as the ERP system was finished, it quickly deteriorated because of three major issues: lack of scalability, flexibility, and low information quality.

Project Failure: Scalability Issue

Like most Chinese companies, the rapid growth has put the company in the state of constant change. Shortly after the project was finished, PB opened 3,000 more retail stores, manufactured over 20,000 models of clothing in its five factories, and established close ties with over 200 companies in Southeast Asia. Because the project was controlled by vendors who did not understand the apparel business, upon completion, PB has already grown out of the capacity that the system was initially designed for. The system could not handle all the traffic, the response time became extremely slow.

Project Failure: Flexibility Issue

Fashion is a highly seasonal and fickle industry. As Chinese consumers' taste for fashion grow more sophisticated, apparel manufacturers need to adapt fast in meeting the changing trend. Frequent structural reorganization to cater to such change is common: several units could be merged into one, only to be split in six months or sooner. The newly finished system was not scalable enough to handle all the traffic, and not flexible enough to accommodate such constant changes, limited company's further growth.

Project Failure: User Experience

Using the newly developed ERP system was not a pleasant experience, it could take 3 to 5 minutes on average to load a simple report. Since the usage was mandatory, employees became increasingly frustrated. Furthermore, information quality was poor. Because the vendor was not familiar with the business process, the system was inflicted with glitches. For example, there were cases that the headquarters sent out 100 pieces of apparel, yet the retail store reported receiving only 90 pieces. Data inconsistancy was common, e.g., the initial inventory data showed 90 pieces in stock, after the sales reported 80 apparels sold by the retail stores, instead of having10 pieces left in inventory, the data indicated only 5. The corporate office did not have timely information, such discrepancy would be found out at either the end of the month or until the end of the accounting cycle, by that time, it was hard to accurately identify the responsible party and find out what had happened. The problem was worsened by the lack of proper procedure in terms of data access, all retail stores could modify their inventory in the system, there were no easy ways to verify whether these numbers were accurate, harder to trace the flow of information, hence thousands of products could be lost at one time and had to be written off.

The New ERP System

Environmental Context: Competitive Pressure

PB limped through the challenges of a highly competitive market with a flawed ERP system for the next few years and found itself in the survival of the fittest mode along with other competitors because of the financial tsunami around 2008. Technology innovation adoption literature have demonstrated that, in a highly competitive environment, companies have more incentives to adopt new technologies such as ERP to gain competitive advantages (Cartman & Salazar, 2011; Huang & Cai, 2005). Even though the first failed ERP project brought a lot of issues, PB decided to try again considering the potential competitive advantage a successful ERP system could bring.

Environmental Context: Government Policies

Responding to the central government's call for developing information technology driven economy, Ningbo government started to routinely invite experts to train reprsentatives from local companies, it also promised to provide 8%-30% subsidies to match companies' IT investment. Starting from 2007, Ningbo government set up funds designed to support information system initiatives in local corporations. The funding information was released on government web sites, which were open and available to the public, any companies or organizations can apply regardless of their industries. Applicants were required to have full disclosure of the company information, e.g., company history, the number of employees, annual financial and accounting reports, purposes of the project, project scope and budget, and background information on the project team members etc. Projects that would have significant impacts on the company and could potentially serve as best practices for other companies were most likely to be awarded with government funds.

Organizational Environment: Financial Readiness

PB applied for the Ningbo city government fund in 2007. In the application package, PB described its 5-year plan and the vision of using the system to total transform the organization, e.g., developing e-commerce, improvement of supply chain, and using business intelligence to penetrate and create new markets etc. PB finally won the $225,000 government fund. This award was based on three grounds: 1) apparel was one of Ningbo's primary industries, 2) PB was one of well known apparel companies, 3) the ERP system that PB proposed was very unique, in addition to traditional functionalities, it also had the surveillance component to monitor system performance and ensure data quality. Once the project was successful, it can serve as a model project to be promoted and be replicated in other organizations. After years of struggling with the failed ERP system, PB was finally ready to develop another one with the blessing from the government.

Organizational Environment: Management Commitment and Support

When PB being the sole sponsor of the first ERP project, management was reluctant to invest more than what was necessary because of the high project failure rate. Since the new project had got blessings from the government, the PB management renewed their optimism. Receiving government support increased the stake of the project, on the one hand, it increased visibility of the company and improved company image; on the other hand, if the project failed, it wold be a high-profile failure. The project result would also impact Ningbo city government. Since the city officials were evaluated based on how they had supported the central government's policy, project success would mean promotion and acknowledgement, whereas failure could bring reprimand and embarrassment to the local officials. This project broght the Ningbo city government and PB together, the project success would be a win-win and failure would be a loss-loss for both. With so much at stake, PB's senior management gave the project the highest priority, the general manager was actively involved in every decision making, which was vastly different from management's hands-off attitude in the previous project.

Technology Context

PB learned from their mistakes and grew more technically savvy. It hired an IT director that has solid technical background and years of manufacturing experience to lead the project. The IT staff have also gained experience from the first ERP project. PB contracted the new project to three companies, based on their technical expertise and experience, each company was to develop one of the three components: ERP, office automation, and ERP control and surveillance system. Once the three components were successfully implemented, PB's IT department did the final system integration. Having multiple vendors working simultaneously can be risky, miscommunications and integration difficulties could jeopardize the system. Nonetheless, PB chose this approach to avoid having one overpowering vendor influencing the project.

Project Success: System Architecture

The new project took over 14 months to finish, it consists of three modules: data acquisition, data storage, and data analysis and business intelligence. The data acquisition module collects daily operational data extracted from disparate systems. These data tend to have a lot of "noises", they come with various formats and errors. This module would first convert these data into proper format, verify and clean them to ensure data consistency and integrity. Once this process is done, it activates the data loader and saves the data onto the data storage module. The data storage module centralizes storage of enterprise data and metadata, from which data warehouses and data marts are built. The data analysis and business intelligence module provides tools to generate reports and conduct OLAP analysis.

Project Success: User Experience

The new system was met with enthusiasm from users upon completion, one of the main reasons was that all users have been through proper training. The training took a top-down approach by having IT department train senior managers first, then having the managers teach their subordinates. Since data entry employees have the highest turnover rate, PB needs to constantly hire and train new employees. With the new system, these employees have fewer tasks and system access privilege, hence their training got much simplified, and they can become proficient with their work quickly.

The new system has proved to be very reliable and robust, it can accommodate thousands of users simultaneously without any delay of service. Employees can access data in real time or in batch daily, they have been thrilled with fast system response and reliable information provided. According to PB's estimation, the return on investment is 20.6%, the new ERP system contributes to over 16% decrease in inventory and 10% increase in annual sales. The management is very pleased with the result.

Project Success: Information Quality

The new system has fixed the glitches in the previous system that caused the data inconsistency problem; users get timely and accurate information. For example, when the inventory in a retail store for certain apparel is supposed to be ten instead of five, the data surveillance and monitoring component would immediately alarm the manager. This helps managers identify problems as they occur. Also, to ensure data integrity, users are classified into three levels with different data access privileges: senior managers and analysts, middle management users, and data entry users. The first group have full access to the system, and data entry users have limited access. Retail stores cannot modify the value of their inventory without corporate approval. Thus, management now has better control of the operational activities, more accurate sales data, and customer information, and can track market trends more accurately. This arrangement not only improves data security and integrity but also makes training easier.

Project Success: Scalability and Flexibility

The new system is also more flexible and scalable to accommodate change. Whenever there are organizational restructuring, the IT department can add a functional module in the system without disrupting the normal operation of the system. This new ERP system has increased PB competitiveness and transformed it into a high fashion corporation that is highly focusing on product R&D with a global reach. Soon after the project is finished, PB launched its e-commerce business, in 2013, it was awarded as the model e-commerce company by the Ministry of Commerce. Now PB launches more than 7,000 models/colors on the market each year at a high frequency. Without the support of its ERP system, such growth is unthinkable.

DISCUSSION

This paper applied the TOE framework to document the journey of a Chinese apparel company's ERP endeavors over the years. From the trials and errors from its first ERP project, PB acquired important managerial and technical skills that eventually contributed to the success of its second project.

Organizational Environment

A successful ERP implementation requires the cooperation and coordination from all stakeholders: management, development team, vendors, and users, and in this case, government support. Resources such as funding, development time, and technical skills need to be available (Cartman & Salazar, 2011; Jia et.al., 2017), and the organizations need to ready for ERP implementation. ERP project is a high reward and high-risk endeavor, having enough financial resources is crucial. Although the amount of financial resource is objective, the perception of financial readiness is subjective. For two companies in a similar financial condition, one may perceive itself financially ready for ERP, whereas the other might consider insufficient and unprepared. Perceived financial readiness weighs more in the decision to adopt

ERP system. In the first ERP project, management did not allocate enough budget to ERP project still considered it financially ready.

Top management commitment has been identified as very important factor for the success of ERP projects (Aloini, Dulmin, & Mininno, 2007; Seyal & Rahman, 2014; Zhang et al., 2005). Because the impact of ERP system is felt across the organization, having blessings from top management to set up proper procedures and resolve issues is crucial for success. Government involvement increased the stake of the second project, it not only secured the much-needed capital and provided PB fringe benefits such as increased visibility of the project and company, but also motivate full support of the senior management.

Technology Readiness

In the first project, PB was not ready technology wise: management did not have good understanding of ERP solutions, had no inhouse talents who knew the technology, yet did not see it a problem. The management team trusted the vendor to make all the project related decisions. Since the vendor was not familiar with the operation of the apparel industry, the completed system got inherent problems.

From this experience, PB has learned the importance of having the "right people" within the company to lead the project. The "right people" are those who have both the technical background, are familiar with the industry that the company is in, and also have managerial experience. Under this guideline, PB hired a new IT director who fits in this profile. It proved to be one of the best decisions that the management team can make. The new IT director played a pivotal role in the project: he represented PB to negotiate successfully with three IT vendors, tracked the project progress, guided the in-house development team to integrate the three separately implemented modules into a seamless system, and headed the training to make sure the users would be properly trained.

PB's second ERP project was an intricate dance among the company, the three vendors, and the government, any missteps would create repercussions that might jeopardize the project. The relationship between vendors and customers in China is fragile and complicated, both sides are cautious about dealing with each other. Companies have a shortage of qualified IT professionals, they are anxious about their projects being hijacked by the vendors, and decisions are made not in their best interests. Also because of fast growth, companies often experience constant structural changes, they prefer to wait to see if the system works before the payment is made. Whereas vendors are pressured to build more flexible and highly scalable systems for their increasingly demanding customers, and it is common for them to complain about customers' procrastination in payment; whereas customers, because of the high risk of system failures and unmet expectations, feel justified in waiting instead of making an on-time payment. According to Park, Im, and Kim (2011), whether the client's IT staffs are competent determines vendor's ability in cooperative learning and knowledge transfer. In the context of Chinese companies, it is even more so. Fortunately, PB has a competent in-house IT team that facilitated the communication between PB and its vendors, it helped to build more flexible and robust system, promote mutual understanding, and manage expectation of both parties.

Environmental Context

Chinese companies have a close relationship with the government, it is hard to discuss the company without mentioning the government policies at the time. China's science and technology policy has been through four phases since the founding of the People's Republic in 1949. During the first phase

(1949 to 1959), the focus was on supporting the creation of heavy industry along Soviet lines; during the second phase up through the end of the Cultural Revolution (1959-1976), the technology policies were mostly ideology drive; the third phase launched "open door" policy reform by Deng Xiaoping in 1978, the policy pushed for the gradual shift to market-oriented, product-driven research. Starting from 2002, the government sees technology as a main engine for sustainable development and has released a series of policies to foster an innovation centered economy (Campbell, 2013; Lee, Xiang, & Kim, 2011). PB has benefited in this favorable environment.

The push of the market competition in the apparel industry and the pull of Chinese government's support have motivated PB to adopt ERP to improve its competitive advantage. Its first effort in 2002 failed because of lack of technical skills, financial sources, organizational readiness to handle a complicated ERP system; Once PB learned their lessons, its second project 5 years later was a success.

CONCLUSION AND FUTURE STUDY

China's fast economic growth and huge demand for information technology have made it an attractive market for ERP. Due to its high risk and high reward nature, organizations that are eager to adopt ERP need to proceed with caution, and to take calculated risk. To maximize the possibility for system success, it is important to have realistic assessment on whether the organization is ready to move forward. Regarding project investment, it is better for organizations make a consistent investment every year, even though the investment might not be massive. Steadiness wins the race.

For vendors who want to better serve the Chinese market, Chinese companies tend to take a pragmatic approach to minimize risk and lower cost: some can have SAP to set up their first ERP system at a branch, then develop the systems in their other branches. And sometimes they use SAP for key functional areas and develop their solutions at the non-key areas. For small and medium-sized companies, it is critical to have their business processes fit their ERP system, and the functions and features for essential tasks geared to the requirements and skill levels of the individual users (Van Velsen et. al., 2008). It would mean a lot of customization and communications with the customers. Spending on software accounted for merely 5% of total IT spending in 2015 in China, hardware investments made up 83% and services the rest according to IDC. This is contrast to the more developed US IT market, whereas software, hardware, and services each accounted for roughly 1/3 of the 2015 IT spending. As China's corporates are growing into a more mature stage and cloud becoming the de facto standard for software delivery, there will be further upward trend to ERP and cloud adoption in China (Chan, Huang, Lynch, Pan, & Yu, 2016). Vendors need to prepare for such change.

Researchers who are interested in conducting information system research in the context of China, it is vital to pay attention to China's ever-growing and ever-changing economic development. The high implementation costs and high risk of ERP project have increased demand for cloud-based ERP. Although cloud-based ERP offers benefits such as low cost, low maintenance, and shorter development time, the lack of a healthy business environment in China would slow down its adoption. Concerned with the relevance of research to practitioners, information system researchers have been calling for studies to focus more on current business issues and offer practical research findings (Benbasat & Zmud, 1999). Instead of studying what has happened, it would be interesting for researchers to study how companies can take advantage of government policies to help their growth. Since Chinese companies are under huge influence of the government policies and regulations, it helps to monitor the political environment.

Using the TOE framework to document the journey of a Chinese apparel company's ERP adoption effort, this study contributes to the literature by providing a comprehensive picture on the struggles and triumphs of Chinese companies' informatization effort. There are some limitations to this study: our data collection for the first ERP project is based on the memory of employees, which may not be accurate after more than 5 years; also a follow up study is needed to track the current status of the second system, a lot of questions remain: how it has handled such rapid growth, and whether any new features were added etc. Although there are some limitations in this study, we believe that the study can help many companies improve the probability of their ERP system success. Our research is also one of the few studies that discuss the role of the local government in organization's ERP project. Since Chinese government has a huge impact on Chinese companies, we call for more studies to include the factor of political environment in their research related to China.

REFERENCES

Agourram, H., Robson, B., & Amine, N. T. (2007). Defining Information System Success in France. *International Journal of Enterprise Information Systems*, *3*(3), 66–69, 71–80. doi:10.4018/jeis.2007070105

Aloini, D., Dulmin, R., & Mininno, V. (2007). Risk management in ERP project introduction: Review of the literature. *Information & Management*, *44*(6), 547–567. doi:10.1016/j.im.2007.05.004

Argyropoulou, M., Ioannou, G., Koufopoulos, D. N., & Motwani, J. (2009). Measuring the impact of an ERP project at SMEs: A framework and empirical investigation. *International Journal of Enterprise Information Systems*, *5*(3), 1–13. doi:10.4018/jeis.2009070101

Benbast, I., & Zmud, R. W. (1999, March). Empirical research in information systems: The practice of relevance. *Management Information Systems Quarterly*, *23*(1), 3–16. doi:10.2307/249403

Brown, D. H., & He, S. (2007). Patterns of ERP adoption and implementation in China and some implications. *Electronic Markets*, *17*(2), 132–141. doi:10.1080/10196780701296287

Campbell, R. R. (2013). Becoming a Techno-Industrial Power: Chinese Science and Technology Policy. *Issues in Technology Innovation*, *23*, 1-15. Retrieved from https://www.brookings.edu/wpcontent/uploads/2016/06/29-science-technology-policy-china-campbell.pdf

Cartman, C., & Salazar, A. (2011). The influence of organizational size, internal IT capabilities, and competitive and vendor pressures on ERP adoption in SMEs. *International Journal of Enterprise Information Systems*, *7*(3), 68–92. doi:10.4018/jeis.2011070104

Cegielski, C. G., Allison Jones-Farmer, L., Wu, Y., & Hazen, B. T. (2012). Adoption of cloud computing technologies in supply chains: An organizational information processing theory approach. *International Journal of Logistics Management*, *23*(2), 184–211. doi:10.1108/09574091211265350

Chan, H., Huang, W., Lynch, J., Pan, J., & Yu, J. (2016). *China Internet and Software: All eyes on cloud and internet finance*. Macquarie Capital Limited.

DeLone, W. H., & McLean, E. R. (1992). Information systems success: The quest for the dependent variable. *Information Systems Research*, *3*(1), 60–95. doi:10.1287/isre.3.1.60

Ebru, E., Duyguy, T., & Ceren, A. (2015). An Analysis of Interdepartmental Relations in Enterprise Resource Planning Implementation: A Social Capital Perspective. *International Journal of Enterprise Information Systems, 11*(3), 68–93.

Hsu, P. F., Yen, H. R., & Chung, J. C. (2015). ERP system quality, information quality, and service quality, user satisfaction, users' individual benefits. *Information & Management, 52*(8), 925–942. doi:10.1016/j.im.2015.06.009

Huang, Z. M., & Cai, S. (2005). Developing Medium and Small Technological Enterprises in China: Informatization Issues and Counter-Measures. *International Journal of Enterprise Information Systems, 1*(4), 20–38. doi:10.4018/jeis.2005100102

Jia, Q., Guo, Y., & Barnes, S. (2017). Enterprise 2.0 post-adoption: Extending the information system continuance model based on the technology-Organization-environment framework. *Computers in Human Behavior, 67*, 95–105. doi:10.1016/j.chb.2016.10.022

Johansson, B., & Newman, M. (2010). Competitive advantage in the ERP system's value-chain and its influence on future development. *Enterprise Information Systems, 4*(1), 79–93. doi:10.1080/17517570903040196

Krishnan, S., Teo, T. S. H., & Lymm, J. (2017). Determinants of electronic participation and electronic government maturity: Insights from cross-country data. *International Journal of Information Management, 37*(4), 297–312. doi:10.1016/j.ijinfomgt.2017.03.002

Lai, I. K. W. (2006). The critical success factors across ERP implementation models: An empirical study in China. *International Journal of Enterprise Information Systems, 2*(3), 24–42. doi:10.4018/jeis.2006070103

Lee, S., Xiang, J. Y., & Kim, J. K. (2011). Information technology and productivity: Empirical evidence from the Chinese electronics industry. *Information & Management, 48*(2-3), 79–87. doi:10.1016/j.im.2011.01.003

Malaurent, J., & Avison, D. (2015). From an apparent failure to a success story: ERP in China - Post implementation. *International Journal of Information Management, 35*(5), 643–646. doi:10.1016/j.ijinfomgt.2015.06.004

Maldonado, M., & Sierra, V. (2013). User satisfaction as the foundation of the success following an ERP adoption: An empirical study from Latin America. *International Journal of Enterprise Information Systems, 9*(3), 77–99. doi:10.4018/jeis.2013070104

Markus, M. L., & Tanis, C. (2000). The Enterprise System Experience – From Adoption to Success. In R. W. Zmud (Ed.), *Framing the Domains of IT Research: Glimpsing the Future Through the Past* (pp. 173–207). Cincinnati, OH: Pinnaflex Educational Resources.

McGaughey, R. E., & Gunasekaran, A. (2007). Enterprise Resource Planning (ERP): Past, Present and Future. *International Journal of Enterprise Information Systems, 3*(3), 23–35. doi:10.4018/jeis.2007070102

Muscatello, J. R., & Chen, I. J. (2008). Enterprise Resource Planning (ERP) Implementations: Theory and Practice. *International Journal of Enterprise Information Systems, 4*(1), 63–77. doi:10.4018/jeis.2008010105

Oliveira, T., Thomas, M., & Espadanal, M. (2014). Assessing the determinants of cloud computing adoption: An analysis of the manufacturing and services sectors. *Information & Management, 51*(5), 497–510. doi:10.1016/j.im.2014.03.006

Park, J. Y., Im, K. S., & Kim, J. S. (2011). The role of IT human capability in the knowledge transfer process in IT outsourcing context. *Information & Management, 48*(1), 53–61. doi:10.1016/j.im.2011.01.001

Ravasan, A. Z., & Rouhani, S. (2014). An Expert System for Predicting ERP Post-Implementation Benefits Using Artificial Neural Network. *International Journal of Enterprise Information Systems, 10*(3), 24–45. doi:10.4018/ijeis.2014070103

Saade, R. G., & Nijher, H. (2016). Critical Success Factors in Enterprise Resource Planning Implementation: A Review of Case Studies. *Journal of Enterprise Information Management, 29*(1), 72–96. doi:10.1108/JEIM-03-2014-0028

Seddon, P. B., Calvert, C., & Yang, S. (2010). A multi-project model of key factors affecting Organizational benefits from enterprise systems. *Management Information Systems Quarterly, 34*(2), 305–328. doi:10.2307/20721429

Seyal, A. H., & Rahman, M. N. A. (2014). Evaluating the Internal and External Factors Toward ERP Success: Examples from Bruneian Businesses. *International Journal of Enterprise Information Systems, 10*(4), 73–95. doi:10.4018/ijeis.2014100105

Tian, F., & Xu, S. X. (2015). How Do Enterprise Resource Planning Systems Affect Firm Risk? Post-Implementation Impact. *Management Information Systems Quarterly, 39*(1), 39–60. doi:10.25300/MISQ/2015/39.1.03

Tornatzky, L. G., & Fleischer, M. (1990). *The processes of technological innovation.* Lexington, MA: Lexington Books.

Tse, E. (2016). *The Rise of Entrepreneurship in China.* Retrieved from https://www.forbes.com/sites/tseedward/2016/04/05/the-rise-of-entrepreneurship-in-china/#51f8b4403efc

van Velsen, L., Huijs, C., & van der Geest, T. (2008). Eliciting User Input for Requirements on Personalization: The Case of a Dutch ERP System. *International Journal of Enterprise Information Systems, 4*(4), 34–46. doi:10.4018/jeis.2008100103

Velcu, O. (2010). Strategic alignment of ERP implementation stages: An empirical investigation. *Information & Management, 47*(3), 158–166. doi:10.1016/j.im.2010.01.005

Venkatesh, V., Morris, M., Davis, G., & Davis, F. (2003). User acceptance of information technology: Toward a unified view. *Management Information Systems Quarterly, 27*(3), 425–478. doi:10.2307/30036540

Wu, Y., Cegielski, C. G., Hazen, B. T., & Hall, D. J. (2013). Cloud computing in support of supply chain information system infrastructure: Understanding when to go to the cloud. *The Journal of Supply Chain Management*, *49*(3), 25–41. doi:10.1111/j.1745-493x.2012.03287.x

Yin, R. (1994). *Case study research - design and methods*. Thousand Oaks, CA: Sage publishing.

Zhang, Z., Lee, M. K. O., Huang, P., Zhang, L., & Huang, X. Y. (2005). A framework of ERP systems implementation success in China: An empirical study. *International Journal of Production Economics*, *98*(1), 56–80. doi:10.1016/j.ijpe.2004.09.004

Zhu, Y., Li, Y., Wang, W., & Chen, J. (2010). What leads to post-implementation success of ERP? An empirical study of the Chinese retail industry. *International Journal of Information Management*, *30*(3), 265–276. doi:10.1016/j.ijinfomgt.2009.09.007

Chapter 9
Consumer Value Trumps Perceived Privacy Risk:
Item–Level RFID Implementation in the FMCG Industry

Wesley A. Kukard
University of Otago, New Zealand

Lincoln C. Wood
University of Otago, New Zealand & Curtin University, Australia

ABSTRACT

This chapter reviews past radio frequency identification (RFID) literature within the fast-moving consumer goods (FMCG) industry and the impact of consumer benefits on the perceived risks of item-level RFID. Two new categories are used to measure this impact; the separation of consumers' interactions with the technology to in-store and after-sales allows the consumers expectation of privacy to changes depending on the surrounding environment. A quantitative survey on primary household grocery purchasers within the USA revealed that while consumers are aware of the associated privacy risks after sale, they would be willing to use the technology, given sufficient benefits. This important step in RFID literature changes the conversation from a privacy risk management focus to a balanced integration of the technology, focusing on consumer benefits to manage the roll-out within the FMCG industry.

INTRODUCTION

As technology moves forward, modern society will see a future where all devices are connected to the Internet – a 'connected future' (Burrus, 2014). While the concept of a connected future remains in its infancy, it is built on an expectation of the future and our way of life. In much in the same way social media networks have evolved to become a fundamental part of day-to-day life, the 'Internet of Things' (IoT) paradigm will soon become embedded as a part of life over the globe, as "by 2025 Internet nodes may reside in everyday things – food packages, furniture, paper documents, and more" (National Intelligence Council, 2008, p. v.).

DOI: 10.4018/978-1-5225-7214-5.ch009

The "Internet of Things" term is used to describe an eco-system of Internet-connected devices that can either send or receive information between one another. This information is gathered, stored and processed over time to create a complex information database to allow the device to produce a more accurate outcome for the end user/business (Morgan, 2014).

To understand the implications for global firms shifting their products and services in recognition of the IoT, there is a focus on implementation opportunities within the Fast Moving Consumer Goods (FMCG) industry. Due to a large number of goods and the way that FMCG touches the lives of everyone, this is likely where the IoT will become a part of everyday life (Kukard & Wood, 2017, p. 22). For FMCG companies to gain the most out of IoT integration, they are going to have to incorporate item-level RFID / Near-Field Communication (NFC) into their packaging, each tag with its electronic product code (EPC). The EPC is a string of numbers, similar to a barcode but much longer. It is this unique identifier that gives the IoT ecosystem its power. Item-level passive RFID and NFC has been chosen as the main focus in this chapter, as opposed to active RFID, Wi-Fi or Bluetooth technology as it has a much lower production cost. As we are looking at the FMCG industry, consumer goods usually have a much lower absolute sales price. Therefore, it is likely a low cost and easily mass-produced technology such as RFID / NFC would be used.

This chapter will focus on the history of RFID research, consumers' perceptions of item-level RIFD and the role it will play in the future of the FMCG industry. The focus on consumers' perceptions remains important as,

One of the major continuing conversations with RFID research is the potential for mass data collection on a level that, in theory, could cause major privacy issues for consumers. When RFID tags are introduced at an item-level, the ability to track objects or consumers through their use of the items could become a lot easier. The introduction could lead to consumers becoming responsible for the objects they purchase, information collection while within stores to build a personalized advertising campaign or objects that punish misbehavior and criminals using the system to their advantage. These types of privacy concerns are well documented. (Kukard & Wood, 2017, p. 23)

This chapter first addresses the background use of RFID in the FMCG industry. The focus is on current RFID research trends and related technologies; there is a strong emphasis on understanding how to implement the technology given consumer concerns about their privacy. Next, several hypotheses are generated and the research method is explained. We then present the research results and discuss the implications.

BACKGROUND

The use of RFID, especially on the scale required for integration into the FMCG industry will require the development of global information databases that will support the adoption of RFID and the IoT. While there are recognized cost barriers to firms seeking to adopt these technologies (Owunwanne & Goel, 2016; Lanfranchi, Giannetto, & De Pascale, 2016), a key challenge will continue to be the consumer acceptance of these changes. Such consumer acceptance of the technology has historically proven difficult with a majority of research highlighting privacy and security concerns (Kukard, 2015). Therefore, an overview of past research on RFID use will be reviewed, focusing specifically on privacy and security issues in RFID adoption. These proposed technology approaches to solve these issues are identified and a review of consumer acceptance literature is conducted.

Current Research Trends in RFID

The potential applications for RFID within the grocery store environment are diverse, with the potential to add value for manufacturers, retailers, and consumers (McHugh, 2004; Östman, 2013). This chapter will highlight some of the applications that could benefit the FMCG industry and their consumers. The conventional industry benefits include inventory management, shrinkage reduction, theft reduction, reduction in food waste or deterioration, and faster checkout processing (Angeles, 2005; Duong, Wood, & Wang, 2016; Jones, Clarke-Hill, Hillier, & Comfort, 2005; Li, Visich, Khumawala, & Zhang, 2006; McHugh, 2004; A. D. Smith, 2005; Taghaboni-Dutta & Velthouse, 2006; Wood, Reiners & Srivastava, 2016). Benefits beyond those within the supply chain are associated with building a better understanding of their customer base to personalize advertising, shopping lists and ultimately sell more goods (Albrecht, 2005; Alt et al., 2009). The main obstacles facing widespread adoption are the perceived privacy and security issues surrounding RFID, both in academic literature and mainstream media. The adoption of NFC – a related, wireless technology – has been far more successful than RFID as a whole, although, they are in essence the same technology. However, NFC has been marketed with a focus on consumer benefits, allowing the quick pairing of devices, thus saving time and being relatively easy to use. NFC's success lays the groundwork for large-scale RFID implementation through benefits promotion.

Past research has focused on privacy and security issues. Major RFID-related research between 2002 and 2007 was primarily (68% of publications) focused on security and privacy mechanisms for RFID, with 97 papers listing end-user privacy as the main motivation for their research (Spiekermann & Evdokimov, 2009).

RFID Privacy and Security

A major continuing conversation within RFID research is the potential for mass data collection on a level that, in theory, could cause major privacy issues for consumers. An overview of factors influencing consumer perceptions of such RFID technologies is provided by Margulis, Boeck, Bendavid, and Durif (2016). The challenges around consumers' privacy concerns raise the important issue that when RFID tags are introduced at an item-level and cross-referenced with consumer demographics, it creates the ability to track objects or consumers through their use of the items they purchase. This introduction could lead to consumers becoming responsible for the items they purchase, information collection while within stores to build a personalized advertising campaign or objects that punish misbehavior and the possibility of criminals using the system to their advantage. These types of privacy concerns are well documented (Bélanger & Crossler, 2011; Lockton & Rosenberg, 2005; Spiekermann & Evdokimov, 2009; Frédéric Thiesse, 2007). Various solutions have been proposed to either curb or completely remove the perceived potential privacy risks (Garfinkel, Juels, & Pappu, 2005; Juels, Rivest, & Szydlo, 2003; Ohkubo, Suzuki, & Kinoshita, 2005). There have also been a range of governmental regulations and industry self-regulation in various formats around the world, yet there are indications that "relying on businesses within the RFID industry to police themselves may not be adequate as there is no way to enforce compliance" (Turri, Smith, & Kopp, 2017, p. 346).

Garfinkel, Juels, and Pappu (2005) present some theoretical scenarios stemming from the implementation of RFID. They identified three main contexts for the use of RFID tags. First, "Inside the Supply Chain" from manufacture until delivered to the final retail outlet. Second, the "Transition Zone," which covers the customer-facing portion of the retail outlet in which the RFID enabled the item, is being sold to the consumer (i.e., what we define as in-store risks). Third, "Outside the Supply Chain," this includes all locations beyond the "Transition Zone" including the consumers' home (i.e., what we define as after-sales risks).

Two of these three main zones provide points of direct interaction between consumers and item-level RFID. According to Garfinkel et al. (2005), this could be a personal privacy nightmare for consumers as tags could be associated with a unique identity. As an example, high-value consumer items (e.g., razor blades), once removed from shelves could engage a security photograph of the consumer to later determine whether shoplifting occurred, despite the fact that most consumers would likely not pose a security threat. A location threat may emerge from individuals carrying unique tags that, once scanned, could reveal their location and provide a connection to a personal profile. A preference threat might be that thieves could identify potential targets by scanning their victim from a distance to identify any high-value items and targeting them.

Rotter (2008) proposes a framework for assessing system security and privacy risks for RFID systems. Possible consumer risks include Eavesdropping, Relay attacks, Unauthorized tag reading, Tag cloning, People tracking, Tag content changes, Malware, RFID systems breakdown, Tag destruction, Tag blocking, Tag jamming and Back-end attacks. A key privacy risk is the connection of information on the tag to an individual's identity (Rotter, 2008). Thus, only items directly associated with an individual's identity pose a privacy risk. Such items could include, RFID tagged items purchased through a retail environment that is somehow linked to the purchaser or a registered identification card. Only in very specific instances do these factors affect a person's security or privacy (Rotter, 2008).

In recent years, alternative methods have emerged that could be incorporated into an item-level RFID ecosystem reducing any potential privacy or security risks. A major alternative comes in the form of Bitcoin and its underlying blockchain technology. Both Bitcoin and blockchain architecture have become a hot topic in both academic and industry research as an excellent alternative to cloud-based database solutions. Bitcoin is a peer-to-peer electronic cash system; the concept, originally published by Satoshi Nakamoto (2008), viewed the technology as a decentralized, accelerated and streamlined international currency transfer without the need for a 3rd party financial institution. A working version of the concept was led to the creation of Bitcoin in 2008. However, the digital currency only found mainstream popularity in 2013 when the currency's market cap quickly ballooned by 1000% to US$12.8b in 3 months (Coin Market Cap, 2017). Although Bitcoin itself has had mixed success, it is the underlying blockchain architecture that is now being repurposed to solve many industry issues as it offers multiple benefits for its integration. Wüst & Gervais (2017) highlight several of these benefits, public verifiability, transparency, privacy, integrity, redundancy and a trust anchor. The integration of blockchain into an item-level RFID ecosystem would create a transparent information trail while also offering consumer privacy. Consumer and item-level tag information are encrypted, only allowing the authorized users/databases to access information. This concept goes beyond the scope of this chapter but provides an interesting insight into the potential future of item-level RFID back-end systems that could help reduce privacy and security risks.

Creating Value for Consumers Through Item-Level RFID

After a comprehensive literature review (Kukard, 2015), only three key papers considered consumer benefits from RFID technology (Lee, Fiedler, & Smith, 2008; J. S. Smith et al., 2013; Frederic Thiesse, Al-Kassab, & Fleisch, 2009). The current academic conversation surrounding consumers and RFID is heavily weighted around the potential privacy risks of the technology, while not considering the potential benefits to consumers.

A novel approach to using RFID to add value is presented in Lee, Fiedler, and Smith (2008), suggesting a customer-facing diffusion model rather than the traditional supply chain efficiency approach. RFID can be used to add intangible value to an item or service, thus increasing customer loyalty or customer satisfaction. Three case studies were presented and examined to develop the model. First, RFID in a public library was used to add a self-checkout service, reducing the number of staff dedicated to checkout and improving the simplicity of the self-checkout service. Second, a road race timing system was automated, decreasing the number of volunteers, and providing runners with more accurate results. Third, a hospital patient tracking system, demonstrated improvements in the check-in of patients, the link between patient medical records and getting the right patient the right asset at the right time. All of these benefits could be considered 'in-store' benefits as they are internal to the organization being studied. There was no examination of benefits external to the organization, the after-sales benefits.

A major European department store participated in two RFID trials, one in 2003 and another in 2008 (Frederic Thiesse et al., 2009). The main objective of the first trial was to examine to what extent RFID could create efficiency within supply chain operations under real-world conditions. The second trial extended the RFID implementation into the retail side of the department store; now offering customers the ability to engage with RFID via smart-shelves, mirrors, monitors and in-store mobile devices. Implementing RFID at a retail level and allowing customers to interact with items before the purchase could create value in a retail environment. A limitation of the study is that all benefits were limited to in the retail environment, and examples were limited to the fashion retail environment. Additionally, no after-sales benefits were examined. The study was one of the first case studies of a large-scale RFID rollout within the retail environment. Of particular interest was the way that they demonstrated that there could be a business case for engaging consumers by adding value to their shopping experience. While privacy considerations were not a part of the case study, the department store noted only three customer complaints of privacy issues during the trial period.

Consumer's acceptance of RFID could be positively impacted through perceived usefulness of the technology (J. S. Smith et al., 2013). The perceived usefulness weighs more heavily on consumers' acceptance than the associated perceived risks and that consumers are still adverse to name RFID when used at an item-level, but a privacy statement from the company could help reduce this negative attitude and therefore improve acceptance of the technology. RFID is explored from consumers' perspectives with three studies.

First, a semi-structured qualitative preliminary study involved 57 Masters of Business Administration (MBA) students who would be familiar with RFID technology. The results indicate that the respondents could see the benefits of the technology, but the study results may be representative of the general public as all respondents were MBA students familiar with RFID.

Second, the promotional and preventative concerns noted by consumers are examined using a survey. The results show that the type of message received related to the technology, either positive or negative, impacts subsequent evaluations.

Third, they focused on the increasing consumer acceptance, by alleviating privacy concerns associated with RFID. The concerns were alleviated by providing consumers with a privacy statement before the survey, allowing the consumers to understand what information is being collected and what will be done with it. A total of 104 general consumers were used as participants. When the results were analyzed, they showed that the consumers presented with the 'new technology' label had higher purchase intentions to those presented with the 'RFID' label. Respondents would be more willing to accept the technology if presented with a privacy statement from the organization.

RESEARCH MODEL, HYPOTHESES, AND TESTING

After reviewing current literature, a research gap is identified, that is to what degree the perceived benefits of RFID at an item-level will affect consumers' perceived risks and whether there a difference between the benefits/risks within a store environment and the benefits/risks after the item has been purchased.

This gap exists, as there has never been a differentiation between the types of potential consumer benefits and their differing associated risks, both in-store and after the sale, the model in Smith et al. (2013), can be expanded to provide further insight into consumer acceptance of RFID after the purchase has been completed. Differentiating between these two types of benefits available to consumers allows for a greater understanding of how consumers might react to RFID at an item-level and to what degree they are willing to accept its integration into their everyday lives. Potential benefits to consumers are split into two separate categories, in-store benefits, and after-sales, as consumers' expectation of privacy would change depending on whether they are using benefits associated with RFID technology in a grocery store or at home. Below are some examples of what would be considered benefits in each of the categories.

In-Store and After-Sales Benefits

Consumer in-store benefits are those, which a consumer would consider of value while in a store environment. For example, smart shopping cart, instant coupons, suggested complementary items, returning an item without a receipt, detailed item information (environmental impacts / nutritional information), rapid self-checkouts, item reviews, and interactive promotional displays.

In contrast, after-sales benefits consist of value-added while at home or otherwise away from the store and are available after purchase. For example, budgeting assistant, recipe suggestion, shopping list generation, real-time access to a kitchen inventory, company promotional interaction (competitions), and a meal planner based on dietary requirements/workout regime. The benefits provided are theoretically possible examples based on RFID implemented at an item-level and coupled with smart appliances and kitchens integrated with medium-range RFID readers.

These In-store Benefits (ISB) and After-Sales Benefits (ASB) will measure the consumer's Perceived Benefits (PB) of RFID within the Fast Moving Consumer Goods Industry (FMCG).

H1: In-store benefits will have a positive influence on consumers' perceived usefulness of RFID
H2: *After-sales benefits will have a positive influence on consumers' perceived usefulness of RFID*

Therefore, this chapter posits that a combination of both in-store and after-sales benefits will indicate the perceived benefits of RFID will provide a similar result when used at the item-level within the fast moving consumer goods industry. PB is a contextualized version of the TAM-based Perceived Usefulness (PU) construct (Davis, 1989). Perceived usefulness (PU) is a well-accepted indicator of consumers' Technology Attitude (TA). This chapter posits that the PB will have a positive influence on consumer's technological attitude towards RIFD for fast moving consumer goods.

H3: Perceived usefulness of RFID will have a positive influence on technology acceptance of RFID

Similarly to the PB, the Perceived Risks (PR) are separated into two types of risks, In-store Risks (ISR) and After-Sales Risks (ASR). This separation is justified as consumers' expectation of privacy within a shopping environment will differ from their expectation of privacy at home. Trocchia and Ainscough (2012) present a compelling argument as to why consumers may be prepared to have a lower expectation of privacy in a grocery store and a much higher expectation of privacy in their home:

Legal [academics] have said that a "reasonable expectation of privacy" exists when a person has "exhibited an actual (subjective) expectation of privacy" and, second, that the expectation is "one that society is prepared to recognize as reasonable. Thus, a man's home is, for most purposes, a place where he expects privacy, but *objects, activities, or statements that he exposes to the plain view of outsiders are not protected, because no intention to keep them to himself has been exhibited*" [...] Similarly, consumers may be less sensitive to such violations in locations in which such expectation would not reasonably exist, such as a grocery store sales floor (Trocchia & Ainscough, 2012, emphasis added)

Therefore, as there are clearly two separate expectations of privacy, then this differential level of sensitivity suggests that while consumers may be more willing to forgo privacy in a shop, they may be more sensitive to forgoing privacy at home.

H4: In-store risks will have a negative influence on consumers' perceived risks of RFID.
H5: After-sales risks will have a negative influence on consumers' perceived risks of RFID.

These hypotheses (H1, H2, H4, and H5) serve as the measure for the PB and PR for this model. As consumers' RFID acceptance is still a relatively untested subject, other higher risk new technology platforms were explored, for example, the adoption of online banking. In the case of our proposed model, Perceived Usefulness (PU) can be equated to Perceived Benefits (PB), which will indicate a positive influence on overall Technology Acceptance (TA).

The perception of risk has been recognized as influencing consumer adoption. For example, Roy, Kesharwani, and Singh Bisht (2012, p. 303) explored the impact of perceived risk on online banking acceptance; the findings were "that perceived risk has a negative impact on the behavioral intention of internet banking adoption." So, it can be assumed that in the proposed model, Perceived Risk (PR) will have a negative influence on Technology Acceptance (TA).

H6: Perceived risks will have a negative influence on technology acceptance of RFID.

Both PB and PR will directly affect the overall Technology Acceptance (TA) of RFID, which as the TAM dictates will have a direct impact on consumers' overall Intention of Use (IOU), giving the final hypothesis as part of the model in Figure 1.

Figure 1. How in-store and after-sales benefits/risks affect consumer's RFID acceptance

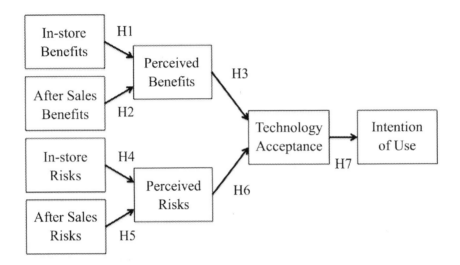

H7: The overall positive or negative perceptions of RFID will affect the intention of use the technology at an item-level

Methodology

Due to the nature of RFID research at an item-level within the FMCG industry, it was anticipated that there might be some consumer privacy concerns (McCullagh, 2003). Therefore, a quantitative approach was used to measure and evaluate acceptance of a hypothetical RFID technology. When people are presented with new technology, in this case, RFID-enabled smart groceries, the novelty of the technology could skew the results. A quantitative survey allowed the questions to be structured in a way to minimize bias and could be conducted through a US-based research company. As this research is using an experimental model with the goal of measuring consumer perceptions to predict potential technology acceptance in a reliable and repeatable manner, the use of quantitative methods to test these hypothetical generalizations is the best solution (J. K. Smith, 1983).

Data Collection

To test the validity of the model, a large-scale data collection was undertaken via an online structured survey. This research sought to improve on the J. S. Smith et al. (2013) questionnaire, which had no differentiation between the consumers' perceived usefulness in-store and after-sales. This differentiation is key to understanding to what degree consumers will accept such an invasive technology on such a large scale. The data in J. S. Smith et al. (2013) was collected from MBA students, of which many already had a good understanding of the workings of RFID; this is limitation means that those results are not necessarily a true reflection of a general consumers' acceptance. For the survey, a five-point Likert-type scale was used, ranging from 1 (indicating strong agreement) to 5 (indicating strong disagreement). The questions were situational, putting consumers in hypothetical scenarios where they would be interacting with this new wireless technology and being told the potential benefits or risks.

While many items were adapted from Smith et al. (2013), new questions for the latent constructs of in-store / after sales benefits/risks, while not previously tested or validated within the literature, were based on the *reasonable expectation of privacy* theory (*Katz v. United States - 389 U.S. 347*, 1967); while in a public place, such a grocery store a person has a lesser expectation of privacy, as opposed to at home, where someone would have a definite expectation of privacy.

The structured survey asked respondents to rate the potential benefits and risks of "a new smart grocery technology." The use of the term 'RFID' was intentionally avoided due to possible consumer negative associations and biases (e.g., as identified by J. S. Smith et al. (2013)). A pilot test of the survey was conducted with 20 postgraduate students to identify any potential biases. Feedback indicated that we should pair of positive and negative questions to reduce bias within the survey from the 'order effect' (Steinberg, 2001).

Data Sources and Analysis

A quantitative approach was taken through a large-scale data collection via an online survey research company. The respondents were based in the United States; this demographic would be likely to be among the first to be exposed to this type of technology, and it allows the results to be more directly compared to existing research (as this often used a US-based sample). 264 initial responses were received from the respondents.

After the data had been collected, it was analyzed using Partial Least Squares Structural Equation Modeling (PLS-SEM) (Henseler, Ringle, & Sinkovics, 2009). PLS-SEM was preferred to accommodate a more exploratory analysis of relationships between attributes have not been previously tested (Ainuddin, Beamish, Hulland, & Rouse, 2007). PLS-SEM estimates the path model relationships that maximize the R^2 value of the endogenous constructs, minimizing unexplained variances, which allows for better theoretical model development (Hair Jr et al., 2013). Therefore, it was a better fit for the objectives than covariance-based SEM (CB-SEM, often used in confirmatory studies). As three indicators were used for each construct, a sample size of 250 should yield an R^2 of 0.10 and a significance level of greater than 1% (Hair Jr, Hult, Ringle, & Sarstedt, 2013).

Demographics and Descriptive Results

In total, there 264 responses; after careful analysis of responses, 16 responses were discarded as they were invalid, leaving a total of 248 responses used in the analysis. The discarded responses were considered invalid for several reasons. Exploratory analysis indicated that there were 13 responses where the same answer was selected throughout the entire questionnaire. One respondent declared they were not the household buyer, invalidating their response. Demographical data is provided in Table 1.

As 56% of young adults aged 18 to 24 still live at home with their parents (Fry, 2013), we, therefore, expected more grocery buyers to be in an older age group. The small number of respondents falling into the 18-25 age range was therefore not a concern.

Overall, the sample was primarily female (66.5%) over the age of 45 (70.9%). There was an even distribution of respondents' level of education, with 25.8% of them had completed high school, 21% had some college education, but no degree and 21% had graduated from a college. 75% of surveyed household income is under $70,000pa. Table 2 compares the sample to the household income of the 2011 United States Census (US Census Bureau, 2012) showing general similarities.

Data Validation

To evaluate the proposed model, the PLS-SEM evaluation process outlined in Hair et al. (2013) was followed to ensure that all necessary measures for validation were met (e.g., internal consistency reliability, convergent validity, and discriminant validity). Validating the proposed model through this process ensured reliable and repeatable results for future research.

Reflective indicators examine an underlying construct that is unobservable as opposed to an indicator in which case it determines the construct (Petter, Straub, & Rai, 2007). Our research model consists of eight reflective constructs including, *in-store benefits* (ISB), *after sales benefits* (ASB), *in-store risks* (ISR), *after sales risks* (ASR), *perceived benefits* (PB), *perceived risks* (PR), *technology acceptance* (TA) *and intention of use* (IOU).

Testing the internal consistency reliability is typically the first criterion to be evaluated. In this instance, composite reliability (CR) was used to test the model. Results vary between 0 and 1; usually, a higher value indicates a higher reliability (Hair Jr et al., 2013). The results indicate a range from 0.856 to 0.977 (Table 3). Most results are all within an acceptable range of 0.70 and 0.90. However, two constructs have an undesirable result of above 0.95 (Hair Jr et al., 2013). Technology acceptance (TA) and intention of use (IOU) indicate 0.965 and 0.977 respectively. However, under these circumstances, the constructs have been derived from Davis (1989), and they have been proven to be solid and reliable constructs.

Convergent validity measures the positive correlation between a construct's indicator and the alternative indicators of the same construct; we tested this by considering the outer loadings of the indicators as well as the average variance extracted (AVE). The recommended acceptable value of the AVE should be 0.50 or higher (Hair Jr et al., 2013). Our results are all within the acceptable value, with AVE ranging from 0.665 to 0.933 (Table 4), suggesting that the convergent validity is confirmed.

Discriminant validity was checked to determine to what extent each of the constructs were distinct from each other. The check was conducted using the Fornell-Larcker criterion (Fornell & Larcker, 1981) that compares the square root of the AVE values with the latent variable correlations. The square root of the AVE value should be higher than that of its highest correlation with any other construct (Hair Jr et al., 2013). Table 5 shows the construct's outer loadings and cross-loadings. In all cases, the outer loadings are higher than the cross-loadings, indicating that each indicator was measuring a unique concept, and there was no need to remove any indicators from the proposed model.

The shaded diagonal values are the square root of the AVE extracted for each construct; in each case, these values exceed the highest correlation with any other construct to fulfill the Fornell-Larcker criterion.

RESULTS

Structural model validation measures proposed model constructs and allow it to be compared with the theoretical measure model and sample data (Hair Jr et al., 2013). Full outputs of the PLS-SEM results are shown in Figure 2. The next step is to assess the statistical relevance of the loadings and path coefficient. The PLS bootstrap procedure was used to draw a large number of additional samples from the original sample at random with replacement. For our bootstrap procedure, 5000 bootstrap samples were used (Hair Jr et al., 2013). Bootstrapping also provides R^2 values, which assesses the reliability of the model; results are shown in Table 6.

The most common method used to evaluate the structural model is the coefficient of determination (R^2 value), measuring the model's predictive accuracy and is calculated as the correlation between a specific construct's actual and predicted values (Hair Jr et al., 2013). The structural model's R^2 values are presented in Table 6; all values exceed the required minimum values of 0.75 as only consumer perceptions and their potential behaviors are being measured (Hair Jr et al., 2013). The strongest relationship is Technology Acceptance (0.775), followed by Intention of Use (0.769), then Perceived Benefits (0.698), and Perceived Risks with the lowest value (0.456).

1. **In-Store Benefits and Perceived Benefits:** Table 6 shows a strong relationship between potential in-store benefits and consumers' perceived usefulness of RFID technology (path coefficient=0.524, t=10.777, p<0.000). These results indicate that H1 is supported.

2. **After-Sales Benefits and Perceived Benefits:** There is a moderate relationship between potential after sales benefits and consumers' perceived usefulness of RFID technology (path coefficient =0.382, t=7.656, p<0.000). Therefore, H2 is supported.

3. **Perceived Benefits and Technology Acceptance:** The relationship between consumers' perceived benefits of RFID and the acceptance of the technology has a significantly strong relationship (path coefficient =0.732, t=22.186, p<0.000). Therefore, H3 is supported.

4. **In-Store Risks and Perceived Risks:** There is a weak relationship between in-store risks and consumers' perceived risks of RFID technology (path coefficient =0.236, t=3.165, p<0.02). This relationship is weaker than the others due to consumers' having a lower expectation of personal privacy while in a public/in-store environment. The weakness of the relationship may mean that either consumers' are unaware of the potential risks or are not as concerned with potential in-store risks. Hence, H4 is supported.

5. **After-Sales Risks and Perceived Risks:** There is a moderate relationship between the after sales risks and the perceived risks of RFID technology (path coefficient =0.475, t=6.800, p<0.000). Therefore, H5 is supported.

6. **Perceived Risks and Technology Acceptance:** There is a moderate inverse relationship between the perceived risks of RFID technology and its technology acceptance (path coefficient =-0.260, t=7.232, p<0.000). Therefore, H6 is supported.

7. **Technology Acceptance and Intention of Use:** There is a strong relationship between the technology acceptance of RFID and the consumer's intention of use (path coefficient =0.878, t=54.666, p<0.000). Therefore, H7 is supported.

DISCUSSION

This chapter focused on the consumer acceptance of RFID implementation at an item level within the FMCG industry and how the perceived benefits of the technology could outweigh any perceived risks. No other research has actively given such consideration to reasons for consumers' desire the adoption of the technology beyond the checkouts.

Previous RFID literature highlighted the privacy / security issues faced by the technology, but have not investigated the relationship between the technology from a consumer lens. Our research hypothesized that consumer's have different expectations of privacy in retail environments and at home and that consumers would be more willing to accept RFID technology, if they felt the potential benefits outweighed the potential risks in the technologies implementation.

The first hypothesis was supported, indicating that consumers within a grocery store environment will view the implementation of RFID as positive as long as they gain a sufficient benefit. The second hypothesis was also supported, meaning, if these benefits continue into the home, consumers will remain positive about RFID, despite the potential risks. They will also have an overall positive view of the technology as the third hypothesis was also supported. These findings are important, as they extended the analysis and recognized the importance of defining perceived benefits outside of a retail environment, as well as recognizing after-sales benefits as a distinct category that needs to be considered in this context and has not been considered in prior research (e.g., Lee et al. (2008)). Indeed, while not as important as the in-store benefits, the after-sales benefits do have a relationship with the consumers' perceived benefits. In contrast to Frederic Thiesse et al. (2009), where few privacy issues were noted – it is important to recognize that these privacy issues might also occur later, after-sales, and it may then be less likely that a consumer would lodge a complaint or register their concern.

The fourth hypothesis was supported although this was a weak relationship. Therefore, consumers may not feel that there are significantly more privacy risks associated with RFID technology within a grocery environment, as there was no reasonable expectation of privacy while shopping in such a public place. While privacy may not be an issue in public place, like a grocery store, the fifth hypothesis showed that consumers would consider RFID a potential privacy risk within their home as there is a reasonable expectation of privacy within your home. Overall, these perceived risks would have a negative influence on the consumer's perception of the technology. Interestingly, this was one of the weaker relationships, and this indicates that consumers are more able to overlook in-store risks and 'discount' these when evaluating the technologies; instead, they perceive the after-sales risks to be more important. Therefore, our results are well aligned with greater expectations of privacy within the home rather than a retail environment, like a grocery store.

However, the after-sales risks as perceived risk have an $R^2 = 0.456$ (Table 6), indicating that this model explains 45.6% of the variance in the construct; therefore, there could be other contributing factors that may affect after-sales adoption other than perceived risk. Overall, the survey results indicate that there is an opportunity to further understand the contributing factors and expand our conceptualization of risks in this model, as there may be other moderating or mediating factors at play.

Hypothesis seven was supported, indicating that the combined benefits and risks would give a good indication of the likelihood of consumers to adopt RFID.

Overall, while consumers seem to be aware that there could be a certain degree of risk while using RFID both in-store and after-sale, they would still be willing to use the technology if there were sufficient benefits. Due to the nature of the survey method, we believe these results draw from a wide range of consumers with differing backgrounds and experiences, giving a more generalized result than a comparable survey attempting to understand the likelihood of consumer RIFD acceptance, where respondents were MBA students with an understanding of RFID technology and its capabilities (Smith et al., 2013). Overall, while Smith et al. (2013) found that privacy risks were negatively impacted, these were not as significant as expected in our study. Given our results, we believe that this may be partly due to how the risks have been measured and evaluated. By splitting risks into in-store and after-sales, we believe the survey instruments and concepts are more clearly defined and measured. Indeed, we find that while there are in-store risks perceived by consumers, it is the perceived after-sales risks that will be most important for item-level RFID implementation and the best method to address these perceptions is through effective communication and education of consumers about what to expect and how to address any concerns.

SOLUTIONS AND RECOMMENDATIONS

The exploration of consumer acceptance through the balancing of the benefits and risks of RFID allows a new conversation to emerge within academic literature. It is worth noting that this has previously been mentioned as a gap in the literature, as there is wide recognition that the TAM model still requires refinement (Müller-Seitz et al., 2009).

The framework is this chapter differentiates between in-store and after-sales measures for consumer benefits and risks. Therefore, this develops insight into the first of two important factors influence consumer acceptance. First, consumers must be aware of a specific usefulness that outweighs the potential disadvantages of the technology. Second, consumers must believe that the novel technology is secure (Müller-Seitz et al., 2009).

The research finds when consumers are given sufficient benefits they can look beyond potential privacy risks associated with RFID technology. This weighting of benefits relative to risk has a major impact on how researchers could create models for RFID integration for a controlled and scalable integration into the supply chain. For example, a bottom-up strategy could be used to test how consumers react to RFID implementation in different item categories. If successful, implementation could be expanded to other item ranges, categories and further up the supply chain, eventually creating an entire RFID enabled eco-system.

Overall, this research expanded RFID literature by questioning the current conversation that focused on privacy risks for consumers and asked what if consumers were able to gain sufficient benefit for RFID at an item-level, that the potential privacy risks were a non-issue. There is now a framework for future researchers to measure consumer acceptance of RFID at an item-level within the FMCG industry.

This chapter suggests that professionals in the FMCG industry should consider an alternative method for the item-level implementation of RFID / NFC. An effective implementation may include a bottom-up approach, including RFID / NFC on certain item-level products, solely for the benefit of the consumer that these benefits should be very visible. For example, promotions, item information, suggested items, or coupons. This approach is scalable, ensuring manufacturers/retailers can control the initial rollout, select the potential value for their businesses and gain an understanding of what benefits are gained from the roll-out as well as the cost of further implementation. This approach gives manufacturers valuable insight into how their consumers use the technology and how they can incorporate consumer benefits into the overall architecture of their RFID system.

This chapter identified the benefits a potential consumer would find most useful, allowing them to overlook the potential privacy issues in exchange for these benefits. Managers can tailor the potential benefits to cater for what consumers' would find most useful, making the roll-out of this new technology much more likely to be accepted.

FUTURE RESEARCH DIRECTIONS

This chapter focused on exploring consumers' perceptions of item-level RFID in both the retail environment as well as within the home environment. Moreover, how consumers' perceived the associated risks of this technology changed depending on the benefits they received in the home environment. However, this study was limited to the primary decision maker for household grocery items, and not other members of the household. An interesting extension of this research would be to understand the what input other members of the household have on the purchasing behavior of the primary household purchaser, for example, if other household members specified a certain brand over another and what would the implications be if one had RFID and the other did not.

CONCLUSION

The research introduces an important consideration into RFID literature and one that should be considered once item-level RFID technology becomes more prevalent, especially with the increased interest in IoT and its potential introduction into the FMCG industry. This research examined an FMCG home-market sample of consumers to understand perceived privacy risks and benefits of the introduction of item-level RFID technology into the FMCG environment. Therefore, this research expanded the conversation within academic literature beyond privacy risks to the consumer by expanding the investigation into consumers' perceived privacy risks using a quantitative survey within this paper. By investigating both in-store and after-sales categories in this research, insights emerge about how consumers may react to item-level RFID implementation and how the inclusion of consumer-focused benefits; both in-store and after-sale could negate consumers' perceived risks towards the technology. We find that consumers' concerns about risks are weighted more heavily to after-sales risks, suggesting that consumers would expect a level of risk while using item-level RFID within a store environment but believe that these can be sufficiently addressed. Therefore, acknowledging after-sales risks and developing a more comprehensive range of consumer benefits would be required to overcome perceived risks. Additionally, this research gives a solid foundation for researchers wanting to understand consumer acceptance of IoT appliances, as they will have a similar privacy risk / benefits balance.

REFERENCES

Ainuddin, R. A., Beamish, P. W., Hulland, J. S., & Rouse, M. J. (2007). Resource attributes and firm performance in international joint ventures. *Journal of World Business*, *42*(1), 47–60. doi:10.1016/j.jwb.2006.11.001

Albrecht, K. (2005). *Spychips: How major corporations and government plan to track your every move with RFID*. Thomas Nelson.

Alt, F., Balz, M., Kristes, S., Shirazi, A. S., Mennenöh, J., Schmidt, A., & Goedicke, M. (2009). *Adaptive user profiles in pervasive advertising environments. In Ambient Intelligence* (pp. 276–286). Berlin, Germany: Springer.

Angeles, R. (2005). RFID technologies: Supply-chain applications and implementation issues. *Information Systems Management, 22*(1), 51–65. doi:10.1201/1078/44912.22.1.20051201/85739.7

Bélanger, F., & Crossler, R. E. (2011). Privacy in the digital age: A review of information privacy research in information systems. *Management Information Systems Quarterly, 35*(4), 1017–1042. doi:10.2307/41409971

Burrus, D. (2014). *The Internet of Things Is Far Bigger Than Anyone Realizes*. Academic Press.

Coin Market Cap. (2017). *Cryptocurrency Market Capatilization – Bitcoin*. Retrieved from https://coinmarketcap.com/currencies/bitcoin/

Davis, F. D. (1989). Perceived usefulness, perceived ease of use, and user acceptance of information technology. *Management Information Systems Quarterly, 13*(3), 319–340. doi:10.2307/249008

Duong, L. N. K., Wood, L. C., & Wang, X. (2016). Review of RFID applications in perishable inventory management. In B. Christiansen (Ed.), *Handbook of Research on Global Supply Chain Management* (pp. 139–146). Hershey, PA: IGI Global. doi:10.4018/978-1-4666-9639-6.ch008

Fornell, C., & Larcker, D. F. (1981). Structural equation models with unobservable variables and measurement error: Algebra and statistics. *JMR, Journal of Marketing Research, 18*(3), 382–388. doi:10.2307/3150980

Fry, R. (2013). *A rising share of young adults live in their parents' home*. Pew Research Center. Retrieved from http://www.pewsocialtrends.org/files/2013/07/SDT-millennials-living-with- parents-07-2013.pdf

Garfinkel, S. L., Juels, A., & Pappu, R. (2005). RFID privacy: An overview of problems and proposed solutions. *Security & Privacy, IEEE, 3*(3), 34–43. doi:10.1109/MSP.2005.78

Hair, J. F. Jr, Hult, G. T. M., Ringle, C., & Sarstedt, M. (2013). *A primer on partial least squares structural equation modeling (PLS-SEM)*. Thousand Oaks, CA: SAGE.

Henseler, J., Ringle, C. M., & Sinkovics, R. R. (2009). The use of partial least squares path modeling in international marketing. *Advances in International Marketing, 20*, 277-319.

Hossain, M. M., & Prybutok, V. R. (2008). Consumer acceptance of RFID technology: An exploratory study. *Engineering Management. IEEE Transactions on, 55*(2), 316–328.

Jones, P., Clarke-Hill, C., Hillier, D., & Comfort, D. (2005). The benefits, challenges and impacts of radio frequency identification technology (RFID) for retailers in the UK. *Marketing Intelligence & Planning, 23*(4), 395–402. doi:10.1108/02634500510603492

Juels, A., Rivest, R. L., & Szydlo, M. (2003). The blocker tag: Selective blocking of RFID tags for consumer privacy. *Proceedings of the 10th ACM conference on Computer and communications security.* 10.1145/948109.948126

Katz v. United States - 389 U.S. 347, 347 - 373 (1967).

Kukard, W. A. (2015). *Consumers' Perception of Item-level RFID Use in FMCG: A Balanced Perspective of Benefits and Risks* (PhD dissertation). Auckland University of Technology.

Kukard, W. A., & Wood, L. C. (2017). Consumer's perceptions of item-level RIFD use in FMCG: A balanced perspective of benefits and risks. *Journal of Global Information Management, 27*(1), 21–42. doi:10.4018/JGIM.2017010102

Lanfranchi, M., Giannetto, C., & De Pascale, A. (2016). Information asymmetry on RFID system in the agrifood sector: A study of consumer behaviour. *Calitatea: Acces La Success, 17*(151), 73–77.

Lee, L. S., Fiedler, K. D., & Smith, J. S. (2008). Radio frequency identification (RFID) implementation in the service sector: A customer-facing diffusion model. *International Journal of Production Economics, 112*(2), 587–600. doi:10.1016/j.ijpe.2007.05.008

Li, S., Visich, J. K., Khumawala, B. M., & Zhang, C. (2006). Radio frequency identification technology: Applications, technical challenges and strategies. *Sensor Review, 26*(3), 193–202. doi:10.1108/02602280610675474

Lockton, V., & Rosenberg, R. S. (2005). RFID: The next serious threat to privacy. *Ethics and Information Technology, 7*(4), 221–231. doi:10.100710676-006-0014-2

Margulis, A., Boeck, H., Bendavid, Y., & Durif, F. (2016). Building theory from consumer reactions to RFID: Discovering Connective Proximity. *Ethics and Information Technology, 18*(2), 81–101. doi:10.100710676-016-9388-y

McCullagh, D. (2003). *RFID tags: Big Brother in small packages*. Retrieved from https://www.student. cs.uwaterloo.ca/~cs492/11public_html/papers/rfid.pdf

McHugh, J. (2004). Attention, shoppers: You can now speed straight through checkout lines. *Wired Magazine, 12,* 135-139. Retrieved from http://www.wired.com/wired/archive/12.07/shoppers.html

Morgan, J. (2015). *A simple explanation of 'the Internet of Things'*. Retrieved from https://www. forbes.com/sites/jacobmorgan/2014/05/13/simple-explanation-internet-things-that-anyone-can-understand/#16567b691d09

Müller-Seitz, G., Dautzenberg, K., Creusen, U., & Stromereder, C. (2009). Customer acceptance of RFID technology: Evidence from the German electronic retail sector. *Journal of Retailing and Consumer Services, 16*(1), 31–39. doi:10.1016/j.jretconser.2008.08.002

National Intelligence Council. (2008). *Disruptive civil technologies: Six technologies with potential impacts on US interests out to 2025*. Conference Report CR 2008-07. Retrieved from https://www.fas. org/irp/nic/disruptive.pdf

Ohkubo, M., Suzuki, K., & Kinoshita, S. (2005). RFID privacy issues and technical challenges. *Communications of the ACM, 48*(9), 66–71. doi:10.1145/1081992.1082022

Östman, H. (2013). Grocery industry operations are facing a real paradigm shift. *RFID Areana*. Retrieved from http://www.rfidarena.com/2013/4/11/grocery-industry-operations-are-facing-a-real-paradigm-shift. aspx

Owunwanne, D., & Goel, R. (2016). Radio frequency identification (RFID) technology: Gaining a competitive value through cloud computing. *International Journal of Management & Information Systems, 20*(2), 37–44.

Petter, S., Straub, D., & Rai, A. (2007). Specifying formative constructs in information systems research. *Management Information Systems Quarterly, 31*(4), 623–656. doi:10.2307/25148814

Rotter, P. (2008). A framework for assessing RFID system security and privacy risks. *IEEE Pervasive Computing, 7*(2), 70–77. doi:10.1109/MPRV.2008.22

Roy, S. K., Kesharwani, A., & Singh Bisht, S. (2012). The impact of trust and perceived risk on internet banking adoption in India: An extension of technology acceptance model. *International Journal of Bank Marketing, 30*(4), 303–322. doi:10.1108/02652321211236923

Smith, A. D. (2005). Exploring the inherent benefits of RFID and automated self-serve checkouts in a B2C environment. *International Journal of Business Information Systems, 1*(1), 149–181. doi:10.1504/IJBIS.2005.007405

Smith, J. K. (1983). Quantitative versus qualitative research: An attempt to clarify the issue. *Educational Researcher, 12*(3), 6–13. doi:10.3102/0013189X012003006

Smith, J. S., Gleim, M. R., Robinson, S. G., & Kettinger, W. J. (2013). Using an old dog for new tricks: A regulatory focus perspective on consumer acceptance of RFID applications. *Journal of Service Research.*

Spiekermann, S., & Evdokimov, S. (2009). Critical RFID privacy-enhancing technologies. *Security & Privacy, IEEE, 7*(2), 56–62. doi:10.1109/MSP.2009.31

Steinberg, L. (2001). The consequences of pairing questions: Context effects in personality measurement. *Journal of Personality and Social Psychology, 81*(2), 332–342. doi:10.1037/0022-3514.81.2.332 PMID:11519936

Taghaboni-Dutta, F., & Velthouse, B. (2006). RFID technology is revolutionary: Who should be involved in this game of tag? *The Academy of Management Perspectives, 20*(4), 65–78. doi:10.5465/amp.2006.23270307

Thiesse, F. (2007). RFID, privacy and the perception of risk: A strategic framework. *The Journal of Strategic Information Systems, 16*(2), 214–232. doi:10.1016/j.jsis.2007.05.006

Thiesse, F., Al-Kassab, J., & Fleisch, E. (2009). Understanding the value of integrated RFID systems: A case study from apparel retail. *European Journal of Information Systems, 18*(6), 592–614. doi:10.1057/ejis.2009.33

Trocchia, P. J., & Ainscough, T. L. (2012). Consumer attitudes toward RFID tracking in the retail environment. *Review of Business Information Systems, 16*(2), 67–72. doi:10.19030/rbis.v16i2.6893

Turri, A. M., Smith, R. J., & Kopp, S. W. (2017). Privacy and RFID technology: A review of regulatory efforts. *The Journal of Consumer Affairs, 51*(2), 329–354. doi:10.1111/joca.12133

US Census Bureau. (2012). *2011 Household income distribution.* Retrieved from http://www.census.gov/hhes/www/cpstables/032012/hhinc/toc.htm

Venkatesh, V., & Morris, M. G. (2000). Why don't men ever stop to ask for directions? Gender, social influence, and their role in technology acceptance and usage behavior. *Management Information Systems Quarterly, 24*(1), 115–139. doi:10.2307/3250981

Wood, C., Reiners, T., & Srivastava, H. S. (2016). Effective use of information can allow operational decisions to be made that minimise costs of the firm and position them to respond more quickly to market changes. *International Journal of Logistics Research and Applications*, *20*(5), 426–443. doi:10 .1080/13675567.2016.1267126

Wüst, K., & Gervais, A. (2017). Do you need a blockchain? *IACR Cryptology ePrint Archive, 2017*, 375-382.

KEY TERMS AND DEFINITIONS

Electronic Product Code (EPC): The number associated to an RFID tag to specifically identify that tag in a group of other tags. Depending on the application, RFID tags could have matching EPCs or all have a unique EPC.

Fast-Moving Consumer Goods (FMCG): The global term for the industry that sells common household consumer products, for example, shampoo, washing powder, deodorant, instant soup, etc.

Internet of Things: An ecosystem of internet-connected devices that can share data to better complete the tasks they were designed for or provide additional value to a consumer/business.

Item-Level RFID: RFID tag with a unique EPC, placed on a product as the SKU or item level. This is the product that the consumer will purchase from the shelf.

Near-Field Communication (NFC): A small wireless passive tag with a frequency of 13.56Mhz, commonly found on most new smartphones and other technology products.

Privacy Concerns: The concern that private information from end-users can be accessed and associated to the specific individuals.

Radio Frequency Identification (RFID): An RFID tag is a small wireless tag with an EPC to uniquely identify it. There are multiple frequencies in which different versions can be accessed, depending on the application.

Technology Acceptance: The likelihood of consumers accepting a new fringe technology.

APPENDIX

Table 1. Demographics data

Demographic	Category	Percentage	Frequency [N=248]
Gender	Male	33.5%	83
	Female	66.5%	165
			[N=264]
Age	18 to 25	0.8%	2
	26 to 34	12.1%	32
	36 to 44	20.5%	54
	46 to 55	31.1%	82
	56 to 65	35.6%	94
			[N=248]
Education	Middle School - Grades 4 - 8	0.4%	1
	Completed some high school	2.0%	5
	High School Graduate	25.8%	64
	Other post-highschool volational training	4.8%	12
	Completed some college, but no degree	21.0%	52
	Associate Degree	12.5%	31
	College Degree (Such as B.A, B.S.)	21.0%	52
	Complete some graduate, but no degree	1.2%	3
	Masters Degree	10.1%	25
	Doctorate Degree	0.8%	2
	Prefer not to answer	0.4%	1
			[N=248]
Household Income	Less than $9,999	4.4%	11
	$10,000 to $19,999	14.1%	35
	$20,000 to $29,999	10.5%	26
	$30,000 to $39,999	12.5%	31
	$40,000 to $49,999	8.9%	22
	$50,000 to $59,999	15.7%	39
	$60,000 to $69,999	8.9%	22
	$70,000 to $79,999	6.0%	15
	$80,000 to $89,999	4.0%	10
	$90,000 to $99,999	4.0%	10
	$100,000 to $124,999	3.2%	8
	$125,000 to $149,999	3.6%	9
	$150,000 to $174,999	0.8%	2
	$175,000 to $199,999	0.4%	1
	Over $200,000	0.4%	1
	Prefer not to answer	2.4%	6

Table 2. Household incomes: Sample vs. 2011 US census

Household Income	Survey	2011 US Census
Less than $9,999	4.4%	7.6%
$9,999 to $19,999	14.1%	11.6%
$20,000 to $29,999	10.5%	11.3%
$30,000 to $39,999	12.5%	10.6%
$40,000 to $49,999	8.9%	8.9%
$50,000 to $59,999	15.7%	7.8%
$60,000 to $69,999	8.9%	6.8%
$70,000 to $79,999	6.0%	5.8%
$80,000 to $89,999	4.0%	4.6%
$90,000 to $99,999	4.0%	4.0%
$100,000 to $124,999	3.2%	7.5%
$125,000 to $149,999	3.6%	4.4%
$150,000 to $174,999	0.8%	3.2%
$175,000 to $199,999	0.4%	1.7%
Over $200,000	0.4%	4.2%
Prefer not to answer	2.4%	N/a

(Data Source: US Census Bureau, 2011)

Table 3. Internal consistency reliability results

Construct	Composite Reliability
After Sales Benefits (ASB)	0.878
After Sales Risks (ASR)	0.875
In-store Benefits (ISB)	0.892
In-store Risks (ISR)	0.856
Intention to Use (IOU)	0.977
Perceived Benefits (PB)	0.929
Perceived Risks (PR)	0.941
Technology Acceptance (TA)	0.965

Table 4. Convergent validity results

Construct	AVE
In-store Benefits (ISB)	0.733
After Sales Benefits (ASB)	0.700
Perceived Benefits (PB)	0.814
In-store Risks (ISR)	0.665
After Sales Risks (ASR)	0.700
Perceived Risks (PR)	0.842
Technology Acceptance (TA)	0.901
Intention to Use (IOU)	0.933

Table 5. Discriminant validity results. The shaded diagonal values are the square root of the AVE extracted for each construct; in each case these values exceed the highest correlation with any other construct to fulfill the Fornell-Larcker criterion.

	After-sales Benefits	After-sales Risks	In-store Benefits	In-store Risks	Intention to Use	Perceived Benefits	Perceived Risks	Technology Acceptance
After Sales Benefits (ASB)	0.840							
After Sales Risks (ASR)	-0.315	0.837						
In-store Benefits (ISB)	0.699	-0.237	0.856					
In-store Risks (ISR)	-0.285	0.800	-0.217	0.815				
Intention to Use (IOU)	0.684	-0.428	0.672	-0.336	0.966			
Perceived Benefits (PB)	0.748	-0.364	0.791	-0.321	0.828	0.902		
Perceived Risks (PR)	-0.437	0.663	-0.292	0.615	-0.543	-0.455	0.917	
Technology Acceptance (TA)	0.751	-0.452	0.693	-0.389	0.878	0.850	-0.593	0.949

Table 6. R^2 value for the constructs

Construct	R^2 Value
Perceived Benefits (PB)	0.698
Perceived Risks (PR)	0.456
Technology Acceptance (TA)	0.775
Intention of Use (IOU)	0.769

Chapter 10
Consumers' Concerns for Reputation and Identity Theft Online Trading

Alan D. Smith
Robert Morris University, USA

ABSTRACT

Although online trading with Amazon, eBay, and many others has its benefits, such as convenience and the ability to compare prices online, there are still many concerns about the integrity of the buyer, the seller, and/or the online action service provider (OASP). The empirical section investigated these relationships via multivariate statistical analysis of a stratified sample of working professionals resulting in 198 usable questionnaires from an initial sampling frame of over 550 professional personnel from five relatively large Pittsburgh, PA firms. It was found that buyers that felt feedback systems were viable were more willing to engage in online trading activities and more willing to pay a premium price for merchandise being sold by a seller with a better reputation, regardless of gender. Customers were especially concerned with the total price, including shipping cost, regardless of gender. In terms of the convenience of payment method, electronic forms were preferred in transacting online trading activities, regardless of age and gender.

INTRODUCTION

Growth of the Online Trading Industry

Online trading has become an increasingly popular source of income used by consumers as well as businesses. However, many factors need to be considered in order to determine the success of the auction including security and fraud safeguards, convenience, selling and buying points, reputation and feedback, and competitive forces surrounding pricing structures. Since 1995, online auctions have been one of the major success stories of the Internet with over 1,600 significant web-based auction websites and still growing (Armes, 2006). The largest online auction websites for business-to-consumers (B2C) are

DOI: 10.4018/978-1-5225-7214-5.ch010

Amazon and eBay. Although Amazon has a huge competitive advantage over many online retailers, they do have significant competition for consumers with eBay. However, Amazon believes they will be able to "level the playing field" with eBay. As for media, competition with Amazon includes Netflix, Apple, Google and Liberty Interactive. Other competitors include Target, Walmart, Sears, Big Lots, Overstock. com, Wayfair.com, Insight Enterprises, etc. Numbers show that Amazon is the largest e-commerce online retailer based on revenue as of May 2017. When it comes to online negotiation, a website named Greentoe provides competition for Amazon. Greentoe recruits vetted online retailers, simplifies the process by showing you the average price and the lowest price for each product currently available online, and then consumers are able to say how much they are willing to pay for the product (Buhr, 2014). One issue with this website is that the retailer will not be revealed until the retailer accepted the offer.

Amazon has been a growing company ever since it began as an online book distributer in 1994. Amazon has grown quite a bit over the last 20+ years and has positioned itself as the number one ecommerce retailer in terms of sales. During 2016 alone, Amazon generated over $94 billion in sales, which is much higher than Apple who came in second place at only US$16 billion in sales ("Online price negotiation …," 2017; Zaczkiewicz, 2017). Amazon has clearly set themselves apart from the rest of the industry in terms of sales as they have produced five times the number of sales as the next closest competitor, Apple (Zaczkiewicz, 2017). With Amazon now offering the ability to "make an offer" on certain products and be able to negotiate the price, the ability is there to strengthen the business. Even though this feature is only limited to a certain number of products as this is only in the initial phases, providing options to their customers is a positive for the business. This feature may provide the opportunity to attract customers who may not have used Amazon before to try and negotiate on the product that they may want to purchase. Expanding this offer to more products in the future is something for Amazon to consider as the opportunity to grow the business even further is there. The "make an offer" feature will help give Amazon and its third-party sellers an idea of what customers will pay for the products; this feature may attract more sellers due to Amazon's position within the market as the number one e-commerce seller. Companies will want to sell through Amazon as their customer reach is so much greater than when companies are only selling in their stores. This feature allows the opportunity for Amazon to attract more sellers to use their website and has the ability to draw in more customers who want to "make an offer" on these products. Amazon has put itself in a great position within the ecommerce industry and the "make an offer" feature can really give them a stranglehold on the market.

Such may online providers has been on a major force in the expanding online auction service provider (OASP) industry since the beginning on the Internet, initially not concerned with banner advertising in its formative years. Coincidentally, the first major business-to-business (B2B) online auction was conducted by FreeMarkets Inc. in 1995, with the company experiencing a slow start for the first two years. but in 1998 they grew at a much higher rate raising US$172.8 million in capital (Emiliani, 2000). FreeMarkets Inc. manufactured industrial parts, raw materials, and commodities. The primarily reasons for their growth in capital was due, in part, to their contracts with General Motors and United Technologies Corp. Ariba, Inc., a company headquartered Sunnyvale, CA, which made its name by providing software and network services to assist corporations in managing their capital, bought TradingDynamics, Inc. in 1999. This acquisition helped make Ariba, Inc. one of the fastest rising companies in the early dotcom era. Ariba acquired a privately-held procurement Business Process Outsourcing provider called Alliente, Inc. and Freemarkets, Inc., which is now the home of the Ariba Pittsburgh, PA office. Ariba has continued to be successful today thanks largely to their partnerships with 40 of the top 100 companies, as well as many other partnerships with smaller companies.

As B2C transactions are the traditional way most consumers view online auctions are utilized and transacted, the growth of e-tailing tied to B2C has been extensive and the B2C auction website, eBay, has become a generic term for e-tailing (Smith, 2009a-b, 2010), as eBay is already a household name for online auctions. Whether management takes advantage of B2B or B2B online auctions, such auctions are rapidly becoming an essential tool that organizations are using to reduce costs and improve margins with a wider supply base. There are different approaches to e-procurement marketplaces, similar to the make or buy options for materials and finished products; namely, one is to establish in-house auction teams and the other is seeking external assistance from specialist auction consultants, namely OASP (Armes, 2006; Hu, Wang, Fetch, & Bidanda, 2008; Jain, Benyoucef, & Deshmukh, 2008; Scherrer-Rathje, Boyle, & Deflorin, 2009).

Typically, the B2B online auction process begins with the formation of a cross-functional team, as this team's responsibility is to analyze a commodity and gather data from existing sources to establish the current condition of the commodity (Smith, 2006). Such team members usually identify suppliers that are capable of performing the work and eventually create a bid list. The bid list typically consists of suppliers that currently do business with the buyer as well as the new suppliers and usually contains 50 to 60 suppliers (Emiliani, 2000). After the bid list is created, a comprehensive request for quote is sent to the suppliers, which usually contains important information concerning the commodity as well as the bid time and date as related information. Suppliers are usually given 15 to 45 days to evaluate the request for quote to develop pricing. By this time, the bid list is down to 25 to 30 interested suppliers, which is dependent on the type of product and initial capital outlays to acquire it. After all interested suppliers have communicated with the cross-functional team about all parts of the commodity, the auction is ready to begin as interested suppliers are instructed to log into the auction on a certain day and time and begin to bid on each commodity. The number of suppliers who actually participates in the auction may be quite small, typically between 10 and 20. In online auctions, the buyer is not obligated to accept a bid, as most may have a reserve price or there are certain exceptions in place, which may complicate the process as the highest bidder may not always win.

Purpose of Present Study

Selected driving forces behind the OASP industry and the acceptability of using B2B and B2C online auctions, as illustrated in Figure 1, have significant and long-term influences on consumer spending and related behavioral patterns. Within the backdrop of current global recession, consumer trust is relatively low and bankruptcy rates are relatively high, although not close to the rates experienced during the Great Recession. It is important for companies to understand these forces and their influences on consumer behavior if management is to formulate successful strategies. These strategies should integrate financial, accounting, and security safeguards against identity theft, control program-costs, provide both tangible and intangible benefits to all stakeholders of online auctions, as well as rebuilding customer trust. In the empirical analysis, an attempt is made to provide at least some informal linkage between financial markets and governmental efforts to improve the transitions inherent in a recessional economy, such as job loss, less disposal income, credit crunch, and depreciation of property values. To accomplish this task, the empirical examination will use specific research hypothesis-testing procedures to help determine if appropriate reputation and feedback systems, convenience, selling and shipping price concerns and related safeguards are important and customers are willing to pay a premium for such services. In terms of the data reduction or exploration portion, via cluster and hypothesis-analysis techniques, it was decided to perform an analysis of selected customer relationship management (CRM)-based initiatives (Anton & Petouhoff, 2002; Smith, 2006, 2007) and perceived protection against identity theft to promote consumer mutual trust in business transactions (Ba & Pavlou, 2002; Looyestyn, et al., 2017). Pathak, 2003). Figure 1 highlights the major elements of the present study, in terms of discussion and generation of actual hypotheses that were eventually tested. The next section provides a belief discussion of the major constructs from a clockwise direction, starting with the construct, Security and Fraud Concerns.

CONSUMER CONCERNS ASSOCIATED WITH ONLINE AUCTION SERVICE PROVIDERS (OASP)

Big Data Analytics and B2B Transactions and Purchasing and Supply Management

Supply chain management (SCM) has recently received considerable attention from IT/IS scholars because of the collection of digitally enabled inter-firm processes that entails global supply chain. The issue at hand in this situation is how the emergence of big data analytics (BDA) has affected the productivity and growth of both manufacturing and service business enterprises. The performance impacts of BDA

Figure 1. Conceptual or activity map on the basic forces driving the acceptability associated with online auction programs (numbers refer to specific sections for more discussion)

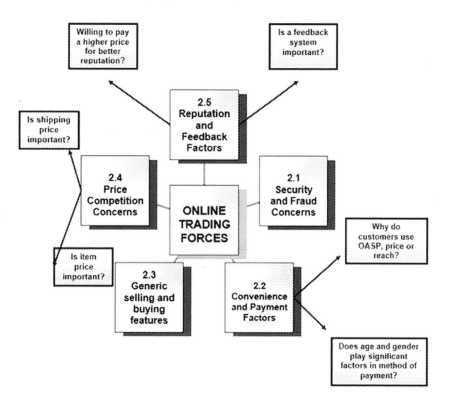

generally have not produce the transactional and relational information that can be drawn from other SCM systems, but may be symptom of it (Chen, Preston, & Swink, 2015). Since the operational, tactical and strategic information are generally shared across all of the supply chain, there is a greater need for business to rationalize the transactional and relational information that they suggest. Most studies on the impact of B2B transactions, especially online, are asset productivity, business growth, environmental dynamism, and the technical drivers of BDA. Noted by Chen et al. (2015), the functionality of dynamic capabilities is likely to be common and similar BDA technologies that can be obtained in the open market. Based on the logic of opportunity, dynamic capabilities are frequently used to build new resource configurations in the pursuit of a continual series of temporary advantages. The potential the long-term competitive advantage through the use of BDA lies in the dynamic capabilities than the need to create a resource configuration that have that advantage. Asset productivity is the primary measure used to assess supply chain performance, describing the extent to which business productivity uses their current assets as well as their fixed assets. It is important to establish indictors of asset productivity.

As stated by Melnyk et al. (2010, p. 36) "Some researchers and managers might be tempted to regard the six basic supply chain outcomes as mutually exclusive. But in practice, effective supply chains are often hybrids - reflecting various combinations of the six." The authors further suggested that this blended model requires trade-offs that some organizations do not want to make. A similar agreement was made by Ponomarov and Holcomb (2009). From the personal and professional work experiences of the author of the present chapter, as with any lean operation, reducing costs, become a paramount objective that may make management to over-emphasize short-term profits over long-term objectives. Many of the research emphasis that SCM is a strategic process (Mateen & More, 2013; Nobari, Khierkhah, & Hajipour, 2018; Park & Min, 2013; Rajapakshe, Dawande, & Sriskandarajah, 2013). As with Melnyk et al. (2010), many organizations think that you need to specialize in one or more of these outcomes as if they are mutually exclusive. In the old days, if was often said that you cannot have high quality at low cost – you either have one or the other, not both. Now, the common statement is that the way to achieve low cost is through high quality. By establishing strong IT systems, responsive systems that are CRM-embedded, etc., management with also reduce waste and become more lean. There is a general changing view of management theory from one of a Newtonian view (i.e., linear systems or trade-offs) to possibly one involving complexity theory (not mutually exclusive, but mutually benefiting) with companies as treating organizations as complex adaptive systems. The present author of this chapter firmly believe that the more traditional Newtonian model of management of trade-offs may now be hopelessly lost. It is increasingly an approach has been embraced by SCM.

As opposed to the traditional model, chaos and complexity theorists common believe that collecting information and taking measurements may blind us to the world of larger possibilities. These theorists believe that instead of attempting to impose structure, leaders should relinquish control. By accepting that SCM is dynamic and all-encompassing with many players and agents, no one metric is sufficient. This seems to be the case in B2B transactions and online auctions used in SCM operations. Therefore, we need a cluster of metrics, certainly more than just cost. If we cannot adequately measure customer satisfaction and utility, we need to have more subjective ways to measure it. Unfortunately, it is unlikely that there is a one-size-fits-all solution, as managers are more prone to try something that has worked elsewhere in times of crisis. This is particularly true if they are afforded a budget to spend without any personal consequences (relative to their take-home pay). SCM requires a more comprehensive approach and with the availability of 3PL and 4PL providers, an organization does not have to do it all.

Purchasing and Supply Management (PSM), which was originally a sub-discipline of manufacturing and operations management, has only recently gained recognition as a separate discipline. This new focus on PSM can be attributed to: Outsourcing, globalization, and e-business. For example, Van Weele and Van Raaij (2005) go into much detail about the six aspects or dimensions of SC in order to pave a path for the future of PSM. They argue that both relevance and rigor in terms of academic research are necessary in order to define a clear theoretical underpinning for the subject of PSM and in order to help those outside of the PSM community to recognize and utilize it. Instead of researchers scouring to find new theories, they should focus more on researching topics that revolve around strategic priorities and a limited number of management theories: stakeholder theory, network theory, the Resource-Based View of the Firm, dynamic capabilities theory, and relational view are all identified by Van Weele and Raaij as interesting candidates. Not only is relevance important, but so is the rigor. Instead of 'one-shot' studies, researchers should focus more on replication studies, longitudinal studies, and meta-analytical studies. Finally, the article argues that in terms of quantitative studies, it is extremely easy to misinterpret p-values (a common validation metric) and instead focus on effect sizes and confidence intervals (a more reliable validation metric).

So what is PSM? PSM can be defined as the discipline that is concerned with the management of external resources - goods, services, capabilities and knowledge - that are necessary for running, maintaining and managing the primary and support processes of a firm at the most favorable conditions. In short, PSM is a vendor-manufacturer connection that results in a mutually beneficial relationship. It is quite interesting to note that the term dates back to the early 19th century in references to wars and economic recessions. The traditional problem is that many applications of SCM, the primary focus of PSM is typically on cost reduction, especially through competitive contracting. This is easily understandable when one considers that PSM has its roots in Transaction Cost Economics (TCE). It is important to understand where a philosophy comes from and what it traditionally focuses on in order to fully understand its implications and how it will evolve in the future. In more recent decades PSM has focused on strategic relationships with suppliers and research has focused on: supplier relationship management, collaborative networks, and early supplier involvement in new product development. It's interesting to note the applicability of some of these ideas; for example, my own company has recently involved itself in a specific supplier relationship known as vendor managed inventory (VMI).

The evolution of PSM in American industry is fascinating. Soon after World War II, the U.S. was focused on securing raw materials and producing. Matter of fact, companies were basically only ordering raw materials and producing virtually everything themselves. Most companies typically produced products related to consumer lifestyle, healthcare, and lighting; during the 1960's the company also produced its own glass and packaging, and even produced its own toilet seats. It is interesting how only a few decades later the American industry, instead on focusing on making everything, begins focusing on core competencies and outsourcing everything else. Focusing on innovation and speed a company could be the first to market with a product, seize market share, and profit from economies of scale. Van Weele and Van Raaij (2005) focused on three different aspects in relation to the relevance and robustness of PSM research: research objectives, data collection methods, and data analysis methods. Research is relevant if it describes a phenomenon and its impact in contemporary context. Research is robust if the methodology through which it is obtained is rigorous.

Chen et al. (2015) suggested that insights developed through BDA, PSM, and SCM usage create opportunities for organizations to reconfigure their resources in ways that are in greater alignment with trends and shifts in both demand and supply markets. Environmental dynamism is a key situational parameter in dynamic capabilities theory, which suggests that the variance of competitive advantage created by organizational capability is contingent upon environmental dynamism. An environment will provide greater opportunity for companies to capitalize on BDA. It is very likely that the influence of BDA use on supply chain performance will be amplified in high velocity markets. It is fairly obvious that companies competing in the global economy need to examine the influence of BDA, PSM, and SCM usage as organizational outcomes, as well as the key factors that facilitate BDA use. Organizational level BDA use has significant impacts on type types of supply chain value creation; asset productivity and business growth. Technological factors have a direct influence on organizational BDA use. It is extremely useful with the proper environmental factors and can have an influence on organizational BDA through the use of top management support. The key organizational BDA factors suggested by Chen et al. (2015) included proper environmental factors, as well as a sound structure can completely revitalize the information sharing, market share, and increase business productivity contributing to the successes of a given firm.

There are a number of independent websites which rate OASPs on a basis of price, security, and many other factors; typically eBay is ranked high as they currently are the largest and most-trusted e-auction web website in operation. Their reputation and name recognition has continued to improve as the company has continually remained at the top of the highly competitive OASP industry, especially in terms of sales, visits, and profits. The integrity of these websites can be questionable if third-party audits and sound security safeguards are not in place. Following proper industrial procedures, policies, and practices as well as becoming familiar with preventative measures will help to safeguard online auction users. These procedures are the first line of defense, especially for newcomers that have yet to familiarize themselves to these numerous safeguards that are designed to protect their personal information and exchanges of finances online. Using more popular and highly reputable websites can help as they usually take the most conservative approaches regarding security due to the sheer traffic volume that they experience on a daily basis. Online auctions are generally as safe as the user will allow, as previously mentioned, risk assessment and its management is at its weakest link in the security chain with the consumer.

Convenience and Payment Factors

As an efficient and flexible sales channel, online auction businesses are becoming an internationally successful phenomenon (Dholakia & Simonson, 2005; Li, Ward, & Zhang, 2007; Smith & Potter, 2010). Customers typically use auction websites as a marketplace to conduct online sales; companies use auction websites to liquidate unwanted inventory, as well as to assist in pricing new products, acquire new markets for low-margin items, and reaching markets that would otherwise be too expensive in the past. All participants using online auctions can get their products in front of millions of people spanning the globe for a fraction of the cost and time of traditional methods. In today's online market, companies like eBay, Yahoo, and Amazon are the major players, with eBay leading the industry with over 50 million users at the time of the present study. These trends are projected to continue to grow, perhaps due to the convenience of the online consumer marketplace. Convenience is becoming an increasingly important issue in modern society as people are attracted to new technologies that trade a small amount of their privacy for greater convenience and speed. A major function of B2B, B2C, and P2P (peer-to-peer) transactions are driven by the convenience in information gathering and processing, ultimately ensuring the success of e-commerce. Another major successful factor when dealing with online auctions is the convenience of payment method.

Payment methods have various levels; for example, a credit card is more convenient for a buyer than a money order or a cashier's check. A credit/debit card can be electronically passed, which makes the transaction quicker and smoother for all partners of the transactions, especially the customer. For the seller, credit/debit cards are more convenient, since the buyer's payments are automatically collected and forwarded to the seller's bank quickly via electronic transmission. Electronic payment systems such as PayPal are emerging as the easiest and most popular method of payment online. From a user's standpoint, when dealing with electronic payment systems, it has been found that ease-of-use, convertibility of funds, and security and trust are among the most important features (Adams, Nelson, & Todd, 1992; Bruner & Kumar, 2005; Burton-Jones & Hubona, 2005; Chau, 1996; Novak, Hoffman, & Yung, 2000).

An important convenience factor for the OASP industry is achieved by strategically positioning themselves within the supply chain (Summers & Scherpereel, 2008; Vinodh, Sundararaj, Devadasan, & Maharaja, 2008). As many OASPs are operationally designed to primarily, provide services have little direct connection to manufacturing process; their supply chains encompass only some of the traditional supply stage. Service provides like eBay, on-the-other-hand, provide sellers with the wholesaler-to-distributor-to-retailer stages as primary contributions to the selling process. The customers, as end users, are the final link in the supply chain. To demonstrate this further, a typical supply chain may be composted of a supplier-to-manufacturer-to-distributor-to-retailer-to-customer model; while the eBay supply chain may be better described as seller-to-OASP-to-bidder model, which further demonstrates the simplicity and convenience that OASPs offer the bidding public.

Generic Selling and Buying Features

One of the most important strategic metric is the reputation of the seller (Dholakia, 2004; Dholakia & Simonson, 2005; Smith, 2010; Smith & Potter, 2010; Smith, Synowka, & Smith, 2010). The peer-evaluation system in which the management at eBay has set in place lets an individual rate another on how well they conducted business on a variety of consumer issues, including shipping cost, clarity of communications, description accuracy, and customer value. Whether it measures how quickly the seller processes the order and ships the items or how quickly the buyer provides the payment for the item, the peer-evaluation system is designed to inform potential and existing future buyers and sellers of the trust-worthiness of conducting business online. A high-reputation plays a very important role in ensuring the integrity of the online auctioning process by allowing the various stakeholders in the eBay community a direct measure of trustworthiness (as defined by the willingness to purchase products and/or services and to engage in financial transaction with bank accounts, debit/credit instruments) and efficiency concerning online transactions. According to Melnik (1997), Melnik and Alm (2005), and Snijders and Zijdeman (2004), a higher reputation leads to better sales and higher profits online.

Hwang and Lee (2016) applied empirical-based research methods when researching how electronic data interchange (EDI) affects the competitiveness of a firm's SCM, B2B, and B2C transactions. By combining previous research efforts, the authors analyze how EDI affects a firm's transactional environment. EDI enables a firm to replace tradition modes of document exchange. It formats the documents according to agreed-to standards and, then, transmits the messages over the Internet using a converter as a translator rather than using email or other conventional methods. The basic issue is whether or not EDI is positively affecting the firm's performance and if it is helping eliminate several different problems related to costs and human information processes. Environmental uncertainty is a major problem in firms and can be defined as a perceived inability to accurately predict an organization's environment due to lack of information or the inability to distinguish between relevant data regarding a firm's external environment and consumer's tastes and preferences. Human decision makers are limited in this sense, because they do not know how to rationalize these processes in a standardized fashion. If a firm fails to overlook these changes or fails to adopt them, it may cause failure, which typically resulted from an information asymmetry through the firm's SCM, B2B, and B2C transactions. Lack of EDI provides exchange parties the opportunity to take advantage of information advantage and they will in turn behave opportunistically, which is bad for a firm. If exchange parties face trading difficulties, this will in turn generate high-transaction costs. Behavioral or internal uncertainty tends to compromise successful performance evaluation processes. Performance is difficult to assess for an individual when there is a shared responsibility in a firm. It is a problem when performance cannot be evaluated properly or easily, as it leads to inefficient use to markets and results in hard to define rewards. Furthermore, when performance is not easy to evaluate, imperfect input measures and a manager's subjective judgments are preferable. Behavioral uncertainty occurs when it is infeasible to accurately record an individual's performance.

If performance itself cannot be a simple and measurable item readily. Firms need to avoid opportunism. This refers to the incomplete or distorted information disclosure between suppliers. When either environmental or behavioral uncertainty is high, transaction costs are high and the supply chain management is effectively decreases easily fixed costs. Transaction costs are the costs of negotiating or writing a contract and monitoring and enforcing the contractual performance. The goal of the firm is to keep these costs as low as possible by eliminating human errors and constantly adapting to what the consumers want and prefer. EDI is a very efficient use of technology to help increase a firm's effectiveness of their supply chain management.

Typical results from the use of EDI it that it substantive tangible and intangible benefits to participating firms. Those who use it have higher performance and competition between firms forces them to adopt EDI. Such applications improve their competitive position with real-time control and forecast errors decrease. Lead time is typically reduced by 50% as EDI reduces negative impact of behavioral uncertainty on performance and moderates the negative impact of environmental uncertainty on it as well. The advantages of using EDI are typically reduction in inventory costs, improved accuracy, speedy communication, increased market share, and elimination of labor-intensive task performed by humans (Hwang & Lee, 2016; Jain, et al., 2008; Kennedy & Widener, 2008; Looyestyn, et al., 2017). In essence, EDI minimizes data entry errors, shortens message length, secures messages, reduces cycle time, increases productivity, and improves overall customer service.

Allowing companies to rely on constant evolving technology to help lower costs and improve communication between suppliers is only beneficial in the long or even short run for a firm. Many OASPs firmly believe that the use of EDI is a blessing, as it helps take the workload off of employees and allows them to be productive in maintain customer retention efforts and other value-added activities. Time management activities are critical to satisfying customers and moving materials and information in an effective and low-cost manner. True, being proactive, a major part of the continuous improvement process, is important. So is it equally important that firms' management must control suppliers, and not let suppliers control the buyer's business. From previous discussions, the importance of to communicate very clearly that the effort of lean to reduce the waste of inventory and time (Basu & Nair, 2012; Mateen & More, 2013) and it is critical to align performance with demand planning. Supplier development requires that your suppliers are willing to listen to the goals of planning for the mutual benefit of all stakeholders. It has been the personal of the author of this chapter that some suppliers will only give the appearance of wanting to participate in a supplier development, only if there is some guarantee that it will increase their share of business with the buyer firm.

For example, Niranjan, Wagner, and Nguyenm (2012), suggested that supplier development may lead to continuous improvement processes and vendor managed inventory (VMI). VMI is when the supplier is in charge of making sure supply levels are proper at each customer location. VMI has its benefits and inefficiencies, and may not be for every company. Depending on the company, improper forecasting and expensive logistics could arise if the inventory style is not designed to be managed by the supplier. Because of this, Niranjan,et al. felt that there should be an evaluation method for management to determine if this style of inventory tracking is tailored to their firm. Wal-Mart and Procter & Gamble, during the 1980s, were two of the largest businesses to begin using VMI and since then more companies, including Campbell Soup and Nestle, have followed their lead. However, success of this system has stalled somewhat, which is what some recent research is trying to understand. Raghunathan and Yeh (2001) discovered that VMI is more valuable for products that are mature and have a high amount of demand. Contrary to that, other research has shown that the volume levels of the product and the value of the product are not drivers for how well the VMI system will work. In addition, the VMI process will work more efficiently if there is a solid relationship between the members in the supply chain.

Niranjan, et al. (2012) found that 10 companies selected varied in their use of VMI (e.g., RUAG, Legacy Pharmaceuticals International, Louis Widmer, Novartis, Ferring Pharmaceuticals, Hilti, Daimler, ODLO International, Merck Serono and Procter & Gamble). RUAG is an international technology group who has chosen not to use VMI because their products are usually only built one time for a customer. Their research suggested that VMI is not recommended for this company. Legacy Pharmaceuticals sources raw materials from around the world and has also not chosen to implement a VMI-based system and were content with their old school IBM method. Their research suggested that Legacy has made the correct choice to not use VMI. Louis Widmer is in the cosmetics industry and has chosen not to use VMI due to the knowledge of the ordering process their workers have and the purchasing power they hold over their suppliers. The research, however, indicated this company should indeed use VMI, but Louis Widmer has not moved in that direction. Novartis, who is in the medical industry, is among the leaders in supply chain management practices, with the help of SAP, has implemented a VMI system prior to the research even though the research supports their decision. Ferring Pharmaceuticals is a proprietary pharmaceuticals company that uses VMI on internal supplies. The research shows that Ferring should highly consider transitioning VMI to its external suppliers. Hilti is in the construction industry which uses VMI, mostly because their Materials Manager had success with it when at a previous employer. Again, the research is consistent with Hilti's decision to use VMI. Daimler, like Hilti, also employs the VMI system with the research greatly supporting their decision. OLDO International produces sportswear that uses VMI with both its suppliers and its customers. Like the previous two companies, the framework of the research states they should be using a vendor managed inventory system. Merck Serono has biopharmaceutical products and uses a VMI system to minimize the levels of inventory throughout the company. Procter & Gamble, the well-known consumer goods manufacturer also uses a VMI system to efficiently serve its customers. The research for both Merck and Procter & Gamble supports their decisions to have implemented a VMI system. Each of the investigated firms, with the exception of Louis Widmer, had consistent VMI implementation choices with the concluded research. The authors understand that their work has not shown if VMI adds to the firms' performance, it merely provided a guide to whether or not a firm should use VMI or not. Therefore, after much proactive research on supplier development by these companies suggested that such proactive approaches, although usually successful, does not guarantee success. Then, the obvious question is that ensuring such benefits can be produced by minimizing risk among partners alone?

It is good to see that scholars understand that supplier development has its risks and may not always be successful. At a company of which the present author of this chapter had done some consulting, they do not use VMI on raw materials or purchased parts, but do use it on shipping materials and consumable shop floor items such as pens and gloves. The firm has a wide variation of products, so keeping inventory on-hand for those that do not get sold often would not make sense. This was mentioned as one of RUAG's reasons for not implementing the VMI system. On-the-other-hand, their shipping materials and shop floor items are standard and can easily be monitored by the vendor with onsite visits. To my knowledge, the VMI system has worked well for these items, and the only time they strayed from the concept is if we anticipate a very large order and require higher amounts of certain shipping items. Ultimately, the purpose of supplier development, VMI in particular, is to integrate key members of the supply chain. When a company implements a supplier development program and VMI system, they are instilling the trust in their supplier is always make sure the inventory levels are kept up to date. If the relationship is not strong, the program will eventually fail and trust will be hard to regain. As previously mentioned, a VMI concept at work has bestowed trust in multiple vendors to manage the inventory levels. This typically saves firm resources to perform other important managerial tasks and allows plant personnel to focus energy on other important actions.

Reputation and Feedback Features

Numerous studies have been conducted about the use of feedback forums to promote trust, to determine whether or not trust leads to higher auction prices and the role that trust plays in relation to risk and the purchase of more expensive products (Bland & Barrett, 2006; Bolton, Katok, & Ockenfels, 2004; Boyd, 2002; Prasad, Bryan, & Reeves, 2007; Roman, 2007; Smith, 2002; Smith & Potter, 2010). Consumer trust measures and security protocols are needed to decrease the temptation for a seller to lure a buyer into a fraudulent transaction. Trust is critical when risk is involved, as buyers have to rely on electronic information without being able to physically inspect the product. One of the aims of the empirical section of the present research effort is to measure this potential impact via the implementation of an online feedback system has on aspects of consumer trust, trustworthiness of financial transactions, trading efficiency, and price. Trust is defined, for the purposes of the present study, as the expectation of payment (seller) and the expectation of delivery of the promised good (buyer); trustworthiness is generally defined as deserving trust and confidence (seller and buyer) within the transaction procedure. A buyer places trust by bidding on an auctioned item and following through with payment whereas a seller places trust by shipping the auctioned item. The primarily sources of trust that are important may be classified as familiarity, calculativeness, and mutually shared values; familiarity stems from repeated transactions, calculativeness stems from an assessment of the other party's cost and benefits of cheating and values are the structures that encourage trustworthy behavior (Bland and Barrett, 2006; Bolton, Katok, & Ockenfels, 2004; Boyd, 2002; Prasad, Bryan, & Reeves, 2007; Roman, 2007).

Growth of E-Applications in Service Sectors

Hansen and Levin (2010) identified a number of reasons why retail managers employ the use of e-learning modules to train their employees. These concepts are useful in preparing successful operation of OASPs. These reasons include flexibility, customizability, self-pacing for employees, and the consistent quality offered by these modules. Since there are no physical classes that employees must attend, e-learning modules offer flexibility around busy schedules. Employees and customers can simply take these modules whenever is convenient for them and they are extremely customizable. They can be adjusted for each user and their specific job requirements simply by adding or subtracting content. This allows such training to be customized quickly and inexpensively. E-learning modules allow for different paces of users. If the user needs to review the previous slide or video segment, he or she can simply rewind. This is not as possible with a live class taught by a live instructor. Such modules are available in many different languages, making them appropriate for large corporations with branches in many countries and multiple users. Simply translating the audio content in the video for each language is easy and inexpensive. Finally, and maybe the most useful aspect of e-learning is the instant assessment offered by these programs. Modules can be designed with quizzes spaced periodically through the material, or with a test at the end. Modules offer immediate feedback on how the user is learning and understanding the material. It is easy for the company to track the progress of its employees/customers in their learning. If the retailer/service provider needs to certify that all employees/customers working in a certain area of OASPs have taken appropriate training and are certified, it can be done in an easy, efficient, and inexpensive manner. There are a number of user intrinsic and extrinsic motivations that directly affect the use of e-learning, the location of use, the value generated by these modules as perceived by the user and the user's perceptions of the module and its value versus the objective outcome of the training module.

In a society where the Internet has taken over many advertising avenues, many corporations are looking to become more e-business, such as OASPs, friendly to counter the seeming overuse of technologies. With increasing competition, management are increasing motivated towards finding innovate ways to generate leads and information on effective business strategies. Many organizations have now begun to turn their attention on information and communication technologies (ICT). Many organizations may have felt the need to reach out and focus their resources on the Internet, that by creating the best website in order to attach more business. However, through research by Martinez-Caro and Cegarra-Navarro (2009), website designs are not enough exposure in the e-commerce to help the organization maximize its e-business needs. The authors focused on finding the best ways to maximize e-business for small to medium-size organizations. Many large organizations have been able to establish empirical data to help find knowledge on the issue of e-business, but for smaller organizations, there is little evidence to help support the claim as to what is the most important in maximization of e-business. Other innovative strategies include groupware and collective applications, as evident in the growth of OASPs. Since there is a lack of empirical evidence, good data, the focus has then turned to capital productivity and how it can be a useful variable to measuring business performance. Capital productivity can be used, "because it reflects the efficiency and effectiveness of resource utilization to create value in the marketplace" (p. 489). Much of the literature in this situation is reliant on case studies, anecdotes, and conceptual frameworks, rather than empirical evidence.

Martinez-Caro and Cegarra-Navarro (2009) used hierarchical regression with hopes of considering three different types of e-business; Internet-based application, groupware application, and collective systems to find evidence of influence of e-business on capital productivity. Their findings suggest that many organizations may be over investing in Internet-based applications because it seems that there is a higher yield in groupware application and collective systems. Alternative approaches, such as cloud computing, may offer significant advantages as e-business search for better, more profitable alterative of delivery and service. Table 1 is an illustration of some of the positive and negative opportunities for these service providers as a function of the attractiveness of three cloud-based market opportunities are outlined.

Table 1. Positive and negative opportunities for service providers based on market attractiveness of cloud-based technologies

Opportunities Analysis framework	Cloud Storage	Cloud Backup	Cloud CPA
Competitive Vulnerability	Negative - big players (i.e. HP, Amazon, and etc.) who have entered into the market.	Negative - big players (i.e. HP, Amazon, and etc.) who have entered into the market.	Natural – weak competitors
Magnitude of Unmet Needs	High- individuals need a centralized place to store their bills, financial statements, and other documents automatically.	Neutral – most customer needs have been addressed	High – smaller firms need to lower their operating costs.
Interaction Between Segments	High –individuals and small businesses are willing to use electronic storages	High - most small and mid-size businesses do not have backup systems. In addition, big corporations own their backup systems.	Negative – the number of smaller firms is limited.
Likely Role of Growth	High –most individuals and small businesses have not assigned for services.	High - most small and mid-size businesses do not have backup systems. In addition, big corporations own their backup systems.	Negative – the number of smaller firms is limited.
Technology Vulnerability	Negative – targeted consumers will be attracted by competitors who adopt new technologies.	Negative – targeted consumers will be attracted by competitors who adopt new technologies.	Negative – targeted consumers will be attracted by competitors who adopt new technologies.
Market Size	High – most individuals and small business have not assigned for services.	High - most small and mid-size businesses do not have backup systems. In addition, big corporations own their backup systems.	Negative – the number of smaller firms is limited.
Level of Profitability	Negative – the competition is intense.	Negative – the competition is intense.	High – it is based on the best customization of the consumer experience

METHODOLOGY

Sample Characteristics

The global recession that was started in 2009 has placed a number of negative consequences in regards to eroding consumer trust, as previously discussed, forcing many customers to significantly change spending and fiscal policies, even to the present day. Ultimately, these negative impacts can have long-term effects on an economy built on consumer confidence and spending. To explore the concepts of customer trust and confidence with the OASP industry, a basic survey instrument was developed for exploratory purposes. This instrument contained 27 items that were grouped on the basis of perceptions of the importance of OASP-related factors tied to building consumer confidence, including reputation and feedback, security and fraud concerns (especially identity theft), convenience, selling and buying promotional points, and pricing concerns, as well as demographic information. A study among working professionals should provide value-added insights concerning such coping strategies in the current economic downturn; hence, a number of specific hypotheses was tested.

A series of paper-based questionnaires were distributed via a stratified sample of employed professionals, representative of the service industry located in the metropolitan area of Pittsburgh, PA, a major corporate headquarters. This procedure resulted in 198 useable questionnaires from an initial sampling frame of over 550 professional personnel from five large area firms. The surveyed personnel, primarily service representing marketing and financial services, were conducted over a three-month period. Pittsburgh was chosen as a classical representative of many rustbelt areas most hit by the global recession and, in part, due to accessibility by the present author.

Statistical Techniques

Using a variety of graphical and data reduction techniques, it was hoped that the constructs and propositions discussed in the precious sections dealing with the professional intellect could be validated. Mostly scale and a few nominal-based scales were used to develop graphs and perform the relevant statistical analyses. The dominant statistical techniques used in the present study were multiple regression and Chi-square analyses for the formal hypotheses testing processes and principal-components analysis (PCA) for the exploratory or data reduction portion of the present study. PCA is a classical linear transform statistical method, which has been widely used in data analysis and compression (Bishop, 1995; Cumming, 1993). In general, if the data are concentrated in a linear subspace, this provides a way to compress data without losing much information and simplifying the representation. Hence, by picking the eigenvectors having the largest eigenvalues, little information as possible in the mean-square sense is lost. The survey questions that were used may be at least partially derived from the frequencies, cross-tabulations, and data reduction techniques found in Tables 1 through 10 and Figures 2 through 6, which are the bulk of the survey questions contained in the data-collection process and ultimately used in the analysis portion of the present study.

RESULTS AND DISCUSSION

Descriptive Comparisons

Table 1 displays frequencies of selected variables to determine intrinsic and extrinsic motivations behind the extensive use of online trading websites and what their concerns or preferences are in regards to online trading. The specific hypothesis-testing section was designed to answer questions concerning selected major forces promoting the acceptability of online trading as found in Figure 1; namely are buyers are willing to pay a higher price if the seller has a better reputation, is shipping price is equally important as item price, and are customers using online auctions for price and/or reach as their primary motivations. The survey instrument originally consisted of the categories of reputation and feedback, security and fraud, convenience, selling and buying points, price factors, and demographics.

Table 2 displays frequencies of selected variable of the 198 professionals' responses to the survey instrument. As evident from an inspection of the table, for example, the majority of respondents were willing to pay higher price if seller has better reputation (51.1%), feedback systems are important (only 9.1% disagreed), seller concerned with buyer's reputation (only 10.1% disagreed), buyer concerned with seller's reputation (only 8.61% disagreed), consider shipping price in bidding (only 15.2% disagreed), pay higher shipping price for higher value (only 22.2% disagreed), and used electronic methods of payment (PayPal 15.2%, credit card, 50.5%, check, 6.6%). The fear of identity theft while engaged in online trading was felt by the majority of respondents (only 18.7% disagreed and 21.2% strongly agreed). Many of the respondents have engaged directly while selling transactions, with 44.4% selling at least US$21 worth, while 8.1% sold over US$500 annually. Figures 2a-b illustrate the cross-tabulations of method of payment with reasons for using online auctions and age level, respectively. As evident by the figures, electronic payments are vastly preferred, especially by younger professionals, and although price is a dominant factor, the value or reach or broadcasting to greater accessibility to other domestic and international markets is very significant as well.

Due in part to this diversity of behavioral and attitudinal patterns, the next two section deals with individual hypotheses as well as cluster analysis and data reduction techniques, with specific hypothesis-testing procedures. These statistical procedures were employed in order to determine existing patterns from a working professional's confidence perspective in terms of the online trading process, general, and, in particular, an OASP's ability to safeguard its clientele against the threat of identity theft.

Hypothesis-Testing Results

From the research-propositions and business literature on the development of the growth of online trading and the major forces driving its acceptability (e.g., feedback systems, price competitiveness, and payment method) both hypothesis-testing and exploratory research procedures were performed to test these relationships. The three specific research hypotheses that were tested are as follows:

H1: Buyers, especially working professionals, that find the feedback systems important are willing to engage in online trading activities and may be willing to pay a higher price for merchandise being sold by a seller with a better reputation, regardless of gender.

H2: Customers, especially working professionals, are concerned with selling price as well as shipping cost or total price, regardless of gender.

Table 2. Selected frequencies of selected variables that measured the constructs identified in Figure 1 and some used as dependent variables in the hypothesis-testing phase

A. Willing to pay higher price if seller has better reputation.				
Coding Scheme	Frequency	Percent	Valid Percent	Cumulative Percent
Strongly Disagree	26	13.1	13.1	13.1
Disagree	28	14.1	14.1	27.3
Neutral	42	21.2	21.2	48.5
Agree	80	40.4	40.4	88.9
Strongly Agree	22	11.1	11.1	100.0
Total	198	100.0	100.0	
B. Feedback systems are important.				
Coding Scheme	Frequency	Percent	Valid Percent	Cumulative Percent
Strongly Disagree	8	4.0	4.0	4.0
Disagree	10	5.1	5.1	9.1
Neutral	37	18.7	18.7	27.8
Agree	102	51.5	51.5	79.3
Strongly Agree	41	20.7	20.7	100.0
Total	198	100.0	100.0	
C. Seller concerned with Buyer's reputation.				
Coding Scheme	Frequency	Percent	Valid Percent	Cumulative Percent
Strongly Disagree	10	5.1	5.1	5.1
Disagree	10	5.1	5.1	10.1
Neutral	58	29.3	29.3	39.4
Agree	79	39.9	39.9	79.3
Strongly Agree	41	20.7	20.7	100.0
Total	198	100.0	100.0	
D. Buyer concerned with seller's reputation.				
Coding Scheme	Frequency	Percent	Valid Percent	Cumulative Percent
Strongly Disagree	6	3.0	3.0	3.0
Disagree	11	5.6	5.6	8.6
Neutral	30	15.2	15.2	23.7
Agree	91	46.0	46.0	69.7
Strongly Agree	60	30.3	30.3	100.0
Total	198	100.0	100.0	
E. Fear of identity theft with online auctions.				
Coding Scheme	Frequency	Percent	Valid Percent	Cumulative Percent
Strongly Disagree	7	3.5	3.5	3.5
Disagree	30	15.2	15.2	18.7
Neutral	49	24.7	24.7	43.4
Agree	70	35.4	35.4	78.8
Strongly Agree	42	21.2	21.2	100.0
Total	198	100.0	100.0	
F. Method of payment.				

continued on following page

Table 2. Continued

Coding Scheme	Frequency	Percent	Valid Percent	Cumulative Percent
PayPal	79	39.9	39.9	39.9
Credit Card	100	50.5	50.5	90.4
Check	13	6.6	6.6	97.0
Other	6	3.0	3.0	100.0
Total	198	100.0	100.0	

G. Sold in a year on online auctions (US$).

Coding Scheme	Frequency	Percent	Valid Percent	Cumulative Percent
0 to 20	110	55.6	55.6	55.6
21 to 50	17	8.6	8.6	64.1
51 to 100	31	15.7	15.7	79.8
101 to 500	24	12.1	12.1	91.9
500+	16	8.1	8.1	100.0
Total	198	100.0	100.0	

H. Days of week shop online.

Coding Scheme	Frequency	Percent	Valid Percent	Cumulative Percent
Monday	23	11.6	11.6	11.6
Tuesday	13	6.6	6.6	18.2
Wednesday	27	13.6	13.6	31.8
Thursday	20	10.1	10.1	41.9
Friday	45	22.7	22.7	64.6
Saturday	45	22.7	22.7	87.4
Sunday	25	12.6	12.6	100.0
Total	198	100.0	100.0	

I. Consider shipping price in bidding.

Coding Scheme	Frequency	Percent	Valid Percent	Cumulative Percent
Strongly Disagree	11	5.6	5.6	5.6
Disagree	19	9.6	9.6	15.2
Neutral	52	26.3	26.3	41.4
Agree	74	37.4	37.4	78.8
Strongly Agree	42	21.2	21.2	100.0
Total	198	100.0	100.0	

J. Pay higher shipping price for higher value.

Coding Scheme	Frequency	Percent	Valid Percent	Cumulative Percent
Strongly Disagree	15	7.6	7.6	7.6
Disagree	29	14.6	14.6	22.2
Neutral	63	31.8	31.8	54.0
Agree	68	34.3	34.3	88.4
Strongly Agree	23	11.6	11.6	100.0
Total	198	100.0	100.0	

Figure 2. Cross-tabulation of method of payment with selected variables: Reasons for using online auctions

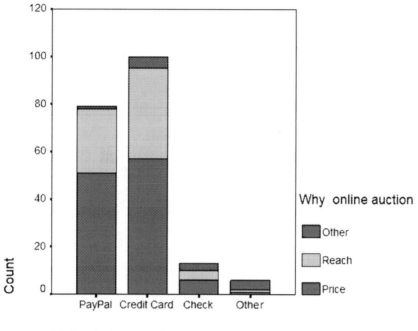

For a more accurate representation see the electronic version.

Figure 3. Cross-tabulation of method of payment with selected variables: Age level (years)

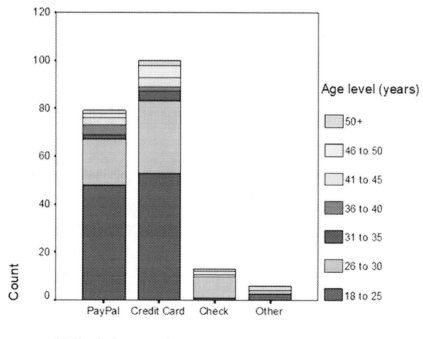

For a more accurate representation see the electronic version.

H3: In terms of the convenience of payment method, electronic forms are preferred by working professionals in transacting online trading activities, regardless of age and gender.

Specific-Research Hypothesis (H1) Results

Based on the derivation of the inherent value of reputation and feedback systems, it was hypothesize those buyers that find the feedback systems important may willing to pay a higher price for an item being sold by a seller with a better reputation. Table 3 is cross-tabulation statistics of willing higher price if seller has better reputation with feedback systems are important with gender status was found to be highly significant at the 0.01 level of a two-tailed test (for males, Chi-square = 60.512, p < .001; for females, Chi-square = 62.886, p < .001). As demonstrated in Table 2, 72.2% of those that find that a feedback system to be important agree or strongly agree that they are willing to pay a higher price if the seller has a better reputation. It was decided to cross-tabulate willingness to pay a higher price if the seller has a better reputation with gender status, as shown in Table 4. The results were equally impressive with males and females equally agreeing on paying a higher price for a better reputation. This relationship was found to be highly significant at the .01 level of a two-tailed test (for males, Chi-square = 153.577, p < .001; for females, Chi-square = 107.282, p < .001). Slightly more males (2.1%) strongly agree that they are willing to pay a higher price for a better reputation over that of females, but that difference is not statistically significant. Figure 3 presents a cross-tabulation of seller's concern with buyer's reputation with buyer concerned with seller's reputation, while Figures 5-7 display the cross-tabulation with degree of importance of feedback systems and gender, respectively. Hence, H1 was accepted, suggesting the strategic advantage value of reputation and feedback systems is very powerful.

Specific-Research Hypothesis (H2) Results

The second hypothesis deals with the construct of competitive pricing structures, which includes the total price and shipping costs. As the results from Table 5 indicates, there is overwhelming evidence and highly significant that buyers that consider the selling price before bidding consider the shipping price of the item they are bidding on (Chi-square = 101.915, p < .001). There are a significant number of buyers who strongly agree that they consider both the selling price before bidding as well as the shipping price of the item; the numbers were significantly lower for those buyers that disagreed on both aspects. Hence, most customers, especially working professionals, who are concerned with the selling price before bidding are consider the total price, including shipping costs; therefore, H2 is formally accepted.

Specific-Research Hypothesis (H3) Results

This hypothesis was in the area of convenience of payment methods, especially in terms of gender and age. The results summarized in Table 6 indicated that the most significant use of payment was PayPal and credit cards and it was significantly related to the reason for use, namely price and/or reach (the extent of accessibility to other marketplaces), with price the most important factor (Chi-square = 45.740, p < .001). In terms of age, Table 7, of the 105 respondents that were from the age 18 to 25 years, 46% used PayPal and 50% used credit cards; the 59 in the age level of 26 to 30 years, 30% used PayPal and 50% used credit cards; while the older age groups predominately used credit/debit cards. These relationships between age and use of electronic means, with younger professionals preferring PayPal over credit/debit

Figure 4. Cross-tabulation of seller's concern with buyer's reputation with buyer concerned with seller's reputation

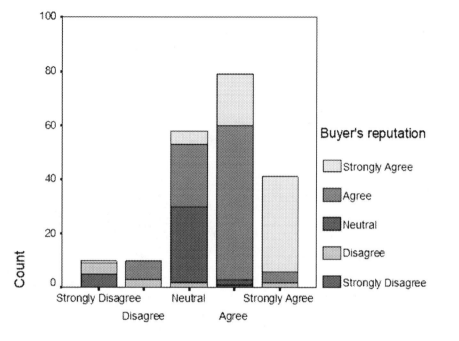

Seller concerned with buyer's reputation

*For a more accurate representation see the electronic version.

Figure 5. Cross-tabulation of willingness to pay higher prices if greater reputation of seller with selected variables: Degree of importance of feedback systems

*For a more accurate representation see the electronic version.

Figure 6. Cross-tabulation of willingness to pay higher prices if greater reputation of seller with selected variables: Gender

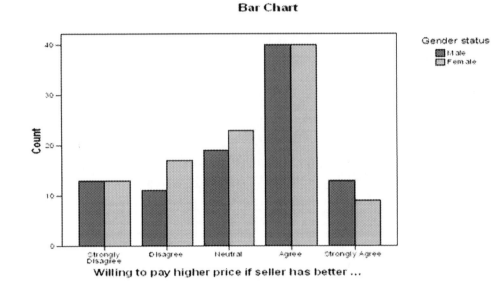

cards, were found to be statistically significant, regardless of gender, although less strong for females (for males, Chi-square = 36.884, p = 0.005; for females, Chi-square = 27.331, p = 0.073). Figure 2 previously illustrated some of these important relationships.

Although PayPal and credit cards are the most popular methods of payment through all age groups, younger professionals tend to use them more frequently and without much hesitation.

Factor-Analysis and Exploratory Results

In the search for validation of the major constructs that are most likely to be associated with fear of identity theft when engaged in online auctions and the basic constructs outlined in Figure 1, namely considerations of reputation and feedback features, convenience, price competition, security and fraud, payment methods, and generic selling and buying features (other factors). CRM-based aspects and the concerns of professional workers' eroded consumer trust due to the current global recession, principal components and factor analyses techniques were selected as the dominant multivariate statistical procedures to be used in the exploratory segment of this research effort. Principal component analysis (PCA) is a classical linear transform statistical method, which has been widely used in data analysis and compression (Bishop, 1995; Cumming, 1993; Oja, 1989). Factor analysis using PCA techniques computed the communalities and common grouped factors in terms of shared variance. The analysis was done by separating the variables into independent factor-based constructs, then completing the PCA techniques, followed by appropriate hypothesis-testing procedures with degree identity theft fears are affected by the major driving forces of acceptability of online trading among the working professional crowd Tables 8 and 9).

It was the basic research assumption of the present study that there are positive steps that management in the OASP industry can undertake to minimize the negative aspects of global recession to rebuild

Table 3. Cross-tabulation statistics of willing higher price if seller has better reputation with feedback systems are important with gender status

A. Actual count.								
Gender status			Feedback systems are important					Total
Coding Scheme			Strongly Disagree	Disagree	Neutral	Agree	Strongly Agree	
Male	Higher price if seller has better reputation	Strongly Disagree	3	3	4	1	2	13
		Disagree	1	1	3	6	0	11
		Neutral	0	0	7	8	4	19
		Agree	0	0	4	30	6	40
		Strongly Agree	0	0	1	4	8	13
	Total		4	4	19	49	20	96
Female	Higher price if seller has better reputation	Strongly Disagree	2	4	2	3	2	13
		Disagree	1	2	4	9	1	17
		Neutral	0	0	8	13	2	23
		Agree	1	0	4	27	8	40
		Strongly Agree	0	0	0	1	8	9
	Total		4	6	18	53	21	102

B. Chi-square test results.					
Gender status	Statistics		Value	df	Asymptotic Significance (two-tailed test)
Male	Pearson Chi-Square		60.512	16	<.001 (HS)
	Likelihood Ratio		55.696	16	<.001 (HS)
	Linear-by-Linear Association		30.253	1	<.001 (HS)
	N of Valid Cases		96		
Female	Pearson Chi-Square		62.886	16	<.001 (HS)
	Likelihood Ratio		53.970	16	<.001 (HS)
	Linear-by-Linear Association		25.208	1	<.001 (HS)
	N of Valid Cases		102		

C. Symmetric measures.				
Gender status	Statistics		Value	Approximate Significance
Male	Nominal by Nominal	Contingency Coefficient	0.622	<.001 (HS)
	N of Valid Cases		96	
Female	Nominal by Nominal	Contingency Coefficient	0.618	<.001 (HS)
	N of Valid Cases		102	

HS denotes highly significant at the .01 level for a two-tailed test.

Table 4. Cross-tabulation statistics of seller concerned with buyer's reputation with buyer concerned with seller's reputation with gender status

A. Actual count.								
Gender status			Buyer concerned with seller's reputation					Total
Coding Scheme			Strongly Disagree	Disagree	Neutral	Agree	Strongly Agree	
Male	Seller concerned with buyer's reputation	Strongly Disagree	3	3	0	0	0	6
		Disagree	0	2	0	3	0	5
		Neutral	0	1	11	11	2	25
		Agree	0	0	1	35	6	42
		Strongly Agree	0	1	0	1	16	18
	Total		3	7	12	50	24	96
Female	Seller concerned with buyer's reputation	Strongly Disagree	2	1	0	0	1	4
		Disagree	0	1	0	4	0	5
		Neutral	0	1	17	12	3	33
		Agree	1	0	1	22	13	37
		Strongly Agree	0	1	0	3	19	23
	Total		3	4	18	41	36	102

B. Chi-square test results.				
Gender status	Statistics	Value	df	Asymptotic Significance (two-tailed test)
Male	Pearson Chi-Square	153.577	16	<.001 (HS)
	Likelihood Ratio	112.503	16	<.001 (HS)
	Linear-by-Linear Association	55.597	1	<.001 (HS)
	N of Valid Cases	96		
Female	Pearson Chi-Square	107.282	16	<.001 (HS)
	Likelihood Ratio	87.434	16	<.001 (HS)
	Linear-by-Linear Association	34.730	1	<.001 (HS)
	N of Valid Cases	102		

C. Symmetric measures.				
Gender status	Statistics		Value	Approximate Significance
Male	Nominal by Nominal	Contingency Coefficient	0.784	<.001 (HS)
	N of Valid Cases		96	
Female	Nominal by Nominal	Contingency Coefficient	0.716	<.001 (HS)
	N of Valid Cases		102	

HS denotes highly significant at the .01 level for a two-tailed test.

Table 5. Cross-tabulation statistics of consider shipping price in bidding with consider selling price before bidding

A. Actual count.							
Coding Scheme		Consider selling price before bidding					Total
		Strongly Disagree	Disagree	Neutral	Agree	Strongly Agree	
Consider shipping price in bidding	Strongly Disagree	9	1	0	1	0	11
	Disagree	1	5	4	9	0	19
	Neutral	4	5	18	14	11	52
	Agree	3	7	10	42	12	74
	Strongly Agree	2	3	5	17	15	42
Total		19	21	37	83	38	198

B. Chi-square test results.			
Statistics	Value	df	Asymptotic Significance (two-tailed test)
Pearson Chi-Square	101.915	16	<.001 (HS)
Likelihood Ratio	71.353	16	<.001 (HS)
Linear-by-Linear Association	34.550	1	<>.001 (HS)
N of Valid Cases	198		

C. Symmetric measures.			
Statistics		Value	Approximate Significance
Nominal by Nominal	Contingency Coefficient	0.583	<.001 (HS)
N of Valid Cases		198	

HS denotes highly significant at the .01 level for a two-tailed test.

consumer trust, especially in the integrity of online trading. Table 9, Part C, displays the communalities among factor loadings results for the creation of the independent-variable factor-based constructs, indicating that there are 8 statistically significant groupings of data clusters at the .05 level among the independent variables for data-reduction purposes. Figures 7 and 8 present cross-tabulation of fear of identity theft conducting online auctions with selected variables.

In terms of the independent-variable constructs, Table 9 displays evidence that the total explained variance from data-reduction techniques of eight major constructs that was statistically significant. The independent factor groups were renamed to suit their description of the independent variables, which loaded into the groupings with at least .5 (Bishop, 1995; Cumming, 1993) and were similar to the labels generated by theoretical constructs from the literature review. As evident from the results, there are eight or less major groupings or data clusters; Table 8, Part A, displays the total explained variance from data reduction techniques of these eight major constructs was 66.955%. The significant variable loadings defining each major factor are highlighted in bold print for easy recognition in Table 9, Part B (rotated component matrix) and C (component transformation matrix). Table 9, Part A lists these factor-based constructs as, in order of the greatest explained variance; namely Reputation and Feedback Features,

Table 6. Cross-tabulation statistics of method of payment with reason for using online auctions

A. Actual count.					
Coding Scheme		Reason for using online auctions			Total
		Price	Reach	Other	
Method of payment	PayPal	51	27	1	79
	Credit Card	57	38	5	100
	Check	6	4	3	13
	Other	1	1	4	6
Total		115	70	13	198

B. Chi-square test results.				
Statistics		Value	df	Asymptotic Significance (two-tailed test
Pearson Chi-Square		45.740	6	<.001 (HS)
Likelihood Ratio		24.498	6	<.001 (HS)
Linear-by-Linear Association		16.348	1	<.001 (HS)
N of Valid Cases		198		

C. Symmetric measures.			
Statistics		Value	Approximate Significance
Nominal by Nominal	Contingency Coefficient	0.433	<.001 (HS)
N of Valid Cases		198	

HS denotes highly significant at the .01 level for a two-tailed test.

Online Auction Usage, Price Factors, Bidding Preference, Demographic Maturity, Security Factors, Convenience Factors, and Other Factors, resulting in eight factor-based scores.

Factor-Analysis Hypothesis-Testing Results

In the testing of factor-based constructs to determine the most important considerations for management of OASP-related industry in characterizing the impact of eroded consumer trust, especially due to the fears of identity theft while engaged in online trading. Table 9 presents the relevant statistics associated with testing these independent constructs derived from PCA results found in Table 9, with the dependent variable, consumer belief that the credit crunch has contributed to consumer insolvency. As displayed Part A, the model summary, a total variance in predicting the dependent variable was a respectable 28.1%. In terms of the hypothesis-testing results, the overall results were not found to be statistically significant (F = 9.294, p < .001). While, as shown in Part C that inspects specific contributions of each component in the hypothesis and 4 independent factor-based constructs were found to be statistically associated with the dependent variable, fear of identity theft with online auctions.

The Reputation and Feedback Features factor-based construct, compositing of highly significant independent variables shown in Table 10 of seller concerned with buyer's reputation (0.860), feedback systems are important (0.789), buyer concerned with seller's reputation (0.757), and higher price if seller has better reputation (0.745), was found to be highly significant and positively related to the dependent

Table 7. Cross-tabulation statistics of method of payment with age level (years) with gender status

A. Actual count.											
Gender status			Age level (years)								Total
Coding Scheme			18 to 25	26 to 30	31 to 35	36 to 40	41 to 45	46 to 50	50+	
Male	Method of payment	PayPal	32	6	0	3	0	1	0	42
		Credit Card	30	9	2	1	2	0	1	45
		Check	0	2	0	0	1	1	1	5
		Other	2	1	0	0	0	0	1	4
	Total		64	18	2	4	3	2	3	96
Female	Method of payment	PayPal	16	13	2	1	3	1	1	37
		Credit Card	23	21	2	1	2	5	1	55
		Check	1	7	0	0	0	0	0	8
		Other	1	0	0	0	0	0	1	2
	Total		41	41	4	2	5	6	3	102

B. Chi-square test results.				
Gender status	Statistics	Value	df	Asymptotic Significance (two-tailed test)
Male	Pearson Chi-Square	36.884	18	0.005 (HS)
	Likelihood Ratio	31.009	18	0.029 S)
	Linear-by-Linear Association	9.237	1	0.002 (HS)
	N of Valid Cases	96		
Female	Pearson Chi-Square	27.331	18	0.073 (MS)
	Likelihood Ratio	18.121	18	0.448 (NS)
	Linear-by-Linear Association	0.308	1	0.579 (NS)
	N of Valid Cases	102		

NS denotes not statistically significant at the .05 level for a two-tailed test, MS denotes marginally significant at the .05 level for a two-tailed test; S denotes significant at the .05 level for a two-tailed test, HS denotes highly significant at the .01 level for a two-tailed test.

C. Symmetric measures.				
Gender status	Statistics		Value	Approximate Significance
Male	Nominal by Nominal	Contingency Coefficient	0.527	0.005 (HS)
	N of Valid Cases		96	
Female	Nominal by Nominal	Contingency Coefficient	0.460	0.073 (MS)
	N of Valid Cases		102	

MS denotes marginally significant at the .05 level for a two-tailed test, HS denotes highly significant at the .01 level for a two-tailed test.

Table 8. Communalities among factor loadings results for the creation of the independent-variable factor-based constructs

Variables used to create Independent Variable Constructs	Initial	Extraction
Higher price if seller has better reputation	1.000	0.640
Feedback systems are important	1.000	0.652
Seller concerned with buyer's reputation	1.000	0.812
Buyer concerned with seller's reputation	1.000	0.711
Involvement in an online auction	1.000	0.671
Likelihood to visit eBay	1.000	0.676
Likelihood to visit UBid	1.000	0.698
Likelihood to visit Amazon	1.000	0.712
Likelihood to visit Yahoo	1.000	0.661
Frequency online auction hours per week	1.000	0.618
Security is important when picking a website	1.000	0.568
Read security policies prior to online signature	1.000	0.713
Compare prices, options and features	1.000	0.500
Spend in a year on online auctions (US$)	1.000	0.670
Sold in a year on online auctions (US$)	1.000	0.777
Number of days shop online	1.000	0.625
Check shipping price before bidding	1.000	0.749
Consider shipping price in bidding	1.000	0.716
Pay higher shipping price for higher value	1.000	0.574
Consider selling price before bidding	1.000	0.599
Paid more in auction than fixed price from other website	1.000	0.659
Education level	1.000	0.710
Age level (years)	1.000	0.785
Income level (US$)	1.000	0.810
Time of day shop online	1.000	0.431

Extraction Method: Principal component analysis.

variable, fear of identity theft with online auctions as expected ($t = 6.317$, $p < .001$), suggesting that reputation of both buyers and sellers are important safeguards in dealing with the fear generated from potential identity theft problems while engaging in online auction activities. The other independent variable constructs of Online Auction Usage ($t = 1.734$, $p = 0.084$), Price Factors ($t = 5.027$, $p < .001$), and Demographic Maturity ($t = 1.810$, $p = 0.072$) were found to be at least marginally significantly related to fears of identity theft. The other independent variable constructs of Bidding Preference ($t = 0.155$, $p = 0.877$), Security Factors ($t = 1.646$, $p = 0.101$), Convenience Factors ($t = 0.211$, $p = 0.833$), and Other Factors ($t = 0.344$, $p = 0.731$) were found not to be significantly related to identity theft fears while engaging in online auction activities. Table 11 displays a summary of the hypothesis-testing results associated with both the original testing phase and the exploratory analysis.

Table 9. Total explained variance from data reduction techniques for creation of independent-variable constructs

Part A. Total explained variance.

Factor-based Components	Initial Eigenvalues			Rotation Sums of Squared Loadings		
	Total	% of Variance	Cumulative %	Total	% of Variance	Cumulative %
Reputation and Feedback Features	5.088	20.351	20.351	3.177	12.710	12.710
Online Auction Usage	2.903	11.614	31.965	3.126	12.505	25.215
Price Factors	1.841	7.362	39.327	2.274	9.095	34.310
Bidding Preference	1.715	6.859	46.186	2.068	8.271	42.581
Demographic Maturity	1.482	5.928	52.114	1.726	6.903	49.484
Security Factors	1.338	5.354	57.468	1.531	6.123	55.607
Convenience Factors	1.218	4.873	62.341	1.494	5.976	61.583
Other Factors	1.153	4.614	66.955	1.343	5.372	66.955

Extraction Method: Principal component analysis.

Part B. Rotated component matrix.

Independent Variables	Factor-based Components							
	Reputation and Feedback Features	Online Auction Usage	Price Factors	Bidding Preference	Demographic Maturity	Security Factors	Convenience Factors	Other Factors
Higher price if seller has better reputation	**0.745**	0.069	-0.123	0.045	-0.037	0.245	0.038	0.035
Feedback systems are important	**0.789**	0.063	0.108	0.109	0.030	-0.012	-0.013	0.034
Seller concerned with buyer's reputation	**0.860**	0.184	0.161	-0.051	-0.078	-0.015	0.053	0.028
Buyer concerned with seller's reputation	**0.757**	0.028	0.173	0.291	0.039	-0.074	0.095	-0.078
Involvement in an online auction	0.149	**0.768**	0.091	0.016	-0.135	0.017	0.056	-0.173
Likelihood to visit eBay	0.120	0.133	0.005	**0.789**	0.004	-0.066	0.100	-0.089
Likelihood to visit UBid	0.015	0.307	-0.394	0.136	0.163	0.024	0.183	**0.608**
Likelihood to visit Amazon	0.057	-0.086	0.173	0.116	0.018	0.038	**0.809**	-0.052
Likelihood to visit Yahoo	0.101	0.094	0.003	0.017	-0.007	-0.034	**0.795**	0.091
Frequency online auction hours per week	0.031	**0.707**	-0.107	-0.084	0.079	0.118	0.003	0.280
Security is important when picking a website	**0.564**	-0.116	0.405	0.112	0.132	0.161	0.133	0.002
Read security policies prior to online signature	0.143	-0.039	0.161	-0.243	0.026	**0.766**	0.032	0.132
Compare prices, options and features	0.034	0.313	0.392	0.443	-0.074	0.083	0.173	-0.095

continued on following page

Table 2. Continued

Spend in a year on online auctions (US$)	0.095	**0.619**	0.176	0.354	0.192	-0.283	-0.065	-0.020
Sold in a year on online auctions (US$)	0.011	**0.864**	0.039	0.027	-0.016	0.095	-0.058	-0.130
Time of day shop online	-0.031	0.067	**0.596**	0.039	0.037	-0.112	0.206	-0.112
Number of days shop online	0.046	**0.703**	0.126	0.166	0.203	-0.059	0.068	0.190
Check shipping price before bidding	0.296	0.072	**0.780**	0.162	-0.036	0.114	-0.050	0.076
Consider shipping price in bidding	0.292	0.140	**0.683**	0.251	-0.059	0.192	-0.006	0.202
Pay higher shipping price for higher value	0.286	-0.006	0.149	0.472	-0.024	0.430	-0.186	0.168
Consider selling price before bidding	0.165	-0.028	0.324	**0.668**	0.075	0.065	0.067	0.076
Paid more in auction than fixed price from other website	-0.014	0.122	-0.067	0.339	-0.042	**0.692**	0.003	-0.208
Education level	-0.015	0.086	-0.174	0.095	0.258	0.014	0.037	-0.771
Age level (years)	-0.028	-0.080	0.025	0.009	**0.881**	-0.009	0.035	0.005
Income level (US$)	0.045	0.265	-0.054	0.019	**0.841**	-0.011	-0.030	-0.164

Extraction Method: Principal component analysis, rotation method was Varimax with Kaiser Normalization; rotation converged in 9 iterations.

Part C. Component transformation matrix.

Factor-based Components	Online Reputation	Online Auction Usage	Price Factors	Bidding Preference	Demographic Maturity	Security Factors	Convenience Factors	Other Factors
Reputation and Feedback Features	0.627	0.423	0.448	0.424	0.057	0.157	0.135	0.047
Online Auction Usage	-0.359	0.830	-0.269	0.028	0.278	-0.174	-0.031	-0.025
Price Factors	-0.376	-0.263	0.343	0.457	0.415	-0.265	0.264	-0.389
Bidding Preference	0.501	-0.165	-0.405	-0.200	0.699	-0.090	0.022	-0.142
Demographic Maturity	-0.111	-0.036	0.006	0.231	0.179	0.541	-0.733	-0.267
Security Factors	-0.233	-0.080	-0.191	0.157	0.237	0.650	0.470	0.424
Convenience Factors	-0.141	0.033	0.626	-0.530	0.397	0.011	-0.164	0.349
Other Factors	-0.007	0.166	0.130	-0.461	-0.109	0.390	0.355	-0.673

Extraction Method: Principal component analysis, rotation method was Varimax with Kaiser Normalization.

Table 10. Relevant statistics associated with exploratory testing results. Part A displays the model summary, Part B the overall results, and Part C inspects specific contributions of each component in the hypothesis (Dependent variable: Fear of identity theft with online auctions).

Part A: Model summary.			
R	R Square	Adjusted R Square	Std. Error of the Estimate
0.531	0.282	0.252	0.944

Predictors: (Constant), Reputation and Feedback Features, Online Auction Usage, Price Factors, Bidding Preference, Demographic Maturity, Security Factors, Convenience Factors, and Other Factors.

Part B: ANOVA results.					
Source of Variation	Sum of Squares	df	Mean Square	F-ratio	Significance
Regression	66.315	8	8.289	9.294	<.001 (HS)
Residual	168.574	189	0.892		
Total	234.889	197			

Part C: Coefficients-testing results.

Independent Factor-based Constructs	Un-standardized Coefficients		Standardized Coefficients	t-test	Significance
	B	Std. Error	Beta		
(Constant)	3.556	0.067		52.976	>.001
Reputation and Feedback Features	0.425	0.067	0.389	6.317	<.001 (HS)
Online Auction Usage	0.117	0.067	0.107	1.734	0.084 (MS)
Price Factors	0.338	0.067	0.310	5.027	0.000 (HS)
Bidding Preference	0.010	0.067	0.010	0.155	0.877 (NS)
Demographic Maturity	0.122	0.067	0.112	1.810	0.072 (MS)
Security Factors	0.111	0.067	0.101	1.646	0.101 (NS)
Convenience Factors	0.014	0.067	0.013	0.211	0.833 (NS)
Other Factors	0.023	0.067	0.021	0.344	0.731 (NS)

Dependent Variable: Fear of identity theft with online auctions. NS denotes not statistically significant at the .05 level for a two-tailed test, MS denotes marginally statistical significant at the .05 level for a two-tailed test, HS denotes highly significant at the .01 level for a two-tailed test.

GENERAL CONCLUSION AND IMPLICATIONS

Basic Summary

After reviewing the results of the present study, it was quite evident that many people use online trading websites for price and convenience based on the accuracy of good measures of reputation through feedback systems. Simultaneously, customers, especially working professional in the current economic downturn, have many concerns regarding security and fraud safeguards, with identity theft ranked highest among those most concerned issue among those engaged with online trading activities. All specific research hypotheses were found to be highly significant. Buyers, especially working professionals that find the feedback systems important, are more willing to engage in online trading activities and more willing to pay a higher price for merchandise being sold by a seller with a better reputation, regardless

Figure 8. Cross-tabulation of fear of identity theft conducting online auctions with selected variables: Gender

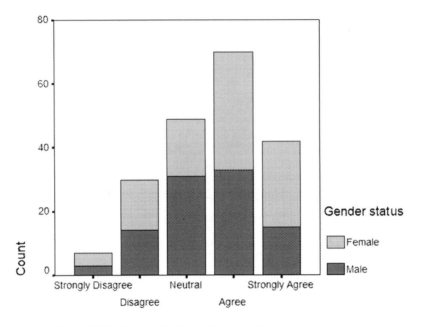

Fear of identity theft with online auctions

Figure 7. Cross-tabulation of fear of identity theft conducting online auctions with selected variables: Method of payment

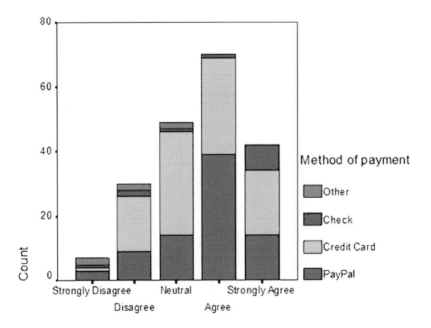

Fear of identity theft with online auctions

*For a more accurate representation see the electronic version.

Table 11. Summary of hypothesis-testing results associated with the exploratory analysis

Hypothesis Number	Description Of Hypothesis	Present Study's Results
H1	Buyers, especially working professionals, that find the feedback systems important are willing to engage in online trading activities and may be willing to pay a higher price for merchandise being sold by a seller with a better reputation, regardless of gender.	HS, accepted (expected)
H2	Customers, especially working professionals, are concerned with selling price as well as shipping cost or total price, regardless of gender.	HS, accepted (expected)
H3	In terms of the convenience of payment method, electronic forms are preferred by working professionals in transacting online trading activities, regardless of age and gender.	HS, accepted (expected)
H4	In terms of exploratory research, there will be a significant predictive relationship between the dependent variable, fear of identity theft with online auctions, with the factor score-based independent construct of Reputation and Feedback Features, a perceived measure of employment experience and knowledge.	HS, accepted (expected)
H5	In terms of exploratory research, there will be a significant predictive relationship between the dependent variable, fear of identity theft with online auctions, with the factor score-based independent construct of Online Auction Usage, a perceived measure of economic support, especially employer-based.	MS, rejected (expected)
H6	In terms of exploratory research, there will be a significant predictive relationship between the dependent variable, fear of identity theft with online auctions, with the factor score-based independent construct of Price Factors, a perceived measure of job experience and respect for education and its affects on employee confidence.	HS, accepted (expected)
H7	In terms of exploratory research, there will be a significant predictive relationship between the dependent variable, fear of identity theft with online auctions, with the factor score-based independent construct of Bidding Preference, a perceived measure of the importance of pursuing educational and/or training opportunities for enhanced economic security and stability on employee confidence.	NS, rejected (expected)
H8	In terms of exploratory research, there will be a significant predictive relationship between the dependent variable, fear of identity theft with online auctions, with the factor score-based independent construct of Demographic Maturity, a perceived measure of job experience and respect for education and its affects on employee confidence.	MS, rejected (expected)
H9	In terms of exploratory research, there will be a significant predictive relationship between the dependent variable, fear of identity theft with online auctions, with the factor score-based independent constructs of Security Factors, a perceived measure of current job satisfaction and employee confidence.	NS, rejected (not expected)
H10	In terms of exploratory research, there will be a significant predictive relationship between the dependent variable, fear of identity theft with online auctions, with the factor score-based independent construct of Convenience Factors, a perceived measure of job experience and respect for education and its affects on employee confidence.	NS, rejected (not expected)
H11	In terms of exploratory research, there will be a significant predictive relationship between the dependent variable, fear of identity theft with online auctions, with the factor score-based independent constructs of Other Factors, a perceived measure of current job satisfaction and employee confidence.	NS, rejected (expected)

NS denotes not statistically significant at the .05 level for a two-tailed test, MS denotes marginally statistical significant at the .05 level for a two-tailed test, S denotes significant at the .05 level for a two-tailed test, HS denotes highly significant at the .01 level for a two-tailed test.

of gender. Customers, especially working professionals, are concerned with the total price, including shipping cost, regardless of gender. Finally, in terms of the convenience of payment method, electronic forms are preferred by working professionals in transacting online trading activities, regardless of age and gender. Interestingly, those with a bachelor's degree rank importance of security the highest out of all levels of the sample of professional workers. This demonstrates that identity theft is a serious concern with online auctioning and it is important for websites to have proper policies and procedures in place to prevent computer crimes. Risk of security breaches in online auctions can be greatly reduced if proper procedures are followed by the user to protect themselves.

Managerial Implications

Presently, there is little doubt that the global economy is in the midst of a total transformation in the management of information flows in the decision-making process for both consumers and businesses. The management of both manufacturing and services that strategically leverages its information technologies of IT is all about linking the various strategic components that add value as defined by its end users. Overall, management must link products to orders and orders to shipments and shipments to payments through proper supply chain management, which has strongly been demonstrated by the OASP industry. The use of the web-enabled and automatic identification and data capture (AIDC)-related systems serve as foundation for management of data flows for strategic purposes and basic transactions that both cause transactions and result from these informational and material flows. OASP industry is characterized by significant strategic efforts concerning customer relations and technological innovations, which points executives toward developing a sustainable competitive advantage. A classic short article by Colvin (1997) lays out his argument that information technology (IT) has revolutionized most industries to the point that what was originally considered an impenetrable advantage is no longer.

Capabilities such as delivery speed, reliability, responsiveness and low-cost distribution are considered critical components for sustained competitive advantage. But Ponomarov and Holcomb (2009) viewed that logistics capability qualifies to be a distinct capability, leading to sustainable competitive advantage, by reviewing characteristics such as added value, rarity and difficulty for imitating. Improving efficiency and effectiveness within a firm, especially in logistics, BDA, PSM, and SCM should lead to long-term profitability and survival in B2B transactions and online trading activities. Such strategic initiative should lead to supply chain resilience, which is a concept that is hard to define and, perhaps, harder to implement. While there are complex features of supply resilience, some successfully practitioners do not agree with that such concepts are not so difficult to understand. They frequently fault that academic scholarly researcher that never really had to manage supply chains, as more routine activities are increasingly becoming more automated and routine. Such strategies can be simply being applied to a B2B transactions in order to increase effectiveness and efficiency. True, a general understanding of supply resiliency can allow managers at a firm to begin to think about different types of situations that can happen and what their plan is to recover from the event, but is it really something new or just a rehash of concepts that is not unique to SCM? What capabilities must management really have an understanding of in order to gain a better understanding of resiliency? Is not adapt or die equally true for all businesses?

Hence, as evident from the empirical section, the future of competitive advantage in the OASP industry is found within people, not machines or processes. As demonstrated by Looyestyn, et al., (2017), Kennedy and Widener (2008), Scherrer-Rathje, Boyle, and Deflorin (2009). Shah, Chandrasekaran, and Linderman (2008), and Sprovieri (2008), there is a fallacy of relying solely on modern production techniques, IT-embedded and big data systems, and incremental process improvements as distinguishing factors for a firm. Since essentially all competitive firms are developing these operational features, such advances cannot be considered to be strategically unique or defendable. Rather, it is intangibles, such as trust and trustworthiness that differentiates the various competitors in the OASP industry. Management should consider the source of future competitive advantage to be somehow contained within the uniqueness within each company, or the ideas and skills their people have, as well as the culture and how it contributes to innovation and service.

Directions for Future Research

As there are numerous literature sources and articles are written about the requirements of nimbleness and quick reaction for modern companies, IT and related technologies have had an enormous impact on this newer marketplace dynamic. The sheer speed and volume of information available for consumers and businesses has had a huge influence on business practices. As customers are web-empowered, comparison-shopping goes beyond mere pricing structures. When innovations are found or patent filed for, the information is readily available for almost anyone who wants it. Fernie and Azuma (2004) suggested that e-businesses need to develop a quick response approach (QR) or model helps the supply chain become more efficient, via by applying an industry standard in information technologies and contractual procedures. This not only enhances one firms supply chain, but this makes supply chains in the entire industry much more efficient. This forces supply chain partners to have a collaborative relationship and makes supply chains more efficient and less expensive. A QR system would be very approach for OASPs and should be a future direction for more research. Hence, providing almost limitless access to data and information that has made a huge impact on how quickly companies now need to react and IT-related technologies are at the core of this changing marketplace dynamic on online actions.

Online trading websites must couple their technology initiatives with sound customer friendly strategies that are designed to alleviate fears of identity theft through proper protection of personal and financial information through related software. These systems provide not only a direct contact between the organization and its customers, but present an opportunity for innovation in both the delivery and selling of these products and services online. It would be interesting to see how companies grow internally with BDA, PSM, and SCM usage in a more detailed and understood study. If a major firm has not adopted these practices uncovered in the empirical portion of the present study, one can only wonder how quickly and rapidly they could grow and increase organizational effectiveness if they did adapt to such processes and usages. This chapter included a number of different studies to show how these processes can directly/indirectly influence the organizational performance in comparison to how they performed if they access to the various metrics outlined and actually tested.

ACKNOWLEDGMENT

I want to thank most heartedly for the valuable contributions by the reviewers for their input into the final paper. Peer reviewing and editing are commonly tedious and thankless tasks.

REFERENCES

Adams, D. A., Nelson, R. R., & Todd, P. A. (1992). Perceived usefulness, ease of use, and usage of information technology: A replication. *Management Information Systems Quarterly*, *16*(2), 227–247. doi:10.2307/249577

Anton, J., & Petouhoff, N. (2002). *Customer Relations Management: The Bottom Line to Optimizing Your ROI*. Prentice Hall.

Armes, D. (2006). Online auctions prove their staying power. *Strategic Direction*, *22*(7), 6–7. doi:10.1108/02580540610669008

Ba, S., & Pavlou, P. A. (2002). Evidence of the effect of trust building technology in electronic markets: Price premiums and buyer behavior. *Management Information Systems Quarterly*, *26*(3), 243–268. doi:10.2307/4132332

Bishop, C. M. (1995). *Neural Networks for Pattern Recognition*. Oxford, UK: Oxford University Press.

Bland, E., & Barrett, R. T. (2006). A measure of the factors impacting the effectiveness and efficiency of eBay in the supply chain of online firms. *The Costal Business Journal, 18*(2), 1–15.

Bolton, G. E., Katok, E., & Ockenfels, A. (2004). Trust among Internet traders: A behavioral economics approach. *Analyse & Kritik, 26*(1), 185–202. doi:10.1515/auk-2004-0110

Boyd, J. (2002). In community we trust: Online security communication at eBay. *Purdue University, 25*(1), 1-25.

Bruner, G. C. II, & Kumar, A. (2005). Explaining consumer acceptance of handheld internet devices. *Journal of Business Research, 58*(5), 553–558. doi:10.1016/j.jbusres.2003.08.002

Buhr, S. (2014). *An e-commerce site where you can haggle down the price*. Retrieved October 7, 2017 from https://techcrunch.com/2014/07/04/an-ecommerce-site-where-you-can-negotiate-the-price-you-want-to-pay/

Burton-Jones, A., & Hubona, G. S. (2005). Individual differences and usage behavior: Revisiting a technology acceptance model assumption. *The Data Base for Advances in Information Systems, 36*(2), 58–77. doi:10.1145/1066149.1066155

Chau, P. Y. K. (1996). An empirical assessment of a modified technology acceptance model. *Journal of Management Information Systems, 13*(2), 185–204. doi:10.1080/07421222.1996.11518128

Chen, D. Q., Preston, D. S., & Swink, M. (2015). How the use of big data analytics affects value creation in supply chain management. *Journal of Management Information Systems, 32*(4), 4–39. doi:10.1080/07421222.2015.1138364

Colvin, G. (1997). The changing art of becoming unbeatable. *Fortune, 136*(10), 299–300.

Cumming, S. (1993). Neural networks for monitoring of engine condition data. *Neural Computing & Applications, 1*(1), 96–102. doi:10.1007/BF01411378

Dholakia, U. M. (2004). The usefulness of bidders' reputation ratings to sellers in online auctions. *Journal of Interactive Marketing, 19*(1), 31–40. doi:10.1002/dir.20029

Dholakia, U. M., & Simonson, I. (2005). The effect of explicit reference points on consumer choice and online bidding behavior. *Marketing Science, 24*(2), 206–217. doi:10.1287/mksc.1040.0099

eBay's bid to win back buyers. (2007). *BusinessWeek*. Retrieved October 7, 2017 from http://www.businessweek.com/print/technology/content/sep2007/tc20070917_75070.htm

Emiliani, M. L. (2000). Business-to-business online auctions: Key issues for purchasing process improvement. *Supply Chain Management, 5*(4), 176–193. doi:10.1108/13598540010347299

Fernie, J., & Azuma, N. (2004). The changing nature of Japanese fashion – Can quick response improve supply chain efficiency? *European Journal of Marketing, 38*(7), 790–808. doi:10.1108/03090560410539258

Gaylord, C. (2007). Why we do what we do on eBay. *The Christian Science Monitor,* 13-14. Retrieved October 7, 2017 from http://www.csmonitor.com/2007/0716/p13s02-wmgn.html

Great tools to help eBay sellers; expert recommends five tools to determine what items to sell on eBay. (2007). *PS Newswire.* Retrieved October 7, 2017 from http://reddog.rmu.edu:2079/pqdweb?index=1& did=1195547291&SrchMode=1&sid=6&Fmt=3&VInst=PROD&VType=PQD&RQT=309&VNam e=PQD&TS=1193760199&clientId=2138

Hansen, J. M., & Levin, M. A. (2010). Retail e-learning assessment: Motivation, location, and prior experience. *International Journal of Retail & Distribution Management,* *38*(10), 789–805. doi:10.1108/09590551011076551

Hu, G., Wang, L., Fetch, S., & Bidanda, B. (2008). A multi-objective model for project portfolio selection to implement lean and Six Sigma concepts. *International Journal of Production Research,* *46*(23), 6611–6648. doi:10.1080/00207540802230363

Huang, X., Radkowski, P., & Roman, P. (2007). Computer crimes. *The American Criminal Law Review,* *44*(2), 285–335.

Hwang, K. M., & Lee, S. J. (2016). How does electronic data interchange (EDI) affect the competitiveness of a firm's supply chain management? *Journal of Marketing Thought,* *3*(2), 13–18.

Jain, V., Benyoucef, L., & Deshmukh, S. G. (2008). What's the buzz about moving from 'lean' to 'agile' integrated supply chains? A fuzzy intelligent agent-based approach. *International Journal of Production Research,* *46*(23), 6649–6678. doi:10.1080/00207540802230462

Kennedy, F. A., & Widener, S. K. (2008). A control framework: Insights from evidence on lean accounting. *Management Accounting Research,* *19*(4), 301–319. doi:10.1016/j.mar.2008.01.001

Lansing, P., & Hubbard, J. (2002). Online auctions: The need for alternative dispute resolution. *American Business Review,* *20*(1), 108–115.

Li, H., Ward, R., & Zhang, H. (2007). Risk, convenience, cost and online payment choice: a study of eBay transactions. *Commerce Center od DuPree College of Management,* *8*(4), 1-36.

Lin, L., & Daim, T. U. (2005). Platform strategy framework for Internet-based service development: Case of eBay. *International Journal of Services Technology and Management,* *11*(4), 334–354. doi:10.1504/ IJSTM.2009.024565

Looyestyn, J., Kernot, J., Boshoff, K., Ryan, J., Edney, S., & Maher, C. (2017). Does gamification increase engagement with online programs? A systematic review. *PLoS One,* *12*(3), 1–19. doi:10.1371/ journal.pone.0173403 PMID:28362821

Martinez-Caro, E., & Cegarra-Navarro, J. G. (2009). The impact of e-business on capital productivity. *International Journal of Operations & Production Management,* *30*(5), 488–507. doi:10.1108/01443571011039597

Mateen, A., & More, D. (2013). Applying TOC thinking process tools in managing challenges of supply chain finance: A case study. *International Journal of Services and Operations Management,* *15*(4), 389–410. doi:10.1504/IJSOM.2013.054882

McPherson, K. (2007). Using eBay as a collection development tool. *Teacher Librarian, 34*(5), 71–73.

Melnik, M. (2005). *Seller reputation, information signals, and prices for heterogeneous coins on eBay.* Retrieved October 7, 2017 from http://reddog.rmu.edu:2079/pqdweb?index=34&did=911359041&SrchMode=1&sid=2&Fmt=3&VInst=PROD&VType=PQD&RQT=309&VName=PQD&TS=1193075203&clientId=2138

Melnik, M. I., & Alm, J. (2005). Seller reputation, information signals, and prices for heterogeneous coins on eBay. *Southern Economic Journal, 72*(2), 305–315. doi:10.2307/20062113

Melnyk, S. A., Davis, E. W., Spekman, R. E., & Sandor, J. (2010). Outcome-driven supply chains. *MIT Sloan Management Review, 51*(2), 3833–3851.

Nobari, A., Khierkhah, A. S., & Hajipour, V. (2018). A Pareto-based approach to optimise aggregate production planning problem considering reliable supplier selection. *International Journal of Services and Operations Management, 29*(1), 59–84. doi:10.1504/IJSOM.2018.088473

Novak, T. P., Hoffman, D. L., & Yung, Y. F. (2000). Measuring the customer experience in on-line environment: A structural modeling approach. *Marketing Science, 19*(1), 22–42. doi:10.1287/mksc.19.1.22.15184

Oja, E. (1989). Neural networks, principal components, and subspaces. *International Journal of Neural Systems, 1*(1), 61–68. doi:10.1142/S0129065789000475

Online price negotiation: How Automation is driving conversion. (2017). Retrieved October 7, 2017 from https://www.pricewaiter.com/2017/03/online-price-negotiation-automation-driving-conversion/

Park, B.-N., & Min, H. (2013). Global supply chain barriers of foreign subsidiaries: The case of Korean expatriate manufacturers in China. *International Journal of Services and Operations Management, 15*(1), 67–78. doi:10.1504/IJSOM.2013.050562

Pathak, J. (2003). Assurance and e-auctions: Are the existing business models still relevant? *Managerial Auditing Journal, 18*(4), 292–294. doi:10.1108/02686900310474307

Ponomarov, S. Y., & Holcomb, M. C. (2009). Understanding the concept of supply chain resilience. *International Journal of Logistics Management, 20*(1), 124–143. doi:10.1108/09574090910954873

Potter, J. A., & Smith, A. D. (2010). Performance appraisals and the strategic development of the professional intellect within non-profits. *International Journal of Management Education, 3*(2), 188–203.

Prasad, N., Bryan, D., & Reeves, D. (2007). Pennies from eBay: The determinants of price in online auctions. *The Journal of Industrial Economics, 25*(2), 223–233.

Rajapakshe, T., Dawande, M., & Sriskandarajah, C. (2013). On the trade-off between remanufacturing and recycling. *International Journal of Services and Operations Management, 15*(1), 1–53. doi:10.1504/IJSOM.2013.050560

Roman, S. (2007). The ethics of online retailing: A scale development and validation from the consumers' perspective. *Journal of Business Ethics, 72*(2), 131–148. doi:10.100710551-006-9161-y

Scherrer-Rathje, M., Boyle, T. A., & Deflorin, P. (2009). Lean, take two! Reflections from the second attempt at lean implementation. *Business Horizons, 52*(1), 79–85. doi:10.1016/j.bushor.2008.08.004

Shah, R., Chandrasekaran, A., & Linderman, K. (2008). In pursuit of implementation patterns: The context of Lean and Six Sigma. *International Journal of Production Research, 46*(23), 6679–6698. doi:10.1080/00207540802230504

Smith, A. A., Synowka, D. P., & Smith, A. D. (2010). Exploring fantasy sports and its fan base from a CRM perspective. *International Journal of Business Innovation and Research, 4*(1-2), 103–142. doi:10.1504/IJBIR.2010.029543

Smith, A. D. (2002). Loyalty and e-marketing issues: Customer retention on the Web. *Quarterly Journal of E-commerce, 3*(2), 149–161.

Smith, A. D. (2005). Accountability in EDI systems to prevent employee fraud. *Information Systems Management, 22*(2), 30–38. doi:10.1201/1078/45099.22.2.20050301/87275.4

Smith, A. D. (2006). Supply chain management using electronic reverse auction: A multi-firm case study. *International Journal of Services and Standards, 2*(2), 176–189. doi:10.1504/IJSS.2006.008731

Smith, A. D. (2009a). The impact of e-procurement systems on customer relationship management: A multiple case study. *International Journal of Procurement Management, 2*(3), 314–338. doi:10.1504/IJPM.2009.024814

Smith, A. D. (2009b). Leveraging concepts of knowledge management with total quality management: Case studies in the service sector. *International Journal of Logistics Systems and Supply Management, 5*(6), 631–653. doi:10.1504/IJLSM.2009.024795

Smith, A. D. (2010). Retail-based loyalty card programs and CRM concepts: An empirical study. *International Journal of Innovation and Learning, 7*(3), 303–330. doi:10.1504/IJIL.2010.031949

Smith, A. D., & Lias, A. R. (2005). Identity theft and e-fraud as critical CRM concerns. *International Journal of Enterprise Information Systems, 1*(2), 17–36. doi:10.4018/jeis.2005040102

Smith, A. D., & Potter, J. A. (2010). Loyalty card programs, customer relationships, and information technology: An exploratory approach. *International Journal of Business Innovation and Research, 4*(1-2), 65–92. doi:10.1504/IJBIR.2010.029541

Snijders, C., & Zijdeman, R. (2004). Reputation and Internet auctions: eBay and beyond. *Analyse & Kritik, 26*(1), 158–184. doi:10.1515/auk-2004-0109

Sprovieri, J. (2008). A Modest Increase. *Assembly, 51*(13), 22–41.

Summers, G. J., & Scherpereel, C. M. (2008). Decision making in product development: Are you outside-in or inside-out? *Management Decision, 46*(9), 1299–1314. doi:10.1108/00251740810911957

Van Weele, A., & van Raaij, E. (2005). The future of purchasing and supply management research: About relevance and rigor. *The Journal of Supply Chain Management, 50*(1), 56–72. doi:10.1111/jscm.12042

Vinodh, S., Sundararaj, G., Devadasan, S. R., Maharaja, R., Rajanayagam, D., & Goyal, S. K. (2008). DESSAC: A decision support system for quantifying and analyzing agility. *International Journal of Production Research*, *46*(23), 6759–6678. doi:10.1080/00207540802230439

Zaczkiewicz, A. (2017). *Amazon, Wal-Mart and Apple top list of biggest e-commerce retailers*. Retrieved October 4, 2017 from http://wwd.com/business-news/business-features/amazon-wal-mart-apple-biggest-e-commerce-retailers-10862796/

Chapter 11
Culture and Internet Banking Technology:
Long-Term Orientation Over the Acceptance

Leelien Ken Huang
Feng Chia University, Taiwan

ABSTRACT

The interaction between the cultural value of long-term orientation and internet banking technology acceptance is examined. A survey involving a total of 376 potential users was conducted in an internet banking setting in Taiwan. The results confirm previous TAM findings that both efficacy and belief variables have significantly positive direct and in-direct effects on the usage, but under the cultural influence of long-term orientation, users remain hesitant to accept internet banking technology because they are more concerned with face-to-face long-term bank relationships to ensure future gratification than with current social status influence to obtain immediate benefits (e.g., convenience). Practitioners may refer this cultural influence on users' behavior in Fin-tech development. The implications of the study are discussed.

BACKGROUND

Despite the benefits of internet banking, its use is controversial because of varying customer perceptions of fund management through branch counters or ATMs (and other electronic devices, such as mobile phones, laptops, and PCs) services, the convenience or inconvenience of banking hours, security risks and privacy issues, technology comprehension issues, and Internet problems (Callaway, 2011; Chuang & Hu, 2012; Chaudhury, Mallick, & Rao, 2001; Proenca, Silva, & Fernandes, 2010). Our primary concern involves the intention of users to conduct financial transactions on a bank's website, as this capability continues to be a fundamental and important issue in promoting internet banking services.

DOI: 10.4018/978-1-5225-7214-5.ch011

Although the TAM can be used in a variety of adoption contexts, prior research indicates that the TAM may not be applicable to all cultures (McCoy, Everard, & Jones, 2005; Wu, 2006). Chinese culture, for example, has often been recognized as differing significantly from Western culture (Ferraro, 2002; Hofstede, 2001). Technology adoption behaviour in the Chinese setting could differ from Western empirical findings for the TAM. It is thus worthwhile to consider cultural issues when studying internet banking technology acceptance in the Chinese context of Taiwan.

Because bank services are often rendered through interactions between customers and bank employees, our cultural research on the TAM focuses primarily on the role of interpersonal relationships in influencing internet banking technology acceptance. Long-term orientation has been viewed as a key cultural factor for such social interactions (Ryu & Kim, 2010), and such an orientation values future interpersonal relationships (Hofstede, 1991; Shore, 2001). This perspective is used to test the effects on the internet banking adoption, which includes "subjective norms" and "computer self-efficacy" as antecedents, to confirm the validity of our cultural influence on internet banking technology acceptance.

Our research objective is to explore how the cultural influence of long-term orientation moderates the effect of the TAM on users' intention to accept internet banking as they consider the appropriateness, timing, and effectiveness of personal financial services. We contribute to identifying the critical role of long-term social relationships in a new model combining the Western TAM and the Chinese culture of long-term orientation in Taiwan, which has not been thoroughly explored in previous work. We also bring the Government attention to the possible long-term orientation's impact on users' acceptance of those hotly debated advanced Fin-tech services since 2016 in Taiwan. This paper is organized as follows. The next section presents the research concept. The research method and data analysis are then presented. Discussions, implications and limitations for both researchers and practitioners are then presented, followed by a discussion of the conclusions of the study.

RESEARCH CONCEPT

Technology Acceptance Model

Based on Ajzen and Fishbein's (1980) theory of reasoned action (TRA), the TAM finalizes two primary psychological states of individual user perceptions, "usefulness" and "ease of use", which affect individuals' beliefs about and attitudes towards technology and in turn determines their behavioural intentions to adopt that technology (Bagozzi, Davis, & Warshaw, 1992; Davis, 1989, 1993).

In past decades, the TAM has been shown to be a more robust model than TRA in predicting the adoption of different technologies under various contexts in terms of their validity, generality, and wide application (King & He, 2006; Lee, Kozar, & Larsen, 2003; Ojha, Sahu, & Gupta, 2009; Venkatesh & Davis, 2000). To alleviate criticism of limited predictivity, the TAM has been extended to TAM 2 by adding antecedents such as a social influence variable (e.g., subjective norms) to improve the specificity and explanatory utility of the model (Venkatesh & Davis, 2000). These antecedents, which have been tested in both voluntary and mandatory settings, have a strong TAM-supported effect (direct or indirect) on perceived usefulness (Chan & Lu, 2004; Venkatesh & Davis, 2000). However, the literature argues that the social influence antecedent of perceived usefulness may affect perceived ease of use via a crossover effect (Venkatesh & Bala, 2008).

To avoid such an effect, antecedents such as computer self-efficacy (e.g., Yu, Li, & Gangnon, 2009) with respect to perceived ease of use are added and combined with TAM 2 to form TAM 3 (Venkatesh, 2000; Venkatesh & Bala, 2008). TAM 3 is believed to reduce the mutual influence of the interaction between perceived usefulness and perceived ease of use because the former is considered an extrinsic variable (i.e., the instrumental belief of an individual), and the latter is considered an intrinsic variable (i.e., the emotion of an individual) (Venkatesh & Bala, 2008).

Long-Term Orientation

Long-term orientation tends to be strong when it reflects a more dynamic and future-oriented view (Hofstede, 1991; Hofstede & Bond, 1988; Wong, 2005). However, the other extreme tends to be weak when it reflects a more static and past-oriented (and/or present-oriented) view (Hofstede, 1994, 2001; Hofstede & Bond, 1988). Long-term orientation is the fifth cultural value of Hofstede's model, and it is the most influential bridge to span the chasm between cultural behaviour and the workplace (Hofstede, 1991, 2001).

To avoid bias resulting from the different thinking between the Chinese and Western contexts and resulting from the tendency of cultural questionnaires to be designed for the Western context (Wu, 2006), the construct of long-term orientation is specifically developed and surveyed in the study of Chinese Culture Connection (1987) using Chinese value questionnaires across 22 countries (later extended to 93 countries [Minkov, 2007]). Most findings are similar to Hofstede's (1980) original four IBM work-related cultural dimensions of power distance, uncertainty avoidance, individualism, and masculinity. However, the results indicate an additional dimension called Confucian dynamism.

Confucian dynamism was subsequently renamed long-term orientation because the unclear and sometimes contradictory nature of Confucian characteristics such as perseverance (in the long term) and respect for tradition (in the short term) can cause confusion (Bearden, Money, & Nevins, 2006; Fang, 2003; Hofstede, 2001). The construct of long-term orientation more clearly focuses on a time-oriented concept that emphasizes a long-term "future-oriented" perspective versus a short-term "past-oriented (and/or present-oriented)" perspective on life and work (Bearden et al., 2006; Ryu, Park, & Min, 2007; Salam, 2011).

With such a time concept, the key characteristics of the long-term "future-oriented" perspective are "schedules not taken seriously", "time is a friend and plentiful", and "long-term social relationships are important" (representing a high score). By contrast, the key characteristics of the short-term "past-oriented (and/or present-oriented)" perspective are "schedules taken very seriously", "time is money and scarce", and "short-term relationships are important" (representing a low score) (Ferraro, 2002). Countries in the Chinese context tend to score high on this construct, indicating a long-term orientation (e.g., 87 for Taiwan, 96 for Hong Kong, 118 for China; Low=1, High=120), whereas Western countries tend to score low, indicating a more short-term orientation (e.g., 29 for USA, 23 for Canada) (Hofstede, 2001).

The Research Model and Hypotheses

Our research adds the cultural value of long-term orientation to the TAM research model in the Chinese context of Taiwan. We believe that our research contributes significantly to the TAM literature. As shown in Figure 1, the research model shows that the use of internet banking services may be treated as a valuable extended market and/or social relationship (e.g., duration, continuity, quality) between users and

Figure 1. The research model

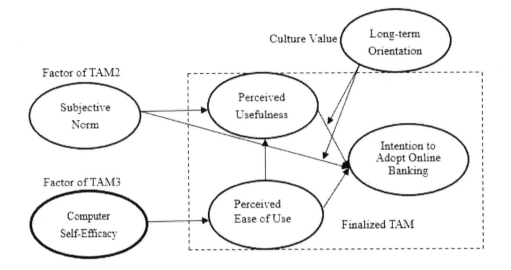

banks (Proenca & Silva, 2005). However, given the possible cultural difference from Western adoption behaviour, the Chinese value of long-term orientation may play a moderating role in users' intentions to accept internet banking, contingent on maintaining that relationship.

In the model, we use the social status influence variable subjective norms that has been adapted from TAM 2. This variable is well researched and is likely to be influenced by culture (McCoy et al., 2005). We propose that subjective norms determine users' belief construct of perceived usefulness and in turn affects their behavioural intention to accept internet banking technology. We further propose that subjective norms directly predict the intention to accept. As noted, the cultural value of long-term orientation reflects one's social interactions (Ryu & Kim, 2010). Given the social status influence of subjective norms on perceived usefulness, we are primarily concerned with how the importance of such social interactions (i.e., long-term social relationships) influences the intention to accept in Taiwan, which has a high degree of long-term orientation (a score of 87, as noted).

We further adapt computer self-efficacy from TAM 3 for the model because the use of online banking for personal financial services requires a certain degree of computer literacy (Chan & Lu, 2004). This adaptation avoids the potential mutual influence between perceived usefulness and perceived ease of use. We propose that computer self-efficacy determines the extent to which customers perceive the ease of using online banking and in turn affects the level of perceived usefulness and intention to accept.

Although the model is parsimonious, the inclusion of antecedents of subjective norms and computer self-efficacy, which respectively affect customers' extrinsic motivation of perceived usefulness and intrinsic motivation of perceived ease of use, avoids the previously criticized weaknesses of the TAM in lacking external forces. That is, with both subjective norms and computer self-efficacy, we test the extended TAM to assure its validity, as evidenced in the literature. Examining the moderating effect of long-term orientation also increases validity (external). Three groups of hypothesized relationships are formulated in the followings.

Subjective Norms and Perceived Usefulness

A subjective norm refers to one's perceived social pressure to engage in a behaviour, which was initially included in the TRA (Ajzen, 1991). This pressure often comes from significant people in an individual's life who think that s/he should accept a new technology (Ajzen & Fishbein, 1980; Venkatesh & Davis, 2000). Perceived usefulness refers to one's perception that using a particular technology would enhance his or her job performance or assist in achieving a certain goal (Davis, 1989). Although subjective norms did not significantly predict perceived usefulness in early TAM studies (e.g., Davis, 1989; Davis, Bagozzi, & Warshaw, 1989), subsequent studies indicated a significantly positive relationship between them (e.g., Thompson, Higgins, & Howell, 1991; Venkatesh & Davis, 2000).

Several recent TAM studies have found a significant positive effect of subjective norms on perceived usefulness (e.g., Chen, Chen, & Chen, 2009; Lee, 2006). A significant direct positive effect of subjective norms on the intention to accept has also been found (e.g., Yang & Zhou, 2011). Other empirical works on the TAM have found that subjective norms have a significant indirect positive effect on the intention to accept through perceived usefulness (e.g., Chi, Yeh, & Yang, 2011; Jones, McCarthy, & Halawi, 2010; McCoy et al., 2005). These results generally demonstrate that when one seeks to achieve a certain purpose, his/her belief in the usefulness of technology acceptance depends on the suggestion of an important person from his/her workplace (e.g., superior/senior colleague), friends, family members (e.g., wife), and others.

Given the setting of Taiwan in the Chinese context, which emphasizes the influence of social status (Hofstede, 2001), we assume that the effects of subjective norms are also evident in Taiwan. We believe that if superior/senior colleagues and important friends and/or family members suggest that a particular banking system might be useful, then a person will likely believe that the system would actually be useful for his/her own personal financial services and in turn accept this tool. Therefore, we propose the first two hypotheses:

Hypothesis 1: Subjective norms positively influence the perceived usefulness of internet banking in Taiwan.

Hypothesis 2: Subjective norms have (a) direct and (b) indirect positive influences on users' intention to accept internet banking in Taiwan.

Computer Self-Efficacy, Perceived Ease of Use, and Perceived Usefulness

Initially used in social psychology, the term "self-efficacy" indicates one's belief in his or her own ability to perform a particular task (Bandura, 1977). Accordingly, Compeau and Higgins (1995) define computer self-efficacy as one's judgement of his or her own capability to use a computer. Computer self-efficacy generally depends on one's weighting, integration, and evaluation of complex cognitive, linguistic, social, and enactive experiences in using a computer (Chan & Lu, 2004). Computer self-efficacy reflects not only one's confidence level required to complete a computing task but also the level expected to support a broader task (Compeau & Higgins, 1995). In a sense, people with strong computer self-efficacy may judge themselves as capable of performing a computer-related task or completing a non-computing task using different software packages and/or systems (Compeau & Higgins, 1995).

Perceived ease of use refers to one's perception that a particular technology is easy to understand and use (Davis, 1989). The literature has identified that computer self-efficacy is a key antecedent to determining perceived ease of use, and in turn, it directly and/or indirectly increases adoption intention through perceived usefulness (e.g., Chan & Lu, 2004; Venkastesh, 2000; Venkatesh & Bala, 2008; Venkatesh & Davis, 1996; Yu et al., 2009). With this support, we can plausibly assume that users with higher levels of computer self-efficacy may not be limited by the knowledge of various software packages and systems required for internet banking technology and may thus evaluate the technology as easy to understand and eventually use it. We believe that this assumption is also applicable in Taiwan because computer competence is viewed as one's fundamental motivation for using computer-based technology (Burkhardt & Brass, 1990; Compeau & Higgins, 1995). We also expect that perceived ease of use may predict the usefulness of internet banking (Chan & Lu, 2004). Therefore, three additional hypotheses are proposed:

Hypothesis 3: Computer self-efficacy positively influences users' perceived ease of use of internet banking in Taiwan.

Hypothesis 4: Computer self-efficacy positively influences users' intention to adopt internet banking based on perceived ease of use in Taiwan.

Hypothesis 5: Perceived ease of use positively influences users' perceptions of the usefulness of internet banking in Taiwan.

Long-Term Orientation and TAM

People in a country that score higher on long-term orientation generally tend to be more future oriented and expect to have plenty of time to socialize because they are capable of multitasking. Such individuals emphasize building and maintaining interpersonal relationships through continuous (long-term) social interactions (Yeung & Tung, 1996). They have a high level of perseverance in the achievement of goals and emphasize the importance of long-term persistence to compensate for current efforts (Ryu & Kim, 2010). Nevertheless, people in a country that score lower in this dimension pay close attention to both the past and the present, as noted (i.e., they are short term oriented), and they treat social interactions as isolated occurrences (Ferraro, 2002; Ryu & Moon, 2009). These individuals believe that the present can control the future, and they consequently emphasize gains in the immediate future rather than rewards in the distant future (Ferraro, 2002).

As such, people from strongly long-term-oriented countries generally engage in activities not for immediate rewards but for the potentially greater benefits realized later. These individuals tend to conduct tasks synchronically and loosely because time is plentiful. In a sense, social relationships are more valued than the maintenance of rigid schedules when meeting someone or conducting business. By contrast, people from short-term-oriented countries generally emphasize immediate gains or accomplishments. Such individuals tend to conduct tasks sequentially and precisely because time is limited. Therefore, the idea that "time is money" (or business relationships [e.g., contracts]) is more valued than having loose schedules. These individuals value immediate gains from those interactions and are not effective in deferring gratification or planning for the future (Ferraro, 2002).

As previously noted, few studies focus on the relationship between long-term orientation and the TAM. However, in Taiwan, which scores high on long-term orientation, the two key characteristics of "long-term social relationships" and "perseverance" are believed to be applicable to the TAM. For example, a subjective norm can be social status, which demonstrates one's social relationship with his or her superiors/senior colleagues, important friends, and/or family members. To maintain long-term social relationships, people in Taiwan might tend to care about or respect the opinions of important people in their lives regarding a new technology and therefore consider using that technology on the basis of those opinions (Ferraro, 2002; Hofstede & Hofstede, 2005).

Perseverance also causes people in Taiwan to defer gratification until the future without the necessity of explaining everything (i.e., they are pragmatic) (Hofstede, 2001). Rather than using a new technology today to complete a certain specific purpose, people in Taiwan might tend to wait and leave more time to foster or maintain long-term social relationships to attain greater benefits from that relationship in the future (Ferraro, 2002; Haapaniemi & Mäkinen, 2009).

In a sense, we can plausibly assume that long-term orientation is likely to increase the influence of subjective norms on the intention to accept internet banking in Taiwan. We also expect that users may perceive that they have plenty of time to build face-to-face relationships with financial service representatives at the branch rather than using internet banking technology to facilitate immediate financial transactions. This expectation is based on the belief that such users are likely willing to wait for financial transactions to be completed or to have their demands fulfilled until they have satisfied the need for social interactions with financial service representatives, which are believed to increase benefits for future financial services and even for investments. Therefore, two additional hypotheses are proposed:

Hypothesis 6: Long-term orientation positively moderates the relationship between subjective norms and users' intention to accept internet banking in Taiwan.

Hypothesis 7: Long-term orientation negatively moderates the relationship between the perceived usefulness of internet banking and users' intention to accept internet banking in Taiwan.

METHODOLOGY

Executive MBA students in Taiwan were selected as our respondents. In addition to answering general demographic questions, the respondents were asked to score perceived characteristics of the overall use of online banking technology and its relation to long-term orientation (5 = *Strongly Agree* to 1 = *Strongly Disagree*).

Measure

The model is based on six hypothetical constructs. The measures for subjective norms (SN, 3 items [SN1-SN3]), computer self-efficacy (CSE, 10 items [CSE1-CSE10]), perceived usefulness (PU, 7 items [PU1-PU7]), perceived ease of use (PEOU, 5 items [PEOU1-PEOU5]), intention to accept internet banking (ITA, 6 items [ITA1-ITA6]), and long-term orientation (LTR, 6 items [LTR1-LTR6]) were operationalized based on previous studies, as shown in Table 1. The development of the questionnaire involved a series of refinements using IS professors and bank practitioners. The wording of certain items was changed to improve clarity and minimize ambiguity. Thirty-eight executive MBA students completed the questionnaires in the pretest (19 reported using online banking less than once a week, 17 reported never using it, and 2 did not specify). A measure of internal consistency was calculated for each construct, generating a range of acceptable Cronbach's alpha values of 0.819-0.912 (Nunnally, 1978) and showing no significant difference from the comments received during the questionnaire refinement.

Table 1. Measurement of constructs

Construct	Indicators	Variables	Sources	Loadings
Subjective Norm (SN)	Adopt online banking is influenced by friends … by my family/relatives … by my colleagues./peers	SN1 SN2 SN3	Taylor & Todd (1995)	0.947 0.957 0.712
Computer Self-Efficacy (CSE)	I would be confident in using Internet banking even if there is no one around to show me how to use it	CSE1	Compeau & Higgins (1995)	0.864
	…even if I have never used a system like it before	CSE2		0.915
	…even if I have only the online instructions for reference	CSE3		0.833
	…if I see someone else using it before I try it myself	CSE4		0.587
	…if I can call someone for help if I get stuck	CSE5		0.615
	…if someone else can help me get started	CSE6		0.841
	…if I have sufficient time to complete the transaction for which the system provides	CSE7		0.685
	…if I have built in online "help" function for assistance	CSE8		0.754
	…if someone show me how to use it first	CSE9		0.870
	…if I had used a similar system before this one to do the same transactions	CSE10		0.758
Perceived Usefulness (PU)	Internet banking makes it easier for me to conduct my bank transactions	PU1	Venkatesh & Davis (2000)	0.735
	…gives me greater control over my finance	PU2		0.722
	…allows me to manage my finance more efficiently	PU3		0.716
	…is a convenient way to manage my finance	PU4		0.754
	…is more user friendly than other existing channels, including bank branches, ATMs, and phone banking.	PU5		0.797
	…eliminate time constraints; thus I can use the baking services at any time I want	PU6		0.807
	…eliminate geographic limitation and increase flexible in mobility; thus I can bank any place that has Internet connection	PU7		0.682

continued on following page

Table 1. Continued

Construct	Indicators	Variables	Sources	Loadings
Perceived Ease of Use (PEOU)	Learning to operate online banking would be easy for me	PEOU1	Venkatesh & Davis (2000)	0.771
	It is easy for me to remember how to perform tasks with online banking	PEOU2		0.795
	I believe it would be easy to get online banking to do what I want it to do	PEOU3		0.899
	Using online banking does not require a lot of mental efforts	PEOU4		0.739
	Online banking provides a clearer interface (visual) than phone banking (audio)	PEOU5		0.749
Intention to Adopt (ITA)	Plan to experiment with or regularly use online banking	ITA1	Venkatesh & Davis (2000)	0.857
	Be interested in using wireless online banking (mobile banking)	ITA2		0.826
	…using securities trading via online banking	ITA3		0.856
	…using insurance via online banking	ITA4		0.704
	…using investment fund services via online banking	ITA5		0.886
	…using fund transfer, payment services via online banking	ITA6		0.812
Long-term Orientation	People have a loose or relaxed schedule (maintaining relationship)	LTR1	Ferraro (2002)	0.620
(LTR)	People are late in the meeting or event	LTR2	Ryu & Moon (2009)	0.090 (Omitted)
	Social relationships (plentiful time) are more valued than punctuality (limited time)	LTR3		0.624
	Willing to wait for bank transaction completed rather than get it done immediately (perseverance)	LTR4		0.779
	Adapt to new technology is important for the future (pragmatism)	LTR5		0.562
	Willing to wait for future returns (gratification deferred))	LTR6		0.740

Data Collection

Over a two-month period, 461 paper and pencil questionnaires were distributed in executive MBA classes at nine universities, and there were no duplicates. 376 questionnaires were returned. After unusable and incomplete questionnaires were removed, 286 valid questionnaires (out of 461 questionnaires) remained, yielding an overall response rate of 62.03%. Approximately 91% of the respondents (including 34.61% who had never used the service) reported that they used online banking less than once a week, and more than 78% of the respondents had at least five years of Internet experience; hence, the results suggested that this sample was appropriate for studying customers' potential acceptance of internet banking. Although 25 respondents (less than 10%) reported using inetrnet banking at least once a week, they were nonetheless considered in the sample because they might expect face-to-face interactions at branches if they embraced multichannel access (McKinsey & Company, 2014).

More than 86% of the respondents reported that they were employed across different industries, indicating an acceptable level of representativeness of the Taiwanese people, who are long term oriented, based on Hofstede's (2001) work-related results of national culture. Similarly, the effective use of working professionals as a sample was shown in studies by Chang (2011) and Chang, Furner, and Zinko (2010) to represent the population's culture orientation. The results revealed no significant difference between the earlier and later respondents over the two months; hence, non-response bias was not an issue (Armstrong & Overton, 1977). Detailed descriptive statistics on the respondents' characteristics are shown in Table 2.

THE MEASUREMENT MODEL

Our model was an exploratory rather than confirmatory study because the new cultural value of LTR was incorporated into the TAM. Therefore, instead of co-variance-based SEM (structural equation modelling), the component-based partial least squares (PLS) approach was used to test the internal consistency reliability, convergent validity, and discriminant validity of the measurement model. An internal consistency reliability of 0.7 or higher is considered adequate (Agarwal & Karahanna, 2000). Convergent and discriminant validity assessed by the average variance extracted (AVE) of a construct should ideally be at least 0.50 and should be greater than that construct's squared correlation with other constructs (Fornell & Larcker, 1981). An item should load higher on the construct that it is intended to measure than it does on another construct (Hwang, 2005).

Table 3 shows the internal consistency reliabilities, AVE, and squared correlations among the constructs. The internal consistency reliabilities were supported by Cronbach's alpha value that were all higher than 0.7. Convergent and discriminant validity were further evidenced because all factors had acceptable AVEs greater than the construct's squared correlation. Moreover, except for the LTR2 item, with a poor loading of 0.090 (omitted), other items with loadings greater than 0.5 significantly loaded on their respective measured constructs (i.e., SN1-SN3 [0.712-0.957], CSE1-CSE10 [0.587-0.915], PU1-PU7 [0.682-0.807], PEOU1-PEOU5 [0.749-0.899], ITA1-ITA6 [0.704-0.886], LTR1 [0.620], LTR3-LTR6 [0.562-0.779], p <= 0.05, Table 3), and no item loaded higher on other constructs than on the construct that it was intended to measure. Thus, the results confirmed the theoretical structure of the measurement model.

Table 2. Characteristics of Respondents (n=286)

	Frequency	Percentage	Accumulated Percentage
Gender			
Male	180	62.93%	62.93%
Female	106	37.07%	100%
Age			
<=30	59	20.62%	20.62%
31-40	76	26.57%	47.19%
41-50	26	9.09%	56.28%
>51	2	0.6%	56.88%
Unknown	123	47.12%	100%
Corporate Experience			
Business Services	38	13.28%	13.28%
Bank and Insurance	50	17.48%	30.76%
Manufacturing	71	24.82%	55.58%
IT and Communications	66	23.07%	78.65%
Government/Education	18	6.29%	84.94%
Real Estate/Developer	5	1.74%	86.68%
Unknown	38	13.32%	100%
Internet Experience			
<=5	52	18.18	18.18%
>5	224	78.32%	96.50%
Unknown	10	3.50%	100%
Frequency of Using Online Banking			
Never Use	99	34.61%	34.61%
<1 per week	162	56.64%	91.25%
>=1 per week	25	8.75%	100%
Reason Not Using Online Banking			
No Direct Contact Bank Tellers	93	32.51%	32.51%
Service Quality Issues	32	11.18%	43.69%
Data Security Issues	111	38.81%	85.50%
Technical Issues	37	12.93%	98.43%
Others	13	1.57%	100%

PREDICTIVE VALIDITY AND MODERATING EFFECT

The predictive validity of the structural model indicates its ability to predict the hypothesized relationships. Table 4 shows that the PLS that analysed the standardized path coefficients (with t-values) for six hypothesized relationships (i.e., H1, H2a, H2b, H3-H5) were positive and that four of the six standardized

Table 3. Internal consistencies reliability, AVE, and squared correlations

Construct	ICR	SN	CSE	PU	PEOU	ITA	LTR
Subjective Norm (SN)	0.898	0.748					
Computer Self-Efficacy (CSE)	0.921	-0.095 (0.009)	0.541				
Perceived Usefulness (PU)	0.907	-0.048 (0.002)	0.445 (0.198)	0.583			
Perceived Ease of Use (PEOU)	0.922	-0.154 (0.023)	0.683 (0.466)	0.562 (0.316)	0.704		
Intention to Adopt (ITA)	0.931	-0.068 (0.004)	0.501 (0.251)	0.688 (0.473)	0.606 (0.367)	0.693	
Long-term Orientation (LTR)	0.730	0.055 (0.003)	0.317 (0.196)	0.351 (0.123)	0.321 (0.103)	0.431 (0.186)	0.541

Note: ICR=internal consistencies reliability, AVE=the number underscored, the numbers in the parenthesis indicate squared correlations

Table 4. Test results of predictive validity

Hypothesis	Path	Path Coefficient (t-value)	Test Results
H1	SN→PU	0.039 (0.386)ns	Not Supported
H2a	SN→ITA	0.005 (0.059)ns	Not Supported
H2b	PU→ITA	0.511 (5.938)***	Supported
H3	CSE→PEOU	0.684 (12.831)***	Supported
H4	PEOU→ITA	0.320 (3.664)***	Supported
H5	PEOU→PU	0.568 (7.987)***	Supported

Note: ns = Non-significant, ***Significant at the 0.001 level (t-value > 3.29)

coefficients were statistically significant. Such strong associations evidenced the predictive validity of the structural model with a coefficient determination (R^2) of 0.571.

As Table 4 shows, although the effect was in the hypothesized direction, no significant path coefficient was found for H1 (SN→PU [$\beta = 0.039$, t-value = 0.386 < 1.96, $p > 0.05$]) or H2a (SN→ITA [$\beta = 0.005$, t-value = 0.059 < 1.96, $p > 0.05$]). H1 and H2a were not supported. However, a significant path coefficient was found for H2b (PU→ITA [$\beta = 0.511$, t-value = 5.938 > 3.29, p < 0.001]). Thus, H2b was strongly supported. Significant path coefficients were found for H3 (CSE→PEOU [$\beta = 0.684$, t-value = 12.831 > 3.29, p < 0.001]), H4 (PEOU→ITA [$\beta = 0.320$, t-value = 3.664 > 3.29, p < 0.001]), and H5 (PEOU→PU [$\beta = 0.568$, t-value = 7.987 > 3.29, p < 0.001]). Therefore, all three hypotheses were strongly supported.

To test the moderating effect of cultural values on the model, we analysed the interaction effects of the long-term orientation construct for H6 and H7. The PLS method was employed and followed a hierarchical process similar to that used in multiple regression analysis by comparing the results of the main effects model and the interaction model, as shown in Figure 2 (Yoon, 2009).

Figure 2. Two models for PLS moderating effect analysis

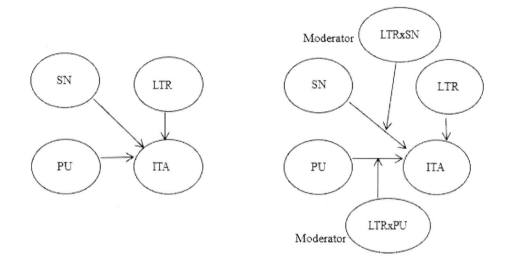

Main Effects Model   Interaction Model

As Table 5 shows, non-significant interactions between subjective norms and the intention to accept were found for H6 (LTR x SN→ITA [interactive $\beta = 0.076$, t-value $= 0.134 < 1.96$, $p > 0.05$]). Although the effect was in the hypothesized direction, H6 was not supported. The negative interactions between perceived usefulness and intention to accept were found to be significant for H7 (LTR x PU→ITA [interactive $\beta = -0.459$, t-value $= 1.972 > 1.96$, $p < 0.05$], $R^2 = 0.531$). Thus, H7 was supported. Our test results are discussed in the following section.

Table 5. Test results of moderating effects of long-term orientation

Hypothesis	Main Effects Model			Interaction Model			
	Path	Path Coefficient (t-value)	R^2	Path	Path Coefficient (t-value)	R^2	Test Results
H6	SN→ITA	0.036 (0.195)[ns]	0.571	SN→ITA	-0.125 (0.221)[ns]	0.192	
	LTR→ITA	0.173 (1.909)		LTR→ITA	0.407 (1.930)		
				LTRxSN→ITA	0.076 (0.134)[ns]		Not Supported
H7	PU→ITA	0.461 (5.038)***	0.574	PU→ITA	0.470 (3.954)***	0.531	
	LTR→ITA	0.173 (1.909)		LTR→ITA	0.387 (2.319)**		
				LTRxPU→ITA	-0.459 (1.972)**		Supported

Note: ns = Non-significant, **Significant at the 0.05 level (t-value > 1.96), ***Significant at the 0.001 level (t-value > 3.29)

DISCUSSION

Effect of Subjective Norms on Acceptance-Related Belief Variables

The results of testing H1, H2a, and H2b showed that subjective norms were less influential than perceived usefulness in determining the intention to accept internet banking. The current ability of the overall social status influence of subjective norms in our respondents may not by itself be sufficiently accurate to predict acceptance (H1 [$\beta = 0.039$, $p > 0.05$], H2a [$\beta = 0.005$, $p > 0.05$]), unless our respondents believed that internet banking services are useful and therefore worthy of acceptance (H2b [$\beta = 0.511$, $p < 0.001$]). Although the evidence of stronger emphasis on perceived usefulness (H2b) is consistent with previous TAM studies (e.g., Venkatesh & Davis, 2000), our results for H1 and H2a are not consistent with the literature.

For example, Chan and Lu's (2004) study reports that subjective norms are significant for potential users in influencing perceived usefulness. As the researchers argue, potential users would evaluate the benefits of internet banking primarily based on the opinions of superior/senior colleagues, important friends, and/or family members because of their own lack of experience. Although our respondents were potential uers, subjective norms were not found to be significant. This finding is not consistent with Chan and Lu's (2004) conclusion. Other examples that conflict with our results are Lee's (2009) and Al-Smadi's (2012) studies, which show a significant influence of subjective norms on acceptance. Possible explanation for such discrepancies may relate to factors such as the influential role of the cultural value of long-term orientation, which was not identified in the past model.

Moderating Effect of Long-Term Orientation

As noted, people with a more long-term orientation tend to be pragmatic when adopting new technology (Hofstede, Hofstede, & Minkov, 2010). Thus, we can plausibly infer that our Taiwanese respondents may consider using internet banking as long as they believe that this new technology will benefit them in their future financial needs (H2b) without necessarily consulting with superior/senior colleagues, important friends, and/or family members (H1, H2a). This inference also echoes the result of H6 ([interactive $\beta = 0.076$, $p > 0.05$]), which shows that the level of social status pressure is not sufficiently strong for our respondents to maintain long-term social relationships with powerful and influential people to influence future acceptance.

Notably, the results for H7 show that although the abovementioned perceptions of the usefulness of internet banking are a critical condition for acceptance (H2b), the effect of perceived usefulness substantially decreases as the cultural value of long-term orientation becomes stronger ([interactive $\beta = -0.459$, $p < 0.05$]). That is, a stronger long-term orientation counterbalances the TAM effect of perceived usefulness, and such respondents are thus hesitant to accept internet banking.

As such, our respondents tended not to emphasize current social status effects on their intention to accept (H2a); they were more concerned with fostering long-term face-to-face social relationships with bank employees (i.e., financial service representatives) before being ready to use (H6 and H7). That is, maintaining good, long-term relationships with their banks is more important than maintaining relationships with influential people (although they may consider the opinions of such individuals). This finding was expected because the perseverant (pragmatic) characteristics of people with a long-term orientation reflect the need for "building long-term social relationships" to ensure future rewards (Ferraro, 2002; Hofstede & Hofstede, 2005). This characteristic also explains why our results contradict the literature arguing that a strong long-term orientation reinforces the influence of social status influence on acceptance (Kim & Kim, 2009).

Therefore, we believe that our respondents prefer to foster familiar and solid relationships with banks by spending time (plenty of time) engaging in social interaction (e.g., talking) with financial service representatives. Such long-term, mature relationships become a relatively important condition when considering internet banking, and they would likely increase respondents' trust and confidence (e.g., security and privacy) in the future use of internet banking systems, which can be treated as an extended financial service channel for users. This finding is supported by the literature demonstrating the positive moderating effect of long-term orientation on the relationship between trust and the intention to adopt a new technology (e.g., Yoon, 2009). The finding implies that trust is socially generated and that it accumulated as our respondents became more familiar with and developed longer-term relationships with banks, and in turn, they considered accepting online banking based on evaluation of its usefulness.

The results for H7 also imply that maintaining a good and persistent relationship with banks to ensure better service benefits in the future is more important than enjoying the immediate benefit of usefulness (e.g., convenience). This finding was expected because "deferred gratification" is also a persistent characteristic of people with a long-term orientation (Ferraro, 2002; Hofstede & Hofstede, 2005). In a sense, although internet banking may be useful to them now in facilitating personal financial transactions, our respondents appear to be willing to wait to accumulate strong and close long-term social relationships with banks. Such relationships would benefit from face-to-face interaction in several ways, such as more fringe service benefits, more reliable personal and/or family financial service advice, and more professional and customized investment consultancy, and other benefits that online banking services cannot provide. The respondents consider this waiting prior to use (i.e., a type of perseverance) to be pragmatic and worthwhile.

Effect of Computer Self-Efficacy on Acceptance-Related Belief Variables

The results of testing H3, H4, and H5 indicate that respondents with higher levels of computer self-efficacy tend to perceive internet banking as an easy and therefore useful tool (H3 [$\beta = 0.684$, $p < 0.001$], H5 [$\beta = 0.568$, $p < 0.001$]). This finding was expected because approximately 78% of our respondents had more than five years of Internet experience. Because they judged themselves as having sufficient computer skills, they were willing to use banking system for personal financial services (H4 [$\beta = 0.320$, $p < 0.001$]). These results are similar to those found in previous TAM studies (e.g., Venkatesh & Bala, 2008; Venkatesh & Davis, 1996).

When we consider which belief force (i.e., extrinsic or intrinsic motivation) is more closely related to the intention to accept, the extrinsic motivation of perceived usefulness (H2b [$\beta = 0.511$, $p < 0.001$]) appears to play a more important role than the intrinsic motivation of perceived ease of use (H4 [$\beta = 0.320$, $p < 0.001$]). This finding indicates that in our model, perceived usefulness alone may constitute a necessary condition for accepting internet banking. The same results are obtained by Pikkarainen (2004) and Chan and Lu (2004), who note that perceived usefulness is more influential than perceived ease of use in predicting the intention to accept. Venkatesh, Speier, and Morris (2002) also report that intrinsic motivation has less influence despite its importance. However, although perceived usefulness alone can be a necessary condition for the intention to accept online banking, it cannot guarantee use, particularly for potential users to which the cultural value of long-term orientation is applied in the model.

IMPLICATIONS AND FUTURE WORK

Our main evidence suggests that respondents anchor their perceptions of the ease of use of the banking system to their perception of computer self-efficacy, which in turn determines whether they evaluate internet banking as useful. However, the results suggest that perceived usefulness plays a greater role than perceived ease of use in significantly predicting the intention to accept. The practical implication is that for voluntary and potential users, computer literacy and perceived ease of use are not sufficient conditions to ensure the intention to accept unless the usefulness of internet banking is demonstrated. In other words, the computer literacy of individuals, which makes them believe that internet banking is easy to use, is only a baseline. Bank practitioners must exert more effort showing the usefulness or benefits (or privileges) of internet banking services while promoting them.

Our main evidence further suggests that potential users would rely not on references from others for internet banking acceptance but on their own evaluation of its usefulness because they are influenced by the cultural value of long-term orientation and thus place greater emphasis on the future potential usefulness of a new technology (pragmatic nature) than on social status influences (subjective norms). However, this cultural influence further suggests that perceived usefulness per se is not sufficient for people to accept internet banking unless comparable efforts are made to foster trusted long-term customer relationships with banks.

A practical implication for the Chinese context of Taiwan is that the usefulness and benefits of time efficiency do not necessarily cause users to accept internet banking. Such users are more concerned about whether their relationship with their banks can continue to be well maintained. Although this relationship would strengthen their confidence and trust in the bank's ability to protect their privacy and security online, users expect additional benefits, such as potential privileges and service upgrades, from that interpersonal relationship.

Our study, as a preliminary exploration of long-term orientation effects on TAM, was limited to a single country. Future research could thus explore the effect of long-term orientation on acceptance across countries. Our study did not consider all aspects of Hofstede's cultural dimensions and their effects on the TAM and its extensions. Future research may examine the relationship between all cultural aspects and TAM antecedents and determine which cultural force can better predict or moderate acceptance.

CONCLUSION

We contribute new findings to the literature. For example, in contrast to previous TAM cultural studies, the "subjective norms" construct actually had no effect, and its interaction with long-term orientation was significantly weak in the ability to improve acceptance intention. Moreover, perceived usefulness alone cannot guarantee usage, although this factor is significant. We contribute to the literature by demonstrating that the cultural influence of long-term orientation in the Chinese context of Taiwan moderates TAM effects. That is, although internet banking may be useful and easy to use and although users may be affected by social status pressure or concern about family relationships, users still hesitate (defer) to accept the service because they value long-term bank relationships to ensure future benefits more than they value the recommendations of other people based on the desire to obtain immediate benefits. We also contribute to gain the Government's attention that long-term orientation may impact users' acceptance of advanced Fin-tech services recently advocated in Taiwan.

Moreover, the literature argues that poor trust may hinder adoption, and our results clearly support this argument in showing that users lack confidence in the absence of solid, long-term relationships. Once customers become familiar with a bank, they gain more trust in banking systems with the proper privacy protections and security in place. As users in Taiwan's retail banking sector tend to favour face-to-face interactions to maintain relationships and prefer to wait for better outcomes, a well-defined and synchronized customer relationship programme (strategy) must be considered to progressively enhance (or encourage) current and/or new customers' willingness to use internet banking technology by positioning such services in a supportive and facilitating service role. We conclude that internet banking can play only a complementary role as a service and/or sales channel in the Chinese context of Taiwan, where interpersonal relationships are key.

REFERENCES

Agarwal, R., & Karahanna, E. (2000). Time flies when you're having fun: Cognitive absorption and beliefs about information technology use. *Management Information Systems Quarterly*, *24*(4), 665–694. doi:10.2307/3250951

Ajzen, I. (1991). The theory of planned behavior. *Organizational Behavior and Human Decision Processes*, *50*(2), 179–211. doi:10.1016/0749-5978(91)90020-T

Ajzen, I., & Fishbein, M. (1980). *Understanding attitudes and predicting social behavior*. Englewood Cliffs, NJ: Prentice-Hall.

Al-Smadi, M. O. (2012). Factors affecting the adoption of electronic banking: An analysis of the perspectives of bank's customers. *International Journal of Business and Social Science*, *3*(17), 294–309.

Armstrong, J. S., & Overton, T. S. (1977). Estimating nonresponse bias in mail surveys. *JMR, Journal of Marketing Research*, *14*(3), 396–492. doi:10.2307/3150783

Bagozzi, R. P., Davis, F. D., & Warshaw, P. R. (1992). development and test of a theory of technological learning and usage. *Human Relations*, *45*(7), 660–686. doi:10.1177/001872679204500702

Bandura, A. (1977). Self-efficacy: Toward a unifying theory of behavioral change. *Psychological Review*, *84*(2), 191–215. doi:10.1037/0033-295X.84.2.191 PMID:847061

Bearden, W. O., Money, R. B., & Nevins, J. L. (2006). A Measure of Long-term Orientation: Development and Validation. *Journal of the Academy of Marketing Science*, *34*(3), 456–467. doi:10.1177/0092070306286706

Burkhardt, M. E., & Brass, D. J. (1990). Changing patterns or patterns of change: The effects of a change in technology on social network structure and power. *Administrative Science Quarterly*, *35*(1), 104–121. doi:10.2307/2393552

Callaway, S. K. (2011). Internet banking and performance. *American Journal of Business*, *26*(1), 12–25. doi:10.1108/19355181111124070

Chan, S., & Lu, M. (2004). Understanding Internet banking adoption and use: A Hong Kong perspective. *Journal of Global Information Management*, *12*(3), 21–42. doi:10.4018/jgim.2004070102

Chang, L. (2011). A comparison of Taiwan and Malaysia in negotiation style. *Journal of International Business Management*, 6(1), 9–17.

Chang, L., Furner, C. P., & Zinko, R. (2010). A study of negotiation within the ethnic Chinese community between Taiwan and Hong Kong. *Management Research and Practice*, 2(4), 329–343.

Chaudhury, A., Mallick, D. N., & Rao, H. R. (2001). Web channels in e-commerce. *Communications of the ACM*, 44(1), 99–104. doi:10.1145/357489.357515

Chen, S., Chen, H., & Chen, M. (2009). Determinants of satisfaction and contiunace intention toward self-service technologies. *Industrial Management & Data Systems*, 109(9), 1248–1263. doi:10.1108/02635570911002306

Chi, H., Yeh, H. R., & Yang, Y. (2011). Applying theory of reasoned action and technology acceptance model to investigate purchase behavior on smartphone. *Journal of International Management Studies*, 6(3), 1–11.

Chinese Culture Connection. (1987). Chinese values and the search for culture-free dimensions of culture. *Journal of Cross-Cultural Psychology*, 18(2), 143–164. doi:10.1177/0022002187018002002

Chuang, C. C., & Hu, F. (2012). Customer adoption of Internet banking: An empirical investigation in Taiwanese banking context. *Information Management and Business Review*, 4(11), 570–582.

Compeau, D. R., & Higgins, C. A. (1995). Computer self-efficacy: Development of a measure and initial test. *Management Information Systems Quarterly*, 19(2), 189–211. doi:10.2307/249688

Davis, F. D. (1989). Perceived usefulness, perceived ease of use, and user acceptance of information technology. *Management Information Systems Quarterly*, 13(3), 318–339. doi:10.2307/249008

Davis, F. D. (1993). User acceptance of information technology: System characteristics, user perceptions and behavioral impacts. *International Journal of Man-Machine Studies*, 38(3), 475–487. doi:10.1006/imms.1993.1022

Davis, F. D., Bagozzi, R. P., & Warshaw, P. R. (1989). User acceptance of computer technology: A comparison of two theoretical models. *Management Science*, 35(8), 982–1003. doi:10.1287/mnsc.35.8.982

Fang, T. (2003). A critique of Hofstede's fifth dimension. *International Journal of Cross Cultural Management*, 3(3), 347–368. doi:10.1177/1470595803003003006

Ferraro, G. P. (2002). *The cultural dimension of international business*. Upper Saddle River, NJ: Pearson.

Haapaniemi, T., & Mäkinen, S. (2009). Moderating effect of national attributes on the role of cultural dimensions in technology adoption takeoff. *Management Research News*, 32(1), 56–63.

Hofstede, G. (1991). *Culture and organization: Software of mind*. London, UK: McGraw-Hill.

Hofstede, G. (1994). *Values survey module 1994 manual*. Maastricht, The Netherlands: Institute of Research On Intercultural Cooperation.

Hofstede, G. (2001). *Culture's consequences: Comparing values, behaviors, institutions, and organizations across nations.* Thousand Oaks, CA: Sage.

Hofstede, G., & Bond, M. H. (1988). The Confucius connection: From cultural roots to economic growth. *Organizational Dynamics, 16*(4), 4–21. doi:10.1016/0090-2616(88)90009-5

Hofstede, G., & Hofstede, G. J. (2005). Cultures and organizations. Software of the mind (2nd ed.). New York, NY: McGraw-Hill.

Hofstede, G., Hofstede, G. J., & Minkov, M. (2010). *Cultures and organizations: Software of the mind* (3rd ed.). New York, NY: McGraw-Hill.

Hwang, Y. (2005). Investigating enterprising systems adoption: Uncertainty avoidance, intrinsic motivation, and the technology acceptance model. *European Journal of Information Systems, 14*(2), 150–161. doi:10.1057/palgrave.ejis.3000532

Jones, C. M., McCarthy, R. V., & Halawi, L. (2010). Utilizing technology acceptance model to assess the employee adoption of information systems security measures. *Journal of International Technology and Information Management, 19*(2), 43.

King, W. R., & He, J. (2006). A meta-analysis of the technology acceptance model. *Information & Management, 43*(6), 740–755. doi:10.1016/j.im.2006.05.003

Lee, M. (2009). Factors influencing the adoption of Internet banking: An integration of TAM and TPB with perceived risk and perceived benefits. *Electronic Commerce Research and Applications, 8*(3), 130–141. doi:10.1016/j.elerap.2008.11.006

Lee, Y. (2006). An empirical investigation into factors of influencing the adoption of an e-learning systems. *Online Information Review, 30*(5), 517–541. doi:10.1108/14684520610706406

Lee, Y., Kozar, K. A., & Larsen, K. R. T. (2003). The technology acceptance model: Past, present, and future. *Communications of the AIS, 12*(50), 752–780.

McCoy, S., Everard, A., & Jones, B. M. (2005). An examination of technology acceptance model in Uruguay and the US: A focus on culture. *Journal of Global Information Technology Management, 8*(2), 27–45. doi:10.1080/1097198X.2005.10856395

McKinsey & Company. (2014). *The Future Role of US Retailing Banking Distribution.* Author.

Minkov, M. (2007). *What makes us different and similar: A new interpretation of the World Values Survey and other cross-cultural data.* Sofia, Bulgaria: Klasika y Stil Publishing House.

Nunnally, J. C. (1978). *Psychometric theory.* New York, NY: McGraw-Hill.

Ojha, A., Sahu, G. P., & Gupta, M. P. (2009). Antecedents of paperless income tax filing by young professionals in India: An exploratory study. *Transforming Government: People. Process and Policy, 3*(1), 65–90.

Pikkarainen, T., Pikkarainen, K., Karjaluoto, H., & Pahnila, S. (2004). Customer acceptance of on-line banking: An extension of technology acceptance model. *Internet Research*, *14*(3), 224–235. doi:10.1108/10662240410542652

Proenca, J. F., & Silva, M. M. (2005). Banking relationships and Internet banking. *IADIS International Journal on WWW/Internet*, *5*(2), 181-192.

Proenca, J. F., Silva, M. M., & Fernandes, T. (2010). The impact of Internet on bank marketing. *Journal of Financial Services Marketing*, *15*(2), 160–175. doi:10.1057/fsm.2010.12

Ryu, S., & Kim, E. (2010). The moderating effect of long-term orientation on the relationship between inter firm power asymmetry and inter firm contracts: The case of Korea and USA. *Journal of Applied Marketing Research*, *26*(6), 135–146.

Ryu, S., & Moon, C. W. (2009). Long-term orientation as a determinant of relationship quality between channel members. *International Business and Economics Research Journal*, *8*(11), 1–9.

Ryu, S., Park, J. E., & Min, S. (2007). Factors determining long-term orientation in inter-firm relation-ships. *Journal of Business Research*, *60*(12), 1225–1233. doi:10.1016/j.jbusres.2006.09.031

Salam, M. A. (2011). Supply chain commitment and business process integration: The implications of Confucian dynamism. *European Journal of Marketing*, *45*(3), 358–382. doi:10.1108/03090561111107230

Shore, B. (2001). Information sharing in global supply chain systems. *Journal of Global Information Technology Management*, *4*(3), 27–50. doi:10.1080/1097198X.2001.10856306

Thompson, R. L., Higgins, C., & Howell, J. M. (1991). Personal computing: Toward a conceptual model of utilization. *Management Information Systems Quarterly*, *15*(1), 125–143. doi:10.2307/249443

Venkatesh, V., & Bala, H. (2008). Technology Acceptance model 3 and a research agenda on interven-tions. *Decision Sciences*, *39*(2), 273–315. doi:10.1111/j.1540-5915.2008.00192.x

Venkatesh, V., & Davis, D. F. (2000). A theoretical extension of the technology acceptance model: Four longitudinal field studies. *Management Science*, *46*(2), 186–204. doi:10.1287/mnsc.46.2.186.11926

Venkatesh, V., Speier, C., & Morris, M. G. (2002). User acceptance enablers in individual deci-sion making about technology: Toward an integrated model. *Decision Sciences*, *33*(2), 297–316. doi:10.1111/j.1540-5915.2002.tb01646.x

Ventakatesh, V., & Davis, D. F. (1996). A model of perceived ease of use: Development and test. *Deci-sion Sciences*, *27*(3), 451–483. doi:10.1111/j.1540-5915.1996.tb01822.x

Wong, L. (2005). Chinese management as discourse: Chinese as a technology of self and control. *Asian Business & Management*, *4*(4), 431–453. doi:10.1057/palgrave.abm.9200142

Wu, M. (2006). Hofstede's cultural dimensions 30years later: A study of Taiwan and the United States. *Intercultural Communication Studies*, *15*(1), 33–42.

Yang, H., & Zhou, L. (2011). Extending TPB and TAM to mobile viral marketing: An exploratory study of American young consumers' mobile viral marketing attitude, intent, and behaviour. *Journal of Targeting. Measurement and Analysis for Marketing, 19*(2), 85–98. doi:10.1057/jt.2011.11

Yeung, I. Y. M., & Tung, R. L. (1996). Achieving business success in Confucian societies: The importance of Guanxi (connections). *Organizational Dynamics, 25*(2), 54–65. doi:10.1016/S0090-2616(96)90025-X

Yoon, C. (2009). The effects of national culture values on consumer acceptance of e-commerce: Online shoppers in China. *Information & Management, 46*(5), 294–301. doi:10.1016/j.im.2009.06.001

Yu, P., Li, H. C., & Gagnon, M. P. (2009). Health IT acceptance factors in long-term care facilities: A cross-sectional survey. *International Journal of Medical Informatics, 78*(4), 219–229. doi:10.1016/j.ijmedinf.2008.07.006 PMID:18768345

Chapter 12
Comprehensive Internet Youth Protection Policies by Private Organizations and Effectiveness Verification:
Efforts by Japan Internet Safety Promotion Association

Nagayuki Saito
Keio University, Japan

Ema Tanaka
Waseda University, Japan

Eri Yatsuzuka
Mirai Factory, Japan

Madoka Aragaki
Business Breakthrough University, Japan

ABSTRACT

Seeking a safer internet environment for minors, the Japanese government enacted a new law in 2008 to promote both protective measures and empowerment activities. Under the law, many entities—including newly established non-profit organizations (NPOs)—are working to bring a safer internet environment to Japan. The Japan Internet Safety Promotion Association (JISPA), one such NPO established in February 2007, has been promoting a safer internet environment for minors by providing non-formal learning opportunities through educational materials and events. Efforts to improve children's online safety have evolved from offering e-learning content and guidelines to holding workshops in the real world. This chapter presents various measures taken by JISPA for the protection of children using the internet and verifies the effectiveness of these measures based on evidence. Measures to be verified are e-learning contents, workshop programs, and internet literacies among young people and parents.

DOI: 10.4018/978-1-5225-7214-5.ch012

BACKGROUND

In recent years, mobile devices that can connect to the Internet, such as mobile phones and smartphones, are spreading among young people. The use of these devices brings not only advantages but also disadvantages in the form of youth problems. In particular, for young people who are less experienced than adults and lacking in good judgment regarding Internet risks, it will be necessary to establish protection as a social system.

Internet problems among young people in Japan include net dependency and cyberbullying, both of which are worsening, so correspondence is important. According to a survey by Higuchi (2013), approximately 6.0% of junior high students and 9.4% of high school students "use the Internet morbidly," so that approximately 520,000 young people are Internet-dependent. On the other hand, according to the survey regarding problem behaviors of students conducted by the Ministry of Education, Culture, Sports, Science and Technology (2016), the number of cyberbullying incidents reported to schools in 2015 was 8,787—the highest number ever since last year. Furthermore, the National Police Agency (2017) reported that the number of crime victims per community Internet site was 1,736, which is about 2.2 times more than the 792 cases reported in 2008 when the Act on Regulation on Soliciting Children by Using Opposite Sex Introducing Service on Internet (the so-called dating site regulation) was revised. Community sites are crime routes, generally used in society and frequently used by elementary, junior high, and high school students. Going forward, self-defense instruction for youth and involvement/management by parents are important issues and include mastering knowledge of various risks resulting from the use of Web services and setting rules for use of the Internet at home.

In view of this situation, in 2009, the Act on Establishment of Enhanced Environment for Youth's Safe and Secure Internet Use (Act No. 79 [2008], hereinafter referred to as the "Youth Internet Environment Improvement Act") became effective in Japan. Article 3 provides as basic objectives: that "young people should acquire skills for independently utilizing information and communication equipment, properly sorting out information available on the Internet and appropriately transmitting information via the Internet" (para. 1), "reducing the chances of young people viewing content harmful … via the Internet as much as possible, by way of improving the performance and disseminating the use of software for filtering content harmful to young people" (para. 2), and "safe and secure Internet use for young people shall be promoted based on the principle that voluntary and independent efforts in the private sector should play a substantial role" (para. 3).

In line with the gist of the Youth Internet Environment Improvement Act, this paper reports on the efforts for improving Internet use by young people in Japan and verifies its impact under the theme of awareness education activities by JISPA and voluntary measures established by the private sector.

NECESSITY OF INTERNET AWARENESS EDUCATION FOR THE DEVELOPMENTAL ENVIRONMENT OF YOUNG PEOPLE

The various risks raised from Internet use are problems faced by all Internet users. However, protective measures are needed for young people in the developmental stage. This section addresses the necessity of protecting youth using *The Ecology of Human Development* (Bronfenbrenner, 1979) as a clue.

Bronfenbrenner (1979) classifies the ecological environments in which humans live into four areas. The microsystem is the area in which one's experiences influence him/her and direct subsequent actions.

The mesosystem includes influences from homes, schools, et cetera, that affect behavior style and roles. The exosystem is the area in which relationships between parents and teachers indirectly influence the microsystem. Finally, the macrosystem is affected by one's living environment and sociocultural factors. Thus, these ecological environments directly and indirectly influence young people in their development (Figure 1).

Next, from the historical point of view and based on the theory of Bronfenbrenner (1979), the authors examine how the development of the media has influenced young people and how the relationships of parents have changed along the way.

Developmental Environment of Young People in the Television Era

In the 1980s, television was the main medium directly affecting youth's microsystems. At that time, harmful information, such as violent scenes transmitted through television and long-time viewing, etc., were regarded as problems (Mukoda, 2003; Yukawa, 2003). Protection of youth in this era was based on broadcasting ethics regulations of television stations, and information that was considered to be harmful to young people was excluded. Content for adults was broadcast during the midnight frame. Therefore, it can be said that broadcast ethics provisions were functioning as a bottleneck system for youth's development of microsystems (Broadcast Ethics and Program Improvement Organization, 2013). In addition, since televisions were installed mainly in places where guardians' eyes would reach (e.g., living rooms), parental control was functioning and parents could control their children's microsystems.

Advent of the Internet Era and Young People's Developmental Environment

Since the introduction of Windows 95 in 1995, the Internet has become easy for the general public to use. The sender and receiver of information have been made identical. Prior to 1995, the originator of

Figure 1. The direction of youth protection measures based on The Ecology of Human Development (Bronfenbrenner, 1979)
Source: Created by the author based on Bronfenbrenner (1979)

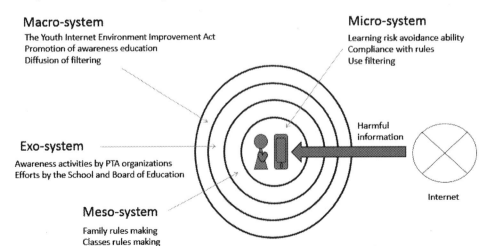

information was limited to television stations and radio stations, which were disseminating information in compliance with ethical regulations (Yoshimi & Mizukoshi, 2004).

However, in the Internet era, measures to protect youth from harmful information based on the sender's ethics are no longer functioning as they were earlier (when the impact of harmful information transmitted via the Internet on the microsystems of youth were limited). Because the main Internet users in the 1980s were adults and college students, the Internet environment was not always connected.

Developmental Environment for Youth During Mass Popularization of the Internet

The media environment for youth changed considerably with the spread of the broadband connection environment through ADSL, optical lines, and the start of IP connection services for the mobile phone in 2000. With the development of the broadband connection environment, the Internet connection environment of users has improved dramatically, and the communication environment for text communications has changed to allow communication using images, movies, voice, etc. Furthermore, communication services, such as blogs, profile sites, and SNSs that provide an online communication environment, have appeared. In addition, with the service of mobile phones, continuous Internet connectivity of users has increased because of the IP connection service provided by each mobile phone company and NTT DoCoMo's i-mode.

The problem of this era is that youth are using the Internet on a daily basis despite the fact that the bottleneck against harmful information is not fully functioning. Furthermore, the factor worsening the situation is that young people have begun to own high-functioning mobile phones, such as feature phones (Cabinet Office, 2006). As a result, they remain in an environment where they can access the Internet daily (out of reach of their parents). Accordingly, it has become apparent that young people using the Internet are involved in troubling activities, such as bullying at informal school sites and encountering criminals via profile sites (Ministry of Education, Culture, Sports, Science and Technology, 2008a; Shimoda, 2008).

Changes in this media environment have not only greatly influenced the development of the microsystems of youth, but they have also caused confusion in their environments. Parents and teachers who construct mesosystems for adolescents have had to determine how to protect and guide them in schools and homes. Schools, school boards, and the PTA, which construct exosystems, have struggled to develop concrete measures thst address the rising problems among youth who use the Internet. Furthermore, governments (national and local) as macrosystems have had to develop national institutions, including communication industry organizations for youth protection, quickly (Ministry of Internal Affairs and Communications, 2009a; Ministry of Internal Affairs and Communications, 2009b; Ministry of Education, Culture, Sports, Science and Technology, 2012b).

As a countermeasure against such a situation at the macrosystem level, the government legislated the Youth Internet Environment Improvement Act in 2008; enforcement began in 2009. The Act stipulates the promotion of filtering use as a technical protection measure to alleviate as many opportunities as possible for adolescents to encounter harmful information (Article 14). It also stipulates the promotion of awareness education for the enhancement of youth's ability to protect themselves from online risks (Article 13). Furthermore, the purpose of this Act is to promote the development of activities to protect youth from harmful elements in the Internet environment by cooperating with multiple stakeholders, such as telecommunication associations, educational institutions, and parents (Article 16). Based on enforcement of this Act as a macrosystem for the media environment of youth, exosystems such as PTA organizations, schools, and school boards are encouraged, as are educational activities that promote awareness for parents and teachers who construct mesosystems.

Developmental Environment of Youth in the Smartphone Era

Since enforcement of the Youth Internet Environment Improvement Act, various efforts by multi-stakeholders have been carried out; however, with the advent of smartphones, it became necessary to review these efforts.

Since the iPhone was introduced, smartphones have swept the mobile phone market, and front-row displays in mobile phone stores and consumer electronics retailers have replaced feature phones with smartphones. From this situation, the ratio of smartphones to mobile phones used by youth became quite large. Along with that, new problems not seen in the era of feature phones became manifest.

In the smartphone era, connection to the Internet has become easier, and continuous connectivity has increased. Furthermore, Web application services made it possible to use sophisticated and attractive products. The attractive features of smartphones brought risks that youth had not experienced with feature phones.

Problems with the smartphone are caused by its high-level user interface and specifications, so young people become immersed in various contents and services provided by the smartphone, including the danger of getting into a situation in which self-control is not effective (Saito & Yoshida, 2013). As a result, this becomes a variable that expands the problems of Internet dependence.

Furthermore, the use of applications has made it possible for youth to connect to SNSs, sometimes posting inappropriate photos/movies/remarks that garner considerable publicity and an inundation of comments. Additionally, youth may expose personal information or a relative's information via the Internet (Kobayashi, 2011).

Some of the applications that have become easy to use are offering closed virtual space communication, and "community in-house bullying," which occurs in a closed communication space that parents and teachers have difficulty accessing in order to protect and supervise young people. Therefore, it is not easy to calm the resulting problems.

Necessity of Awareness Educational Policy

As mentioned above, the media have the ability to directly affect the developmental microsystems of youth. In addition, development of the media increases ease of access to the Internet, and youth with inadequate self-control are in a state whereby they cannot properly control use of the media. Under these circumstances, it can be said that the factor that makes parental involvement difficult is personalization of the media.

When returning to the developmental theory of Bronfenbrenner, an important measure for counteracting the influence of the media on the development of youth microsystems will be effective parental control in the home (mesosystem environment). In addition, it will be important for the PTA to conduct awareness-raising activities in the exosystem and for school staff to provide awareness education. Furthermore, it will be necessary to tackle effective youth protection measures, such as technical measures by Internet-related operators in the macrosystem. It is also important for governments at the national and local levels to design effective social systems and awareness policies for citizens (i.e., youth macrosystem).

DEVELOPMENT PROCESS FOR MOBAMI'S E-LEARNING CONTENT

In August 2009, JISPA started to develop educational content to raise awareness of safer mobile Internet usage and promote rulemaking for Internet access and use at home. The program, Mobami, was opened to the public in February 2010. Its web-based e-learning program targeted new mobile-phone users between the ages of six and 15 and their parents. The program was designed to be entertaining so that children and their parents could both benefit from its use. It was also intended to help families set rules for their children's mobile usage.

Although there are several activities online that provide learning materials, most of the content and materials are static ones that provide information. On the other hand, Mobami has some features that reflect a non-formal learning style, which are a result of its being an outcome of a public-private partnership and an interactive e-learning program based on instructional design theory targeted at both children and parents.

Mobami was developed through the cooperation of mobile carriers and content providers and reflected their experience and knowledge of Internet safety under the coordination of the council (Japan Internet Safety Promotion Association, 2010). It is composed of two main sections: one for minors and one for parents. Parents can create family rules suitable for their desired usage and level of understanding of Internet safety with reference to the results of a self-check test, which both they and their children can take (Figure 2).

Mobami as a Support Tool to Make Family Rules on Mobile Usage of Children

In addition to the skill-check program, the site provides a rulemaking navigation program for families. The categories for rulemaking correspond to the five categories of the skill-check program: basic rules, call rules, e-mailing rules, Internet access rules, and application rules (see Table 1). The main purpose of the section entitled "Navigation for making *Kei-tai* rules" is to support parents and children in setting

Figure 2. Mobami's content image and characters
Source: Japan Internet safety Promotion Association (JISPA) (https://www.good-net.jp/)

family rules for mobile usage. When they start making rules, the site requires that the family enter each child's nickname, sex, and birth year and month. There are 63 prepared rules across five categories of rulemaking: basic rules (14 rules), call rules (10 rules), e-mailing rules (12 rules), Internet access rules (16 rules), and application rules (11 rules) (Table 2). The 14 basic rules are required, but users may select the rules they want from the other four categories before they begin.

The rulemaking program helps families decide which rules are suitable for their own situation. The navigation system allows users to choose from a variety of possible rules and to enter details for the rules, such as time zones for *Kei-tai* usage and maximum charges allowed. The customized rules made using the program are summarized as "family rules lists" at the end of the rulemaking program. Figure 3 is an example of a family rules list made using the rulemaking navigation program.

Results of Family Rulemaking Analysis

This section illustrates the tendency of family rulemaking to focus on popular rules according to age groups, as well as rulemaking differences based on children's grade in school, which were found using data collected from the rulemaking log. The rule making result was retrieved as CSV format with data of the age, nickname and sex of children, the data of rules that the families made and access day and time as the rule making content requires the database functionality. As the data contains the attributes of child and rules, this paper shows the result of the analysis on the relationships between these factors to investigate the need of non-formal learning content.

It was necessary to clean the original CSV data because of missing values and incomplete answers. We selected data from 136 cases (out of a total of 191 cases) for analysis after eliminating incomplete cases and adopting the latest available case when several cases appeared to be linked to the same family. We judged the duplication by the age of the child, their nicknames and nearness of access time zone as it seemed that some families restarted their rulemaking activities.

As shown in Figure 4, rulemaking activity was most active for families with children in elementary school grades 5-6 (50 cases), followed by junior high school grades 1-3 (44 cases) and elementary school grades 3-4 (28 cases). There were more than twice as many female cases (94 cases) as male ones (42 cases), which indicates that more attention is given to girls' mobile usage by parents and society since girls tend to be victimized by sexual offenders using mobile communications (Figure 4).

Further Challenges for Promoting Non-Formal Learning

This paper examines family rulemaking tendencies using case data obtained from the site. The results of this analysis show that Mobami seems to be used as a supplemental program for junior high school children's needs, especially girls and their parents. Additionally, families who use the site appear to regard it as a supportive tool for setting basic rules to ensure safer mobile service usage, as intended in the site design.

However, Mobami seems to be an insufficient resource as an instructive e-learning program for high school students, who are already actively using mobile services, as Mobami is targeted at elementary and junior high school students, who tend to have rules that are more restrictive. To address these points, further cooperation among public- and private-sector groups and new approaches for improving the program are required.

Table 1. Rulemaking categories and examples of rules

Related Skill Category	Rule Category (Number of rule choices)	Examples of Rules
Basic Skill	Basic Rules (14)	Treating *Kei-tai* carefully so it does not break
		Contacting the mobile carrier immediately if you lose *Kei-tai*
		Not using *Kei-tai* while walking or riding a bicycle
		Setting *Kei-tai* to silent mode except where ringing is allowed
		Turning off *Kei-tai*'s power when it is necessary to shut it down
Call Skill	Call Rules (10)	Making phone calls only to persons who are designated beforehand
		Using a landline, not *Kei-tai*, when you make phone calls from home
		Not answering calls from strangers if you do not know the number
		Consulting with parents or seniors in your family before giving your phone number to someone
		Not giving family phone numbers or numbers of friends without asking their permission
E-mailing Skill	E-mailing Rules (11)	Not writing slanderous things about people in e-mails
		Deleting e-mail from strangers without clicking the URL in the e-mail or replying to the e-mail
		Consulting with parents or seniors in your family before giving your email address to someone
		Not giving email addresses of family members or friends without asking their permission
		Not forwarding chain e-mail
Internet Access Skill	Internet Access Rules (16)	Not accessing websites except those permitted
		Consulting with parents or seniors in your family when you want to use services that include charges, such as music download services or online games
		Consulting with parents or seniors in your family when you want to shop online
		Not writing down personal information or uploading photos of yourself or others without their permission
		Not meeting offline with persons you get to know online
Application Skill	Application Rules (11)	Asking permission when you take a photo of someone or something using a *Kei-tai* camera
		Consulting with parents or seniors in your family when you want to upload pictures you have taken
		Only using the payment function attached to *Kei-tai* at previously approved shops
		Making sure the payment function of *Kei-tai* is locked using a password
		Watching mobile television (one-episode TV) only in specific places

Figure 3. A sample family rules list
Source: Japan Internet safety Promotion Association (JISPA) (https://www.good-net.jp/)

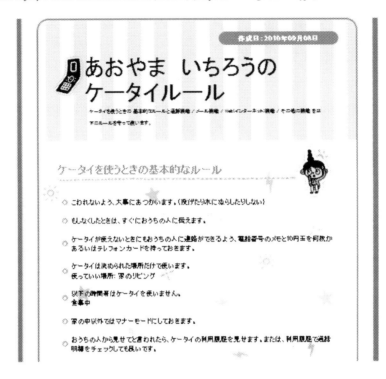

Figure 4. Frequency distribution graph of rulemaking cases

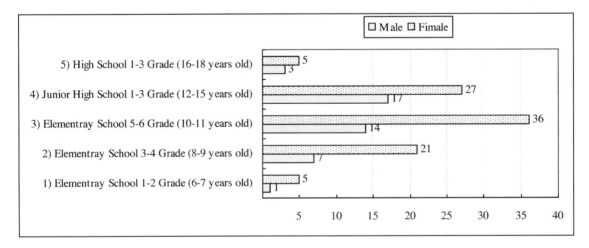

The remaining issues for further research on the program have two dimensions: the consideration of desirable measures for promoting usage of the program by successive adoption using the action research method and the investigation of how conscious children and parents who utilized the program are of the need to make their own rules about mobile Internet access.

ENLIGHTENMENT PROGRAMS FOR PARENTS

In 2012, JISPA and the Sports and Youth Bureau of MEXT jointly started a new type of workshop program for parents to facilitate their awareness of online safety. This workshop program was based on social constructionism and was a kind of revolutionary in the online safety educational program, as most of the previous programs for parents were one-way lectures held at Parent-Teacher Association meetings, etc. Saito was one of the program development members and joined the workshop as a facilitator (Ministry of Education, Culture, Sports, Science and Technology, 2012a).

Outline of "Kei-Tai Moral Caravan" and Its Research Aim

The program "Kei-tai Moral Caravan" was developed as a research project funded by the Sports and Youth Bureau of MEXT. JISPA and experts in public sectors formed a committee for the research project. Saito participated in the committee from the early stage of planning. He also worked to design the workshop-style learning program for parents, to develop a questionnaire for program assessment, and to implement the workshop events (Figure 5). The field experiment of this research project was conducted in six cities using the following three types of courses: workshop-style, talk session style, and workshop style. The outcomes of each course were analyzed and compared for optimizing upcoming policies of enlightenment education on safer Internet use. Table 3 shows the detail of six research projects which were conducted in six cities.

Figure 5. The Kei-tai Moral Caravan course
Source: Ministry of Education, Culture, Sports, Science and Technology (2012a), p. 43.

Table 2. The detail of six research projects of "Kei-tai Moral Caravan"

City	Date and time	Event type	Capacity of participants	Number of participants
Sanjo city, Niigata	Nov. 12 2011, pm 13:30-16:00	Talk Session	300	220
Kyoto city, Kyoto	Dec. 10 2011, pm13:30-16:20	Panel Discussion	750	300
Yuki city, Ibaragi	Jan. 14 2012, pm13:30-16:20	Workshop	120	110
Tokushima city, Tokushima	Jan. 28 2012, pm13:30-16:00	Talk Session	200	130
Karatsu city, Tokushima	Jan. 28 2012, pm13:30-16:15	Panel Discussion	150	120
Aomori city, Aomori	Feb. 18 2012, pm13:30-16:00	Talk session	300	140

Source: Ministry of Education, Culture, Sports, Science and Technology (2012a), p. 3.

Assessment of the Kei-Tai Moral Caravan Course Through Participant Evaluations

The research team distributed a questionnaire to the course participants. The team adopted a four-point Likert scale to measure the course benefits. Four points were allocated to the answer "very useful" in response to the question "How useful was the course for you?" Three points were given for "useful," two points for "not so useful," and one point for "useless." The course consisted of three parts, and the evaluation results for each part are shown in Table 3. The participants highly valued the workshop-style course, as it was rated an average of 3.59 points, compared to 3.35 on the panel discussion course and 3.29 on the talk session course (p=0.001) (Table 3).

The participants' level of satisfaction was also assessed using a four-point Likert scale. Four points were allocated to the answer "very satisfied," three points to "satisfactory," two points to "somewhat unsatisfactory," and one point to "unsatisfactory." Again, the workshop-style course gained the highest mark of 3.48, in comparison with 3.20 for the panel discussion course and 3.21 for the talk session course (p=0.002) (Table 4).

Table 3. Evaluation of the course usefulness by parent participants. Question: "How useful was the course for you?"

Group	Sample Size	Sum	Average	Variance
Panel discussion	149	499	3.35	0.39
Talk session	276	908	3.29	0.34
Workshop	66	237	3.59	0.25

Table 4. Evaluation of the satisfaction level of parent participants by course. Question: How satisfied are you with each course?

Group	Sample Size	Total	Average	Variance
Panel discussion	136	435	3.2	0.32
Talk session	266	853	3.21	0.33
Workshop	62	216	3.48	0.32

The results of the above analysis show that the workshop-style course was more effective in terms of usefulness than the other types of courses in promoting the online safety consciousness of parents. The cost, however, of holding workshops is more expensive, as it requires small group discussions with facilitators who specialize in the field. The facilitator has the role of stimulating the group, navigating the discussion, and coordinating interactions. Therefore, an experienced organizer should take a workshop for a successful orientation. On the other hand, courses that use panel discussions or talk sessions can handle more participants at one time.

Challenges to the Workshop-Style Course Offerings

The assessment of courses for parents indicates that the workshop-style course is effective for online safety education. There are, however, several challenges to providing this type of course, according to the posteriori questionnaire survey of six course lecturers who played the facilitator role (Ministry of Education, Culture, Sports, Science and Technology, 2012a). The survey used a free description method to ask about "issues on holding workshop-style programs in the future." Three of the lecturers pointed out tasks related to the workshop operation: the need to cultivate facilitators, to enhance understanding for workshops in areas where participants are not familiar with the style, and to inform participants of the differences between a seminar style and workshop.

Their opinion on the need for facilitators suggests the importance of obtaining the human resource of facilitators to offer the workshops. Generally, a lecture-style program needs just one lecturer. However, the workshop style requires one lecturer for handling whole program and a facilitator for each discussion group.

The second and third points raised suggest the need for pre-instruction for the participants. Parents who attend workshops might have psychological barriers to contributing to the workshop discussion, as they may be unfamiliar or uncomfortable with the format. Because some have never experienced the style, which is not a common learning method in Japan, there is a need to remove this barrier before the workshop begins. Furthermore, some staff of the online safety program also lack experience participating in workshops. In this case, the program organizer should offer pre-instruction on workshops to the program staff. This will increase the time and human resources needed.

DEVELOPMENT OF INDICATOR FOR ASSESSING THE INTERNET LITERACY OF YOUTHS AND PARENTS

Development of ILAS JISPA

To discuss effectively the protection of youths online, it is essential to evaluate and analyze the ability of youths and parents to use the Internet appropriately. The research group of this study collaborated with the JISPA to develop the Internet Literacy Assessment Indicator for Students (ILAS JISPA) in 2014, for evaluating the Internet literacy of both youths and their parents. In this study, by analyzing the nationwide the ILAS JISPA data, the Internet literacy of youths and parents was evaluated to discuss future policy making for providing support to parents.

Online literacy is systematically collected by the ILAS JISPA. It defines 3 online abilities as follows: The ability to cope appropriately with illegal and harmful contents on the Internet, the ability to communicate appropriately on the Internet, and the ability to protect privacy and security on the Internet. Online risks are classified into major 3 categories: I. Illegal and harmful Information risks, II. Inappropriate usage risks, and III. Privacy and security risks. In addition, 7 medium categories and 13 sub-categories are defined (Table 5). The indicator contains 21 questions to evaluate the level of online literacy (Table 6) (Japan Internet Safety Promotion Association, 2015).

The Data Which Was Collected for Analysis

This study uses the data which was collected from the survey conducted by Japan Internet Safety Promotion Association in 2015. The sample was collected from all over the Japan. Guardian's sample number was 1,327 (valid response 1,261) which were collected from 4 areas in Tohoku district and 2 areas in Kanto district. High school student's sample number was 365 (valid response 350) which were collected from 1 area in Tohoku district, 1 area in Kanto district, and 1 area in Kansai district. Junior high school

Table 5. The Internet literacy risk categorization list

Major category	Medium category	Sub-category
I. Illegal and harmful Information risks	A. Illegal information	1. Copyrights, portrait rights, criminal threats, dating sites, etc.
	B. Harmful information	1. Content offensive to public order and morality, adult-only content, etc.
II. Inappropriate usage risks	A. Inappropriate contact	1. Libel
		2. Anonymous social networking site (SNS)
		3. Non-anonymous SNS
		4. Spam
		5. Applications
	B. Improper transactions	1. Fraud, sale of improper products, etc.
	C. Inappropriate usage	1. Excess Internet consumption
		2. Dependence
III. Privacy and security risks	A. Privacy risks	1. Leakage of private and/or personal information, inappropriate disclosure
	B. Security risks	1. Impersonation through unauthorised access, etc.
		2. Viruses

Source: Japan Internet Safety Promotion Association (2015)

Table 6. Sample questions

Category	Sample Questions
1a	I posted my favorite singer's lyrics on my personal page of the SNS. Which of the following describes best on this action? 1. If it was a part of the lyrics, no problem at all. 2. It's illegal to post lyrics without permission regardless how much I love the singer. 3. No problem, because I released it only for my friends. 4. I don't understand words/contents of the question.
1b	Which of the following describes best when minors play portable game? 1. There is no concern about compromising your personal information when you use a portable gaming console. 2. You should use filtering when you connect to internet with your portable gaming console. 3. It's safe because the online network of portable game is designed for children. 4. I don't understand words/contents of the question.
2a	Which of the following describes best on online bullying? 1. It can be a crime even though the bullying occurred online. 2. You can make a snide remark about someone because nobody can detect your name when you hide your name online. 3. There is no possibility that you bully someone online without your intention. 4. I don't understand words/contents of the question.
2b	When you were using a smartphone, you clicked a link by mistake. Then it showed "This is a paid site. Please pay 5,000 yen as soon as possible". Which of the following is the best solution? 1. Mailing to the showed address that you won't pay for it. 2. Paying for that to avoid collecting. 3. You can ignore it. You can discuss about it with your family to ease your anxiety. 4. I don't understand words/contents of the question.
2c	Some games can be connected to internet to play with someone online. Which of the following is the best way when you play the online game? 1. You can trust the online gaming buddy because the person is your genuine friend. 2. You shouldn't get out from the game for taking meals because it is rude for gaming buddy. 3. When you play online games, you should decide when to quit it beforehand. 4. I don't understand words/contents of the question.
3a	I want to introduce my 3 friends by posting their picture on my blog. Which of the following is the best solution? 1. I don't need my friends' permission if the picture was taken by myself. 2. I should get permission from all of them. 3. I don't need my friend's permission if the picture shows their side face. 4. I don't understand words/contents of the question.
3b	Using smartphone by walking/ riding a bicycle may be very dangerous. Which of the following describes best to avoid accident? 1. Avoid busy street when you use smartphone by walking. 2. Avoid controlling it, and you can just watching the display by walking. 3. You can be charged when you use smartphone by riding a bicycle. 4. I don't understand words/contents of the question.

student's sample number was 601 (valid response 560) which were collected from 1 area in Kanto district, and 1 area in Tokai district. The total number was 2,293 (valid response 2,171) (Table 7).

Comparison on Literacy Scores Between Students and Parents

The Average Percentages Which Were Answered Correctly and Kruskal Wallis Test Results

The average percentages which were answered correctly on total 21 questions of ILAS JISPA test were calculated on parents, high school students, and junior high school students. The average percentage of parents was highest (90.6%). It was followed by high school student (83.1%), and junior high school students (81.2%). Significant difference was shown between these 3 average percentages by Kruskal Wallis test ($p < 0.01$) (see Table 2 And Figure 1).

Table 7. Overview of ILAS JISPA survey in 2015

Date	Sep. 1, 2015 to Jan. 30, 2016
Research area	Parents: 4 areas in Tohoku district and 2 areas in Kanto district
	High school students: 1 area in Tohoku district, 1 area in Kanto district, and 1 area in Kansai district
	Junior high school students: 1 area in Kanto district, and 1 area in Tokai district
Sample number	Parents: 1,327 (valid response 1,261)
	High school students: 365 (valid response 350)
	Junior high school students: 601 (valid response 560)

Source: Japan Internet Safety Promotion Association (2015)

Next, the average percentages which were answered correctly on sub-total of each 7 medium categories of ILAS JISPA test were also calculated on parents, high school students, and junior high school students. The result showed that average percentages of parents' were higher than that of youths in all 7 medium categories (see Table 2 and Figure 1). On the other hand, the average percentages of junior high school students' were higher than that of high school students in "Harmful information (1b)", "Inappropriate usage (2c)", and "Privacy risks (3a)". Significant difference of average percentages between parents, high school students, and junior high school students were shown in all 7 medium categories by Kruskal Wallis test ($p<0.01$, $p<0.01$, $p<0.01$, $p<0.01$, $p<0.05$, $p<0.01$, $p<0.01$) (see Table 8, Figure 6).

Comparison of Average Percentages of Students and Parents Who Answered Questions Correctly

The aforementioned results showed that the average percentages of parents who answered correctly were significantly higher than those of youths in all seven medium categories. However, a previous study suggested that parents did not have confidence in providing proper guidance to youths at home (Japan Internet Safety Promotion Association, 2015). Therefore, the average percentages of students and parents who answered each question correctly were compared in the present study to identify the literacy areas in which parents have a disadvantage.

Table 8. Average percentage which was answered correctly in ILAS JISPA test

Average percentage	Parents (n=1,261)	High school students (n=350)	Junior high school students (n=560)	P value
total 21 questions	90.6	83.1	81.2	<0.01
1a. Illegal information	77.0	73.3	70.7	<0.01
1b. Harmful information	90.6	77.5	77.9	<0.01
2a. Inappropriate contact	96.2	89.9	88.4	<0.01
2b. Improper transactions	96.8	87.3	83.0	<0.01
2c. Inappropriate usage	87.2	82.7	83.1	<0.05
3a. Privacy risks	95.4	85.7	86.7	<0.01
3b. Security risks	89.4	81.9	76.2	<0.01

Figure 6. Average percentage which was answered correctly in each category

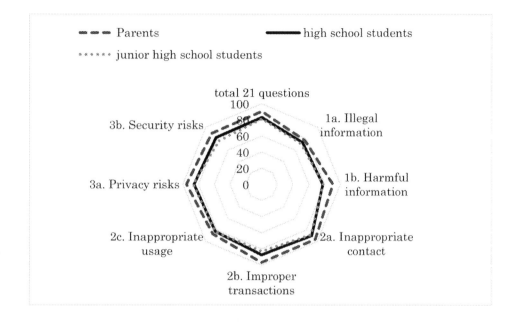

The comparison results showed that the average percentages of parents who answered correctly were higher than those of youths for most questions, except for questions 10 and 11. For question 10, "Online game billing and coping strategies," the average percentages for answering correctly yielded the following ranking: high school students (77.6%), junior high school students (75.7%), and parents (72.8%). For question 11, "Understanding of the 'Act on Regulation on Soliciting Children by Using Opposite Sex Introducing Service on Internet,'" the ranking was as follows: high school students (72.6%), parents (66.3%), and junior high school students (61.1%) (see Table 9).

The χ square test was then performed on the average percentages of participants who answered questions 10 and 11 correctly. First, the χ square test was performed on the average percentages of parents (72.8%) and high school students (77.6%) who answered question 10 correctly. The P value was not significant at the 5% level (p=0.07), but high school students tended to answer this question correctly more than parents did, at the 10% level. Next, the χ square test was performed on the average percentages of parents (72.8%) and junior high school students (75.7%) who answered question 10 correctly. The result yielded no significant difference (p=0.20).

Second, the χ square test was performed on the average percentages of parents (66.3%) and high school students (72.6%) who answered question 11 correctly. The result showed that high school students answered this question correctly significantly more than parents did (p=0.02). Next, the χ square test was performed on the average percentages of parents (66.3%) and junior high school students (61.1%) who answered question 11 correctly. The result showed that parents answered this question correctly significantly more than junior high school students did (p=0.03) (see Table 10).

Therefore, parents had attained higher general Internet literacy compared with youths. However, for question 11, "Understanding of the 'Act on Regulation on Soliciting Children by Using Opposite Sex Introducing Service on Internet,'" they had significantly lower understanding than high school students did; and for question 10, "Online game billing and coping strategies," they tended to have lower understanding compared with high school students.

Table 9. Comparison of average percentages of students and parents who answered questions correctly

Question number	Category	Contents	Parents	High school students	Junior high school students
1	2c	Appropriate time to spend on online games	91.50%	79.80%	85.90%
2	1b	Importance of filtering settings	94.80%	86.10%	84.50%
3	1a	Illegal downloads of copyrighted material	89.10%	83.00%	80.60%
4	2a	Understanding of online bullying	96.70%	91.10%	87.40%
5	3a	Understanding of online applications	95.90%	85.30%	85.50%
6	3a	Taking pictures and obtaining permission	98.20%	92.00%	92.30%
7	3b	Smartphone use while walking	94.50%	82.50%	82.30%
8	1b	Message board use that needs ID exchange	89.70%	76.70%	79.40%
9	1a	Understanding of copyrights of lyrics	75.60%	64.00%	70.10%
10	2c	Online game billing and coping strategies	72.80%	77.60%	75.70%
11	1a	Understanding of the "Act on Regulation on Soliciting Children by Using Opposite Sex Introducing Service on Internet"	66.30%	72.60%	61.10%
12	2c	Understanding of Internet addiction	97.30%	90.80%	87.60%
13	2a	Coping strategies for online troubles	94.40%	87.20%	87.60%
14	1b	Understanding of the "Act on Establishment of Enhanced Environment for Youth's Safe and Secure Internet Use"	87.00%	69.40%	68.50%
15	3a	Coping strategies for message boards	91.80%	79.80%	81.50%
16	2b	Coping strategies for improper transactions	96.80%	89.40%	84.80%
17	2a	Risks of inappropriate posts	97.40%	91.40%	90.20%
18	2b	Understanding of credit card holders	95.80%	82.20%	74.70%
19	3b	Knowledge of security software	79.60%	77.20%	65.70%
20	2b	Coping strategies for fraud	98.00%	89.40%	89.60%
21	3b	Knowledge of Internet viruses	94.10%	86.10%	80.40%

Table 10. Comparison of average percentages of students and parents who answered questions 10 and 11 correctly

		Question 10			Question 11		
		Parents	**High school students**	**Junior high school students**	**Parents**	**High school students**	**Junior high school students**
Wrong answer	N	355	81	142	443	99	227
	%	27.2	22.4	24.3	33.7	27.4	38.9
Correct answer	N	952	280	442	870	262	357
	%	72.8	77.6	75.7	66.3	72.6	61.1
Total	N	1307	361	584	1313	361	584
	%	100.0	100.0	100.0	100.0	100.0	100.0

Discussion on Analysis Results

The results yielded the following ranking of Internet literacy: parents, high school students, and junior high school students, with the overall Internet literacy of parents' being significantly higher than that of youths. In addition, parents showed significantly higher Internet literacy than that of youths in all seven medium categories systematically defined by the ILAS JISPA.

The Japanese policy on awareness education for parents is based on the assumption that parents have lower Internet literacy than that of youths; thus, providing educational opportunities to enhance support for parents has been a primary challenge (Ministry of Internal Affairs and Communications, 2009c). However, the present study obtained evidence to overturn the prevailing orthodoxy.

On the other hand, for all questions defined by the ILAS JISPA, this study found that parents showed higher literacy than youths did. Parents tended to have lower understanding compared with high school students for "online game billing and coping strategies." In addition, parents had significantly lower understanding than high school students did for "understanding of the 'Act on Regulation on Soliciting Children by Using Opposite Sex Introducing Service on Internet.'" Thus, parents have higher Internet literacy in general than youths do, despite having limited literacy regarding unfamiliar risks.

Therefore, it will be necessary for parents, who must provide appropriate guidance to their children, to become apprised of emerging troubles caused by the latest applications and acquire the skills necessary to monitor Internet use without their continual attendance. Therefore, in addition to knowledge-based instruction, awareness education for parents must present cases of typical troubles caused by the latest devices and applications, enhance coping strategies, and instill best practices in order to improve the Internet literacy of parents.

SUMMARY AND CONCLUSION

This paper provides an overview of the practice of information morals education in Japan, focusing on the activities of JISPA. Information morals are a different concept from information literacy or media literacy. The idea includes having appropriate knowledge, skills, and attitude in cyber space. Due to the rapid growth of Internet use, especially mobile Internet access. On the other hand, parents, who are responsible for providing social skills training, have not benefited from formal learning programs on information morals because of their generational difference. Aiming to improve this situation, the newly enacted Youth Internet Environment Improvement Act sets up a legal framework for providing educational opportunities for teaching information morals to both children and parents. Moreover, the act encourages voluntary activities to provide non-formal learning materials and opportunities.

This paper focuses on JISPA activities and the assessment process using various data analyses and field research data. Mobami, one of the non-formal learning programs for children and parents, introduces the concept of instructional design and composition to facilitate information morals education and mobile literacy. Mobami was developed by JISPA with the support of private-sector companies. Additionally, the paper examines the rulemaking tendencies by analyzing the program's rulemaking data. The results of the rulemaking data analysis show that junior high school students and their parents are more conscious of the necessity of making rules at home than elementary school students and their parents. The popularity of certain rules reveals parents' high level of attention to their children's communications via e-mails from mobile phones.

The above analysis also revealed the further challenges of learning opportunities for high school students, who become more active and varied in their Internet service usage. As it becomes difficult to limit their usage, JISPA expanded their non-formal learning opportunities to real events such as Keitai Moral Caravan for parents. Starting new events, JISPA joined a comparative field research study to examine effective approaches to promoting online safety. The results of the field research showed that the workshop style was more effective at deepening the knowledge of parent participants.

As this paper discussed, JISPA's efforts to improve children's online safety have evolved from offering e-learning content and guidelines to holding workshops in the real world. JISPA's activities are characterized by its evolving process, in which changes are made based on feedback and assessments of their activities, such as e-learning content from Mobami and discussion workshops for high school students. Furthermore, JISPA has become a hub among the concerned parties including telecom carriers, IT companies, and individuals; it has 186 members as of November 2013.

Based on the results of this analysis, it would be desirable for non-formal learning activities to support formal learning activities. Data analysis and feedback from non-formal learning experiences should be used to improve formal learning practices. As the areas of information education and mobile literacy are new to the formal education system, this would require that additional and continuous research be done to identify areas for improvement in both formal and non-formal educational content and methodologies.

Moreover, this study sought to derive evidence in order to discuss effective policy making for providing support to parents who must monitor Internet use and protect youths against various online troubles. Because Article 3 of the supplementary provision of the Youth Internet Environment Improvement Act aims to review continually the development of the protection policy for youths and the improvement of the policy based on evidence provided, the evidence must be made available throughout Japanese society.

This study evaluated the Internet literacy of youths and parents based on data collected by a nationwide survey of the ILAS JISPA, to obtain evidence for effective policy making for youth protection. The results showed that parents had significantly higher Internet literacy than that of youths in all seven risk categories systematically defined by the ILAS JISPA. However, parents had significantly lower understanding of several risks.

The limited understanding of parents was related to the risks that have emerged from smartphone use. Therefore, the challenge of providing support to parents must be overcome to improve understanding of these types of emerging problems. For its sake, providing information on lacked online risks through awareness education, and it will be important to enhance social system which can play enough roles.

ACKNOWLEDGMENT

This research was partially supported by the Ministry of Education, Science, Sports and Culture, Grant-in-Aid for Scientific Research (C), 2017-2020 (17K00467, Nagayuki Saito).

This study could not have been completed without the cooperation with Japan Internet Safety Promotion Association (JISPA). We take this opportunity to thank them.

REFERENCES

Broadcast Ethics and Program Improvement Organization. (2013). *Broadcast Ethics and Program Improvement Organization Agreement.* Retrieved from http://www.bpo.gr.jp/wp/wp-content/themes/codex/pdf/bpo/20130529BPOkiyaku.pdf (in Japanese)

Bronfenbrenner, U. (1979). *The ecology of human development: experiments by nature and design.* Cambridge, MA: Harvard University Press.

Cabinet Office. (2006). *5th Annual Survey Report on Information Society and Young People.* Retrieved from http://www8.cao.go.jp/youth/kenkyu/jouhou5/index.html (in Japanese)

Higuchi, S. (2013). *Net Dependency.* PHP Laboratory. (in Japanese)

Japan Internet Safety Promotion Association. (2010). *Mobile family Mobami.* Press release. Retrieved from http://good-net.jp/modules/news/uploadFile/2010020334.pdf (in Japanese)

Japan Internet Safety Promotion Association. (2015). *ILAS2015 Final Report.* Japan Internet Safety Promotion Association. (in Japanese)

Kobayashi, N. (2011). *Cases of Social Media Flame Incidents.* Nikkei Digital Marketing. (in Japanese)

Ministry of Education, Culture, Sports, Science and Technology. (2008). *Survey Report on Unofficial School Informal Sites Used by Students.* Retrieved from http://www.mext.go.jp/a_menu/sports/ikusei/taisaku/1262855.htm (in Japanese)

Ministry of Education, Culture, Sports, Science and Technology. (2012a). *The Kei-tai Moral Caravan course.* Retrieved from http://www.mext.go.jp/a_menu/seisyounen/moral/1313273.htm (in Japanese)

Ministry of Education, Culture, Sports, Science and Technology. (2012b). *Research Report of the Promoting Measures to Harmful Informations to Face the Youth.* Retrieved from http://www.mext.go.jp/a_menu/seisyounen/moral/1328093.htm (in Japanese)

Ministry of Education, Culture, Sports, Science and Technology. (2016). *Survey on Problems Related to Student Guidance to Problematic Behavior of Students in FY2008*. Retrieved from http://www.mext.go.jp/b_menu/houdou/29/10/__icsFiles/afieldfile/2017/10/26/1397646_001.pdf (in Japanese)

Ministry of Internal Affairs and Communications. (2009a). *Survey Research on Trouble Cases in the Internet Usage - Internet Troubles Case Study* (Vol. 3). Retrieved from http://www.soumu.go.jp/main_content/000173733.pdf (in Japanese)

Ministry of Internal Affairs and Communications. (2009b). *Program for the Development of Safe and Secure Internet Environment - Safety Network Promotion Program*. Retrieved from http://www.soumu.go.jp/menu_news/s-news/2009/pdf/090116_2_bs.pdf (in Japanese)

Ministry of Internal Affairs and Communications. (2009c). *Final report of Study Group on Measures to Illegal and Harmful Information on the Internet: Internet Safety Promotion Program*. Tokyo: Ministry of Internal Affairs and Communications. (in Japanese)

Mukoda, K. (2003). *TV and cognitive abilities. In Media and Human Development - Psychological Impact of TV, TV Game, Internet, and Robots* (pp. 23–40). Gakubunsha. (in Japanese)

National Police Agency. (2017). *Current Situation and Countermeasures of Offenses Arising from Community Sites etc. in the First Half of FY2017*. Retrieved from https://www.npa.go.jp/cyber/statics/h29/H29_siryou.pdf (in Japanese)

Saito, N., & Yoshida, T. (2013). The Policy Issues for the Environmental Improvement of Smartphone Usage for Youth: Examination of Policy Issues by Analysis of Empirical Data. *Information and Communications Policy Review*, 6, 1–21.

Shimoda, H. (2008). *School Back Site*. Toyo Keizai Inc. (in Japanese)

Yoshimi, T., & Mizukoshi, S. (2004). *Media theories*. The Open University of Japan. (in Japanese)

Yukawa, S. (2003). *TV and Violence. In Media and Human Development - Psychological Impact of TV, TV Game, Internet, and Robots* (pp. 41–57). Gakubunsha. (in Japanese)

KEY TERMS AND DEFINITIONS

E-Learning Content: Educational materials offered online.

Family Rules: Rules that should be held by family members.

ILAS JISPA: An indicator developed to measure the internet literacy of young people and parents.

Media Literacy: The ability to use media properly with sufficient knowledge, skill, and moral conscience.

Mobile Phone: A wireless device which has several communication functions such as call, website access, e-mail, and so on.

Non-Formal Learning: Learning practices conducted outside of formal learning in schools.

Chapter 13
Play It Like Burberry!
The Effect of Reputation, Brand Image, and Social Media on E–Reputation – Luxury Brands and Their Digital Natives Fans

Insaf Khelladi
ICN Business School, France

Sylvaine Castellano
Paris School of Business, France

ABSTRACT

Some firms and industries were not willing to take full advantage of the internet and its endless opportunities, mainly because they rather focused on the inherent risks and challenges. However, when taking into consideration the specificities of the connected generation, the question is not anymore whether to go online or not, but rather to understand how, when, and where, especially in a luxury context. More specifically, the digital natives represent tomorrow's customers. This new market segment represents a main reason for luxury firms to adopt online strategies. Still, further analysis is needed to uncover the main objectives when firms decide to engage in digital activities. The authors herein investigate the concept of e-reputation. The authors expand on their initial study that focused on brand image and social media as determinants of online reputation. Recommendations and future research directions are suggested.

INTRODUCTION

Social media is the phenomenon of our era. In 2015, more than 211 well-known social media websites were accounted (Erkan, 2015). The number of social networking users attained 2.46 billion in 2017, and is expected to reach 2.95 billion by 2020, which would represent about 40% of the Earth overall population (Statista, 2017a). Social media is also the place where almost every Internet user can be reached as well. More than 94% of digital consumers have at least an account in one social network site (GlobalWebIndex, 2017). Last but not least, social media is the place where people spend almost one third of their daily Internet time on social networking and messaging (GlobalWebIndex, 2017). But,

DOI: 10.4018/978-1-5225-7214-5.ch013

more importantly, social media is becoming paramount for marketing activities. Indeed, more than 70% of consumers have visited social networking sites to collect information; nearly half of them decide to purchase based on the information gathered through social media sites (DEI Worldwide, 2008). Moreover, 60% of consumers stated their likelihood to use social media websites to pass along the online information they got; and two-thirds of them confirm the influence of the online Word-of-Mouth on their perceptions of a brand and on their purchase decision (DEI Worldwide, 2008).

Social media and the luxury business were long term foes. On the one hand, social media is known for its immediacy, extreme speed and widespread sharing (Kaplan and Haenlein, 2010). Also, thanks to its versatile and unpredictable nature, social media serves as virtual brand and anti-brand community, rendering positive and negative UGC (User-Generated Content) simultaneously co-exiting (Annie Jin, 2012). Moreover, customers are more and more using wikis, blogs and social networking to create, modify, and discuss Internet content, thus dramatically impacting companies' reputation and growth (Kietzmann et al., 2011). On the other hand, the luxury world is known for its heritage, immutability and exclusivity (Kapferer & Bastien, 2009). Luxury brands are unique, selective and exclusive (Chevalier & Mazzalovo, 2008); such attributes are evoked through high quality, premium pricing and a strictly controlled distribution (Annie Jin, 2012). Hence, nothing is fast in luxury; everything is held on to in time, is preserved or is aged. Nothing is shared, and everything is exclusive, secret and reserved for a selected clientele. Furthermore, while social media involves facts, delivering raw contents without any artifice, luxury involves fantasy, in which the luxury brand *"[…] goes beyond the object: it is constructed from the reputation."* (Kapferer, 2012, p.142), delivering products on a silver dish with the required ceremony. All in all, social media and luxury seem being part of two opposite worlds. Yet, one can wonder why Chanel is Instagramming, Dior is twitting, and Burberry is snapchatting!

The luxury business is the one of the mature sectors that has resisted the best to the economic decline, and where companies are demonstrating strong growth figures, whether in volume or in value. Indeed, the luxury market is a high-value-added industry (Kim & Ko, 2012), in which luxury brands still represent a noteworthy portion of consumer product sales, especially in emerging markets such as India, China and the Middle East. The sales revenue of LVMH, the world's largest luxury group owning around 50 of the most well-known luxury brands worldwide, have reached €37.6 billion in 2016, exhibiting a 5% growth progress (LVMH, 2017). Also, LVMH's operating margin is more than 18% and the net profit reached more than 3.9 billion, an 11% increase (LVMH, 2017). Moreover, the global personal luxury goods market, the core of luxury, is expected to reach almost €260 billion in 2017, and to gain 3-4% growth per year, by 2020 (Bain & Company, 2017). Nevertheless, the luxury sector is becoming more and more competitive with the recent arrival of many luxury and premium brands. Hence, traditional luxury brands can no longer rely on their brand symbol, but need to better emphasize their brand legacy, quality, aesthetic value, and trustworthy customer relationships in order to prosper (Kim & Ko, 2012).

One major reason explaining luxury brands' engagement in digital activities is to reach their future consumers, namely, the digital natives (Kennedy et al., 2008). Indeed, luxury brands' future success will be built on the younger generation, as millennials and Gen Z will represent 45% of the global personal luxury goods market by 2025 (Bain & Company, 2017). Still, this young generation is complex and requires additional insight (Hargittai, 2010).

Although reputation and image are inherent to the luxury industry (Kapferer & Bastien, 2009), and social media represents a major challenge for luxury brands especially among digital natives (Hargittai, 2010), previous research has not explored their influence on e-reputation. Hence, further research regarding the activities on social media in a luxury context is needed, especially to analyze the reputation of luxury brands online and to better understand the behavior of digital natives who represent their future core consumers. The aim of this chapter is threefold (1) understand reputation, brand image antecedents of e-reputation and the underlying role of social media, (2) investigate the perception of digital natives of luxury brands' image, reputation and e-reputation, and (3) propose recommendations and futures directions on how to manage e-reputation, social media and digital natives, as well as the future role of Gen Z in the luxury world.

In the next paragraphs, we explore e-reputation and brand image in a social networks context. Then, we investigate the growing importance of social networks in the luxury industry in general and the specific case of the French context. The chapter concludes with key recommendations and future research areas on e-reputation and digital natives' management.

E-REPUTATION AND CORPORATE BRAND IMAGE IN A SOCIAL MEDIA CONTEXT

Reputation Offline and Online

Reputation is "a perceptual representation of a company's past actions and future prospects that describe the firm's overall appeal to all its key constituents when compared to other leading rivals." (Fombrun, 1996, p.72). It reflects the aggregate opinion of the company's internal and external stakeholders' perceptions (Dutot & Castellano, 2015). Past research assessed reputation in terms of signals of quality, esteem, image, prestige, goodwill, hence to favorable aspects (Deephouse, 2000).

E-reputation has often been viewed as an extension of online reputation, although it refers to the "elements of reputation which is derived from electronic contacts." (Chun & Davies, 2001, p.316). E-reputation results from the perception of the evaluating online communities, their intrinsic motivations, and their retention of online content.

Firms face new challenges especially when they need to build, manage, or restore their reputation online (Dutot & Castellano, 2015). On the one hand, reputation is built over time and summarizes the past assessments of evaluators. One the other hand, e-reputation is immediate and reflects evaluators' instant perceptions. On another note, reputation is co-created and co-managed when it appears online (Castellano et al., 2014).

Differentiating reputation and e-reputation is even more important when it comes to specific types of reputation. Of particular interest is media reputation, which is "the representation of a person or organization in the media - from the standpoint of complex systems." (Murphy, 2010). When going online, one can wonder if media reputation becomes a social media reputation. Also, as highlighted by Forman and Argenti (2005), reputation drives from the image of the different constituencies and audiences that evaluate the firm. Investigating the role of brand image as an underlying determinants of e-reputation is therefore of interest.

Brand Image

Corporate brand image is the way a company presents itself to the public. Corporate brand image derives from corporate identity and is closely connected to corporate reputation. The link between image and reputation is further presented by Forman and Argenti (2005). Image is the link between a firm's identity and a firm's reputation. While firms may have a direct control on their identity and their reputation, it seems more challenging and problematic regarding the perception from different stakeholders.

Brand image is the stakeholders' perception of a firm's reputation (Alwi & Da Silva, 2007). The Internet challenged the way that corporate branding is built, managed and understood (Alwi & Da Silva, 2007). E-reputation mirrors the image that Internet users have concerning a company and considers the online available information and other people's opinions of the company. Also, corporate brand image is a determinant of e-reputation (Dutot & Castellano, 2015).

Therefore, to which extent are the reputation and the image of a firm impacted when audiences evolve online? In order to better unveil the challenges that firms face, we hereafter present social media.

Social Media

Social media is defined as "[…] a group of Internet-based applications that build on the ideological and technological foundations of Web 2.0 and that allow the creation and exchange of User Generated Content." (Kaplan and Haenlein, 2010, p.61). Social media encompasses various types of media and represent new opportunities. Kaplan and Haenlein (2010) distinguished between collaborative projects (e.g., Wikipedia), blogs and micro blogs (e.g., Twitter), content communities (e.g., YouTube), social networking sites (e.g., Facebook), virtual game worlds (e.g., World of Warcraft) and virtual social words (e.g., Second Life). Social media displays many contents. Each content has a specific role. For example, YouTube displays movies and attractive images that attempt to go viral. Facebook allows creating informative content that can be shared with a community. Twitter acts as an instant messenger and disseminates words and pictures, as well as advertising and YouTube and Facebook contents, which create a phenomenon. Furthermore, it is currently insufficient to have a dedicated brand Facebook page. Companies must also provide interesting content regarding animation, news and interactions with people (Phan, 2011).

The web itself has become a complex stakeholder difficult to manage from reputation perspective. The building blocks of e-reputation previously identified help us understand the specificities of reputation online and its inherent challenges which can occur on three levels (see Figure 1), which are presented hereafter.

- The first online challenge is connected with the perception of the firm's identity, which encompasses the brand dimension. It relates to the e-character (personality of the company), the e-identity (website's structure and ergonomics) and e-experience (online user experience) (Chun, 2005). Online audiences might not perceive correctly the corporate identity developed by the firm. Consumers are no longer mere information receivers; they become active transmitters which extends their power. Thus, consumers can no longer be content with a unique speech, and they currently compare and cross reference information to shape their proper opinions.

Figure 1. E-reputation processes and challenges
(adapted from Forman & Argenti, 2005)

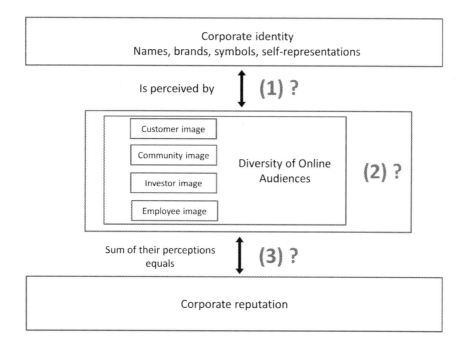

- The second online challenge is related to the social media, also called "*Consumer-Generated Media*" (Blackshaw & Nazzaro, 2004), which reflects new online information sources that are created, initiated, distributed and used by diverse audiences. The heterogeneity of online audiences combined with the speed, proximity, and endless sharing links that characterize the Internet create additional layers of complexity to manage. Overall, the firm is no longer defined by what it says or does but by what other people say, amplify or distort thanks to the Internet (Larkin, 2003).
- The third online challenge is linked to the biases and alterations that can exist between the perception of online audiences and the e-reputation granted. Social media can bring many advantages if firms are able to manage the above-mentioned challenges. Similarly, if they fail to tackle any of these issues, firms will face reputational concerns. Social media changes the way individuals communicate with one another (Aula, 2010) and influence reputation (Kietzmann et al., 2011). Through their connected devices such as laptops and smartphones, consumers search easily, participate openly, publish instantly and network quickly, which makes them dynamic stakeholders.

These three challenges encompass the four dimensions of e-reputation – brand characteristics; quality of website; quality of service; and social media – identified in past studies (Dutot & Castellano, 2015).

All in all, social media provide many advantages. Nevertheless, their biggest drawback is the brand image damage in the case of poor social media management (Phan et al., 2011). Consequently, social media challenges the traditional corporate reputation concerning (1) corporate communication's interaction and influence, (2) looking good compared with being good and (3) managing the subjective, collective truth regarding what a corporation is and what it should be (Aula, 2010). We hereafter analyze such challenges in the context of luxury firms aiming at targeting digital natives.

THE GROWING IMPORTANCE OF SOCIAL MEDIA IN THE LUXURY INDUSTRY

Kapferer and Bastien (2009, p.311), pointed out that nowadays "luxury is everywhere. Everyone wants his products to be luxury. The concept of luxury is attractive and fashionable […] there is confusion today about what really makes a luxury product, a luxury brand or a luxury company." Therefore, as emphasized by Bernard Arnault, the CEO of LVMH, "[…] a brand is built over time and patience is an essential virtue." (LVMH Letter to shareholders, 2013, p.2).

One key aspect of a luxury brand is to control all aspects of the business. From product design to the procurement of raw materials, distribution and marketing, luxury brands have maintained strict control of all activities. However, the introduction of the Internet has shaken the luxury industry. The Internet has greatly influenced how the luxury industry works and how consumers interact, especially the digital natives.

The Luxury Industry

The overall luxury industry encompasses several markets such as luxury automobiles, leather goods, ready-to-wear and haute couture, cosmetics, real estate, hotels and spas, wine and spirits, gastronomy, design and art. Such industry reached €1.08 trillion in retail sales in 2016, with luxury cars, luxury hospitality and personal luxury goods, accounting together for about 80% of the total market (Bain & Company, 2016). Moreover, the global luxury consumer population is also facing an upraise, moving from 90 million in 1995 to 330 million in 2013, and is forecasted to reach 400 million by 2020 and 500 million by 2030 (Bain & Company, 2014). The luxury goods industry in France reached around €20 billion in 2017, which is the 4th largest market worldwide, behind the U.S., China, and Japan (Statista, 2017b). Luxury firms can be independent (i.e., Hermes) or controlled by large luxury global groups such as LVMH and Kering (Formerly PPR) in France, Richemont in Switzerland and Luxottica in Italy.

Previous studies have shown the complexity of the luxury industry in terms of categorization. For instance, Castarède (1992) suggests three circles that are based on a classification of luxury objects – a 1st circle that links to heritage, a 2nd circle that links to image, and a 3rd circle that links to quality and wellness. Allérès (1995) distinguishes luxury brands based on social class hierarchy – accessible, inter-mediary and not accessible. Sicard (2003) differentiates between classical, modern and contemporary luxury brands and considered the time and degree of the democratization dimensions. Each category might require different online strategies to better interact with their audiences on the digital sphere.

In recent years, the luxury industry has faced major changes because of new trends in consumer expectations. Among them, there is the growing importance of the digital and the digital natives, the next generation of luxury consumers. Indeed, such consumers are "younger, digital-savvy and have higher expectations of brands. Not only do they expect brands to be available online, but they also expect a seamless experience to go with it." (Blackden, 2016). This target is mainly composed by HENRY's (High-Earners-Not-Yet-RICH). They are aged between 25-34 years old, and represent as much a vast opportunity as a massive distortion for luxury brands. HENRY's prefer to spend on experience and lifestyle enhancing products, more than on investing or on statutory consumption. This new generation of High-Net-Worth (HNW) individuals has "[…] a desire to be spontaneous, without the pressure of permanent ownership. Whether that's flying via private jet to Ibiza one weekend, staying in a luxury ski chalet the next, or hopping on a yacht a few weeks later – all with a luxurious wardrobe to match." (Blackden, 2016).

The Digital Market

The digital market has been growing by 8% year-on-year in terms of global users. Nowadays, the market accounts 3.8 billion Internet users, representing half of the total population worldwide (Hootsuite, 2017), in which about 2.5 billion are active social media users, i.e. almost 40% of the world population (Statista, 2017a). Such growth offers great opportunities for all businesses, including luxury firms. In France, individuals connect several times daily, either through their computers, tablets or smartphones. As of June 2017, France has more than 56.3 million Internet users and ranks 17th in the world, in terms of Internet users, with almost 87% penetration rate (Internet World Stats, 2017).

The digital dimension challenges traditional media, such as magazines and newspapers, and has become the first communication channel for businesses and even big luxury houses. Nowadays, businesses need to 'think digital native' in order to be able to target the hashtag generation which is consuming digital and ready to pay for its consumption (Bain & Company, 2015). Indeed, in 2016, the online sales of luxury goods accounted for 8% of the total sales, which makes digital sales the 3rd largest global market in the world for personal luxury goods, after the U.S. and Japan (Bain & Company, 2016).

The Internet is currently the channel on which luxury brands engage more proactively. Consumers need interactivity, and luxury brands must adapt to these new consumer trends. There is no doubt; the 21st century is digital, even though luxury actors took time to realize it. Actually, the Gen Y wanted to buy more luxury via Internet but felt that luxury brands were by far lagging behind (Bain & Company, 2014).

When Luxury Brands Meet Social Media

Social media has been challenging luxury companies in creating the right balance between (1) maintaining their brand integrity and exclusive reputation, and (2) exploiting the power of user-generated content (UGC) and social networking sites, while keeping up with the social media trends (Annie Jin, 2012).

This research builds on past studies that aim at offering a comprehensive understanding of the role of social media in luxury brands (Arrigo, 2018). Luxury brands started to seriously use social media in 2009, with Gucci creating its multicultural social network site (Guccieyeweb.com), constantly updating its Facebook and twitting in order to attract the digital generation customers. Also, November 2009 saw the launch of Burberry's social network site "Artofthetrench.com" in order to stimulate the trench's adoration feeling among Burberry fans while narrating the company's stories. As well, Dolce & Gabbana started to invite bloggers to its fashion shows. These bloggers were diffusing their feedbacks on the brand's Twitter and Facebook accounts, in order to get closer to the fans and customers (Kim and Ko, 2012).

Currently, luxury brands are present on almost every type of social media, which may suggest that an online presence becomes very important to luxury brands' image and reputation (Hennigs et al., 2012). For instance, past study sought to identify and characterize social media engagement behaviors of luxury consumers (Pentina et al., 2018). Furthermore, social media marketing is evaluated as a genuine business take-off activity for luxury firms (Kim and Ko, 2012), where luxury brands' company-generated contents and consumer-generated contents are learning to co-exist (Annie Jin, 2012). Such digital transformation impetus is currently remodeling the luxury sector, and online sales are expecting to be the leading channel in the upcoming years (Bain & Company, 2017).

STUDIES ON LUXURY BRANDS AND SOCIAL MEDIA IN THE FRENCH CONTEXT

Luxury brands are pursuing a new clientele through their digital activities: young and dynamic individuals who are very active on social media. The new challenge for luxury houses is to attract and retain this particular target via digital communication. To be active in the digital arena, luxury brands are now having their own website and dedicated pages on social media, such as Facebook, Instagram, and Twitter, which allow consumers to follow the trends anywhere and anytime from any type of device. As such, the latest data of Iconosquare Index Brand (2017) reveals the top ten of the most influential French brands on Instagram are from the luxury sector.

An initial study explored the determining roles of reputation, image and social media on e-reputation and analyzed the moderating role of digital natives in shaping e-reputation. Throughout an online questionnaire, the objective was to investigate the determinants of e-reputation. Among the 141 respondents, 25% were male, and 75% female; 66% were digital natives (below 25 years) and 34% were not (14% between 26 and 35 years old, 10% between 36 and 45 years old, and 10% above 45 years old).

Because the concepts of reputation and image are inherent to the luxury world, the authors found interesting to further investigate traditional versus modern luxury brands. In the initial study, Christian Dior, Louis Vuitton, Burberry and Chanel are considered as traditional luxury brands. Alternatively, Gucci, Dolce & Gabbana, Ralph Lauren and Calvin Klein are perceived to be modern luxury brands. These brands mainly originate from Western European countries (3 from France, 3 from Italy, 1 from England), and 2 brands are from the U.S. These brands were established between 1854 and 1985, and possess different governance structure as they are either independent (i.e., Chanel) or subsidiaries of large luxury multinationals (i.e., Kering, LVMH).

A presentation of digital natives is necessary to better capture the findings of the study and to discuss the results in the luxury contexts.

Digital Natives: Who Are They?

Digital natives or the Net generation are labels for the young people who have been exposed to digital media all their lives (Hargittai, 2010). Also called Generation Y or Millennials, this cohort represents the second largest group of consumers after the Baby Boomers because of their important purchasing power (Kennedy et al., 2008).

Digital natives are multitasking-oriented and active learners; they like to obtain information and process it rapidly, and they rely mostly on Information and Communication Technology (ICT) to access information or manage their professional and social lives (Kennedy et al., 2008). Digital natives' behavior is unique, and they are not greatly influenced by traditional media (Bellman et al., 2009). Also, digital natives are brand switchers, and they seek product variety, convenience and personalization (Sweeney, 2006). They fear bad brand experiences and consider trust as vital (Gurau, 2012). Overall, digital natives are seen as a complex target that is highly influenced by the Internet and new ICT (Lester et al., 2005). Therefore, understanding their specific online behavior through the analysis of e-reputation is paramount.

Online and Offline Reputation for Traditional vs. Modern Luxury Brands

Previous studies have emphasized the differences between reputation and e-reputation. In fact, the perception of consumers may vary, as the authors found that reputation and e-reputation differ for modern luxury brands but not for traditional luxury brands.

The initial results showed that traditional luxury brands possess a greater perceived reputation in comparison to modern brands. Reputation takes time, and once established, it endures in the minds of consumers. The authors also found that traditional luxury brands benefit from higher levels of brand image in comparison with their modern counterparts. Consequently, consumers do not perceive reputation and image similarly, especially when they compare traditional and modern luxury firms.

On another note, even though that traditional luxury brands were first hesitant to engage in digital activities, they then decided to fully be part of the virtual world. This explains the fact that the authors found no differences between the two types of reputation for traditional luxury firms as the two are aligned in the mind of digital natives. In contrast, they differentiate between the offline and e-reputation of modern luxury brands. Surprisingly, even though modern luxury brands were proactive in engaging in digital activities, digital natives do not consider the offline reputation and e-reputation of modern luxury brands to be equivalent.

Digital natives represent a new type of stakeholder consumer with specific behaviors. Contrary to Gen X who followed the way Baby Boomers consumed, digital natives are installing a cross-generational mindset, which is *"[…] influencing the evolution of the whole luxury customer base."* (Claudia D'Arpizio, in Bain & Company, 2017). Instead of being a mere question of demographic, this new 'state of mind' is a genuine psychographic phenomenon, setting the tone for the next transformation stage of the luxury industry, as the one seen during the '70s and the '80s (Bain & Company, 2017).

The Role of Social Media in the Luxury World

Although most firms recognize the importance of an online presence, they find it much more difficult to choose the most appropriate social media, what to post, when to post it and through which media. Indeed, the digital challenge for luxury firms emerged long ago, and the decision to engage in digital activities has been difficult (Hansen, 2011).

The dilemma for luxury firms lies in finding the right balance between exclusivity and broader visibility on the digital sphere. Digital media can dilute the brand image, but ignoring them can exclude the luxury firm from the conversation with its diverse communities, which ultimately hampers the brand image (Dubois, 2013). Also, the interactions among Internet users seem to be the most pertinent mechanism, even though firms cannot control what is said about them.

Still, the question remains regarding what to post, when, and where. The analysis of social media is complex. Our results showed that the most effective media appears to be microblogging when luxury firms aim to increase their online reputation. In addition, media content (image and video) and external links (to other content) are more effective in influencing e-reputation. Further investigation is still needed to unveil the complex nature of the links between luxury firms and social media, which we present hereafter.

SOLUTIONS AND RECOMMENDATIONS

E-Reputation, Image and Social Media: One Size Does Not Fit All

Luxury firms have different strategies when using the diverse digital platform. They post a variety of content on each social media in order to target consumers with different profiles. As different categories of luxury firms compete, and a variety of social media co-exist in order to reach different types of targets, it seems necessary to capture, illustrate and summarize such complexity. One strategy does not fit all online challenges. As shown in Table 1, luxury firms aim at connecting with different types of customers when engaging on social media such as Facebook, Instagram, through their blog, etc.

Several luxury brands are shifting from traditional mass-market and advertising to social media marketing (Phan et al., 2011). However, social media itself is becoming a stakeholder with which luxury brands need to understand how to deal with (Dubois, 2014). Hence, any shift envisaged by luxury brands would need to be anchored in a customer-focused brand strategy in order to be beneficial to the brands (Phan et al., 2011). Such shift will push luxury brands to mediate their online identity with social media. Such mediation will require to constantly redefining, balancing, and evolving (1) the image deal (i.e. how the brands' image will be represented?); (2) the content deal (i.e. what content will build brands' stories?); and (3) the people deal (i.e. who will spread and communicate brands' values?) (Dubois, 2014).

Table 1. Use of alternative digital platforms

Social Media Platform	Strategy	Example	Target
Facebook	Product driven	Small accessories & items (wallets, clutches, sunglasses)	Actual and potential customers interested in the life of the brand & its products
Instagram	Backstage driven	Scenes of London Behind the scenes photo shoots Live pictures from runway shows	Visual and artistic customer Craving instant gratification from staying updated & plugged in real-time
Blog	Lifestyle driven	Posts on styling influences, travel stories, events & food recipes	Individuals and communities interested in creativity, aesthetics and values exerted by luxury brands Consciousness and inspiration (e.g., health, sustainability)
Twitter	Real-time driven	Exclusive behind-the-scenes images of fashion shows Purchase accessories directly from runways	Reward for engagement with the content Discover and buy products
Pinterest	Personalization driven	Create customized make-up boards Showcase ways to use products with beauty tips	Customized beauty experience Provide posts to individuals though personalized and monogrammed content
Snapchat	Story driven	Seasonal product launch Sharing previews of campaigns or new products	Create stories around key events Offer a rough-cut, edgy view into the 'behind the scenes' reality of a brand

(adapted from Dubois, 2013; Moth, 2013; Prakash, 2016; Rein, 2017)

Let us explore the pioneering case of Burberry, the brand viewed as the early-adopter of social media, among luxury brands. Burberry is "*161 year-old global brand with a distinctly British attitude.*" The brand is a flagship of luxury British fashion, founded in 1856 by Thomas Burberry, a former draper's apprentice. Initially fabricating outdoor clothing, Burberry became famous thanks to the invention of the gabardine and its trench coat (Burberry.com, 2017).

Burberry went through some troubles and started to be viewed as 'stodgy nonentity' in the fashion world (Collins 2009). After the 'chavs' (i.e. anti-social and loutish youth subculture), the mass-market and the counterfeiting episodes, the brand needed to purify its message (Collins 2009). Mario Testino's photographs of aristocrats and famous fashion models were diffused on social media websites, which worked on radically changing Burberry's image, especially among young women (Collins 2009).

Burberry made a successful shift from a so-called brand for 'chavs' to a social media marketing trendsetter (Phan et al., 2011). It was the first luxury brand heavily investing in digital communication and social media. In 2010, Burberry was also the first in broadcasting live and in using 3D in its fashion shows from London to Paris, Dubai, Tokyo, New York and Los Angeles (Phan et al., 2011).

Furthermore, Burberry understood, far before other luxury brands, how to consider the consumer as an ally not only as a mere audience (Phan et al., 2011). Accordingly, the brand launched in 2009 its proper social networking site ('Art of the Trench'). The site asked consumers to post pictures mirroring their personal trench coat stories. The brand then selected, on a regular basis, some of these pictures to display a worldwide patchwork of styles posted on the front page of the company's website. Such social site became so popular that the brand prolonged it to its social media accounts (Facebook, Instagram, Twitter, and Pinterest), adding millions of followers worldwide (Tea, 2016).

Likewise, Burberry understood social media platforms' specificities. The brand opened its Facebook account in 2009, and has reached almost 17 million followers. The page is used to display the product ranges as well as music influences (i.e. the Acoustic Campaign). The brand has an Instagram account with about 10 million followers, and is used to post behind the scene photo shoots or live pictures from runway shows (Dubois, 2014). Burberry is also present on Twitter since 2009, reaching nowadays more than 8 million followers. This account is viewed as the most active Burberry's social accounts, with an average of 5 posts per day (Tea, 2016). The brand diffuses mainly a content related to its products and various musicians, while standing aloof from the followers. The brand does not mix between the marketing messages and the customer queries. Instead, Burberry's social team creates and diffuses personalized messages to reward the followers who engaged (i.e. retweeting) with the content, creating a personal attachment with the brand (Moth, 2013). Last but not least, Burberry was one of the first brands using Twitter's 'Buy Now' function in 2014 (Tea, 2016). This features allowed the followers to discover and buy products on Twitter. Such device will allow Burberry to change the relationship with its audience, turning followers to purchasers.

All in all, Burberry's social media strategy helped the brand to rejuvenate toward a more fashionable and aspirational positioning, hence increasing its appeal to young and digital-savvy consumers (Phan et al., 2011).

Adapt to the Digital Natives Behaviors

The benefits of engaging on digital activities outweigh the risks, especially for the younger generation comprised of digital natives (Dubois, 2013). Indeed, digital natives are seen as different, whether in their way of thinking as well as in their way of shopping. They are "*[...] the first generation to approach adult life in less favorable economic condition than their parents. They have inherited a secular vision of the world: for example, 'family' and 'religion' are no longer indispensable elements of one's life, but they are possible choices among many. They are also part of the digital revolution, which leads to a different perception of 'time,' 'space' and 'possibilities.' Everything is possible, here and now."* (Claudia D'Arpizio, in Bain & Company, 2017). Digital natives are also seen as different in the meaning they give to their consumption. Indeed, for such generation *"[…] consuming products and brands is not just a way to say who you are but a way to define who you are […] this is why they are more engaged than previous generations with self-expression."* (Claudia D'Arpizio, in Bain & Company, 2017). Last but not least, digital natives are genuinely global, being *"highly digital and having disposable income to invest in education, travels and connectivity, such luxury consumers are exposed to very similar stimuli and can participate in the same global conversations and experiences […] even in those countries that were historically less open to other cultures, they have the opportunity to share experiences with people from all over the world. No culture is impermeable to the Digital Natives wave."* (Claudia D'Arpizio, in Bain & Company, 2017).

Digital natives rely on different determinants of e-reputation in comparison to the perceptions of non-digital native. Initial results showed that brand image has no influence on online reputation for them.

Also, as digital natives display specific behaviors compared to older generations, luxury firms are required to use particular strategies for this target. For instance, the use of specialized social media such as YouTube increases the e-reputation of luxury brands among digital natives. These results are not surprising as YouTube represent their favorite provider of video content. Millennials are *"highly-engaged, highly-loyal YouTube users."* (Heltai, 2016). Which factors can explain such behavior, and what are the implications for luxury brands?

Recent studies showed that digital natives consider YouTube their preferred destination, not only to watch videos uploaded by people (72%), but also to watch "current season TV shows". In addition, one third of millennials binge-watch daily and YouTube is perceived to be the most appropriate platform to that end (Heltai, 2016). Interestingly, even though digital natives are perceived as being highly skeptical regrading brands communications, they exert some loyal behavior and are deeply engaged once the brand appears relevant to them (Heltai, 2016). Luxury brands can benefit from such behavior if such resonance is created choosing the most pertinent digital platform and sending the right message at the most appropriate time.

Back to the Burberry case, the brand's social media use allowed reaching and connecting with the young consumers and mass audiences, while controlling the luxury image through well-crafted contents and messages (Phan et al., 2011). Indeed, Burberry displays some stout numbers in the social media arena, making it to be the top performer on Instagram, the most followed brand on Twitter, and among the top 10 most influential brands among FTSE100 companies (Battenhall, 2017). The brand is also ranked second in Fashion Index (L2 Digital IQ Index, 2016), recognizing its digital competences and more specifically as a genuine social media leader.

Burberry excelled in creating contents while optimizing the features of each social media platforms, such as using live streaming abilities of Facebook, exhibiting artfully minimalist photos for Instagram, and posting the right material that foster audience engagement on Twitter (Tea, 2016). Also, Burberry opened, in 2016, a Pinterest account which totalizes nowadays more than 200.000 subscribers. The brand was besides the first luxury brand to partner with Pinterest to launch a customized beauty board offering (Prakash, 2016). Needless to mention the fact that Pinterest is the largest beauty platform worldwide with more than 38 million monthly unique beauty viewers, and the 'luxury pins' are the highest among digital natives ages 18-34 (Prakash, 2016).

All in all, luxury brands need to understand how to converse with their digital publics. Such publics are part of the social web where consumers freely meet, connect and exchange, in a way that either excludes luxury brands' input or online magazines' influence (Okonkwo, 2009). But above all, luxury brands need to know who their new customers (i.e. digital natives) are and how they are using social media. Indeed, in today's world *"[…] the question that brands ask is not whether to have a presence on social media, but how to have a strong and engaging presence on social media. The reality is that social media is a big part of people's lives, including our customers' and fans."* (Erica Kerner, Tiffany & Co's Asia-Pacific vice-president for marketing, in Cheong, 2016).

FUTURE RESEARCH DIRECTIONS: EXPLORING THE COMING GENERATION Z

Gen Z is the new generation of individuals who were born after 1995, when Internet and smartphones were being fully integrated to people's everyday lives. Such individuals are viewed as the genuine (first) digital natives (Jennings, 2017). More than being digital, Gen Z are social media natives (Granados, 2017), having Facebook, Instagram, Twitter and Snapchat, among others, taking a bigger place in their lives (Patel, 2017).

Getting to Know the Generation Z

Generation Z represents more than two billion individuals, or 27% of the population worldwide (Jennings, 2017). Zers came to a world with a tenacious economic crisis, with no full safety guarantee from terrorism, making them becoming more realistic, independent, and self-ware about their lives, compared to Yers (Wolinski, 2016). Gen Z people praise product individuality, customization and personalization, allowing them to exhibit their uniqueness (Patel, 2017). Zers are innovative and creative, and have a higher entrepreneurial spirit than Yers (Jenning, 2017). They want to act, to make a difference and not just to obey and accept what is given (IPSOS, 2017). They don't fear the risk if the reward is worth the shot, and constantly adjust the parts of their social lives that are not harmonious with their values and social mindsets (Patel, 2017). Last but not least, Zers are multitaskers, fast learners and fast information absorbers. Being surrounded with numerous screens and digital devices helped them to learn how to juggle with multiple information channels and sources since their childhood (Jennings, 2017).

Gen Z is known of its hyper connectivity and all-inclusive communication through social media. The most famous digital platform for Generation Z is Facebook (IPSOS, 2017), while Instagram is second, with 800 million active users per month (Statista, 2017c). Also, digital platforms are Gen Z's favorite device to share their creative work and hence exhibiting their individuality (Wolinski, 2016). This explains why platforms such as Snapchat, Instagram and Pinterest are so popular among this generation (IPSOS, 2017). The fact that some of these platforms (i.e. Snapchat) offer ephemeral experiences and hence no traceability is applied, at least officially, also explains their success among Zers (Jennings, 2017). Last but not least, Zers greatly master the art of forming multiple 'curated selves'. Such digital personas of themselves are built to suit each social media platform in a specific moment in time (Ben-Shabat, 2017). They also shop heavily online, and consider a brand's social stance and policies in their purchasing decisions (Ben-Shabat, 2017).

Generation Z and the Luxury World

Luxury brands have been heavily sending signals to the members of the Gen Z cohort. Among emblematic examples, one can recall Calvin Klein's latest campaign with Kendall Jenner (about 84 million followers on Instagram) and Justin Bieber (respectively 84 million and 92 million followers on Instagram), or Louis Vuitton's featuring Jaden Smith (son of Will Smith and Jada Pinkett Smith), or Burberry who hired Brooklyn Beckham (son of David and Victoria Beckham, more than 10 million followers on Instagram), as the photographer for its 'This is Brit' fragrance advertising campaign, and live documented through Snapchat and Instagram (Arthur, 2016).

Hence, it seems that luxury brands are more and more turning to Gen Z. They are striving to drive Zers' engagement in platforms such as Snapchat, relying on influencers such as Kendall Jenner, while moving away from Facebook, as the latter is growing more among the 55+ years old (Arthur, 2016). Indeed, Gen Zs most popular social media platform is Snapchat because it's fun, allowing texting and sending pictures in a fast and easy way, seeing stories of friends and peers, and above all, avoiding the parents and friends' parents (Kosoff, 2016).

Back to Burberry case and its campaigns, virtual kisses send through Google+ in 2013, personalized virtual bottles for the 'My Burberry' perfume, launched with Cara Delevingne (40 million followers on Instagram) in 2014, and the 'This is Brit' campaign shot by Brooklyn Beckham in 2016. The latter provoked the outrage of the established fashion photographers, calling the hiring of Brooklyn Beckham as a "sheer nepotism" (Cartner-Morley, 2016). But, Instagram and Snapchat feeds got more than 15 million views during the eight hours the shoot was going (Cheong, 2016). Nevertheless, *"[...] proficiency with a light meter is not necessarily a more important skill than the ability to create an image and a caption that works on social media. Thirty years of experience, or millions of Instagram followers? No contest."* (Cartner-Morley, 2016).

Moreover, Burberry was the first luxury brand to experiment with Snapchat, applying the platform for a seasonal product launch (Tea, 2016). More specifically, Burberry was the first brand who published its 2016 Spring/Summer adverting campaign shot by the photographer Mario Testino, live through Snapchat, and premiered its Spring 2016 collection via the platform, a day before its London Fashion Week launch, garnering 200 million views (Cheong, 2016). Last but not least, Burberry uses the Snapchat's Discover channel, a feature usually favored by online media outlets such as Buzzfeed and Vice to generate original content (Cheong, 2016). It is worth to mention that Snapchat was targeted because it reflects *"[...] a mix of reality, intimacy and inclusivity that other platforms don't really capture in the same way."* (Christopher Bailey, Burberry's chief creative officer and president, in Cheong, 2016).

The luxury industry is notorious for its innovation, avant-gardism and creativity (Okonkwo, 2009). Indeed, luxury brands know how to produce best quality products. Hence, it is expected from them to know how to develop best contents and platforms for their social media strategy, while safeguarding brand consistency and keeping their brand DNA (Phan et al., 2011). Also, luxury brands need to generate desirability among the young generation, through creating aspiration on affordable luxury products to motivate this generation to consider buying higher products in the future (Arthur, 2016).

On another note, Gen Z's social media consumption is a lifestyle not just entertainment (Granados, 2017). For such generation, social media is the major way to engage with their communities. Hence, luxury brands need to build on their specificities to attract Gen Z. As such, being artistic and creative, while providing unique and customizable products of great quality, are highly acclaimed features by Zers (Jennings, 2017). Luxury brands need also to speak the future generation's values, while being more engagement driven. For that, these brands will have to evolve from good storytellers to co-creators of narratives through involving the Zers, and hence, empathizing with their fans (Ben-Shabat, 2017). Moreover, luxury brands should put aside some of the 'exclusivity' feature and focus more on workmanship, quality and durability, greatly praised features by Gen Z (Cheong, 2016). Finally, as it was rightly put by Christopher Bailey (Burberry's chief creative officer and president), *"Fans want to know how our things are made and the stories behind the scenes. They want more access and more authenticity, and, if that's what they are demanding, then we need to listen and find new and exciting ways of democratically bringing them into our world."* (in Cheong, 2016).

CONCLUSION

In this chapter, the authors aimed at analyzing the factors that influence the perception of luxury firms' e- reputation, which is mainly observed on social media.

As well put by Okonkwo (2009, p. 302): *"Luxury is neither a product, an object, a service nor is it a concept or a lifestyle. It is an identity, a philosophy and a culture."* Hence, the decision for luxury firms to engage in digital activities is complex. The luxury world is characterized by rarity, exclusivity, and reputational effects take time for established firms. Alternatively, the Internet is defined by its immediacy, mass appeal and global reach. Even though the luxury world and the digital sphere might a priori seem irreconcilable, further examination was needed. We used these initial findings to provide insightful recommendations.

First, based on an initial study, the authors found that such complexity depends on the type of luxury firms. Audiences do not perceive traditional and modern luxury brands similarly. Stakeholders are sensitive to the characteristics of the firms they follow online, which can ultimately influence their perception. Therefore, when going online, modern luxury firms need to pay attention to their reputation offline and to they need to guaranty some alignment between their activities both offline and line. This is particularly true for digital natives who do not grant their trust easily. However, once granted, they display stronger levels of engagement towards a trusted brand.

Second, the type of social media and the type of content posted also influence e-reputation. An online presence is far from being sufficient for luxury firms to be well perceived by their audiences. Each market segment requires a particular message / video / post on a specific platform.

Third, the results showed that digital natives perceive e-reputation differently in comparison to other generations. For luxury brands to reach this specific target, they need to master their online strategies. The type of content and the type of platform are of great important. In addition, digital natives are comprised of sub-segments with their own specificities. Generations Y and Z exert different behaviors. If luxury firms minimize or ignore such differences, the market verdict is immediate on social media.

Finally, luxury firms have to keep up with the constant changes on the Internet. Because the digital sphere is at the core of its activities, Burberry has created a transformational team. The firm does not aim at adapting to the Internet; its objective is to anticipate and to shape it.

Overall, the right balance for luxury firms to succeed online is based on 3 pillars: (1) knowing yourself. What works for other brands will not necessarily fit you, isomorphic behaviors will damage your reputation and brand image; (2) Internet platforms are not equivalent, and social media content are not interchangeable. Stakeholders perceive differently a post, a video or an image, and interacting with them on Twitter, Facebook or Instagram has different reach and outcomes; (3) knowing your audience precisely. Digital natives are not homogeneous. Identifying and understanding their specificities is a key to succeed online and manage your e-reputation and brand image.

Complementary research can enrich the present findings and discussion. Further analysis could examine more precisely the type of objective sought using different social media, especially based on the types of consumers targeted (new vs. loyal; millennials vs. older generations, etc.). In addition, new insight can be brought by investigating other industries with dissimilar dynamics. For instance, online reputation is critical in the food industry, as well as in the transportation industry with Uber, or in hospitality management, especially through the rise of business models with community based online platforms such as AirBnB.

ACKNOWLEDGMENT

The authors would like to thank Hélène SCHMITT, Nicolas TROCHOUX, Margot FASSOLETTE (ICN Business School Master Students), and Lucile LECLERCQ, Marie MASSIAS (PSB Paris School of Business Master Students), for their valuable input and contribution to the chapter.

REFERENCES

L2 Digital IQ Index. (2016). *Digital IQ Index Fashion 2016*. Author.

Allérès, D. (1995). *Luxe: un management spécifique*. Paris: Economica.

Alwi, S. F. S., & Da Silva, R. V. (2007). Online and offline corporate brand images: Do they differ? *Corporate Reputation Review*, *10*(4), 217–244. doi:10.1057/palgrave.crr.1550056

Annie Jin, S. A. (2012). The potential of social media for luxury brand management. *Marketing Intelligence & Planning*, *30*(7), 687–699. doi:10.1108/02634501211273805

Arrigo, E. (2018). Social media marketing in luxury brands: A systematic literature review and implications for management research. *Management Research Review*. doi:10.1108/MRR-04-2017-0134

Arthur, R. (2016). *The Risk Of Generation Z: Let's Talk About Luxury's Obsession With Teen-Endorsed Snapchat Campaigns*. Retrieved October 4th, 2017, from https://www.forbes.com/sites/rachelarthur/2016/02/03/the-risk-of-generation-z-lets-talk-about-fashions-obsession-with-teen-endorsed-snapchat-campaigns/#7b0b1772633b

Aula, P. (2010). Social media, reputation risk and ambient publicity management. *Strategy and Leadership*, *38*(6), 43–49. doi:10.1108/10878571011088069

Bain & Company. (2014). *Luxury Goods Worldwide Market Study, Fall-Winter 2014: The rise of the borderless consumer*. Bain & Company for Fondazione Altagamma. Retrieved September 20th, 2017, from http://www.bain.com/publications/articles/luxury-goods-worldwide-market-study-december-2014.aspx

Bain & Company. (2015). *Génération #hashtag 2015: l'ère du numérique natif*. Bain & Company. Retrieved September 20th, 2017, from http://www.bain.fr/Images/2015_Etude%20Generation_Hashtag.pdf

Bain & Company. (2016). *Luxury Goods Worldwide Market Study, Fall-Winter 2016: As Luxury Resets to a New Normal, Strategy Becomes*. Bain & Company for Fondazione Altagamma. Retrieved September 20th, 2017, from http://www.bain.com/publications/articles/luxury-goods-worldwide-market-study-fall-winter-2016.aspx

Bain & Company. (2017). *Bain Luxury Study 2017 Spring Update*. Retrieved September 20th, 2017, from http://www.bain.com/about/press/press-releases/global-personal-luxury-goods-market-expected-to-grow-by-2-4-percent.aspx

Battenhall. (2017). *FTSE100 Social Media Report. An analysis of the use of social media for brand and corporate communications by the FTSE 100 companies*. Academic Press.

Bellman, L. M., Teich, I., & Clark, S. D. (2009). Fashion accessory buying intentions among female millennials. *Review of Business*, *30*(1), 46–57.

Ben-Shabat, H. (2017). *Gen Z and the Paradox of Luxury*. Retrieved October 4th, 2017, from http://www.therobinreport.com/gen-z-and-the-paradox-of-luxury

Blackden, E. (2016). *6 Key Luxury Trends That Will Make Or Break Brands In 2016*. Retrieved September 20th, 2017, from https://luxurysociety.com/en/articles/2016/01/6-key-luxury-trends-that-will-make-or-break-brands-in-2016

Blackshaw, P., & Nazzaro, M. (2004). *Consumer-Generated Media (CGM) 101: Word-of-mouth in the age of the Web-fortified consumer*. Nielsen BuzzMetrics White paper.

Cartner-Morley, J. (2016). *Brooklyn Beckham, Burberry and the new celebrity aristocracy*. Retrieved October 4th, 2017, from https://www.theguardian.com/fashion/2016/feb/01/brooklyn-beckham-burberry-celebrity-artistocracy-16-photography-snobbery-instagram-followers

Castarède, J. (1992). *Le luxe*. Presses universitaires de France.

Castellano, S., Khelladi, I., Chipaux, A., & Kupferminc, C. (2014). The Influence of Social Networks on E-Reputation: How Sportspersons Manage the Relationship with Their Online Community. *International Journal of Technology and Human Interaction*, *10*(4), 65–79. doi:10.4018/ijthi.2014100105

Cheong, G. (2016). *How Luxury Brands are Using Social Media to Woo A New Generation of Customers*. Retrieved October 4th, 2017, from http://thepeakmagazine.com.sg/fashion-watches/how-luxury-brands-are-using-social-media-to-woo-a-new-generation-of-customers

Chevalier, M., & Mazzalovo, G. (2008). *Luxury brand management: a world of privilege*. John Wiley & Sons.

Chun, R., & Davies, G. (2001). E-reputation: The role of mission and vision statements in positioning Strategy. *Journal of Brand Management*, *8*(4), 315–333. doi:10.1057/palgrave.bm.2540031

Collins, L. (2009). Check Mate. Burberry's working-class hero. *The New Yorker*. Retrieved October 4th, 2017, from https://www.newyorker.com/magazine/2009/09/14/check-mate

Deephouse, D. L. (2000). Media reputation as a strategic resource: An integration of mass communication and resource-based theories. *Journal of Management*, *26*(6), 1091–1112. doi:10.1177/014920630002600602

Dubois, D. (2013). *Why Social Media Is Luxury's Best Friend*. Retrieved October 4th, 2017, from https://knowledge.insead.edu/strategy/why-social-media-is-luxurys-best-friend-2951

Dubois, D. (2014). *"Social Media New Deal" for Luxury Brands*. Retrieved October 4th, 2017, from https://knowledge.insead.edu/marketing-advertising/the-social-media-new-deal-for-luxury-brands-3649

Dutot, V., & Castellano, S. (2015). Designing a measurement scale for e-reputation. *Corporate Reputation Review*, *18*(4), 294–313. doi:10.1057/crr.2015.15

Erkan, I. (2015). Electronic word of mouth on Instagram: Customers' engagements with brands in different sectors. *International Journal of Management, Accounting and Economics*, *2*(12), 1435–1444.

Fombrun, C. (1996). *Reputation*. John Wiley & Sons, Ltd.

Forman, J., & Argenti, P. A. (2005). How Corporate Communication Influences Strategy Implementation, Reputation and the Corporate Brand: An Exploratory Qualitative Study. *Corporate Reputation Review*, *8*(3), 245–264. doi:10.1057/palgrave.crr.1540253

GlobalWebIndex. (2017). *Social summary. Quarterly report on the latest trends in social networking*. Author.

Granados, N. (2017). *Gen Z Media Consumption: It's A Lifestyle, Not Just Entertainment*. Retrieved October 4th, 2017, from https://www.forbes.com/sites/nelsongranados/2017/06/20/gen-z-media-consumption-its-a-lifestyle-not-just-entertainment/#15f4a2da18c9

Gurau, C. (2012). A life-stage analysis of consumer loyalty profile: Comparing Generation X and Millennial consumers. *Journal of Consumer Marketing*, *29*(2), 103–113. doi:10.1108/07363761211206357

Hansen, R. (2011). How Fashion Brands Learned to Click–A Longitudinal Study of the Adoption of Online Interactive and Social Media by Luxury Fashion Brands. In IRIS (No. 34). Akademika forlag.

Hargittai, E. (2010). Digital na (t) ives? Variation in internet skills and uses among members of the "net generation". *Sociological Inquiry*, *80*(1), 92–113. doi:10.1111/j.1475-682X.2009.00317.x

Heltai, G. (2016). *What Millennials' YouTube Usage Tells Us about the Future of Video Viewership*. Retrieved October 4th, 2017, from https://www.comscore.com/ita/Insights/Blog/What-Millennials-YouTube-Usage-Tells-Us-about-the-Future-of-Video-Viewership

Hennigs, N., Wiedmann, K. P., & Klarmann, D. O. C. (2012). Luxury brands in the digital age–exclusivity versus ubiquity. *Marketing Review St. Gallen*, *29*(1), 30–35. doi:10.100711621-012-0108-7

Hootsuite. (2017). *Digital in 2017 Global Overview. A Collection of Internet, Social Medial, and Mobile Data from around the World*. Retrieved September 20th, 2017, from https://hootsuite.com/fr/newsroom/press-releases/digital-in-2017-report

Iconosquare Index Brand. (2017). *Top Brands*. Retrieved September 20th, 2017, from https://index.iconosquare.com/category/luxury

Internet World Stats. (2017). *Top 20 Countries with the Highest Number of Internet Users*. Retrieved September 20th, 2017, from http://www.internetworldstats.com/top20.htm

IPSOS. (2017). *Génération Z, les nouveaux partenaires de consommation*. Retrieved September 20th, 2017, from https://www.ipsos.com/fr-fr/generation-z-les-nouveaux-partenaires-de-consommation

Jenning, J. (2017). Generation Z: Two billion people coming of age. *Business Today*. Retrieved September 20th, 2017, from http://www.businesstoday.co.om/Issues/Top-companies-on-MSM/Generation-Z-Two-billion-people-coming-of-age

Kapferer, J. N. (2012). *The luxury strategy: Break the rules of marketing to build luxury brands*. Kogan Page Publishers.

Kapferer, J. N., & Bastien, V. (2009). The specificity of luxury management: Turning marketing upside down. *Journal of Brand Management*, *16*(5), 311–322. doi:10.1057/bm.2008.51

Kaplan, A. M., & Haenlein, M. (2010). Users of the world, unite! The challenges and opportunities of social media. *Business Horizons*, *53*(1), 59–68. doi:10.1016/j.bushor.2009.09.003

Kennedy, G. E., Judd, T. S., Churchward, A., Gray, K., & Krause, K. L. (2008). First year students' experiences with technology: Are they really digital natives? *Australasian Journal of Educational Technology*, *24*(1). doi:10.14742/ajet.1233

Kietzmann, J. H., Hermkens, K., McCarthy, I. P., & Silvestre, B. S. (2011). Social media? Get serious! Understanding the functional building blocks of social media. *Business Horizons*, *54*(3), 241–251. doi:10.1016/j.bushor.2011.01.005

Kim, A. J., & Ko, E. (2012). Do social media marketing activities enhance customer equity? An empirical study of luxury fashion brand. *Journal of Business Research*, *65*(10), 1480–1486. doi:10.1016/j.jbusres.2011.10.014

Kosoff, M. (2016). *Dozens of teenagers told us what's cool in 2016 — these are their favorite (and least favorite) apps*. Retrieved October 4th, 2017, from:www.businessinsider.com/teens-favorite-apps-in-2016-2016-1+&cd=1&hl=fr&ct=clnk&gl=fr&client=firefox-b

Larkin, J. (2003). *Strategic reputation risk management*. Palgrave McMillian.

Lester, D. H., Forman, A. M., & Loyd, D. (2005). Internet shopping behavior of college students. *Services Marketing Quarterly*, *27*(2), 123–138.

LVMH. (2017). *LVMH Résultats 2016 records*. Retrieved September 20th, 2017, from https://www.lvmh.fr/actualites-documents/communiques/resultats-2016-records

Moth, D. (2013). *How Burberry uses Facebook, Twitter, Pinterest and Google+*. Retrieved October 4th, 2017, from https://econsultancy.com/blog/62897-how-burberry-uses-facebook-twitter-pinterest-and-google

Murphy, P. (2010). The intractability of reputation: Media coverage as a complex system in the case of Martha Stewart. *Journal of Public Relations Research*, *22*(2), 209–237. doi:10.1080/10627261003601648

Okonkwo, U. (2009). Sustaining the luxury brand on the Internet. *Journal of Brand Management*, *16*(5-6), 302–310. doi:10.1057/bm.2009.2

Patel, D. (2017). 10 Tips For Marketing To Gen Z On Social Media. *Forbes*. Retrieved September 20th, 2017, from https://www.forbes.com/sites/deeppatel/2017/08/08/10-tips-for-marketing-to-gen-z-on-social-media/#54651b422718

Pentina, I., Guilloux, V., & Micu, A. C. (2018). Exploring Social Media Engagement Behaviors in the Context of Luxury Brands. *Journal of Advertising, 47*(1), 55–69. doi:10.1080/00913367.2017.1405756

Phan, M. (2011). Do social media enhance consumer's perception and purchase intentions of luxury fashion brands. *The Journal for Decision Makers, 36*(1), 81–84.

Phan, M., Thomas, R., & Heine, K. (2011). Social media and luxury brand management: The case of Burberry. *Journal of Global Fashion Marketing, 2*(4), 213–222. doi:10.1080/20932685.2011.10593099

Prakash, R. (2016). *Burberry partners with Pinterest to create a customized beauty experience*. Retrieved October 4th, 2017, from https://business.pinterest.com/en/blog/burberry-partners-with-pinterest-to-create-a-customized-beauty-experience

Rein, G. (2017). *How luxury brands should engage on Instagram and Snapchat*. Retrieved October 4th, 2017, from http://www.retaildive.com/ex/mobilecommercedaily/how-luxury-brands-should-engage-on-instagram-and-snapchat

Sicard, M.-C. (2003). *Luxe, mensonge et marketing, Mais que font les marques de luxe*. Paris: Village Mondial.

Statista. (2017a). *Number of social media users worldwide from 2010 to 2021 (in billions)*. Retrieved September 20th, 2017, from https://www.statista.com/statistics/278414/number-of-worldwide-social-network-users

Statista. (2017b). *Market value of luxury goods in France from 2012 to 2017 (in million euros)*. Retrieved September 20th, 2017, from https://www.statista.com/statistics/494154/luxury-goods-france-market-value

Statista. (2017c). *Number of monthly active Instagram users from January 2013 to September 2017 (in millions)*. Retrieved October 4th, 2017, from https://www.statista.com/statistics/253577/number-of-monthly-active-instagram-users

Sweeney, R. (2006). Millennial behaviors and demographics. Newark, NJ: New Jersey Institute of Technology.

Tea, B. (2016). Case Study: Is Burberry's Social Media Use the Best Amongst Luxury Brands? *Socialwall. me*. Retrieved October 4th, 2017, from https://socialwall.me/en/burberry-social-media-use-luxury-brands

Wolinski, C. (2016). They're Post-Millennial, Pre-Myopic Digital Natives...How Will You Connect With Gen Z? *Vision Monday*. Retrieved September 20th, 2017, from http://www.visionmonday.com/eyecare/optometry/article/theyre-postmillennial-premyopic-digital-natives

Worldwide, D. E. I. (2008). *The impact of social media on purchasing behavior. Engaging Consumers Online. The impact of social media on purchasing behavior*. Retrieved September 20th, 2017, from https://themarketingguy.files.wordpress.com/2008/12/dei-study-engaging-consumers-online-summary.pdf

Chapter 14
Social Media and Motivational Complexities Associated in Promoting Professional Soccer Engagement

Alan D. Smith
Robert Morris University, USA

Amber A. Ditizio
Independent Researcher, USA

Steven R. Clinton
Robert Morris University, USA

ABSTRACT

The purpose of this chapter is to examine and determine factors that lead to increased television ratings for soccer in the U.S. Undoubtedly, the topic of fantasy sports and the various roles it plays with types of fan involvement and their need for enhanced engagement with a complex social media landscape has intrigued scholars from a number of disciplines. How the various motivational factors, both intrinsically and extrinsically, impact the degree of fan involvement and loyalty have been investigated several times. The overall results have been mixed to say the least. The current chapter primarily focuses on fantasy soccer participation, involvement in soccer, presence of a local professional team, and social media interaction. After providing a brief history of soccer television ratings in the U.S., a conceptual model based on these factors is developed and explained. The factors of this conceptual model are tested through statistical analysis.

DOI: 10.4018/978-1-5225-7214-5.ch014

INTRODUCTION

Growth of Soccer in the U.S.

There is little doubt that when Major League Soccer (MLS) played its initial 1996 season, it could not expect in the short-term to compete with the advertising budget and player-related expenses with its big business professional football. As the 2014 World Cup games played on, many spectators hope for a strong competitive showing of the young U.S. soccer team. During this time, the Internet was taking a foothold in the general public and allowed an avenue or communication channel for sport organizations to directly create relationships and influence the hearts and minds of its potential fan base. The MLS handles the initial contracts for individual players to help owners take on a lesser financial burden that had crippled previous attempts at professional sport organizations such as the North American Soccer League (NASL) and the USA Football League. These organizations mainly failed due to an excessive expenditure in the largest markets (Zimmerman, Clavio, & Lim, 2011). This study explores a few areas, from fantasy sports to involvement in sports, which may or may not contribute to increased television ratings in the soccer market. By understanding these aspects, decision makers can increase their e-commerce approaches or target specific viewers to increase television ratings in the U.S. Increasing television ratings can generate many forms of increased revenues, including online streaming and advertisement revenue.

When discussing television ratings, within a 6-year span from 2007-2012, MLS grew over 50% from 12 teams to 19 teams. This period of expansion is shown in Table 1. Expansion in recent years has been well executed into popular markets and helped improve everything league-wide from global exposure to a bigger salary cap to superb attendance figures. With MLS's young age and the recent upswing overall of soccer in the U.S., very little research has been done on why Americans are now tuning into soccer at a higher rate than ever before. With the domestic league now spanning so many large cities and the increased availability for Americans to watch foreign soccer, research on how and why television ratings increase for soccer is vital to decision makers in the global marketplace.

MLS has a niche market in the U.S. with per-game attendance figures surpassing both the National Hockey League (NHL) and the National Basketball Association (NBA). These 2 leagues are generally referred to as the arena leagues because they are played indoors with smaller capacity stadiums. None of these three leagues (e.g.; MLS, NBA, or NHL) play in venues nearly as big as Major League Baseball (MLB) or the National Football League (NFL). With proper expansion, MLS broke above the arena leagues and sits nicely in the middle of the pack in per-game attendance. Most recent per-game season attendance figures are listed below in Table 2. Although these numbers are great for soccer in the U.S.,

Table 1. Expansion 2007-12 in MLS

Year	Expansion Team(s)
2007	Toronto FC
2008	San Jose Earthquakes
2009	Seattle Sounders FC
2010	Philadelphia Union
2011	Portland Timbers, Vancouver Whitecaps
2012	Montreal Impact

Table 2. MLS attendance vs. major sport leagues

League	Average Attendance per Game
NFL	67,358
MLB	31,368
MLS	18,732
NBA	17,273
NHL	17,455

it is important to note that MLS teams do not play as many games as any other U.S. major sport league, except for the NFL.

While these leagues and tournaments will compete against one another for television ratings, this research paper just focuses on soccer as a sport and combines all of the leagues/competitions into a single group. This research looks to fill a specific void in examining a set of characteristics and determining if these items have any effect on whether or not a person decides to watch soccer on television. If the decision makers of soccer programming can pinpoint these characteristics, they may be able to focus their broadcasts better or increase ratings in the long-term through better preparation of a few topics including various e-commerce opportunities.

The former first-division soccer league of the U.S. was the North American Soccer League. With similar characteristics to MLB (i.e., unlimited spending for large market teams, little parity, minimal revenue sharing), the league quickly failed. MLS from its beginning planned and promised to never follow the business structure of the former NASL, but rather a slow-and-steady growth approach to avoid failure of the league. Overexpansion was a huge reason for the failure of NASL and must be avoided in MLS. Average attendance of the NASL never broke 15,000 and while some teams were very successful because of their big market ability to spend, others were left with horrible teams in poor stadiums with barely any people watching. To avoid this and past problems of the NASL, MLS has achieved a relative parity. With a salary cap, individual player cap, revenue sharing, and single-entity business structure, MLS has created one of the most competitive league structures in the world. Most recently, Columbus Crew became the best team in the league in 2008 after being one of the worst teams in both 2006 and 2007. This parity is a unique attribute to MLS that provides an opportunity for all firms to maximize their potential both on and off the pitch.

There has been an effort to apply operational and mathematical techniques (Bhurjee, Kumar, & Padhan, 2018; Chaturvedi & Chakrabarti, 2018; Gothwal & Raj, 2018; Hossain & Hossain, 2018; Jain & D'lima, 2018; Oey & Nofrimurti, 2018) in scheduling and managing professional soccer. For example, Durán, Guajardo, and Wolf-Yadlin's (2012) research used in scheduling Chile's Second Division soccer league is an interesting application of such efforts. For at least 40 years, experts in operations research (OR) and related fields have studied the application of optimization techniques, if is only logical to apply such techniques to managing and scheduling sports league seasons. This scheduling was an extension of previous studies on scheduling in order to optimize certain aspects of the season for teams. There have been fewer studies on soccer using this scheduling and, therefore, less former research.

In order to help mitigate the travel of teams from home and away games, location strategies were implemented into the linear programming models (Durán, Guajardo, & Wolf-Yadlin, 2012). The first model in the 2 linear programming models generates the clubs' (i.e., teams') home-away patterns. The second model then determines the match date assignments. This procedure allows the researchers to rapidly generate solutions for all instances encountered. The application of the 2 models to the Second Division provides significant qualitative and quantitative benefits to the league and the teams. These techniques have replaced the traditional methodology in the league. Factors such as location, economics, scheduling fairness, and attractiveness to fans are included in the integer linear programming (ILP) model. The league defines in advance the dates on which the various rounds will be played. Basic constraints are that each team play a match in each round and each pair of teams plays each other m times, the actual number depending on the type of tournament. Other constraints related to breaks, locations, and game dates are included in the linear programming models. Given 2 teams and a round, the main decision variable is a binary one, which equals one if these teams play each other in that round. In tournaments with an odd number of teams, byes are expressed as a match against a dummy team added to the model during implementation (e.g., the scheduling conditions for this team include only the basic constraints).

The Second Division scheduling problem used an ILP model that they have termed the match-scheduling model (MSM). These schedules had positive qualitative and quantitative impacts. The financial savings to teams based in the far north and south of the country, which stem from scheduling good trips, are particularly relevant. Each tournament scheduled included approximately five such trips. This compares favorably with the last manually generated schedules, which had no good trips. The league estimates that each of these trips represents a savings to the associated team of almost $4,000- about 13% of a Second Division team's monthly payroll. The use of incorporating factors related to location strategies has had a positive impact on leagues costs and impact of schedule. Another impact is the more even distribution of trips over the length of the tournament, enabling the teams to better spread their expenses over the year. By using the OR models, it greatly helps facilitate implementation of key changes that are made by the league from season to season. The modifications are designed to ensure attractive tournaments for fans while reducing road trips from one end of the country to the other, easing the strain on the team budgets and alleviating player travel fatigue. Since the schedules being created were more favorable to fans, the Second Division saw about a 10% increase in average match attendance over the previous seasons when the traditional method of random scheduling was still used. The qualitative impacts of the OR scheduling since 2007 have taken various forms. The league is more transparent primarily due to the requirements incorporated into the models are known to all the teams. The league accepts requests for the incorporation of requirements from all the teams, thus making the system fairer. The flexibility provided will be beneficial in the future as the league continues to modify itself and adapted to fan preferences.

Based on the results of implementing the ILP for scheduling the Second Division in Chile, the methods used and strategic management decisions incorporated are successful in producing a competitive but fair schedule in the league. The appropriate scheduling of matches through the application of OR methodologies has made the tournaments more attractive to the fans. I think a major factor for the success of the implementation of the new scheduling system stems from the relationship these researchers have with the league. The trust and relationship that was created initially when developing the First Division schedule made the transition for the Second Division scheduling much easier.

LOOKING FOR PARITY WITH OTHER PROFESSIONAL TEAM SPORTS

The parity found in MLS is one of the items that helps make this study so interesting. Not only are there numerous leagues and tournaments for fans to watch on television, their local team always has the opportunity to be competitive and bring attention to their city. Everything in this survey directly ties back to an e-commerce concept of online television viewership. Streaming of soccer matches is one of the most-used forms of streaming on the Internet, because it is impossible to show every team's games throughout the year. So, if managers and executives can drive up soccer television ratings, they will ultimately drive up the page views on their websites and the views of online matches. This study focuses on a few other concepts of e-commerce like social media interaction and participation in fantasy sports. It is important to determine whether any of these items truly increase television ratings or if they are not a cause of an increase television ratings. The growth and popularity of women's soccer, for example, have explored in recent years to the success of the USA women's soccer team (Coche, 2016). As noted by Baxter (2017), "as the pool of women's soccer talent in the U.S. expands and diversifies, that bar will only be pushed higher" (p. 1), resulting in a new generation of motivated female soccer players and fans.

Coates and Humphreys (2010) tried to find a correlation between the uncertainty of the outcome and attendance in the National Football League (NFL). Previous studies were conducted to find the relationship between viewers and different variables in a particular week's game, however there were no studies completed to find the exact correlation between uncertainty and attendance in the NFL. By analyzing the relationship between game day attendance, uncertainty of outcome, and team and facility quality in the NFL. These data were composed from the game day attendance of 5,495 regular season games, which went over a span of 1985-2008. The arguments are, does the success of the teams playing and their quality have an effect on the attendance? The primary argument is that uncertainty is the key factor in determining attendance for a regular season game. By taking the point spread for the game, they were able to determine how intriguing of a matchup it would be.

More competitive games would in return mean more interest to fans and greater attendance. Most sport managers believe that the outcome of attendance for a game is dependent on the quality of the 2 teams that are playing. Other important factors involved include when the game is being played, how good those teams are performing, and the projected outcome of the game. For example, the NFL schedule is created based on past seasons' results. The teams that win the division and advance in the playoffs, will be scheduled to play against other division winners and teams that advanced in the playoffs. The thought process behind this is that, these teams have proven themselves to be competitive and among the elite, in return having a higher game day attendance and viewer rating.

Another factor that is involved is the league's salary cap that they have implemented. Basically, the purpose of the salary cap is to keep teams on an equal playing field. Perhaps, the reasoning behind this practice is to allow all teams to have a respected chance to win, whoever the opponent is. Coates and Humphreys (2010) determined that the uncertainty of outcome played a key factor in the attendance. The uncertainty of outcome can be calculated using the winning percentage of the teams, which in return capture the quality of the team. The results show that high scoring home teams do not attract a greater attendance, though high scoring visiting teams do. Home teams that let up a lot of points have lower attendance as well. Interestingly, the outcome is about 2% less attendance for each 5 points per game extra a team. As a result, defensively strong teams attract more fans. Ultimately, it is intriguing that there is such a large difference in attendance when a team is expected to win, as opposed to being relevant to the uncertainty of the game. Brown, Billings, and Ruihley (2012), in dealing with the change in motivational factors for participants of fantasy sports throughout their life cycles, fans are demanding more engagement and meaning interactions.

RECENT TRENDS IN SOCCER TELEVISION RATINGS AND CONTRACTS

Domestic Acceptance and Growth Trends

Soccer television ratings in the U.S. have been improving in recent years, especially in major tournaments, including the World Cup, which is the largest sporting event in the world. On a smaller scale, teams in the U.S. and MLS have also signed more lucrative television contracts. Improving television ratings is really the last major step MLS needs to compete with the other major sports in the U.S. As mentioned earlier, gate revenue from attendance, one of the biggest revenue drivers in any sport, is already at a great level for the league and surpasses some of the other major sports in the U.S. Simon Evans explained after speaking with MLS Commission Don Garber that "breaking through on television remains the missing link" (Evans, 2012). To increase ratings, MLS released an iPad/iPhone app that allows its users to watch the league website's live games and highlights on their mobile devices (Dure, 2011). With a mixture of increased television partnerships and the availability to stream over 200 matches each year online, MLS is combating their television ratings in a couple different ways.

Other tournaments, such as the World Cup and the European Championship, have seen drastic increases in television ratings during the 2 most recent tournaments. The average viewing attendance for all 31 matches at Euro 2012 was 1.3 million viewers, which represented a 51% increase on the numbers from the 2008 edition of the tournament (Matchett, 2012). These numbers are even more impressive when realizing when the games were broadcast. The majority of the games were shown during weekday working hours in the U.S. as the tournament was played live during peak times in Poland and Ukraine. Similarly, television ratings for the most recent World Cup in 2010 were just impressive, even though they faced a similarly bad time slot for American viewing audiences. It was the most-watched World Cup ever in the U.S., with more than 3.2 million average viewers per game. This total resulted in an increase of 41% over the previous World Cup in 2006 (Seidman, 2010). The U.S. will likely continue this trend and crush the record in 2014, as the tournament will be hosted in Brazil and many games will start during a more lucrative television timeslot. Not only did television ratings increase in the U.S., but American online websites who covered the tournaments also posted record numbers (Tidey, 2012).

Similarly, companies have begun to pay more for these tournaments' broadcast rights. ESPN is now paying US$100 million for the rights for 2 World Cups and 2 women's World Cups through 2014, which is up significantly from US$11 million in 1994 and US$22 million in 1998 (Sandomir, 2010). Soccer has quickly become a major player in sports, television deals, and online revenue, which have all attributed to its place in the forefront of this study.

Internet and Spectator Engagement

MLS has significantly benefited from the immediacy and engaging nature of the Internet; hence allowing fans to become more engaged in their favorite sports. These trends allow fans to become a more active spectator rather than a passive one. The Internet has a vast variety of tools and channels for this enhanced interaction to occur. The almost universal acceptance of YouTube has become a significant tool in measuring how users display an individual clip and allowing input from its users. Such information can be used to collect fans' thoughts on the individual video and the effects of brand marketing and team logos on game attendance and team-related merchandising behaviors. As suggested by Zimmerman, et al., (2011). The communication and marketing channels created by YouTube was become the industrial standard among newly created websites in terms of options, engagement, and collecting users' feedback on company-based initiatives in such popular social media as Facebook, Tweeter, and Wikipedia. The exponential growth of social media and its various communication channels makes it an excellent platform to increase the exposure and fan loyalty without the huge financial and marketing budgets of more traditional professional sport organizations. Many well-known professional sports leagues have just begun to explore the power of social media, it is interesting to note that management of MLS teams have more embraced YouTube and social media platforms, allowing the MLS as a lesser known sports league to maximized its regular use of essential free websites to become more competitive in attracting a loyal fan base.

On top of these significant contracts and increases for major tournaments, the U.S.' domestic product, MLS, has also benefited recently from big contracts. The most significant of these new contracts, and a big headline grabber for the league, was the recent three-year contract signed with NBC and the NBC Sports Network. This contract was formerly with the Fox Soccer Channel (FSC), but NBC bid and won the contract for US$30 million over three years to broadcast 45 league matches. In just half a season since obtaining this contract, NBC Sports has nearly doubled the ratings from FSC on their networks attracting roughly over 120,000 viewers per match. In addition to this national contract, local teams have also signed many new lucrative contracts e.g., (many of those amounts are undisclosed due to league policies) that will help increase television ratings. The Los Angeles Galaxy signed a 10-year US$55 million deal with Time Warner to broadcast their matches locally (Becker, 2011). Similarly, Columbus Crew signed a contract with Fox Sports Ohio to broadcast all 32 of their non-nationally televised games in high-definition ("Fsohio and Columbus," 2012). Each of these contracts, slightly smaller in games to NBC's contract and only locally, gives the league and soccer in general more exposure in the country and will likely lead to higher television ratings. Figure 1 displays a conceptual model or map of the major trends indirectly/directly impacting domestic soccer TV ratings that will be examined in the present study.

Concepts in Figure 1 highlight some of potential driving factors and/or importance of soccer television ratings is illustrated above. This survey addresses the four potential factors that could lead to higher soccer television ratings: fantasy sports, social media interaction, involvement in soccer, and the presence of a local professional team. The importance of improved soccer television ratings is emphasized by the four outward points (i.e., television contracts, online streaming, advertisement revenue, and merchandise and ticket sales). This entire group of outward points drive up the bottom line for the various soccer party entities involved in increasing soccer television ratings. A few of these were mentioned in the preceding

Figure 1. Conceptual model

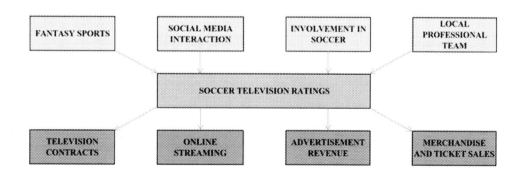

sections, including the increased revenue from television contracts and ticket sales, both of which have skyrocketed in recent years.

Online Customization for Goods and Services

Internet and digital technologies, in general, have completely broadened the boundaries of service and manufacturing customizations or e-personalization. Typically, elements of website usability, technology acceptance, and transaction costs are major considerations in creating a positive impact or link between the customization of online purchase processes in e-retailing that enhances customer satisfaction. Sport entertainment venues are increasing relying on fan engagement to promote a team's services and merchandise. Thirumalai and Sinha (2011) discussed the need for customization when it comes to online shopping. The authors focus on 2 types of customization; namely the decision for customization and the transaction customization, which they believe play an important role in determining the quality of service and translate into customer satisfaction and repeat business. In essence, they found that that personalized product recommendations and transaction customizations are indeed positively associated with customer satisfaction. When purchasing online, the quality of the product is not the only element that matters as the quality of the purchasing process has significant implications to the customers' ultimate purchase decision. This premise is equally true with judging the quality of sport entertainment as well. Moreover, it has ramifications into customer satisfaction and loyalty in e-retailing as retailers typically look to enhancing each customer's shopping experience by offering superior products, being responsive, offering convenience and e-personalization. Although, the direct benefits associated with customization to be inconclusive (Beldona & Tsatsoulis, 2010; Long, 2010; Zopounidis, Baourakis, & Niklis, 2010), probably the ultimate goal of such research is to take a step toward the answer to the question: Does customization matters when dealing with a customer's online shopping experience? Most recent research has suggested that customization does play a major role in customer satisfaction and returning business. Thirumalai and Sinha (2011) suggested that the idea of online purchase customization into the decision-making process (e.g., which identifies customer needs) and the transaction process (e.g., the stage in which the customer concludes the purchase and interacts with the retailers' customer service regarding the purchase), is an excellent place to begin such research into the inherent value of e-personalization.

In order to achieve e-personalization, Thirumalai and Sinha (2011) suggested that retailers follow a 5-stage process consisting of collecting customer data; creating customer profiles; matchmaking to established the personalized products; services and content that best suits each customer; delivering these personalized products and recommendations to each customer; and measuring customer response toward the personalized offerings. Ultimately, their research found that decision customization, which includes presenting customers with recommendations and pre-selected items, avoids information overload and increase the ease of purchasing online. Transaction customization, which includes storing customer information such as address, bank account number and other preferences, increases ease of purchase online. Combined, such customization can have substantial positive impact on customer satisfaction. Decision customization and transaction customization were determined as the independent variables. The dependent variables included product information, ease of ordering, customer support, order tracking, shipping and handling, and retailer performance. The control variables in the study are price, product selection, product variety, number of years the retailer has had an Internet domain, number of customers visiting the retailer online and whether the retailer has an offline presence. The authors found that decision customization has a significant effect how customers perceive the dependent variables product information, ease of ordering, customer support, order tracking, shipping and handling, and retailer performance. They further found that that transaction customization has a significant effect on the same variables.

Hence, online sales are no longer a competitive advantage to retailers wishing to reach their customers on the Web, it is a necessity. Many types of retailers make their products and services available online and knowing how to make the process easier and more enjoyable for each individual customer is indispensable. Online retailers need to offer customers personalized products and support each purchase in a convenient, responsive and personalized way. Therefore, such research efforts support the view that the quality of a product and well as how the service and/or good is delivery is equally important when dealing with online sales. Hence, as noted by Thirumalai and Sinha (2011), "the quality of the service, the relevance of the digital content, the convenience of the online purchase process, and the overall purchase experience are as critical as the product quality (p. 485).

Social Media Interaction

Social media is a powerful tool that has grown in importance significantly over recent years. Twitter and Facebook have taken nearly a daily role in millions of peoples' lives. It is a way to follow your favorite things, including sports teams and professional athletes. Recent research on social media and its impact on attracting new customers has suggested that Facebook, Twitter, and active communication channels created through live-blogging have fueled viewer interest in television (Larkin & Fink, 2016; Pookulangara & Koesler, 2011; Smith, 2012; Wu, Wang, & Tsai, 2011). In particular, Larkin and Fink examined the role of fear from a psychological process perspective and tested a model of highlighting fear of "missing out" of fantasy sport and social media involvement with team identity salience during gaming activities. From a team sponsor/provider perspective, there are some fears that these social media sites and other websites would actually hurt television ratings. Social media has been deemed a hybrid element of the promotion mix in the sense that it not only allows companies to communicate with their customers, but also allows for customers to talk directly to one another (Mangold & Faulds, 2009). Probably due to the timeliness of media access online, managers are able to strategically use the Internet as a way to promote different sport organizations, athletes, events, and marketing products. When sport and office pooling information comes from a trus2rthy source, consumers and fans are more likely to pay attention to the information being presented to them, even from social media. There will continue to be an ethical component in dealing with social media associated with office pooling activities and their corporate sponsors in terms of trus2rthiness. Although research studies can be designed to look at the individual behavior level, there needs to be a renewed focus on understanding the strategic goal of a sports' organization, both in its formulation and implementation, and how best to utilize the various media channels available to convey the messages that sport organizations want to project.

Consumers of sport-related materials are redefining how organizations' leverage of media attempts to communicate with them in the most effective ways. Sometimes this communication occurs at a tacit level, even without our conscious consent, as in the case of eye-tracking methodologies. A message's reach (i.e., broadcast to multiple audiences) and richness (i.e., personalized content) via mass media and its research seems to have gone beyond simple content analyses of sport websites. Such analysis has often failed to consider a user's goal-direction (Green, Murray, & Warner, 2011), a more long-term or strategic direction of the organization. Hence, it appears that a number of Internet technology's impacts on sports are driven by media, is of the most successful tactics, "The press may not be successful much of the time in telling people what to think, but it is stunningly successful in telling its readers what to think about" (Cohen, 1963, p. 177). Still, principles of strategic management, namely mission and vision statements and the role of leadership (Evans & Smith, 2004), are important in research efforts to understand and model media theory and sport-related communications.

Most competitive businesses (e.g., for-profit and nonprofit organizations) have successfully employed mission and vision statements for years; not having an official Internet vision illustrates a significant organizational weakness and misalignment of business and marketing strategies. Understanding these dynamics is essential if an organization is to understand the impacts of any regulation of sport-related programming and engagement activities within the workplace environment, such as office pooling and gambling activities.

Local Professional Teams

MLS currently has 19 teams in 15 U.S. markets (Los Angeles has 2 teams) and three Canadian markets. This is a little less than 2-thirds of the market coverage found in other professional sports leagues (NHL, NFL, NBA, and MLB) in the U.S. While this lower market coverage likely leads to lower television ratings as people do not have a team in as close of proximity to follow as other sports, the idea is an interesting component of my study. Not only does this mean less markets have soccer teams, it also means less markets have interest in the league overall as parts of the U.S. do not have a team anywhere nearby (i.e.; Southeast). The map below, Figure 1, shows the markets covered by MLS in the U.S. and Canada. A key component in this study is whether people are willing to follow sports teams outside of their market, but maybe even more importantly it is determining whether people follow leagues that are not represented in their market (which includes MLS and foreign leagues).

As explained by Tainsky and McEvoy (2011), it is extremely important for leagues such as the NFL to attract television viewers from large markets without professional teams. The importance of television ratings from markets without professional teams because television contracts are a huge revenue source, but are not as valuable when the only market interested is the local market. They found that "demand is positively associated with team age as well as the presence of select franchises or the closest team geographically, suggesting that familiarity with the teams featured is especially important to these fans" (Tainsky & McEvoy, 2011). If these results carry to MLS, they likely work against the league for a few key reasons. First, the league is very young and does not have the history of other sports. Leagues from around the world are much older (along with specific franchises in MLS) so this may not necessarily impact soccer television ratings completely. Second, local teams are far away from some major markets. Some states, such as Florida, Georgia, and Alabama, do not have teams anywhere nearby.

Television Contracts

Television contracts is one of the first positive impacts felt from increases soccer television ratings and the first of four result items of the conceptual model. Television contracts and their growing revenues were discussed earlier in this paper. These included significant revenue increases for television contracts relating to the World Cup, Euro Championship, and MLS. All of these contracts have significantly increased year-over-year or competition-over-competition. MLS is poised for what is likely another increase in their bargaining power during the next round of television contract negotiations. During the 2012 season, MLS was on pace for their best season ever on ESPN, up 12% during the same period in 2011, and is off to a great start during their first year with NBC and the NBC Sports Network (Karp, 2012).

Fox Soccer had the same contract as NBC last year, and NBC was having 78% better ratings during the same time period. Both of these statistics, along with the increased viewership for the Euro Championship and World Cup, mean larger and more profitable television contracts in the future for soccer.

Online Streaming

With the availability of live broadcasts to be shown online, it is likely that as interest grows towards a program online (in this case, soccer) that the corresponding ratings of online streaming will increase as well. Online streaming provides companies the ability to make advertisement revenue online and increase viewership overall when a television is not available or the market is not covering a specific channel or program (Smith, 2013; Smith & Rupp, 2013; Smith, Synowka, & Smith, 2014). Online streaming is on the rise and becoming just as important to companies as the traditional television market. Generally, a firm or program should see online viewing increase in stride with television ratings. This survey asks people about their willingness and tendency to stream sports and stream soccer online, but the focus is not to prove whether the characteristics of a person increase either of the 2. To understand the new importance of online streaming, it is easiest to look at the growth of Netflix. For example, subscribers watched more than one billion hours of video in June, 2012, which made the service more popular than any traditional U.S. cable network ("Netflix just became," 2012). The same demand functions that possibly lead to increased soccer television ratings may lead to increased online streaming ratings. However, the characteristics of users of the traditional television market in comparison to online streaming users may be vastly different.

Advertisement Revenue

An increase in soccer television ratings can relate directly to an increase in advertisement revenue for all parties involved in soccer on television. Soccer, as it is unique in many aspects, is also unique in advertising opportunities. Besides commercial revenue and online advertisements, soccer teams also have very lucrative sponsorship deals for advertisements on their jerseys. Like other sports, they also receive revenue for stadium sponsorships. All of these forms of advertisement can generate more revenue when the various leagues and teams can prove that their reach to a television audience is greater. Bloxsome, Voges, and Pope (2011) suggested that the rewards of sport sponsorship are relatively clear via audience reach, which is specifically measured through attendance and television rating metrics. When these metrics improve, the revenue generated through sponsorships increases with it. Another unique aspect to soccer television advertisements is a running advertisement that runs alongside the scoreboard graphic during each half of play, as soccer has no television breaks or timeouts during the 2 halves of the match. If television ratings improve, the audience grows, and this advertisement space increases significantly in value.

Sustainable competitive advantage through quality initiatives is the goal of most business enterprises throughout the global economy (Ali & Alolayyan, 2013; Bhamu, Khandelwal, & Sangwan, 2013; Chiarini, Vagnoni, & Chiarini, 2018; Dharamdass & Fernando, 2018; Franceschini & Mastrogiacomo, 2018). Ultimately, management must make a decision to reach out globally when they feel they have hit a roadblock with expansion in their country or they just want to make the big step and go international. Once the decision is made to internationalize their products, the company must decide what products they are going to offer and how will they have to modify their products to appeal to the market they are trying to reach. The timing of when a company tries to go international can have a tremendous impact on their success. If a company tries to enter another country during a recession or slow times, that can prove very fatal to their success in that country.

Abdi, Awan, and Bhatti (2008) tried to answer the question of whether quality management is a big factor for companies to make the decision to go international or not. It also looks at companies who have made the decision to go with the ISO-9000 standard. It seems as though many companies use the ISO standard as a stepping stone to get to Total Quality Management. Using a quality management system shows customers that the company cares about the products they are putting out in the market and that they have been tested to make sure they are not going to break or malfunction right away. Also with quality comes a safety check to be sure that products are not dangerous or that safe-guards are put in place. Customers prefer to purchase merchandise they know has been tested for quality and safety. When so much money has been paid for a product, the customer does not want to get it home and it not work, or it breaks the first few times it is used.

Commercialization of Sport and Issues in the Workplace

It is apparent from the previous literature cited from the business, physiological, and sport-marketing research areas, there are several possible options to formally pursue a theoretical background for the justification of empirical section of the present study. In fact, Jonasson and Thiborg (2010) suggested that simple mentioning of computer gaming via e-sport as a form of sports is "subversive, according to public health and media discourses" (p. 287). The nature of sport activities is often regarded as a type of virtue, while computer gaming is often perceived as a vice, a corruptor of youth; then leads to crime and possibly terrorist training. So, what is the future evolution of e-sports? The popularity of e-sports is gaining equally with other types of Internet-based activities, such as social networking and Internet gambling. As these online activities continue, what are the possible impacts on sports in general? Are we on the evolutionary threshold of a new generation or phase of sports?

Just as the origins of sports broadcasting and the revenues associated with it were in the U.S. and received world-wide acceptance, American sports are rapidly becoming part of a global entertainment network, as noted by Helland (2007) and Lever & Wheeler (1993). Although the beginning of com-mercialization in sports had a humble beginning, now the astronomical costs associated with this new sports/media complex are being justified as part of giving valuable exposure to new series/entertainment specials through advertising spots and products. The great transformational changes in both technology and society's need for mass consumption (both services and goods), has led to an almost insatiable ap-petite for sports to be treated as a consumable product for the general commodification of leisure time. Many of the changes in global sports are the direct result and reflection of the existing pattern of growth through consumerism; or in other terms, a growth of consumerism over socially responsible behavior or citizenship. Unfortunately, it is natural for economic incentives to take over virtually all sectors of tra-ditional life and turn them into methods for growth. Hence, sport-related media have inevitably become commercialized with both positive and negative consequences.

The commercialization of sport, especially television and the broadcasting rights associated with it has manifested itself in the corporate world, where increased competition for audiences in a new media market, has left a moral gap in the ideals of independent sports coverage and professionalism in news reporting. Helland (2007) and Szymanski (2006) suggested that this economic liberalism in sport broad-casting initially began in the technological modernization of the sports/media complex, but soon moved to business processes founded in the principles of competitive marketplaces and promotions of sport products (i.e., commercial sports, sponsorship, and media-product). As highlighted by Szymanski (2006), the large capital flows from commercialization through the increase media accessibility of sports has become commonplace with sponsors, managers and teams. Unfortunately, as noted by Helland (2007), the growth and power of media is too weak to provide the journalistic safeguards that the general public needs to protect citizens' rights to fair coverage. Commercial interests have dominated sports coverage, which threatens the social role of broadcasting and journalism.

Commercialization is a double-edged sword; in that it provides for corporations' need for increased visibility and a place that may win the attention of fans. Many managers believe that the emotional meaning of the game or the team was transferred to the sponsoring company. On the other hand, the reverse may also be true; emotional meaning is just as easily transferred from the company to the club that it sponsors. The same mutually beneficial relationship may exist when management allows certain sport-related activities, such as gambling and office pooling, to co-exist, even if there are organizational policies that do not formally support such activities. Many people have an emotional need for bonding within the workplace environment and, although sport promotion is highly commercialized, such activities allow for such engagement and a sense of belonging to occur (Dees, 2011; Hutchins, 2011; Schirato, 2012; Weeks, Cornwell, & Drennan, 2008).

METHOD

Specific Research Hypotheses

The three hypotheses presented in this paper dealing with the interplay of online social networking, work assignments, and office layouts, as derived from the review of relevant operations literature (Durán, Guajardo, & Wolf-Yadlin, 2012; Jain & D'lima, 2018; Oey, & Nofrimurti, 2018; Rego, Kumar, & Mukherjee, 2018) and from applying the basic tenants of Uses and Gratification Theory are as follows:

H1: Participation in online fantasy soccer leads to increased television ratings for soccer.
H2: A local professional soccer team leads to increased television ratings for soccer.
H3: Respondents who are more athletically or programmatically involved in soccer are more likely to watch soccer on television.

The basic conceptual model, Figure 1, was designed to serve as an aid to display the interplay of the three major areas of focus and how they relate to firms dealing with intrinsic and extrinsic fan satisfaction issues. It is further research assumption that management needs to properly manage these elements in order to promote a more satisfying and engaging environment.

Sample and Statistical Techniques

A basic survey instrument was developed for exploratory purposes. The survey instrument consists of items that were developed from the sport business literature and media applications. Through personal and confidential connections on the part of the researcher, a focused stratified sample of employed professional management (typically at the lower to middle-levels) was created and collected. The sample chosen was representative of the service industry located in the metropolitan section of Pittsburgh, PA. Pittsburgh was chosen as the site of the study as a classic rebirth urban area that historically a low unemployment, technically advanced, and economically strong within an area of declining manufacturing, but a very strong professional sport following.

This procedure resulted in 129 submitted useable questionnaires from an initial sampling frame of approximately 500+ professional personnel from several large area marketing and financial service firms. The surveyed personnel, primarily service representing marketing and financial services, were conducted over a three-month period. The rationale for selecting employed and relatively well-educated people was to gauge the sense of the impact of communication technology in a knowledge-based environment on television of MLS ratings theme. The following section on results will address the previously mentioned hypotheses and also considers a few other interesting results that came out of the 25 question survey. The primary goal of the survey and these tests was to find any useful media interconnection for soccer business decision-makers in regards to television ratings and increase the dividends these ratings create, as discussed in the earlier conceptual model.

Mostly scale (interval) measurements, with a few nominal-based questions, were used to develop graphs and perform the relevant statistical analyses; the actual instrument is available upon request. Most perceptual questions were based on a 5-point scale (i.e., 5 = strongly disagree, 1 = strongly agree). The dominant statistical techniques used in the present study were descriptive statistics, means testing, and regression analyses. The following survey questions that were used in the analysis may be at least partially derived from the descriptive statistics and the cross-tabulations found in Table 3 and the resulting cross-tabulations.

RESULTS AND DISCUSSION

Descriptive Comparisons

Table 3 displays the descriptive statistics of the 129 management professionals' responses to the survey instrument. As evident from an inspection of the table, the majority of respondents were relatively frequent users of social media websites, view social media at the workplace regardless of management's approval, and ranked cell phone as the preferred technology to access social media (e.g., followed by tablet, MP3, and other category). There was moderate agreement on the use of social networking sites streamline communication in the workplace, somewhat split on whether social media sites at work positively affect worker productivity, and generally felt that social networking sites increase expertise/ information sharing.

In terms of management's perceived degree of strong personal face-to-face communication with co-workers cross-tabulated with strong personal electronic communication with co-workers, Figure 2- Figure 9 illustrate a strong relationship among the various cross-tabulation of customer preferences of television and social media programming options with age. As expected, younger age groups have a greater affinity for social media and fantasy league inactions/engagements than older groups that have greater preferences for fan-based face-to-face skills/sport participation to more electronic forms of communication/social networking.

Table 3. Basic descriptive statistics of the major scaled variables in the present study

Variable Description and Coding Schema	N	Mean	Std. Deviation	Skewness	Kurtosis
Age of respondent (years) (1 = less than 20, 6 = 60+)	129	3.16	1.372	.822	-.641
I'm more likely to watch sports on TV if personally involved in a fantasy sports league (5 = strongly disagree, 1 = strong agree)	129	3.16	1.247	-.250	-.891
Regularly follow sports teams from different cities (5 = strongly disagree, 1 = strong agree)	128	3.20	1.358	-.170	-1.239
Regularly follow sports leagues not represented in my local city like following the NBA in Pittsburgh (5 = strongly disagree, 1 = strong agree)	128	2.96	1.416	.138	-1.357
Watch the majority of my local sports teams' games on television (if not attending in person) (5 = strongly disagree, 1 = strong agree)	128	3.91	1.157	-1.193	.630
Regularly stream sports matches online like ESPN3 (5 = strongly disagree, 1 = strong agree)	129	2.26	1.289	.644	-.877
Regularly stream soccer matches online (5 = strongly disagree, 1 = strong agree)	129	1.79	1.273	1.510	.993
Involvement in soccer throughout your life (e.g., player, coach) (1 = never, 5 = lifetime)	129	2.47	1.490	.658	-1.007
Involvement in ALL sports throughout your life (e.g., player, coach) (1 = never, 5 = lifetime)	129	3.90	1.211	-.903	-.101
Based on sports teams' social media updates, more likely to turn on TV and watch a live sporting event (5 = strongly disagree, 1 = strong agree)	129	2.75	1.173	-.005	-.849
Valid N	128				

Figure 2. Cross-tabulation of selected customer preferences of television and social media programming options with age and Fantasy soccer

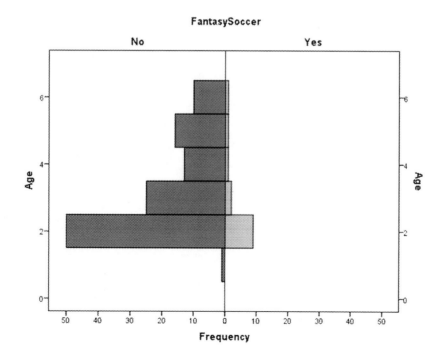

Figure 3. Cross-tabulation of selected customer preferences of television and social media programming options with age and Soccer on TV

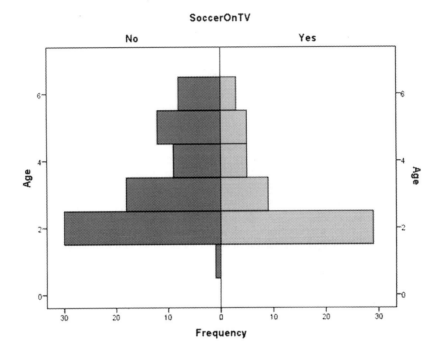

Figure 4. Cross-tabulation of selected customer preferences of television and social media programming options with age and Sports on TV

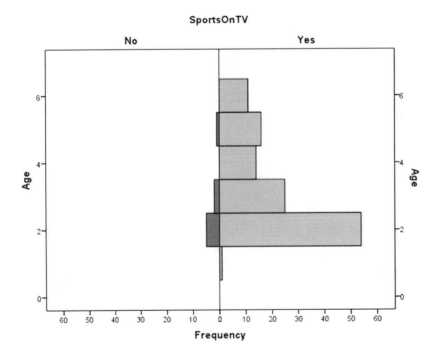

Figure 5. Cross-tabulation of selected customer preferences of television and social media programming options with age and Fantasy sports

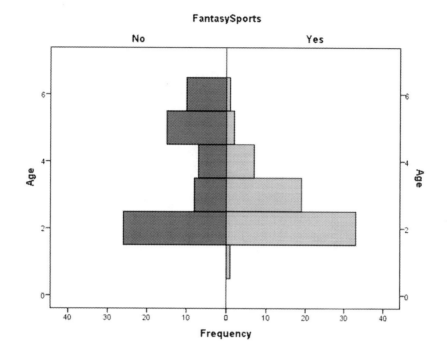

Figure 6. Cross-tabulation of selected customer preferences of television and social media programming options with age and Fantasy sports viewed on TV

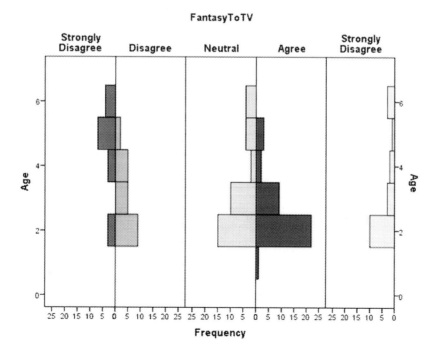

Figure 7. Cross-tabulation of selected customer preferences of television and social media programming options with age and Fantasy sports

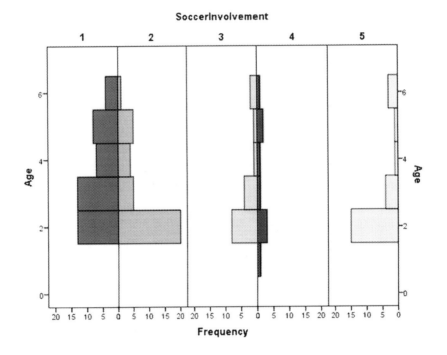

Figure 8. Cross-tabulation of selected customer preferences of television and social media programming options with age and Sports involvement

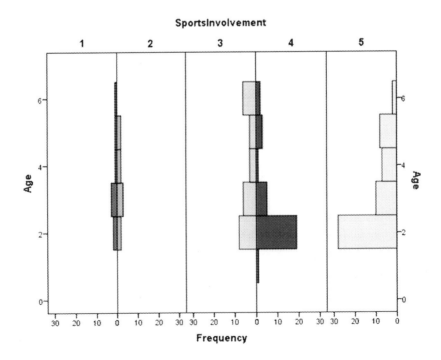

Figure 9. Cross-tabulation of selected customer preferences of television and social media programming options with age and Use social media

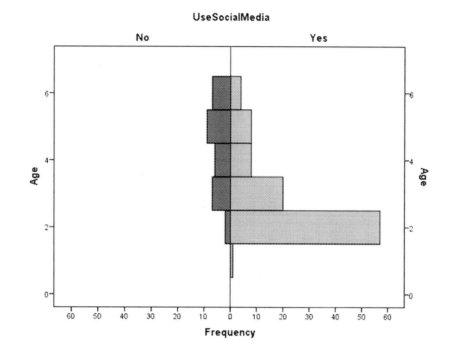

HYPOTHESIS-TESTING RESULTS

Results of Specific Hypothesis (H1)

H1: Participation in Online Fantasy Soccer Leads to Increased Television Ratings for Soccer

The first stated hypothesis is that managerial employees with greater access to mobile and online social media technologies, as measured in various forms of passive/active participation with fantasy soccer leagues generally leads to increased ratings for televised soccer participation/viewing. In order to properly test this hypothesis, a series of Chi-square tests were decided as a legitimate option to inspect these apparent differences of qualitative and quantitative variables for comparing the willingness to engage in these efforts. As noted in the conceptual model, Figure 1, and a review of the literature, fantasy sports, especially participation in fantasy football, have been linked to an increase in people watching the NFL on television. There may be a similar case for people who participate in fantasy soccer. While fantasy soccer participation is so much lower in the U.S. than other sports, this is likely an opportunity for soccer decision makers to help stimulate new and improved television ratings even further in the U.S. It is important to determine whether people who participate in fantasy sports also watch sports on television and those who participate in fantasy soccer also watch soccer on television. Of relative importance would also be finding the correlation between those who participate in fantasy soccer and attend live soccer matches. Without monitoring the amount of games a person watches, the survey simply asks if people are more likely to follow sports when they are involved in fantasy sports.

Fantasy sports and fantasy soccer was discussed in three specific questions in the survey determining whether people participate in fantasy soccer, other fantasy sports, and if their participation in fantasy sports leads them to watch more sports on television. Nearly half of the people surveyed participate in some form of fantasy sports. However, only about 10% of those surveyed participate in fantasy soccer. Generally, people who participate in fantasy sports believe that they do watch more sports and are more interested in tuning into sports on television because of fantasy sports. Figure 10 illustrates the cross-tabulation between watching sports on television because of fantasy sports with participation with fantasy sports.

As illustrated in Tables 4 and 5, a series of cross-tabulation statistics associated with watching soccer on TV with participation in any soccer fantasy sports games with more likely to watch sports on TV if involved in a fantasy sports league (H1), factoring degree of social media usage, can be found. It is realtively clear that people who participate in fantasy sports feel they are more likely to watch television because of of their participation. With such low fantasy soccer participation, this trend may suggest a significant opportunity for the soccer industry to help improve overall television ratings. As the results point to roughly 28% of those who watch soccer on television also participate in fantasy soccer. With only 14 people participating in fantasy soccer, it was harder to get sufficient data results, so it is just as important to look at television viewing of those who participate in all fantasy sports, as shown below. Overall fantasy sports participation is extremely important to look at when predicting the success of increasing fantasy soccer participation. Only one person did not watch sports on television that participates in fantasy sports, but over 50% of those who watch sports on television participate in fantasy sports (Chi-Square = 24.018, p < .001).

Figure 10. Watching sports on television because of fantasy sports with participation with fantasy sports

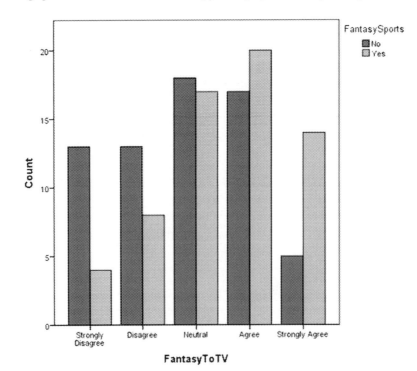

Participating in fantasy sports has a significant relationship with people watching sports on television. With low fantasy soccer participation, this is a significant opportunity for soccer (or any sport) to increase their television ratings. These results provided support for the hypothesis that online fantasy sports participation leads to increased television ratings. On a whole, the evidence looks promising that participating in fantasy soccer leads to increased television ratings, which also supports previous research done in other major sports (Davis & Duncan, 2006; Lee, Kwak, Lim, Pedersen, & Miloch, 2011; Schirato, 2012). Hence, H2 was accepted.

Results of Specific Hypothesis (H2)

H2: A Local Professional Soccer Team Leads to Increased Television Ratings for Soccer

As previously mentioned, MLS only has 15 major markets within the U.S., easily the lowest number of markets among the major professional sports leagues. This low representation will likely result in a negative impact on TV ratings for soccer in the U.S., since each marketing segment is further away from

Table 4. Cross-tabulation statistics associated with Watch soccer on TV with Participate in any soccer fantasy sports games with more likely to watch sports on TV if involved in a fantasy sports league (H1)

Part A. Actual count					
I'm more likely to watch sports on TV if Personally involved in a fantasy sports league			*Participate in any soccer fantasy sports games*		*Total*
			No	*Yes*	
Strongly Agree	Watch soccer on TV	No	12	0	12
		Yes	5	0	5
	Total		17	0	17
Agree	Watch soccer on TV	No	11	0	11
		Yes	8	2	10
	Total		19	2	21
Neutral	Watch soccer on TV	No	25	0	25
		Yes	7	3	10
	Total		32	3	35
Disagree	Watch soccer on TV	No	18	0	18
		Yes	12	7	19
	Total		30	7	37
Strongly Disagree	Watch soccer on TV	No	12	0	12
		Yes	5	2	7
	Total		17	2	19
Total	Watch soccer on TV	No	78	0	78
		Yes	37	14	51
	Total		115	14	129

321

Table 5. Part B: Chi-square test results

I'm more likely to watch sports on TV if Personally involved in a fantasy sports league		Value	df	Asymptotic Significance (2-sided)	Exact Sig. (2-sided)	Exact Sig. (1-sided)
Strongly Agree	Pearson Chi-Square	.[c]				
	N of Valid Cases	17				
Agree	Pearson Chi-Square	2.432[d]	1	.119		
	Continuity Correction[b]	.664	1	.415		
	Likelihood Ratio	3.201	1	.074		
	Fisher's Exact Test				.214 (NS)	.214 (NS)
	Linear-by-Linear Association	2.316	1	.128		
	N of Valid Cases	21				
Neutral	Pearson Chi-Square	8.203[e]	1	.004		
	Continuity Correction[b]	4.822	1	.028		
	Likelihood Ratio	8.258	1	.004		
	Fisher's Exact Test				.018 (S)	.018 (S)
	Linear-by-Linear Association	7.969	1	.005		
	N of Valid Cases	35				
Disagree	Pearson Chi-Square	8.179[f]	1	.004		
	Continuity Correction[b]	5.954	1	.015		
	Likelihood Ratio	10.885	1	.001		
	Fisher's Exact Test				.008 (HS)	.005 (HS)
	Linear-by-Linear Association	7.958	1	.005		
	N of Valid Cases	37				
Strongly Disagree	Pearson Chi-Square	3.832[g]	1	.050		
	Continuity Correction[b]	1.399	1	.237		
	Likelihood Ratio	4.411	1	.036		
	Fisher's Exact Test				.123 (NS)	.123 (NS)
	Linear-by-Linear Association	3.630	1	.057		
	N of Valid Cases	19				
Total	Pearson Chi-Square	24.018[a]	1	<.001		
	Continuity Correction[b]	21.265	1	<.001		
	Likelihood Ratio	28.659	1	<.001		
	Fisher's Exact Test				<.001 (HS)	<.001 (HS)
	Linear-by-Linear Association	23.832	1	<.001		
	N of Valid Cases	129				

a. No cells (0.0%) have expected count less than 5. The minimum expected count is 5.53.

b. Computed only for a 2x2 table

c. No statistics are computed because Participate in any soccer fantasy sports games is a constant.

d. 2 cells (50.0%) have expected count less than 5. The minimum expected count is 0.95.

e. 2 cells (50.0%) have expected count less than 5. The minimum expected count is 0.86.

f. 2 cells (50.0%) have expected count less than 5. The minimum expected count is 3.41.

g. 2 cells (50.0%) have expected count less than 5. The minimum expected count is 0.74.

NS denotes not statistically significant at the .05 level for a 2-tailed test; S denotes statistically significant at the .05 level for a 2-tailed test; HS denotes significant at the .01 level for a 2-tailed test.

Table 6. Part C: Symmetric measures

I'm more likely to watch sports on TV if Personally involved in a fantasy sports league			Value	Approximate Significance
Strongly Agree	Nominal by Nominal	Phi	.c	NA
	N of Valid Cases		17	
Agree	Nominal by Nominal	Phi	.340	.119 (NS)
		Cramer's V	.340	.119 (NS)
		Contingency Coefficient	.322	.119 (NS)
	N of Valid Cases		21	
Neutral	Nominal by Nominal	Phi	.484	.004 (HS)
		Cramer's V	.484	.004 (HS)
		Contingency Coefficient	.436	.004 (HS)
	N of Valid Cases		35	
Disagree	Nominal by Nominal	Phi	.470	.004 (HS)
		Cramer's V	.470	.004 (HS)
		Contingency Coefficient	.425	.004 (HS)
	N of Valid Cases		37	
Strongly Disagree	Nominal by Nominal	Phi	.449	.050 (S)
		Cramer's V	.449	.050 (S)
		Contingency Coefficient	.410	.050 (S)
	N of Valid Cases		19	
Total	Nominal by Nominal	Phi	.431	<.001 (HS)
		Cramer's V	.431	<.001 (HS)
		Contingency Coefficient	.396	<.001 (HS)
	N of Valid Cases		129	

NS denotes not statistically significant at the .05 level for a 2-tailed test; S denotes statistically significant at the .05 level for a 2-tailed test; HS denotes significant at the .01 level for a 2-tailed test.

other sport-related markets, making it harder to find coverage on a team and drive interest in a positive direction. It would be equally interesting to determine if a relationship existed if people are following leagues and teams outside of their local market. By looking at people's interest in teams outside of their local market and looking at whether people generally follow their local teams, perhaps useful insights can be made on the importance of league expansion. U.S. league expansion and relocation have traditionally been an important topic in all professional leagues, as picking the right locations can mean success or failure for a league and its bottom line.

Potentially, one way to create higher television ratings is just to expand the league further, as they have done over the past few years. The survey focused on a few key questions surrounding local teams and people's willingness to follow teams and leagues that are not locally represented. Since that vast majority of the respondents are located within or around Pittsburgh, it is unlikely that most people have a local MLS team. The closest teams to Pittsburgh are Columbus, OH, Philadelphia, PA, and Washington, DC. However, the results are a fairly good indicator to show the difference between people with a

Table 7. Cross-tabulation statistics associated with watch soccer on TV with participation in any soccer fantasy sports games with more likely to watch sports on TV if involved in a fantasy sports league by use of social media sites like Facebook, Twitter (H1).

Part A. Actual count					
Use social media sites like Facebook, Twitter			**Participate in any soccer fantasy sports games**		**Total**
			No	**Yes**	
No	Watch soccer on TV	No	21	0	21
		Yes	9	1	10
	Total		30	1	31
Yes	Watch soccer on TV	No	57	0	57
		Yes	28	13	41
	Total		85	13	98
Total	Watch soccer on TV	No	78	0	78
		Yes	37	14	51
	Total		115	14	129

Table 8. Part B: Chi-square test results

Use social media sites like Facebook, Twitter		Value	df	Asymptotic Significance (2-sided)	Exact Sig. (2-sided)	Exact Sig. (1-sided)
No	Pearson Chi-Square	2.170ᶜ	1	.141 (NS)		
	Continuity Correctionᵇ	.149	1	.700 (NS)		
	Likelihood Ratio	2.334	1	.127 (NS)		
	Fisher's Exact Test				.323 (NS)	.323 (NS)
	Linear-by-Linear Association	2.100	1	.147 (NS)		
	N of Valid Cases	31				
Yes	Pearson Chi-Square	20.837ᵈ	1	<.001 (HS)		
	Continuity Correctionᵇ	18.173	1	<.001 (HS)		
	Likelihood Ratio	25.493	1	<.001 (HS)		
	Fisher's Exact Test				<.001 (HS)	<.001 (HS)
	Linear-by-Linear Association	20.625	1	<.001 (HS)		
	N of Valid Cases	98				
Total	Pearson Chi-Square	24.018ᵃ	1	<.001 (HS)		
	Continuity Correctionᵇ	21.265	1	<.001 (HS)		
	Likelihood Ratio	28.659	1	<.001 (HS)		
	Fisher's Exact Test				<.001 (HS)	<.001 (HS)
	Linear-by-Linear Association	23.832	1	<.001 (HS)		
	N of Valid Cases	129				

a. No cells (0.0%) have expected count less than 5. The minimum expected count is 5.53.

b. Computed only for a 2x2 table

c. 2 cells (50.0%) have expected count less than 5. The minimum expected count is 0.32.

d. 0 cells (0.0%) have expected count less than 5. The minimum expected count is 5.44.

NS denotes not statistically significant at the .05 level for a 2-tailed test; S denotes statistically significant at the .05 level for a 2-tailed test; HS denotes significant at the .01 level for a 2-tailed test.

Table 9.

Part C. Symmetric measures				
Use social media sites like Facebook, Twitter			*Value*	*Approximate Significance*
No	Nominal by Nominal	Contingency Coefficient	.256	.141 (NS)
	N of Valid Cases		31	
Yes	Nominal by Nominal	Contingency Coefficient	.419	<.001 (HS)
	N of Valid Cases		98	
Total	Nominal by Nominal	Contingency Coefficient	.396	<.001 (HS)
	N of Valid Cases		129	

NS denotes not statistically significant at the .05 level for a 2-tailed test; S denotes statistically significant at the .05 level for a 2-tailed test; HS denotes significant at the .01 level for a 2-tailed test.

local team and people without one. The majority of people surveyed have local sports teams (119/128). The question really now is whether the people with a local professional soccer team are more likely to watch soccer on television. A simple Chi-square (Table 10) test should provide evidence to accept/reject H2. As shown in the previous hypothesis (H1) test, 51 respondents watch soccer on television (while only 21 have a local MLS team) so it may be safe to assume that that a local team is not necessary for a person to watch soccer on television. However, it is reasonable to expect that the ratio of people who watch soccer on television with a team in a local market to be higher. Figure 4 graphically displays this cross-tabulation as well.

Surprisingly, the presence of a local team does not have a significant relationship to people watching soccer on television (Chi-square = 1.465, P = .833). Only 11 of 21 (52%) people with a local professional soccer team watch soccer on television. Comparatively, 40 out of 107 (37%) people without a local professional soccer team watch soccer on television. While the percentage of people watching in local markets is higher than the ratings in markets without local teams, the results of the current study does not find this to be a significant factor in increasing television ratings. The majority of people agreed that they followed most of their local teams on television, which contradicts the findings that a local professional team is not important to television ratings. A local team and that market is extremely important to television ratings.

Table 10. Cross-tabulation statistics associated with having a local professional soccer team (MLS) with watching the majority of local sports teams' games on television (if not attending in person) (H2)

A. Actual count							
Independent Variables		*Watch the majority of my local sports teams' games on television (if not attending in person)*					*Total*
		Strongly Agree	*Agree*	*Neutral*	*Disagree*	*Strongly Disagree*	
Have a local professional soccer team (MLS)	No	6	10	5	47	39	107
	Yes	2	2	2	10	6	22
Total		8	12	7	57	45	129

Table 11. Part B: Chi-square test results

Statistics	Value	df	Asymptotic Significance (2-sided)
Pearson Chi-Square	1.465	4	.833 (NS)
Likelihood Ratio	1.371	4	.849 (NS)
Linear-by-Linear Association	.756	1	.385 (NS)
N of Valid Cases	129		

Note, 3 cells (30.0%) have expected count less than 5. The minimum expected count is 1.19. NS denotes not statistically significant at the .05 level for a 2-tailed test.

Part C. Symmetric measures			
Statistics		Value	Approximate Significance
Nominal by Nominal	Contingency Coefficient	.106	.833 (NS)
N of Valid Cases		129	

NS denotes not statistically significant at the .05 level for a 2-tailed test.

Therefore, as illustrated in Figure 11, many sport fans had mixed opinions on whether they would follow a team outside of their local market. Similarly, respondents are also mixed in whether they would follow a league not represented in their local market, as shown in the chart below. Both of these findings, relating to non-local teams and non-local leagues, show support to the hypothesis that a local professional team would increase television ratings. Hence, H2 was rejected.

Figure 11. Watching majority of local sports teams on television with having a local professional soccer team

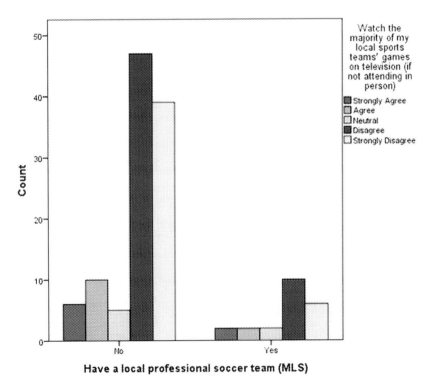

Results of Specific Hypothesis (H3)

H3: Respondents Who Are More Athletically or Programmatically Involved in Soccer Are More Likely to Watch Soccer on Television

Many respondents in the U.S. follow sports that they have never participated in or been involved in, especially the NFL. However, respondents often have interesting reasons for not following soccer, which includes not understanding the game. These same reasons are often given for reasons why respondents do not follow the National Hockey League (NHL), as well (Fortunato, 2011; Nesbit & King, 2010). This is an important concept for decision makers to understand, since it could theoretically help marketers target an audience, whether involvement in soccer matters or not and how they can attract new viewers to soccer programming. Of course, being physically involved in a highly competitive and demanding sport like soccer would be relatively rare for most fans of soccer; therefore, engagement in fantasy soccer was analyzed in the formal testing of H3 (Table 12), and basically the same test with selecting only those respondents that also watch soccer on television (Table 14). As evident from both tables, only the independent variable involvement in soccer throughout one's life (e.g., player, coach) was statistically significant ($t = 2.297$, $p = .023$), but not statistically significant when the population was limited to those fans who also watched soccer on television ($t = 1.112$, $p = .272$). As illustrated in Table 16, the results of the Chi-square analysis

An observation that has not been fully researched on any sport is the likelihood that direct involvement in sports leads to respondents who follow the sport and watch the sport on television. With the infancy of soccer in the U.S., the enormous amount of youth players, and the complexities of any sport, it would be interesting to explore the topic of soccer involvement would be beneficial research to the subject of television ratings in the U.S. While it is not the sole determining factor, as we will see later in the survey results, it is important to know if soccer broadcasts should only be targeted at a market who is full of soccer knowledge or if respondents need to learn and understand the game, as the NFL explains during many of their broadcasts and shows. Recently reported by ESPN analyses (Karp, 2012; Matchett, 2012; Sandomir, 2010), soccer has the youngest average age of fans in the U.S. among major professional sports. It may be an indicator that the sport is continuing to grow. If one inspects in further detail at soccer involvement's ability to increase soccer television ratings, respondents involved in soccer (e.g., player or coach) may be more likely to watch soccer on television. To test this assumption, hypothesis, Table 16 inspects the distribution of those who are involved in soccer and whether they watch soccer on television.

Table 12. Relevant statistics associated with specific hypothesis-testing results (H3). Part A displays the model summary, Part B the overall results, and Part C inspects specific contributions of each component in the hypothesis (Dependent variable: More likely to watch sports on TV if personally involved in a fantasy sports) Part A. Model summary.

R	R Square	Adjusted R Square	Std. Error of the Estimate
.354	.125	.067	1.209

Table 13. Part B: ANOVA results

Source of Variation	Sum of Squares	df	Mean Square	F-ratio	Significance
Regression	24.944	8	3.118	2.133	.038 (S)
Residual	173.931	119	1.462		
Total	198.875	127			

S denotes statistically significant at the .05 level for a 2-tailed test.

Part C. Coefficients-testing results

Independent Variables	Unstandardized Coefficients		Standardized Coefficients	t-test	Significance
	B	Std. Error	Beta		
(Constant)	2.559	.555		4.613	<.001
Involvement in soccer throughout your life (e.g., player, coach)	.206	.090	.246	2.297	.023 (S)
Involvement in ALL sports throughout your life (e.g., player, coach)	-.096	.105	-.093	-.913	.363 (NS)
Follow favorite sports teams on social media sites	.197	.233	.079	.845	.400 (NS)
Regularly follow sports teams from different cities	.069	.129	.075	.539	.591 (NS)
Regularly follow sports leagues not represented in my local city	.197	.117	.223	1.688	.094 (NS)
Watch the majority of my local sports teams' games on television (if not attending in person)	-.088	.096	-.081	-.914	.363 (NS)
Regularly stream sports matches online like ESPN3	.102	.138	.105	.741	.460(NS)
Regularly stream soccer matches online	-.291	.138	-.297	-2.118	.036 (NS)

Dependent Variable: I'm more likely to watch sports on TV if personally involved in a fantasy sports league. NS denotes not statistically significant at the .05 level for a 2-tailed test; S denotes statistically significant at the .05 level for a 2-tailed test.

Table 14. Relevant statistics associated with specific hypothesis-testing results (H3). Part A displays the model summary, Part B the overall results, and Part C inspects specific contributions of each component in the hypothesis (Dependent variable: More likely to watch sports on TV if personally involved in a fantasy sports, when Watch soccer on TV = Yes Selected). Part A: Model summary.

Watch soccer on TV = Yes (Selected)			
.358	.128	-.038	1.237

Table 15. Part B: ANOVA results

Source of Variation	Sum of Squares	df	Mean Square	F-ratio	Significance
Regression	9.449	8	1.181	.772	.629 (NS)
Residual	64.238	42	1.529		
Total	73.686	50			

NS denotes not statistically significant at the .05 level for a 2-tailed test.

Part C. Coefficients-testing results					
Independent Variables	Unstandardized Coefficients		Standardized Coefficients	t-test	Significance
	B	Std. Error	Beta		
(Constant)	.444	1.434		.310	.758
Involvement in soccer throughout your life (e.g., player, coach)	.151	.136	.186	1.112	.272 (NS)
Involvement in ALL sports throughout your life (e.g., player, coach)	.229	.202	.170	1.136	.262 (NS)
Follow favorite sports teams on social media sites	.447	.387	.178	1.154	.255 (NS)
Regularly follow sports teams from different cities	.181	.205	.201	.885	.381 (NS)
Regularly follow sports leagues not represented in my local city	-.019	.200	-.021	-.095	.925 (NS)
Watch the majority of my local sports teams' games on television (if not attending in person)	.058	.168	.052	.343	.734 (NS)
Regularly stream sports matches online like ESPN3	.127	.246	.149	.518	.607 (NS)
Regularly stream soccer matches online	-.266	.228	-.339	-1.167	.250 (NS)

Dependent Variable: I'm more likely to watch sports on TV if personally involved in a fantasy sports league, Selecting only cases for which Watch soccer on TV = Yes. NS denotes not statistically significant at the .05 level for a 2-tailed test.

Table 16. Cross-tabulation statistics associated with soccer involvement (e.g., player, coach) with watching soccer on television (H3)

Part A. Actual count				
Independent Variables		Watch soccer on TV		Total
		No	Yes	
Involvement in soccer throughout your life (e.g., player, coach)	never involved	39	6	45
	little involvement	26	9	35
	somewhat involved	10	6	16
	more involvement	2	7	9
	lifetime involvement	1	23	24
Total		78	51	129

Table 17. Part B: Chi-square test results

Statistics	Value	df	Asymptotic Significance (2-sided)
Pearson Chi-Square	53.076	4	<.001 (HS)
Likelihood Ratio	58.876	4	<.001 (HS)
Linear-by-Linear Association	50.649	1	<.001 (HS)
N of Valid Cases	129		
a. Only 1 cell (10.0%) has expected count less than 5. The minimum expected count is 3.56.			

Table 18. Part C: Symmetric measures

Statistics		Value	Approximate Significance
Nominal by Nominal	Contingency Coefficient	.540	<.001 (HS)
N of Valid Cases		129	

Even by viewing this relatively simple table, it is very easy to see that respondents who are moderately to highly involved in soccer are more likely to watch soccer on television. The target audience for soccer television is respondents very familiar with the sport. This table supports H3, namely that respondents involved in soccer are more likely to watch soccer on television, although not necessarily those engaged actively in fantasy sports, especially fantasy soccer (Table 16). Overall, respondents are more likely to watch soccer when they are involved in soccer as a player or a coach. Hence, H3 was formally accepted.

GENERAL CONCLUSION AND RECOMMENDATIONS

General Summary and Conclusion

As suggested by Hutchins (2011), there is little doubt that communication via networked personal computers as well as mobile devices has become the dominate form of communication, domestically and globally. With Internet-connected devices, particularly mobile devices and smart phones, social networking via Facebook and Tweeter has added chaotic and highly unpredictable consequences of how fans enhance a sense of engagement in terms of expression and promotion associated with spectator sport and its media coverage. This has certainly been the case with U.S. soccer. Soccer in the U.S. has made great strides over the past decade, as evident by the massive showing on television viewing the of 2014 World Cup in Brazil. One of the most important and often most overlooked areas of profitability when discussing MLS and other professional soccer is what drives and can increase soccer television ratings. As discussed in the conceptual model, increased soccer television ratings can lead to significant profit increases through sponsorships, advertisements, and increase merchandise sales. While the empirical evidence presented in the present study explored a number of areas and driving factors of soccer television ratings, the hypotheses focused on a few main areas that may present opportunities to decision makers in the professional soccer industry.

First, by increasing fantasy soccer participation, soccer probably will drive television viewers up, and increase their financial investments. Second, local professional teams are a driving force that increase and virally promote a sport in big markets on a regular basis. MLS is definitely behind other professional sports leagues in the U.S. when it comes to acquiring a large number of major television markets. MLS has some very large and important markets of the U.S. without a local team, which ultimately may be keeping television ratings relatively low. Respondents in these areas typically do not hear viral campaign messages in relation to the league and can likely put their interest to many other sports that are local enough to be involved in. Third, respondents heavily involved in soccer tend to watch soccer on television more than those who have never been involved in the sport in their life. With one of the largest youth sport programs in the country, soccer in the U.S. has the ability to turn many casual viewers into regular viewers. Keeping players involved will likely increase television ratings throughout adulthood. In most areas, there are already adult leagues, both recreational and competitive so this would not be as big of an area to improve ratings, but an adult league in underrepresented areas would also be a smart move.

Recommendations

Soccer has a lot of room for growth in television and social media ratings, but prior research and the results of the present study illustrate that the ratings are already becoming significant. MLS and other leagues and tournaments have opportunities in the U.S. to increase television ratings through fantasy sports, social media interaction, soccer involvement, and smart expansion. All of these items lead to increases in soccer television ratings, which will help increase television contracts, online streaming revenue, advertisement revenue, and merchandise and ticket sales. Undoubtedly, recent data and television revenue for soccer show one thing is clear: soccer in the U.S. is here to stay and it is important for decision makers to capitalize on this quickly growing market.

Directions for Future Research

A potential area for future research related to the growth of communication technologies in major soccer venues centers around strategic framing of sport issues. Strategic framing activities highlighted by Entman (2007) are often perceived as placing agenda-setting activities at heart of the political process and serves as a primary aid in defining problems that require public and government attention, but within a sport environment. As noted by Zimmerman, et al. (2011), theoretical aspects of agenda-setting activities manipulate the messages the public receives and learns from the media. In the case of soccer, the higher levels of exposure brought about more media options made the sport more important in society. It may have caused the traditional media (e.g., print, radio, TV) to increase their coverage to match online sources. Hence, cultural biases are reinforced and accelerated throughout the media options available for the message. If one applied the conceptual model of Entman (2007) to sport coverage, the slant of a specific news item is primarily a function of facts and the ability of news managers to place their "word spin" on the facts as opposed to their opposition.

ACKNOWLEDGMENT

The authors wish to thank most heartedly for the valuable contributions by the reviewers for their input into the final paper. Peer reviewing and editing are often tedious and thankless tasks.

REFERENCES

Abdi, S., Awan, H., & Bhatti, M. (2008). Is quality management a prime requisite for globalization? Some facts from the sports industry. *Quality & Quantity*, *42*(6), 821–833. doi:10.100711135-007-9135-x

Ali, K. A. M., & Alolayyan, M. N. (2013). The impact of total quality management (TQM) on the hospital's performance: An empirical research. *International Journal of Services and Operations Management*, *15*(4), 482–506. doi:10.1504/IJSOM.2013.054904

Baxter, K. (2017). Diversity, talent on the rise in U.S. women's soccer. *Los Angeles Times*. Retrieved September 18, 2017 from http://www.latimes.com/sports/soccer/la-sp-soccer-baxter-20170121-story.html

Becker, J. (2011). *La galaxy announce $55 million TV contract*. Retrieved March 1, 2018 from http://losangeles.sbnation.com/los-angeles-galaxy/2011/11/15/2565118/la-galaxy-55-million-TV-contract-time-warner

Beldona, S., & Tsatsoulis, C. (2010). Identifying buyers with similar seller rating models and using their opinions to choose sellers in electronic markets. *International Journal of Information and Decision Sciences*, *2*(1), 1–16. doi:10.1504/IJIDS.2010.029901

Bhamu, J., Khandelwal, A., & Sangwan, K. S. (2013). Lean manufacturing implementation in an automated production line: A case study. *International Journal of Services and Operations Management*, *15*(4), 411–429. doi:10.1504/IJSOM.2013.054883

Bhurjee, A. K., Kumar, P., & Padhan, S. K. (2018). Solid transportation problem with budget constraints under interval uncertain environments. *International Journal of Process Management and Benchmarking*, *7*(2), 172–182. doi:10.1504/IJPMB.2017.083104

Bloxsome, E. L., Voges, K. E., & Pope, N. K. (2011). Sport sponsorship: Appeal and risks. *The International Journal's Research Journal of Social Science and Management*, *1*(8), 133–145.

Brown, N., Billings, A. C., & Ruihley, B. (2012). Exploring the change in motivations for fantasy sport participation during the life cycle of a sports fan. *Communication Research Reports*, *29*(4), 333–342. doi:10.1080/08824096.2012.723646

Chaturvedi, S., & Chakrabarti, D. (2018). Operational efficiency in manufacturing process using design of experiments. *International Journal of Process Management and Benchmarking*, *7*(2), 249–261. doi:10.1504/IJPMB.2017.083111

Chiarini, A., Vagnoni, E., & Chiarini, L. (2018). ERP implementation in public healthcare, achievable benefits and encountered criticalities - an investigation from Italy. *International Journal of Services and Operations Management*, *29*(1), 1–17. doi:10.1504/IJSOM.2018.088460

Coates, D., & Humphreys, B. R. (2010). Week to week attendance and competitive balance in the national football league. *International Journal of Sport Finance*, *5*(4), 239–252.

Coche, R. (2016). Promoting women's soccer through social media: How the US federation used Twitter for the 2011 World Cup. *Soccer and Society*, *17*(1), 90–101. doi:10.1080/14660970.2014.919279

Cohen, B. C. (1963). *The Press and Foreign Policy*. Princeton, NJ: Princeton University.

Davis, N. W., & Duncan, M. C. (2006). Sports knowledge is power: Reinforcing masculine privilege through fantasy sport league participation. *Journal of Sport and Social Issues*, *30*(3), 244–253. doi:10.1177/0193723506290324

Dees, W. (2011). New media and technology use in corporate sport sponsorship: Performing activational leverage from an exchange perspective. *International Journal of Sport Management and Marketing*, *10*(3/4), 272–285. doi:10.1504/IJSMM.2011.044795

Dharamdass, S., & Fernando, Y. (2018). Contact centre service excellence: A proposed conceptual framework. *International Journal of Services and Operations Management*, *29*(1), 18–41. doi:10.1504/IJSOM.2018.088470

Durán, G., Guajardo, M., & Wolf-Yadlin, R. (2012). Operations research techniques for scheduling Chile's second division soccer league. *Interfaces*, *42*(3), 273–285, 326, 328. doi:10.1287/inte.1110.0608

Dure, B. (2011). Getting bigger, major league soccer seeks better TV ratings: New clubs add buzz, but getting more viewers to tune in is trick. *USA Today*. Retrieved March 1, 2017 from http://www.usatoday.com/SPORTS/usaedition/2011-03-14-mls14_st_U.htm

Entman, R. M. (2007). Framing bias media in the distribution of power. *Journal of Communication*, *57*(1), 163–173. doi:10.1111/j.1460-2466.2006.00336.x

Evans, D. M., & Smith, A. C. T. (2004). The Internet and competitive advantage: A study of Australia's four premier professional sporting leagues. *Sport Management Review*, *7*(1), 27–56. doi:10.1016/S1441-3523(04)70044-3

Evans, S. (2012). *Soccer-television ratings missing link for growing major league soccer*. Retrieved July 9, 2017 from http://www.reuters.com/article/2012/03/09/soccer-mls-television-idUSB67913220120309

Fortunato, J. (2011). The relationship of fantasy football participation with NFL television ratings. *Journal of Sport Administration and Supervision*, *3*(1), 74–90.

Franceschini, F., & Mastrogiacomo, L. (2018). Service gap deployment: A framework to link quality gaps to service activities. *International Journal of Services and Operations Management*, *29*(1), 85–99. doi:10.1504/IJSOM.2018.088474

FSOhio and Columbus crew announce television agreement. (2012). Retrieved March 1, 2018 from http://www.foxsportsohio.com/02/22/12/FSOhio-and-Columbus-Crew-announce-televi/landing_crew.html?blockID=671512

Gothwal, S., & Raj, T. (2018). Prioritising the performance measures of FMS using multi-criteria decision making approaches. *International Journal of Process Management and Benchmarking, 8*(1), 59–78. doi:10.1504/IJPMB.2018.088657

Green, B. C., Murray, N., & Warner, S. (2011). Understanding website useability: An eye-tracking study of the Vancouver 2010 Olympic Games website. *International Journal of Sport Management and Marketing, 10*(3/4), 257–271. doi:10.1504/IJSMM.2011.044793

Helland, K. (2007). Changing sports, changing media: Mass appeal, the sports/media complex and TV sports rights. *Nordicom Review, 28*(2), 105–119.

Hossain, M. S., & Hossain, M. M. (2018). Application of interactive fuzzy goal programming for multi-objective integrated production and distribution planning. *International Journal of Process Management and Benchmarking, 8*(1), 35–58. doi:10.1504/IJPMB.2018.088656

Hutchins, B. (2011). The acceleration of media sport culture. *Information Communication and Society, 14*(2), 237–257. doi:10.1080/1369118X.2010.508534

Jain, N., & D'lima, C. (2018). Organisational culture preference for gen Y's prospective job aspirants: A personality-culture fit perspective. *International Journal of Process Management and Benchmarking, 7*(2), 262–275. doi:10.1504/IJPMB.2017.083122

Karp, A. (2012). *Final ratings: Major League Soccer on pace for best season on ESPN; Strong first year on NBCSN.* Retrieved March 1, 2018 from http://m.sportsbusinessdaily.com/Daily/Issues/2012/07/20/Media/Final-Ratings.aspx

Larkin, B., & Fink, J. (2016). Fantasy Sport, FoMO, and Traditional Fandom: How second-screen use of social media allows fans to accommodate multiple identities. *Journal of Sport Management, 30*(6), 643–655. doi:10.1123/jsm.2015-0344

Lee, W.-Y., Kwak, D. H., Lim, C., Pedersen, P. M., & Miloch, K. S. (2011). Effects of personality and gender on fantasy sports game participation: The moderating role of perceived knowledge. *Journal of Gambling Studies, 27*(3), 427–441. doi:10.100710899-010-9218-9 PMID:20865303

Long, J. (2010). Do what yourself: Reevaluation of the value created by online and traditional intermediary. *International Journal of Information and Decision Sciences, 2*(3), 304–317. doi:10.1504/IJIDS.2010.033453

Matchett, K. (2012). *ESPN TV ratings for Euro 2012: New record viewings in US for soccer final.* Retrieved March 1, 2018 from http://bleacherreport.com/articles/1244834-espn-TV-ratings-for-euro-2012-new-record-viewings-in-us-for-soccer-final

Nesbit, T. M., & King, K. A. (2010). The impact of fantasy sports on television viewership. *Journal of Media Economics, 23*(1), 24–41. doi:10.1080/08997761003590721

Netflix just became cable's biggest TV network. (2012). Retrieved March 1, 2018 from http://www.textually.org/TV/archives/2012/07/030853.htm

Oey, E., & Nofrimurti, M. (2018). Lean implementation in traditional distributor warehouse - a case study in an FMCG company in Indonesia. *International Journal of Process Management and Benchmarking*, *8*(1), 1–15. doi:10.1504/IJPMB.2018.088654

Pookulangara, S., & Koesler, K. (2011). Cultural influence on consumers' usage of social networks and its impact on online purchase intentions. *Journal of Retailing and Consumer Services*, *18*(4), 348–354. doi:10.1016/j.jretconser.2011.03.003

Rego, S., Kumar, N., & Mukherjee, P. N. (2018). Impact of policy implementation on telecommunication diffusion in India. *International Journal of Process Management and Benchmarking*, *8*(1), 16–34. doi:10.1504/IJPMB.2018.088655

Sandomir, R. (2010). For ESPN and Univision, the US is a soccer country. *The New York Times*. Retrieved March 1, 2018 from http://www.nytimes.com/2010/06/08/sports/soccer/08sandomir.html

Schirato, T. (2012). Fantasy sport and media interactivity. *Sport in Society: Cultures, Commerce, Media. Politics*, *15*(1), 78–87.

Seidman, R. (2010). *World cup ratings: Out of home viewing adds 14%, non-TV platforms add 32%.* Retrieved March 1, 2018 from http://TVbythenumbers.zap2it.com/2010/07/18/world-cup-ratings-out-of-home-viewing-adds-14-non-TV-platforms-add-32/57429/

Smith, A. A., Synowka, D. P., & Smith, A. D. (2014). E-commerce quality and adoptive elements of e-ticketing for entertainment and sporting. *International Journal of Business Information Systems*, *15*(4), 450–487. doi:10.1504/IJBIS.2014.060397

Smith, A. D. (2012). Social media and online dating service providers: Re-examining the new face of romance in the current global economic recession. *International Journal of Business Information Systems*, *9*(2), 127–148. doi:10.1504/IJBIS.2012.045166

Smith, A. D. (2013). Online social networking and office environmental factors that affect worker productivity. *International Journal of Procurement Management*, *6*(5), 578–608. doi:10.1504/IJPM.2013.056173

Smith, A. D., & Rupp, W. T. (2013). Data quality and knowledge/information management in service operations management: Regional supermarket case study. *International Journal of Knowledge-Based Organizations*, *3*(3), 35–52. doi:10.4018/ijkbo.2013070103

Szymanski, S. (2006). The economic evolution of sport and broadcasting. *The Australian Economic Review*, *39*(4), 428–434. doi:10.1111/j.1467-8462.2006.00432.x

Tainsky, S., & McEvoy, C. D. (2011). Television broadcast demand in markets without local teams. *Journal of Sports Economics*, *13*(3), 250–265. doi:10.1177/1527002511406129

Thirumalai, S., & Sinha, K. K. (2011). Customization of the online purchase process in electronic retailing and customer satisfaction: An online field study. *Journal of Operations Management*, *29*(5), 477–487. doi:10.1016/j.jom.2010.11.009

Tidey, W. (2012). *ESPN ratings for Euro 2012 demonstrate soccer's growing reach in America*. Retrieved July 9, 2014 from http://bleacherreport.com/articles/1245475-us-audience-for-euro-2012-demonstrates-soccers-growing-reach-in-america

Weeks, C. S., Cornwell, T. B., & Drennan, J. C. (2008). Leveraging sponsorships on the Internet: Activation, congruence, and articulation. *Psychology and Marketing*, *25*(7), 637–654. doi:10.1002/mar.20229

Wu, J. H., Wang, S. C., & Tsai, H. H. (2011). Falling in love with online games: The uses and gratifications perspective. *Computers in Human Behavior*, *26*(6), 1862–1871. doi:10.1016/j.chb.2010.07.033

Zimmerman, M. H., Clavio, G. E., & Lim, C. H. (2011). Set the agenda like Beckham: A professional sports league's use of YouTube to disseminate messages to its users. *International Journal of Sport Management and Marketing*, *10*(3/4), 180–195. doi:10.1504/IJSMM.2011.044789

Chapter 15
Ethical Dilemmas Associated With Social Network Advertisements

Alan D. Smith
Robert Morris University, USA

Onyebuchi Felix Offodile
Kent State University, USA

ABSTRACT

A significant amount information can be relayed on Facebook, MySpace, and Twitter, but the question remains whether or not organizations are using this to their advantage, especially in the era of big data. The present study used a sample of working professionals that were knowledgeable in the various options of social networking to test these assumptions. The three hypotheses dealt with the interplay of online social networking, advertising effectiveness, gender and age trends, and remaining the interplay with positive comments of the use of the "like" function and its impacts on consumer behavior, as derived from the review of relevant operations literature and from applying the basic tenants of uses and gratification theory. All three specific research hypotheses were accepted in the null form.

INTRODUCTION

Popularity of Social Media, Branding, and Consumer Tribalism

Social networking systems are relatively new to our society and clarification on certain aspects of the system can be obtained through further research. There are many positive aspects of social networks, such as Facebook, that organizations could benefit from including stronger CRM-embedded techniques. On the-other-hand, questions are raised as to whether or not an organization who advertises on social networking systems experiences an increase in sales as a result. It is unclear whether or not these advertisements actually deter individuals from further using these types of social networking systems. If individuals who spend a large amount of time on social networking sites are deterred from further us-

DOI: 10.4018/978-1-5225-7214-5.ch015

age due to these advertisements, are there any benefits to them? An increasing number of individuals are utilizing social networking sites, such as Facebook on a daily basis. As Taylor, Lewin, and Strutton (2011) pointed out, both Facebook and Twitter reported an increase in users in the triple digits in 2009. Founded in 2004 by Mark Zuckerberg, Facebook's mission is to "give people the power to share and make the world more open and connected" (Facebook). Facebook began by being exclusive to college students only, but through the years has opened memberships up to everyone over the age of 13 with an email address. Facebook helps people stay connected with friends and family, learn what is happening around them, as well as share moments. Fernandez (2009) noted that a recent study found that 35% of all adults, 75% of adults in the range of 18-24 years old, and 65% of teenagers utilize a social networking site. It has been noted that individuals have increased their time spent on these sites. Social networking sites can be categorized as web-enabled services that engage users to create and maintain openly or partially open profiles, create and update preferred list of users that they want to personalize connections with, and view and interact their list of preferred connections with other lists within the networking system (Greenhow, 2011). Under the recent congressional hearings that concluded April 11, 2018 concerning Mark Zuckerberg's testimony on privacy violations of Facebook data, renewed scrutiny on the public value of social media platforms have surfaced. Much of the publicity surrounding Cambridge Analytica, a political data mining enterprise hired by President Trump's 2016 election campaign, illegally gained access to private information on more than 50 million Facebook users via offering tools that could identify the personalities of American voters and influence their voting behavior (Granville, 2018). That number of affected Facebook users was updated to over 80 million. Recent trend involving fake news and questionable ads have rekindled a debate if social platforms are really a force for good, but can be used to undermine democratic societies.

Social network sites allow consumer to interact and enhance self-expression and self-presentation. One tool to achieve enhancement is self-expression via brands. Hence, consumer with greater social network influence may be more likely to express themselves via brands. Brands are an extension of the consumer's self-concept, allowing consumers to express and define them. Brands enable consumers to become a part of a group membership. Tribes facilitated collective social actions within members of the group. Brands offer more than the product itself, they offering value through self-expression and linking value. This paper aims to examine brand loyalty and word-of-mouth (WOM) as an outcome of self-expression tribal consumption.

Existing literature suggest that self-expressing brands positively affect WOM and brand loyalty and improve brand success. Yet, little is known about the relationship between the role of the brand for the self and consumers' purchase motivation. In addition, little is also known about consumer tribes and their influence on consumer behavior. Brand-supporting consumer tribes reflect a strategic resource for brand managers. A tribe refers to a loose network of heterogeneous persons who share passion and emotions for a product. Such groups of empowered consumers boost brand loyalty through creating exit barriers. Additionally, WOM is also considered to be an outcome of tribal membership. Brand passion enhances relationships within the tribe and increases information sharing. Tribe members tend to evangelize the brand to others. However, due to the loose connection, consumer tribes are short-living. This paper explores the influence of tribal membership on WOM and brand loyalty. This study analyzed the influence of reference groups on self-expressive brands because the role of reference groups on tribal behavior towards brands is not fully understood. Further, the research focuses on the influence of online social networks on the susceptibility to interpersonal influence (SUSCEP). Finally, the paper examines the impact of SUSCEP and SNI on consumers' self-expressive brand consumption and brand tribalism.

Brands act as an enabler for consumers to express themselves through creating meaningful association and help them to reinforce their self-concept. The motivation of expressing oneself is often the stimulus that influences the purchase decision. "Self-expressive brands reward consumers with certain social benefits that allow them to enhance their self-concept, make a social impression and display the group they belong to" (Ruane & Wallace, 2015, p. 334). Consumer tribalism refers to the connectedness of consumers to brands. Brand tribalism are networks of social micro-groups with shared emotional links, a common sub-culture and a vision of life. This paper considers the influence of consumer tribes and examines their influence on brand choices of their members.

The results show that SUSCEP and SNI had a positive effect on self-expressive brands as well as brand tribalism. Hence, there was a positive impact of self-expressive brands on brand tribalism, brand loyalty and WOM. In contrast, there was a negative relationship between brand tribalism and both brand loyalty and WOM. Ruane and Wallace (2015) provided evidence that consumers who are more influenced by others brand choices are more likely to choose more self-expressive brands. Hence, SUSCEP drives tribal membership as consumers who seek self-expression engage on social network sites are more likely to consume self-expressive brand as well as are part of consumer tribes. In contrast to previous research, it was demonstrated that consumers express greater brand tribalism when they have a high motivation for self-expression and engagement on social network sites. Further, they discovered that tribe members were less loyal and practiced less WOM. In contrast, self-expressive brand users who are not part of a consumer tribe were the loyalist and have offered the most WOM. Consumer tribes may not be loyal to a specific brand. It is more likely that the members are loyal to the group.

Such research efforts illustrate to manager of self-expressive brand how important other consumers are on an individual's consumer decision and that social media campaigns have an effect on consumption. Managers should also be aware of the fact that consumers may not be loyal to the brand rather to the tribe they are a part of. To increase brand loyalty and WOM, they should consider brand endorsers. Lastly, managers should be aware of the different types of consumers and should be able to separate them according to their needs. There are two main types of consumers, those who use a brand for differentiation and those who use their brand to belong to a group.

Corporate Social Responsibility

Essentially, the goal of every firm is to maintain viability through long-run profitability. Until all costs and benefits are accounted for, however, profits may not be claimed. In the case of Corporate Social Responsibility (CSR), costs and benefits are both economic and social. While economic costs and benefits are easily quantifiable, social costs and benefits are not. Managers therefore risk subordinating social consequences to other performance results that can be more straightforwardly measured. The dynamic between CSR and success (as measured in profits) is complex. While one concept is clearly not mutually exclusive of the other, it is also clear that neither is a prerequisite of the other. Rather than viewing these two concepts as competing, it may be better to view CSR as a component in the decision-making process of business that must determine, among other objectives, how to maximize profits.

Social responsibility is a broad and encompassing term that can be broken down in to a number of responsibilities. Economic responsibilities are the duty of managers, as agents of the company owners, to maximize stockholder wealth. Legal responsibilities are the firm's obligations to comply with the laws that regulate business activities. Ethical responsibilities are the strategic managers' notion of right and proper business behavior. Discretionary responsibilities are the responsibilities voluntarily assumed by a business, such as public relations, good citizenship, and full corporate responsibility.

In addition to a commonsense belief that companies should be able to "do well by doing good," at least three broad trends are driving businesses to adopt CSR frameworks: the resurgence of environmentalism, increasing buying power, and the globalization of business. The most prevalent forms of environmentalism are efforts to preserve natural resources and eliminating pollution, often referred to as the concern for "greening". Consumers are becoming more interested in buying products from socially responsible companies. There has also been a dramatic increase in the number of people interested in supporting socially responsible companies through their investments. It is difficult enough to come to a consensus on what constitutes socially responsible behavior within one culture, let alone determine common ethical value across cultures.

The rise of the consumer movement has meant that buyers – consumers and investors – are increasingly flexing their economic muscle. Consumers are becoming more interested in buying products from socially responsible companies. Organizations such as the Council on Economic Priorities (CEP) help consumers make more informed buying decisions through such publications as *Shopping for a Better World*, which provides social performance information on 191 companies making more than 2,000 consumer products. CEP also sponsors the annual Corporate Conscience Awards, which recognize social responsible companies. One example of consumer power at work is the effective outcry over the deaths of dolphins in tuna fisherman's nets.

Investors represent a second type of influential consumer. There has been a dramatic increase in the number of people interested in supporting socially responsible companies through their investments. Membership in the Social Investment Forum, a trade association serving social investing professionals, has been growing as a rate of about 50 percent annually. As baby boomers achieve their own financial success, the social investing movement has continued its rapid growth. For example, firms such as ice cream maker Ben & Jerry's have successfully argued that CSR and profits do not clash; their stance was that doing good lead to making good money, too. Managed properly, CSR programs can confer significant benefits to participants to participation in terms of corporate reputation; in terms of hiring, motivation, and retention; and as a means of building and cementing valuable partnerships. The benefits extend well beyond the boundaries of the participating organizations, enriching the lives of many disadvantages communities and individuals and pushing back on problems that threaten future generations, other species, and precious natural resources.

Research suggests that such single-minded devotion to CSR may be unrealistic for larger, more established corporations. Companies need to view their commitments to corporate responsibility as one important part of their overall strategy but not let the commitment obscure their broad strategic business goals. A balance has to be reached however, because if the broad strategic goals of a business do not follow what is expected of a corporation's social responsibility, the response can be very negative. While some corporations may have gotten away with past discrepancies, advances in technology have changed not only the competitive landscape but the landscape in which companies are looked at from under a microscope. CSR strategies can also run afoul of the skeptics, and the speed with which information can be disseminated via the web – and accumulated in web logs – makes this an issue with serious ramifications for reputation management.

Implementing CSR-embedded programs have some promotional barriers to overcome as for all their resources and capabilities, corporations will face growing demands for social responsibility contributions far beyond simple cash or in-kind donations. Aggressive protesters will keep the issues hot, employees will continue to have their say, and shareholders will pass judgment with their investments – and their votes.

Perhaps, many of the recent mergers and acquisitions by Internet and mobile technology industry leaders are at least partially geared to control these corporate images and reputations. Figure 1 highlights some of these features that social networking providers are concentrating on promoting in order to attract and retain customers (e.g., advertising promotions, market segmentation and targeting, open and semi-secured communications, promoting newer forms of communication technologies and mobile applications) through a more ethical viewpoint.

Purpose of Study

The purpose of this study is to determine whether or not social networking advertisements should continue to be utilized by organizations. Social networking systems are relatively new to our society and clarification on certain aspects of the system can be obtained through further research. Questions are raised as to whether or not an organization who advertises on social networking systems experiences an increase in sales as a result. This paper will explore the following three issues surrounding social networking advertisements: Do advertisements used on social networking systems deter individuals from using these sites? Do consumer purchases increase as a result of social networking advertisements? Is the "like" function on organizations' Facebook pages being utilized to the full extent and influential in consumer behavior?

Figure 1. Conceptual framework for present study dealing with social networking

BACKGROUND

Advertising Promotion

Companies are realizing that social network advertisements are an easy way to reach their target market and get promotional information to consumers quickly. In general, online advertisements are a cost-effective way for organizations to get information about their products or services to the community. "Online advertising reduces costs, increases efficiency, provides more flexibility and as a global medium, the Internet enables buyers and sellers to interact and manage business transactions" (Alijani et al, 2010, p.1). Todor (2016) examined the current strategies of marketing that are being used to target consumers in the current market by comparing traditional print marketing such as magazines, newspapers, and billboards in comparison to the more modern use of digital marketing. What is the best way to reach consumers and create a campaign that create new customers, as well as maintaining loyal customers? What is right combination of both digital and traditional marketing?

Digital marketing, commonly known as online marketing, Internet marketing, and/or Web marketing, is considered to be the targeted, measurable, and interactive marketing methods used to reach customers through a type of digital technology in order to create and maintain customers for either a good or service (Todor, 2016). Inbound marketing, while similar to digital marketing, is a more embedded marketing tool. Inbound marketing is when a company promotes it products or services through a blog, eBook, video, social media campaign, and podcasts. Digital and inbound marketing have many advantages in terms how and when they reach the consumer. Digital marketing comes with many advantages as well as some disadvantages. One large advantage to digital marketing is that it is more cost efficient. When digital marketing campaigns are deployed on websites that generate traffic on their own, the cost to market on this website is much lower than it would be to use a marketing strategy that requires the campaign to drive its own traffic. The cost advantage also closely ties into the advantage that web can reach an unlimited number of consumers, whether the campaign be driven worldwide or locally.

An advantage to digital marketing is that the online user is generally in control of their exposure to the ad. This allows the user to turn off the ad if they are not interested, which reduces the chance that the ad will become associated with annoyance rather than a positive opinion. User-controlled exposure is also great because it allows the consumer to immediately pursue the product being marketed to them. A significant advantage over traditional marketing is that digital marketing has is that it is easily changed. Digital marketing can be adaptable almost immediately and either displayed or taken down with a matter of minutes. This is great for situations such as marketing sports championship apparel. Companies like Dick's Sporting Goods immediately switched their marketing from saying they had Pittsburgh Penguins Eastern Conference Championship memorabilia to Pittsburgh Penguins Stanley Cup Champion memorabilia. Lastly, digital marketing can be made personal, or be directly at very distinct groups of people. This way the marketing budget is spent on those consumers who are the most likely to become or remain loyal customers. With advantages, come disadvantages and digital marketing has a few significant ones to control. A large disadvantage to digital marketing is the risk of copyright infringement. Marketing campaigns can easily be copied or be falsely created in order to defraud customers.

Digital marketing is not always as successful, is with products that consumers are still interested in seeing in person, touching, experiencing prior to making the actual purchase. This is a great disadvantage because there is no way for digital marketing to recreate the physical sensations require to eliminate this part of the purchasing process. There may be significant distrust in the conduction business over the Internet by many consumers. Distrust effects the success of digital marketing because many people, particularly those who have had negative experiences previously and those from older generations are still not willing to purchase online. Many people are skeptical of anything online that is too "personal" and may be deterred by marketing strategies that are to tailored to them or that require them to make a purchase online using electronic payment. As digital marketing evolves the advantages will become greater, as the disadvantages are mended through new technological advances.

The underlying assumption brand loyalty goes beyond the name of a particular brand and the type of media that serves to promote it. A general definition of brand as being a frame of mind towards a particular perceived notion of loyalty in general. As suggested by Yee and Sidek (2008), although their research was related to brand loyalty among sports apparel manufacturers, brand loyalty can come in the form of loyalty towards the notion of the product or what the product symbolizes. This can include a lifestyle, such as the subculture of those who identify with a particular brand, as well as what implications the brand has on the subculture. Identifying with a brand based on the attributes the brand is merely a preference for that type of product and the values that the product instill upon the user. Loyalty towards the specific brand carry over into the lifestyle of the user and the identity that the user can establish with the brand as it relates to the subculture of the users of that brand.

Amine (1998) suggests that brand loyalty has two main approaches: the behavioral approach is that repeat purchases over time expresses their loyalty to the brand, and; the attitude assumes that it must be complimented with a positive attitude towards the brand to ensure that the behavior will be further pursued. This suggests that behavior and attitude are both functions of brand loyalty. Image is a key determinant in the lifestyle selection among a subculture group. Displaying the correct image to your peers relies on the brand selected in a continuous pattern, as a form of social acceptance. Prestigious brand names and their associated images promote repeat purchases if the subculture feels that these brands and images portray the desired attitude towards the lifestyle of the group, linking the emotional and self-expressive benefits for differentiation Cadogan and Foster (2000) suggested that differentiation, as it relates to those outside the group, are key factors of inclusion by the group. This creates an image of the consumer that can relate to the consumer tribe who views the brand as a symbol of the subculture; hence differentiating the consumer from those outside the subculture as evident from the divisiveness of social media platforms that emphasizes people identify with their unique characteristics and not overall inclusiveness.

Other attributes include quality, price, store environment, promotion, and service quality, usually do not apply when the brand loyalty is generated from lifestyle choices of the subculture. If these attributes were more of a key factor of social acceptance within the subculture, the subculture lifestyle would reflect a more consumer conscious attitude, thus defeating the rebellious nature of the group. It is important to acknowledge that image is an important aspect of choice in brand loyalty, especially when choice of selection relates to subcultures. Many typical attributes that the general consumer feels are vital are less important when peer pressure is involved. Quality is a key determinant to brand loyalty and should be an important factor when making a choice, whereas image may not be as important as other attributes. However, many consumers feel that image is vital when brand loyalty is selected, making the consumer appear to be one of the followers instead of having value-seeking qualities, especially on many social media platforms. If the attributes suggested for the factors that influence consumers' brand loyalty towards a specific brand created positive relationships that encourage brand loyalty, marketers would have a better understanding of what creates brand loyalty. This seems to be not quite the revelation that one would expect based on the notion that hedonic principles suggest that more pleasure is desirable as opposed to less pleasure.

Todor (2016) explored the value in the advantages of traditional marketing, as well as the disadvantages that are holding it back from being a superior choice for brands. Traditional marketing is categorized as marketing delivered through tangible items such as print ads from newspapers or magazines, business cards, commercials delivered through radio or television, billboards, posters, and brochures. Traditional marketing however is not limited to these examples as it includes anything that is not considered to be digital marketing. Traditional marketing is its ability to produce fast results. Traditional marketing ads that are placed well for their targeted audience often have the ability to reach the audience faster than digital marketing which could take a few weeks to reach the audience. An example of this is with sales flyers. A store that displays its sales flyers in the entrance is more likely to reach the audience than they would if they only posted their flyer digital online. The other main advantage listed is trust. With so much mistrust and misuse online, traditional marketing is generally more widely accepted by those who are skeptical of digital marketing. Traditional marketing reduces many opportunities for fraud to occur making it a safer option for consumers.

The ultimate recommendation is to find a balance between the use of traditional marketing and digital marketing. While consumers are increasingly becoming more involved with the internet and often exposed to digital marketing, traditional marketing still has much to offer in order to balance the advantages and disadvantages of both strategies. Todor (2016) suggested that many believe that digital marketing is overtaking traditional marketing, however others believe that the balance is essential and currently very much in place.

Target Market Segmentation

In addition to being cost effective, Schroeder (2004) explains that companies have found that online advertisements were able to reach a large audience when no other form of advertisement does; during work hours. Individuals who work in an office setting during the day spend the majority of their day in front of the computer rather than watching television. Online advertisements are a way for organizations to reach a larger percentage of their target market. Ankeny (2011) explores how organizations including movie theaters, restaurants and photographers do this. It is not just about putting advertisements on their own Facebook page; it is about reaching out to the individuals that they consider part of their target market. Advertising within these social networking systems is unique due to the fact that the majority of the information used to qualify an organization's target market is often times readily available on their consumers' personal webpages. For example, Ankeny (2011) pointed out that a photographer targeted females who were 24-30 years old with their profiles indicated as being engaged. Ankeny (2011) indicated that this individual became one of the busiest photographers in their local area as their target market was successfully reached through the use of social networking sites.

Open Communication and Technologies

In order to clarify what affect social networking advertisements have, we must first explore the reasons why these sites, such as Facebook and Twitter, are so popular. Ankeny (2011) explains that one reason for the sites' popularity is because they allow open communication between individuals as well as with organizations. Ankeny (2011) outlined that today's society is more geared towards open communication between consumers and businesses rather than the latter guessing what their consumers want. Social networks allow companies to not only compete with other companies that are located down the road from them, but also with ones that are located across the country. "Users desire social interaction and connectivity and disclosing information plays an essential role; yet users may not wish to have their information publicly accessible to unknown parties" (Bateman, Pike, & Butler, 2010, p. 79).

Operational and Big Data Applications

The emergence of networked businesses through social media and the associated analytics has dramatically enhanced the volume, variety, and velocity of information available to management. This relatively recent trend is often referred to the emergence of big data. Big data analytics (BDA), if properly organized, can result in many positive (Mateen & More, 2013; Nobari, Khierkhah, & Hajipour, 2018; Park & Min, (2013) as negative outcomes. Positive outcomes can influence business productivity and growth, which are the key drivers of organization usage of BDA. In terms of operational and supply chain management (SCM) that has recently received much attention is the collection of digitally enabled interfirm processes. The basic issue at hand is how the emergence of BDA can positively affect the productivity and enhanced customer benefits from tapping into this wealth of transactional and personal information through data mining activities. In general, performance impacts of BDA may not produce the transactional and relational information that can be drawn from other SCM systems (Rajapakshe, Dawande, & Sriskandarajah, 2013; Rajeev, Rajagopal, & Mercado, 2013; Senthilmurugan, Jegadheesan, & Devadasan, 2018). Since the operational, tactical and strategic information are generally shared across all of the supply chain there is a greater need for business to rationalize the transactional and relational information that can be collected.

The types of operational that are readily available from BDA are typically classified as asset productivity, business growth, and environmental dynamism (Chen, Preston, & Swink, 2015). The functionality of dynamic capabilities is likely to be common and similar BDA technologies that can be obtained in the open market. Based on the logic of opportunity, dynamic capabilities are frequently used to build new resource configurations in the pursuit of a continual series of temporary advantages. The potential the long-term competitive advantage through the use of BDA lies in the dynamic capabilities than the need to create a resource configuration that have that advantage (Chen, et al., 2015; Sharma & Sharma, 2018; Verma, Sharma, & Kumar, 2018; Xu, Tiwari, Chen, & Turner, 2018; Yazdi & Esfeden, 2018). Asset productivity is the primary measure used to assess supply chain performance, describing the extent to which business productivity uses their current assets as well as their fixed assets. It is important to establish indictors of asset productivity.

In general, there are number of insights developed through BDA usage that create opportunities for organizations to reconfigure their resources in ways that are in greater alignment with trends and shifts in both demand and supply markets. As opposed to the traditional operational models of data collection tied to continuous improvement of specific processes. Many chaos and complexity theorists commonly believe that collecting information and taking measurements may blind us to the world of larger possibilities. These theorists believe that instead of attempting to impose structure, leaders should relinquish control. By accepting that SCM is dynamic and all-encompassing with many players and agents, no one metric is sufficient. This situation may well be the case in SCM. Therefore, we need a cluster of metrics, certainly more than just cost. If we cannot adequately measure customer satisfaction and utility, we need to have more subjective ways to measure it. Unfortunately, it is unlikely that there is a one-size-fits-all solution. Typically, in times of crisis, many managers are more prone to try something that's worked elsewhere. This is particularly true if they are afforded a budget to spend without any personal consequences (relative to their take-home pay). Operational and SCM applications requires a more comprehensive approach and with the availability BDA, 3PL (third-party logics providers), and 4PL (fourth-party logistics providers) applications, an organization does not have to do it all.

Environmental dynamism is another key situational parameter in dynamic capabilities theory, which suggests that the variance of competitive advantage created by organizational capability is contingent upon environmental dynamism (Chen, et al., 2015). An environment will provide greater opportunity for companies to capitalize on BDA. It is very likely that the influence of BDA use on operational and supply chain performance will be amplified in high velocity markets. Hence, there is little doubt that the influence of BDA on organizational outcomes, as well as the key factors that facilitate BDA use are well entrenched in many global service and manufacturing firm.

Examining the Roles of Advertising on Social Media Websites

McCormick (2006) indicates that not only do people feel this type of advertising is a violation to their privacy, the advertisements were sometimes misdirected. It was found that MySpace was allowing gambling advertisements to be seen by children that were younger than sixteen years old. Morimoto and Chang (2009) further look into the intrusiveness of advertisements. Their research explores consumers' attitudes on unsolicited advertisements in emails, which could also be felt regarding unsolicited advertisements on social networking systems. Morimoto et al (2009) indicated that approximately 86% of consumers felt that these unsolicited advertisements were seen as being a big problem or annoying. In order to determine how consumers will react to advertising, the level of intrusiveness must be addressed. The research completed by Morimoto et al. (2009) indicated that individuals not only felt that unsolicited advertisements were a big problem when there was intrusion into their personal affairs, but also when their thought process was interrupted as it would be with pop up advertisements or banners.

Further research is needed in order to determine how social network advertisements affect the acceptance of these sites. Although social network advertisements have a lot of positive outcomes for the companies who are utilizing them, excessive advertisements may deter individuals from using the sites. According to Taylor et al (2011), it is widely believed that MySpace usage deteriorated due to the increased commercialization in the form of advertisements, specifically pop-up advertisements. "The Federal Trade Commission found that more than 40% of consumers who experienced pop-up ads believe the Web site they were on – not the pop-up advertiser – had permitted the ad to appear" (Zaney, 2004, p.42). In this same study completed by the Federal Trade Commission, one-third of the consumers that participated in the research indicated that the pop-up advertisements caused them to view the Website they were on unfavorably.

In order to understand whether or not advertisements will deter individuals from utilizing social networking sites, we must first look into what motivated them to go online in the first place. A study referenced in the article written by Taylor et al (2011) indicates that the motives for going online include filling up one's time, entertainment or informational value, and to connect with others. Social networking systems are designed to help individuals to connect with others. "They are online forums in which users with common interests or connections 'can gather to share thoughts, comments, and opinions. There are other aspects of social networking systems such as Facebook that meet the consumers' criteria of educational or informational value as well as simply to help them pass the time. Due to the fact that Facebook and Twitter have a majority of the aspects described above, they are widely accepted in today's society. As social network advertisements increase, the question remains whether or not these sites will remain accepted and this paper will research this question further. Taylor et al (2011) indicates that Facebook will remain accepted by today's society as it has TOCAS, which stands for Targeted Opt-in Customer Ads. The advertisements are only shown to individuals who have 'liked' the organization's Facebook page, therefore the general public is not bombarded with unwanted advertisements in their newsfeeds. This seems to be the big difference regarding the success of Facebook and MySpace and my research will look into this aspect further.

Relationships Between Purchases and Social Networking Advertisements

The research second question that will be explored in the present study is whether social networking advertisements actually increase an organization's sales. There are a lot of articles and research completed that takes the point of view of the organization doing the advertising. As indicated in the article written by Goldie (2007), social networks now have strategies in place to generate high levels of advertising revenues from their sites. Jaffe (2009) explored ways that organizations can maximize their advertising budgets such as obtaining a computer program to track consumers' purchases, email advertising and the use of social networking advertisements. When it comes to social networks, the article indicates that organizations are not likely to obtain new customers. In spite of this, the author recommended organizations obtain social networking sites due to the fact that marketers continue to research how these sites could be used to acquire new customers. Booth and Matic (2011) indicated that companies that do not currently participate in social networking sites, such as Facebook, feel the need to establish a presence. "Establishing a presence on Twitter or Facebook without the due diligence required to make the effort worthwhile will produce few worthwhile results" (Booth et al, 2011, p.185). Another aspect of social media advertising that affects consumers' purchases is the idea of group sales such as Groupon and Living Social. Ham (2011) explores how Jump on it Deal, which is similar to the two sites previously mentioned, enables bigger discounts for the consumer. Organizations have found that these programs have added to their sales and have brought customers through their doors that were not familiar with their product or service prior to participating in these programs.

Is the "like" function on organizations' Facebook pages being utilized to the full extent? Engagement of consumers on the computer has been difficult to measure. Howell (2009) references a report that indicates less than 5% of social network users have ever clicked on a banner site. Even if the banner is clicked on, it does not mean that the customer was engaged with the brand or was motivated to make a purchase. Shields (2009) explores the fact that Facebook users are less likely to click on an advertisement that takes them away from the site they were originally on. Therefore, Facebook advertisements encourage users to actually interact with the brand by posting comments near a video advertisement or reading what their friends had posted. As Shields (2009, p. 8) indicates, "the idea is to build ad products that users can interact with in the same way they do with other things on the site." Ang (2011) explains that when a social media user 'likes' an organization on Facebook, this information is saved in their profile where other people can see this information. The research indicated by Ang (2011) found that an ad will achieve 30% higher recall if the social media user sees that their friends have either 'liked' it or commented on it. The question remains whether or not this increases the consumers' purchases. Ang (2011) references a time when Honda Japan decided to launch a new car. The organization created a social networking site and also ran a competition. If users of the social networking site added CRZ on the end of their username, their names were entered for a chance to win a new car. Research indicated that this helped increase brand awareness prior to the launch and orders reached 4500 units during the prelaunch period.

The "like" function on Facebook is an easy way for an organization to focus on which aspect of their corporate strategy they need to focus on. It is a basic assumption of the present study that by businesses being able to keep an open means of communication with their consumers, they will be able to quickly react and switch their focus according to their consumers' needs.

METHOD

Specific Research Hypotheses

Large portions of society use social networking systems regularly, creating potential for both consumers and businesses to benefit from social networking advertisements. This paper will further explore three specific issues previously outlined to more fully understand the effects of social networking advertisements on both consumers' acceptance of the systems as well as the effect on their purchases. The three hypotheses presented in this paper dealing with the interplay of online social networking, advertising effectiveness, gender and age trends, and remaining the interplay with positive comments of the use of the 'like' function and its impacts on consumer behavior, as derived from the review of relevant operations literature and from applying the basic tenants of Uses and Gratification Theory (Papacharissi & Mendelson, 2011; Smock, Ellison, Lampe, & Wohn, 2011) are as follows:

H1: There should be no statistical relationship between the use of social networking advertisements on Facebook and related social networking sites and users' feelings toward the site.

H2: Social networking advertisements will not have an effect on consumers' purchases.

H3: Users of social networks primarily utilize such systems to stay connected with their personal connection. The "like" function is used, but it is not a major reason that individuals utilize social networking sites.

A combination of statistical techniques that were deemed appropriate to analysis the survey data included Chi-square, multiple linear regression, and independent t-test among means.

Derivation of H1

There will be no relationship between the use of social networking advertisements on Facebook and individuals' feelings or personal attachment toward the site, since it is a mutual business transaction. The reason being is that the only advertisements that appear in a user's newsfeed are from organizations that this individual has shown an interest in. People are not bombarded with unwanted advertisements. In fact, individuals may 'like' an organization so that they will be kept up-to-date on any sale items or services that this organization may offer.

Derivation of H2

Social networking advertisements will not have an effect on consumers' purchases. The main reason is that Facebook seems to be utilized primarily to spread brand awareness and word of mouth advertising rather than to increase consumers' purchases. Some individuals may choose to 'like' an organization's page because they see that their friends are interested in the company. This is a way for organizations to spread the awareness for their products or services and reach individuals who would normally not follow their organizations. It is unlikely that consumers' purchases will increase based on receiving these advertisements on Facebook.

Derivation of H3

The "like" function on organizational Facebook pages is not a major function used by individuals. Organizations have yet to master all of the benefits that social networks have to offer. Users of social networks, such as Facebook, primarily utilize the systems to stay connected with their friends and family. The "like" function is used, but it is not a major reason that individuals utilize Facebook.

Sample Selection and Instrument

In order to test the hypotheses listed above, individuals were questioned from various age groups who currently utilize Facebook by sending them a questionnaire on the site as well as questioning co-workers. The research concentrates on Facebook/LinkedIn as this is the most widely used social networking system that most working business professionals (as well as the general public) are familiar with and, hence, should be able to reach a larger sample of individuals to complete the research. The collected variables of the present research effort include the demographics of the participants involved in the research such as their age and gender. The variables that are randomized deal with whether or not the participants utilize the 'like' function on Facebook regularly, and whether or not they actually have advertisements appear in their newsfeeds as a result. The questionnaire was electronically distributed to individuals within a business professional setting as well as users of the Facebook and LinkedIn that one of the authors of the present study has developed over the past two years.

The individuals chosen to be included in the research are from a comprehensive selection of users from the friends list of the present study's authors who currently use Facebook and/or LinkedIn, comprising of individuals within associated professional work groups. In regards to the individuals that participated, they ranged in age from 20 to 63. There is a mix of individuals from every age group as well as both males and females. Not only did this sample enable the researchers to have a relatively large portion of individuals participate in the research, but it may also help to clarify whether there are certain trends within the age groups or whether males and females are affected differently by social networking advertisements.

In order to question the participants, they were a link to the questionnaire to individuals from the friends list on Facebook/LinkedIn who were preselected based on business professional status. Although there were a few who did not wish to participate in the study, the response rate was over 86% and it was felt that there were enough collected responses from this sample of individuals to obtain the statistical power data needed to formally test the specific research hypotheses. The survey has questions to clarify the participant's demographic information as well as questions dealing with their thoughts on social networking advertisements. The answers are in a multiple choice format and a majority utilized the Likert scale. The Likert scale has been the preferred format with public surveys that typically deals with the measurement of opinions or attitudes (Ridinger & Funk, 2006; Robinson & Trail, 2005; Seguin, Richelieu, & O'Reilly, 2008; Smock, Ellison, Lampe, & Wohn, (2011). Since a majority of individuals who utilize social media tend to be in the younger age groups, it is important to understand the participant's age. By using this information, it was a simple task to group the participants' answers according to their age in order to clarify whether trends exist within the certain age groups.

Another demographic that is important to clarify is the gender of the participant involved. By determining whether an individual is male or female aids in determining whether they are affected by advertisements utilized on Facebook. Are females more likely to purchase a product or service after viewing an advertisement in their newsfeed? Are males less likely to 'like' a business? By asking how many organizations a participant has 'liked' on Facebook, it was possible to determine the extent to which this function is utilized on average, among the participants.

The questionnaire was sent to the participants via links embedded in common social media platforms, such as Facebook and LinkedIn, to business professional within the Pittsburgh area workplaces. As the participants responded to the survey, the data collected was entered into a spreadsheet to enable me to keep track of the various answers. Within two weeks of sending the survey out to a representative group of potential participants on Facebook/I\LinkedIn, it was reassessed whether additional surveys should be sent in order to receive a proper sample size.

RESULTS

Descriptive Analysis

The data collected were then categorized according to the controlling variables. The men's answers were separated from the females' answers to determine if there any statistically significant gender biases present in the present study. The same procedure was applied to the different age ranges, since the majority of the participants lie into two separate age groups. Accordingly, there are two subgroups under the men's category and two subgroups under the women's category. A total of 102 participants answered the survey that was sent via the message function on Facebook/LinkedIn. As evident in Table 1 and Figure 1, a majority of the participants, 81.4% (n = 83), were in the 31-40 years of age range. Clemmitt (2006) outlined that most individuals who utilize social networking sites are between the ages of 12 and 25 years. Given the results of this study are not consistent with this demographic, it is a possibility that the numbers were skewed due to the participants that were targeted for this study. On-the-other-hand, the study did reach a significant number of business professionals who were 41 years of age or older, 15.7% (n = 16). Of the 102 participants, an overwhelming 72.5% were female.

H1 Results

The findings seem to support H1, which stated that there will be no relationship between the use of social networking advertisements on Facebook and individuals' feelings toward the site. A majority of the questions relating to H1 were answered with a split decision. As indicated earlier in this paper, there is evidence that the usage of MySpace dropped primarily due to the use of excessive advertising. In order

Table 1. Basic frequencies of selected variables used in the present study

A. Age (years).				
Variable Coding Scheme	Frequency	Percent	Valid Percent	Cumulative Percent
20 or younger	3	2.9	2.9	2.9
21-30	40	39.2	39.2	42.2
31-40	43	42.2	42.2	84.3
41-50	8	7.8	7.8	92.2
51-60	7	6.9	6.9	99.0
Older than 60	1	1.0	1.0	100.0
Total	102	100.0	100.0	
B. Gender Status.				
Variable Coding Scheme	Frequency	Percent	Valid Percent	Cumulative Percent
Female	75	73.5	73.5	73.5
Male	27	26.5	26.5	100.0
Total	102	100.0	100.0	
C. Frequency of Facebook use.				
Variable Coding Scheme	Frequency	Percent	Valid Percent	Cumulative Percent
Daily	84	82.4	82.4	82.4
Weekly	11	10.8	10.8	93.1
Bi-weekly	3	2.9	2.9	96.1
Monthly	4	3.9	3.9	100.0
Total	102	100.0	100.0	
D. Average social networking hours per week.				
Variable Coding Scheme	Frequency	Percent	Valid Percent	Cumulative Percent
1-2	54	52.9	52.9	52.9
2-6	33	32.4	32.4	85.3
6-8	8	7.8	7.8	93.1
8+	7	6.9	6.9	100.0
Total	102	100.0	100.0	
E. Major purpose to stay connected with friends, family, co-worker.				
Variable Coding Scheme	Frequency	Percent	Valid Percent	Cumulative Percent
Strongly Agree	52	51.0	51.0	51.0
Agree	36	35.3	35.3	86.3
Neutral	13	12.7	12.7	99.0
Disagree	1	1.0	1.0	100.0
Total	102	100.0	100.0	

continued on following page

Table 1. Continued

F. Number of organizations liked on Facebook.				
Variable Coding Scheme	Frequency	Percent	Valid Percent	Cumulative Percent
1-5	47	46.1	46.1	46.1
5-10	35	34.3	34.3	80.4
10-15	10	9.8	9.8	90.2
15+	10	9.8	9.8	100.0
Total	102	100.0	100.0	

G. Major use to obtain information on savings on potential purchases.				
Variable Coding Scheme	Frequency	Percent	Valid Percent	Cumulative Percent
Strongly Agree	2	2.0	2.0	2.0
Agree	10	9.8	9.8	11.8
Neutral	21	20.6	20.6	32.4
Disagree	32	31.4	31.4	63.7
Strongly Disagree	37	36.3	36.3	100.0
Total	102	100.0	100.0	

H. Would continue using social media if banners and pop-ups common.				
Variable Coding Scheme	Frequency	Percent	Valid Percent	Cumulative Percent
Strongly Agree	3	2.9	2.9	2.9
Agree	21	20.6	20.6	23.5
Neutral	32	31.4	31.4	54.9
Disagree	29	28.4	28.4	83.3
Strongly Disagree	17	16.7	16.7	100.0
Total	102	100.0	100.0	

I. Advertisements newsfeed are distractive and annoying.				
Variable Coding Scheme	Frequency	Percent	Valid Percent	Cumulative Percent
Strongly Agree	22	21.6	21.6	21.6
Agree	38	37.3	37.3	58.8
Neutral	32	31.4	31.4	90.2
Disagree	9	8.8	8.8	99.0
Strongly Disagree	1	1.0	1.0	100.0
Total	102	100.0	100.0	

J. Major reason to like company is due to their products/services.				
Variable Coding Scheme	Frequency	Percent	Valid Percent	Cumulative Percent
Strongly Agree	4	3.9	3.9	3.9
Agree	26	25.5	25.5	29.4
Neutral	35	34.3	34.3	63.7

continued on following page

Table 1. Continued

Disagree	25	24.5	24.5	88.2
Strongly Disagree	12	11.8	11.8	100.0
Total	102	100.0	100.0	

K. Formally searched a company before following on social network.

Variable Coding Scheme	Frequency	Percent	Valid Percent	Cumulative Percent
Strongly Agree	8	7.8	7.8	7.8
Agree	24	23.5	23.5	31.4
Neutral	26	25.5	25.5	56.9
Disagree	31	30.4	30.4	87.3
Strongly Disagree	13	12.7	12.7	100.0
Total	102	100.0	100.0	

L. Made purchases after seeing advertisements in newsfeed.

Variable Coding Scheme	Frequency	Percent	Valid Percent	Cumulative Percent
Yes	12	11.8	11.8	11.8
No	90	88.2	88.2	100.0
Total	102	100.0	100.0	

M. Purchases per month based on advertisements on social media.

Variable Coding Scheme	Frequency	Percent	Valid Percent	Cumulative Percent
0-2	101	99.0	99.0	99.0
2-4	1	1.0	1.0	100.0
Total	102	100.0	100.0	

to determine if individuals would continue to utilize Facebook if pop up advertisements were to begin to be used, participants were asked to rate the degree to which they agree with that statement. Slightly more of the individuals agreed they would continue using Facebook regardless of whether or not pop up advertisements were to begin to be used; 51% of the participants were either neutral on the subject or agreed that they would continue using Facebook, while 46% either strongly disagreed or disagreed. Again, this result indicates that users are unsure whether or not pop up advertisements would deter them from further utilizing the site. Slightly more than half of participants did not seem to like the current form of advertisements on Facebook wherein the advertisements appear in their newsfeed. When asked whether these types of advertisements annoy the participants, 59.4% either strongly agreed or agreed. This was an unexpected result due to the fact that the advertisements only appear in their newsfeeds if the individual 'likes' the organization. Random advertisements do not appear unless the user shows an interest in the organization. This result may be further explained in the discussion that follows later in this paper regarding the other hypotheses.

In order to further explain the results regarding H1, an analysis was completed by separating the participants further into the variables of gender and age groups. When inspecting the male participants (27.5% or sample), 39% were 31-40 years of age, while 35.7% were 21-30 years of age. Overall, there

Figure 2. Age range of respondents

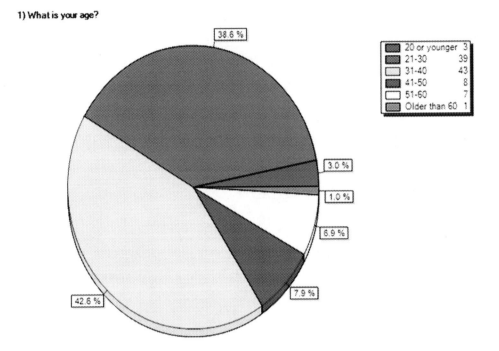

For a more accurate representation see the electronic version.

did not seem to be a difference in these two age groups regarding males. The variable of age in the male participants did not seem to affect their answers when asked if they would continue to utilize the site if pop up advertisements were to begin to appear. 60% of males 21-30 years of age either strongly disagreed or disagreed that they would continue to use Facebook, while 72.4% of males 31-40 years of age answered the same. The advertisements appearing in the participants' newsfeed seem to annoy approximately 80% of males ranging in age from 21-40 years. Overall, the males seem to not care for the social networking advertisements, whether they are in the form of pop up advertisements or ones that appear in their newsfeed.

The results are similar when dealing with females within the age groups of 21-30 and 31-40 than with males of the same age groups. When asked whether or not the females would continue using Facebook if pop up advertisements began, 68.9% of the women ages 21-30 and 62% of women ages 31-40 either are neutral or disagree. In order to determine if the current form of social networking advertisement troubles the women participants, it was decided to analysis their responses answers to the question of whether or not the advertisements appearing in their newsfeeds were considered a distraction. It was found that 72.4% of females, aged 21-30 and 63.7% aged 31-40 either were neutral or disagreed with this statement. This result is similar to that of the male participants within the same age groups.

Due to the small amount of participants that were outside of the age groups previously discussed in this study, it was decided to focus on an analysis of respondents that were 41-50 years of age to determine if there trends in their answers. This group represents only 7.9% of the total participants, but it was thought it would give an insight as to whether there are trends within the older age group. Interestingly, the 41-50 age group had exactly 50% male and 50% female responses, therefore, the gender variable should not be a factor in a sample of a majority of female respondents. The participants in this age group reported similar results as compared to the previously discussed groups when asked whether they use Facebook primarily to connect to friends and family; 50% of these participants strongly agreed with this statement. This group also indicated that 25% of them disagreed with the fact that Facebook is utilized to obtain information on products or services that organizations were offering. Where the results differ is when these participants were asked whether or not they would continue to use Facebook if pop up advertisements began on the site; 37.5% stated they agreed. This differs from the other groups previously analyzed as a large percentage of the other groups, which included males and females who were 40 years old or younger, indicated they would actually stop using Facebook if the pop up advertisements were to start appearing. Participants in the 41-50 age groups also did not seem to care about advertisements appearing in their newsfeed; 62.5% of these individuals were either neutral or disagreed with the current form of advertising on Facebook.

In in an effort to formally test H1, a series of statistical tests were performed. Tables «tbc2»2 and «tbc3»3 displays the relevant independent test for differences among means for traditional and non-traditional aged groups for variables associated with consumer behavioral and social networking and advertising preference characteristics as a function of gender status (i.e., as shown in Table 3, the mean differences were completed as female's mean less male's mean). As evident from an inspection of Tables 2 through Table 3, there were no significant differences among the various factors due to differences between equal or not equal variance assumptions. The same was true that there were on statistically significant difference among the various factors as a function of gender. Hence, even though there were more females represented in the same than females, there was no evidence of a gender bias in the sample.

A multiple linear regression analysis was conducted, with number of organizations liked on Facebook used as the dependent variable. As shown in Table 4, a relatively moderate portion [24.7% (15.5% adjusted)] of the total variance in number of organizations liked as the dependent variable was explained by the independent variables used in the analysis. The overall relationship was found to be highly significant, as expected ($F = 2.684$, $p = 0.005$).

Not surprisingly, if assuming H1 to be true, the independent variables of average social networking hours per week ($t = 4.275$, $p < 0.001$), and advertisements newsfeed are distractive and annoying ($t = 2.114$, $p = 0.037$) were found to be statistically significant. As hypothesized, critical consumer behavior-related success factors of major purpose to stay connected with friends, family, co-workers ($t = 1.110$, $p = 0.270$), major use to obtain information on savings on potential purchases ($t = 1.441$, $p = 0.661$), would continue using social media if banners and pop-ups common ($t = 0.828$, $p = 0.410$), major reason to like company is due to their products/services ($t = -0.856$, $p = 0.394$), formally searched a company before following on social network ($t = -0.139$, $p = 0.890$), majority of companies on social network page obtained from friends' pages ($t = -0.351$, $p = 0.726$), purchases per month based on advertisements on social media ($t = 0.146$, $p = 0.885$), as well as others studied. As these professionals have undoubtedly experienced, there will be no relationship between the use of social networking advertisements on Facebook and individuals' feelings or personal attachment toward the site, since it is a mutual business transaction. Based on the statistical analysis associated with the formal testing of H1; hence, it was accepted in the null form. The overall results show that individuals who currently utilize Facebook do not seem to be affected by the use of social networking advertisements in terms of liking or being personally attached to the companies providing the advertisements.

Table 2. Group statistics in terms of selected variables and gender (H1)

Variable Description	Gender Status	N	Mean	Std. Deviation	Std. Error Mean
Age (years)	Female	75	2.85	.954	.110
	Male	27	2.63	.967	.186
Frequency of Facebook use	Female	75	1.23	.649	.075
	Male	27	1.44	.847	.163
Average social networking hours per week	Female	75	1.77	.924	.107
	Male	27	1.44	.751	.145
Number of organizations liked on Facebook	Female	75	1.88	.999	.115
	Male	27	1.70	.869	.167
Major use to obtain information on savings on potential purchases	Female	75	3.85	1.099	.127
	Male	27	4.04	.980	.189
Would continue using social media if banners and pop-ups common	Female	75	3.35	1.033	.119
	Male	27	3.37	1.214	.234
Advertisements newsfeed are distractive and annoying	Female	75	2.31	.885	.102
	Male	27	2.30	1.103	.212
Major reason to like company is due to their products/services	Female	75	3.12	1.052	.121
	Male	27	3.22	1.086	.209
Formally searched a company before following on social network	Female	75	3.12	1.196	.138
	Male	27	3.30	1.068	.205
Majority of companies on social network page obtained from friends' pages	Female	75	2.71	.897	.104
	Male	27	2.67	.961	.185
Purchases per month based on advertisements on social media	Female	75	1.01	.115	.013
	Male	27	1.00	.000	.000

H2 Results

The results of the survey emphatically support H2, which stated that social networking advertisements will not have an effect on consumers' purchases. If one inspects the results of all the participants, essential the same amount of individuals, 25.5%, both agreed and disagreed that the reason they 'like' an organization is to purchase the organization's products or services, with 40.4% liked an organization merely because they saw that their friends had done the same, whereas 23.5% searched for organizations to like. This result seems to indicate that the 'like' function on Facebook is used primarily because people are curious about what their friends are interested in. This result also brings us back to a point made in the analysis of the results as they pertain to H1. It was surprising that participants reported being bothered by the advertisements that appear in their newsfeed when these advertisements only show up when the individual shows an interest in the organization by liking the organization's page. The analysis of the results as they pertain to both H1 and H2 seems to indicate that individuals 'like' an organization for reasons other than to purchase their products. Therefore, individuals are somewhat bothered by any advertisements that appear in their newsfeeds, regardless of whether or not they show an interest in the

Table 3. Equality of means tests results compared variables as a function of gender (H1) (note mean differences were completed as female's mean less male's mean)

Independent Variables and Variance Assumptions		t-test	df	Sig. (2-tailed)	Mean Difference	Std. Error Difference
Age (years)	Equal variances	1.041	100	.300 (NS)	.224	.215
	Not equal variances	1.035	45.476	.306 (NS)	.224	.216
Frequency of Facebook use	Equal variances	-1.375	100	.172 (NS)	-.218	.158
	Not equal variances	-1.214	37.545	.232 (NS)	-.218	.179
Average social networking hours per week	Equal variances	1.661	100	.100 (NS)	.329	.198
	Not equal variances	1.831	56.176	.072 (NS)	.329	.180
Number of organizations liked on Facebook	Equal variances	.812	100	.419 (NS)	.176	.217
	Not equal variances	.868	52.484	.390 (NS)	.176	.203
Major use to obtain information on savings on potential purchases	Equal variances	-.765	100	.446 (NS)	-.184	.240
	Not equal variances	-.808	51.195	.423 (NS)	-.184	.227
Would continue using social media if banners and pop-ups common	Equal variances	-.098	100	.923 (NS)	-.024	.243
	Not equal variances	-.090	40.370	.928 (NS)	-.024	.262
Advertisements newsfeed are distractive and annoying	Equal variances	.049	100	.961 (NS)	.010	.212
	Not equal variances	.044	38.716	.965 (NS)	.010	.236
Major reason to like company is due to their products/services	Equal variances	-.429	100	.669 (NS)	-.102	.238
	Not equal variances	-.423	44.744	.674 (NS)	-.102	.242
Formally searched a company before following on social network	Equal variances	-.675	100	.501 (NS)	-.176	.261
	Not equal variances	-.712	51.154	.480 (NS)	-.176	.248
Majority of companies on social network page obtained from friends' pages	Equal variances	.195	100	.846 (NS)	.040	.205
	Not equal variances	.189	43.379	.851 (NS)	.040	.212
Purchases per month based on advertisements on social media	Equal variances	.598	100	.551 (NS)	.013	.022
	Not equal variances	1.000	74.000	.321 (NS)	.013	.013

NS denotes not statistically significant at the .05 level for a two-tailed test; S denotes statistically significant at the .05 level for a two-tailed test; HS denotes significant at the .01 level for a two-tailed test.

organization. H2 is further confirmed by the fact that an overwhelming 88% of individuals never made a purchase as a result of seeing an advertisement in their newsfeed. For the small percent of participants that actually did make a purchase, 99% of the individuals purchased only two products or less.

Female participants' answers were inspected in the same age groups, 21-30 and 31-40, as they related to H 2. It was found that 31% of the female respondents who were 21-30 years of age 'liked' an organization in order to purchase the product or service offered by that organization. Similarly, 25% of the female participants who were 31-40 years of age also agreed with this statement. Females of both age groups consistently answered with both the overall results and the male participants when asked if they searched for organizations to 'like'. On-the-other-hand, the female participants seemed more concerned with what their friends were interested in than the male participants were; 55.2% of females who were

Table 4. Relevant statistics associated with specific hypothesis-testing results (H1). Part A displays the model summary, Part B the overall results, and Part C inspects specific contributions of each component in the hypothesis (Dependent variable: Number of organizations liked on Facebook).

Part A. Model summary.				
R	R Square	Adjusted R Square	Std. Error of the Estimate	
.497	.247	.155	.888	

Part B. ANOVA results.						
Source of Variation		Sum of Squares	df	Mean Square	F-ratio	Significance
	Regression	23.263	11	2.115	2.684	.005 (HS)
	Residual	70.903	90	.788		
	Total	94.167	101			

Dependent Variable: Number of organizations liked on Facebook.

Predictors: (Constant), Purchases per month based on advertisements on social media, Frequency of Facebook use, Age (years), Majority of companies on social network page obtained from friends' pages, Advertisements newsfeed are distractive and annoying, Major purpose to stay connected with friends, family, co-workers, Formally searched a company before following on social network, Would continue using social media if banners and pop-ups common, Major use to obtain information on savings on potential purchases, Average social networking hours per week, Major reason to like company is due to their products/services. HS denotes significant at the .01 level for a two-tailed test.

Part C. Coefficients-testing results.					
Independent Variables	Unstandardized Coefficients		Standardized Coefficients	t-test	Significance
	B	Std. Error	Beta		
(Constant)	.269	1.358		.198	.843
Age (years)	-.077	.098	-.076	-.782	.436 (NS)
Frequency of Facebook use	-.012	.144	-.009	-.085	.932 (NS)
Average social networking hours per week	.520	.122	.479	4.275	>.001 (HS)
Major purpose to stay connected with friends, family, co-workers	.141	.127	.108	1.110	.270 (NS)
Major use to obtain information on savings on potential purchases	.049	.110	.054	.441	.661 (NS)
Would continue using social media if banners and pop-ups common	.077	.093	.086	.828	.410 (NS)
Advertisements newsfeed are distractive and annoying	.234	.111	.228	2.114	.037 (S)
Major reason to like company is due to their products/services	-.098	.114	-.107	-.856	.394 (NS)
Formally searched a company before following on social network	-.013	.092	-.015	-.139	.890 (NS)
Majority of companies on social network page obtained from friends' pages	-.037	.104	-.034	-.351	.726 (NS)
Purchases per month based on advertisements on social media	.146	1.000	.015	.146	.885 (NS)

Dependent Variable: Number of organizations liked on Facebook. NS denotes not statistically significant at the 0.05 level for a two-tailed test; S denotes statistically significant at the 0.05 level for a two-tailed test; HS denotes significant at the 0.01 level for a two-tailed test.

21-30 years of age agreed that they typically 'liked' an organization due to the fact that they saw their friends had done the same and 43.8% of females in the 31-40 age group also agreed with this statement. As in the other groups analyzed, females did not typically make purchases based on seeing advertisements in their newsfeeds. 86.2% of the females ages 21-30 and 83.9% of the females ages 31-40 never made a purchase as a result of seeing a social networking advertisement. Out of the small percentage that did make a purchase, 96.6% of the participants purchased two products or less.

As with H1, the answers of the participants were also analyzed, male and female, who were 41-50 years of age. The results were consistent with the overall results as well as with the results of the age groups analyzed that were 40 years of age and younger. Specifically regarding the amount of purchases made as a result of social networking advertisements, 87.5% of the participants 41-50 years of age indicated that they never made a purchase. Similarly, out of the small percent of participants that did make a purchase, 100% of them purchased two or less products.

To further test these research assumptions associated with H2, Chi-square analyses were conducted, with cross-tabulation statistics associated with made purchases after seeing advertisements in newsfeed and major reason to like company is due to their products/services (Table «tbc5»5), and gender added to the same mix of variables (Table «tbc6»6). As shown in Table «tbc5»5, the vast majority of respondents felt that liking and organization based on its products/services had little to do with completing purchases after seeing advertisements in newsfeed (Chi-square = 11.802, p = 0.019). The same overall relationship has found to be statistically true for females (Chi-square = 14.338, p = 0.006), but not true for males (Chi-square = 3.536, p = 0.472). Males were apparently more indifferent to the concept of madding of purchases after seeing advertisements in newsfeed and it acting as the major reason to like a company. Hence, as stated earlier, the results of this study suggest that H2 is accepted as the statistical evidence supports that fact that social networking advertisements do not have a significant positive impact or effect on consumers' purchases. If fact, it might well be the complete opposite.

H3 Results

Finally, the results of the formal testing of H3 suggested that there is evidence to support the claim that the "like" function on organizational Facebook pages is not a major function used by individuals. As previously suggested, the format of all the specific research hypotheses were stated in the null form. The reasons that many individuals use social networking sites, like Facebook and LinkedIn, are less about commercial and consuming motivations, and more about maintaining personal connections. Krivak (2008) suggested that Facebook started in 2004 as a way for individuals to stay connected with friends and family, even if they were considerable distances apart. The results of this study indicate that this very basic fact remains to be true, even though commercialism seems to drive the profits of the social networking industry. Of the 102 participants, 86.3% either strongly agreed or agreed with the fact that that they participated in Facebook mainly to stay connected to friends and family. When asked whether or not they utilized Facebook primarily to obtain information on deals available through different organizations, 58.6% of the participants either strongly disagreed or disagreed. Regarding the 'like' function, 46.1% indicated that they have only 'liked' five organizations or less. This finding further confirms that Facebook is primarily used to stay connected with friends and family, rather than to benefit from the social networking advertisements. The amount of time the participants spent on Facebook was important to measure. The longer an individual is on Facebook, the more likely they would take advantage of all of the site's features, such us 'liking' an organization. A majority of the participants, 82.4%, included

Table 5. Cross-tabulation statistics associated with Made purchases after seeing advertisements in newsfeed and Major reason to like company is due to their products/services (H2)

Part A. Actual count.							
Variable Descriptions		Major reason to like company is due to their products/services					Total
		Strongly Agree	Agree	Neutral	Disagree	Strongly Disagree	
Made purchases after seeing advertisements in newsfeed	Yes	1	8	1	2	0	12
	No	3	18	34	23	12	90
Total		4	26	35	25	12	102

Part B. Chi-square test results.			
Statistics	Value	df	Asymptotic Significance (2-sided)
Pearson Chi-Square	14.338	4	.006 (HS)
Likelihood Ratio	14.275	4	.006 (HS)
Linear-by-Linear Association	8.064	1	.005 (HS)
N of Valid Cases	102		

Note, 6 cells (60.0%) have expected count less than 5. The minimum expected count is 0.47. HS denotes significant at the 0.01 level for a two-tailed test.

Part C. Symmetric measures.			
Statistics		Value	Approx. Sig.
Nominal by Nominal	Contingency Coefficient	.351	.006 (HS)
N of Valid Cases		102	

HS denotes significant at the .01 level for a two-tailed test.

Facebook and other social networking sites as part of their daily routine. Not only do individuals utilize such sites on a daily basis, they spend multiple hours per day on Facebook, as 85.3% spent six hours or less on the site, which is close to what many working adults may spend working daily for a full-time position.

As with H1 and H2, a further breakdown of the respondents was performed in terms of gender status and age groups, using the same age groups, 21-30 and 31-40, when analyzing whether the 'like' feature was a major function used on Facebook. It was found that 100% of the males that were 21-30 years of age indicated that they either strongly agreed or agreed that they utilize Facebook primarily to stay connected with friends and family while 81.8% of males that were 31-40 years of age either strongly agreed or agreed with this statement. When the males were asked whether they primarily utilize Facebook to obtain information pertaining to deals from different organizations, 90% of the male participants in the 21-30 age group either strongly disagreed or disagreed while 63.7% in the age group of 31-40 did the same. Of the 72.5% female participants, 39.7% were 21-30 years of age while 43.8% were 31-40 years of age. When asked if Facebook is used primarily to stay connected with friends and family, 75.9% of females ages 21-30 either strongly agree or agree while 80.7% of females ages 31-40 answered the same. Accordingly, the same percentage, 34.5%, in both age groups of females disagree that they use Facebook primarily to obtain information on products or services that are for same.

Table 6. Cross-tabulation statistics associated with Made purchases after seeing advertisements in newsfeed and Major reason to like company is due to their products/services and Gender Status (H2)

Part A. Actual count.								
Gender Status			Major reason to like company is due to their products/services					Total
			Strongly Agree	Agree	Neutral	Disagree	Strongly Disagree	
Female	Made purchases after seeing advertisements in newsfeed	Yes	1	6	1	1	0	9
		No	2	13	27	15	9	66
	Total		3	19	28	16	9	75
Male	Made purchases after seeing advertisements in newsfeed	Yes	0	2	0	1	0	3
		No	1	5	7	8	3	24
	Total		1	7	7	9	3	27
Total	Made purchases after seeing advertisements in newsfeed	Yes	1	8	1	2	0	12
		No	3	18	34	23	12	90
	Total		4	26	35	25	12	102

Part B. Chi-square test results.				
Gender Status		Value	df	Asymptotic Significance (2-sided)
Female	Pearson Chi-Square	11.802[b]	4	.019 (S)
	Likelihood Ratio	11.411	4	.022 (S)
	Linear-by-Linear Association	7.446	1	.006 (HS)
	N of Valid Cases	75		
Male	Pearson Chi-Square	3.536[c]	4	.472 (NS)
	Likelihood Ratio	4.182	4	.382 (NS)
	Linear-by-Linear Association	.883	1	.347 (NS)
	N of Valid Cases	27		
Total	Pearson Chi-Square	14.338[a]	4	.006 (HS)
	Likelihood Ratio	14.275	4	.006 (HS)
	Linear-by-Linear Association	8.064	1	.005 (HS)
	N of Valid Cases	102		

a. 6 cells (60.0%) have expected count less than 5. The minimum expected count is 0.47; b. 6 cells (60.0%) have expected count less than 5. The minimum expected count is .36; c. 7 cells (70.0%) have expected count less than 5. The minimum expected count is 0.11.
NS denotes not statistically significant at the .05 level for a two-tailed test; S denotes statistically significant at the .05 level for a two-tailed test; HS denotes significant at the .01 level for a two-tailed test.

Part C. Symmetric measures.				
Gender Status			Value	Approx. Sig.
Female	Nominal by Nominal	Contingency Coefficient	.369	.019 (S)
	N of Valid Cases		75	
Male	Nominal by Nominal	Contingency Coefficient	.340	.472 (NS)
	N of Valid Cases		27	
Total	Nominal by Nominal	Contingency Coefficient	.351	.006 (HS)
	N of Valid Cases		102	

NS denotes not statistically significant at the .05 level for a two-tailed test; S denotes statistically significant at the .05 level for a two-tailed test; HS denotes significant at the .01 level for a two-tailed test.

To formally test H3, Table 7 illustrates the cross-tabulation statistics associated with major purpose to stay connected with friends, family, co-workers and age (years) and gender status. As presented in the table, all relationships with staying connected with friends, family, co-workers and age did not statistically differ as a function of gender [male (Chi-square = 5.848, p = 0.664), female (Chi-square = 8.292, p = 0.912)], with the vast majority of respondents accepting, regardless of gender status and age. Once again, the testing of H3 supports the fact that Facebook is primarily utilized to stay connected with friends and family, although the males in the 31-40 age groups showed some interest in what the organizations had to offer through the 'liking' feature. Therefore, H3 is formally accepted in the null form.

Table 7. Cross-tabulation statistics associated with Major purpose to stay connected with friends, family, co-workers and Age (years) and Gender Status. (H3)

Part A. Actual count.									
Gender Status			Age (years)						Total
			20 or younger	21-30	31-40	41-50	51-60	Older than 60	
Female	Major purpose to stay connected with friends, family, co-workers	Strongly Agree	1	15	16	2	4	1	39
		Agree	0	7	15	1	2	0	25
		Neutral	0	6	3	1	0	0	10
		Disagree	0	0	1	0	0	0	1
	Total		1	28	35	4	6	1	75
Male	Major purpose to stay connected with friends, family, co-workers	Strongly Agree	1	4	4	3	1	0	13
		Agree	1	7	3	0	0	0	11
		Neutral	0	1	1	1	0	0	3
	Total		2	12	8	4	1	0	27
Total	Major purpose to stay connected with friends, family, co-workers	Strongly Agree	2	19	20	5	5	1	52
		Agree	1	14	18	1	2	0	36
		Neutral	0	7	4	2	0	0	13
		Disagree	0	0	1	0	0	0	1
	Total		3	40	43	8	7	1	102

Part B. Chi-square test results.					
Gender Status		Value	df	Asymptotic Significance (2-sided)	
Female	Pearson Chi-Square	8.292[b]	15	.912 (NS)	
	Likelihood Ratio	9.978	15	.821 (NS)	
	Linear-by-Linear Association	.624	1	.429 (NS)	
	N of Valid Cases	75			

continued on following page

Table 7. Continued

Male	Pearson Chi-Square	5.848[c]	8	.664 (NS)
	Likelihood Ratio	7.776	8	.456 (NS)
	Linear-by-Linear Association	.636	1	.425 (NS)
	N of Valid Cases	27		
Total	Pearson Chi-Square	8.638[a]	15	.896 (NS)
	Likelihood Ratio	10.689	15	.774 (NS)
	Linear-by-Linear Association	1.138	1	.286 (NS)
	N of Valid Cases	102		

a. 18 cells (75.0%) have expected count less than 5. The minimum expected count is 0.01.
b. b. 20 cells (83.3%) have expected count less than 5. The minimum expected count is 0.01.

c. 14 cells (93.3%) have expected count less than 5. The minimum expected count is 0.11.
NS denotes not statistically significant at the .05 level for a two-tailed test.

Part C. Symmetric measures.

Gender Status			Value	Approx. Sig.
Female	Nominal by Nominal	Contingency Coefficient	.316	.912 (NS)
	N of Valid Cases		75	
Male	Nominal by Nominal	Contingency Coefficient	.422	.664 (NS)
	N of Valid Cases		27	
Total	Nominal by Nominal	Contingency Coefficient	.279	.896 (NS)
	N of Valid Cases		102	

NS denotes not statistically significant at the .05 level for a two-tailed test.

MANAGERIAL RECOMMENDATIONS

The general findings of the present study provide some insight to the understanding of communication and analytical power of social platforms and BDA usage in modern societies. It also provides guidance regarding what managers should expect from using this technology. It describes that the organizational level BDA use has significant impacts on type types of supply chain value creation; asset productivity and business growth. Also, technological factors have a direct influence on organizational BDA use. It is extremely useful with the proper environmental factors and can have an influence on organizational BDA through the use of top management support.

Although there is overwhelming evidence based on the statistical testing of the three specific research hypotheses that consumers' purchases do not increase as a result of seeing advertisements in their newsfeeds on social networking sites (e.g., Facebook/LinkedIn), there is still some inherent benefits to organizations who do utilize social networking advertisements. The results of this study indicate that 48.5% of all participants indicated that the primary reason that they 'liked' an organization was because they saw that their friends had done the same. This is a great form of free advertisement for an organization known as positive word-of-mouth (WOM) advertisements. There is considerable evident that positive WOM influences consumers to more likely to purchase a product if they see that their friends or relatives have also shown an interest in the organization (Brown, Broderick, & Lee, (2007; Cafferky, 1995; Chang, Hsieh, & Tseng, 2013). WOM advertising can me defined as "a personal referral from someone whose opinions are trusted by others" (Arya, 2010, p. 3). Mulvihill (2011) further outlined the importance of advertising on social networking systems by commenting on the value of an individual 'liking' an organization on Facebook or having a Facebook fan. It is not only about whether or not the individual purchases the organization's product or service, it is about spreading brand awareness. Perhaps, "Facebook's potential for building brand-to-customer relationships is priceless" (Mulvihill, 2011, p. 8). It was further discussed that organizations need to learn how to use these social networking systems to have more meaningful interactions with their consumers or target market. Facebook and other social networking sites should be utilized by businesses of essentially all categories as a way to communicate with their consumers openly and freely. These organizations can obtain immediate feedback from their target consumers and react more swiftly to their concerns. Managers can locate their target market through the information provided by their consumers on such networking sites. This is an easy way for managers to analyze trends within their target market.

GENERAL CONCLUSION AND IMPLICATIONS

The transformation power of the Internet has greatly impacted and revised theoretical frameworks for research, especially concerning media coverage and content of social media-related activities. As web-based technological innovations increase, so have empirically-based methodologies to measure their impacts on consumers of such social media. Mass communication, coupled with technical innovations that promote ease-of-use and greater accessibility, has significantly changed the commercial landscape of social media-related information and marketing gathering by its consumers. The results, in general, indicate that there is no relationship between the use of social networking advertisements and individuals' feelings toward the site.

Although there is indication that individuals do not care to see the advertisements appear in their newsfeeds, it does not bother them enough to discontinue utilizing the site. Interestingly, the majority of working professionals indicated they would discontinue using Facebook/LinkedIn if pop-up advertisements were to begin to be used. Organizations must be mindful of this as social networking sites continue to evolve and grow to meet the expectations of its user base. The information and form of communication found on social networking sites are priceless to an organization and can help these businesses increase their market share. By establishing strong IT systems, responsive systems that are CRM (customer relationship management)-embedded, etc., there is still a need to reduce waste and become more lean. There is a general changing view of management theory from one of a Newtonian view (i.e., linear systems or trade-offs) to possibly one involving complexity theory (not mutually exclusive, but mutually benefiting) with companies as treating organizations as complex adaptive systems. Social media and BDA are becoming for mainstream and an excepted part of the business landscape.

Directions for Future Research

There are many opportunities in SCM, customer relationships, that social network advertisements can have a major impact. In particular, sport-related advertisement is especially promising for future research. According to Pedersen (2013), has an enviable position in that it has a universal significance, ubiquitous presence, and overall importance to its growth and viability in society. Unfortunately, this popularity greatly influences what is considered relevant themes or research threads, especially among doctorial students. Both Frisby (2005) and Pederson (2013) have commented that much research in sport management has been done at the micro-level, catering to new and emerging issues that have caught the attention of the public. Although some attempt to explain the results of the study have been made at the macro-level (e.g., Stakeholder theoretical and ethical orientation/belief systems), micro-level theoretical considerations still dominate as the major factor in explaining participants' views on sport-related gambling and office pooling within the workplace environment. Future studies need to be aware of such issues.

Various theories at the marketing segment or individual level, such as Uses and Gratifications Theory (i.e., used in the present dissertation effort) and Social Learning theories, have been employed with various methodologies, such as experimental design studies, content analyses, and case studies) to investigate sport-related scientific inquiries. Pederson (2013) went a step further to suggest that, based on his experience working with the next generations of doctorial students, because of the limited publication outlets for sport communication research, their work is often published in sport management instead of communication journals.

Both Frisby (2005) and Pederson (2013) have written their essays after the advent of the Internet and social networking and advertising have become main stream avenues for research in studying the impact of social media platforms for increasing involvement in sport management activities. Pederson, for example, suggested that even contemporary studies in sport communication have used primarily content analysis to take mere snapshots of social media and its impact on sport. He suggested doing further research by examining the audience consumption and effects, framed by a strategic communication perspective. Morgan (1983), on-the-other-hand, framed sport research in historical terms at the macro level via Neo-Marxist and Utilitarian Theories of the continuous struggle of the masses on economic and/or political dominance. Both Morgan and Frisby have implied that consumerism and capitalism are at least partially responsible for sport research to be framed in a materialistic lifestyle that related self-esteem to consumption of goods, resulting in exploitation, pollution, and increased poverty. Sport research should be based on understanding the wider and more fundamental questions of utility at the society level. Perhaps commercialization and influence of big business are the greatest limitations associated with this dissertation, as money and self-esteem are important factors that were not investigated. Again, future studies can more effectivity deals with such pressing considerations in social media advertising.

ACKNOWLEDGMENT

The authors wish to thank most heartedly for the valuable contributions by the reviewers for their input into the final paper. Peer reviewing and editing are often tedious and thankless tasks.

REFERENCES

Alijani, G. S., Mancuso, L. C., Kwun, O., & Omar, A. (2010). Effectiveness of online advertisement factors in recalling a product. *Academy of Marketing Studies Journal, 14*(1), 1–11.

Amine, A. (1998). Consumers' true brand loyalty: The central role of commitment. *Journal of Strategic Marketing, 6*(4), 305–319. doi:10.1080/096525498346577

Ang, L. (2010). Community Relationship Management and Social Media. *Database Marketing & Customer Strategy Management, 18*(1), 31–38. doi:10.1057/dbm.2011.3

Ankeny, J. (2011). Face lift. *Entrepreneur, 39*(1), 56–59.

Arya, D. P. (2010). Advertisement effectiveness: Role of 'word-of mouth' in success of educational institutes in non-metro cities. *IUP Journal of Management Research, 9*(1), 1–20.

Bateman, P. J., Pike, J. C., & Butler, B. S. (2010). To disclose or not: Publicness in social networking sites. *Information Technology & People, 24*(1), 78–100. doi:10.1108/09593841111109431

Bennett, S. (2014). Pinterest, Twitter, Facebook, Instagram, Google+, LinkedIn – Social Media Stats 2014 [INFOGRAPHIC]. *AllTwitter*. Retrieved July 8, 2017 from http://www.mediabistro.com/alltwitter/social-media-stats-2014_b5424.3

Bonson, E., & Flores, F. (2010). Social media and corporate dialogue: The Response of global financial institutions. *Online Information Review, 35*(1), 34–49. doi:10.1108/14684521111113579

Booth, N., & Matic, J. A. (2011). Mapping and leveraging influences in social media to shape corporate brand perceptions. *Corporate Communications, 16*(3), 184–191. doi:10.1108/13563281111156853

Brown, J., Broderick, A., & Lee, N. J. (2007). Word of mouth communication within online communities: Conceptualizing the online social network. *Interactive Marketing, 21*(3), 2–20. doi:10.1002/dir.20082

Cadogan, J. W., & Foster, B. D. (2000). Relationship Selling and Customer Loyalty: An Empirical Investigation. *Marketing Intelligence & Planning, 18*(4), 185–199. doi:10.1108/02634500010333316

Cafferky, M. E. (1995). *Let your customers do the talking: 301 + WOM Marketing Tactics Guaranteed to Boost Profits*. Chicago, IL: Upstart Publishing Co.

Chan, C. (2010). Using online advertising to increase the impact of a library Facebook page. *Library Management, 32*(4/5), 361–370. doi:10.1108/01435121111132347

Chang, A., Hsieh, S., & Tseng, T. H. (2013). Online brand community response to negative brand events: The role of group eWOM. *Internet Research, 23*(4), 486–506. doi:10.1108/IntR-06-2012-0107

Chen, D. Q., Preston, D. S., & Swink, M. (2015). How the use of big data analytics affects value creation in supply chain management. *Journal of Management Information Systems, 32*(4), 4–39. doi:10.1080/07421222.2015.1138364

Clemmitt, M. (2006). Cyber socializing. *CQ Researcher, 16*(27), 625–648.

Clemmitt, M. (2010). Social networking. *CQ Researcher, 20*(32), 749–772.

Fernandez, P. (2009). Balancing outreach and privacy in Facebook: Five guiding decisions points. *Library Hi Tech News*, *26*(3/4), 10–12. doi:10.1108/07419050910979946

Finn, G. (2014). Still the One: Facebook gains ground as the leader in social logins. *Marketing Land*. Retrieved July 9, 2017 from http://marketingland.com/still-one-facebook-gains-ground-leader-social-logins-81115

Frisby, W. (2005). The good, the bad, and the ugly: Critical sport management research. *Journal of Sport Management*, *19*(1), 1–12. doi:10.1123/jsm.19.1.1

Gans, H. (2009). Public ethnography: Ethnography as public sociology. *Qualitative Sociology, 33*(2010), 97-104. Retrieved August 4, 2017 from http://herbertgans.org/wp-content/uploads/2013/11/Public-Ethnography.pdf

Goldie, L. (2007). Social networks build up brand opportunities. *News Analysis,* 16.

Granville, K. (2018). Facebook and Cambridge Analytica: What you need to know as fallout widens. *The New York Times*. Retrieved April 12, 2018 from https://www.nytimes.com/2018/03/19/technology/facebook-cambridge-analytica-explained.html

Greenhow, C. (2011). Online social networks and learning. *On the Horizon*, *19*(1), 4–12. doi:10.1108/10748121111107663

Ham, L. (2011). Chasing a bargain: Who pays? *Media Watch,* 7-8.

Howell, N. (2009). If click-through isn't a measure, what's engagement? *New Media Age, 2*.

Jaffie, B. (2009). Getting more bang for your marketing buck – leveraging technology to help your effectiveness. *Proofs,* 62-63.

Krivak, T. (2008). Facebook 101: Ten things you need to know about Facebook. *Information Today,* *25*(3), 42-44.

Mateen, A., & More, D. (2013). Applying TOC thinking process tools in managing challenges of supply chain finance: A case study. *International Journal of Services and Operations Management*, *15*(4), 389–410. doi:10.1504/IJSOM.2013.054882

McCormick, A. (2006). Everyone needs to keep an eye on the ball. *News Analysis,* 16.

Morgan, W. J. (Ed.). (1979). *Sport and the humanities: A collection of original essays.* Knoxville, TN: University of Tennessee.

Morimoto, M., & Chang, S. (2009). Psychological factors affecting perceptions of unsolicited commercial email. *Journal of Current Issues and Research in Advertising*, *31*(1), 63–73. doi:10.1080/106 41734.2009.10505257

Mulvihill, A. (2011). Measuring the value of a 'like.'. *EContent (Wilton, Conn.), 34*(6), 8–12.

Nobari, A., Khierkhah, A. S., & Hajipour, V. (2018). A Pareto-based approach to optimise aggregate production planning problem considering reliable supplier selection. *International Journal of Services and Operations Management*, *29*(1), 59–84. doi:10.1504/IJSOM.2018.088473

Park, B.-N., & Min, H. (2013). Global supply chain barriers of foreign subsidiaries: The case of Korean expatriate manufacturers in China. *International Journal of Services and Operations Management, 15*(1), 67–78. doi:10.1504/IJSOM.2013.050562

Pedersen, P. M. (2013). Reflections on communication and sport: On strategic communication and management. *Communication and Sport, 1*(1/2), 55–67. doi:10.1177/2167479512466655

Pookulangara, S., & Koesler, K. (2011). Cultural influence on consumers' usage of social networks and its impact on online purchase intentions. *Journal of Retailing and Consumer Services, 18*(4), 348–354. doi:10.1016/j.jretconser.2011.03.003

Raice, S., & Ante, S. (2012). Insta-Rich: $1 Billion for Instagram. *The Wall Street Journal*. Retrieved July 9, 2017 from http://online.wsj.com/news/articles/SB10001424052702303815140

Rajapakshe, T., Dawande, M., & Sriskandarajah, C. (2013). On the trade-off between remanufacturing and recycling. *International Journal of Services and Operations Management, 15*(1), 1–53. doi:10.1504/IJSOM.2013.050560

Rajeev, V. (2013). Impact of service co-creation on performance of firms: The mediating role of market oriented strategies. *International Journal of Services and Operations Management, 15*(4), 449–466. doi:10.1504/IJSOM.2013.054885

Ridinger, L. L., & Funk, D. C. (2006). Looking at gender differences through the lens of sport spectators. *Sport Marketing Quarterly, 5*(3), 155–166.

Robinson, M. J., & Trail, G. T. (2005). Relationships among spectator gender, motives, points of attachment, and sport preference. *Journal of Sport Management, 19*(1), 58–80. doi:10.1123/jsm.19.1.58

Ruane, L., & Wallace, E. (2015). Brand tribalism and self-expressive brands: Social influences and brand outcomes. *Journal of Product and Brand Management, 24*(4), 333–348. doi:10.1108/JPBM-07-2014-0656

Schroeder, C. (2004). Online ads. *Campaigns and Elections, 25*(1), 38–39.

Seguin, B., Richelieu, A., & O'Reilly, N. (2008). Leveraging the Olympic brand through the reconciliation of corporate and consumers' brand perceptions. *International Journal of Sport Management and Marketing, 3*(1/2), 3–22. doi:10.1504/IJSMM.2008.015958

Senthilmurugan, P. R., Jegadheesan, C., & Devadasan, S. R. (2018). Improving the quality and yield in the casting of compressor pulley through the application of total failure mode and effects analysis. *International Journal of Services and Operations Management, 29*(1), 42–58. doi:10.1504/IJSOM.2018.088472

Sharma, A., & Sharma, R. K. (2018). Modelling and analysis of enablers for successful implementation of cellular manufacturing system. *International Journal of Process Management and Benchmarking, 8*(1), 103–123. doi:10.1504/IJPMB.2018.088659

Shields, M. (2009). Facebook friends' brands. *Media Week, 18*(30), 8.

Smock, A. D., Ellison, N. B., Lampe, C., & Wohn, D. Y. (2011). Facebook as a toolkit: A uses and gratification approach to unbundling feature use. *Computers in Human Behavior, 27*(6), 2322–2329. doi:10.1016/j.chb.2011.07.011

Taylor, D. G., Lewin, J. E., & Strutton, D. (2011). Friends, fans, and followers: Do ads work on social networks? *Journal of Advertising Research*, *51*(1), 258–275. doi:10.2501/JAR-51-1-258-275

Todor, R. D. (2016). Blending traditional and digital marketing. *Bulletin of the Transilvania University of Brasov. Series V, Economic Sciences*, *9*(1), 51–56.

Verma, P., Sharma, R. R. K., & Kumar, V. (2018). The sustainability issues of diversified firms in emerging economies context: A theoretical model and propositions. *International Journal of Process Management and Benchmarking*, *7*(2), 224–248. doi:10.1504/IJPMB.2017.083107

Xu, Y., Tiwari, A., Chen, H. C., & Turner, C. J. (2018). Development of a validation and qualification process for the manufacturing of medical devices: A case study based on cross-sector benchmarking. *International Journal of Process Management and Benchmarking*, *8*(1), 79–102. doi:10.1504/IJPMB.2018.088658

Yazdi, A. K., & Esfeden, G. A. (2018). Designing robust model of Six Sigma implementation based on critical successful factors and MACBETH. *International Journal of Process Management and Benchmarking*, *7*(2), 158–171. doi:10.1504/IJPMB.2017.083103

Yee, W. F., & Sidek, Y. (2008). Influence of brand loyalty on consumer sportswear. *International Journal of Economics and Management*, *2*(2), 221–236.

Zaney, K. (2004). Down with pop-ups. *Education Week*, *21*(1), 41–42.

Zimmerman, M. H., Clavio, G. E., & Lim, C. H. (2011). Set the agenda like Beckham: A professional sports league's use of YouTube to disseminate messages to its users. *International Journal of Sport Management and Marketing*, *10*(3/4), 180–195. doi:10.1504/IJSMM.2011.044789

Chapter 16
Strategic Planning for Information Technology:
A Collaborative Model of Information Technology Strategic Plan for the Government Sector

Wagner N. Silva
Federal University of Rio de Janeiro, Brazil

Marco Antonio Vaz
Federal University of Rio de Janeiro, Brazil

Jano Moreira Casa de Oswaldo Cruz
Federal University of Rio de Janeiro, Brazil

ABSTRACT

Information technology (IT) is strategic for organization management, although many companies lack IT governance and planning, skilled people, defined and institutionalized methods and procedures, internal controls and indicators, and structures for agreement service levels and information security, legality, and economy. In this scenario, a minimum organization and control in the use of resources is needed to boost technical and administrative efficiency, with a focus on IT governance. An information technology strategic plan (ITSP) aims at discovering the resources and IT in an organization to direct the technological and information architecture to its strategic objectives. The Brazilian government issued a normative instruction (NI04) for public organizations to develop IT strategic plans so that they can purchase products and services. In order to help organizations develop, control, and manage their ITSPs, a model was created that defines a set of auxiliary steps in the construction of the ITSP.

DOI: 10.4018/978-1-5225-7214-5.ch016

INTRODUCTION

Over the years, many public and private organizations have had their areas of Information Technology undervalued, generally confined to the supporting role (Doherty, Marples & Suhaimi, 1999; Blili & Raymond, 1993).

The increasing demand for the use of Information Technology (IT), allied to the transformation of IT in strategic assets, created the need to improve the management of technology in these institutions. Typically, organizations use their technological resources on a very poor level of planning where IT decisions are taken in an isolated way, for different reasons and by different people in their structures.

Still, as a consequence of this scenario, the following situations are experienced: lack of continuity in projects due to constant change of priorities and objectives, or a need to attend to emergency situations, especially those arising from decisions by individual managers; bad design of computational and human resources for the Information Technology unit; information systems deployed without adequate regard to compliance requirements, creating more problems than solutions; lack of motivation of the professionals involved in the process, and leaders who often decide to reduce investments in technology (Chan, 2005).

Nevertheless, IT strategic planning is still placed in the background and, to reverse this, it is necessary to develop a plan that allows the combination of strategic guidelines and organizational intelligence with IT actions (Burn & Szeto, 2000).

There are several ITSP development models, including the one proposed by Microsoft (Microsoft, 2011), named Microsoft Methodology Consulting Service (MCS) which is based on the technical recommendations of COBIT, and developed jointly with partners who specialize in this practice. This model is divided into five stages where each stage has activities related to its responsibility. The first stage deals with the generation of the IT strategic plan, the second includes a survey of IT needs, the third one maps the desired situation, the fourth prepares the strategic IT plan, and the fifth one is for ITSP implementation and monitoring.

The model proposed by some authors considers three steps in ITSP development. The first one is preparation, generated throughout the framework to create a ITSP, the second step diagnoses the current situation, where the body has an exact notion of the stage, and the needs are raised. The final step is to plan the situation whose attainment is planned, at which point the ITSP is produced (Hazan, 2010; Fagundes, 2011; Cruz, 2009; Rezende, 2003).

The Brazilian Planning, Budget and Management Department (BPBMD) issued a Normative Instruction (NI04) stating that IT acquisitions (Products and Services) should be preceded by an ITSP (Normative Instruction 04, 2008).

The ITSP provides a full view of the current environment and of Information Technology, according to current and future needs, and allows direct information architecture and technology aligned with the strategic objectives of the institution (Weill, Ross & Robertson, 2006).

The ITSP consists primarily of the knowledge of its resources (services, business processes, information systems, infrastructure, and technology) from an analysis based on the purpose of the organization, definition and planning of a strategy for IT growth. An administration concerned with ITSP is a company that uses modern principles of rationality, consistency and quality, creating a policy for success.

The IT strategic plan must reflect business needs. Therefore, aligning the IT strategy with the business plan is essential to helping the business achieve its goals through IT solutions. Before defining initiatives and projects, you must determine what the business needs are. A scan of available technologies will identify possible solutions for business requirements. Once you've identified the business elements, IT must develop a model of its business—namely, its mission, goals, and critical success factors—so that they align with the business elements (Hong, 2009).

In this scenario, in order to manage an annual budget of about R$ 4.5 billion, the Brazilian government edited a Normative Instruction. This norm dictates the elaboration of an IT Strategic Plan for all public federal offices that plan to hire IT "services". Although, according to studies from Ministry of Planning, the offices don't seem to be prepared to attend the norm. This work looking to improve the construction process and its monitoring of the ITSP, an idea arose for the development of a model to provide direction, control and monitor the development of ITSPs and, after their production, to allow their effective management and monitoring (Fagundes, 2011).

MOTIVATION

Developing a strategic plan in this manner can help ensure the alignment of business needs and IT activities. Having such a plan can benefit the enterprise in several ways. First, the plan provides a clear roadmap for important items. IT projects should fall into one of the initiatives identified in the plan, thus eliminating unnecessary projects. Second, everyone will be "rowing" in the same direction. When people row in opposite directions, little or no progress is made in moving the boat forward. Third, the business financial team will have a high-level view of IT funding needs each year. Finally, a strategic plan is a great way to motivate user departments to buy into the strategy because they're intimately involved in the strategy development process. (Hong, 2009)

The plan also helps guide an organization as it formulates its overall IT strategy. While an IT strategy focuses on how IT will help the business succeed, an IT strategic plan is a roadmap to help the business implement those strategies. The plan outlines areas where IT can contribute business value and where an organization can gain competitive advantage by making the best use of technology resources. The objectives outlined in an organization's IT strategic plan align with the organization's goals and mission but are pliable enough to accommodate new business priorities and technologies that have the potential for driving business growth. It is important for an organization's IT team to know its priorities and identify the IT projects that the business should invest in Rouse (2016).

The IT strategic plan should outline a mission statement that states what it plans to achieve and how the IT strategy relates to the organization's overall business objectives. Often the first step to creating an effective IT strategic plan is to start with reviewing the organization's strategic plan, which helps in identifying the areas where the use of technology can improve operations (Rouse, 2016).

ITSP planning is a guiding management process for the execution of the IT actions of the organization. The need to manage IT investments and the difficulty in having an agile process to support this management pointed to the lack of a model with a tool that assists managers in this task. The goal of this model is to define a set of steps that can help IT managers in the Central Government in the construction, monitoring, and management of its ITSP. In the following sections we will detail the development and management of the ITSP.

The model of design and construction of an ITSP was split into two parts:

1. Preparation, including the steps of Preparation, Diagnosis, and Planning (Actions and Risks);
2. Management and Control.

Figure 1. Model for ITSP preparation and management

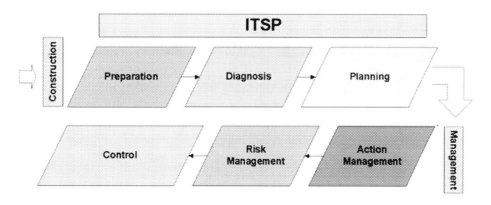

CONSTRUCTION STAGE

The Model for the Development of an ITSP aims at establishing a simple and succinct construction, serving as a tool to aid in the diagnosis, planning and management of IT resources and processes in an agency or entity (DOU 254. 2008; SISP, 2012; Vicente, C.; Celia, et al. 2005; Hazan, 2010; Fagundes, 2011). Below are the steps that make up the development model for the ITSP.

PREPARATION

Information technology (IT) is an essential part of any organization, and with rapidly changing technologies, funding challenges, and conflicting priorities, it's essential for organizations to have an effective plan or roadmap to follow.

Many organizations utilize consultants to undertake the process of creating a plan. This helps ensure objectivity and dedicates resources that can efficiently create a plan, usually within a three- to four-month timeframe depending on the scope of the project and the size of the organization. If an organization believes it has the expertise and resources to undertake the plan creation in-house, it's important that stakeholders outside of IT are directly involved in the plan's creation, as this will help with objectivity and buy-in across the organization. The IT strategic plan should include a SWOT analysis of its strengths, weaknesses, opportunities and threats to identify both internal and external factors that can affect IT's

Figure 2. ITSP preparation model

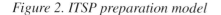

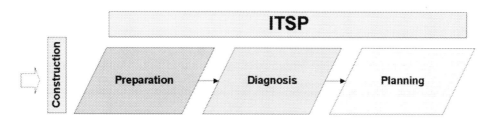

ability to contribute to an organization's success. This process will also help analyze the gap between where the IT department currently is in achieving its goals and what it wants to achieve. The department can then identify the barriers and the resources needed to bridge the gap (Rouse, 2016).

The Preparation Stage represents the beginning of the ITSP development project. The project starts with the IT Committee defining the scope of the ITSP, period and showing the team a draft for the ITSP. This indication is formalized by means of an instrument which confers powers to members, for example, an ordinance designation. Then activities are conducted to define the ITSP preparation methodology, the identification of reference documents, principles, and guidelines, which form a proposed Work Plan to be approved by the IT organization and the maximum authority at the end stage.

Therefore, this stage brings together decision-making aspects of a higher character, document approval and activities directly aimed at preparing the Work Plan, which will guide the conduct to draft the ITSP. There are the team's participation in drafting the ITSP, the IT Committee and Minimum Authority of the Organization.

Before starting the actual development of the ITSP, one should observe the following tasks that make up the first stage of developing the ITSP, which is the preparation stage (SISP, 2012):

- Defining a validity period for the ITSP;
- Defining the scope;
- Defining the construction team and participants in the ITSP;
- Defining the methodology;
- Defining the mission and vision of the institution;
- Defining the documents used as references;
- Aligning the ITSP with the documents of the agency.

The alignment of the ITSP with other planning instruments is to make them compatible, listing requirements already contained in them to prevent inconsistencies and unnecessary expenses, and to boost efficiency.

DIAGNOSTIC

The process followed to develop an IT strategic plan can be just as important as the plan itself. Successful IT strategic plan development should follow a comprehensive process focused on obtaining full stakeholder involvement in all stages.

After the preparation stage, which was organized in the main activities of the project development of ITSP, the second stage of the process begins: the diagnostic stage. This stage is marked by the effort to understand the current state of IT in the organization, in line with this framework, identifying needs (problems or opportunities) whose solution is expected.

This analysis includes processes related to the previous planning, strategic analysis and needs assessment. The analysis of previous planning aims at assessing the status of actions previously planned: the ones is in progress, cancelled, being held now or those in need of re-alignment with the goals of the agency and with IT. Strategic analysis is done to position the IT body in its organizational context. The needs assessment focuses on those related to information and unfolds in all other IT associated elements: services, infrastructure, and hiring staff (SISP, 2012).

It is important to note that this stage requires great interaction with other areas of the organization, as it does extensive data collection and document analysis. One of the key artefacts produced in this stage, and very important in the whole ITSP preparation process is the Needs Inventory. The inventory is consolidated at the end of the stage, from needs assessment to basically all the processes that make up the diagnostic stage.

In the diagnostic stage, the implementation of most of the processes responsible for the development of ITSP team comes up. The IT Committee also acts but specifically to carry the approval of the inventory of needs, after the consolidation from the team preparing the ITSP.

The diagnostic stage seeks to identify internal or external needs that the IT area has to meet. One should remember to include the needs raised during the alignment. The assessment of the needs can be done through questionnaires, interviews, appraisals, a history of the inventories, amongst others.

The following tasks form the IT diagnosis stage (SISP, 2012):

- Raising current IT situation in the body;
- Identifying requirements to be met;
- Evaluating services provided;
- Inventories;
- Filling evaluation forms and interviews with deadlines for replies;

Service evaluation aims at contributing to the improvement of services and giving the IT manager a management tool to make decisions. We suggested the evaluation of the contracted services such as those performed by its own IT area; diagnosing people. Diagnosing people is the identification of HR needs and IT training.

PLANNING

Effective strategic plans help ensure that limited resource and funding can be prioritized for the projects and initiatives that provide the greatest benefit to the organization. Most IT strategic plans are three to five year plans containing goals, objectives, and guiding principles. Some plans are very specific, detailing costs, resources, and timeframes, while others can be more general, leaving it up to the department manager or senior management to determine the specifics to fulfill the goals and objectives.

After the diagnostic stage, in which we analyzed the current situation of the IT organization and identified the IT needs, the third and final stage of the process begins: planning. This stage is marked by planning to meet the needs, setting up plans and actions appropriate to achieve the expected goals. For this purpose, it includes processes related to prioritizing needs and planning goals and actions, covering aspects of personnel, budget and risks (Mcnurlin & Sprague, 2003).

The IT Committee also acts but specifically to perform the update of the criteria for prioritization and risk acceptance, to approve the plans and ultimately towards the adoption of the ITSP draft. The last stage of this process is the publication of the ITSP.

At this stage, a priority has to be set for each requirement, and one or more actions to meeting each one. These actions may involve the contracting of services, equipment acquisition or the use of one's own resources, including human, for its development.

The following tasks form the IT diagnosis stage (SISP, 2012):

- Defining actions to be taken to meet needs;
- Defining the execution mode for the actions;
- Action planning. Identifying, for each requirement listed in the previous stage, the priority goals and actions needed to achieve them;
- People planning. Identifying HR needs arising from activities not addressed in execution planning;
- Execution Planning. Seeks to identify the human and budgetary resources needed to carry out the planned action to meet the needs and estimate the deadlines for start and completion of the actions.

One of the key artefacts produced in this stage, very important to the whole process of preparing the ITSP is the Planning of Goals and Actions. It has data on the indicators, the responsible for each action, deadlines and resources (human and budgetary) to be used by the actions. At the end of this stage, the draft ITSP is consolidated by the ITSP development team, as approved by the Committee and published by the Higher IT Authority. At the planning stage, the ITSP development team is accountable for the implementation of many of the processes (Lutchen, 2004).

MANAGEMENT STAGE

Critical success factors (CSFs) influence whether IT can achieve its stated goals. CSFs are normally point-in-time items, meaning they can change depending on the criticality they have on the current business and IT environments. The environment keeps changing, so CSFs may also change accordingly. Some CSFs that could affect a strategy's implementation include the following (Hong E. K, 2009):

- **Customer Satisfaction:** IT must establish formal partnerships with its customers, understand their business requirements, and consistently exceed customer service expectations.
- **Funding:** As long as there's a demonstrable value to the business, funding must be available for technology initiatives. The business must explicitly define priority-setting criteria to help IT formulate its initiative plans.
- **Culture Change:** IT must focus on providing better services and communications to customers by instilling a sense of urgency, ownership, teamwork, responsibility, and pride in daily activities.
- **Continuous Process Improvement:** IT must continually improve its management processes so that it can deliver responsive, outstanding service to its customers.
- **Buy-in to a Clearly Articulated Strategy:** Buy-in from senior management, business units, and the IT organization is critical to achieving the goals, strategies, and initiatives outlined in this plan.

The IT business model provides the high-level technology direction for the company. It's the basis for formulating the strategic-plan initiatives.

The management model addresses the above-mentioned factors and has three stages, Action Management, Risk Management, and Monitoring, the latter being responsible for managing the other stages. The management of an ITSP should be planned as to facilitate its monitoring and execution (Heeks, 2006; Applegate, Austin & McFarlan, 2007).

Figure 3. ITSP management model

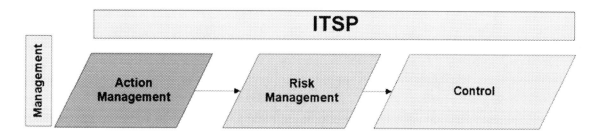

ACTION MANAGEMENT

In the Action Management Stage, it is necessary to identify, for each action, its guardian, its replacement guardian, the terms, and the risks. The planning in this stage is done towards the monitoring and implementing of the actions set out in the ITSP. The preparation of the action management plan can be made by observing the following tasks (SISP, 2012):

- For each action, identify a person responsible and a substitute;
- For each action, set out start and completion deadlines the Execution Plan;
- For each action, a plan can be made separately, a document of which will be referred to as 'detailing' of the action;
- For each action, list the estimated budget resources for its development.

RISK MANAGEMENT

Risks can come from various sources including uncertainty in financial markets, threats from project failures (at any phase in design, development, production, or sustainment life-cycles), legal liabilities, credit risk, accidents, natural causes and disasters, deliberate attack from an adversary, or events of uncertain or unpredictable root-cause. There are two types of events i.e. negative events can be classified as risks while positive events are classified as opportunities. Several risk management standards have been developed including the Project Management Institute, the National Institute of Standards and Technology, actuarial societies, and ISO standards. Methods, definitions and goals vary widely according to whether the risk management method is in the context of project management, security, engineering, industrial processes, financial portfolios, actuarial assessments, or public health and safety.

Strategies to manage threats (uncertainties with negative consequences) typically include avoiding the threat, reducing the negative effect or probability of the threat, transferring all or part of the threat to another party, and even retaining some or all of the potential or actual consequences of a particular threat, and the opposites for opportunities (uncertain future states with benefits).

Planning Risk Management is the identification of each action, the main risks that could result from their full or partial non-performance. For each risk identified, one should set one or more preventive measures and contingency plan, as well as their caretakers. For an effective monitoring identification of the actions, time, responsible human resources involved, type, and value budget. It is necessary to create control points through indicators (Grembergen, 2004).

CONTROL

The ITSP establishes a set of Strategic Objectives and Strategic Guidelines to guide IT management. To achieve this new IT management position, we established a set of actions to be carried out by the Strategic Guidelines and by the associated Strategic Objectives.

ITSP monitoring is based on the execution of these actions, to establish a relationship with the Objectives and Strategic Guidelines (Gottschalk, 1999). The advice from Action Planning monitors the progress of actions where the information is obtained from the actual start and finish projects.

METRICS AND MONITORING

The metrics of the actions will be used to evaluate the progress of the ITSP. The goal is to guide ITSP development to achieve the goals set by the institution in adapting their strategies for IT.

The metrics are defined based on the following schedule parameters (ITSP BH, 2010):

- Percent Complete (%) = Display value after completion of the project or values calculated from actual start date and Actual End of project;
- Variation of Completion (Days) = Conclusion - Conclusion Baseline;
- Variation of Begin (Days) = Begin - Begin Baseline;
- Variation of Duration (Days) = Duration - Duration Baseline.

The Variation Analysis at Start and End can be done with the following parameters (ITSP BH, 2010):

- If Variation of Completion and Variation of Begin is larger than zero it means that there were delays in projects that make up the guidelines;
- If Variation of Completion and Variation of Begin is less than zero it means that there was an anticipation of the projects that make up the guidelines;
- If the Variation of Completion is greater than zero and Variation of Begin is less than zero it means that more time has been spent for projects that make up the guidelines;
- If the Variation of Completion is less than zero and Variation of Begin is larger than zero, it means that less time was spent for projects that make up the guidelines.
- If the dispersion is concentrated in the quadrant in which the variation of completion is less than zero, it indicates better performance in project development;
- Variation of the Duration indicates how much time was spent, whether more or less, in the development of a project.

It is the information that supplements the Variation of Completion and Begin.
Time variation analyses can be:

- If the Variation of Duration is greater than zero, it indicates that more time was spent developing the project;
- If the Variation of Duration is less than zero, it indicates that less time was spent developing the project.

The Percentage Complete (%) indicates how a strategic direction has been met, and the execution of the guidelines indicates how a Strategic Goal is met.

EVALUATION (CASE STUDY)

To support the construction and development of the ITSP a computational tool was designed and built, whose goal is to implement the collaborative model presented in this work. A tool split into two modules, construction module and ITSP management module.

Systems that support ITSP development and management are rare and similar solutions were not found, only some portals or sites serving as hosts for artefacts and documents related to ISTP development, available for reading without any interaction.

This chapter presents the design, implementation and analysis of the case study conducted to evaluate the model of collaborative development and management of the Master Plan for Information Technology built into the tool. This study aims to qualitatively analyze the model proposed model and validate our hypotheses and identify possible flaws and/or paths to improvement.

The goals is to present a brief assessment and demonstrate how this collaborative model can provide improvements in the process to create and manage an ITSP in Government institutions. It is important to point that the participants in this who used and evaluated the model and tool are IT committee members and have participated in the development and management of other ITSPs.

This review involves the study of a real case in the whole process of developing and managing an ITSP in a federal institution. The reason why the identity of the public corporation is preserved is the fact that the institution would not like to see their strategic information publicized. It will therefore be referred to as Institution X.

The team selected is part of the company's IT Committee and all have participated in the ITSP preparation and management before, which makes the assessment tool and results considerable. The table below shows the profile of the team chosen in the case study.

Table 1. Team profile

Profile	Quantity
Director	2
Manager	9
Advisor	6
Analyst	3
Total	**20**

CASE STUDY PROJECT

The project consists of the following steps:

- Definition of the team;
- Train staff to use the tool and the knowledge model;
- Preparation of Master Plan for Information Technology;
- Management Master Plan for Information Technology;
- Assessment Tool;
- Evaluation of results.

The expectation for the case study is that the collaborative model and the tool meet the objectives of the IT committee, assisting in its preparation and management.

The assessment tool and model were also done according to a series of questions designed in a discussion forum with the committee where people talked about how they might be evaluating the model and tool.

Data collection was done through this questionnaire answered by the team drafting the ITSP, also in a survey to identify the period where the activities were performed.

STRENGTHS

Employees engaged in work, tech staff with high degree of technological expertise, interest of the institution in adapting its technology direction to facilitate goals, experienced employees, strong technological structure, good work environment, reference in technology, despite the loss of professionals, employees who believe in the company, training for professionals, expertise in Government work, and an ability to overcome challenges.

WEAKNESSES (NEEDS)

Understanding business drivers, management expectations, and customer requirements for IT solutions is important. IT goals and strategies must align with business needs. As the business environment changes, the IT strategy must also change so that it always aligns with the business.

This activity, based on the evaluations of the previous activity, the ITSP design projects a map of IT needs. TheITSP team should first list the information are exchanged with external organs manually or partially automated, since the listed items are candidates to turn into automation demands. For this, it is necessary to determine how the information is generated internally and which characteristics of the data exchanged.

Another way to identify IT needs is to use issues associated with the systems, carried out in each department. In this way, each system, it is possible to tabulate information on several factors, such as: interface, usability, security, reliability, suitability of the infrastructure that supports the systems, strengths, common problems, processes attended and not, demands of new systems and additions of functionalities to the systems. This tabulation enhances the perception needs. (Fagundes, 2011)

Lack of uniformity in IT standards, failure to plan mid and long-term technology in government changes, lack of staff to meet IT demands, insufficient processes, documentation, and workflows, dispersion of resources at the front desk, making it difficult to work, lack of technological forecasting, no ownership and no project cost estimate to allow a comparison between doing the work internally or outsourcing it, lack of tools for more productive work (hardware and software).

OVERALL ASSESSMENT

A general evaluation of the collaborative model and tool as regards productivity, strategic alignment, diagnosis, outcome and ITSP management proved to be efficient and effective mainly due to the perfect alignment provided, strategic plan, and requiring less effort from the team to act on its activities identification of IT strategies, needs, goals, actions, diagnosis, and ITSP management. The graph below shows the results achieved in terms of needs, goals and actions identified by the use, before and after the model.

CONCLUSION

The implementation of governance mechanisms to the present model has the objective of establishing an environment for the definition of rules and decision making to increase the capacity to execute and monitor the results of the ITSP, making possible the transparency in the application of resources and obtaining results of the institution.

The ITSP aims at guiding an organization in the use of their information technology resources, leading to focus on continuous improvement processes of governance. An institution with an ITSP in place is based on the principles of rationality, economy, uniformity and standardization, creating the technological basis to perform, with enhanced efficiency and effectiveness, of public policies.

Figure 4. Results achieved with the model

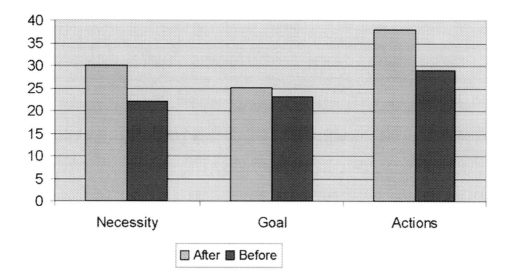

A lack of IT planning can produce an insufficient understanding of the external and internal environment of the organization and emerging technologies that can add value to customer services. This situation can lead to inadequate investments in IT, considering the need of the organization to overcome their challenges. Indeed, an ITSP is a strategic tool to direct and manage Information Technology resources aligned with the strategic priorities of the organization.

It is important to point the dynamism of strategic planning due to the fact of the instability of technology environments, which are constantly evolving. Thus, the ITSP should be reviewed annually to align the strategies with the organization's mission, considering the action of the body, as well as issues related to technological evolution.

The development of an ITSP brings many benefits, such as a complete view of the Information Technology environment, more accurate decision-making, focus on the needs of end-affairs of the institution, amongst others. In addition, the work done in evaluating the model allowed the following benefits:

- A set of data elements that allows a consistent view of the IT environment in the institution;
- Enabling interaction between different areas in the institution and other units in aligning objectives and efforts to IT development;
- Creating an initial portfolio of programs (projects) to guide consolidated investments in IT, and therefore its growth and evolution.

Given this scenario, we see the importance of a methodology that supports ITSP development, while contributing to add value to a business organization, public or private.

To check the feasibility of the model we decided to make a practical application, and the results demonstrate that the proposed model boosts the ability of adaptation to the specific characteristics of organizations, facilitates communication between different levels, and presents a harmonic thread between each layer.

Also important, to follow the process proposed in the model, the development team had little difficulty in understanding why the acceptance of the model was quick. Thus, the positive impact is seen in the motivation and commitment of those involved in drafting the ITSP.

With the establishment of an organized and structured process of ITSP drafting, organizations gain benefits ranging from the implementation process organized logically to the expansion of self-organization. Thus, budget projection, planning of hiring or taking proactive actions can now be grounded in knowledge generated by ITSPs and strategic planning, increasing the competitive edge of the institution.

FUTURE WORKS

According to Tonelli (2015), Information and Communication Technology - ICT every day shows its ability to revolutionize administrative practices and processes and to bring the relationship between State and Public Institutions closer together. ICT reduces bureaucratization of public administration, also serving as an instrument of transparency.

The General Information and Communication Technology Strategy (EGTIC) of the Ministry of Planning, Budget and Management comprises a management tool for the Information Technology Resources Management System (SISP), which outlines the directions of Information Technology and Communication (ICT).

EGTI defines a reference model that aims to promote continuous improvement of ICT management and governance, support for infrastructure, as well as subsidize public institutions in the development of Information Technology Planning.

However, the reference model, along with the model presented in this article, provides PDTI with an approach focused on IT procurement planning, needs assessment (IT inventory), and prioritization of IT needs, including the identification of an estimate budget to meet the needs that are prioritized (Brasil, 2014). It is necessary to align the goals and projects resulting from the ITSP to the strategies and objectives of the organization involving the top management in the decisions, besides adopting practices of governance that allow the delivery of value to the institution adding more intelligence and rationality to the processes related to the TIC, allowing economies scale and resource savings (Kooper, 2011). In the IT governance context, processes involve the organization's approach to monitoring results of IT assessment and setting directions, rules, and recommendations related to IT (Tonelli, 2015).

There is a general consensus in the literature that IT governance arrangements are implemented by mechanisms on structural, procedural and relational level (Winkler, 2013). The COBIT 5 aims to provide a comprehensive framework (good practices) that helps organizations reach their goals and deliver value with effective governance and IT management strategies (ISACA, 2012).

As future work, we suggest the introduction to the presented model a strategic dimension with IT governance processes having COBIT 5 (ISACA, 2012) as a common base implemented by mechanisms on structural, procedural and relational level will enable to guide the strategic decisions with the support of the ITSP results. These governance processes will may improve the targeting of planning, development, implementation and monitoring of ITSP.

This strategic dimension will align the institution strategy and plans with the ITSP plan aiming at stimulate the rational use of information technology to improving the quality and productivity of the IT services. These processes will contribute to alignment between ITSP results and strategic plan as they aim to ensure that identified IT projects and services are delivered the expected value to the public administration. These processes will be vital for IT governance practices such as technology acquisition and approval process and major system prioritizing in the Public Organizations (Demand and Supply).

REFERENCES

Applegate, L. M., Austin, R. D., & McFarlan, F. W. (2007). *Corporate Information Strategyand Management: Text and Cases* (7th ed.). McGraw-Hill Irwin Publishers.

Blili, S., & Raymond, L. (1993, December). Information technology: Threats and opportunities for small and medium-sized enterprises. *International Journal of Information Management*, *13*(6), 439–448. doi:10.1016/0268-4012(93)90060-H

Brazil. (2014). *General Strategy of Information Technology and Communications 2014-1015*. Ministry of Planning, Budget and Management – Brasília.

Burn, J. M., & Szeto, C. (2000). A comparison of the views of business and IT management on success factors for strategic alignment. *Information & Management*, *37*(4), 197–216. doi:10.1016/S0378-7206(99)00048-8

Chan, J. O. (2005). Enterprise Information Systems Strategy and Planning. *The Journal of American Academy of Business, Cambridge, 6*(2), 148–153.

Da Silva Cruz, C. (2009). *Elaboration The Information Technology Strategic Plan - ITSP*. Brasília, Brazil: ENAP.

Doherty, N. F., Marples, C. G., & Suhaimi, A. (1999). The relative success of alternative approaches to strategic information systems planning: An empirical analysis. *The Journal of Strategic Information Systems, 8*(3), 263–283. doi:10.1016/S0963-8687(99)00024-4

DOU 254. (2008). Brazilian Federal Official Gazette, No. 254 of Dec 31st, 2008.

Fagundes, V. (2011). *PDGovTI – A Model of The Information Technology Strategic Plan: Based on Enterprise Architecture and IT Governance the Government*. Federal University of Rio de Janeiro.

Gottschalk, P. (1999). Strategic information systems planning: The IT strategy implementation matrix. *European Journal of Information Systems, 8*(8), 107–118. doi:10.1057/palgrave.ejis.3000324

Grembergen, W. V. (2004). Strategies for Information Technology Governance. Idea Group Publishing. doi:10.4018/978-1-59140-140-7

Hazan, C. (2010). Definition of a Methodology for Development the ITSP based on Zach Framework. *WCGE*.

Heeks, R. (2006). *Implementing and Managing eGovernment: An international text*. London: SAGE Publications.

Hong E. K. (2009). Information Technology Strategic Planning. *IT Professional, 11*(6).

ISACA. (2012). *COBIT 5. Corporate Model for IT Governance and Management of the Organization*. ISACA.

ITSP BH. (2010). *Information Technology Strategic Plan*. Available at: http://itsp.pph.com.br

Kooper, M. N., Maes, R., & Roos Lindgreen, E. E. O. (2011). On the governance of information: Introducing a new concept of governance to support the management of information. *International Journal of Information Management, 31*(3), 195–200. doi:10.1016/j.ijinfomgt.2010.05.009

Lutchen, M. D. (2004). *Managing IT as a business: a survival guide for CEOs*. John Wiley & Sons, Inc.

Mcnurlin, B. C., & Sprague, R. H. (2003). *Information Systems Management in Practice (6th ed.)*. Prentice Hall.

Microsoft. (2011). *Governance Manual*. Available at http://www.microsoft/brasil/setorpublico/governanca/pdti

Normative Instruction 04. (2008). MPOG (Ministry of Planning and Budget) – SLTI (Department of Logistics and Information Technology).

Rezende, D. A. (2003). Computing and Information Systems Planning. Atlas.

Rouse, M. (2016). *IT strategic plan (information technology strategic plan)*. Available at https://searchcio. techtarget.com/definition/IT-strategic-plan-information-technology-strategic-plan

Silva, W. N., Vaz, M. A., & Souza, J. M. (2012). A Collaborative Model of Information Technology Strategic Plan for the Government Sector. IADIS Collaborative Technologies.

SISP. (2012). *Guide for Preparation of Information Technology Strategic Plan. System Administration Resources Information Technology*. SISP.

Stair, R., & Reynolds, G. (2005). *Principles of Information Systems* (7th ed.). Boston: Course Technology, Cengage Learning.

Tonelli, A. O., Bermejo, P. H. S., Santos, P. A., Zuppo, L., & Zambalde, A. L. (2015). IT governance in the public sector: A conceptual model. *Information Systems Frontiers*.

Vicente, C. (2005). *ITCSP – Information Technology and Communication Strategic Plan*. Available at http://www.macmt.com.br/Arquivos/Livro%20PDTIC%20Registrado%20na%20Biblioteca%20Nacional.pdf

Weill, P., Ross, J. W., & Robertson, D. C. (2006). *Enterprise Architecture as Strategy: Creating a Foundation for Business Execution*. Harvard Business School Press.

Winkler, T. J. (2013). IT Governance Mechanisms and Administration/IT Alignment in the Public Sector: A Conceptual Model and Case Validation. *Wirtschaftsinformatik Proceedings*. Retrieved from http://aisel.aisnet.org/wi2013/53

KEY TERMS AND DEFINITIONS

Brazilian Planning, Budget, and Management Department (BPBMD): A ministry of Brazil. Its function is to plan a government administration, plan costs, analyze a project feasibility, control budgets, release funds to states and government projects.

COBIT (Control Objectives for Information and Related Technologies): A good-practice framework created by international professional association ISACA for information technology (IT) management and IT governance. COBIT provides an implementable set of controls over information technology and organizes them around a logical framework of IT-related processes and enablers.

Information Technology Planning: A discipline within the information technology and information systems domain and is concerned with making the planning process for information technology investments and decision-making a quicker, more flexible, and more thoroughly aligned process.

Chapter 17
The Role of Innovative and Digital Technologies in Transforming Egypt Into a Knowledge-Based Economy

Sherif H. Kamel
The American University in Cairo, Egypt

Nagla Rizk
The American University in Cairo, Egypt

ABSTRACT

Digital technology, artificial intelligence, the internet of things, and innovative technology applications are gradually transforming businesses and governments in emerging markets making them more competitive and offering opportunities for economic growth and prosperity. This chapter demonstrates Egypt's potential to enable a knowledge society through the deployment of emerging technology tools and applications across different sectors of the society. The chapter analyzes the critical success factors that are necessary for the realization of a digitally driven society where information is seamlessly exchanged for the optimal utilization of resources for decision-making purposes at the government, public, and private sector levels. The chapter highlights the need for the formulation of a nation-wide entrepreneurial ecosystem that promotes a tech-startup culture that can effectively contribute to transforming the society by enabling inclusion, universal access to the internet, more diversified educational opportunities and a comprehensive and conducive environment to development.

DOI: 10.4018/978-1-5225-7214-5.ch017

OVERVIEW

Emerging information and communication technologies are transforming the global marketplace into becoming more competitive, agile and dynamic. Consequently, these technologies represent an invaluable vehicle for business and socioeconomic development. They are also providing platforms and innovative organizational structures that are not constrained by distance or time barriers. Egypt, as an emerging economy, has strived to achieve the potentials of ICT since the 1960s and has increasingly invested in building its infostructure and infrastructure in an effort to expand the economy's disposition as an important player in both the regional and global economies. In addition, with the growing influence of the millennials and their tech-savvy, passionate, connected, engaged and exposed young generation, the digital transformation and the impact on the economy in specific and the society at large represents an invaluable opportunity for Egypt (Rizk & Kamel, 2013).

This chapter highlights Egypt's progress towards a knowledge society through assessing the socio-economic implications of the diffusion of ICT. It demonstrates the steps that Egypt has taken towards transforming itself into becoming a knowledge-based society through answering a set of questions. This includes how have the ICT for development policy, strategy formulation and infrastructure deployment evolved? How ICT has become a platform to access knowledge and a vehicle for development towards a knowledge society? What are the challenges hindering the realization of a knowledge society? How can an innovative and entrepreneurial tech-startup contribute in the development of a knowledge society in an emerging economy? What are the human capital requirements needed as an integral element in the development of a nation-wide entrepreneurial ecosystem that can transform the economy? What are the skillsets required to enable the community to be ready for a digital society that is connected and driven by innovation technology platforms?

The Evolution of Information, Knowledge, and Technology Diffusion in Egypt

Through its ancient history that extends over 3000 years B.C, Egypt has witnessed massive information flows from the Rosetta stone and papyrus papers, to the establishment of the Library of Alexandrina. During the middle ages, Arabic manuscripts became one of the most common means for information and knowledge dissemination. In the early 19th century, Egypt witnessed the publishing of the first journal and the establishment of the first national archive system (Kamel, 1998a). However, until late in the 20th century and prior to 1985, Egypt was perceived as being rich in data but poor in information. Computers were viewed as ends and not means; accumulated bureaucracy through red tape and the existence of islands of innovation with no connecting bridges restrained the production of information (Kamel, 1998b).

Moreover, the government focus was more on technical issues and not on decision outcomes; multi-sector coordination was poor and synergy between information and socioeconomic development strategies was lacking. Given how important and useful ICT has proven to be to socioeconomic development especially for emerging markets; building the required information infrastructure for Egypt was a necessity and surely innovative ICT presented a good opportunity. The strategy deployed had to have a two-tier approach where society with its different stakeholders can contribute in shaping the infostructure, which in turn effectively contributes in the socioeconomic development and growth. Table 1 demonstrates the evolution of the information society in Egypt over the last four decades (Kamel, 2007).

Table 1. The development of the information society in Egypt

Programs	Year
Open door policy	1974
Economic reform program	1985
Information project cabinet of ministers (IPCOM)	1985
Information and decision support program (IDSC)	1985
National information and administrative reform initiative	1989
Egypt information highway	1994
Ministry of communications and information technology (MCIT)	1999
National information and communications technology master plan	2000
Egypt information society initiative (EISI)	2003
Extending information and communication technology to public services	2004
Information society	2005
Information and communication technology 2007-2010 strategy	2007
Information and communication technology 2013-2017 strategy	2013
The cloud strategy	2014
Information and communication technology 2030 strategy	2017

As the impact of ICT on socioeconomic development became apparent, governments around the globe directed investments towards national information infrastructures (Petrazzini & Harindranath, 1996). Accordingly, Egypt has heavily invested in its technology infrastructure and national infostructure to become the platform for the economy's development and growth (Kamel, 2005a). This effort is still in-progress in terms of infrastructure deployment and regular upgrades are taking place to be able to optimally and effectively use ICT as an impact-driven vehicle for development and growth. It is worth noting that it is an evolving process that is iterative and changing all the time to be able to keep pace with the continuous developments taking place in innovative technology applications and platforms. An invaluable component of the infrastructure that Egypt has focused on over the last few decades was investing in human capital with a focus on information and communication technology knowhow and skillset required to compete at the highest level.

In the 1980s, Egypt launched a nationwide strategy towards its socioeconomic development objectives to address national challenges such as debt, a high illiteracy rate, poor infrastructure and reforms. ICT was perceived as a catalyst for the strategy design, development and implementation (Rizk and Kamel, 2013). In 1985, the government of Egypt established the Information and Decision Support Center (IDSC); a think tank affiliated with the cabinet of Egypt. The objective was to develop and implement, using a supply-push strategy, large nation-wide informatics projects to support socioeconomic development using state-of-the-art ICT.

During the period 1985-1995, a government-private sector partnership had a remarkable impact on the build-up of Egypt's infostructure through establishing hundreds of informatics projects and centers in different public and private sector organizations targeting socioeconomic development (Kamel, 1998a). Such projects were considered as major building blocks necessary to establish a full-fledged infostructure capable of keeping pace with global developments. In 1999, ICT was identified as a priority at the highest policy level and consequently a new cabinet office was established; the Ministry of Communication and Information Technology (MCIT). During that period, the ICT sector was perceived as having transformed itself from a sector looking for support and subsidies to a sector contributing tangibly and intangibly to the economy with a total of 5.2 billion US dollars received by the treasury since early 2006 through establishing and expanding the Internet, ADSL and mobile services as well as upgrading the fixed lines infrastructure. Table 2 demonstrates the Internet as well as the telephone subscriptions including mobile and fixed lines and the evolution between 2011 and 2017 (MCIT, 2017; MCIT, 2011a; and MCIT, 2011b).

Building a Knowledge-Based Society

The definition of a knowledge-based society is not a fixed one. It constantly evolves to reflect developments in the field as they unfold. Indeed, the world has seen the multiple evolutions in this domain such as the digital society, digital economy and shared economy to mention a few with more developments and changes expected as a result of the growing implications of the fourth industrial revolution on the digitization of different societies. Therefore, we are already witnessing the development and implications of cloud computing, drones, artificial intelligence, robotics and 3D printing on our daily lives, all have the potential, tools and applications to affect elements of the knowledge economy, including but not limited to sectors such as education, healthcare, real estate, infrastructure and more (Schwab, 2016).

The term *"knowledge society"* was first used in 1969 by Peter Drucker, at the same time where similar notions evolved such as *"learning societies"* and *"lifelong education for all"* (UNESCO, 2005). The concept of a knowledge society is wider in scope than the concept of an information society, in that the latter is based on technological advances, while the former embraces broader dimensions including social, ethical and political ones (UNESCO, 2005). The commission of the European Union characterizes the knowledge society by a number of interrelated trends, including diffusing the use ICTs; increasing emphasis on innovation in the corporate and national context; and developing knowledge-intensive business services. In recent years, this has created a variety of untapped opportunities for different markets both emerging and developed especially with the evolution of platforms that enable the development

Table 2. Egypt Internet and telephone statistics

Indicators	September 2011	September 2017	Percentage (+/-)
Internet subscribers	29.75 million	33.7 million	+ 13.27%
International internet bandwidth	134.72 Gbps	1213.86 Gbps	+ 801.02%
ADSL subscriptions	1.65 million	4.92 million	+198.18%
Percentage of households using internet	34.83%	41.2%	+18.28%
Telephone subscribers			
Mobile subscriptions	78.99 million	99.50 million	+26.96%
Mobile phones penetration	97.93%	110.34%	+12.67%
Fixed lines subscriptions	8.96 million	6.27 million	-30.02%
Fixed lines penetration	11.28%	6.8%	-39.71%

and proliferation of co-development spaces of knowledge including the wikis coupled with the growing digitization trends that are contributing to the democratization of information and knowledge across different communities.

Innovative ICTs for Knowledge Diffusion

Knowledge has the characteristics of a public good; it is non-rival and is arguably non-excludable. As such, knowledge should be available to everyone. Through knowledge, present and future generations practice integration and solidarity. The focus on human rights in the emerging knowledge society emphasizes basic relevant rights such as freedom of opinion and expression, the right to universal and free basic education, the right to freely to participate in the cultural life of the community and to enjoy the arts and to share in scientific advancement and its benefits (UNESCO, 2005). From here comes the role of ICT as an essential platform in developing a knowledge society and allowing for exercising freedom of opinion and expression and of knowledge sharing. This has clearly contributed to the growing digital transformation of different societies including the growing use of smart-phones, mobile-based applications, access to the Internet on the go as well as the growing global penetration and role of social media applications including facebook, twitter, YouTube, Google+ and Instagram where Egypt as a sample emerging economy has seen massive growth since 2010 (Kamel, 2014a and Kamel, 2014b).

A knowledge society requires a certain enabling environment where education fosters innovation, good governance allows for transparency and accountability, and progress in economic freedoms (Arab Knowledge Report, 2009). Universities, education and training institutions from both the public and private sectors need to cooperate to realize the knowledge society paradigm. This is an effort that should start at the school level and should be integrated into the curriculum to impact the mindset of the growing and upcoming generations. The needs of the local and global markets should be met by different education providers where there is urgency for innovative and creative, problem solvers and critical thinkers who are not affected by rote learning and memorization. It is no more about the quantity studied but rather about the quality of the content, the delivery approach and the impact that could be created that could be sustainable and scalable (Kamel, 2016). An integral element in the transformation process to a knowledge-based society is to avail an education system that promotes discovery, innovation and creativity through in-class and extracurricular activities and that encourages freedom of expression and freedom of speech of younger generations so they can express themselves, share their perspectives and engage with the community.

Moreover, culture serves as another important factor in formulating the knowledge society. Basic enablers such as high gross national product per capita, adequate basic infrastructure, lower rates of illiteracy and familiarity with information sources such as newspapers, television and the Internet factor greatly in the propensity of a society to process, produce and consume knowledge (ESCWA, 2007). The gradual move towards a knowledge society is irreversible and regularly expanding, involving massive developments in information and communication technologies that have revolutionized knowledge production and sharing. Moreover, peer collaboration and participation has remarkably democratized innovation and promoted user generated content (Von Hippel, 2005). As the world approaches the third decade of the 21st century, the enterprise business model is changing drastically where innovation is taking center stage and effectively as well as expeditiously contributing to knowledge creation and sharing. For example, Uber the largest transportation company in the world do not own cars; Airbnb, a massive accommodation platform is not involved in real estate; Ali Baba, arguably the largest eCommerce platform globally does not have an inventory and facebook, the 2+ billion users' platform do not generate content. ICTs have been the catalyst for this transformation from vertical to horizontal platforms of collaborative knowledge production becoming a key characteristic of evolving and dynamic knowledge societies and reflecting an integrated innovative entrepreneurial ecosystem that is changing the dynamics in the global marketplace (Kamel, 2016).

The evolution of innovative ICT tools and applications to encompass the different aspects of the knowledge society reflect its growing impact on business and socioeconomic development. Indeed, information has become a basic need of humankind, along with food, clothing and shelter. Technology innovations could have remarkably positive implications for developing nations if they are properly implemented. Therefore, ICTs must never be marginalized in the development process where the main objective should be to improve the everyday lives of community members, fight poverty and advance the development and growth agenda of different societies.

The Digital Divide: Challenges and Opportunities for Emerging Economies

It is commonplace in the development literature that the developing world lacks sufficient access to ICT, a condition often dubbed as the *"digital divide"* that refers to the gap between the *"haves"* and the *"have-nots"*, correlating the possession of ICT resources by individuals, schools and libraries to variables such as income level, age, ethnicity, education, gender and rural-urban residence (Kamel, 2005b). Unaffordable personal computers, poor or limited telecommunications infrastructure (including mobile and Internet access) especially in remote locations, and high illiteracy rates coupled with poor educational systems are a few of many factors that cripple the digital economy in developing countries, Egypt included (Kamel and Tooma, 2005). Characterized by an inequitable diffusion of technology and expertise from North to South and lacking contribution to the creation of knowledge and technologies necessary for development, the digital divide thus affects countries' ability to develop their local economies and compete on the global platform. In the domain of education and learning, digitization, MOOCs and blended learning approaches over an invaluable opportunity to meet the challenges faced by the growing population and consequently enable access universally within emerging economies and especially among underprivileged communities.

There is a clear correlation between countries that score high on the NRI (Networked Readiness Index) and high on the Human Development Index (HDI). World economies have been classified into three tiers based on the degree of progress of ICT deployment from 2001 to 2008 (Dirks, Keeling, & Lyons, 2008). Tier 1 countries include 20 countries from Western Europe, North America and Asia-Pacific. These countries are amongst the top 20 in United Nations human development index; they have strong competitive global economies; solid legal and political structures and their governments adopt efficient eGovernment strategies. Egypt is classified as a tier 3-country on grounds of starting the new century with inadequately developed social, economic, political and legal infrastructures. Moreover, ICT influences a very small part of their economies (Dirks, Keeling, & Lyons, 2008). This has been growing in recent years, especially with the proliferation of hundreds of startups that are primarily tech-startups, yet the scale is still moderate to realize the scalable impact given the size of the market and the population growth rate in Egypt that exceeds 2.1% and growing (Kamel, 2016).

Egypt together with other tier 3 countries such as Jordan, India and Thailand suffer from poor social infrastructure reflected in low educational attainment together with wide income variation, high population growth rates, high barriers to market entry and challenges in adopting or developing ICT laws.

Example of which is that according to the Ease of Doing Business Index, Egypt ranked in 2017 128th out of 190 countries worldwide (Doing Business Report, 2018) indicating the changes that need to be introduced to encourage business development, innovation, creativity, and foreign direct investment, all contributing to the creation of an open knowledge society. These shortcomings hinder the level of ICT deployment and use that could realize the effective impact targeted. Dirks, Keeling and Lyons explain that Egypt is a good example of a country that continues to direct efforts to developing its digital tele-communications infrastructure and on developing an enabling environment for ICT adoption to allow widespread efficient ICT deployment. However, low performance in areas such as encouraging consumer and business adoption of ICT continues as a socioeconomic obstacle hindering deployment (Dirks, Keeling, and Lyons, 2008). It is worth noting that the maturity and penetration of technology utilization in Egypt at the individual level is more advanced than the private sector and government agencies. For example, in the space of small and medium-sized enterprises (SMEs) in Egypt, only 7% have presence online (Kamel & Abouseif, 2015).

The challenge for developing countries lies in having a clear, implementable vision of how to harness the power of ICT in socioeconomic development. Clearly, the digital divide can and does extend beyond the inequality in access to technology. ICT is but one component of the knowledge society; inequality in technology access can be seen as part of a wider digital divide that is itself a developmental divide (Rizk and Kamel, 2013). Egypt's current policies and strategies are geared towards addressing the connectivity obstacles. However, attention also needs to be directed towards improving the legal and regulatory environment, to capacity development and raising awareness. Moreover, there is a need to focus on the development of efficient mechanisms to strengthen collaboration between different sectors in the economy and to facilitate the deployment of ICT to the benefit of sustainable development through cultural adaptation and localization. One challenge is using ICT as a platform for knowledge dissemination in both major and peripheral cities as well as underprivileged communities. Universal access is an integral element in enabling a societal transformation and the creation of a knowledge society.

Building Egypt's Knowledge Society

With the latest estimates of Egypt population of more than 100 million, Egypt is the most populous country in the Middle East (CAPMAS, 2018). About 30% of its population is enrolled in educational programs, schools and universities accordingly, 58% are under the age of 25. Today, SMEs employ the majority of the workforce in Egypt, around 75%, and account for 80% of the nation's GDP; many are led by women and 90% of the total volume of establishments are family businesses. The economy is increasing at a rate of 4.1% (The World Bank, 2017). However, such challenge is always challenged by the population growth that exceeds 2.1% (Kamel, 2016). Egypt's liberalization of its public sector involves investing heavily in its human capital, encouraging foreign direct investment and using ICT as a platform for business and socioeconomic development. Public-private sector partnerships have been introduced in several economic sectors such as education and health, and government reform is targeting both inter and intra digital divides in an aim to promote social inclusion. However, since 2011, there has been a number of setbacks economically for a few years but the numbers, including tourism figures started to see some promising improvement since 2016.

Information is power, and it is a factor in the manipulation of discourse about socioeconomic reform (Stiglitz, 2002). Historically in Egypt, the government has dominated the supply of information. However, the number of entities generating information is expanding and the quality of their service is improving.

Social media is playing a major role in that domain as part of the growing global trends in the access and democratization of knowledge. Over the last two decades, the government has steadily opened more information to the public, as indicated earlier through the experience of IDSC. The process of information sharing and dissemination was orchestrated by a number of public and private sector organizations led by the Central Agency for Public Mobilization and Statistics (CAPMAS), considered the official source of data in Egypt (El-Mikawy and Ghoneim, 2005). Established by a presidential decree number 2915 in 1964, CAPMAS has since been the official source of data collection in Egypt, collating field data and data from other government agencies.

Over the years, CAPMAS made information publicly available to researchers and businesses in conjunction with other research centers like the Center for Economic and Financial Research and Studies (CEFRS), the Egyptian Center for Economic Studies (ECES) and the Economic Research Forum for Arab Countries, Iran and Turkey (ERF); in addition to IDSC, and other private players that are driven by advanced and innovative technology platforms that transformed information from being a pull to being a push commodity. Moreover, since its inception, MCIT was charged with the task of leading the charge in creating an information society, beginning with the preparation of the national ICT plan which paved the way for Egypt's information society initiative (EISI), which is structured around seven major tracks, each one of them is designed to help bridge the digital divide and progress Egypt's evolution into an information society (MCIT 2005a and 2005b). Table 3 demonstrates the different initial EISI building blocks; however, they were amended and restructured over the years to reflect the developments taking place in the technology space as well as in the society (Rizk and Kamel, 2013).

Creating an Enabling and Conducive Environment for Tech-Startups

The transformation towards a digitized knowledge society in Egypt necessitates the creation of an enabling environment including the design of laws and regulations related to telecommunications, electronic commerce, intellectual copyrights and industry development; investments in human resources; and promoting discovery, innovation as well as research and development. This is an ongoing process as ICT-empowered products and services call for continuous monitoring, evaluation, adoption, diffusion and adaptation since there is no one size that fits all. Furthermore, MCIT took concrete steps like establishing the National Telecommunications Authority (NTRA) and the IT Industry Development Agency (ITIDA) and radically modernizing the Egypt National Postal Organization (ENPO). The continuous collaboration between these institutions and the ICT private sector reflects the invaluable role ICT plays in the economy (Rizk & Kamel, 2013).

It is worth noting that the World Bank outlines the requirements necessary to adopt a knowledge economy which include; (a) a sound institutional and economic regime, (b) an effective educational system, necessary to produce a workforce a qualified workforce (c) establishing and regularly upgrading a telecommunications' infrastructure, an area in which Egypt has made most progress comparatively. Increasingly the availability of information technologies as a public policy objective in Egypt serves in providing the momentum towards establishing a cohesive framework for a balanced, knowledge-producing society. However, these activities and initiatives are at present fragmented and dispersed. It is more of a series of islands with no bridges. To ensure a greater accommodation and use of knowledge in advancing development, these initiatives must accompany public policies that target the creation of an enabling environment that supports the interaction of education, culture, freedom of expression and governance

Table 3. Egypt information society initiative

eReadiness *"Equal access for all"* – Easy and affordable access to emerging technologies – Developing a crucial robust communication infrastructure	**eLearning** *"Nurturing human capital"* – Promoting the use of ICT in education and lifelong learning – Shaping a new generation of citizens who understand ICT and are comfortable with its use in their daily lives both personally and professionally
eGovernment *"Government now delivers"* – Delivering high quality digital government services – Offering citizens, the opportunity to share in the decision-making process – Increasing the level of transparency and efficiency – Combating corruption through digital platforms	**eBusiness** *"A new way of doing business"* – Promoting tech-startups – Improving the human capital skillset – Using electronic platforms – Developing ePayment infrastructure – Using ICT as a catalyst to increase employment, create new jobs and improve competitiveness and agility
eHealth *"Increasing healthcare availability"* – Improving citizens' quality of life and healthcare workers' work environment – Using ICT to reach remote communities to provide medical services – Providing continuous training and development for medical staff – Developing the infrastructure of tools and applications for building a national health network	**eCulture** *"Promoting Egyptian culture"* – Documenting Egyptian cultural identity by using innovative ICT tools to preserve manuscripts, archives and index materials – Offering worldwide access to cultural and historical materials through digitization – Generating and promoting interest in Egyptian civilization and cultural heritage
ICT export initiative *"industry development"* – Fostering the creation of an export-oriented ICT industry – Promoting Egypt as a destination for outsourcing and call centers – Developing an ICT industry that will be a powerful engine for export growth and job creation	

(Arab Knowledge Report, 2009). Commitment to complementary investments in these spheres implies a number of related policy choices that would induce greater value to knowledge-based activities.

Critical to realizing socioeconomic development in the information age is the existence of a win-win partnership between the government and the private sector, not to mention the invaluable role of the civil society. While the framework is not yet defined, the private sector would provide information-based services while the government constructs a supporting regulatory framework based on the greater public participation, engagement and consensus essential for a knowledge society. The development of the knowledge society cannot be left to market forces. Governments, Egypt's included, are responsible for taking a strategic approach to the demands of an information-intensive global environment. This approach should include creating a shared vision of the emerging ICT trends and directions, intensifying the process of information acculturation, generating the necessary human capacities, accelerating the development and deployment of ICT infrastructure, and building a digitally-enabled community including suppliers and users from across the society.

The diffusion of PCs, notebooks and tablets in schools and universities is expected to produce a new larger generation of computer literate users who are different, more willing to take risks, venture into new endeavors and willing to be digital creators rather than just digital consumers. It is important to make use of ICTs across different curriculums that cater to the young population soon to enter the workforce. The pace of technology-driven change creates multiple challenges for using ICT for socioeconomic development in Egypt. With the rapid globalization of trade in services, Egypt should take all necessary steps to profit from opportunities in IT service outsourcing, call centers and more. In addition, the explosive growth in Internet traffic volume and density demands a new cyber-security and governance framework. Moreover, the global shortage of ICT skills represents an employment opportunity for the annual quarter of a million plus university graduates in Egypt (Rizk and Kamel, 2013).

With the development of the Egypt 2030 vision, there is a need to enable an environment that is competitive, agile, and balanced supported by a diversified economy and driven by creativity, innovation, discovery and knowledge dissemination. One of the primary elements to consider moving forward is the participation, engagement and inclusion of the younger generation which represents for Egypt, a unique and invaluable opportunity. Human capital and especially talent empowering is important to enable the digital workforce of the future. This could help transform Egypt into a digital society, develop a more competitive ICT industry and position Egypt as a global digital hub (MCIT, 2015).

Youth, Innovation, Knowledge, and the Impact-Driven Entrepreneurial Ecosystem

Information, technology and innovation are precursors for the knowledge society. The evolution of society towards a knowledge economy therefore heralds a new socioeconomic order characterized by the development and exploitation of ICT within all spheres of human endeavor. Against that background, Egypt has recognized the need to develop its information and knowledge base through substantial investments in ICT and human capacity development, improving access to higher and quality education, professional development and training with an emphasis on creating digital content accessible to the society. Moreover, over the last decade, there has been a growing number of initiatives and players including government agencies, civil society organizations, private sector establishments and universities who collectively have been supporting the development and growth of an entrepreneurial ecosystem with an emphasis on tech-startups through mentorship, financial support, advice, education and more.

It is worth noting that such evolution was the culmination of a number of projects and initiatives that were introduced since 1999 that represented key steps in advancing the nation's economy and society at large to become more information-rich and knowledge-based, which would in turn promote social and economic development. These projects and initiatives include a variety of programs that Egypt has embarked on to further its developmental objectives. Following are some sample examples of these projects and initiatives.

ICT Universal Access to All Egyptians

ICT for all Egyptians is an objective to get everyone connected regardless of their social or economic demographics. It is an an effort launched by the government represented by MCIT to encourage the use of ICT across the nation at the individual, private and government levels. The program had a number of strategic objectives (a) to assist the government policy to integrate ICT in different public services, (b) to foster the inclusion in the knowledge society, and (c) to facilitate the access for all citizens by expanding the reach of mobility, Internet connectivity and broadband to all communities. Sample projects included PC for every home where local and international brand PCs offered from simple models for beginners to high-end desktops and laptops to the entire population through facilitated banking prodecures. The objective was to focus on improving computing distribution across all provinces, with an emphasis on underprivileged communities. The project was realized through a set of public-private partnerships that empower civil society organizations to play a leading role, working with the private sector represented by Internet Service Providers and the government was represented by MCIT which was responsible for policy formulation, strategic planning and building the required capacities.

Another project was the IT clubs which was designed to help in community awareness and developmenty. The clubs are accessible by small businesses, local organizations and individuals and aim to provide different users with the opportunity to become computer literate and electronically ready, regardless of their initial skillset level, gender or income. Some of the clubs were established in universities to bring up-to-date technologies, concepts and trends within reach of all university faculty, staff and student. These clubs were the product of another successful PPP model where all stakeholders contributed. Accordingly, while MCIT provided all necessary equipment, infrastructure and training, civil society organizaitons and universities provided the space and took the responsibility for managing the IT clubs and local ICT companies and multinationals contributed with the training courses curriculum and the training of trainers of different subjects. In addiiton to the mobile units project, and the broadband initiative.

ICT for Education and Lifelong Learning

One of the key piorities of the government has always been deploying state-of-the-art ICT for education, including the optimization of ICT investments to avail the required infrastructure for promoting education and lifelong learning; satisfying the ICT industry training requirements; creating an open learning environment by connecting the education community through broadband; and increasing the efficiency and effectiveness of education institutions by embedding ICT in the curriculum from the schools to the higher education levels. To those ends, MCIT worked closely and strategically with the Ministry of Education (MOE) and Ministry of Higher Education and Scientific Research (MOHE) on a number of projects (MCIT, 2015).

The projects included the Egyptian Education Initiative, a public-private partnership launched in 2006 between the government, the World Economic Forum (WEF), the IT community and different ICT multinationals and organizations operating in Egypt. Bilateral agreements were signed with Microsoft, Intel, IBM, Oracle, Cisco, Computer Associates, HP and Siemens, as well as more than 25 local partners, such as the British Council and the American University in Cairo, in technology sectors from connectivity infrastructure to electronic content development. The overall strategic objective of EEI was to better prepare students to engage in the digital economy by improving the educational content and delivery mechanisms in local schools and universities. The main goals of EEI was to prepare the students and the teachers for the digital workforce by enhancing their effective and creative use of ICT and leveraging national government commitment and corporate citizenship to build an educational reform model that can be exported and replicated throughout the Arab region.

Another project was the Smart Schools Network which aimed to transform the teacher's role from being an information provider to being a facilitator, a moderator by providing a gateway for different schools to the World Wide Web. As well as the ICT for Illiteracy Eradication project which produced electronic content for teaching Arabic and elementary mathematics, based on the General Authority for Literacy and Adult Education curriculum. In addition, MCIT established training of trainers programs in 15 different provinces to serve the growing demand for basic literacy training. One of the most successful partnerships was forged between ICT4IE and Resala Association, a community-based NGO, to CD-based illiteracy eradication courses in different locations. The project has attracted illiterates in remote locations to enroll in the program. With the growing interest in self-education and regular improvement of the tools, CDs and online platforms are meant to shorten the time required for illiteracy eradication.

It is worth noting though that despite the multiple efforts, and the significant progress Egypt realized in achieving its eReadiness objectives, its eLearning programs are generally still at the pilot stage. According to a regional report, Egypt's ICT for education implementation was ranked at a maturity level of two out of four, indicating a number of sporadic projects and initiatives that had concrete impacts, but lacking the consistency and long-term vision for successful implementation and sustainability (ESCWA, 2007).

ICT for Government

MCIT is leading the introduction of eGovernment infrastructure and remains as the ICT advisory vehicle platform for the governemnt and the primary agent for handling partnerships and agreements. The government is attempting to deliver high quality services to the public. eGovernment services ranging from paying telephone bills to enquiring about car license fines and obtaining high school examination results save people time and effort. Yet, the potential for effectiveness of eGovernment in Egypt is strongly limited by low literacy rates. With the digital strategy being introduced and the push for digital transformation, more penetration of digital services offered to the community is expected in the years to come. Recently, there has been a growing interest in digital transformation which could be a game changer for Egypt. However, it requires a different culture and mindset that that should start with proper awareness, education and the proper infrastructure and an enabling and conducive ecosystem nationwide.

Digital Transformation

The digital transformation requires the develoment of digital content that encompasses the creation, design, management and distribution of digital products and services and the technologies that support it. There is a lot of effort that need to be exerted in that direction. The objectives of a digital content platform is to develop an impact-drive added-value Arabic digital content industry and the necessary associated Arabic applications; the use of such platform for socioeconomic development; and the creation of an environment conducive to the sustainable and scalable expansion of this platform to universally spread its use and penetration across the society.

Moving Forward

Despite the progress in technology deployment, there is still some room for acceleration to reach the critical mass of ICT users and level of ICT utilization. Only then can Egypt effectively use ICT as a catalyst for socioeconomic development. Universal access and effective use is mandatory. Therefore, the government of Egypt through MCIT and its different local and international partners continues to amend and iterate its plans and programs to build a knowledge-based society that can help boost socioeconomic development and entice economic growth. Despite the recent accomplishments, Egypt is still an emerging nation in terms of ICT deployment. More time is needed for the efforts exerted to generate a payoff, especially given the size of the population and the different socioeconomic pressures and challenges. Based on the experience of the last few years, attention in the coming phase should be focused on increasing the role of the private sector, addressing priority needs in the education and health sectors, and focusing on digital transformation.

The ICT industry needs more attention on innovation, research and development. ICT is not only a catalyst for development but it is itself an expanding global industry in which Egypt can play an active role. During the last few years, many partnerships have been created with ICT multinationals such as Microsoft, Oracle, Intel and IBM to use Egypt as a hub for exporting services, creating employment opportunities and enabling an inflow of knowledge and research and development. Through specialized centers, these MNCs offer a wide variety of services, including medical, financial and marketing services (Rizk and Kamel, 2013). Egypt has taken commendable steps in advancing ICT with the purpose of utilizing ICT for development. While focusing on ICT is important for the development of a knowledge society, there are other realms that Egypt like many other Arab countries is still considerably behind. The need for an enabling environment remains vital to foster a knowledge society (Arab Knowledge Report, 2009).

There are three pillars that form the core of ICT development that will continue to advance all MDGs. The first pillar is ICT research, which will continue to push the private sector as a world competitor and create new employment opportunities; the second pillar is continuing deregulatory policy that will allow free markets to flourish; and the third pillar is disseminating information access at all levels in the society which will allow the successful delivery of public services, such as eGovernment. The use of public-private partnerships will continue to be instrumental for the government's strategy. The private sector is pioneering new infrastructure foundations such as telecom and wireless technology and the human capital remains the most invaluable element in building a scalable, effective and impactful knowledge society.

CONCLUSION

The role of innovative technologies is undoubtedly impacting the society at large and rendering it more accessible, more knowledgeable, more agile and more competitive. This chapter attempted to share the experience of Egypt in building its infrastructure and infostructure as primary building blocks for the development of a knowledge-based society. The chapter emphasized the integral role that needs to be played by the government, the private sector and the civil society. It is these aligned efforts coupled with a robust, innovative, dynamic educational ecosystem that can help grow an engaged, connected, tech-savvy, and entrepreneurial society which is the platform for a knowledge-based society. To conclude, moving forward Egypt's 2030 ICT strategy should support the development of an ICT infrastructure by thinking, designing and developing programs that can help maximize technology-driven contributions to the economic growth of the country. The strategy could help Egypt be driven and focused by a competitive, balanced and diversified economy, dependent on innovation, creativity and knowledge and based on justice, social integrity, inclusion and participation.

REFERENCES

Central Agency for Public Mobilization and Statistics. (2018). *Population in Egypt*. Cairo: CAPMAS publications.

Dirks, S., Keeling, M., & Lyons, R. (2008). Lessons from global e-readiness trends of national economies. *Proceedings of the VI Globelics Conference*.

Doing Business. (2018). *Reforming to create jobs.* Washington, DC: A World Bank Group Report.

Economic and Social Commission for Western Asia. (2005). *Measuring the information society.* ESCWA.

Economic and Social Commission for Western Asia. (2007). *The Information Society from declaration to implementation.* ESCWA.

El-Mikawy, N., & Ghoneim, A. (2005). *The information base, knowledge creation and knowledge dissemination in Egypt.* Bonn: Center for Development Research, University of Bonn.

Kamel, S. (1998a). Building the African information infrastructure. In P. Banerjee, R. Hackney, G. Dhillon, & R. Jain (Eds.), *Business Information Technology Management: Closing the International Divide* (pp. 118–144). New Delhi: Har-Anand Publications.

Kamel, S. (1998b). Building an information highway. *Proceedings of the 31st Hawaii International Conference on System Sciences*, 31-41.

Kamel, S. (2005a). Assessing the impacts of establishing an internet café in the context of a developing nation. *Proceedings of the 16th International Information Resources Management Association conference on managing modern organizations with information technology*, 176-181.

Kamel, S. (2005b). *The evolution of information and communication technology infrastructure in Egypt.* In G. Hunter & A. Wenn (Eds.), *Information Systems in an e-World* (pp. 117–135). The Information Institute.

Kamel, S. (2007). *The evolution of the ICT industry in Egypt.* In A. Ahmed (Ed.), *Science, Technology and Sustainability in the Middle East and North Africa* (pp. 65–79). Brighton, UK: Interscience Enterprises Limited.

Kamel, S. (2014a). The value of social media in Egypt's uprising and beyond. *The Electronic Journal on Information Systems in Developing Countries, 60*(5), 1–7. doi:10.1002/j.1681-4835.2014.tb00426.x

Kamel, S. (2014b). Egypt's ongoing uprising and the role of social media: is there development? *Journal of Information Technology for Development, 20*, 78-91.

Kamel, S. (2016). Startup, *Global Focus. The European Foundation for Management Development Business Magazine, 10*(3), 52–55.

Kamel, S & Abouseif, M. (2015). *A study of the role and impact of cloud computing on small and medium size enterprises (SMEs) in Egypt.* Microsoft Corporation.

Kamel, S & Tooma, E. (2005). *Exchanging debt for development: lessons from the Egyptian debt-for-development swap experience.* Cairo: Economic Research Forum and Ministry of Communications and Information Technology, September.

Ministry of Communications and Information Technology. (2005a). *Egypt information society initiative* (4th ed.). Cairo: MCIT Publications.

Ministry of Communications and Information Technology. (2005b). *Building digital bridges: Egypt's vision of the information society.* Cairo: MCIT Publications.

Ministry of Communications and Information Technology. (2011a). *ICT Indicators in Brief September Issue*. Retrieved from http://www.mcit.gov.eg/Publications

Ministry of Communications and Information Technology. (2011b). *Information and Communications Technology Indicators Bulletin June Issue*. Retrieved from http://www.mcit.gov.eg/Publications

Ministry of Communications and Information Technology. (2015). *ICT Indicators in Brief December Issue*. Retrieved from http://www.mcit.gov.eg/Publications

Ministry of Communications and Information Technology. (2017). *ICT Indicators in Brief September Issue*. Retrieved from http://www.mcit.gov.eg/Publications

Petrazzini, B. H. G. (1996). Information infrastructure initiatives in emerging economies: the case of India. In The National Information Infrastructure Initiatives. Cambridge, MA: Massachusetts Institute of Technology Press.

Arab Knowledge Report. (2009). *Towards productive intercommunication for knowledge*. Dubai: Mohammed bin Rashid Al-Maktoum Foundation and United Nations Development Programme.

Rizk, N., & Kamel, S. (2013). ICT and building a knowledge society in Egypt. *International Journal of Knowledge Management*, 9(1), 1–20. doi:10.4018/jkm.2013010101

Schwab, K. (2016). *The fourth industrial revolution*. London: Penguin Random House.

Stiglitz, J. (2002). *Transparency in government. In The right to tell: the role of mass media in economic development* (pp. 27–44). Washington, DC: World Bank Publications.

UNESCO. (2005). *Towards knowledge societies*. Paris: United Nations Educational, Scientific and Cultural Organization.

Von Hippel, E. (2005). *Democratizing innovation*. Cambridge, MA: MIT Press.

World Bank. (2017). *Egypt's economic outlook*. Washington, DC: World Bank publications.

Chapter 18
Utilizing the Technology–Organization–Environment Framework to Examine the Adoption Decision in a Healthcare Context

Colleen Carraher Wolverton
University of Louisiana at Lafayette, USA

Patricia A. Lanier
University of Louisiana at Lafayette, USA

ABSTRACT

For several decades the information systems field has studied the individual-level information technology (IT) adoption decision. With the mounting pressure to invest in updated technologies and governmental pressure to implement electronic medical records (EMR), the healthcare industry has searched for factors which influence the adoption decision. However, the adoption rate of ERM has been low due to resistance. In this study, the authors examine why traditional models of adoption which focus on the perceptions of the individual towards the innovation (or a micro-level of analysis) have been inadequate to explain ERM adoption issues. Thus, they examine the broader context within which the adoption/non-adoption decision takes place (or a macro-level of analysis), which incorporates the environmental pressures playing a role in the adoption decision. In this study, the authors adopt the technology-organization-environment framework to examine the context of a physician's decision about whether or not to adopt electronic medical record (or EMR) technology.

DOI: 10.4018/978-1-5225-7214-5.ch018

INTRODUCTION

For some time now, the information systems field has studied the individual-level decision to adopt Information Technology (IT) with the chief aim of making it easier for organizations to derive value out of IT by increasing their effective and efficient use of the deployed IT (Venkatesh et al. 2012). In fact, extant research into the adoption of IT has focused greatly on the enhanced features that users engage with when using these innovations and the resulting benefits of these enhancements (Perez et al. 2017). This exploration has resulted in a broad set of theories such as the Unified Theory of Acceptance and Use of Technology (UTAUT) (Venkatesh et al. 2003; Venkatesh et al. 2012), the Task-Technology Fit (TTF) (Goodhue & Thompson 1995), the Perceived Characteristics of Innovations (PCI) (Moore & Benbasat 1991), and others (Schwarz et al 2014). However, since these adoption theories sought to explain how and why users adopt technology, little is known about the behavior of non-adoption.

Although the topic of non-adoption has been discussed within the literature (Bhattacherjee & Hikmet 2007; Lapointe & Rivard 2005; Schwarz et al. 2012), previous work has utilized a micro-level analysis focusing primarily upon the perceptions of the individual towards the innovation while neglecting the broader context within which the adoption/non-adoption decision takes place (or a macro-level of analysis). The micro-level focus on individual-level adoption (as exemplified by UTAUT) concentrates attention on how an individual perceives an innovation and the role of this perception on the decision regarding whether or not to adopt the innovation. In many technology adoption contexts this view will adequately address the key factors influencing adoption; however, conceivably there could be situations in which institutional pressure influences an adoption decision. We suggest that institutional pressure external to an organization may alter the directionality and outcome of the decision. Specifically, in situations in which there is strong institutional pressure, we propose that macro-level factors (organizational and environmental considerations) will be significantly stronger than micro-level factors (innovation-level perceptions) in the adoption decision.

In this study, we adopt the Technology-Organization-Environment (TOE) framework to examine the context of a physician's decision concerning adoption of Electronic Medical Record (EMR) technology. Despite the demonstrated efficiencies of EMR technology, most physicians still express great concern regarding its adoption and implementation (Gregg 2013), Based on these concerns and given the pressure from the United States government for physicians to adopt health record technology), we will examine the impact of this institutional pressure upon the adoption decision, theorizing that this pressure has shifted the salient factors away from the innovation (or micro) level to the organizational and environmental (or macro) level. This study will demonstrate the influence of the institutional impact of government mandated dogma and industry standards on adoption of the EMR technology. Thus, we address a gap in the literature, specifically, a lack of understanding of the relationship between the environmental considerations, the organizational structure, and the individual level attitudes and decisions regarding the adoption/non-adoption decision of the individual.

THEORETICAL DEVELOPMENT

The Technology-Organization-Environment Framework

While many theories exist to explain adoption behavior, few researchers examine macro-level influences on micro-level behaviors. One notable exception is the Technology-Organization-Environment (or T-O-E) framework proposed by Tornatzky and Fleischer (1990). According to the T-O-E framework (Figure 1), there are three elements that influence the adoption decision: the organizational context, the technological context, and the environmental context. Within each of these contexts are specific constructs that determine whether an innovation is adopted.

T-O-E has been utilized as a broad framework to study both individual and organizational level adoption decisions. As summarized in Table 1, aspects of the framework have been employed across a variety of contexts, including cloud computing (Carr 2017; Kasim & Aziati 2016; Liu et al. 2016; Moktar et al. 2016), e-business (Lin & Lin 2008; Oliveira & Martins 2010; Zhu et al. 2003; Zhu & Kraemer 2005; Zhu et al. 2006), ERP (Schwarz and Schwarz 2014; Pan & Jang 2008), Knowledge Management Systems (Lee et al. 2009), e-commerce (Liu 2008; Oliveira & Martins 2009; Teo et al. 2006), EDI (Kuan & Chau 2001), MHRS (Wang et al. 2016), and open systems (Chau & Tam 1997). Furthermore, a review of the literature reveals, constructs within the elements have been conceptualized using a variety of theoretical lenses in order to understand various aspects of each of the environments.

However, the framework is not flawless. As Baker (2012) notes "the majority of the theoretical development that has taken place related to the TOE framework has been limited to enumerating the different factors that are relevant in various adoption contexts" (p. 237). Nevertheless, although it has not been utilized in the most effective manner, we theorize that the framework still provides a valuable lens with which to view technology adoption. Thus, there are two gaps in previous T-O-E framework research that we seek to overcome: (1) A lack of theoretical consistency with the original constructs and (2) A lack of understanding the framework in different environmental settings.

Figure 1. Technology organization environment framework

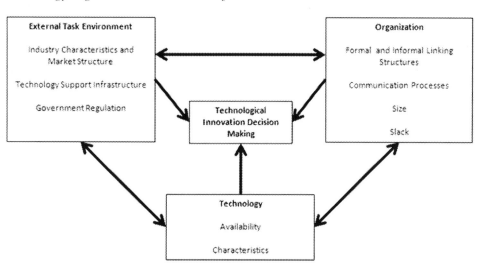

The first identified gap in the literature with the T-O-E framework is the original constructs. We argue that the strength of the framework, namely that it is broad in defining the three contexts has also contributed to the difficulty of the development of a cumulative research stream in this area, namely that there has been little theoretical consistency in the implementation of the constructs. Our analysis of Table 1 highlights that, within each of the dimensions, there has been little consistency in how the technology, organization, and environmental contexts have been enacted, thus contributing to minimal evolution of the theory since the framework was proposed. Awa et al. (2017) reason that the TOE framework often fails due to a lack of clearly defined contexts. Specifically, the original T-O-E framework detailed specific dimensions within each of the contexts (i.e. availability and characteristics within the technology context; formal and informal linking structures, communication processes, size, and slack within the organizational context; and industry characteristics and market structure, technology support infrastructure, and government regulation within the environmental context), yet none of the literature within Table 1 addressed all of the dimensions within each of these contexts. To overcome this limitation, we utilized the original definitions of the constructs and included every dimension within the contexts of the framework to guide the development of our research model.

Table 1. Review of previous literature utilizing the TOW framework

Article	Technology Factors	Organization Factors	Environment Factors	Context
(Chau and Tam 1997)	Perceived Benefits; Perceived Barriers; Perceived importance of compliance to standards, interoperability, and interconnectivity	Complexity of IT infrastructure; satisfaction with existing systems; formalization of system development and management	Market uncertainty	Open systems
(Kuan and Chau 2001)	Perceived Direct Benefits; Perceived Indirect Benefits	Perceived Financial Cost; Perceived Technical Competence	Perceived Industry Pressure; Perceived Government Pressure	EDI
(Lee et al. 2009)	Organizational IT competence; KMS characteristics	Top management commitment; hierarchical organizational structure	With external vendors; among internal employees	Knowledge Management Systems
(Lin and Lin 2008)	IS infrastructure; IS expertise	Organizational compatibility; expected benefits of e-business	Competitive pressure; trading partner readiness	e-business
(Liu 2008)	Support from technology; human capital; potential support from technology	Management level for information; firm size	User satisfaction; e-commerce security	e-commerce development level
(Oliveira and Martins 2009)	Technology readiness; technology integration; security applications	Perceived benefits of electronic correspondence; IT training programs; access to the IT system of the firm; internet and e-mail norms	Internet competitive pressure; web site competitive pressure; e-commerce competitive pressure	Internet Web site E-commerce
(Oliveira and Martins 2010)	Technology readiness; technology integration; security applications	Perceived benefits of electronic correspondence; IT training programs, access to the IT system of the firm; internet and e-mail norms	Web site competitive pressure	E-business
(Pan and Jang 2008)	IT Infrastructure; technology readiness	Size; perceived barriers	Production and operations improvement; enhancement of products and services; competitive pressure; regulatory policy	ERP
(Teo et al. 2006)	Conceived as inhibitors, namely: unresolved technical issues; lack of IT expertise and infrastructure; lack of interoperability	Conceived as inhibitors, namely: difficulties in organizational change; problems in project management; lack of top management support; lack of e-commerce strategy; difficulties in cost-benefit assessment	Conceived as inhibitors, namely: unresolved legal issues; fear and uncertainty	Deployment of B2b e-commerce
(Zhu 2003)	IT infrastructure; e-business know-how	Firm scope, firm size	Consumer readiness; competitive pressure; lack of trading partner readiness	E-business
(Zhu and Kraemer 2005)	Technology competence	Size; international scope; financial commitment	Competitive pressure; regulatory support	E-business
(Zhu et al. 2006)	Technology readiness; technology integration	Firm size; global scope; trading globalization; managerial obstacles	Competition intensity; regulatory environment	E-business

The second gap in the literature that we identify concerning the T-O-E framework is the limited environmental settings utilized to understand the adoption decision. A review of the literature reveals that prior work has examined the T-O-E framework by focusing upon volitional decisions made by adopting firms rather than within the context of heavy institutional pressure. Yet, although firms are constantly under pressure to adopt new operating practices due to environmental influences such as competitive or customer demands, none of the previous studies examined technologies mandated by an external institution. We submit that heavier institutional pressure will alter the salience of environmental factors, while simultaneously altering the influence of the technology and organizational contexts. Specifically, we consider that institutional pressure from the environment could be more significant in driving adoption than assessment of the technology. Nevertheless, without understanding this environmental context, this postulation remains a gap in our understanding of adoption. In an attempt to overcome this void, we applied the T-O-E framework within a context that is currently undergoing significant institutional pressure – the adoption of Electronic Medical Records.

Empirical Context: EMR Adoption

Physicians have experienced strong institutional pressure to adopt Electronic Medical Record (EMR) technology in the United States of America. The American Recovery and Reinvestment Act (ARRA) of 2009 invested nearly $20 billion to facilitate the widespread adoption and use of health information technology (HIT) (Blumenthal 2009). This funding provides incentives for physicians who are early adopters of interoperable HIT, but it also enacts penalties in future years for physicians not demonstrating "meaningful use" of EMRs (Miller 2011). In IT adoption theory, these pressures would be deemed coercive (in the case of the payments/penalties) and mimetic (in the case of interoperable network technologies among physician organizations). Institutional theory (macro-level) applied to technology adoption clearly identifies these pressures (Robey and Boudreau 1999; Scott 1987; Van de Ven 2005). Remarkably, although physicians are aware of both the incentives for adoption and the potential penalties for non-adoption, they have been slow to adopt the technology (DesRoches et al. 2008). As of 2017, only 67% of office-based physicians had adopted an EMR systems that at least met the criteria for a basic system (SK&A 2017). Moreover, some states' adoption rates were as low as 58%. These results suggest that institutional theory drivers (i.e. coercive pressures) were attempted with policy imperatives yet more than 8 years later, they are still inadequate to motivate total adoption.

Yet, with performance expectancy as the most noteworthy driver of adoption (Venkatesh et al. 2003) in combination with the pervasive assumption that EMRs provide numerous benefits once adopted, one would predict high adoption rates. Early findings have provided a variety of rationales for non-adoption of the technology (See Table 2 below). Therefore, we suggest that other factors, such as macro-level considerations, must be influencing the adoption decision. For instance, financial considerations, not included in traditional adoption models, could be causing organizations to pause or struggle in their decision (Reardon & Davidson 2007). Thus, this study seeks to determine the impact of macro-level factors on the adoption decision.

Table 2. Review of previous literature within EMR

Level of Analysis (Most Closely Associated IS Theory Rationale)	Factor	Studies
Macro-Level: (Diffusion of Innovations)	Financial barriers	(Anderson 2007; Ash and Bates 2005; Bates et al. 2003; DesRoches et al. 2008; Gans et al. 2005; Miller and Sim 2004; Reardon and Davidson 2007; Simon et al. 2007)
Micro-Level: (UTAUT: Effort Expectancy)	EMR technology factors	(DesRoches et al. 2008)
Micro-Level: (UTAUT: Facilitating Conditions)	Organizational factors (within hospital or practice)	(Burt and Sisk 2005; Simon et al. 2007)
Macro-Level: (Institution Theory: Normative Pressure)	Lack of standards between EMR systems	(Bates et al. 2003; Simon et al. 2007)
Micro-Level: (UTAUT: Moderators)	Physician characteristics	(DesRoches et al. 2008)
Micro-Level: (UTAUT: Performance Expectancy)	Perceived loss of productivity and time with the patient	(Ash and Bates 2005; DesRoches et al. 2008; Gans et al. 2005)
Micro-Level: (UTAUT: Effort Expectancy)	Concerns over ability to use the EMR system	(Gans et al. 2005; Miller and Sim 2004; Simon et al. 2007)]
Micro-Level: (UTAUT: Effort Expectancy & Performance Expectancy)	Incompatibility with physician work flow	(Miller and Sim 2004)

A Perception-Based Model of the EMR Technology Adoption Decision Using the Technology-Organization-Environment Framework

We propose a model of EMR adoption utilizing the T-O-E framework. This model includes the technology context, the organization context, and the environmental context. In our adaptation of T-O-E, we theorize that each of these contexts are perceived – that the physician possesses an awareness of the role of each of these factors, but that this awareness is focused upon two distinct levels of analysis. From the vantage point of the physician, we theorize that the technology context are micro-level perceptions based upon the narrowly targeted area of the specific technology under consideration. In contrast, we theorize that the organization and environmental perceptions are macro-level perceptions outside the scope of the technology, but that play a role in the EMR adoption decision. A discussion of each of these follows.

The Technology Context

The technology context includes micro-level assessments made by physicians in considering their EMR adoption decision. This context includes both the *characteristics* and *availability* of the technology (Tornatzky and Fleischer 1990). Within our setting, we theorize the technology context as the *perceived characteristics* and the *perceived availability* of an EMR technology. Perceived characteristics focus on how the actors in the firm perceive the technology (an internally-oriented assessment), while the perceived availability is focused on whether there are viable solutions available in the marketplace (an externally-oriented assessment).

We contextualize the characteristics of the technology as the perceived attributes of the EMR technology. While robust theories (e.g. UTAUT, PCI, TTF, et al) define a broad set of potential factors, we selected *quality* since it has been touted as a key characteristic in the adoption of EMR systems (Øvretveit et al. 2007; Shekelle et al. 2006). Systems quality has been found to be a key driver of IS usefulness (Saeed and Abdinnour-Helm 2008) within the IS adoption community, with the argument that a technology that offers a high quality experience will be perceived as more useful and, thus, more utilized (Davis 1993). The importance of systems quality has been codified within the DeLone and McLean model of success (DeLone and McLean 1992) and demonstrated to be important in both a pre and post-adoption context (Nelson et al. 2005). Extending these arguments, we theorize that systems quality will also influence the likelihood of adoption for a physician of an EMR technology. These arguments lead us to the following hypothesis:

Hypothesis 1$_a$: Higher Levels of Perceived Quality of EMR Technology Will Positively Affect the Likelihood of EMR Adoption

The second technology context is the availability of the technology, described as the extent of a firm's technical opportunities in the external marketplace. Research into human behavior has examined the individual's difficulty in making decisions under complex market conditions. For example, Heiner (1983) suggests that an individual will make sub-optimal decisions in a marketplace that is overly complex for the consumer (See also De Palma et al. (1994). Theoretically, the roots of market complexity affecting human behavior can be traced to the argument of bounded rationality (March 1978; Simon 1955). Despite the empirical evidence outside of IS for market complexity influencing human choice, to our knowledge, little work has examined the impact of market complexity on adoption. Therefore, we suggest that if a physician, due to bounded rationality, perceives the EMR vendor marketplace to be complex, he/she will not adopt an EMR system. This logic leads us to the following hypothesis:

Hypothesis 1$_b$: Higher Levels of Perceived Availability of EMR Technology Will Positively Affect the Likelihood of EMR Adoption

The Organization Context

The organization context includes macro-level assessments made by physicians in considering their EMR adoption decision including the following four components: formal and informal linking structures; communication processes; and size and slack. In totality, the organization context includes the processes, structures, and profile of the organization that will facilitate the adoption of the innovation. The focus of the organization context is how the actors in the firm perceive these aspects of the organization (Tornatzky and Fleischer 1990).

The first component of the organization context is *formal and informal linking structures*. These structures are the processes that exist external to the firm to facilitate scanning the environment for information about needs and opportunities for technological change, and to process and transfer the information so that it can support adoption decisions. We contextualize formal and informal linking structures as the formal relationships that facilitate the flow of data about patients from other medical facilities (i.e., hospital and physician practices) to the physician. Researchers and practitioners recognize the need for organizations to integrate both internal and external firm data(Goodhue et al. 1988; Goodhue et al. 1992), with these external sources providing a mechanism through which physicians learn about EMR systems. We therefore theorize that it is through these relationships that a physician discovers information about EMR solutions. This leads us to the following hypothesis:

Hypothesis 2$_a$: Higher Levels of Data Integration With Other Practices and Hospitals Will Positively Affect the Likelihood of EMR Adoption

The second component of the organization context is *communication processes*. While the formal and informal linking structures are external to the firm, communication processes are the business processes internal to a firm referring to how the information about an innovative technology diffuses throughout the organization. We contextualize communication processes as the business processes within firms facilitating the sharing of information. Considerations of information flow are not necessarily new to the IS discipline, yet the focus has been mainly within the context of an Enterprise Resource Planning (or ERP) solution. Previous research within ERP has argued that information flow is crucial in order to facilitate success (Scott 2003). Therefore, if a physician perceives that an EMR will facilitate information sharing[1], then we theorize that the conditions are conducive to the adoption of the innovation. This leads to the following hypothesis:

Hypothesis 2$_b$: Higher Levels of Data Integration Within a Practice or Hospital Will Positively Affect the Likelihood of EMR Adoption

The third component of the organization is the firm size. Scholars lack consensus on the appropriate method to evaluate firm size. However, T-O-E argues that size refers to the amount of work done in an organization and previous studies demonstrate that organizational size influences the adoption of technological innovations (Damanpour 1992; Hage 1980; Kimberly and Evanisko 1981). We contextualize size as the number of patients seen, arguing that a physician who sees more patients will be more likely to adopt an EMR to better control practice workflow. This leads us to the following hypothesis:

Hypothesis 2$_c$: Higher Number of Patient Visits Per Day Will Positively Affect the Likelihood of EMR Adoption

The fourth component in the organization is the slack. The T-O-E framework identifies both financial and human resources as slack resources. The presence of financial slack affords an organization the ability to adopt an innovation and integrate the technology into the firm. It has been found to be a significant driver of adoption (Aiken and Hage 1971; Miller and Friesen 1982). Additionally, it is the least absorbed form of slack and, thus, the easiest to redeploy (Greve 2003; Miller 2003). In our context, we theorize that the availability of financial resources provides the physician the means necessary to adopt an EMR solution. This leads to the following hypothesis:

Hypothesis 2$_d$: Higher Levels of Financial Slack Will Positively Affect the Likelihood of EMR Adoption

Within the context of T-O-E, human resource slack refers to specialized and skilled human resources that are rare and absorbed (Mishina et al. 2004). Specifically, human resource slack is absorbed because "the resources are tied up in the organization's current operations" (Voss et al., 2008 p. 151). In our context, we theorize that the availability of physicians and staff with more free time (or slack) will provide the users with the ability to learn the EMR software. Thus, the presence of human resource slack will give the physician the capability to adopt an EMR solution. This leads us to the following hypothesis:

Hypothesis 2$_e$: Higher Levels of Human Resources Slack Will Positively Affect the Likelihood of EMR Adoption

The Environmental Context

The environmental context includes macro-level assessments made by physicians in considering their EMR adoption decision and includes three components: the industry characteristics and market structure; the technology support infrastructure; and government regulation (Tornatzky & Fleischer 1990).

The first component of the environmental context is the industry characteristics and market structure which refers to differences in competitive and market conditions. We theorize that these differences materialize in the form of mimetic pressure. According to Sherer (2010), mimetic pressure exists when an organization imitates the actions of similarly structured organizations operating in the same economic network and industry Institutional theory suggests that the imitation behavior enables an entity to reduce search costs and is typically more prevalent when questions of relative advantage are present (Shi et al. 2008; Son and Benbasat 2007; Teo et al. 2003; Urgin 2009). Therefore, given the concerns over the advantages that derive from EMR systems and the high degree of search costs with EMR technology, we theorize that the presence of mimetic pressure will lead a physician to adopt an EMR system. Specifically, we suggest that a positive perception of mimetic pressure will lead to adoption. It is the presence of this pressure that leads us to the following hypothesis:

Hypothesis 3$_a$: Higher Levels of Adoption by Other Physicians and Hospitals That Offer Services Similar to the Physician Will Positively Affect the Likelihood of EMR Adoption

The second component of the environmental context is the technology support infrastructure. The technology support infrastructure refers to the constraints or opportunities that a firm must consider when developing its technology acquisition strategy. This strategy depends on labor costs, skills of the available labor force, and access to suppliers of technology-related services. According to the theory of situational normality, when an individual believes that the environment in which a product is purchased is in proper order, success in acquiring and being satisfied with a product is likely because the situation in the purchasing environment is normal or favorable (Baier 1986; Garfinkel 1963; Lewis & Weigert 1985). As example, physicians who possess positive views towards situational normality believe that, in general, vendors offering EMR systems are competent, benevolent, and have integrity (McKnight et al. 2002). In our context, however, we selected one of these three dimensions: whether the physician perceives that there is a vendor who is capable of meeting customer needs (McKnight et al. 2002) in the marketplace. Thus, we theorize that adopters will have a more positive assessment of vendors than non-adopters, leading us to the following hypothesis:

Hypothesis 3$_b$: Higher Levels of Perceived Positive Assessments of EMR Vendors Will Positively Affect the Likelihood of EMR Adoption

The third component of the environmental context is government regulation. Government regulation refers to the pressure imposed upon firms to induce a search for technical alternatives to current practice. In our context, we theorize that government regulation refers to the coercive pressure from state and federal governments to adopt EMR technology. Coercive pressures are defined as formal or informal pressures exerted by other organizations upon which they are dependent (DiMaggio and Powell 1983; Son and Benbasat 2007). Drawing upon institutional theory, we therefore posit that institutions with which physicians are dependent can coercively exert pressure upon him/her to influence adoption. By linking physician service re-imbursement rates to the EMR adoption decision, both government and insurance companies are relying upon formal, financial pressure to influence adoption. We therefore theorize that these forms of coercive pressure will lead a physician to adopt an EMR system. Specifically, we submit that a positive perception of coercive pressure will lead to adoption, while a negative view will lead a physician to reject an EMR system. It is the presence of this pressure that leads us to the following hypothesis:

Hypothesis 3$_c$: Higher Levels of Perceived Government Regulation Will Positively Affect the Likelihood of EMR Adoption

RESEARCH MODEL

Based upon our theoretical development, we propose the research model in Figure 2.

Item Development

With a proposed research model, we will now discuss the creation of our research items. Based upon the definitions of our constructs, we developed items to measure the constructs identified. Where possible, we utilized extant scales to measure each construct. In Table 3 below, we have outlined the construct,

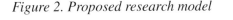

Figure 2. Proposed research model

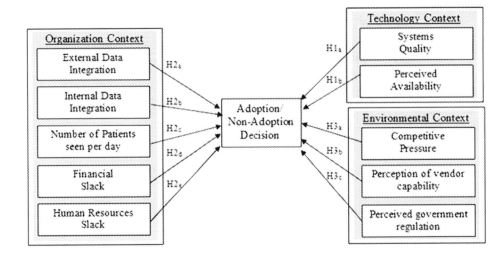

the definition of the construct, the items employed to measure each construct (for both adopters and non-adopters), and the source of the measurement. The dependent variable (i.e. the adoption/non-adoption decision) was based upon whether or not the physician was currently using (i.e. made the decision to adopt) or not currently using (i.e. made the decision not to adopt) an EMR system. The dependent variable was thus binary – with 0 being non-adoption and 1 being adoption.[2]

Sample

In order to test our research model, a survey was conducted with physicians within four regions of the United States, each representing differing levels of EMR adoption. We began by analyzing the adoption of EMR technology by state, focusing upon the adoption of a basic EMR system (based upon the report issued by the Robert J. Woods Foundation (2012). We divided the adoption rates into four groups through a systematic analysis of the adoption rate. First, we divided the states into two groups – those above the mean (20 states) and those below the mean (30 states). Then, within each of the two groups, we divided the groups again. This approach resulted in four groups: Low adoption rate (15.9% to 28.2%), low to medium adoption rate (28.4% to 33.3%), medium to high adoption rate (33.9% to 40.4%), and high adoption rate (41.2% to 60.9%). We then selected one state from each group to analyze in this study and contacted state medical societies to offer an opportunity to be included in the study. Thus, we collected data from physicians within each of these four groups.

Each state in America has its own medical society, which is a voluntary association that provides advocacy and education for physicians within the state. By working with medical societies we have access to a more comprehensive group of physicians, including physicians from various hospitals, rural physicians, physicians across a wide range of specialties, and physicians in private practice, who may otherwise be difficult to locate. We have blinded the specific state names and will refer to each state by its adoption rate. The adoption rates were as follows: the low adoption rate state: 25.8%; low to medium: 31.1%; medium to high: 37%; and high: 54.5%. Table 4 below presents the number of respondents from each state included in the study.

For three of the four states, the medical society for the state distributed the survey to the membership utilizing an e-mail invitation distributed by the leadership of the organization. In the medium to high adoption rate state, the researchers were provided with a one-time use of e-mail addresses from the medical society database, but no contact information was included with this list. In each of the four states, an initial invitation to participate was distributed, along with a follow-up reminder. All physicians were given two weeks to complete the survey.

The invitation directed the respondents to a web-based survey containing our research items. Non-adopters and adopters were distinguished based upon their answer to whether or not their practice (or hospital) had adopted an EMR system. Based upon the answer to this question, respondents were provided with either the non-adopter or adopter items.

Research Analysis

Given that our dependent variable was binary (adoption/non-adoption), we selected binary logistic regression for our analysis. We specified each of the items in Table 3 above as independent variables, with our dependent variable defined as whether or not the physician had adopted the technology. We also included one control variable – the state in which the physician operated, so as to control for geographic location. The results are displayed in Table 6.

Table 3. Research items

Construct		Definition	Non-Adopter Items	Adopter	Source
Technology Characteristics					
Systems Quality		User perceptions of the quality of the EMR system (Nelson et al. 2005)	Overall, I would give the quality of EMR systems a high rating	Overall, I would give the quality of my EMR system a high rating	Nelson et al. (2005
Perceived availability		The degree to which a physician perceives the vendor marketplace to be too complex	The EMR marketplace has too many systems		New item
Organization Characteristics					
External data integration		The degree to which a physician is concerned that other organizations they need to share information with will be unable to integrate with their EMR systems	At this point in time, EMR systems will facilitate the sharing of information between physicians from different practices hospitals	At this point in time, my EMR system facilitates the sharing of information between physicians from different practices hospitals	Adapted from Nelson et al. (2005
Internal data integration		The degree to which a system facilitates the combination of information from various sources internal to the firm (Nelson et al. 2005)	EMR systems effectively combine data from different areas of my practice	My EMR system effectively combines data from different areas of my practice	Adapted from Nelson et al. (2005
Patients seen		An indicator of organizational size, measured as the number of patients seen per day	During your last full week of work, approximately how many patients did you see?		New item
Financial Slack		The extent to which a physician perceives the total cost of an EMR system to be reasonable and should be afforded financial slack	All things considered, the total cost of an EMR system is reasonable considering what you receive	All things considered, the total cost of my EMR system was reasonable considering what I received	New item
Human Resources Slack	Physicians [R]	The extent to which the human resources would be tied up in the organization's operations to engage the new EMR solution (extending Voss et al. (2008)	The time that it will take for me to learn how to use an EMR is significant	The time that it took for me to learn how to use my EMR is significant	New item
	Staff [R]		The time that it will take for my staff to learn how to use an EMR is significant	The time that it took for my staff to learn how to use my EMR is significant	
Environmental Characteristics					
Competitive Pressure		The prevalence of a practice in the focal organization's industry that have adopted an EMR solution (Scott 1987)	What is the extent of EMR adoption by physicians in your area that offer services similar to yours? (None have adopted: 7 - All have adopted)		New item
Perception of vendor capability		The extent to which EMR vendors are competent (i.e. the vendors can do what the physician needs) (McKnight et al. 2002)	Most EMR vendors do a capable job of meeting customer needs	My EMR vendor does a capable job of meeting customer needs	McKnight et al. (2002
Perceived government regulation	Federal government	Formal penalties exerted on organizations by other organizations upon which they are dependent. In our case, we define these organizations as the state and federal government (Scott 1987).	Penalties from the federal government for not adopting an EMR by the deadline will play a critical role in whether or not I adopt an EMR	Penalties from the federal government for not adopting an EMR by the deadline played a critical role in my EMR adoption decision	New item
	State government		Penalties from the state government for not adopting an EMR by the deadline will play a critical role in whether or not I adopt an EMR	Penalties from the state government for not adopting an EMR by the deadline played a critical role in my EMR adoption decision	New item

The [R] indicates that an item is reverse coded

Table 4. Profile of four state contexts

State	Non-Adopter	Adopter	Total
Low Adoption Rate	34	86	120
Low to Medium Adoption Rate	20	66	86
Medium to High Adoption Rate	35	106	141
High Adoption Rate	45	155	200
Total	134	413	547[1]

Table 5. Profile of respondents

Gender	%
Male	72
Female	23
Decline	5

Payment Source	Average Percent
Medicare	34.6
Medicaid	20
Insurance	44.2
Patient	12
Other	21.5

Table 6. Results of binary logistic regression analysis

Variable	B	S. E.	Wald	Df	Sig.	Exp(B)
Systems Quality	.490	.113	18.662	1	.000	1.633
Competitive pressure	.455	.094	23.631	1	.000	1.576
Financial Slack	.408	.127	10.348	1	.001	1.504
Perceived government regulation: federal	.377	.105	12.835	1	.000	1.457
HR Slack: Doctor [R]	.094	.172	.300	1	.584	1.099
External Data Integration	.023	.093	.063	1	.802	1.024
Number of Patients seen per day	-.001	.000	1.565	1	.211	.999
HR Slack: Staff [R]	-.069	.184	.141	1	.707	.933
Perception of vendor capability	-.160	.120	1.771	1	.183	.853
Internal Data Integration	-.222	.088	6.383	1	.012	.801
Perceived Availability [R]	-.231	.093	6.236	1	.013	.794
Perceived government regulation: state	-.292	.115	6.463	1	.011	.747
State			1.005	3	.800	
State (1)	-.306	.330	.857	1	.355	.736
State (2)	-.236	.328	.519	1	.471	.790
State (3)	.234	15684.701	.000	1	1.000	1.264
Constant	17.760	15026.184	.000	1	.999	51674851.385

Note: bolded items refer to the factors that are significant at the level of p < 0.05
[R] refers to items that were reverse coded

[1] Due to the privacy concerns of the medical societies, the link to the web-based survey was distributed by the medical society to their membership database. As membership in a medical society is not restricted to just physicians, an accurate number of practicing physicians (the target population) within the database is unknown or was not provided. While the medical societies indicated to us that the response rate we received was typical, an actual response rate was unable to be calculated.

The results indicate that there were seven significant factors in predicting the adoption of EMR technology, namely perceived quality (0.490), competitive pressure (0.455), financial slack (0.408), and penalties from the federal government (0.377). These results signify that if a physician perceives EMR systems to be of high quality and reasonably priced, another physician similar to him/her adopts an EMR, and the penalties from the federal government are perceived as significant, then a physician is likely to adopt an EMR. Furthermore, perceptions regarding the effectiveness of the integration of the EMR technology within the firm differentiate between adopter and non-adopter physicians of EMR technology (-0.222). Furthermore, if the marketplace is viewed as too complex, then the physician is more likely to not adopt the EMR (-0.231). Moreover, in contrast to the significant impact of federal government penalties, if penalties are from the state, the physician is less likely to adopt the technology (-0.292).

Beyond the interpretation of the beta weights, logistic regression offers the opportunity to determine the extent to which the independent variables can be utilized to discriminate between the two categories. In the table below, the "observed column" indicates the number of individuals who were within each category (i.e. 134 non-adopters and 413 adopters). The "predicted" column displays the number of individuals who were classified into each category, with the numbers in bold indicating the number that were *correctly* classified. As the results in Table 7 below indicate, the independent variables are able to correctly categorize adopters 92.5% of the time and non-adopters 49.3%, for an overall correct percentage of 81.9%. Therefore, these results demonstrate a significant ability to predict the adoption decision.

The results of the classification table indicate that the factors from the Technology-Organization-Environment framework are able to classify adopters at a higher rate than non-adopters. While the model was able to correctly classify non-adopters only half the time, it provides the ability to correctly classify adopters in over 90% of cases.

The factors that are most significant in predicting adoption can be found in Figure 3 below, with the significant paths highlighted. Our results demonstrate that systems quality, competitive pressure, financial slack, perceived government regulation, internal data integration, and perceived availability contribute to the EMR adoption decision, while the other factors are non-significant.

Discussion

Physicians are currently under heavy institutional pressure from both federal and state government to adopt EMR technology. The presence of this strong external pressure provided us with an opportunity to examine how external environmental pressure influences the adoption/non-adoption decision. Utilizing the T-O-E framework, we specified and studied constructs that assess the technological, organizational, and environmental contexts.

Table 7. Classification table

	Observed	Predicted		
		Non Adopters	Adopters	Percentage Correct
Non Adopters	134	**66**	68	49.3
Adopters	413	31	**382**	92.5
Overall Percentage	547			81.9

Figure 3. Results research model

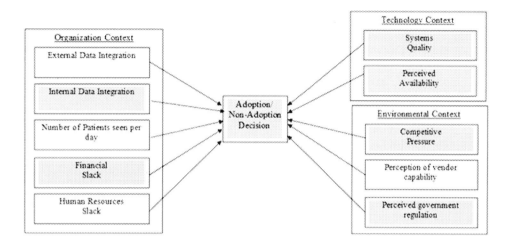

Our results indicate that each context exerts significant pressure on the adoption decision. Specifically, the technological factors of quality and availability, the environmental factors of competitive pressure and government regulation, and the organizational factors of financial slack and effective internal integration[3] are all significant drivers of adoption. Thus, by expanding our view of the factors influencing the adoption decision, we discovered that users want not only a high quality, reasonably priced systems but they also want the system to integrate effectively with other areas of the organization. Moreover, users are influenced by the extent to which competitors have adopted new technology, and they desire more availability of these systems in the marketplace. Government regulation, both from the state and federal government, has also been effective in inducing adoption. Therefore, this study demonstrates the importance of incorporating macro level factors when studying the adoption decision in a context with heavy institutional pressure.

The environmental pressures materialized not from the institutions that are currently seeking to pressure adoption (namely the federal and state governments), but more significantly from other physicians. Competitive pressure was a stronger factor in influencing adoption than either of these two key institutions. This finding suggests that additional work is necessary to understand the nexus of competitive and institutional pressures in organizational decision making. Furthermore, the positive beta weight for penalties from the federal government and the negative for penalties from the state government demonstrate that physicians want EMR adoption to be handled as a component of a broader national HIT strategy as opposed to a more limited statewide initiative. Our findings indicate that driving this initiative at a more localized level is not an approach favored by physicians and may result in lower adoption rates.

Moreover, the findings indicate that while users desire the system to combine data within their organization, they are not concerned about whether the system shares data across different organizations. As internal compatibility is typically a requirement for new technology now, users have developed an expectation that any new IT will seamlessly integrate into the organization. However, integration across organizations is not yet the norm, and users have not developed expectations that technology should be able to seamlessly integrate data between external entities. Thus, users are pragmatic about the limitations of current technology, and they are willing to wait for inter-organizational integration. We posit that users especially in a medical context realize that if a complex technology like the one necessary for external data integration is not yet established and stable, then utilization of it may cause more problems than it may fix. Instead, they desire the more mature and stable technology and do not yet need the untested cutting-edge technology.

When examining slack, we included two forms of slack, namely financial slack and human resources slack. While financial slack was found to influence adoption, human resources slack was unrelated to adoption. Thus, while physicians wanted to see a reasonable cost for the technology, the amount of time it would take to learn the new system was not a factor in their adoption decision. One may surmise that if the physician and his/her staff are spending their time learning the new system, then they have less time to see patients and make money to pay for the new system. However, this finding indicates that physicians believe that it will not take an inordinate amount of time to learn the new system, and that the value of the system is greater than the monetary cost.

Limitations

Our work, however, does not come without limitations. First, we have limited our study to four states within the United States. By utilizing a theoretically-based sampling technique, we seek to overcome this limitation by altering the influence of the environment (a chief motivation for the current study). Furthermore, as most previous EMR studies were conducted within one state or one hospital context, we posit that this study represents a broader study of adoption. Next, we were unable to calculate an accurate response rate for our physicians. However, the medical societies indicated to us that the response rate we received was typical. Third, while the original Technology-Organization-Environmental framework included reciprocating relationships between the constructs, we instead opted to focus upon the direct effects. This decision was made in order to focus attention upon our main constructs and the ability of these factors to explain the adoption/non-adoption decision. Finally, while we have included formal and informal linking relationships as one, we encourage other researchers to examine these two separately to determine their impact (including the role of social contagion). Despite these limitations, the work has some important implications for both researchers and practitioners.

IMPLICATION FOR RESEARCHERS AND PRACTICE

For our colleagues-in-practice, our model demonstrates that with an understanding of seven factors, we can predict the adoption/non-adoption decision correctly 82% of the time. For physicians and EMR providers, quality and internal data integration are the two practice-focused factors that are salient. For policy makers, we urge careful consideration of the role of penalties, the availability of financial slack, and the presence of pressure from other physicians in order to influence the adoption decision.

For researchers, these findings demonstrate the need to move beyond simple models that focus upon micro-level factors to incorporate the broader context under which the adoption decision occurs. In the motivation for our work, we enumerated two limitations of prior work: (1) A lack of consistency in understanding the constructs within the T-O-E framework and (2) Not utilizing the framework where environmental considerations differ. By returning to the original framework, we proposed a model that was theoretically consistent with the original theory. While we recognize that contextualization is necessary, we urge other researchers to utilize the richness of the original theory and to refine the theory rather than simply drawing upon its' broad nature to amalgamate current theoretical approaches under an umbrella framework.

Our second critique was that the environment would influence the adoption decision. Our results validate this critique. However, our findings also demonstrate that the mechanisms that underpin institutional theory are more nuanced – namely that the institutions that seek to exert pressure upon organizations may not be the most salient in influencing that behavior. In our context, one would expect that the penalties from the government (the institution seeking to encourage adoption) would be the most significant influencers of the adoption behavior. However, our findings demonstrate that the competitive pressure that had the strongest impact. The chasm between the institution exerting the pressure and the institution having the most significant impact is an interesting and exciting area of research that we urge others to pursue.

Beyond our critiques, our findings provide a pathway for future research in three main areas. The first is in the domain of non-adoption. As our factors could only classify half of the non-adopters correctly, more work is necessary in order to understand the behavior of non-adoption. An attempt to understand only the enablers (or positively valenced factors) in the adoption decision in the context of non-adoption inhibits us from adequately understanding why a physician (or user) choses to not adopt a technology. According to Inhibitor Theory, inhibitors are worthy of their own investigation (Cenfetelli and Schwarz, 2011), and we urge other researchers to pursue this line of study.

Second, while we have organized our sample into two groups based upon the adoption decision, we acknowledge that the differences in organizational structure and the resulting impact on control may also influence the adoption decision. Thus, a physician in private practice may have control over the adoption decision, while in a hospital, a physician may tend to have less control over (or input into) the decision. We urge adoption researchers to further examine the organizational variables that can explain the differences between organizational contexts as a mechanism to begin to understand the complexity of the adoption and non-adoption decision.

The third implication for future research is for researchers who are interested in the intersection between technology, organization, and environment. We urge other researchers to utilize this framework to begin to understand the intersection of these factors. We argue that the focus on the IT artifact has come at the expense of understanding the organizational artifact and the impact of the environment. The T-O-E framework is designed to incorporate these often-overlooked contexts to provide insights into the broader role of the organization and environment in the adoption decision. We encourage others to utilize this lens to understand how varying organizational and environmental contexts influence the adoption decision.

FUTURE RESEARCH

Researchers have demonstrated that context impacts EMR adoption (Carraher Wolverton, and Thomas, 2018). As the organizational structure in which adoption decisions are made is shifting, our research models must evolve to address these structural changes. Extant EMR adoption work has traditionally examined mainly hospitals, although entrepreneurship is increasing in healthcare. Thus, Carraher Wolverton and Thomas (2018) developed a model demonstrating the differences between EMR adoptions with various related constructs. We encourage other researchers to examine EMR adoption in similar physician-owned practices.

Furthermore, recent research has adopted several lenses by which to examine EMR adoption. One approach has been to study how EMRs influence relationships. For example, Alkureishi et al (2016) demonstrated that EMR use objectively exerts a negative impact on patient-doctor communication. However, patients did not perceive an impact on the level of patient-doctor communication when EMR were implemented. This relationship will continue to transform as technology continues to infiltrate healthcare and dramatically transforms the industry. The assimilation of technology to facilitate the efficiency of routine doctor visits will continue to impact the patient-doctor relationship. EMRs have begun the revolution, but as technology has become ubiquitous throughout business, it will likewise permeate the healthcare industry. Researchers should examine the shifting nature of the patient-doctor relationship and the impact of technology. We posit that an increased understanding of EMR adoption will facilitate an understanding of additional technology disruption in the healthcare industry.

Other researchers have applied novel theories to the context. For example, researchers have applied institutional theory to EMR adoption and found that mimetic forces impact adoption when there is uncertainty (Sherer et al 2016). Our studies should continue to apply novel theories to better understand this unique context.

CONCLUSION

In conclusion, understanding the adoption/non-adoption decision is an important research and organizational-level topic that merits further investigation. In our study, we examined the impact of institutional pressure upon the adoption decision, examining whether the pressure escalates the salient factors away from the innovation (or micro) level to the organizational and environmental (or macro) level of analysis. We have discovered that there is some evidence that this is occurring; specifically, when heavy institutional pressure is present, environmental and organizational factors do matter. However, this shift towards the macro-level should not diminish micro-level factors. Instead, it presents an opportunity for the incorporation of both sets of factors in a more comprehensive examination of the decision to adopt or not to adopt.

ACKNOWLEDGMENT

This work was funded in part through a grant from the Physicians Foundation

REFERENCES

Aiken, M., & Hage, J. (1971). The Organic Organization and Innovation. *Sociology*, *5*(1), 63-82.

Alkureishi, M. A., Lee, W. W., Lyons, M., Press, V. G., Imam, S., Nkansah-Amankra, A., … Arora, V. M. (2016). Impact of Electronic Medical Record Use on the Patient–Doctor Relationship and Communication: A Systematic Review. *Journal of General Internal Medicine*, *31*(5), 548-560.

Angst, C. M., Agarwal, R., Sambamurthy, V., & Kelley, K. (2010). Social Contagion and Information Technology Diffusion: The Adoption of Electronic Medical Records in Us Hospitals. *Management Science*, *56*(8), 1219-1241.

Baier, A. (1986). Trust and Antitrust. *Ethics*, *96*(2), 231-260.

Baker, J. (2012). The Technology–Organization–Environment Framework. In *Information Systems Theory* (pp. 231–245). Springer. doi:10.1007/978-1-4419-6108-2_12

Bhattacherjee, A., & Hikmet, N. (2007). Physicians' Resistance toward Healthcare Information Technology: A Theoretical Model and Empirical Test. *European Journal of Information Systems*, *16*(6), 725-737.

Blumenthal, D. (2009). Stimulating the Adoption of Health Information Technology. *New England Journal of Medicine*, *360*(15), 1477-1479.

Carraher Wolverton, C., & Thomas, D. (2018). The Development of an Integrated Model of Emr Adoption: Incorporating the Organization Artifact. *Journal of Information Technology Theory and Application*. (in press)

Chau, P. Y. K., & Tam, K. Y. (1997). Factors Affecting the Adoption of Open Systems: An Exploratory Study. *MIS Quarterly*, *21*(1), 1-24.

Damanpour, F. (1992). Organizational Size and Innovation. *Organization Studies*, *13*(3), 375-402.

Davis, F. D. (1993). *User Acceptance of Information Technology: System Characteristics*. User Perceptions and Behavioral Impacts.

De Palma, A., Myers, G. M., & Papageorgiou, Y. Y. (1994). Rational Choice under an Imperfect Ability to Choose. *The American Economic Review*, 419–440.

DeLone, W. H., & McLean, E. R. (1992). Information Systems Success: The Quest for the Dependent Variable. *Information Systems Research*, *3*(1), 60-95.

DesRoches, C. M., Campbell, E. G., Rao, S. R., Donelan, K., Ferris, T. G., Jha, A., ... Shields, A. E. (2008). Electronic Health Records in Ambulatory Care—a National Survey of Physicians. *New England Journal of Medicine*, *359*(1), 50-60.

DiMaggio, P. J., & Powell, W. W. (1983). The Iron Cage Revisited: Institutional Isomorphism and Collective Rationality in Organizational Fields. *American Sociological Review*, *48*(2), 147–160. doi:10.2307/2095101

Foundation, R. J. W. (2012). *Health Information Technology in the United States: Driving toward Delivery System Change, 2012*. Retrieved from http://www.rwjf.org/content/dam/farm/reports/reports/2012/rwjf72707

Garfinkel, H. (1963). A Conception of and Experiments with" Trust" as a Condition of Concerted Stable Actions. The production of reality: Essays and readings on social interaction, 381-392.

Goodhue, D. L., Quillard, J. A., & Rockart, J. F. (1988). Managing the Data Resource: A Contingency Perspective. *Management Information Systems Quarterly*, *12*(3), 373–392. doi:10.2307/249204

Goodhue, D. L., & Thompson, R. L. (1995). Task-Technology Fit and Individual Performance. *Management Information Systems Quarterly, 19*(2), 213–236. doi:10.2307/249689

Goodhue, D. L., Wybo, M. D., & Kirsch, L. J. (1992). The Impact of Data Integration on the Costs and Benefits of Information Systems. *Management Information Systems Quarterly, 16*(3), 293–311. doi:10.2307/249530

Greve, H. R. (2003). A Behavioral Theory of R&D Expenditures and Innovations: Evidence from Shipbuilding. *Academy of Management Journal, 46*(6), 685-702.

Hage, J. (1980). *Theories of Organizations: Form, Process, and Transformation*. Wiley New York.

Heiner, R. A. (1983). The Origin of Predictable Behavior. *The American Economic Review, 73*(4), 560-595.

Kimberly, J. R., & Evanisko, M. J. (1981). Organizational Innovation: The Influence of Individual, Organizational, and Contextual Factors on Hospital Adoption of Technological and Administrative Innovations. *Academy of Management Journal, 24*(4), 689-713.

Kuan, K. K. Y., & Chau, P. Y. K. (2001). A Perception-Based Model for Edi Adoption in Small Businesses Using a Technology-Organization-Environment Framework. *Information & Management, 38*(8), 507-521.

Lapointe, L., & Rivard, S. (2005). A Multilevel Model of Resistance to Information Technology Implementation. *MIS Quarterly, 29*(3), 461-492.

Lee, O.-K., Wang, M., Lim, K. H., & Peng, Z. (2009). Knowledge Management Systems Diffusion in Chinese Enterprises: A Multistage Approach Using the Technology-Organization-Environment Framework. *Journal of Global Information Management, 17*(1), 70-84.

Lewis, J. D., & Weigert, A. (1985). Trust as a Social Reality. *Social Forces, 63*(4), 967-985.

Lin, H.-F., & Lin, S.-M. (2008). Determinants of E-Business Diffusion: A Test of the Technology Diffusion Perspective. *Technovation, 28*(3), 135-145.

Liu, M. (2008). Determinants of E-Commerce Development: An Empirical Study by Firms in Shaanxi, China. In *Wireless Communications, Networking and Mobile Computing, 2008. WiCOM'08. 4th International Conference on*. IEEE. 10.1109/WiCom.2008.2143

March, J. G. (1978). Rationality, Ambiguity, and the Engineering of Choice. *The Bell Journal of Economics, 9*(9), 587–608. doi:10.2307/3003600

McKnight, D. H., Choudhury, V., & Kacmar, C. (2002). Developing and Validating Trust Measures for E-Commerce: An Integrative Typology. *Information Systems Research, 13*(3), 334-359.

Miller, C. (2003). Hidden in Plain Sight: Understanding Nonprofit Capital Structure. *The Nonprofit Quarterly, 10*(1), 1-7.

Miller, D., & Friesen, P. H. (1982). Innovation in Conservative and Entrepreneurial Firms: Two Models of Strategic Momentum. *Strategic Management Journal, 3*(1), 1-25.

Miller, R. K. (2011). *Healthcare Business Market Research Handbook*. Loganville, GA: Richard K. Miller and Associates.

Mishina, Y., Pollock, T. G., & Porac, J. F. (2004). Are More Resources Always Better for Growth? Resource Stickiness in Market and Product Expansion. *Strategic Management Journal, 25*(12), 1179-1197.

Moore, G. C., & Benbasat, I. (1991). Development of an Instrument to Measure the Perceptions of Adopting an Information Technology Innovation. *Information Systems Research, 2*(3), 192-222.

Nelson, R. R., Todd, P. A., & Wixom, B. H. (2005). Antecedents of Information and System Quality: An Empirical Examination within the Context of Data Warehousing. *Journal of Management Information Systems, 21*(4), 199-235.

Oliveira, T., & Martins, M. F. (2009). *Determinants of Information Technology Adoption in Portugal.* ICE-B.

Oliveira, T., & Martins, M. F. (2010). Firms Patterns of E-Business Adoption: Evidence for the European Union- 27. *The Electronic Journal Information Systems Evaluation Volume, 13*(1), 47-56.

Øvretveit, J., Scott, T., Rundall, T. G., Shortell, S. M., & Brommels, M. (2007). Improving Quality through Effective Implementation of Information Technology in Healthcare. *International Journal for Quality in Health Care, 19*(5), 259-266.

Petrescu, M. (2013). Marketing Research Using Single-Item Indicators in Structural Equation Models. *Journal of Marketing Analytics, 1*(2), 99-117.

Reardon, J. L., & Davidson, E. (2007). An Organizational Learning Perspective on the Assimilation of Electronic Medical Records among Small Physician Practices. *European Journal of Information Systems, 16*(6), 681-694.

Robey, D., & Boudreau, M. C. (1999). Accounting for the Contradictory Organizational Consequences of Information Technology: Theoretical Directions and Methodological Implications. *Information Systems Research, 10*(10), 167–185. doi:10.1287/isre.10.2.167

Saeed, K. A., & Abdinnour-Helm, S. (2008). Examining the Effects of Information System Characteristics and Perceived Usefulness on Post Adoption Usage of Information Systems. *Information & Management, 45*(6), 376-386.

Schwarz, A., Chin, W., Hirschheim, R., & Schwarz, C. (2014). Toward a Process-Based View of Information Technology Acceptance. *Journal of Information Technology, 29*(1), 73–96. doi:10.1057/jit.2013.31

Schwarz, A., Schwarz, C., & Cenfetelli, R. T. (2012). A Profile of Rejecters of Electronic Medical Record Technology. AMCIS 2012 Proceedings.

Schwarz, C., & Schwarz, A. (2014). To Adopt or Not to Adopt: A Perception-Based Model of the Emr Technology Adoption Decision Utilizing the Technology-Organization-Environment Framework. *Journal of Organizational and End User Computing, 26*(4), 57-79.

Scott, W. R. (1987). The Adolescence of Institutional Theory. *Administrative Science Quarterly, 32*(4), 493–511. doi:10.2307/2392880

Scott, W. R. (2003). *Organizations: Rational, Natural & Open Systems.* Prentice Hall.

Shekelle, P., Morton, S. C., & Keeler, E. B. (2006). *Costs and Benefits of Health Information Technology*. Academic Press.

Sherer, S. A., Meyerhoefer, C. D., & Peng, L. (2016). Applying Institutional Theory to the Adoption of Electronic Health Records in the U.S. *Information & Management, 53*(5), 570–580. doi:10.1016/j.im.2016.01.002

Shi, W., Shambare, N., & Wang, J. (2008). The Adoption of Internet Banking: An Institutional Theory Perspective. *Journal of Financial Services Marketing, 12*(4), 272-286.

Simon, H. A. (1955). A Behavioral Model of Rational Choice. *The Quarterly Journal of Economics, 69*(1), 99-118.

Son, J.-Y., & Benbasat, I. (2007). Organizational Buyers' Adoption and Use of B2b Electronic Marketplaces: Efficiency- and Legitimacy-Oriented Perspectives. *Journal of Management Information Systems, 24*(1), 55-99.

Teo, H. H., Wei, K. K., & Benbasat, I. (2003). Predicting Intention to Adopt Interorganizational Linkages: An Institutional Perspective. *Management Information Systems Quarterly, 27*(1), 19–49. doi:10.2307/30036518

Teo, T. S., Ranganathan, C., & Dhaliwal, J. (2006). Key Dimensions of Inhibitors for the Deployment of Web-Based Business-to-Business Electronic Commerce. *Engineering Management, IEEE Transactions on, 53*(3), 395-411.

Tornatzky, L. G., & Fleischer, M. (1990). *The Processes of Technological Innovation*. Lexington, MA: Lexington Books.

Urgin, J. C. (2009). The Effect of System Characteristics, Stage of Adoption, and Experience on Institutional Explanations for Erp Systems Choice. *Accounting Horizons, 23*(4), 365-389.

Van de Ven, A. H. (2005). Running in Packs to Develop Knowledge-Intensive Technologies. *Management Information Systems Quarterly, 29*(2), 365–377. doi:10.2307/25148683

Venkatesh, V., Morris, M. G., Davis, G. B., & Davis, F. D. (2003). User Acceptance of Information Technology: Toward a Unified View. *Management Information Systems Quarterly, 27*(3), 425–478. doi:10.2307/30036540

Venkatesh, V., Thong, J. Y. L., & Xu, X. (2012). Consumer Acceptance and Use of Information Technology: Extending the Unified Theory of Acceptance and Use of Technology. *MIS Q., 36*(1), 157-178.

Zhu, K., Kraemer, K., & Xu, S. (2003). Electronic Business Adoption by European Firms: A Cross-Country Assessment of the Facilitators and Inhibitors. *European Journal of Information Systems, 12*(4), 251-268.

Zhu, K., & Kraemer, K. L. (2005). Post-Adoption Variations in Usage and Value of E-Business by Organizations: Cross-Country Evidence from the Retail Industry. *Information Systems Research, 16*(1), 61-84.

Zhu, K., Kraemer, K. L., & Xu, S. (2006). The Process of Innovation Assimilation by Firms in Different Countries: A Technology Diffusion Perspective on E-Business. *Management Sciences, 52*(10), 1557-1576.

ENDNOTES

[1]   We acknowledge that physician may have concerns with data integration regarding potential problems with data security and potential power differentials that could come as a result (Angst, et al 2010).

[2]   The issue of single-item versus multiple-item constructs is debated within the measurement community, with proponents on both sides of the issue (Petrescu, 2013). However, we have selected single item constructs for contextual reasons, namely that in the case of long and complicated surveys, for hard to reach populations (such as physicians), single item scales are appropriate and justifiable without a loss in reliability or validity (Wanous & Reichers, 1996; Drolet & Morrison, 2001; Bergkvist & Rossiter, 2007).

[3]   While the negative beta weight for internal data integration may appear counter-intuitive, we theorize that this finding was due to the word "effectively" in our research item. We suggest that physicians were responding over skepticism that an EMR solution would *effectively* integrate their firm, not about the overall goal of integration per se. We encourage additional research into this factor.

Chapter 19
User–Driven Innovation in E–Health Change Processes

Synnøve Thomassen Andersen
The Arctic University of Norway, Norway

ABSTRACT

This chapter describes a user-driven innovation project in psychiatric services for children and adolescents in rural areas in Norway. The researcher applies a multilayer and dialectic perspective in the analysis of the user-driven innovation process that designed new ICT solution in compliance with a new decentralized treatment model with required treatment model. The researchers' findings suggest that contradiction appeared at material, cognitive, and organizational layers are crucial for path creation in such e-health projects. The contradiction in one layer leads to new contradictions in others, which together facilitate changes. Human actors, especially user groups in innovation processes, play an active role in leading the break from the existing path. Thus, this chapter contributes to the understanding of how user-driven innovation might help in deconstructing existing power structures across different layers in the change processes.

INTRODUCTION

Use of technology in Northern Norway is widely known for early adoption of ICT services to serve the population living in rural and remote areas in the Arctic (Antonsen, 1988). Today, use of ICT has become the solution in offering decentralized health services in sparsely populated area. However, it entails a number of challenges, not least in the field of psychiatric care. Since 1987, the organised work on telemedicine services in Norway, was initiated by visionary politicians and researchers, who saw the potential of using telecommunication, to improve the accessibility of health care specialists to the rural areas of Northern Norway (Hartvigsen & Pedersen, 2015). Northern Norway has a scattered population with less than 4 persons per km2. In the northernmost county, Finnmark County, the population density is 1,5 persons per km2., (Hartvigsen & Pedersen, 2015). Through the last 25-30 years, it has been continuously focus on the implementation of telemedicine services in specialist health care in Northern Norway, including building an ICT infrastructure for decentralized health. The broadband and

DOI: 10.4018/978-1-5225-7214-5.ch019

mobile infrastructure in the north is unevenly distributed; some areas well covered by both broadband networks and telephone networks, while others are practically without any coverage at all. Health care is not primarily a matter of technology. Close collaboration with health care providers and between health professionals and patients is essential for achieving better health care (Andersen, 2013). The primary focus is that close collaboration with health care providers and between health professionals and patients is essential for achieving better health care (Ringard, Sagan, Sperre & Lindahl, 2013).This include mobilizing the patients' own resources, as well as family and community resources. Such focus can contribute significantly to the patient´s healing process (Brennan and Safran, 2003; Ball and Lillis, 2001). It is important to provide patients with adequate care and support in order to manage their health problems themselves as much as possible.

This paper is based on the work of Andersen and Jansen (2011), and their research "Innovation in ICT-based health care provision", published in *International Journal of Healthcare Information Systems and Informatics*. Their work presents an innovative eHealth program in Finnmark County[1] based on the Parent Management Training-Oregon (PMT-O) model. PMT-O model is a treatment and prevention program for families with children displaying antisocial behaviour.[2] Andersen and Jansen (2011) present in their research, the development and implementation of an appropriate technical solution based on mobile technology in psychiatric healthcare along with the organizational changes required to support the implementation of the PMT-O treatment model. Andersen and Jansen (2011), describe how the technical solution helps both the care providers and the patients in their communication and information handling routines supporting the psychiatric treatment. The project involved the users largely in this design work. The term "users" in the project means several different users; health care workers, team members and "CYP" specialists (clinics for Children- and Youth Psychiatry), as well as parents, adolescents and children. The focus in Andersen and Jansen´s (2011) research is the innovation process that has taken place in the developmental work. By use of the concept of path creation (Garud & Karnøe 2003), combined with a multi-layered dialectics perspective (Henfridsson, Yoo and Svahn 2009), Andersen and Jansen (2011) explain the critical factors that gave rise to this innovation.

The researchers of this article improve and increase the original article of Andersen and Jansen (2011) and include the recent findings on the coverage of the topic. By improve the analysing of a multi-layered dialectics perspective; the researchers can explain more exactly the innovation outside the product development context in which it originally was applied. The researchers thus pose the same research question as Andersen and Jansen (2011), in the following manner: *How can a multi-layered dialectics perspective explain innovation processes in ICT-supported health care?*

In what follows, the authors first outline the theoretical framework; next, a short description of the research settings, followed by findings and discussions. Section 6 present conclusions and recommendations.

THEORETICAL FRAMEWORK

For decades, there have been an ongoing discussion related to research about extension of ICT innovation. Traditionally, research on such extension as sequential processes unfolding over specific periods of time (see e.g. Attewell 1992; Cooper & Zmud 1990), while other studies highlight that innovation often does not consist of sequential actions, but rather of an interplay of several concurrent processes (Van de Ven et al., 1999). ICT is the target of innovation; it is also the source and means in pulling and shaping innovation processes (Swanson, 1994). Some studies highlight the need to understood ICT innovations as network- and socially constructed, and not as occurring in homogenous and stable social ether among autonomous adopters (Damsgaard, Rogaczewski, & Lyytinen 1994). The sources of knowledge and innovation are both inside and outside of organizations (von Hippel, 1995), while social drivers of innovation are important (von Hippel, 1995; Tuomi, 2002, p.23-25). Based on this, users have a central role in shaping innovation processes, as they have strong influence on the social side of innovations, modifying and improving the products, helping to shape technology in all its phases (Tuomi, 2002, p.4). von Hippel (1988), presented the terms «user-centred innovation» and «lead users» in studies on «the democratization of innovation» (von Hippel 2005). The so-called «lead users» with special competence and interest assume an active role themselves in developing technology or work methods for their own use.

An innovation space, in this sense, is dynamic and volatile, which includes multi-layered influences across the network's different agents. In other words, organizations and individuals seldom innovate alone, but rather in interaction with a network of heterogeneous agents, such as other agents, service providers, universities, technologies centers, customers / service users, and many other agents, who engaged in reciprocal, preferential, and supportive actions (Brown & Duguid, 2017; Henfridsson et al., 2009; Tuomi, 2002). Increased network diversity promotes new combinations, fosters learning and enables faster diffusion (Tuomi, 2002). However, at the same time, it can build thicker boundaries that inhibit innovation spread (Boland Jr, Lyytinen, & Yoo, 2007). A wider variety of ICT artifacts can enable and mediate the interaction among different agents associated with innovation (Carlile, 2002). Therefore, ICT is not just a target of innovation, but is also an engine of innovation because it increases knowledge permeability across boundaries, thereby enabling new knowledge to be created, and distributing it in new ways (Boland Jr et al., 2007). Through the last 15-20 years there has been developed models for understanding the innovation process included focus like knowledge, product processes, design, user participation, organizational change, economy etc. Path-creation is one research current, which influence technology adoption in organizations. Miller and Morris (1999), present one conceptualisation of the innovation process, which acknowledges an appreciation of knowledge as part of the process of creating new products and processes. Kaplan (1998), present a social interactionist framework based on Rogers' work (Rogers, 1995). Kaplan's framework is influenced by theoretical models of several factors; organizational change, adoption and use of innovation, user resistance and evaluation of information systems. This perspective may be useful in evaluating information system research that takes account of organizational issues and traditionally economic oriented innovation processes. Similar research related to the innovation process has to be aware the underlying economic importance to organizations, so it might be utilized in practice.

Andersen and Jansen (2012), describe a different focus that has made it possible to get more insight in how to organize innovation, new ways of thinking, and new alternative ways to organize design and implement new technical solutions. Thus in order to fully account for the complex innovation phenomenon the authors examine in this article, there will be given a theoretical insights that allows us to explain how multiple agents deploying resources can co-shape a successful innovation path.

Path Dependency and Path Creation

As a dynamic system view to technology innovation studies, David (1985), and Arthur (1989), introduced the concept *path dependence*. Path dependency does not separate technological innovation from past developments but assumes some kind of continuity in the process of technological change. Innovation always lines up with earlier technological change; they have historical novel antecedents (Arthur, 1996).

Continuous accumulation of knowledge leads to the formation of a technological trajectory, which delimits the options for the further development (Schienstock, 2007). However, organizations are said to follow a path dependent pattern whenever they are constrained to an increasingly narrow scope of actions and have no other alternative, which refers as lock-in (Garud, Kumaraswamy, and Karnoe, 2010). This lock-in is the result of self-reinforcing mechanisms that foster the adoption of initially and potentially inefficient path (Law, 2017). These self-mechanisms might involve positive feedback processes such as coordination, complementarity, and learning or adaptive expectation effects (Sydow et al., 2009). Or these mechanisms might include negative feedback processes which rely on negative externalities such as constraints in terms of budget, space, or time that will prevent organizations from selecting other choice and directly impose a path on organizations (Law, 2017).

Garud and Karnoe (2001) introduced the concept of *path creation* that complements the concept of path dependence. In contrast to path dependence, path creation are influenced by human agents, which are in structure from which they attempt to depart. Garud and Karnoe (2001) argue that path creation is proactive innovation. It emphasizes human agents who are *"knowledgeable agents with capacity to reflect and act in ways other than those prescribed by existing social rules and taken-for-granted technological artefacts"* (p.2). Path creation, thus, is seen as a process whereby these human agents can and will mindfully deviate from what appears to be the common expectation in order to sample new experience, explore new forms of practice and create new resources (Garud et al., 2010). Path dependence and path creation together in this study present a structure perspective to understand innovation processes. Traditionally, researchers have examined path dependence and path creation largely in isolation. However, an increasing number of recent literature draw upon both perspectives to explain how history and human agency may intertwine during technological innovation (Henfridsson et al., 2009; Sydow, Windeler, Schubert, and Möllering, 2012). As Henfridsson et al. (2009) argue, path dependence and path creation are related and mutually dependent processes; without path dependency, there is no ability to recognize the deviance in path creation, and innovators engage in path creation in hopes of establishing new stable sets of path dependence. Both path dependency and path creation can occur at different layers.

Andersen and Jansen (2011), illustrate how path dependency was linked to the existing way of providing health services through the telemedicine infrastructure, while path creation originated through the break with that socio-technical structure and thereby developed both an alternative technical platform and a new way of providing health services.

Multi-Layered and Dialectic Perspective

Andersen and Jansen (2011) based their studies on both Henfridsson et al. (2009) and Sydow et al. (2012), to apply a multi-layered perspective, for understanding the dynamics and structure of paths that the eHealth project they analyzed created. Henfridsson et al. (2009) argues that technology innovation involves not only the creation of artifacts with new material properties, but also the modification of the existing cognitive model of the product and organizational structure of design tasks and responsibility. There are three broad layers of structures that need to be interrelated during innovation process (Sydow et al., 2012); the material, cognitive and organizational layers (Baldwin and Clark 2000; Henfridsson et al., 2009). The material layer refers to *"the tangible instantiation of a particular design"* (Henfridsson et al., 2009, p. 4), the artefact that performs a set of specific functions that create value for its user, which refer as the specific technical solution that shall support the provision of health services in this case. The cognitive layer is *"a logical design of artifact"* that indicates the *"mental schema underpinning the structure and functions of the artefact being designed"* (Henfridsson et al., 2009, p. 4). For instance, it specifies the hierarchical relationship and interdependences among design elements, which in Andersen and Jansens (2011) study is described by the mobile phone infrastructure and application systems structure as an alternative to the Norwegian Health Network and its support services. The final, upper layer of structure, the organizational layer, specifies *"activities performed by various designers and their interrelationships"* (Anderson & Jansens, 2011, p. 5), which in Andersen and Jansens (2011) research indicates the interrelation and interaction among different agents in the projects, including the project team and its affiliated organization, different user groups, suppliers and regional health authoritative institutions. Furthermore, in order to explore multi-layered path creation as a process involving human agency, Andersen and Jansen (2012) also adopted a dialectical view of institutional organization. As existing literature argue, the core of dialectical perspective is to see designers in organizations as agents who are situated in contractor and multi-layer structures which embedded in a larger socio-technical system that constrains design choice (Benson,1977; Yoo et al., 2006; Henfridsson et al., 2009, Henfridsson, et al. 2013). Innovation, in dialectical view, is a process when agents actively and artfully exploit contradictions in different layers of structures in order to break away from the powerful and systematic force of path dependencies (Henfridsseon et al., 2009).

RESEARCH SETTINGS

The objective of this paper is to use Andersen and Jansen (2011) case study methodology to explore multi-layered and dialectical perspectives within process of path creation in an ICT innovation project in more detail. Andersen and Jansen (2011) based their study on a three-years project called "Come Here! – ambulant teams and technology" which introduced a new health program in Finnmark based on the PMT-O model. The study is thus process-oriented, as it has observed the actors, their project setting and technical development work over time including the innovation processes in the design of mobile application and organizational changes. The research reflects the interpretive tradition of IS research (Myers, 1997; Myers & Avison, 2002; Walsham, 1993, 2006), with its qualitative approach. See Andersen and Jansen (2011) for fully detail information of the project and the data collection analysis.

FINDINGS

Material Layer

The technical artefact in the case refers to the specific solution that supported the provision of psychiatric health services, based on the PTM-O model. The first contradiction in the material layer raised at very beginning of the project and lasted over almost one year. In detail, before the project was established in 2006, the health authority contacted the Norwegian Centre for Telemedicine (NST) for advice on the choice of the technical platform for the project. NST proposed the use of videoconferencing technology and PC-based technology on the existing broadband infrastructure. However, during the initial meeting among researchers and representatives of user groups, another technical alternative was identified, i.e. the artefact that comprises both an application on a mobile phone and PC. Both alternatives suggested by NST and end-users were under a series of evaluation in the period of innovation preformation, and the steering group and the project team eventually decided that mobile technology based on 3G was the only feasible choice based on following facts. First, it would be considerably expensive to use videoconference technology rather than the mobile phone. In addition, videoconferencing technology might also require costly upgrades of the different studios in the outpatient clinics. Not least, since the ambulance teams would be travelling a lot, mobile phones would therefore be more practical for interpersonal communication than portable PCs. Furthermore, the extension of the broadband network in the northern part of Norway is not as good as the coverage of the mobile network. Lastly, the training required for children, families and ambulant teams in order to use the videoconferencing solution would be considerable, while the use of mobile phones is widespread in all age groups and social strata of the population.

The decision upon the adoption of mobile technology and the development of a mobile treatment application was eventually made due to tensions emerged in organizational layers that will be explained later. Over more than one-year efforts, the mobile application (called *Come Here – Mobile*) that support the PMT-O model was developed with user participation at the end of the project. This application (based on J2ME, version midp2.0) was implemented on Nokia E65 phones that were distributed to project participants. This application is a replication of the paper forms used to register the results on specific action points regarding the child's problems. The application is general, but adaptable in order to give every child and family the possibility to adapt it to the individual case management. The data are sent from the phone (e.g. a list of scores or report on behavior during meal time is transmitted over the mobile phone network). The CYP workers have access to the information from the server through Internet and VPN- channels. As this is outside the secure health-care network, there is no direct import into the main patient record application, but it is possible to cut and paste information from the application into the "CYP Data", which is the main patient record application in use in the health care sector.

Cognitive Layer

The cognitive layer of structure are related to the structure and the functions of the chosen technology and the specific design solutions, which in this case indicates the mobile phone infrastructure and tailored applications, as an alternative to the Norwegian Health Network and its support services. The significant contradiction in cognitive layer appeared when the project team proposed their initial decision on the choice of mobile phone as the technical platform to support the development of new ICT-based service. This decision, however, was followed by unexpected reluctance from the Regional IT department, the local authoritative telemedicine organization that this project initially worked with. One participant from the Regional IT department was appointed to the project group, but was not active in providing information requested. For instance, despite multiple requests, the project team failed to receive technical information about the existing regional information infrastructure, known as Norwegian Health Network, which is a broadband network connecting all health institutions in Finnmark. Further, the whole IT department formally withdrew from the project in January 2007, nearly a year after the project started. The argument for withdrawal was related to the reorganization from January 1, 2006, in the regional health authority (Northern Norway Regional Health Authority, which manages health care in Finnmark and two other counties). During this reorganization, the IT divisions of the health authorities for the counties were centralized into one Regional IT department. As this project was initiated on a county level, the Regional IT department required extra resources for further participation in the project. The project had no extra resources to offer, and eventually the project team decided to continue their design work without supports from the Regional IT department as initial planned. Such situation led this project being alone in choosing and shaping the technical solution and its supportive systems. This had certain important consequences. On the one side, it allowed a lot of room for adapting to the wishes and needs of the users in terms of communication patterns and functionality. On the other side, the project explicitly emphasized building a flexible solution; this was due to the lack of information about the existing technical infrastructure. However, due to the contradiction in cognitive layer, the designed application cannot integrate into the national network, but exist as a stand-alone system outside this network. It means that the operational capabilities of new technical solution and the support functions were separated from the health services provided by the Regional Health Authority.

Organizational Layer

The organizational layer of structure specifies activities performed by various designers and their inter-relationships (Henfridsson et al., 2009). In this case, it refers as interrelation among different agents in the projects, such as the project team and its affiliated organization, different user groups, service suppliers, and local health authoritative institutions. The contradiction emerged at very beginning of the project and eventually became the driving force for the changes in both material and cognitive layers. Specifically, there was a reorganization in the regional health authority from 2006 when this project started. The reorganization resulted in the centralization of the IT divisions from three county health authorities into one big Regional IT department. Such reorganization broke up the initial cooperative relation between the project team and small IT divisions. As mentioned earlier, due to the inefficient interaction with Regional IT department, this project team eventually had to break from this authoritative IT divine in 2007. The steering and project group was formally subordinate to the Northern Norway Regional Health Authority. The reference group were mandated by the steering team, while the Regional IT department was part of County Health Authority that responsible for technical support and services. However, the conflict between Regional IT department and the steering and project groups, which lead to termination of financial and design support from Finnmark's authoritative telemedicine department. To cope with such relationship termination, the project team established its own techno group in 2007 (figure of project organization), which included the project manager and representatives from CYP teams, user organizations, patient families, and the system suppliers. The users were represented in steering, project, reference and techno groups, and they were involved in all parts of the development work, from planning to design, prototype and test the solution.

Dominant and Emergent Structure in the Layers

Over a period of 3 years, the project team had gone through significant technical and administrative challenges within innovation process and resulted in crucial shifts in the choice of technical solution and the structure of organization. Consistent with path creation literature (Boland et al., 2007; Henfridsson et al., 2009), this project team faced contradictions between the ongoing production of new ICT-based solution for delivering psychiatric service and the established sociotechnical order in Finnmark region as they attempt to break away. As analyzed, the path was not a single line, it was more like a thread that consists of multiple layers across material, cognitive and organizational dimensions. Furthermore, although designer experienced contradictions at each layer separately in different point of time, these contradictions across layers still interact with each other and together became important force in the path creating process. As Henfridsson et el. (2009) argues, the new path was never swiftly created on the basis of a clear design vision. This study shows that shift in the material layer of technical solution reveals a set of contradictions at other two layers of structure, cognitive and organizational. In detail, the tension among the County Health Authority, project steering group and Regional IT department led to an inefficient cooperation among different agents within organizational layer. This eventually forced the project team ceased its existing relation with Regional IT department and established its own techno team which can better address a decentralized care model by involving end-users (ambulance team and patient families) into the whole design process.

By breaking the traditional centralized development model in regional telemedicine organization in Finnmark, the project team, on the one hand, successfully moved away from the hierarchical control over telemedicine and suppliers. This supported further path creation in cognitive and material layer, i.e. the establishing of a mobile treatment application with stand-alone network system. The new solution indeed demonstrated remarkable characteristics in user-centered (see Andersen & Jansen, 2012) and generativity which refers as the ability for further innovation and use (see Andersen & Aanestad, 2008). However, the contradictions within organizational layer continuously bought new challenges for the project team. The techno team and design work were still under management of the health authority in Finnmak, which means Regional IT department still exerted its supervising power over the designing and assessment process. For example, In January 2008, the Regional IT department responded with an evaluation of the project's solution. Several critical comments were expressed; most of them related to security and confidentiality issues. In addition, County Health Authority later also implied that necessary changes related to administrative routines. These changes were not trivial and were related to defining new contract types, new models for purchase agreements and new types of service models (from centralized to decentralized).

DISCUSSION

The multi-layer framework helped to illustrate and understanding path creation at three layer across the project time. This analysis support the conclusion draw by recent studies, claiming that contradictions appeared at a particular layer (Henfridsson et al., 2009; 2013) and decisions within one layer influenced the others and further affected the innovation paths within the project (Wang, Hedman &Tuunainen, 2016). The contradictions within each layer in general were crucial force to facilitate path creation process. In addition, contradictions and subsequent path creation in one layer led to new contradictions in other layers that bought further changes (Henfridsson et al., 2009). Also, human agents as path creator, played an active role in leading the break from the existing path (Garud et al., 2010), although such path break at all layer did not happen at the same time (Van de Ven, Polley & Garud, 2008). Finally, new innovation paths are never created in a vacuum or isolated from already existing sociotechnical arrangements. Design agency during the innovation process need to involve a critical reflection of sociotechnical reality as presented in the form of established orders in the layers of structure, and active reshaping of those existing order to create alternative structures (Hanseth, 2000; Garud et al., 2010). In detail, designers in this project resolved the contradiction at the organizational structure layer by ending the corporation with Regional IT department and forming its own techno team, which involved users into the whole designing process. However, the embracing of new organizational structure caused certain chasm. With the realization of new possibility of using mobile technology and its 3G network, the project team took the identify of rebels, breaking away from the established norms - designing upon the broadband infra-structure that integrated with National Health Network. Here, the contradiction in organizational layer effectuated the path creation at the cognitive and material layer. This led the innovation team to find a new and flexible mobile-based solution to cater the needs from different agents involved in the project. In addition, the adoption of mobile technology in this case further resulted continuously contradiction in cognitive and organizational layer when designers address Norwegian Health Network's evaluation on developed solution in respect its security and confidential issues.

The users in the project, as co-designer, also involved critical reflection towards contradiction within different layers and further became the crucial part of the driving force for innovation. These individuals were transformed from passive participants in the reproduction of the existing sociotechnical order, into active agents of change (Seo & Creed, 2002). However, although understanding and co-operating with users is key in path creation, it also requires particular skills and competencies and the devotion of time and effort (Heiskanen, Lovio & Jalas, 2011). In Norway, the design of user participation must comply with laws and regulations. In this project, to support user groups' interests and rights, adequate procedures were set up for the involvement of different user groups and consultation process. Different strategies were adopted to support user involvement (see Andersen & Jansen, 2012). Tuomi (2002) claims that technology exists as technology-in-use in the context of a specific practice, and that the starting point for innovation studies therefore must be on the social practical level (p.21).

SOLUTIONS AND RECOMMENDATIONS

This paper has improved the paper based on Andersen and Jansen (2011), by update the theory and examination of the innovation processes. By improving, the analysis related to the contradictions within material, cognitive and organizational layers across the whole project period, the researchers have highlighted how the use of an multi-layered and dialectic perspective can help us to understand how agents in an project team can overcame existing thinking (path dependency), and thereby trigger of new thinking and action (path creation). New studies shows that decisions within one layer influenced the others and further affected the innovation paths within the project (Wang, Hedman and Tuunainen, 2016).The creation of a new technical and organizational path were made possible through a better negotiation of the contradictions that emerged across layers. This results help us to understand how new innovations may be introduced in existing organizations. The health sector faces huge challenges related the implementation of new technical solutions that require changing organizational structures and work practices. One important clue can be to unveil existing contradictions and dialectic views, in particular related to existing task structures. This study analyze how to apply new mobile technology in service provision in psychiatric treatment. The researchers do believe that the findings are relevant for introducing new technology in other types of health services, and that it in this way may contribute to a better understanding of how to change organizational structures by addressing the different layers of structures in the design process. It is important to get more insight into how to stimulate innovative thinking in the design of new technical and organizational solutions to be used in the eHealth sector. In this analysis, the researchers explore the contradictions that existed between the previous and emerging organization of health care service provision, and in particular the tensions between different ICT platforms and their support infrastructure. This research has improved the question of how to break with the fundamental isomorphism between task structure and design structure. The researchers have found that this multi-layered path creation perspective may help in understanding the innovation processes leading to the development of a new technical solution, and corresponding organizational change processes in health care provision in general.

User innovation processes grew and evolved from work practices. The analysis highlights three levels in the information infrastructure; the technical information infrastructures, functional and organizational levels. The new analysis shows that active user-centered innovation can be a rational driving force for meeting the challenges faced by complex organizations in the change processes, and that the strategic foundation of radically new ways by which to deliver health services can be robust. It is, therefore, necessary to understand the significance of the concrete organizational context as defined here. The researchers use the path creation perspective to illustrate the interaction between the information infrastructure technical, organization and institutional level in user-centered processes related to infrastructure. The path dependency perspective is associated with the existing way by which health services are offered and is related to the existing infrastructure, whereas path creation is applied as an enabler. The limitations of the study are that it included just one specific case, the introduction of mobile technology in psychiatric treatment. The findings can accordingly not be generalized without reservations, but it shows at least the relevance of the research framework. More research is thus needed in order to illustrate how this framework may be relevant in other fields in the health sector, and furthermore, to what extent it may offer a conceptual thinking related to changing larger organizations. This type of research is transcending the disciplinary boundaries in that it examines the relationship between organizational design and "product" (artefact) design and illustrates the fruitfulness of a multidisciplinary approach.

Future Works

The researchers claim that if existing health services are to be maintained, and new services developed, it is important to facilitate, profitably, new creativity or innovations. It is important that innovation takes place in interaction with the surrounding environment in order to effect desirable changes. The focus on innovation that is user-centered in a network, is important to get more precise knowledge about innovation and organizational changes, while at the same time highlights the role of users at various levels, as well as organizational changes associated with work practices through the aid of ICT. Future innovation research include interaction within a network of heterogeneous agents (other agents, service providers, universities, technologies centers, customers/service users, and many other agents), who engaged in reciprocal, preferential, and supportive actions (Brown & Duguid, 2017; Henfridsson et al., 2009; Tuomi, 2002).

Future technological development affects many processes in the daily life. Innovation can also be regarded as a process in which organizations seldom innovate alone, but rather in collaboration with other enterprises, networks, formal knowledge-generating organizations (research institutes, universities), legal systems and regulatory statutes (Tuomi, 2002). Nambisian et al. (2017), seek to offer a broader foundation for reinventing innovation management in a digital world. At the same time, it is more important than ever to include users in innovations (Andersen, 2013; Andersen & von der Velden, 2010). In user innovation, users have an active role, as they help in the development process thus helping to create a product that they ultimately are the users of. This study may contribute to further research related to fostering better health-related decisions related to the procurement and use of technology. Further, the study can be useful, as the study has examined the interaction between the social (human), the technological and political (organizational) elements in the health sector. The balance between a central standardization and the closing of the network is a challenge for further innovation in the health care sector. According to Andersen (2013), infrastructures and innovation contributes towards knowledge concerning project management that enables one to influence or make changes, both visible and invisible, in organizations in order to achieve the desired development.

REFERENCES

Andersen, S. T. (2013). *User-centered innovation in psychiatric healthcare by using mobile technology (PhD-thesis)*. Oslo: University of Oslo.

Andersen, S. T., & Van der Velden, M. (2010). Mobile phone-based healthcare delivery in a Sami area: Reflections on technology and culture. *CATAc International Conference*.

Andersen, S. T., & Aanestad, M. (2008). Possibilities and challenges of transition to ambulant health service delivery with ICT support in psychiatry. *IFIP TC8 WG8.2 International Working Conference*. 10.1007/978-0-387-09768-8_9

Andersen, S. T., & Jansen, A. (2011). Innovation in ICT-Based Health Care Provision. *International Journal of Healthcare Information Systems and Informatics*, 6(2). doi:10.4018/jhisi.2011040102

Andersen, S. T., & Jansen, A. (2012). Installed base as a facilitator for user-driven innovation? How user innovation can challenge existing institutional barriers. *International Journal of Telemedicine and Applications*. doi: 10.1155/2012/673731

Antonsen, T. (1988). *Telemedisin i Nord-Norge: forprosjekt* [Telemedicine in North Norway: a pilot study]. Tromsø: FORUT.

Arthur, W. B. (1989). Competing Technologies: Increasing Returns, and Lock-In by Historical Events. *Economic Journal (London)*, 99(394), 116–131. doi:10.2307/2234208

Arthur, W. B. (1996). Increasing Returns. *Harvard Business Review*, 74(4), 100–109. PMID:10158472

Attewell, P. (1992, February). Technology diffusion and organizational learning: The case of business computing. *Organization Science*, 3(1), 1–19. doi:10.1287/orsc.3.1.1

Baldwin, C. Y., & Clark, K. B. (2000). *Design Rules - The Power of Modularity*. Cambridge, MA: MIT Press.

Ball, M. J., & Lillis, J. (2001). E-health: Transforming the physician/patient relationship. *International Journal of Medical Informatics*, *61*(1), 1–10. doi:10.1016/S1386-5056(00)00130-1 PMID:11248599

Benson, J. K. (1977). Organizations: A Dialectical View. *Administrative Science Quarterly*, *22*(1), 1–21. doi:10.2307/2391741

Boland, R. J. Jr, Lyytinen, K., & Yoo, Y. (2007). Wakes of innovation in project networks: The case of digital 3- D representations in architecture, engineering, and construction. *Organization Science*, *18*(4), 631–647. doi:10.1287/orsc.1070.0304

Brennan, P., & Safran, C. (2003). Report of conference track 3: Patient empowerment. *International Journal of Medical Informatics*, *69*(2-3), 301–304. doi:10.1016/S1386-5056(03)00002-9 PMID:12810134

Brown, J. S., & Duguid, P. (2017). *The Social Life of Information: Updated, with a New Preface*. Harvard Business Review Press.

Carlile, P. R. (2002). A pragmatic view of knowledge and boundaries: Boundary objects in new product development. *Organization Science*, *13*(4), 442–455. doi:10.1287/orsc.13.4.442.2953

Cooper, R. B., & Zmud, R. W. (1990). Information Technology Implementation research: A technological Diffusion Perspective. *Management Science*, *3*(1), 60–95.

Damsgaard, J., Rogaczewski, A., & Lyytinen, K. (1994). How Information Technologies Penetrate Organisations. An Analysis of Four Alternative Models. In I. Levine (Ed.), Diffusion, transfer and Implementation of Information Technology. North Holland.

David, P. (1985). Clio and the Economics of QWERTY. *Economy and History*, *75*, 227–332.

Garud, R., & Karnøe, P. (2001). Path Creation as a Process of Mindful Deviation. In Path Dependence and Creation. Lawrence Erlbaum Associates.

Garud, R., & Karnøe, P. (2003). Bricolage versus Breakthrough: Distributed and Embedded Agency in Technology Entrepreneurship. *Research Policy*, *32*(2), 277–300. doi:10.1016/S0048-7333(02)00100-2

Garud, R., Kumaraswamy, A., & Karnøe, P. (2010). Path dependence or path creation? *Journal of Management Studies*, *47*(4), 760–774. doi:10.1111/j.1467-6486.2009.00914.x

Hanseth, O. (2000). The Economics of Standards. In From Control to Drift - The Dynamics of Corporate Information Infrastructures. Oxford University Press.

Hartvigsen, G., & Pedersen, S. (2015). Lessons learned from 25 years with telemedicine in Northern Norway. University Hospital of North Norway Norwegian Centre for Integrated Care and Telemedicine.

Heiskanen, E., Lovio, R., & Jalas, M. (2011). Path creation for sustainable consumption: Promoting alternative heating systems in Finland. *Journal of Cleaner Production*, *19*(16), 1892–1900. doi:10.1016/j.jclepro.2011.02.005

Henfridsson, O., Yoo, Y., & Svahn, F. (2009). *Path Creation in Digital Innovation: A Multi-Layered Dialectics Perspective*. Sprout Working papers on Information Systems. Retrieved from http://sprouts.aisnet.org/9-20

Henfridsson, O., & Bygstad, B. (2013). The generative mechanisms of digital infrastructure evolution. *Management Information Systems Quarterly, 37*(3), 907–931. doi:10.25300/MISQ/2013/37.3.11

Kaplan, B. (1998). *Social Interactionist Framework for Information Systems Studies: The 4Cs IFIPWG8.2&WG8.6 Joint Working Conference on Information Systems: Current Issues and Future Changes.* International Federation for Information Processing.

Law, F. (2017). Breaking the outsourcing path: Backsourcing process and outsourcing lock-in. *European Management Journal.*

Nambisian, S., Lyytinen, K., Majchrzak, A., & Song, M. (2017). Digital innovation Management: Re-inventing innovation management research in a digital world. *MIS Quarterly, 41*(1), 223-238.

Miller, W. L., & Morris, L. (1999). *Fourth Generation R & D: Managing Knowledge, Technology and Innovation.* John Wiley & Sons, Inc.

Myers, M. (1997). Qualitative Research in Information Systems. *MISQ Discovery, 2.*

Myers, M., & Avison, D. (Eds.). (2002). Qualitative Research in Information Systems. London: Sage. doi:10.4135/9781849209687

Ringard, Å., Sagan, A., Sperre, S. I., & Lindahl, A. K. (2013). Norway: Health system review. *Health Systems in Transition, 15*(8), 1–162. PMID:24434287

Rogers, E. M. (1995). *Diffusion of innovations* (4th ed.). New York: Free Press.

Schienstock, G. (2007). From path dependency to path creation: Finland on its way to the knowledge-based economy. *Current Sociology, 55*(1), 92–109. doi:10.1177/0011392107070136

Seo, M.-G., & Creed, W. E. D. (2002). Institutional Contradictions, Praxis, and Institutional Change: A Dialectical Perspective. *Academy of Management Review, 27*(2), 222–247. doi:10.5465/amr.2002.6588004

Swanson, E. B. (1994). Information systems innovation among organizations. *Management Science, 40*(9), 1069–1092. doi:10.1287/mnsc.40.9.1069

Sydow, J., Schrey, G., & Koch, J. (2009). Organizational Path Dependence: Opening the Black Box. *Academy of Management Review, 34*(4), 689–709.

Sydow, J., Windeler, A., Schubert, C., & Möllering, G. (2012). Organizing R&D consortia for path creation and extension: The case of semiconductor manufacturing technologies. *Organization Studies, 33*(7), 907–936. doi:10.1177/0170840612448029

Tuomi, I. (2002). *Networks of innovation.* Oxford University Press Oxford.

Van de Ven, A. H., Polley, D., & Garud, R. (2008). *The innovation journey.* Oxford University Press.

Von Hippel, E. (1988). *Sources of Innovation.* Oxford, UK: Oxford University Press.

Von Hippel, E. (1994). Sticky Information and the Locus of Problem Solving: Implications for Innovation. *Management Science, 40*(4), 429–439. doi:10.1287/mnsc.40.4.429

Von Hippel, E., & Tyre, M. J. (1995). How learning by doing is done: Problem identification in novel process equipment. *Research Policy, 24*(1), 1–12. doi:10.1016/0048-7333(93)00747-H

Von Hippell, E. (2005). *Democratizing Innovation*. Retrieved from http://web.mit.edu/evhippel/www/books.htm

Walsham, G. (1993). *Interpreting Information Systems in Organizations*. Chichester, UK: Wiley.

Walsham, G. (2006). Doing Interpretive Research. *European Journal of Information Systems, 15*(3), 320–330. doi:10.1057/palgrave.ejis.3000589

Wang, J., Hedman, J., & Tuunainen, V. K. (2016). Path creation, path dependence and breaking away from the path: Re-examining the case of Nokia. *Journal of Theoretical and Applied Electronic Commerce Research, 11*(2), 16–27. doi:10.4067/S0718-18762016000200003

Yoo, Y., Boland, R. J. Jr, & Lyytinen, K. (2006). From Organization Design to Organization Designing. *Organization Science, 17*(2), 215–229. doi:10.1287/orsc.1050.0168

ENDNOTES

[1]   Finnmark is the northernmost and largest county in Norway, although with a population of fewer than 73 000 citizens.

[2]   PMT-O is based on "social interaction learning theory", developed by Patterson and co-workers at Oregon Social Learning Center. PMT-O is a detailed program designed to improve parenting practices and indirectly reduce antisocial behaviour in the children.

Chapter 20

Management and Operations of Transfusion Medicine:
Impact of Policy, Planning, and Leadership on Bridging the Knowledge Gap

Cees Th. Smit Sibinga
IQM Consulting, The Netherlands

Maruff A. Oladejo
University of Lagos, Nigeria

ABSTRACT

Healthcare includes supportive services like blood transfusion. To manage blood supply and transfusion services, leadership development is paramount. E-learning has become a common global approach in teaching. However, there are limitations. Some are difficult to influence and eliminate. E-learning packages are promoted to effectively deliver education but are still not penetrated in clinical transfusion. Most clinicians have little knowledge of risks and benefits of hemotherapy. E-learning found its way into the field of blood transfusion. However, audits of clinical transfusion practice have demonstrated deficiencies in knowledge and practice that impact patient safety and in some cases result in death. WHO initiated a post-academic master course, "Management of Transfusion Medicine," focused on leadership in restricted economy countries. This chapter focuses on bridging the knowledge gap in management and operations of transfusion medicine.

DOI: 10.4018/978-1-5225-7214-5.ch020

INTRODUCTION

To manage blood supply centres or establishments and hospital blood transfusion services, leadership development is paramount especially in the area of e-learning. However, there are still limitations of which some are difficult to influence and eliminate, because they are an integral part of less developed societies.

E-learning packages are increasingly being promoted as an effective way of delivering training within the National Health Service in Europe (especially the UK), North America and Australia. One alternative to the traditional lecture format is the use of online technology in continuing nursing education, also known as eLearning continuing nursing education (Gerkin, Taylor & Weatherby, 2009). This is because technology has revolutionized the ability to facilitate professional clinicians and nursing competence through the use of online education. In fact, the use of e-learning in the staff development environment has only recently been explored (Benson, 2004; Bernhardt, Runyan, Bou-Saada & Felter, 2003). Although they are being promoted increasingly as an effective way of delivering education, they have still not really penetrated the clinical transfusion practice illustrating that the importance of adequate knowledge and competence of blood prescribing clinicians is still not well recognized (Smit Sibinga & Oladejo, 2013).

According to Lundvall and Borras (1999), the global on-going revolution in Information and Communication Technologies (ICTs) has given rise to a learning economy wherein the capability to learn how to create new knowledge and adapt to changing conditions now determines the performance of individuals, institutions, regions, and countries. This has led to an increase in the demand for e-learning both in the organizational and the educational sector. Thus, the biggest growth in the Internet, and the area that will prove to be one of the biggest agents of change, will be in e-learning (Rosenberg, 2001). In view of this, the demand for a well-educated workforce has driven many countries to rethink their education systems towards e-learning. E-learning is defined as learning facilitated and supported through the utilization of information and communication technologies (Jenkins & Hanson, 2003). Thus, e-learning includes use of ICTs (e.g., Internet, computer and tablet, mobile phone and video) to support teaching and learning activities.

TRANSFUSION MEDICINE

Transfusion Medicine is a bridging science dealing with the vein-to-vein events of blood transfusion. From the public oriented marketing and motivation sciences through the technical provision of acquiring source material, manufacturing, and distribution to the clinical science of bedside transfusion practice and handling adverse events.

Smit Sibinga and Pitman (2011) presented a broad overview of the various states of development of Transfusion Medicine. The focus is on how to bridge the existing knowledge gaps. Observations in various countries in different parts of the world have demonstrated the need for adequate and competent human capacity development and retention. A state of development in Transfusion Medicine is not in the first place dependent on upgraded equipment, technologies and methodologies, but on the accessibility of education (teaching and training) – a competent human capacity. Globally, clinicians prioritize clinical work, and extra time away would be a serious imposition. However, the need for education in clinical use of blood (in-hospital transfusion chain) is not only restricted to low and medium Human Development Index (HDI) countries, but stretches well into high and even very high HDI countries (UNDP HDI).

The Knowledge Gap in Transfusion Medicine

Since the United Nations' (UN) Declaration of Human Rights was proclaimed in 1948 (UN, 1948), much has improved. However, the fundamental right of health and education is still lacking behind in large parts of the world. Since the outbreak of the HIV/AIDS epidemic, WHO has put enormous effort in controlling the epidemic. In particular, much energy has been invested in the development of safe and sustainable blood supply systems as an integral part of the health care. The Global Status Report on Blood Safety and Availability 2016 (WHO, 2017) provides a far from cheerful picture: 19% of the global population belongs to the more developed world with access to 47% (47.3 million) of all blood collected for transfusion which complies with all modern requirements of safety, and is provided by good organisations according to international standards of quality. The remaining 81% of the global population lives in countries that still have to go a long way to development. Here, only 53% (53.3 million) of the blood is collected, which often does not meet even basic requirements of safety - unsafe and unreliable donors, over 7% is not tested at all, and 32% only partially and often with poor quality reagents and inconsistent methodologies. Most important problems encountered include: lack of political will and vision, insufficient or inadequate legislation and regulations, lack of infrastructure and education, lack of voluntary regular donors, but also a lack of coordinated and structured support and development, human capacity and education, and competency of leadership. Since the 2012 UN Resolution 67/81, WHO has launched the Universal Health Coverage programme which includes availability of and access to safe blood and blood products for all in need. The programme is supported by the inclusion in 2013 of blood and blood components on the WHO Model List of Essential Medicines (EM) with Guidelines on management of blood and blood components as essential medicines (WHO Technical Report Series 1004;67, 2017) which includes ensuring the appropriate use of blood and blood components by clinicians.

Transfusion Medicine has gained much attention since the HIV/AIDS epidemic outbreak mid-1980s. For instance, WHO has developed teaching and training materials, largely based on distance learning (WHO Distance Learning Materials). The focus has been on various elements of the vein-to-vein transfusion chain – donor selection and blood collection, processing blood, testing, clinical use and quality management. However, specific educational material for potential leadership has not been developed. Additionally, the target audience has been the primary blood procurement process involved staff at various levels. These include donor motivators, nurses and laboratory technicians, and blood prescribing clinical specialists. Unfortunately so far, little attention was given to leadership development at senior managerial and executive management level and clinical use.

Clinical Use of Blood

One particular area in which e-learning has been promoted is for clinical blood transfusion training. The use of blood and blood components in treating patients who are deficient in one or more blood constituents is the ultimate goal of transfusion medicine. So far, most attention has been given to the procurement of blood – collection, processing and testing, storage and distribution, but the clinical use at the bedside has been grossly neglected. Most clinicians, nursing staff and hospitals have little knowledge of the risks and benefits of supportive hemotherapy such as indication and prescription, use of alternatives, sample collection and positive identification, compatibility testing, vital signs and ultimate transfusion at the bedside, compatibility of intravenous fluids, medication and giving sets with blood, and the necessary documentation to allow traceability and hemovigilance.

Blood prescribing clinicians and residents are deprived from valuable information that could help them close the knowledge gap, come abreast of current transfusion practices and the need to master proper prescription and bedside practice. This could result in a reduction of the current transfusion related morbidity and mortality, and the development of a balanced and evidence-based Transfusion Medicine driven by identified and established proper clinical demand and the implementation of Patient Blood Management (PBM) (AuBuchon, Puca, Saxena, Shulman & Waters, 2011; Murphy, Saxena & Smit Sibinga, 2012; Frank & Waters, 2016; Eichbaum Q, Murphy M, Liu Y, et al., 2016). Although, e-learning has found its way into the field of blood transfusion, Peterson, Robinson, Verall, Quested and Saxon (2007) reported that audits of clinical transfusion practice have consistently demonstrated deficiencies in knowledge and practice that impact on patient safety and in some cases even result in death. These deficiencies, according to Smit Sibinga (2009) include transfusion being prescribed inappropriately, administration of blood products using poor bedside practices, poor documentation and inadequate identification of potential transfusion recipients. Narayanan, Kirk and Lewis (2008) observed that one of the greatest challenges to the National Health Service in the UK at present is the delivery of effective and up-to-date training to large numbers of staff.

Programmes offered can be divided into two categories – tools and courses. Tools comprise a diversity of guidelines and instructive e-documents as well as apps for consultation of e.g., literature, differential diagnosis. EU strives to develop a series of tools to support clinicians and blood bank professionals in the development of a common quality and quality management system. The main tool is a Manual with guidelines and resources to begin the development of a quality system for the clinical transfusion process (EuBis). Aim is to improve safety and efficacy of the clinical transfusion process and promote rational use of blood products across the EU through sharing of information and best practices.

Courses are largely interactive and modular with inbuilt e-tests and exams. Aims are to improve patient care, reduce risk, create competent practitioners through learning about safe transfusion practice. On-line recording and assessment systems (ORAS) have been designed to allow participants to record their scores on completion of a module assessment and even print a certificate as evidence of theoretical (knowledge) and/or clinical competence. Such ORAS also allows authorized personnel of clinical care institutions to issue reports from the system that show usage, assessment and modules completed by clinical specialty, staff group or different grades. The Australian BloodSafe e-learning program (Blood-Safe eLearning Australia) focuses on transfusion practice and patient blood management education with five courses – 1) Clinical transfusion practice; 2) Collecting blood specimens; 3) Transporting blood; 4) Postpartum haemorrhage; 5) Iron deficiency anaemia.

The eLearning Australia clinical transfusion practice course consists of five e-learning modules; 1) Risks and benefits – decision to transfuse, risks, benefits and informed consent; 2) Pre-transfusion samples – importance of patient identification and specimen labelling; 3) Picking up blood – transporting and storage of blood (in-hospital cold chain); 4) Administering blood; 5) Monitoring and reactions – recognizing and responding to acute adverse events. USA Blood Systems e-Learning Center promotes continuous education through a tracking system of self-study courses on Blood Banking (six courses) and Compliance (three courses). Each course has a post-test and evaluation leading to PACE[1] credits (Blood Systems).

However, in spite of the challenges faced by healthcare institutions, Gerkin, Taylor and Weatherby, (2009) still maintained that the use of online technology (e-learning) to demonstrate competency for prescribing clinicians and practicing nurses in the acute care environment has just only recently been explored. For instance, an analysis of data from the World Health Organization Global Database on Blood

Safety (2011) indicates that, globally 72% of countries cannot meet identified training needs, usually because of limited budgets, inadequate facilities, technological advancement (which the authors believe includes e-learning) and insufficient numbers of experienced teachers and trainers. Consideration of these challenges and informal needs analysis defined a web-based or online learning tool (e-learning) as being a suitable mechanism to assist hospitals to increase knowledge of staff. There is therefore, the need to explore e-learning as a means of bridging the knowledge gap in clinical transfusion medicine. This is the motivating factor to carry out the present observations with a view to extending the frontier of knowledge in the aspect of e-learning usage in clinical transfusion medicine.

NEEDS ASSESSMENT

Health care includes supportive services such as laboratory, radiology and blood transfusion. These supportive services are an essential part of the health care system and need a careful and balanced integration in the health care system. As they operate in the demand-supply chain, proper and intellectually well-equipped leadership is needed to manage these services adequately. Globally, blood safety and sustainability of the blood supply is increasingly organized. WHO (Blood Safety, 2002) and World Health Assembly (WHA63.12, 2010) advocate a nationally supported principle where regional blood procurement centres supply hospitals with safe blood and blood products. The advocated organizational structure is based on the principles of product liability (procurement of blood – collection, processing and testing, storage and distribution) and consumer rights protection (rational use of the products produced and supplied by the blood procurement organization or blood centres).

In most parts of the world, the service offered by blood procurement centres is still supply driven where the actual clinical needs should be met in a demand driven way to avoid shortages and logistic problems of supply and allow the development of rational and appropriate use of supportive haemotherapy. These parts of the world are characterized by the UN classification of Low and Medium Human Development Index (L-HDI and M-HDI). Of the 112.5 million blood donations collected globally, approximately half of these are collected in high-income countries, home to 19% of the world's population. (Blood Safety and Availability, 2017)

Management of Transfusion Medicine (MTM)

At the turn of the 20st century, the need for an educational development programme for potential managers and leadership in blood transfusion was recognized by WHO. The question asked was how to create a specific curriculum that would provide both knowledge and managerial/leadership skills in Transfusion Medicine and also provide access to such potential all over the world without the need for a longer absence from the base in the home country. Most countries are still in a transition and have initiated developments at national level based on the Millennium and Sustainable Development Goals, WHO recommendations and the WHO Essential Health Technology Department Blood Safety Strategic Plan 2000-2003 (Blood Safety and Clinical Technology, 2001). In such situation, identified and appointed competent leadership needs to be on the spot and not so much sent abroad for a period of 2 to 3 years.

In 2000, WHO requested the Faculty of Medical Sciences, University of Groningen to create an Academic Institute for International Development of Transfusion Medicine that would develop a post-academic Master course for Management of Transfusion Medicine (MTM), focused on potential leadership and senior management staff in particular in economy restricted countries. The second objective of this Academic Institute would be the development of transfusion medicine-oriented health sciences research. The concept did match the then WHO Department of Essential Health Technologies initiative to develop an educational e-Health programme (Aide Mémoire e-Health for Health-care Delivery, 2006). Supported by Exencia Pharma Academy Ltd, the Academic Institute has developed an E-Academy to offer the desired post-academic MTM Master course that includes health sciences research in the field of transfusion medicine to be presented as a post-academic thesis for graduation. Since 2012 this course has been integrated in the Graduate School of Medical Sciences (GSMS) of the Faculty of Medical Sciences at the University of Groningen. The course is designed to accommodate advanced higher education for academically qualified potentials largely on an e-learning basis. The e-Academy started with an operational e-coordinator and an MTM course leader who communicated electronically with the fellows; e-questions and comments are responded to within 24 to 48 hours. The technical structure was built by Exencia Pharma Academy Ltd, a firm with an excellent track record in e-learning at higher educational level (Exencia Pharma Academy). The design is based on a meticulous analysis of steps, laid down in a flow chart (Figure 1), and followed two closely related pathways –

- Technical construction or architecture of the e-Academy, and the electronic flow and control of the educational programme;
- Composition of the e-books, self-tests and e-exams.

The architecture itself and its operational access seem to be more important than the contextual module configuration and lay-out to secure a satisfying e-learning environment conveniently. A local infrastructure needed for a smooth and uninterrupted electronic communication is paramount for a successful e-learning programme in a stimulating virtual environment.

However, most of the preparation time was spent on design and writing of modules, and structuring the self-test and e-exam questions in a sound multiple choice fashion. Transformation of this material into e-books, however, took relatively short time. Once an e-book has been created, a structured validation is performed in two or three rounds before opening the e-book to any registered and authorised fellow. A growing e-Academic Library was offered, besides an electronic access to the academic library of the University Medical Centre Groningen for electronic access to references and books to be studied. Since September 2007, the first fellows from economy restricted countries that had registered electronically, have entered the course.

A web site that accommodates a public domain with all basic information about the Academic Institute, and the e-Academy as a restricted access domain was constructed and is currently replaced by the e-access system of the GSMS.

The Master course is spread over two years and composed of 8 modular e-books, each for a study period of 4-6 weeks, followed by an e-exam, that can be repeated maximally two times (at two weeks intervals). The modules were written by a selected academic faculty of experts and transformed into e-books.

The current 8 e-modules (12 months) are organized in an introductory module and two specific clusters –

- Four general managerial elements, e.g. organization and structure, legal and regulatory aspects, human resource management, and economical aspects and costing.

- Four managerial aspects of the core business in transfusion medicine, e.g. societal interface, clinical interface, process and quality management.

Being a higher education programme at post-academic level, the threshold for passing the exams is set relatively high. However, fellows are allowed to repeat the e-exams two more times with a two week interval. When the second re-exam also fails, the module has to be repeated completely. The fellow applies electronically for an e-exam, which has to be done within two weeks, following the completion of the module. This is monitored and communicated automatically and electronically. The material is user friendly organized: off-line e-books can be studied and e-exams taken.

The steps towards the final thesis are threefold –

1. Preparation of the research question, preferably focused on an existing problem in the home country;
2. Research proposal and start of data collection, writing;
3. Completion of data collection, analysis, final writing and presentation of the thesis.

Following the completion of the e-modules and successful e-exams, the fellow is invited to continue for a real-time exposure in an operational blood centre environment, while following 4 more modules in a classic face-to-face tutorial system. The MTM course is completed with a Master Thesis and a final graduation ceremony. The construction of the e-Academy took relatively little time as it followed the standard design of such e-Academies developed by Exencia Pharma Academy Ltd. Over the first years, the public domain was further extended to accommodate a mature website with the necessary public information about the Academic Institute and its activities. However, the Academic Institute has closed its website and offered the domain name for sale.

This post-academic Transfusion Medicine Masters course, focussed on management and based largely on e-learning, has to comply with a number of requirements, such as sufficiently high academic level of the modular contents; a coverage of all aspects of management, a local learning environment that allows an easy access and exploration of the material offered; a user friendly ambiance and appetising presentation of the course; reliability of, and access to supportive technical services for the electronic structure; a guaranteed distance communication with the e-book teachers through an e-tutorial mechanism; and full access to an e-library to study references and literature.

Impact on the Quality of the Medical Education

Factors that do have an impact on personal success when following such electronic distance learning education focussed on management rather than medical-technical and operational aspects, require the ability of the fellow to think and work at a more abstract level. The experience has learned that an academic graduate master degree is no guarantee to such abstract level of thinking and working, particularly not when the learning is done through an electronic medium, rather than in a face-to-face setting. Combined with a different education culture and related personal discipline to self-work with material that in principle is not fully familiar to the participant, creates a special challenge for both the consumer as well as the provider of the course contents. This implicates the embedding of the e-learning environment in an adequate and alert communication setting to allow prompt and supportive communication between teachers, course management and fellow. Teachers and course management need to understand the restrictive conditions in many a developing situation that should be met with flexibility and elasticity.

Figure 1. Flow chart of the MTM process
Source: Smit Sibinga & de Gunst (2008)

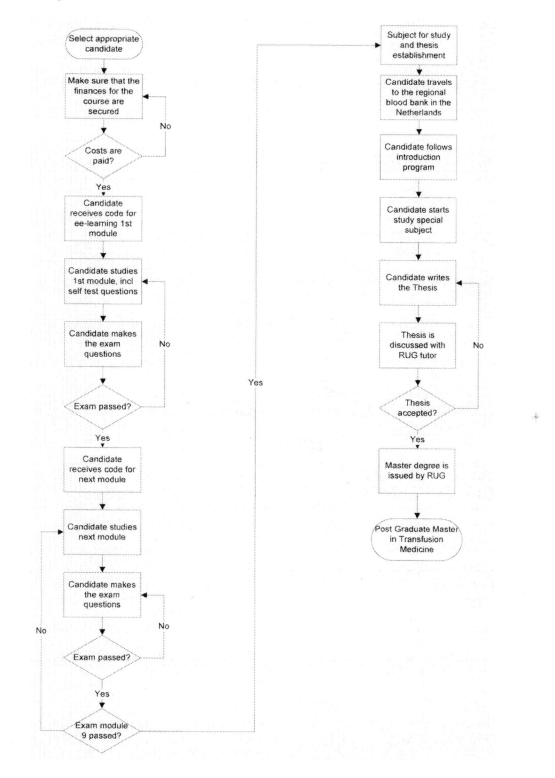

The technical support involved in the architecture of the e-academy and e-library should also be familiar with the technical restrictions at local level and act with creativity and professionalism to rapidly identify and solve problems that may arise, whatever remote the situation might be. A delayed or non-response to a request for help does have an immediate de-motivating effect and therefore a loss of interest and sustained discipline in the learning phase. In some instances, it was observed that the expectations of fellows of the course were distinctly deviating from the course objectives and based on indirect or direct personal experiences with 'advanced' education (Smit Sibinga, 2009).

Local constraints in available time to spend on the e-learning modules and preparation for the e-exams form another limiting factor. These constraints quite often are experienced as a different priority and therefore, not communicated with the course management. The consequence is a lapse of time before a question on progress is communicated and responded to. Some of these constraints are caused by budget problems, especially when the admission to the course is part and parcel of a donor financed project. Shortages of staff due to unexpected moving around of personnel from one position in the health care (e.g., a blood centre) to another (e.g., a hospital laboratory) due to lack or absence of control over staff of the employing institution has also contributed to a slow-down of expected progress.

A variety of relatively known factors such as changes in personal hardware (Laptop and PC) used; changes in internet providers and their nationally controlled and sometimes censored access criteria; and most frequently, fluctuations and unpredictable interruptions of power supply, especially during the on-line e-exam episodes were experienced, and were not really observed in the set up and validation of the course system and structure. In particular, the problem of electronic incompatibility when a change in hardware has occurred, created a technical puzzle for the electronic support service offered. When service has been provided to solve problems, it is of importance to have an inbuilt verification and confirmation protocol for the restoration of the operations, documented to allow analysis and evaluation.

There have been no serious technical problems encountered. Fellows are able to access through internet once they have received their personal e-book or e-exam access code. However, one experience encountered was caused by introduction of a local firewall system in Eritrea, which blocked access to e-books and e-exams. This problem was solved through the technical guidance and advice of the technical coordinator.

MAJOR OBSTACLES EXPERIENCED

Accessibility and awareness are not yet really developed (Smit Sibinga, 2010, Smit Sibinga, Oladejo, Adejumo, et al. 2017). Most of the fellows come from developing parts of the world, predominantly Sub-Saharan Africa, where financing was provided through the PEPFAR programme of the US HHS Department. There are distinct differences in country infrastructure and e-environment which contribute to the access and operational continuity of an e-learning based programme. Although, academically qualified (in-country University diploma's), a majority of fellows is not familiar with e-technology and computer handling other than some internet browsing and basic office functions like Word and PPT. Besides, differences were experienced in personal attitudes and culture once the e-learning has started (Smit Sibinga, 2010). Hardware used is not always guaranteed and in many a situation of second or even more hand nature. The e-learning programme is not public but highly individualised with an electronic match between the master system and e-academy and the personal laptop or PC at home. Changes in hardware need a renewal of the match to allow smooth continuation of the access.

In different countries, different grades of e-learning environmental and climate conditions were observed, but these are essentially variations of the same theme. One element needs to be added based on the observations, and that is the personal discipline of the fellows, caused by a variety of conditions e.g., limited career perspectives; micro-economical situation (family income); and paucity of academic interest and motivation. The differences observed can be classified into differences in academic level of the fellows (Smit Sibinga, 2010) and differences in environment and climate needed for a smooth and problem free operation and performance of the e-learning part of the cours. The prime entrance criterion is an academic education to be evidenced by a University Masters of Science diploma and the period over which the academic education has been followed. All fellows have met this criterion. However, during the e-learning period, it was observed that the education levels differ. Most of the fellows (e.g., Eritrea, Uganda, Tanzania, Qatar, Zambia, but also Singapore) have a difficulty with the post-academic level of the module contents and this is particularly demonstrated in the level of comprehension of the modules on Organisation and Structure and on Finance and Economy. Also, the module on Process and Quality Management showed some difficulties of comprehension at intellectual level. This was more prominent with those from the African continent and Qatar than with the fellow from Singapore.

Major obstacles encountered are –

1.   Inconsistent internet access due to supplier problems;
2.   Unreliable power supply and poor infrastructure;
3.   Virus contamination of laptops and pcs due to frequent uncontrolled use of memory sticks in internet cafés and through friends and relatives;
4.   Poor and not maintained firewall conditions;
5.   Mediocre computer literacy, particularly when skills beyond basic office functions are required; and
6.   Laptop and pc breakdown due to uncontrolled working conditions and improper working environments.

Besides, the differences in levels come very clearly to life with the design of the thesis project, the project proposal and the applied scientific work to be done for the thesis. Some fellows are acceptably familiar, but others show quite some difficulties in the design and writing of the research proposal (e.g., Uganda, Zambia, Tanzania and Qatar). Apparently, the academic education in these countries does not prepare for an academic level attitude and curiosity, and does not foresee in basic intellectual training for scientific research work to be done.

E-Environment and E-Climate

Despite the presence and availability of modern communication technology, there are differences in accessibility of particularly internet due to inconsistent and unreliable providers of internet services. Some countries (e.g., Eritrea) allow only one supplier, controlled through the authorities, others have more local suppliers. As the services depend on power supply, this factor becomes a key in the access to internet. With the exception of Singapore, the countries where most of the fellows live (Sub-Sahara Africa, Middle East and the Caribbean) experience regular and unpredictable power supply problems. These power supply problems also are unpredictably long, sometimes even a full day or more, which happens particularly in the tropical raining season. A variety of virus contaminations has been observed which has an impact the software and therefore, the operations and performance of the e-learning programme.

Most of these contaminations are picked up when the laptop is used in internet cafés or through exchange of USB memory sticks and diskettes. Most of these have been observed in Uganda and Zambia, but also in Eritrea and Tanzania. Fellows lack the knowledge and discipline about virus contamination prevention and elimination. USB memory sticks are regularly exchanged without scanning for contamination. Most of the fellows do not have a fire wall system on their laptop or PC. If so, there are scarcely updates done and regular scanning does not belong to the cyber culture of most of the fellows, particularly in Africa, the Middle East and the Caribbean. Given the diversity of questions asked to the help desk, there is a limited computer literacy with most of the fellows. The laptop and/or PC have become part of modern life, but without sufficient knowledge of even the basics of information technology, leaving them with poor to absent literacy of how to handle basic computer programmes, e-mail and electronic documents. Another observation is in the quality and operations of the hardware used. Most common laptops and PC are bought on the market without reference and second or even more hand, with as a consequence poor quality batteries, limited memory capacity and technical failures, including breakdowns and crashes. Absence of repair and maintenance services aggravate the situation as do limited working space. In one situation, a laptop was placed in front of an open window. When a sudden rain shower took place, the laptop was soaked and evidently no longer usable. In another situation, fellows who had registered and been accepted into the course, suddenly claimed the right to be given for free a laptop and appropriate software.

STRATEGIC APPROACHES

Post-graduate continuing education of medical, nursing and other staff involved in the in-hospital transfusion chain can be difficult when there is inadequate access to the much needed knowledge. Consideration of this difficulty might pave the way for a web-based or on-line learning tool (e-learning) as being a suitable mechanism to assist hospitals to increase knowledge of staff. Such programmes have been developed in advanced situations like the US (AABB), Australia (ARC) and the UK (BBTS). Therefore, additional focus has been on critical examination of possible contributions of e-learning in bridging the knowledge gap in clinical transfusion medicine with its attendant policy implications. The combination of classroom computers and the Internet is often considered together broadly within the concept of e-learning. As highlighted in Expression of Interest Integrated Project (2003), e-learning is where the knowledge is delivered via electronic media (Internet, intranets, extranets, satellite broadcast, audio/video tape, interactive TV, CD-ROM). The use of the Australian eLearning to provide continuing medical education has many benefits, including user convenience; programme design flexibility; easy access to information; adherence to adult learning principles; and accommodation of multiple learning styles. However, an extensive internet search showed that most of the e-learning programmes identified focus on the procurement part of the transfusion chain with limited attention on the in-hospital bedside practice. Also, there were limited programmes detected that focus exclusively on the bedside practice to support prescribing clinicians. Given the paucity of non e-learning programmes, except World Health Organization's few distance learning materials on clinical use of blood on CD-ROM, it illustrates that the importance of adequate knowledge and competence of blood prescribing clinicians as a specific supportive haemotherapy is still not well recognized. E-learning as an easy to access and universal education tool has not yet penetrated the clinical transfusion practice.

Globally the clinical interface and in-hospital transfusion practice still are the weakest link in the vein-to-vein transfusion chain. Since the mystery of incompatibility was unveiled by Karl Landsteiner (1901), attention was driven away from the direct patient treatment into immuno-haematology and in particular blood group serology as the major key to blood safety. With the recognition of transmissibility of infectious agents by blood, starting with syphilis in the 1940s, followed by Malaria, Hepatitis B and non-A non-B or C, in the early 1980s HIV and HTLV, and prions in the 1990s, many more have emerged (Smit Sibinga & Dodd, 2002). That initiated an epoque with a focus on laboratory detection and technical quality control, and assumed inactivation of these infectious agents driven by the hypothetic paradigm of zero-risk. During the last decades more focused attention for the bedside aspects of Transfusion Medicine has started to develop as reflected in the publication of textbooks on clinical practice of blood transfusion and the development of specific teaching material such as the WHO DLM on clinical use of blood (DL Module 2002; Aide Mémoire, 2003; Aide Mémoire, 2010; WHO Distance Learning Materials; WHO/BTC/BTS/01.3, 2001; Handbook, 2002) published in different languages, and the series of proceedings (since 1980) of the Groningen Symposia on Blood Transfusion published (Martinus Nijhoff, Kluwer Academic Publishers and Springer) between 1980 and 2004 in the series Developments in Hematology and Immunology (Springer). These symposia always concluded with a session on the clinical application of the highlighted theme. The obvious reason was in the globally observed and experienced knowledge gap in the peer group of prescribing clinicians and transfusion involved nursing staff. Despite the fact that over these decades an increasing volume of printed and e-learning education material has been published and offered, and a rapidly spreading dogma on patient blood management is occurring, key weaknesses still are awareness, accessibility and utilization of the material. This is reflected in the outcome of the survey, with differences between the clinical transfusion practitioners in the various HDI clusters of countries (Smit Sibinga et al. 2017).

Policy Considerations

Smit Sibinga and Pitman (2011) and Abdella, Hajjeh and Smit Sibinga (2017) observed that in many developing countries, blood transfusion in the vein-to-vein concept is still in its first or second generation stage. This means that blood is most often collected and transfused in the absence of a formal policy environment and without adequate regulatory controls or standards. There should therefore be some clear cut policy statements that will promote an effective e-learning environment in the field of transfusion medicine. Findings from the present observations have certain policy implications for future e-learning practice in Transfusion Medicine as it has an impact on young clinicians. Essentially, there should be a policy formulation that will address:

- Development of competency assessment software for different skills;
- Introduction and accessibility of advanced technology;
- Proper e-training of prescribing clinicians and transfusion safety officers (tsos);
- Development of a uniform management information system (MIS) for blood programs in all blood prescribing and consuming hospitals;
- The clinical risk management committee, through the Hospital Transfusion Committee, needs to oversee, develop and implement all issues and procedures related to blood transfusion.

To ensure effective implementation of these policies, Smit Sibinga and Pitman (2011) recommended the establishment of Hospital Transfusion Committees and a system for reporting adverse transfusion reactions in each hospital to implement the national policy and guidelines, and to monitor the safe and rational use of blood and blood products at the local level.

How to Move Forward

The WHO initiated idea to create a special management oriented higher education for potential leadership in Transfusion Medicine has come to a stage of maturation- e-learning combined with real time exposure to match the academic theoretical knowledge in detail with the day-to-day management of a large blood supply organisation. In principle the e-Academy course did fill the gap observed around the year 2000 and provided an easy accessible e-learning environment at post-academic level to potential leadership in economy restricted countries. The impact of such policy, planning and leadership development will certainly contribute to the creation of an important intellectual capacity and network paramount to achieve sustainability of the ultimate care in Transfusion Medicine as a respectable element in Universal

Health Coverage

E-learning has become a common approach in teaching and training in many parts of the world. However, there are still limitations of which some are difficult to influence and eliminate, because they are an integral part of less developed societies in different parts of the world. To guarantee continuous motivation and discipline of a fellow prerequisites are paramount. Ideally, there should be a personal and local contact and face familiarity between the course management and the fellow, to allow optimal communication in mutual understanding and respect. As fellows are scattered around the world, and live largely in developing societies with a limited e- and ICT teaching infrastructure and culture, it would be appropriate to include in the e-learning package an instructive e-module on how to handle and manage the e-learning tools, how to manage day-to-day problems of access and downloading, as well as re-access for e.g. e-exams and access to new modules in the course. Such instructive e-module would contribute to a better accessibility and awareness leading to a much easier and customer friendly e-access. It would also be appropriate to stimulate the development of essential computer literacy among this group of academics that were not exposed during their academic education at the respective universities or medical schools. The design, validation and implementation of a high level advanced post-academic e-learning programme focussed primarily on developing countries, needs more background information and analysis of the real learning environment and conditions than originally anticipated. A tailor-made and personal guidance and advice of the fellow by an academic and experienced course management is highly recommendable, besides a competent and technically creative and inventive back up service to allow a minimum of operational interruption of the course progress.

Regarding the clinical use of blood, clinicians are confronted with the challenge of acquiring relevant and effective basic and continuing education programmes in an increasingly complex healthcare environment. Although, the challenge of ensuring competence for clinicians and nursing staff might appear complex, educational programmes that are designed using an online format provide a positive educational medium for learning. The developments underscored that the e-learning medium provides a satisfactory and effective alternative for clinicians to bridge the knowledge gap in Transfusion Medicine. The observations provide further support for existing literature which confirms that clinicians and nursing staff can benefit maximally in an online environment to acquire more knowledge and keep abreast of the latest developments in their profession if certain policies are put in place.

PROSPECTS FOR THE FUTURE

It is important to develop similar e-learning courses for the clinical staff with self-tests and e-exams to further develop knowledge and managerial information. This is to optimize the clinical transfusion chain including the introduction of a patient centred blood management system (PBM) (AuBuchon, Puca, Saxena, Shulman & Waters, 2011; Murphy, Saxena & Smit Sibinga, 2012; Frank & Waters, 2016; Eichbaum Q, Murphy M, Liu Y, et al., 2016).

To accommodate the earlier expressed needs that come largely from Anglophone countries, so far English has been used predominantly. However, an initial explorative study to accommodate the Chinese market of higher education in Transfusion Medicine has been done in partnerships with the Chinese authorities, Universities and blood centres. By the time this exploration is completed and the road map for implementation designed, the e-Academy will have to host a Chinese section to accommodate the Mandarin speaking community. Next on the list would then be the development of a Francophone, Russian, Spanish and Arabic section of the e-Academy and the e-learning material.

Simultaneously, an electronic monitoring and evaluation tool that will give room for the assessment of the opinions and critics of those interested as well as those who follow and have completed a course could be developed. Such tool could best be built into the public domain of an institutional website and should have an automatic electronic statistical package to allow immediate update of the outcome.

Equally important is a strategy for funding selected potential fellows needs to be designed to explore the major funding agencies that focus on higher education and human capacity building (leadership development) in restricted economy countries.

REFERENCES

AABB Education. (n.d.). Retrieved August 15, 2017, from http://www.aabb.org/development/education/Pages/default.aspx

Abdella, E.Y., Hajjeh, R., & Smit Sibinga, C. T. (2018). Availability and safety of blood transfusion during humanitarian emergencies. *EMHJ,24 (3),* (in press)

Aide Memoire for eHealth for Health-care Delivery. (2006). Retrieved August 15, 2017, from http://www.who.int/eht/areas/eHealthFlyerAideMemoire.pdf

Aide Mémoire for National Health Authorities and Hospital Management, Clinical Transfusion Process and Patient Safety. (2010). WHO/EHT/10.05. World Health Organization.

Aide Mémoire for National Health Programmes. (2003). The Clinical Use of Blood. WHO/EHT/04.07. World Health Organization.

AuBuchon, J. P., Puca, K., Saxena, S., Shulman, I. A., & Waters, J. H. (2011). *Getting started in Patient Blood Management*. Bethesda, MD: AABB Press.

Benson, E. P. (2004). Online learning: A means to enhance professional development. *Critical Care Nurse*, *24*(1), 60–63. PMID:15007894

Bernhardt, J. M., Runyan, C. W., Bou-Saada, I., & Felter, E. M. (2003). Implementation and evaluation of a Web-based continuing education course in injury prevention and control. *Health Promotion Practice*, *4*(2), 120–128. doi:10.1177/1524839902250758 PMID:14610981

BloodSafe elearning Australia. (n.d.). Retrieved August 15, 2017, from https://bloodsafelearning.org.au/our-courses/

Safety, B. (2002). Aide Mémoire for National Blood Programmes. WHO/BCT/02.03.

Blood Safety and Availability, fact sheet reviewed June 2017. (n.d.). Retrieved August 15, 2017, from http://www.who.int/mediacentre/factsheets/fs279/en/

Blood Safety and Clinical Technology. Strategy 2000-2003. (2001). WHO/BCT/01.01.

Systems, B. (n.d.). Retrieved August 15, 2017, from http://www.bloodsystemseducation.org/

Module, D. L. (2002). *The Clinical Use of Blood in Medicine, Obstetrics, Paediatrics, Surgery & Anaesthesia, Trauma & Burns*. WHO.

Eichbaum, Q., Murphy, M., Liu, Y., Kajja, I., Abrahao, H. L., & Smit Sibinga, C. (2016). Patient blood management: An international perspective. *Anesthesia and Analgesia*, *123*(6), 1574–1581. doi:10.1213/ANE.0000000000001597 PMID:27870740

EuBis. (n.d.). Retrieved August 15, 2017, from www.eubis-europe.eu/objectives.ph

Exencia Pharma Academy Ltd. (n.d.). Retrieved August 15, 2017, from http://www.volgopleidingen.nl/almere/exencia-pharma-academy

Expression of Interest Integrated Project. (2003). *E-Learning- the cultural and societal impacts on the design and perception of e-learning solutions*. Call for Expression of Interest. Retrieved August 15, 2017, from http://kmr.nada.kth.se/papers/SemanticWeb/EOI_PAeLLA_fainal.pdf

Frank, S. M., & Waters, J. H. (2016). *Patient Blood Management: Multidisciplinary Approaches to Optimize Care*. AABB Press.

Gerkin, K. L., Taylor, T. H., & Weatherby, F. M. (2009). The Perception of Learning and Satisfaction of Nurses in the Online Environment. *Journal for Nurses in Staff Development*, *25*(1), E8–E13. doi:10.1097/NND.0b013e318194b6a4 PMID:19182548

Global Database on Blood Safety (GDBS). (2008). Report 2004-2005. Retrieved August 15, 2017, from http://www.who.int/bloodsafety/global_database/GDBSReport2004-2005.pdf?ua=1

GSMS. (n.d.). Retrieved August 15, 2017, from http://www.rug.nl/research/gradschool-medical-sciences/master-programme/

Handbook. (2002). *The Clinical Use of Blood*. WHO.

Jenkins, M., & Hanson, J. (2003). *E-learning Series: A Guide for Senior Managers, Learning and Teaching Support Network (LSTN)*. Generic Centre.

Landsteiner, K. (1901). Uber Agglutinationsverscheinungen normalen menschlichen Blutes. *Wiener Klinische Wochenschrift*, *14*, 1132.

Lundvall, B.-Å., & Borras, S. (1999) The Globalising Learning Economy: Implications for Innovation Policy. Academic Press.

Murphy, M. F., Saxena, S., & Smit Sibinga, C. T. (2013). Patient Safety and Quality Management at the Clinical Interface. In Quality Management in Transfusion Medicine (pp. 283-314). Nova Science Publ. Inc.

Narayanan, R. P., Kirk, P., & Lewis, S. (2008). Uptake and perceptions of an e-learning package on blood transfusion by trainees in Wales. *Journal of the Royal College Physicians Edinburgh*, *38*, 298–301.

Peterson, D., Robinson, K., Verall, T., Quested, B., & Saxon, B. (2007). E-learning and Transfusion Medicine. *ISBT Science Series*, *2*(2), 27-32.

Rosenberg, M. J. (2001). *E-learning: Strategies for building online learning in the digital age*. New York: McGraw-Hill.

Safe Blood and Blood Products: Establishing a distance learning programme in blood safety: a guide for programme coordinators. (2009). WHO/BCT.

Smit Sibinga, C. Th. (2009). Filling a gap in transfusion medicine education and research. *Transfusion Medicine Reviews*, *23*(4), 284–291. doi:10.1016/j.tmrv.2009.06.003 PMID:19765517

Smit Sibinga, C. Th. (2010). Post-academic Masters in Management of Transfusion Medicine (MMTM): An evaluation of the e-learning part of the course. In *Proceedings of the 9th European Conference on e-Learning* (pp. 826-828). Academic Publ. Ltd.

Smit Sibinga, C. Th., & Dodd, R. Y. (2002). Transmissible Diseases and Blood Transfusion. Kluwer Academic Publ.

Smit Sibinga, C. Th., & de Gunst, R. (2008). E-academy for international development of transfusion medicine – a unique institution. In *Proceedings of the 7th European Conference on e-Learning* (pp. 479-484). Academic Publ. Ltd.

Smit Sibinga, C. (2013). Bridging the Knowledge Gap in Management and Operations of Transfusion Medicine: Planning, Policy and Leadership Issues. *Journal of Cases on Information Technology*, *15*(1), 69–82. doi:10.4018/jcit.2013010105

Smit Sibinga, C. Th., Oladejo, M.A., Adejumo, O.H., Midori, K., Shuichi, K., Zolfaghari, S., ... Satti, M.M.H. (2017). Clinicians' Awareness, Accessibility, Utilization of E-Learning and Continous Education Programs; A Global Survey. Quality and efficacy of clinical use of blood: Policy considerations. *International Journal of Clinical Transfusion Medicine.*, *5*, 69–82. doi:10.2147/IJCTM.S136047

Smit Sibinga, C. Th., & Pitman, J.P. (2011). Transmission of HIV Through Blood – How To Bridge the Knowledge Gap. In HIV and AIDS – Updates on Biology, Immunology, Epidemiology and Treatment Strategies (pp. 583-618). InTech.

United Nations. (2012). Resolution 67/81 Global Health and Foreign Policy.

United Nations Universal Declaration of Human Rights. (1948). Retrieved August 15, 2017, from www.un.org/en/documents/udhr/nde.shtml

UNDP Human Development Index. (n.d.). Retrieved August 15, 2017, from http://hdr.undp.org/en/content/human-development-index-hdi

World Health Organization. (2011). Global Database on Blood Safety. In *Blood transfusions safety*. WHO. Retrieved August 15, 2017, from http://www.who.int/bloodsafety/global_database/en/

WHA63. (2010). *12 – Availability, safety and quality of blood products*. Geneva: WHA Resolution.

WHO/BTC/BTS/01.3. (2001). *Developing a National Policy and Guidelines on the Clinical Use of Blood. Recommendations*. World Health Organization.

WHO. (n.d.). *Distance Learning Material, accessible through Education and training in blood transfusion safety*. Retrieved August 15, 2017, from www.who.int/bloodsafety/publications/en/index.html

WHO. (2013). *Global Database on Blood Safety, Summary Report 2013*. Retrieved April 08, 2017, from http://www.who.int/bloodsafety/global_database/GDBS_Summary_Report_2013.pdf?ua=1

WHO Global Status Report on Blood Safety and Availability 2016. (2017). Geneva: WHO.

WHO. (2017). *Technical Report Series no. 1004:67, 2017 – Annex 3. Guidelines on management of blood and blood components as essential medicines*. WHO.

WHO Universal Health Coverage. (n.d.). Accessed on April 08, 2018 from http://www.who.int/universal_health_coverage/en/

ENDNOTE

[1]   PACE is a registered trademark of the American Society for Clinical Laboratory Science.

Chapter 21
What Will Entail Adoption of a Mobile Coaching Service?
The Case of Smoking Cessation Services

Silvia Cacho-Elizondo
IPADE Business School, Mexico

Niousha Shahidi
EDC Paris Business School, France

Vesselina Tossan
EDC Paris Business School, France

ABSTRACT

There is a growing tendency to use smartphones or other mobile devices for healthcare purposes, which offers a huge opportunity to improve public health worldwide and at the same time generates cost efficiencies and higher performance. In that vein, mobile devices make it easier to provide enhanced coaching and follow-up services through text or video messages and also through two-way interaction via social networks (e.g., Facebook) or virtual reality devices (e.g., Oculus). This delivery mode supports individuals or patients trying to break addictions, such as smoking or drinking. The authors propose and validate an explanatory model for the intention to adopt a mobile coaching service and applied it in the context of helping people in their smoking cessation efforts. This chapter uses the concepts of vicarious innovativeness, social influence, perceived monetary value, perceived enjoyment, and perceived irritation as key variables explaining the adoption patterns of this type of mobile coaching service.

DOI: 10.4018/978-1-5225-7214-5.ch021

INTRODUCTION

Addictions to tobacco, alcohol, drugs, over-eating, caffeine and pathological gambling are a serious problem for society. Breaking the habit takes enormous willpower, and in many cases the help of therapists or support groups. The rising popularity of smartphones, has led to a dramatic increase in mobile services through apps. The current tendency to use cell phones or other mobile devices for health offers a very interesting opportunity to improve public health worldwide (Stanford Social Innovation Review, 2011).

A study reported that a great number of smokers in Anglo-Saxon countries had downloaded and used health apps (Borelli et al, 2015). But research also suggests that a big proportion of users stop using health apps soon after they have been downloaded (Krebs & Duncan, 2015). App developers should include more engagement features (Ubhi et al., 2016) such as the use of gamification (Lister, et al. 2014) defined as the use of game design elements in non-game contexts (Detering et al., 2011).

One such service could provide support for giving up smoking. According to the report of PwC (2013), by 2017, mHealth has the potential to save 2.6 billion EUR by helping people quit smoking. This type of service is relatively new in France, hence the relevance of studying the profile of potential adopters.

In France, almost 78,000 deaths each year are directly attributable to smoking (about 6 million in the World, one death every 6 seconds). Tobacco consumption is the most significant cause of premature death in the EU. Around 50% of smokers die on average 14 years earlier (European Union, Public health 2017). From the overall European population, 28% are smokers and 29% of young Europeans aged 15-24 smoke. Across the whole French population 16 million smoke. A third aged 15-85 smoke at least once in a while (36% men, 28% women). The proportion of daily smokers rose from 26.9% to 28.7% between 2005 and 2010 and has been stable since.

Also, cigarette sales saw a slight upturn between 2008 and 2009 (from 53.6 billion to 55 billion packets) after dropping significantly between 2001 and 2004 (from 82.5 billion to 54.9 billion, due to substantial increases in the price of tobacco products). At 7 euros the pack, French smokers already pay one of the highest price in the European Union, surpassed only by Britain and Ireland. Around 80% of the cost of a pack goes to the government in tax, bringing in €14 billion in revenue each year. In 2016, the government introduced neutral cigarette packets covered with graphic health warnings. By 2017, the government is considering increasing the price to 10 euros the pack (The French government launched in November 2017 the "One month without tobacco event", Appendix 2).

However, the proportion of smokers that smoke more than ten cigarettes a day is diminishing. The French smokers are usually very young and represent 50% of the smoker people (about 94% of the smokers in EU start smoking before they turn 25). Considering 16 million of French smokers (more than 100 million in the world), more than half would like to stop smoking. Only 750 000 (nearly 5% of the smoker people) people stop smoking each year. More than 2 million of smokers used skin patches, nicotine substitute or pharmacological processing in 2010. But a research suggests that smokers who buy nicotine replacement medicine over-the-counter without any professional help have similar odds of stopping smoking as those who try to stop smoking without any aid (Kotz et al., 2014).

Tobacco companies are investing in a new generation of smokeless alternatives to cigarettes as the industry faces growing regulatory threats across the globe. The world's four biggest tobacco companies outside China –Philip Morris International, British American Tobacco, Japan Tobacco International and Imperial Tobacco – are positioning themselves for an increasingly smoke-free future as they seek to entice smokers to non-combustible substitutes such as electronic cigarettes, tobacco vaporizers and nicotine inhalers over the next decade (Wembridge & Thompson, 2012). Nevertheless, the benefits of electronic cigarettes are still controversial.

Coaching people to avoid taking a cigarette or an e-cigarette seems to be a better option. According to PcW estimates, out of the 102 million smokers, 48.8 million can potentially use mHealth solutions regularly and 3.9 million smokers could quit smoking successfully. Since January 2010, Health & Human Services (HHS) has invested $5 million dollars to develop its eHealth / mHealth smoking cessation resources aimed at increasing quitting attempts among teens, young adults and adults (Merrill, 2011a).

This chapter concerns a mobile coaching service providing support for people trying to stop smoking. The service takes the form of short text messages (SMS or MMS) sent to cell phones to help individuals in a range of situations or anti-smoking activities. In their research Oosterveen and colleagues (2017) in their systematic review suggest that eHealth interventions are more effective in asserting behavioral change in the short-term, however they identified very few studies comparing eHealth intervention to more traditional modes of delivery such as face-to-face coaching. The principal objective of this study is to identify drivers fostering the intention to adopt a mobile coaching service for the young smokers segment in France.

Firstly, the conceptual framework is presented and after that the model of the intention to adopt the mobile coaching service is introduced. The methodology is then described along with the operationalization of the underlying hypotheses. After reporting the main findings, the authors present the limitations, avenues for future research and a conclusion with some final thoughts.

CONCEPTUAL FRAMEWORK

The effectiveness of a mobile coaching service has already been tested in various countries, including New Zealand where a program to stop smoking was developed and tried out (Whittaker et al., 2008). Several content analyses in the anglo-saxon countries have been conducted to evaluate the quality of smoking cessation apps/platforms that are available in the leading app stores. These studies found that most were not customised to users' needs, especially they didn't contain behaviour change techniques (BCTs) which have been found to be effective in face-to-face support for smoking cessation. The fact is that it is challenging to keep users/smokers active on the apps because the benefits of using them may not be immediately apparent (to the contrary of apps in which you share photos for example).

There are five BCTs that were expected to be effective in aiding smoking cessation (West et al., 2010):

1. Strengthening ex-smoker identity i.e. for example establishing a very clear mental image of the goal of becoming an ex-smoker, constructing clear boundaries, good role model of the non-smoker.
2. Providing rewards like praise when stopping successfully.
3. Advising on changing routines.
4. Counselling and helping with ways of coping with urges to smoke.
5. Guiding on the use of stop-smoking medication.

Ubhi et al. (2016) compared specific behaviour change techniques prevalence in 137 free smoking cessation apps downloaded on Apple store in UK in 2014 to apps of 2012 (only 27 were the same) and found that while prevalence of supporting identity change, rewarding abstinence, advising on changing routines dropped, advising on coping with cravings and especially advising on medication use increased.

This may be attributed to the fact that pharmaceutical companies are developing smoking cessation apps with the objective of marketing their drugs rather than with the intent of improving the quality of smoking cessation apps.

It can be highlighted that 55% of the apps assessed in 2014 had no evidence-based content, no BCTs present, while 31% had only up to two BCTs present. It also was observed that some of the free apps only revealed part of the information required for quitting and then directed users to buy additional material (books, DVDs, e-coaching) for additional support. This means that the users of free apps may not be receiving end-to-end support. But specified ease-of-use features that were used in the apps in 2012 and that were already high (82,6%) increased in 2014 (94,5%).

Such mobile coaching services are relatively little used in France, and this is why they are considered as an innovation for the purposes of this study. Several definitions of an innovation have been proposed. The one used here is by Rogers (1962), who defines an innovation as an idea, practice or object perceived as new by the individual.

Diffusion of an innovation is the process by which it is communicated through certain channels over time among the members of a social system (Rogers, 1962). Rogers identifies three factors that explain how an innovation spreads and is adopted: 1) the features of the product or service, 2) the characteristics of consumers and 3) the profiles of different adopter categories through the innovation diffusion process.

Adoption of an innovation can be defined as the initial purchase or repeated purchase of the innovation, depending on the context. For frequent-purchase products, repetition of the purchase is necessary to consider a product adopted, and the threshold of three purchases appears to be an acceptable threshold for judging whether a product has been adopted by the consumer (Cestre, 1996), whereas for durable goods and services, adoption is generally considered to take place from the very first purchase, regardless of regular use or replacement purchases (Le Nagard-Assayag & Manceau, 2011).

Gatignon and Robertson (1985) propose a general model of innovation diffusion, taking the conceptual bases proposed by Rogers (1983) (which include the concept of innovation, diffusion over time, influence of interpersonal communication and opinion leaders, the adoption process, the role of innovators and other adopter categories, and the social system in which the diffusion takes place) and adding the influence of marketing campaigns and competitors' actions.

D'Hauteville (1994) develops an attitudinal model of factors that enhance the acceptability of an innovation for consumers that he seeks to explain not only by consumer characteristics but also by product attributes. His empirical studies confirm the results of other studies on innovation, particularly the finding of Ostlund (1974) that perceived attributes play a decisive, more important role in the acceptability of a new product than individual variables, including the specific variable of innovativeness. He also confirms the predominant role of consumer habits in forming attitudes.

Consumer Innovativeness

The concept of consumer innovativeness is not unanimously accepted among researchers (Cestre, 1996; Masson, 2010). Some (Hurt, Joseph & Cook, 1977; Foxall & Haskins, 1986; Venkatraman & Price, 1990) see it as a core personality trait, possessed to varying degrees by all individuals. Midgley and Dowling (1993), Roehrich (1994) and Le Louarn (1997) consider it at the level of all consumer products as a consumer's *generalized unobservable predisposition to purchase new products and brands* rather than sticking to habitual choices and models (Midgley & Dowling, 1993). Others (Goldsmith & Hofacker,

1991; Goldsmith, d'Hauteville & Flynn, 1998) see innovativeness at the level of a product category as a combination of personality traits and attitudes.

For Subin, Mason and Houston (2007), empirical studies paint an inconsistent picture of the relationship between the consumer's innovative predisposition and an innovative behavior (adoption of a new product). They demonstrate that innate innovativeness does not influence adoption behavior *directly*, but *indirectly* through two of the three components of indirect or vicarious innovativeness (defined later), namely modeling and involvement in word of mouth, but not exposure to advertising.

Hirschman (1980) identifies three types of innovativeness: *adoptive innovativeness*, *indirect innovativeness* or *vicarious innovativeness* and *use innovativeness*. Adoptive innovativeness concerns the actual adoption of a new product. Vicarious innovativeness can be defined as *openness to information on new products of any kind*. This vicarious innovativeness is followed by adoptive innovativeness when consumers actually adopt the product.

Finally, use innovativeness involves solving consumer problems with products already available to the consumer. In other words, the consumer invents new uses for an existing product. For the purposes of this study the focus is on the vicarious innovativeness specific to a given field, i.e. the consumer's attitude to new services, namely *mobile coaching services via cell phone*.

Intention to Adopt a Mobile Coaching Service

It is established that intention is a good predictor of actual behavior (Davis, Bagozzi & Warshaw 1989; Ajzen, 1991; Venkatesh & Brown, 2001). Intention is determined by the attitudes to that behavior, and by subjective norms (Ajzen & Fishbein, 1980). Subjective norms relate to the way the subject perceives the opinion of people important to him/her about his/her decision to engage or not engage in a certain behavior.

When an information technology-based service is in the early stages of diffusion, as is the case for mobile coaching services to help people stop smoking, the intention to adopt appears a more appropriate object of study than adoptive behavior (Hong & Tam, 2006). This is why the authors seek to explain the intention to adopt rather than adoptive behavior.

The Technology Acceptance Model (TAM) constructed by Davis (1989) is an adaptation of the theory of Reasoned Action (Fishbein & Ajzen, 1975) designed to model the intention to adopt information systems. Perceived usefulness is defined as the degree to which a person believes that using a particular technology would enhance his or her job performance (Davis, 1989). It determines both the attitude and the intention to use. Although TAM has been widely used, this model has also been criticized. Among TAM´s main criticisms as a "theory", the authors can mention its lack of falsibiality and limited explanatory and predictive power (Riffai et al., 2012).

The perceived ease-of-use is defined as the degree to which a person believes that understanding and using a particular technology would be free from effort (Davis, 1989). This leads the individual towards a perceived usefulness but also to an attitude that directly affects the intention to use (Davis, Bagozzi & Warshaw, 1989, p. 985). Later, Hong & Tam (2006) showed that the perceived usefulness exercises a direct positive influence on the intention to adopt multi-purpose information services. Information services are devices or instruments that are used to supply users with various types of information: data, video, images (Bergman, 2000).

Hong and Tam (2006) define multi-purpose information services as information technology (IT) artifacts that: 1) improve the personal, individual link with the user, 2) offer mobile services and 3) supply a suite of functions for both work and leisure needs. These authors also demonstrate that the perceived monetary value exerts a positive influence on the intention to adopt these services, and that the perceived enjoyment has a positive influence on the intention to adopt. Their study also confirms that the perceived enjoyment has a positive influence on perceived usefulness and perceived ease-of-use, and that social influence has a positive influence on the intention to adopt.

WHAT ARE EXPLANATORY FACTORS FOR THE INTENTION TO ADOPT A MOBILE COACHING SERVICE?

Vicarious Innovativeness

Vicarious innovativeness towards cell phone coaching services should influence the intention to adopt a specialist service such as help with stopping smoking. Therefore, the authors propose the following hypothesis:

H1: Vicarious innovativeness towards coaching services exerts a direct, positive influence on the intention to adopt a text-message based mobile coaching service to stop smoking.

Apart from the innovativeness related to the above field, other variables may influence the adoption process. In this study, the authors consider social influence, perceived monetary value, perceived enjoyment, perceived irritation and demographic profile. Future research could examine the influence of other variables.

Social Influence

This is defined as the measure of a subject's belief of whether significant referents will approve or disapprove of the subject adopting a certain behavior (Ajzen, 1991). This social influence is exerted through messages and signals that help to form perceptions concerning the value of a product or activity (Venkatesh & Brown, 2001).

Various studies confirm that peers, superiors and family members all influence consumer behavior and the decisions associated with adoption of products or services (Venkatesh & Brown, 2001; Hong & Tam, 2006).

In the theory of planned behavior, intention, as a determinant of behavior, is conditioned by attitude, subjective norms (or social influence) and perceived behavioral control, which is a kind of perceived ease of adoption (Ajzen, 1991). Mathieson (1991) developed a scale to measure this social influence that was used by Hong & Tam (2006) to demonstrate that social influence has a direct, positive effect on the intention to adopt mobile data services. They define such services as a set of digital data services accessed by a mobile device across a vast geographical zone that can be used to exchange messages, pictures and emails, check flight times, book concert tickets and play games, making no distinction between the services and the devices used to access them.

Mobile coaching services, such as support with stopping smoking, are services in which messages of encouragement are sent at random intervals to users, and are therefore a specific category of mobile services. Based on past studies, the authors propose the following hypothesis:

H2: Social influence (SOCIAL) has a direct, positive effect on the intention to adopt a text-message based mobile coaching service to stop smoking.

Perceived Monetary Value

Most consumers encode prices along a scale and classify products as "expensive" or "cheap" even when they are not familiar with the products concerned. This happens because individuals call on references associated with similar experiences. In general, consumers mentally consider the perceived quality and perceived sacrifice associated with a price. This consideration brings about a perceived monetary value in the consumer's mind, which has an effect on the consumer's intention to adopt a product (Dodds, Monroe, & Grewal, 1991).

When the consumer attaches high importance to the use value, he is willing to make a greater monetary sacrifice. If the consumer who intends to stop smoking perceives the mobile coaching services as having a higher use value than other methods of stopping smoking then he will have the intention to adopt them. Based on these premises, the authors propose the following hypothesis:

H3: The perceived monetary value (MONEY) exerts a positive influence on the intention to adopt a text-message based mobile coaching service to stop smoking.

Perceived Enjoyment

Seeking pleasurable, fun experiences is a typical personal desire (Rokeach, 1973). The value of enjoyment as regards use of an innovation is conceptualized as the extent to which use of an innovation is agreeable in itself, independently of the expected consequences of its performance.

The variables of enjoyment and irritation are rooted in study of the affect and its influence on behavior in general and innovative behavior in particular. Several studies show that the perceived enjoyment value explains adoption of information technologies (Hong & Tam, 2006). Venkatesh and Morris (2000) and Venkatesh and Brown (2001) argue in their research that perceived enjoyment can have an indirect impact on intention through the perceived ease-of-use.

Hong and Tam (2006), meanwhile, suggest that services such as downloadable games, horoscopes or videos can help to pass the time agreeably while a person is waiting for a train. They show that the perceived enjoyment has a positive influence on the intention to adopt mobile data services. In this view, the "fun" aspect of the mobile service will facilitate its adoption and have a positive effect on attitudes. But other researchers such as Chowdhury et al. (2006) find that the influence exerted by perceived enjoyment on the attitude towards mobile advertising is negative and non-significant. To verify this, the authors propose the following hypothesis:

H4: The perceived enjoyment (ENJOY) exerts a positive influence on the intention to adopt a text-message based mobile coaching service to stop smoking.

Perceived Irritation

Based on the fact that mobile advertising may be perceived by the consumer as invasive, irritating or boring, Chowdhury et al. (2006) propose a scale of perceived irritation, which is not the same thing as the absence of perceived enjoyment. They set out to demonstrate that this construct is negatively associated with the consumer's attitude to mobile advertising.

However, their research leads to the opposite finding, namely that the *influence of irritation on the attitude to mobile adverting is positive but non-significant*. As regards the intention to adopt a mobile coaching service for support while stopping smoking, this leads us to propose the following hypothesis:

H5: Perceived irritation (IRRITA) exerts a negative influence on the intention to adopt a text-message based mobile coaching service to stop smoking.

Considering the conceptual framework developed above, the authors propose the following model in Figure 1.

It is intuitive to think that light smokers (who smoke less than 5 cigarettes a day) and heavy smokers (who smoke more than 10 cigarettes a day) won't have the same intention to adopt a smoking cessation device. The light smokers don't feel so dependent, and medical research shows that the more you smoke the more dependent you are. They may feel they can stop at any moment. They may have the intention to do so for different reasons (social influence, savings). As they think that 5 cigarettes or less is "nothing" they may also feel it is not dangerous for their health. The following hypotheses compare different groups of individuals:

Figure 1. Model of adoption of a text-message based mobile coaching service

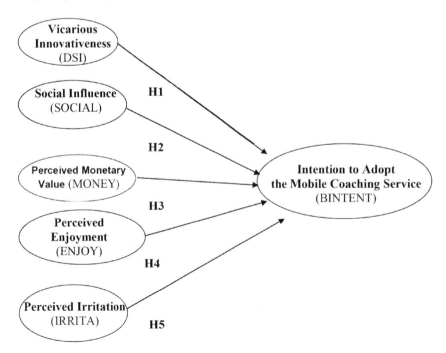

H6a: The intention to adopt the Mobile Coaching Service differs between light and heavy smokers.
H6b: The effect of perceived enjoyment is greater in light smokers than in heavy smokers because these ones know how difficult it may be to stop.

Adolescents may feel less concerned for their health as at their age cancer seems a very far possibility and more subject to social influence than adults

H7: The intention to adopt the Mobile Coaching Service differs between adolescent and adult smokers.

METHODOLOGY

This research was initially originated through a collaborative project with a French start-up company called *e-Medicis*, which was considering introducing a new service to provide support for people who wanted to stop smoking. The study took the form of a face-to-face survey with a convenience sample of 113 people in several Paris locations (Cacho-Elizondo, Shahidi & Tossan, 2013). The objectives were to measure vicarious innovativeness as regards mobile services, to measure the intention to adopt the mobile coaching service for stopping smoking, and to validate the hypotheses. The analysis also covered the demographic profile of participants, their smoking behavior (heavy smokers/medium smokers/light smokers/non-smokers).

Measures

Below is the analysis of the data collected through the face-to-face survey with smokers. The description of the mobile coaching service tested in the survey is provided in Appendix 3. The analysis done used the structural equations method. Six 5-point Likert scales from "totally disagree" to "totally agree" were used to measure the variables in the model. The scales are described, together with the authors that inspired them, in Table 1.

Intention to Adopt the Mobile Coaching Service (BINTENT)

To measure this construct, the authors used a French adaptation of the scale proposed by Davis et al (1989), itself adapted from Ajzen and Fishbein (1980). This scale consists of three items: (1) I intend to use this mobile coaching service to stop smoking in the future. (2) I would be prepared to use this mobile coaching service to stop smoking in the future. (3) To stop smoking, I will use this service.

Vicarious Innovativeness (DSI)

Goldsmith and Hofacker (1991) distinguish global innovativeness from domain-specific innovativeness that can be applied to a specific category of products or services. They propose a scale to measure consumers' tendency to be among the first to try out new products in a specific field. This 5-point scale consists of six items that capture the following constructs: *involvement, usage, intention to adopt, opinion seeking, perceived knowledge* and *need for change*. The scale has been validated for durables and other goods as well as for services.

In 2007, Pagani added two further indicators to this scale. The first, *ease of use*, is an indicator that emerges from the theory of reasoned action and the Technology Acceptance Model (TAM) constructed by Davis (1989). The second, the *need for cognition*, is an indicator drawn from psychological studies. Pagani (2007) uses this scale to measure the vicarious innovativeness regarding third generation (3G) mobile music services, which use technology to generate voice, images and video in any place, soc or terminal.

Pagani showed in her research that the scale gained reliability when the *opinion seeking* and *usage* items were eliminated. Her final modified scale consists of 6 items measuring involvement, intention to adopt, perceived knowledge, ease of use, need for change and need for cognition. In addition to these items, the authors include a *price* item (I will adopt a mobile coaching service if the price is right, an item used by Pagani (2007) to test the nomological validity of her scale).

Social Influence (SOCIAL)

Following Mathieson (1991), three items were used: (1) People who are important to me would want me to use this mobile coaching service. (2) People who influence my behavior would think I should use this mobile coaching service. (3) People whose opinions I value would prefer me to use this mobile coaching service.

Perceived Monetary Value (MONEY)

Following Dodds et al. (1991), three items were used: (1) I expect this mobile service would have a reasonable price. (2) This mobile service would offer good value for money. (3) I believe that at the right price, this mobile service would be good value.

Perceived Enjoyment (ENJOY)

The authors adopt the scale devised by Chowdhury et al. (2006). Three items were used: (1) I expect that using this mobile service would be enjoyable. (2) I expect that using this mobile service would be pleasing. (3) I expect that using this mobile service would be entertaining.

Perceived Irritation (IRRITA)

As previously, the authors use the scale devised by Chowdhury et al. (2006). Three items were used: (1) I feel that this mobile service is irritating. (2) I feel that mobile coaching services are everywhere and, there is no need for another. (3) This mobile service looks annoying.

The following Table 1 summarizes our measurement scales.

Control Variables

The model includes the classification of smokers by number of cigarettes smoked by day and age. There are heavy smokers who smoke more than 10 cigarettes a day and light smokers who smoke fewer than 5 cigarettes a day. The control variables are used in the section "Analysis of Subsamples" in order to test the hypothesis H6a, H6b and H7.

Table 1. Measurement scales

Concept	Label	Items	Adapted from
Intention to Adopt the Mobile Coaching Service	BINTENT	1. I intend to use this mobile coaching service to stop smoking in the future. 2. I would be prepared to use this mobile coaching service to stop smoking in the future. 3. To stop smoking, I will use this service	Davis (1989)
Vicarious Innovativeness	DSI	1. **Involvement:** If I heard a new mobile coaching service was available, I would be interested in using it. 2. **Intention to adopt:** I would consider adopting a new mobile coaching service even if I had not yet heard about it. 3. **Perceived knowledge:** I know more about new mobile coaching services than other people do. 4. **Ease of use:** If I heard that a new mobile coaching service was available and easy to use, I would be interested enough to adopt it. 5. **Need for change:** I adopt a new mobile coaching service because of the advantages it offers me. 6. **Need for cognition:** Before adopting a new mobile coaching service I consider the benefits provided by innovation and its relationship to the status quo. 7. **Price:** I would adopt the mobile coaching service if the price was right (intention to adopt if you have to pay and at what price level, or if the service is free, sponsored by a private or public organization).	Pagani (2007)
Social Influence	SOCIAL	1. People who are important to me would want me to use this mobile coaching service. 2. People who influence my behavior would think I should use this mobile coaching service. 3. People whose opinions I value would prefer me to use this mobile coaching service.	Mathieson (1991)
Perceived Monetary Value	MONEY	1. I expect that this mobile service would have a reasonable price. 2. This mobile service would offer good value for money. 3. I believe that at the right price, this mobile service would be good value.	Dodds, Monroe & Grewal (1991)

STATISTICAL ANALYSES AND RESULTS

Descriptive Analysis

The sample shows a homogeneous distribution between men (52%) and women (48%). Among the participants, 42% are adolescents, 34% of them are aged between 18 and 21 years old, 19% between 22 and 25 years old and 5% were over 25 years old. More than 80% of participants (N=92) stated that they smoke every day or nearly every day. Smokers can be grouped into three categories according to the number of cigarettes smoked per day: *light smokers* (N=32, 28.3%), *medium smokers* (N=40, 35.4%) and *heavy smokers* (N=41, 36.3%) (see Table 2). A statistic test demonstrated that the category of smokers varies according to the age range. Herein, 50% of smokers tried at least once to quit smoking (38% are adolescents and 62% are adults). A test showed that this did not depend on the categories of smokers.

Several types of messages were proposed to help smokers to stop smoking and evaluated by the respondents. The averages by type of message have been compared (Challenge / Fear / Humor), there are no differences across them. The authors notice that Fear messages could help more people intend to stop smoking with a higher rate of success.

Of the 113 participants in the study, only 37 stated that they intended to stop smoking in the next 12 months; 76 did not share that intention. However, the average intention to adopt the service does not differ significantly between the two groups, i.e. between people who say they want to stop smoking and the rest (F=2.62 (0)). The analysis shows that the variable Intention is low on average (see Table 4), while the perceived monetary value is high.

Among the people who intend to stop smoking in the next 12 months (N=37), most were Heavy Smokers (more than 10 cigarettes a day) and Light Smokers (fewer than 5 cigarettes a day). Medium Smokers (5 to 9 cigarettes a day) have proportionally less intention of giving up smoking; probably because, according to the arguments collected in the exploratory study they are less worried about their budget and their health, or are under less pressure from their entourage.

One of the barriers to adopting the service that emerges from the study is the lack of human contact in the coaching service. This is observed more with individuals over 18 than individuals under 18. The reason may be that the latter who are digital natives and so more used to digital services without human contact.

Analysis of the variance shows a significant difference between the averages for the two groups of individuals (F=2.969 and p-value=0.088). Of the 43 individuals who would not use this service because of the lack of human contact, 22 think it could help someone else to stop smoking. This is consistent with extant literature that shows that consumer acceptance of the mobile Internet is linked with a low desire for social contact (Koenigstorfer & Groeppel-Klein, 2012), the mobile Internet being a replacement of social contact (Syed & Nurullah, 2011).

Hypotheses H1 to H7 (except H6a) were tested using the structural equations technique. The maximum likelihood fit function was applied. A two-stage approach was used as recommended by Anderson and Gerbing (1988). First, the measurement instruments for the constructs were assessed by examining the reliability and validity of scales. Then, the relationships were tested.

Table 2. Categorization of smokers based on Cigarettes consumed

Category	Adolescent	Adult
Light (< 5 cigarettes)	18	14
Medium (5-9 cigarettes)	20	20
Heavy (>10 cigarettes)	10	31

Table 3. Evaluation of text messages

Items	Mean
Challenge messages	
Hello you are able to follow your plans[1]	1.88
In spite of the effort you didn't give up	2.91
Refusing to smoke when you want is a sign of strenght and maturity	2.60
Your will is enough	2.56
An additional evidence of strenght of will!	2.53
I knew you would succeed	2.66
Fear messages	
Only you can do something for your health	2.81
Your lungs are worthwhile	2.89
It is cigarette or your skin	2.72
Your blood circulation is worthwhile	2.10
A lung is so useful	2.94
Hello! Today they are 200 French people that are going to die directly because of tobacco	3.02
Humor messages	
Take some fresh air...I hope it is not raining	2.12
Don't think of it!!!What are you doing next week-end?	2.61
You can do it	2.96
A day won, it is cool!	2.70
For real success in love quit cigarette	2.36
Tell me please:3X3/2=...nothing to do with...think of something else..., you will hold on!	2.40

NB: A 5-point Likert scales from
"will not help me a all" (1) to "will help me a lot" (5) is used to measure each items

Scale Reliability and Validity

The reliability of all instruments was tested by the Cronbach's alpha reliability coefficient (see Table 5). All coefficients are acceptable, except those associated with the perceived irritation construct ($\alpha=0.56$). Consequently, the IRRITA construct was eliminated from the model and hypothesis H5 was not tested. As Table 5 shows, the Jöreskog ρ values are high (except for the IRRITA construct).

Each item is better explained by the construct it relates to than by chance. Concerning convergent validity, the influence of relationships (between the measures and their construct) is statistically different from 0. The average extracted variance between a construct and its measures is always above 0.5 (except for the IRRITA construct).

Table 4. Scores of variables

Variables	Full Sample
DSI	2.79 (1) 0.99 (2)
SOCIAL	2.37 1.18
MONEY	3.29 1.31
ENJOY	2.46 1.16
BINTENT	2.23 1.22
IRRITA	2.82 1.12

NB: (1) The mean (2) The standard deviation

To test discriminant validity, the authors conducted a Chi squared difference test (by reference to the difference in degrees of freedom). To test the discriminant validity, the analysis recommended by Bagozzi and Yi (1991) relies on a comparison between the χ^2 values of a model that leaves the correlations between the different constructs free, and a model in which the correlations between constructs are fixed at 1. If the difference is significant in view of the difference in degree of freedom, it can be concluded that the model tested is better than the constrained model and that the constructs are different. The results for the indicators used in our study are satisfactory *(difference of Chi squared= 22 and difference of dof =6).*

Estimation of the Model

Having established that the goodness of fit is satisfactory, interpretation of the estimations of linear relationships can begin. Our model has two sub-models one to measure independent variables, one to measure dependent variables and a structural model connecting the latent dependent variables to the latent independent variables. There are several observed independent variables that depend on 4 latent variables. These latent variables are correlated. There are also 3 observed dependent variables (3 items

Table 5. Scale reliability and validity

	DSI	SOCIAL	MONEY	ENJOY	IRRITA	BINTENT
Cronbach's alpha	0.86	0.76	0.76	0.83	0.56	0.84
Standardized item loading (> 0.5)						
Item 1	0.64	0.80	0.84	0.76	0.56	0.86
Item 2	0.84	0.84	0.87	0.79	0.72	0.89
Item 3	0.87	0.83	0.74	0.90	0.48	0.85
Item 4	0.72					
Item 5	0.50					
Item 6	0.50					
Item 7	0.76					
Average extracted variance (ρvc>0.5)	0.50	0.53	0.55	0.67	0.35	0.64
Jöreskog ρ (>0.70)	0.86	0.77	0.78	0.86	0.62	0.84

concerning intention) that depend on a latent variable. The indicators are fairly satisfactory (see Table 6). The data thus show a satisfactory goodness of fit for the theoretical model.

This model explains 69% of the variance in intention (R^2). As shown in Table 7, the "perceived enjoyment", "vicarious innovation" and "social influence" variables make a significant contribution to the intention to adopt the mobile coaching service (critical ratio>1.96 or very similar).

Consequently, hypotheses H1, H2 and H4 are validated. However, the direct influence of the "perceived monetary value" variable on intention to adopt the mobile coaching service is not significant, and consequently hypothesis H3 is not validated.

Table 6. Goodness of fit

RMSEA (< 0.08)	0.07
NFI	0.77
CFI (> 0.90)	0.90
TLI (> 0.90)	0.82

Table 7. Effects of variables on the intention to adopt the mobile coaching service

Relationships to Test			Estimation	Critical Ratio
Vicarious Innovativeness	→	Intention	0.26	2.32
Social Influence	→	Intention	0.22	1.90
Perceived Monetary Value	→	Intention	-0.17	-1.43
Perceived Enjoyment	→	Intention	0.75	4.73

The validated model is illustrated in Figure 2.

COMPARISON OF RELATIONSHIPS BETWEEN VARIABLES IN THE SUBSAMPLES

Light and Heavy Smokers

The model tested is now split by type of smoker depending on the number of cigarettes smoked per day. According to Table 8, the means differ between the two samples but the differences are not significant (H6a is not validated). However, the mean of vicarious Innovativeness of light smokers is significantly greater than that of heavy smokers.

Table 9 shows the standardized effects of the model's variables on the intention to adopt the mobile coaching service in each of the two subsamples.

For reasons of clarity, only estimations significant at the 0.05 level are shown. Some variables are significant in one sample but not the other. The greater the perceived enjoyment, the greater is the intention to adopt the mobile coaching service of heavy smokers. Hypothesis H6b is thus confirmed.

Vicarious innovativeness has a significant effect on the intention to adopt the mobile service in individuals who are light smokers.

Adolescent and Adult Smokers

According to Table 10, Vicarious innovativeness is high for adolescents. The means differ between the two samples but the differences are not significant.

Perceived enjoyment has shown a significant effect on the intention to adopt the mobile service in both samples, however, the effect is higher for adolescents than for adults but this difference is not significant (Hypothesis H7 is not validated).

Figure 2. Result of the model tested

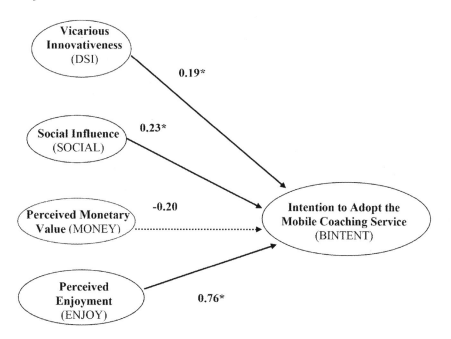

Table 8. Comparison of variables between light and heavy smokers

Variables	Sample 1 *Light smokers* (N=32)	Sample 2 *Heavy smokers* (N=41)	F (df=1)	p	Eta²
DSI	2.88 *(1)* 0.87 *(2)*	2.62 1.01	1.347	.251	.018
SOCIAL	2.42 0.97	2.41 1.21	0.001	.969	.0
MONEY	3.52 1.32	3.33 1.34	0.355	.553	.005
ENJOY	2.75 1.2	2.62 1.20	0.218	.642	.003
BINTENT	2.35 1.26	2.38 1.33	0.008	.928	.0

NB: (1) The mean (2) The standard deviation (3) If the p-value related to the value of statistic F is greater than the significance level 0.05, then the hypothesis H0 (the mean of sample 1 is equal to the mean of sample 2) is not rejected otherwise H0 is rejected. (4) A unilateral test was also done for each variable. The test is significant for the variable DSI. As the Student statistic value z is closed to 1.96, then H'0 (the mean of light smokers is superior than the mean of heavy smokers) is not rejected.

Table 9. Standardized effects on the intention to adopt the mobile coaching service for light and heavy smokers

Variables	Sample 1 Light smokers (N=32)	Sample 2 Heavy smokers (N=41)	Critical Ratios for Differences between Parameters (*)
DSI	0.498		-0.63
SOCIAL			
MONEY			
ENJOY		0.733	2.1

NB: Only significant coefficients (5%) are reported. (*) Comparison of two regression weights: the difference of the regression weights between the two groups is significant (0.05) if the absolute value of the critical ratio is over 1.96.
This table shows only variables which obtain at least one significant statistic test for clarity.
The difference between the two samples is significative for perceived enjoyment.

Table 10. Comparison of variables between adolescents and adults

Variables	Sample 1 Adolescents (N=48)	Sample 2 Adults (N=65)	F (df=1)	p	Eta²
DSI	2.85 (1) 0.94 (2)	2.74 1.03	0.295	.588	.003
SOCIAL	2.40 1.21	2.34 1.18	0.068	.795	.001
MONEY	3.17 1.40	3.37 1.24	0.613	.435	.005
ENJOY	2.63 1.23	2.34 1.11	1.621	.206	.014
BINTENT	2.36 1.28	2.13 1.18	0.955	.331	.009

NB: (1) The mean (2) The standard deviation (3) If the p-value related to the value of statistic F is greater than the significance level 0.05, then the hypothesis H0 (the mean of sample 1 is equal to the mean of sample 2) is not rejected otherwise H0 is rejected. (4) A unilateral test was also done for each variable. The tests are not significant.

Table 11. Standardized effects on the intention to adopt the mobile coaching service for adolescents and adults

Variables	Sample 1 *Adolescents* (N=48)	Sample 2 *Adults* (N=65)	Critical Ratios for Differences between Parameters *(*)*
DSI			
SOCIAL			
MONEY			
ENJOY	0.934	0.433	-1.249

NB: Only significant coefficients (here 1%) are reported. (*) Comparison of two regression weights: the difference of the regression weights between the two groups is significant (0.05) if the absolute value of the critical ratio is over 1.96.
This table shows only variables which obtain at least one significant statistic test for clarity.
The difference between the two samples is not significant.

MAIN CONTRIBUTIONS AND MANAGERIAL IMPLICATIONS

This study has broad social and managerial implications. The field of mobile health services is providing opportunities to make improvements and reduce costs in the French and worldwide health sector. Worldwide, the mobile health market has an estimated value of $50 billion (Ascari et al., 2010). However, attention should not be focused solely on the business opportunities offered by the market, but rather on the social impact of these initiatives. Because these mobile health services can offer continuous "24/7" monitoring and have no geographical barriers, thus, mobile coaching services are open to a larger range of benefits. If they are positioned as accessible services complementing other medical and psychological methods, they could also offer a less formal approach to support in the fight to break addictions.

The intention to adopt the text message-based mobile coaching service to help stop smoking was tested with a mostly young target. This is precisely the group with the greatest risk of developing tobacco-related illnesses in the long term, since the lower the age at which people start smoking, the higher their risks of serious tobacco-related illnesses. Yet the study observed that these young smokers do not always intend to stop smoking in the short term. Explanations may be that they don't fear possible dependence nor illness.

It is important to find new innovative and challenging ways to motivate smokers to try and start the process of giving up smoking. With this in mind, mobile services can play an important role because young people are generally heavy users of cell phones and generally find new technologies attractive (Syed & Nurullah, 2011).

Two factors of influence should be taken into consideration: peer influence and the enjoyment generated by this type of remote coaching service, habitually perceived as a game. The more enjoyment consumers get out of using these services, the more they will be prepared to use them in the future. The designers of this type of service need to develop amusing messages to convince early adopters to talk about the effectiveness of the service and how much fun it was to use. They may mix them with messages including fear as these seem the most effective to intend to stop smoking. They may use artificial intelligence in order to design a chatbot holding a conversation with the user.

Furthermore, if the service is perceived to be at a reasonable price or free because sponsored by a government health organization or by a private insurance company, the potential user will get more enjoyment out of trying it. The influence exercised by smokers' families and general entourage can also play a decisive role in diffusion of these services by their word of mouth. For a private insurance company, offering this service is a way to reach people's engagement and preferences in a very competitive world, where customers are more and more sensitive to companies´ social responsibility. It is also a mean to reduce risks of lung disease and corresponding associated cost.

The above findings also underline the fact that stimulating curiosity and the smokers' intrinsic interest seem to be more important factors than the perceived monetary value. Therefore, it would be judicious to ensure that the most favorable techniques and functions are selected, to give the consumer a higher level of perceived enjoyment and intrinsic inter-user motivation.

LIMITATIONS AND AVENUES FOR FUTURE RESEARCH

The limitations of this study are mainly related to the sample size of the convenience sample and the overrepresentation of young people, which limits its external validity. Larger-scale studies with samples of different population types (multi-country, different age brackets, different types of smokers) will still be required for closer examination of each segment's needs and preferences. Another possible bias is the low number of participants who had stated a clear intention of stopping smoking in the next 12 months. In future research, a much greater effort should be made to recruit people with a concrete intention to stop smoking.

Future studies should be undertaken with a broader sample comprising subjects of all ages, to determine how the desire (or lack of desire) to stop smoking influences the smoker's perception of the mobile coaching service. Some experience of the service would also be advisable in more advanced stages of the research, once the beta version is available, because the measure of attitude to these new services used in this study is based on respondents' own statements and does not involve them much. A measure that allows closer observation of a behavior could be more effective. It would also be useful to test the perceived enjoyment of this type of service, in order to increase numbers giving up other addictions and/ or pay greater attention to other illnesses.

Another interesting avenue to explore is the impact of mobile coaching service in conjunction with e-cigarettes (Wang et al. (2018) showed that e-cigarette users did seem more likely to have tried to quit smoking than never users) which could grow as greater regulation looms. This impact could also be measured with for example, plain packaging proposals that would remove brands from cigarette packs (Wembridge & Thompson, 2012).

In their research Andrews, Cacho-Elizondo, Drennan and Tossan (2013) showed that perceived usefulness continually proves to be the most important predictor of intentions to use a mobile assisted smoking intervention. Based on this, health practitioners offering an m-health service must consider its design and delivery to ensure its usefulness to the target group. For Andrews and her colleagues, this could include whether it is used as an additional component to a web-based intervention or a standalone mobile phone-based intervention. For example, the consumer could use this service anytime he or she desperately longs for the pleasure of a cigarette, and the playfulness and novelty of every service "response" is so exciting that he or she really forgets the desire to smoke.

New technologies are clearly changing the digital and healthcare ecosystem and need to be fully incorporated into this type of interventions. For instance, the growing diffusion of Internet of Things (IoT), which represents the intersection between physical and digital, worlds, will allow the design of products/services better adapted to smokers'needs in real time. *Wearable Tech* allowing a more dynamic and direct two-sided communication with the smoker, will facilitate for example the measurement and monitoring of vital signs overtime.

Also, *Internet of Things (IoT), connected objects, augmented, diminished* and *virtual realities* could provide closer and more efficient communications between smokers and counselors. Nevertheless, few studies have been done on connectedness and its impact on behaviors (Touzani et al., 2017).

Furthermore, *Social Media* (Merrill, 2011a,b) also contributes to the success of cessation processes by facilitating the interaction among the smoker´s closest circles of people (ex. family and friends) and offers new spaces for sharing experiences among smokers. Lakon et al. (2016) suggested potential for Twitter (Tweet2Quit) as a platform for adult smoking-cessation interventions. The growing capability to combine all these technologies promotes new digital platforms which are highly appealing for young smokers as they can provide more immersive experiences.

A multi-country online study could measure how intending (or not intending) to give up smoking in the short term influences the perception of a mobile coaching service to help people stop smoking. It could also measure the impact of cultural and socio-economic factors, including isolation.

In addition, it would be interesting to replicate this study with people who want to break other addictive habits such as excessive consumption of medicines, drugs or food or alcohol, or people suffering from health problems such as depression. Support could be provided through prerecorded messages sent by cell phone alone, or in conjunction with other media, for instance as a complement to an internet application, personalized coaching, or treatments such as nicotine patches to stop smoking. As Oosterveen and colleagues (2017) suggested in their systematic review of eHealth interventions (see Appendix 4), the long-term efficacy of this type of interventions is still to be tested in future research. In a more advanced stage of research, the service itself could be tried out, to determine the value of using theoretical approaches to examine factors influencing the perceptions and attitudes of participants who use the service, app, device and/or platform.

CONCLUSION

This chapter has explored the factors that determine the intention to adopt a mobile coaching service designed to help people stop smoking. The authors obtained a fairly robust model in which vicarious innovativeness, social influence and the perceived enjoyment exert a positive influence on the intention to adopt the mobile coaching service. For the authors, this framework could be used as a starting point to explore adoption patterns of other mobile counseling and mentoring services.

At the methodological level, this research contributes with an improved approach to test the acceptance and potential adoption of new services, not yet available, through the use of a scenario script where the mobile coaching service to quit smoking is described (Appendix 3).

Kihyun et al. (2009) concluded in their research that adoption of an amusing mobile service is a direct reflection of users' way of life insofar as that adoption is in line with socio-economic conditions. In future research, it would be interesting to explore further both the enjoyment aspect of the service and the socio-economic conditions of potential adopters. On this point, male-female differences also require more attention, as our model turned out to be more suited to women. One possible explanation for this could be the level of curiosity associated with this segment, and its usage of mobile applications.

Steenkamp and Gielens (2003) found in their study that the probability of trying an innovation is higher in individuals with a high degree of innovativeness than those with a low degree of innovativeness. These authors compared consumer innovativeness as measured by the attitude scale with innovativeness as measured by actual purchasing behavior for new products, and observe that the results by either measure are equivalent.

Another factor for consideration is the level of the individual´s involvement. Bloch (1982) and Valette-Florence (1989) noted that a high-involvement individual will have a greater propensity to adopt an innovative behavior than a low-involvement individual. An additional lesson to be drawn is the discovery of smokers' preference for multimedia communications including images and videos. This trend would certainly help to compensate for the lack of real human contact that has often been considered as one of the weaknesses of this type of remote coaching service.

The future of mobile health or m-health services is promising, it is necessary to continue encouraging further interdisciplinary research to improve them and spread their adoption and wide application in the health sector worldwide. Special focus should be given to developing countries where m-health services could have a significant impact on low-income vulnerable groups. Research suggests that individuals with different cultural backgrounds may respond differently to adoption of new technologies and services (Hall, 1976, Hofstede. 1984; Bourdieu, 1984).

ACKNOWLEDGMENT

The authors acknowledge the helpful comments and suggestions of Professor Jean-Pierre Helfer, Professor Emeritus at IAE de Paris, Paris Panthéon Sorbonne University, Dean of Professors and President of the Scientific Committee at EDC Paris Business School. The authors would additionally like to thank two anonymous referees for their comments, which strengthened this chapter and the support received from our institutions.

REFERENCES

Ajzen, I. (1991). The Theory of Planned Behavior. *Organizational Behavior and Human Decision Processes*, *50*(2), 179–212. doi:10.1016/0749-5978(91)90020-T

Ajzen, I., & Fishbein, M. (1980). *Understanding Attitudes and Predicting Social*. Englewood Cliffs, NJ: Prentice-Hall.

An, L. C., Klatt, C., Perry, C. L., Lein, E. B., Hennrikus, D. J., Pallonen, U. E., & Ehlinger, E. P. (2008). The RealU online cessation intervention for college smokers: A randomized controlled trial. *Preventive Medicine*, *47*(2), 194–199. doi:10.1016/j.ypmed.2008.04.011 PMID:18565577

Anderson, J. C., & Gerbing, D. W. (1988). Structural Equation Modeling in Practice: A Review and Recommended Two-step Approach. *Psychological Bulletin*, *103*(3), 411–423. doi:10.1037/0033-2909.103.3.411

Andrews, L., Cacho-Elizondo, S., Drenna, J., & Tossan, V. (2013). Consumer Acceptance of an SMS-assisted Smoking Cessation Intervention: A Multi Country Study. *Journal of Health Marketing Quarterly*, *30*(1), 47–62. doi:10.1080/07359683.2013.758015 PMID:23458481

Ascari, A., Bakshi, A. & Grijpink, F. (2010). *mHealth: A New Vision for Healthcare*. McKinsey & Company, Inc.

Bagozzi, R. P., & Yi, Y. (1991). Multitrait-Multimethod Matrices in Consumer Research. *JMR, Journal of Marketing Research*, *17*, 426–439.

Bloch, P. H. (1982). Involvement beyond the Purchase Process: Conceptual Issues and Empirical Investigation. *Advances in Consumer Research. Association for Consumer Research (U. S.)*, *9*(1), 413–417.

Borelli, B., Bartlet, Y. K., Tootley, E., Armitage, C. J., & Wearden, A. (2015). Prevalence and frequency of mHealth and eHealth use among US and UK smokers and differences by motivation to quit. *Journal of Medical Internet Research*, *17*(7). PMID:26149323

Bourdieu, P. (1984). *Distinction: A Social Critique of the Judgement of Taste*. Harvard University Press.

Cacho-Elizondo S., Shahidi N. & Tossan V. (2013). Intention to adopt a text message-based mobile coaching service to help stop smoking: which explanatory variables? *International Journal of Technology and Human Interaction*, (4).

Cestre, G. (1996). Diffusion et Innovativité: Définition, Modélisation et Mesure. *Recherche et Applications en Marketing*, *11*(1), 69–88. doi:10.1177/076737019601100105

Chowdhury, H. K., Parvin, N., Weitenberner, C., & Becker, M. (2006). Consumer Attitude toward Mobile Advertising in an Emerging Market: An Empirical Study. *International Journal of Mobile Marketing*, *1*(2).

d'Hauteville, F. (1994). *Un Modèle d'Acceptation du Nouveau Produit par le Consommateur: Cas du Vin allégé en Alcool* (Unpublished Doctoral Dissertation). Université Montpellier II, France.

Davis, F. D. (1989). Perceived Usefulness, Perceived Ease of Use, and User Acceptance of Information Technology. *Management Information Systems Quarterly*, *13*(3), 319–340. doi:10.2307/249008

Davis, F. D., Bagozzi, R. P., & Warshaw, P. R. (1989). User Acceptance of Computer Technology: A Comparison of Two Theoretical Models. *Management Science*, *35*(8), 982–1003. doi:10.1287/mnsc.35.8.982

Dodds, W. B., Monroe, K. B., & Grewal, D. (1991). Effects of Price, Brand, and Store Information on Buyers' Product Evaluations. *JMR, Journal of Marketing Research*, *28*(3), 307–319. doi:10.2307/3172866

Foxall, G., & Haskins, C. G. (1986). Cognitive Style and Consumer Innovativeness: An Empirical Test of Kirton's Adaptation-Innovation Theory in the Context of Food Purchasing. *European Journal of Marketing*, *20*(3/4), 63–80. doi:10.1108/EUM0000000004755

Gatignon, H., & Robertson, T. S. (1985). A propositional Inventory for New Diffusion Research. *The Journal of Consumer Research*, *11*(4), 849–867. doi:10.1086/209021

Goldsmith, R. E., d'Hauteville, F., & Flynn, L. R. (1998). Theory and Measurement of Consumer Innovativeness. *European Journal of Marketing*, *32*(3/4), 340–353. doi:10.1108/03090569810204634

Goldsmith, R. E., & Hofacker, C. H. (1991). Measuring Consumer Innovativeness. *Journal of the Academy of Marketing Science, 19*(3), 209–221. doi:10.1007/BF02726497

Hall, E. T. (1976). *Beyond Culture*. Anchor Doubleday Press.

Hebden, L., Cook, A., van der Ploeg, H. P., King, L., Bauman, A., & Allman-Farinelli, M. (2013). A mobile health intervention for weight management among young adults: A pilot randomised controlled trial. *Journal of Human Nutrition and Dietetics, 27*(4), 322–332. doi:10.1111/jhn.12155 PMID:23992038

Hofstede, G. (1984). *Culture's Consequences: International Differences in Work-related Values*. Sage Publications.

Hong, S., & Tam, K. Y. (2006). Understanding the Adoption of Multipurpose Information Appliances: The Case of Mobile Data Services. *Information Systems Research, 17*(2), 162–179. doi:10.1287/isre.1060.0088

Hurt, H. T., Joseph, K., & Cook, C. D. (1977). Scales for the Measurement of Innovativeness. *Human Communication Research, 4*(1), 58–65. doi:10.1111/j.1468-2958.1977.tb00597.x

INPES (French National Health Prevention and Education Institute). (2007). Le tabac tue un fumeur sur deux. L'industrie du tabac compte sur vous pour les remplacer. *Espace Presse*. Retrieved April 4, 2015 from: www.inpes.sante.fr/70000/cp/07/cp070820.asp

Kihyun, K., Gyenung-Min, K., & Eun Sook, K. (2009). Measuring the Compatibility Factors in Mobile Entertainment Service Adoption. *Journal of Computer Information Systems*, (Fall): 141–148.

Koenigstorfer, J., & Groeppel-Klein, A. (2012). Consumer Acceptance of the Mobile Internet. *Marketing Letters, 23*(4), 917–928. doi:10.100711002-012-9206-1

Kothe, E. J., & Mullan, B. A. (2014). A randomised controlled trial of a theory of planned behavior to increase fruit and vegetable consumption. *Fresh Facts Appetite, 78*, 68–75. doi:10.1016/j.appet.2014.03.006 PMID:24656949

Kotler, P., & Armstrong, G. (2006). *Principles of Marketing* (11th ed.). Pearson Prentice-hall.

Kotz, D., Brown, J., & West, R. (2014, March). "Real-world" effectiveness of smoking cessation treatments: A population study. *Addiction (Abingdon, England), 109*(3), 491–499. doi:10.1111/add.12429 PMID:24372901

Krebs, P., & Duncan, D. T. (2015, November). Health app use among US mobile phone owners: A national survey. *JMIR mHealth and uHealth, 3*(4), e101. doi:10.2196/mhealth.4924 PMID:26537656

Lakon, C. M., Pechmann, C., Cheng, W., Li, P., Delucchi, K., & Prochaska, J. J. (2016). Mapping Engagement in Twitter-Based Support Networks for Adult Smoking Cessation. *American Journal of Public Health, 106*(8), 1374–1380. doi:10.2105/AJPH.2016.303256 PMID:27310342

Le Louarn, P. (1997). La Tendance à Innover des Consommateurs: Analyse Conceptuelle et Proposition d'une Échelle de Mesure. *Recherche et Applications en Marketing, 12*(1), 3–19. doi:10.1177/076737019701200101

Le Nagard-Assayag, E., & Manceau, D. (2011). *Le Marketing de l'Innovation, de la Création au Lancement de Nouveaux Produits* (2nd ed.). Paris: Dunod.

Lister, C., West, J. H., Cannon, B., Sax, T., & Brodegard, D. (2014, August 4). Just a fad? Gamification in health and fitness apps. *JMIR Serious Games*, *2*(2), e9. doi:10.2196/games.3413 PMID:25654660

Mason, M., Benotsch, E. G., Way, T., Kim, H., & Snipes, D. (2014). Text messaging to increase readiness to change alcohol use in college students. *The Journal of Primary Prevention*, *35*(1), 47–52. doi:10.100710935-013-0329-9 PMID:24114551

Masson, J. (2010). *Effets de la Modification d'un Attribut Constitutif d'un Produit Alimentaire sur son Adoption par les Consommateurs: Le cas du Vin à teneur réduite en Alcoo.* (Unpublished Doctoral Dissertation). Montpellier Supagro, Centre International d'Etudes Supérieures en Sciences Agronomiques, France.

Mathieson, K. (1991). Predicting User Intentions: Comparing the Technology Acceptance Model with the Theory of Planned Behavior. *Information Systems Research*, *2*(3), 173–191. doi:10.1287/isre.2.3.173

Merrill, M. (2011a). HHS mHealth initiatives target smoking cessation. *Healthcare IT News*. Retrieved April 4, 2015 from www.healthcareitnews.com/news/hhs-mhealth-initiatives-target-smoking-cessation

Merrill, M. (2011b). Study finds potential in social media tools for smoking cessation. *Healthcare IT News.* Retrieved April 4, 2015 from www.healthcareitnews.com/news/study-find-potential-social-media-health-tools-smoking-cessation

Midgley, D. F., & Dowling, G. R. (1993). A Longitudinal Study of Product Form Innovation: The Interaction between Predispositions and Social Messages. *The Journal of Consumer Research*, *19*(4), 611–625. doi:10.1086/209326

Napolitano, M. A., Hayes, S., Bennett, G. G., Ives, A. K., & Foster, G. D. (2013). Using facebook and text messaging to deliver a weight loss program to college students. *Obesity (Silver Spring, Md.)*, *21*(1), 25–31. doi:10.1002/oby.20232 PMID:23505165

One month without tobacco event. (n.d.). Retrieved from http://mois-sans-tabac.tabac-info-service.fr/

Oosterveen, E., Tzelepis, F., Ashton, L., & Hutchesson, M. (2017). A systematic review of eHealth behavioral interventions targeting smoking, nutrition, alcohol, physical activity and/or obesity for young adults. *Preventive Medicine*, *99*, 197–206. doi:10.1016/j.ypmed.2017.01.009 PMID:28130046

Ornes, L., & Ransdell, L. B. (2007). Web-based physical activity intervention for college-aged women. *International Electronic Journal of Health Education*, *10*, 126–137.

Ostlund, L. E. (1974). Perceived innovation attributes as predictors of innovativeness. *The Journal of Consumer Research*, *1*(2), 23–29. doi:10.1086/208587

Pagani, M. (2007). A Vicarious Innovativeness Scale for 3G Mobile Services: Integrating the Domain Specific Innovativeness Scale with Psychological and Rational Indicators. *Technology Analysis and Strategic Management*, *19*(6), 709–728. doi:10.1080/09537320701711207

PwC (PricewaterhouseCooper). (2013). *Socio-economic impact of m-health, An assessment report for the European Union*. Retrieved November 2014, from http://www.pwc.fr/socio-economic-impact-of-mhealth-an-assessment-report-for-the-european-union.html

Riffai, M. M. M. A., Grant, K., & Edgar, D. (2012). Big TAM in Oman: Exploring the promise of on-line banking, its adoption by customers and the challenges of banking in Oman. *International Journal of Information Management, 32*(3), 239–250. doi:10.1016/j.ijinfomgt.2011.11.007

Roehrich, G. (1994). Innovativités Hédoniste et Sociale: Proposition d'une Échelle de Mesure. *Recherche et Applications en Marketing, 9*(2), 19–42. doi:10.1177/076737019400900202

Rogers, E. M. (Ed.). (1962). *Diffusion of Innovations*. New York: The Free Press.

Rogers, E. M. (Ed.). (1983). *Diffusion of Innovations* (3rd ed.). New York: The Free Press.

Rokeach, M. (1973). *The Nature of Human Values*. New York: The Free Press.

Schwerdtfeger, A. R., Schmitz, C., & Warken, M. (2012). Using text messages to bridge the intention-behavior gap? A pilot study on the use of text message reminders to increase objectively assessed physical activity in daily life. *Frontiers in Psychology, 3*. PMID:22876237

Simmons, V. N., Heckman, B. W., Fink, A. C., Small, B. J., & Brandon, T. H. (2013). Efficacy of an experiential, dissonance-based smoking intervention for college students delivered via the internet. *Journal of Consulting and Clinical Psychology, 81*(5), 810–820. doi:10.1037/a0032952 PMID:23668667

Sriramatr, S., Berry, T. R., & Spence, J. C. (2014). An Internet-based intervention for promoting and maintaining physical activity: A randomized controlled trial. *American Journal of Health Behavior, 38*(3), 430–439. doi:10.5993/AJHB.38.3.12 PMID:25181763

Steenkamp, J.-B. E. M., & Gielens, K. (2003). Consumer and Market Drivers of the Trial Probability of New Consumer Packaged Goods. *The Journal of Consumer Research, 29*(December), 368–384. doi:10.1086/378615

Subin, I., Mason, C. H., & Houston, M. B. (2007). Does Innate Consumer Innovativeness relate to New Product/ Service Adoption Behavior? The Intervening Role of Social Learning via Vicarious Innovativeness? *Journal of the Academy of Marketing Science, 35*(1), 63–75. doi:10.100711747-006-0007-z

Suffoletto, B., Kristan, J., Callaway, C., Kim, K. H., Chung, T., Monti, P. M., & Clark, D. B. (2014). A text message alcohol intervention for young adult emergency department patients: A randomized clinical trial. *Annals of Emergency Medicine, 64*(6), 664–672. doi:10.1016/j.annemergmed.2014.06.010 PMID:25017822

Syed, S. F., & Nurullah, A. S. (2011). Use of Mobile Phones and the Social Lives of Urban Adolescents: A Review of Literature. *Trends in Information Management, 7*(1), 1–18.

Thompson, C., & Wembridge, M. (2012, August 12). Big Tobacco Push for Cigarette Alternatives. *Financial Times*.

Touzani, M., Charfi, A. A., Boistel, P., & Niort, M.-C. (2017). *Connecto ergo sum*! An Exploratory Study of Motivations behind the Usage of Connected Objects. *Information & Management*.

Ubhi, H. K., Kotz, D., Michie, S., Van Schayck, O. C. P., Sheard, D., Selladurai, A., & West, R. (2016). Comparative analysis of smoking cessation smartphone applications available in 2012 versus 2014. *Addictive Behaviors*, *58*, 175–181. doi:10.1016/j.addbeh.2016.02.026 PMID:26950256

Valette-Florence, P. (1989). Conceptualisation et Mesure de l'Implication. *Recherche et Applications en Marketing*, *4*(1), 57–78. doi:10.1177/076737018900400104

Venkatesh, V., & Brown, S. (2001). A Longitudinal Investigation of Personal Computers in Homes: Adoption Determinants and Emerging Challenges. *Management Information Systems Quarterly*, *25*(1), 71–102. doi:10.2307/3250959

Venkatesh, V., & Morris, M. (2000). Why don't Men ever Stop to Ask for Directions? Gender, Social Influence and their Role in Technology Acceptance and Usage Behavior. *Management Information Systems Quarterly*, *24*(1), 115–139. doi:10.2307/3250981

Venkatraman, M. P., & Price, L. (1990). Differentiating between Cognitive and Sensory Innovativeness: Concepts, Measurement, and Implications. *Journal of Business Research*, *20*(4), 293–315. doi:10.1016/0148-2963(90)90008-2

Wang, X., Zhang, X., Xu, X., & Gao, Y. (2018). Electronic cigarette use and smoking cessation behavior among adolescents in China. *Addictive Behaviors*, *82*, 129–134. doi:10.1016/j.addbeh.2018.02.029 PMID:29522934

Wembridge, M., & Thompson, C. (2012). Big Tobacco bets on e-cigarette future. *Financial Times*. Retrieved November, 2014, from http://www.ft.com/cms/s/0/cb76997ee0a511e1b46500144feab49a.html#ixzz23RJXFAJZ

West, R., Walia, A., Hyder, N., Shahab, L., & Michie, S. (2010). Behavior change techniques used by the English stop smoking services and their associations with short-term quit outcomes. *Nicotine & Tobacco Research*, *12*(7), 742–747. doi:10.1093/ntr/ntq074 PMID:20478957

Whittaker, R., Maddison, R., McRobbie, H., Bullen, C., Denny, S., Dorey, E., & Rodgers, A. (2008). A Multimedia Mobile Phone-Based Youth Smoking Cessation Intervention: Findings from Content Development and Piloting Studies. *Journal of Medical Internet Research*, *10*(5), e49. doi:10.2196/jmir.1007 PMID:19033148

Ybarra, M. L., Holtrop, J. S., Prescott, T. L., Rahbar, M. H., & Strong, D. (2013). Pilot RCT results of stop my smoking USA: A text messaging-based smoking cessation program for young adults. *Nicotine & Tobacco Research*, *15*(8), 1388–1399. doi:10.1093/ntr/nts339 PMID:23348969

KEY TERMS AND DEFINITIONS

Mobile Health or M-Health: It considers all the declinations of healthcare using mobile portable or wireless devices.

Perceived Enjoyment: The fun you may have while playing with an application.

Perceived Irritation: Based on the fact that mobile advertising may be perceived by you as invasive, irritating, or boring.

Perceived Monetary Value: The value you obtain according to the price quality ratio.

Social Influence: Influence of the people who matter to you towards your behavior.

APPENDIX 1

Tobacco Control Measures in the European Union

(https://ec.europa.eu/health/tobacco/policy_en)

- The regulation of tobacco products on the EU market (e.g. packaging, labelling, and ingredients)
- Advertising restrictions for tobacco products
- The creation of smoke-free environments
- Tax measures and activities against illicit trade
- Anti-smoking campaigns

APPENDIX 2

Some Examples of Smoking Cessation

- **Smokitten**: It is the first video game to stop smoking. See https://www.smokitten.com and also http://www.dowino.com.

Smokitten *is a serious game to encourage smokers to break the habit and prevent children from ever starting! It is aimed both at adult smokers who want to end their addiction and at raising children's awareness of tobacco-related risks and harm. The player can fight their urge to smoke through plenty of activities that are simple and engaging and/or relaxing (running, yoga, angling…), but they can also get support from a whole community, with whom they can share their doubts and successes!*

It is proposed by Dowino, an independent studio developing serious game which is already specialised in social issues such as disabilities and also sustainable development.

This video game is partially financed by a crowdfunding campaign on Ulule, which is the 1st European Crowdfunding site.

- The French government launched in November 2017 the "One month without tobacco event"(see http://mois-sans-tabac.tabac-info-service.fr/) that is advertised on Tv: The idea is that if you stop one month the odds to stop definitively are multiplied by 5. A community is created via Facebook and Twitter. You can either participate or support a person. Because everything is easier when you are involved in a team you can join a geographic or a lifestyle team or even create your team and exchange with it for support. A famous TV animator coached by a physician that has many TV shows appear as role model.

APPENDIX 3

Description of the Mobile Coaching Service Provided in the Interviews

We are now going to describe the main characteristics of a SMS assisted smoking cessation service which allows you to receive SMS or MMS message on your mobile phone to help you quit smoking:

Every morning you would receive an SMS or MMS message on your mobile phone to encourage you to not smoke all day.

If during the day, you feel that you will break your effort to not smoke, you can send an SMS message to a special mobile phone number to ask for help.

You will receive a supportive SMS message back immediately that would be specifically adapted to your needs.

In the middle or at the end of the day, if you haven't sent any alert messages, you'll receive an SMS or MMS message of congratulations and encouragement.

You would be able to modify the timing of receiving the messages to suit the times of day that are most convenience for you.

APPENDIX 4

See Table 12.

Table 12. Examples of SNAPO (smoking rates, nutrition behaviors, alcohol intake, physical activity levels, and/or obesity) studies

Healthy problem	Type of eHealth intervention	Studies	Improvement to control group	eHealth vs Non eHealth	eHealth vs other delivery mode
Smoking	Website and email	An et al. (2008)	+	No differences (Simmons et al., 2013)	No differences (Buller et al., 2014)
	Website and text messages	Ybarra et al. (2013)	+		
	Website	Simmons et al. (2013)	+		
Nutrition	Email	Kothe and Mullan (2014)	=		
Alcohol	Website and computer	Simmons et al. (2013)	+	No differences (Alfonso et al., 2013)	Computer with personal assistance better than only computer (Wagener et al., 2012)
	Text messages	Suffoletto et al. (2014)	+		
	Text messages	Mason et al. (2014)	=		
Physical Activity	Website and email	Ornes and Ransdell (2007)	+	No differences (Sriramatr et al., 2014)	
	Website, email and telephone	Sriramatr et al. (2014)	+		
	Text messages and face-to-face group session	Schwerdtfeger et al. (2012)	+		
Obesity	Text message, mobile app, website, email, telephone, and printed materials	Partridge et al., (2015b)	+	No differences (Lachausse, 2012)	Facebook, e-mail, and text messages intervention, better than Facebook and email only group. (Napolitano et al., 2013)
	Text messages and email	Napolitano et al. (2013)	+		
	Text messages, mobile app, website, face-to-face, and printed materials	Hebden et al. (2013)	=		

NB: Highlights of different studies for each health problem obtained from Oosterveen et al. (2017)

Chapter 22
Novelty on the Matrices of Weighing

María J. García G.
Minimax Consultores, Venezuela

Gilberto J. Hernández G.
Minimax Consultores, Venezuela

José G. Hernández R.
Minimax Consultores, Venezuela

ABSTRACT

This chapter relates some social aspects, such as playfulness, customer service, and citizen safety with one of the simplest multicriteria techniques to implement, matrixes of weighing (MOW, matrices de ponderación [MDP]). Taking as starting point the work matrixes of weighing and catastrophes, a brief review is made of the MOW, highlighting new applications of the same, as well as new concepts that have emerged from its use. The objective of this work will be to present some applications of the matrixes of weighing, while explaining what they are and how they apply, the multilayer matrix of weighing with multiplicative factors (ML-MOWwMf). To achieve this general objective and secondary objectives, this chapter will make use of the integrated-adaptable methodology for the development of decision support system (IAMDSS [MIASAD])

INTRODUCTION

To beginnings of the second decade of the XXIst century, it was commented, in the work Matrixes Of Weighing and catastrophes (Hernández, García & Hernández, 2011), that the Matrixes Of Weighing (MOW [MDP]), although, undoubtedly, one of the multicriteria models, simpler to implement, does not produce many quotations in the specialized literature. They may even be confused with other decision making methods, which make use of matrices, as is the case of the linguistic decision matrix (Xu, Wu & Zhang, 2014; Wu, Xu & Xu, 2016), or the meta-matrix with which she works Gaspars-Wieloch (2017), or the extreme case of Chow et al. (2015), who mention the transition matrix, the stochastic matrix, and

DOI: 10.4018/978-1-5225-7214-5.ch022

the perturbation matrices, but when they use the abbreviation MDP, are referring to Markov Decision Process and not to Matrixes Of Weighing (MOW, Matrices De Ponderación [MDP].

Different is the situation in relation to the decision matrix presented by Jassbi, Ribeiro & Dargam (2014), which in its structure coincides with the MDP, differing in the management and subsequent use made by their authors. A similar situation occurs in the work of Li, Kou & Peng (2016), where the initial individual decision matrix practically coincides with a MDP, only that it follows another series of steps, including fuzzy logic, which leads to very different results.

In recent years, in the sense of missed appointments and cross quotes, the situation has not varied much, however, if new possible applications of the MDP are found, as well as new ways of expressing them.

This paper discussed the Matrixes Of Weighing with multiplicative factors (MOWwMf [MDPcFm]), which had already been mentioned in the work of Hernández, García & Hernández (2011) and are discussed the Multilayer Matrix Of Weighing with Multiplicative factors (ML-MOWwMf [MDPcFm-MC]), which have been presented in more recent works (García et al., 2017; Hernández, García & Hernández, 2012; Jeney, 2014).

At the same time comments are made on MDP applications in different fields of human endeavor, such as the Sports fantastic leagues (SFL [LFD]) (Hernández et al., 2014), the location of vehicles to protect the population (García, Hernández & Hernández, 2014) and in the effects, that can have on the citizens the control of inventories (García et al., 2017).

From the above the objective of this work is to present some applications of the Matrixes Of Weighing, while explain what they are and how they apply, the Multilayer Matrix Of Weighing with Multiplicative factors (ML-MOWwMf).

In pursuing this overall objective, the following specific objectives arise:

Present an update of the Matrixes Of Weighing (MDP), including a discussion of the Multilayer Matrix Of Weighing with Multiplicative factors (MDPcFm-MC).

Examine some situations where MDP can be useful: participate in Sports fantastic leagues (SFL [LFD]), Location of vehicles to handle emergencies (LVHE [UVAE]) and to face measures that affect the control of inventories (IC [CI]).

Construct three MDPcFm-MC to solve, each one, of the previously mentioned situations: the LFD, the UVAE and the CI.

Methodology

In order to achieve the general objective and the specific objectives arising from it will use, the Integrated-Adaptable Methodology for the development of Decision Support System (IAMDSS, in Spanish, Metodología Integradora-Adaptable para desarrollar Sistemas de Apoyo a las Decisiones [MIASAD]), which, mainly for its flexibility, has been shown to be very useful, to complete research in different fields of knowledge (García, Hernández & Hernández, 2014; Jeney, 2014; Schwarz & Schwarz, 2015; Schwarz et al., 2016).

Similar to what was done in other works (García et al., 2017; Hernández, García & Hernández, 2011; Jeney, 2014; Schwarz & Schwarz, 2015), for this investigation the following steps were followed:

1. Define the problem, which as highlighted in the objectives is to present some applications of the Matrixes Of Weighing, while explain what they are and how they apply, the Multilayer Matrix Of Weighing with Multiplicative factors (ML-MOWwMf [MDPcFm-MC]);

2. Elaborate a first prototype, which, among its main functions, is to offer a clear vision of what will be the result of the research, so one of the first aspects to be carried out is to identify the users of the final product, which, in this case, because it is a scientific article, will be the readers of the same. Thus, among the main readers of this article, should be all interested in the application of mathematical tools, to solve social problems, in particular all those students of the multicriteria models and especially those who are attracted by the MDP, they are joined by those who are interested in each of the fields of knowledge studied here: Sports fantastic leagues (LFD), Location of vehicles to handle emergencies (UVAE) and the inventories control (CI). On the other hand, the first prototype, serves as a starting point to establish the structure of the article, which in addition to this introduction and the background, consists of two central sections, the first is devoted to a brief review on the MDP, at the same time some novelties of the same are presented, emphasizing the MDPcFm-MC and the second is dedicated to show applications of the MDPcFm-MC, in the fields of knowledge previously mentioned: LFD, UVAE and CI. To close the work will show possible lines of future research and some conclusions and will present the references of the works cited;

3. Obtain data, in particular on the developments that have arisen around the MDP, as well as the problems to be studied: UVAE, CI and LFD;

4. Establishing alternatives, in this specific case, is to identify all possible new alternatives of management of the MDP and the problems to which they can be applied;

5. Evaluate alternatives, attending mainly to the novelty offered by each alternative and to the facility, offered by each of them, to be able to explain it in a few words;

6. Select the alternative, according to the previous evaluation and considering the secondary objectives, whether tacit or explicit;

7. Implementing the chosen alternative, although it is not an implementation as such, must guarantee the completion of the article, meeting the proposed objectives and

8. Establish controls, mechanisms, that allow to recognize if the solution obtained, remains valid in the course of time.

As a limitation and scope, it should be emphasized that no field work will be done, but the examples used as an illustration will be hypothetical, which will allow to give, to the study, a greater generality.

BACKGROUND

As already mentioned in the introduction, this work is, in a way, a deepening of Matrixes Of Weighing and catastrophes (Hernández, García & Hernández, 2011), so it will be the main starting point, for the development of the same.

Moreover, as other background a set of works which have been carried out will have applications of the Matrixes Of Weighing (MDP). Among these works they stand out of the García, Hernández & Hernández (2014), on vehicle location, for emergency management (UVAE), of García et al. (2017), which handles the problems that society can suffer, when the government imposes measures that hinder the control of inventories (CI) and of Hernández et al. (2014), where they comment the application of mathematical models, on the Sports fantastic leagues (LFD).

Based on this background, then, at the next session, some news related to MDP will be discussed and it ends with a session dedicated to presenting examples of practical applications thereof, particularly the Multilayer Matrix Of Weighing with Multiplicative factors (ML-MOWwMf [MDPcFm-MC]).

REVIEW AND NOVELTY ON MATRIXES OF WEIGHING

As already mentioned, it is taken as a starting point the work Matrixes Of Weighing and catastrophes of Hernández, García & Hernández (2011), therefore, to comment on some basic aspects of the Matrixes Of Weighing (MOW [MDP]) the reader will be referred directly to that work.

The MDP are simply a numerical arrangement of rows and columns, which allow hierarchy and even facilitate the selection of alternatives, according to a set of criteria established (García et al., 2017; Hernández, García & Hernández, 2011), as can be seen in the Table 1. This structure makes them one of the simplest multicriteria models to construct and implement. But despite its simplicity, they can offer very robust solutions when it comes to prioritize and, above all, to select alternatives.

In addition, there are a set of situations that can be handled as MDP, as well as direct variants thereof, which can be reviewed in the works of Hernández, García and Hernández (2011) and Hernández et al. (2014).

As shown in the work of Hernández, García & Hernández (2011), to make decisions with MDP a series of equations is used:

$$\text{Total } Ak = \sum_{j=1, n} vj * P_{k, j} \tag{1}$$

In this equation (1) Total Ak, reflects for each alternative k its valuation reached, which comes from the sum of the valuations of the alternative k, for each of the criteria j, the $P_{k, j}$, which in turn are multiplied by each one of the multiplicative values (vj).

$$1 = \sum_{j=1, n} v_j \tag{2}$$

The equation (2) is used for variations 5 and 6 of the MDP (see Hernández, García & Hernández (2011)), in which the sum of the vj is required to be equal to 1.

Table 1. General characteristics of a MOW

		Criteria (C$_j$) and its weights				Multiplicative factors (fg$_h$)	Total
		Criterion 1	...	Criterion n-1	Criterion n		
	Weight	PC$_{1i}$ to PC$_{1f}$		PC$_{n-1i}$ to PC$_{n-1f}$	PC$_{ni}$ to PC$_{nf}$	---	---
Alternatives (A$_k$)	A$_1$	P$_{1,1}$	...	P$_{1, n-1}$	P$_{1, n}$	fm$_1$	Total A$_1$
	A$_2$	P$_{2,1}$	...	P$_{2, n-1}$	P$_{2, n}$	fm$_2$	Total A$_2$
	..	...	P$_{k, j}$	...	...	---	...
	A$_{m-1}$	P$_{m-1,1}$	...	P$_{m-1, n-1}$	P$_{m-1, n}$	fm$_{m-1}$	Total A$_{m-1}$
	A$_m$	P$_{m,1}$	...	P$_{m, n-1}$	P$_{m, n}$	fm$_m$	Total A$_m$

Source: García et al. (2017).

The MDP are transformed into Matrix Of Weighing with Multiplicative factors (MOWwMf [MDP-cFm]), incorporating the concept of multiplicative factors, which has been taken from the Multiatributte Models with multiplicative factors (MMwMf [MMcFm]) (García, Hernández & Hernández, 2015).

$$\text{Total } Ak = \prod_{h=1, H} fgh * \sum_{j=1, n} vj * P_{k, j} \tag{3}$$

Equation (3) become the general expression of the MDP and in addition to the terms presented in (1), multiplicative factors appear, fgh, whose product from 1 to H, where H is the total number of multiplicative factors, is multiplied by the sum of the products of the $P_{k, j}$ by the vj.

If further details on these equations and the various elements of Table 1 are desired, it is recommended to review García et al. (2017) and Hernández, García & Hernández (2011). In particular, in the latter, the work that serves as the starting point to the present, is more detailed information on: the MDP in group decision making, MDP with multiplicative factors (MDPcFm) and steps to build and apply an MDP.

Likewise, it is recommended to review these works to have details of the six variants of the MDP. It will only be added that there is a sub-variant for the first four variations and consists in demanding that a constant value be obtained from the sum of major values of the ranges, usually one or one hundred. That is, we want to ensure that no alternative exceeds a predetermined value. At least directly, without the application of the vj.

These sub-variants of the MDP leads to comment, that exist, some approximations to them.

Approaches to the Matrix of Weighing

In addition to being little quoted formally in the literature on multicriteria models, the Matrix Of Weighing (MOW [MDP]) compete with a series of techniques, which without fully adapting to their structure are very close to them.

Of these cases, which can be called, not very formal applications of the MDP, are some voting systems, in particular can be mentioned (Hernández et al., 2014):

1. Distribution of fixed points. It consists in distributing a fixed sum of points among the alternatives, presenting itself under two variants: 1a. With repetition and 1b. Without repetition. For either variant, when this system is applied, some of the alternatives may be left without receiving points. In the case where it is required that all the alternatives must receive point, it coincides with the sub-variants of the MDP, indicated at the end of the previous section, when it is required that the total sum of points, of the criteria, be a fixed amount.
2. Distribution points for the m alternatives. 2a. Among the alternatives are distributed a number of points ranging from 1 to m, where m is the number of alternatives. Each alternative is assigned a different amount between 1 and m. Of the case 2a. a variation arises 2b. When k points are distributed, with k < m, so there are alternatives that left without points. This variant is very similar to case 1a, when there are alternatives without receiving points, only here it is not fixed the sum of points to be distributed but the number of alternatives that will receive punctuation.
3. Distribution weighted by the evaluators. More than one variant is a complement, and is used with multiple evaluators. First, all evaluators weigh all alternatives across all criteria, in most cases following a type one MDP (see Hernández, García & Hernández (2011)). Of all the values obtained, for each criterion the best evaluation is taken. This higher value for each criterion becomes an

upper bound (in general it is taken as one hundred percent) and from these new limit values, all alternatives are reevaluated, through this normalization, to obtain more homogeneous values. The evaluation process is not usually repeated, but proportional values are assigned and the final sum is made.

These cases mentioned are usually found in beauty contests and music festivals, in particular to choose the winning song in the former festival of the Iberoamerican Television Organization (Organización de Televisión Iberoamericana [OTI]), each country assigns a fixed number of votes, without repetition, which causes some countries to be left without obtaining votes, for which it is an example of type 2b, previously indicated.

But there is a case that deserves mention separately, it is the Vectors Of Weighing (VOW [VDP]), which can be considered a single row MDP. They are used, not to hierarchize alternatives, but to have a clear knowledge of the goodness of the analyzed alternative. The vector is usually type five, this is all criteria are valued with the same scale and multiplicative values (vj) are used whose sum is equal to one (see Hernández, García & Hernández (2011)).

By the latter condition they are usually associated with the Decreasing digits (Dd) or the Decreasing primes (Pd) (García, Hernández & Hernández, 2015).

Although they are not directly a multicriteria technique, their simultaneous use on several alternatives would have the same effect of an MDP, gaining with it, one of the main strengths of the MDP, which is to offer a clear numerical value, about the goodness or not of an alternative.

With recent comments, it is given terminating the review of the MDP and then will go to present the Multilayer Matrix Of Weighing with Multiplicative factors (ML-MOWwMf).

The Multilayer Matrix of Weighing With Multiplicative Factors

To present the Multilayer Matrix Of Weighing with Multiplicative factors (ML-MOWwMf [MDPcFm-MC]), it will essentially follow García et al. (2017).

When it uses a Matrix Of Weighing with Multiplicative factors (MOWwMf [MDPcFm]), what is common is that it is desired to rank a series of alternatives and in the final case choose the best of them. For it is available, or should establish appropriate criteria. But whether these criteria in turn need to be evaluated, it will require using a MDPcFm-MC.

To better understand the operation of the MDPcFm-MC, it is recommended to review the work of Hernández, García and Hernández (2012) and of Jeney (2014), but especially the of García et al. (2017).

And following García et al. (2017), we make some comments, by way of illustration, that allow us to have a better idea of how, where and when the MDPcFm-MC can be applied.

A first situation is when it is desired to evaluate the cashierss in a branch of an auto market and for this a series of criteria are available. By way of illustration are taken as criteria: punctuality, customer service (kindness), speed and efficiency in terms of the minimum of mistakes made. If interest only focuses on prioritizing tellers a branch, MDPcFm be enough. But if it also has the need to evaluate the cashierss of several branches and both know what the criteria is having better performance, these four criteria mentioned above, at the same time become a kind of alternatives to be evaluated, which would be making use of an MDPcFm-MC.

In this second scenario proposed, it would not only be evaluating each of the tellers, each branch, but would evaluate all the cashierss and one could see the overall performance per branch and what is more important would be evaluating the criteria with which the comparison is being made.

Another situation where it may be necessary to use an MDPcFm-MC is when decisions are conditioned to different scenarios.

To illustrate this application, making use of the hypothetical situation presented above, suppose it works seven days a week and are interested in the performance of the cashierss each day of the week, separately and at the same time it is interesting to measure this performance during the months of greatest sale, understood December and the months of least number of clients, to say something, the summer months or school holidays.

In situations like this, each scenario can be seen as a layer. Although the MDPcFm-MC, presented through rows and columns, in two dimensions, for situations like the above it is preferred to speak of multiple layers, rather than double layer.

For the structure of an MDPcFm-MC, there is no difference with respect to a normal MDPcFm, nor is there any difference with respect to the steps to carry out the valuation (see Hernández, García & Hernández (2011)).

The fundamental difference is visualized in the criteria, which, continue to maintain their valuation range and usually have multiplicative values (vj), but more important, is that now, additionally, there is interest in the overall result that these criteria may be offering.

With these statements about the MDPcFm-MC, these general comments on the MDP are culminated and we will now go on to illustrate possible applications of these MDPcFm-MCs.

APPLICATIONS OF THE ML-MOWwMf (MDPcFm-MC)

Three examples are presented where the MDPcFm-MC are applied, although in two of the original applications normal MDPcFm were used, some minor modifications are made, so that all three cases are performed with MDPcFm-MC.

It will be illustrated how it can choose the players that integrate a squad in a Sport fantastic league (SFL [LFD]), supported on an MDPcFm-MC, it will be shown how an MDPcFm-MC is used to select the places, from a population, from location of vehicles to handle emergencies (LVHE [UVAE]) and finally the application of an MDPcFm-MC will be shown, to help an organization analyze alternatives to confront governmental measures that affect its inventories control (IC [CI]). These three illustrations, although starting from real situations, will be done through hypothetical cases, which will allow to obtain a greater generalization of the application of the MDPcFm-MC.

Multilayer Matrix of Weighing and the Sport Fantastic League

Of the three illustrations of the Multilayer Matrix Of Weighing with Multiplicative factors (ML-MOWwMf [MDPcFm-MC]) that are going to present, this is, perhaps, where the multiple layers have less relevance. The matrix itself is a normal MDPcFm, only that, from it, assessment will be made of the criteria, posteriori. It analyzes how, for each of the selected players participated each of the criteria, it will be seen which of them presents a greater percentage, with respect to the greater attainable value, this will allow to know, in fact, which was the criterion that most influenced in the selection.

But before showing the MDPcFm-MC, it should make some general comments about the Sport fantastic leagues (SFL [LFD]).

The Sport Fantastic Leagues (SFL [LFD])

Comments on LFD and other aspects of the illustration of the application of the MDPcFm-MC in such leagues will be taken mainly from Hernández et al. (2014) and of Hernández, García & Hernández (2014).

Sport is a business and is one of the businesses with the best return on investment. (Bonacin, Bonacin & Bilić, 2015) and the LFD are a new way of living sports (Hernández et al. (2014), which have millions of fans, distributed around the world and participating in almost all the most popular sports, especially team sports.

Given that transactions are made of millions of dollars in the sports industry (Ebrahimi & Fadaei, 2016), the participants of the LFD, which are in permanent growth (Hyatt et al., 2013), from the point of view of marketing, have become a very important objective. Hence it is interesting to study the application of mathematical tools to the LFD.

In the LFD, the participants compete with each other, following the performance of the athletes in real life, which are translated into points, which allow them to become the winners of a day, or league, at the end of the season. This competition, makes participants in the LFD sit on the playing field, although in reality they are in different places, sometimes quite distant from each other, and very far from the sports arena (Hernández, García & Hernández, 2014).

In the works of Hernández, García & Hernández (2014) and Hernández et al. (2014), mathematical model applications were used to the LFD through soccer. Specifically, La Liga was used, which corresponds to the first division of Spanish football and in which each season participate twenty teams. One of the first problems presented to the participant of the LFD is the formation of their squad. It is in this conformation of his list of players, which each participant performs, where he makes use of the MDPcFm-MC.

Each LFD has its own rules, which, as it supposes, depend mainly on the sport with which it is participating.

Simplifying and in accordance with what is indicated by Hernández, García & Hernández (2014), in this work, the main rules to follow are: each participant can have up to 15 players, the total investment cannot exceed US$ 100 million, it cannot have more than three players from the same team and with respect to positions will not have more than 2 goalkeepers (GK), 5 defenders (DF), 5 midfielders (MI) and 3 forward (FO).

Regarding the points system, through which the participants in the LFD, seek to be the winners, Hernández et al. (2014), express that includes among other aspects: goals of DF or GK = 6; goals of MI = 5; goals of FO = 4; assistance = 3; clean sheet for DF or GK (at least 60 minutes) = 4; clean sheet for MI (at least 60 minutes) = 1; goals against = -2.

It is these points, which define the execution of a player in a LFD, performance, which does not always match their performing in real life. Hence the situation is presented that a relatively modest player in real life is a star for an LFD.

This system of points allows hierarchizing players and this at the same time influences the price that each player has for a given LFD. This price is related to the points of the player, but it is not a direct relation, since in the price of a player usually intervene other factors as, the equipment, for which it plays, the position that plays and there is a somewhat curious factor, the sympathies that arouses the player itself. Normally they have higher price the GK and FO, then DF and finally the MI.

Selection of the Squad Through a MDPcFm-MC

With all the previous information and considering the multiple criteria that could be used, Hernández et al. (2014) took: Performance in the previous season (PPS [RTP]) (1 - 100), Direct cost (DCT [CTD]) (1 - 80) and Percentage of money it consumes (PMC [PDC]) (1 - 40), where the numbers in parentheses represent the valuation range of the respective criterion.

In addition, two multiplicative factors are considered, which in fact only served as control elements: the multiplicative factor of the equipment (MFE [FME]) and the multiplicative factor of the position (MFP [FMP]).

As the team of each club, in real life, is composed of twenty players, we will be talking about 400 players available, for which it is usually prepared a first list of the best players, in this case the top nine or ten of each team, which reduces the list to about 180 to 200 players.

For reasons of space, these lists are not usually presented in research on this subject, however, for this work, a list of the top 200 players is available to readers. Those who require it, should only write to the correspondence author.

In Table 2, only the thirty first players, respect to their performance, of the list are shown, these players identify, according to their equipment, by a letter (from A to V, since neither O nor Q are used) and within each team for the importance that has the player (01 to 20, with 01 the most important) and also shows the position in which it performs, following the previously mentioned nomenclature (DE, FO, GK, MI).

For each player, the parameters are calculated:

RTP = (player performance / performance of the highest performance player) * 100

The performance of a player is measured on a scale of 1 to 100, where among nearest to 100, a player is best rated.

CTD = (cost of the player / cost of the highest performance player) * 80.

It is multiplied by 80, to express it in the desired range.

PDC = (20 - player cost) * 2.

In the latter case, all players are under US$ 20 million, and it is desired that a less expensive player, more points, of their 20 minus its cost and the multiplication by 2 to express it in the desired range.

FME and FMP, will always be 1 and become 0, when the respective quota has been fulfilled.

In Table 2, reflects the player, his performance and cost. With the performance and the cost, the three parameters mentioned above are calculated, RTP, CTD and PDC, which are reflected in Table 3, which corresponds to the MDPcFm-MC, to choose the squad, to participate in an LFD.

In this Table 3, a column has been included to reflect the costs of the players, who become part of the squad, this in order to be able to carry out a rapid review, that the budget has not been exceeded, for

Table 2. List of the top thirty players, available to be selected

Player	Performance	Cost	Player	Performance	Cost
R01FO	97	19,90	R04DF	27	13,50
D01FO	94	18,80	R05FO	26	13,40
D02FO	60	16,60	T02FO	25	13,35
C01FO	58	16,90	R03GK	25	14,20
R02FO	50	16,00	C04MI	25	13,15
B01FO	38	15,40	C06MI	25	13,10
C02GK	35	16,00	C03DF	25	13,00
F01FO	35	15,00	H02GK	24	13,80
H01FO	33	14,90	C07MI	24	12,60
S01FO	32	14,70	D03DF	24	12,50
I01FO	32	14,65	C08DF	23	12,40
V01FO	30	14,00	R06DF	22	12,50
M01FO	28	13,95	L01FO	22	12,40
T01FO	28	13,90	R07DF	21	11,95
C05DF	27	13,70	C09MI	21	11,90

Table 3. MDPcFm for the selection of players, a squad of LFD

Player	Cost	Team	Position	RTP	CTD	PDC	FME	FMP	Total K
				(1 - 100)	(1 - 80)	(1 - 40)	0 or 1	0 or 1	
D02FO	16,60	D	FO	61,86	66,73	6,80	1	1	135,39
C01FO	16,90	C	FO	59,79	67,94	6,20	1	1	133,93
R03GK	14,20	R	GK	25,77	57,09	11,60	1	1	94,46
N07GK	7,00	N	GK	4,12	28,14	26,00	1	1	58,26
P08FO	6,10	P	FO	3,09	24,52	27,80	1	1	55,41
E09DF	4,70	E	DF	3,09	18,89	30,60	1	1	52,58
N09MI	4,50	N	MI	3,09	18,09	31,00	1	1	52,18
P07MI	4,45	P	MI	3,09	17,89	31,10	1	1	52,08
G10DF	4,40	G	DF	3,09	17,69	31,20	1	1	51,98
E10MI	4,40	E	MI	3,09	17,69	31,20	1	1	51,98
L10MI	4,35	L	MI	3,09	17,49	31,30	1	1	51,88
N08DF	4,30	N	DF	3,09	17,29	31,40	1	1	51,78
J10DF	4,20	J	DF	3,09	16,88	31,60	1	1	51,57
P09DF	3,90	P	DF	2,06	15,68	32,20	1	1	49,94
Suma	**100,00**			181,41	402,01	360,00			943,42
%				**31,88**	**46,89**	**79,79**			62,89

Source: Modified of Hernández et al. (2014).

similar reasons, to verify that the limit imposed has not been exceeded, a column has been included to identify the team of each player, as well as another column to identify their position.

Some comments, about the results expressed in Table 3, can be seen in Hernández et al. (2014). Here only it calls attention to the outstanding values in bold.

The 100,00 of the sum row, in the cost column, indicates that the available budget has been consumed, for this reason the squad, was only with fourteen players. In this case, the participant prefers to lose an MI, but maintain players of higher cost in other positions.

The three quantities highlighted in bold in row %, are the ones that convert the MDPcFm into an MDPcFm-MC, since through them it is possible to see which of the criteria used, results of greater relevance for the selection. In this case the most relevant was the PDC with a 79,79% range with respect to the maximum possible, while the RTP, that one could think a priori the most important, it only reached the 31,88%. For the calculation of these percentages we used the first n players, of each position, that offered the maximum attainable value, being n, the maximum of players allowed for that position and that in total they complete the fifteen.

Made these comments, the discussion about the use of a MDPcFm-MC in an LFD is closed. It will then be reviewed, as these matrices can also be used, to define the location of a vehicle that can assist the population in case of a specific emergency.

Multilayer Matrix of Weighing and Emergency Vehicles

Same as the previous case, the original model, used in the work, on which this section will be based (García, Hernández & Hernández, 2014), is a normal MDPcFm, to which small adjustments are made to make it a Multilayer Matrix Of Weighing with multiplicative factors (ML-MOWwMf [MDPcFm-MC]).

In the cities of great extent, which generally tend to have strong traffic problems, it may be desirable the location of vehicles to handle emergencies (LVHE [UVAE]) at specific locations, so that they can go faster where they are required. Of these vehicles for emergencies, mainly include ambulances (Boukioudi et al., 2016), fire trucks and police vehicles. Just to mention a few very particular situations, is the case of the emergency medical services (EMS) in India (Garg, 2012) and the use of emergency vehicles in case of disasters (Chu et al., 2012; Eide et al., 2013), that, although it is a different situation, in general, the mathematical algorithms used, are usually the same, or at least similar.

In this case we work with police vehicles, following, as has been said, the work of García, Hernández and Hernández (2014).

And as in the previous case, before showing the MDPcFm-MC that will help in the location of police vehicles, some comments should be made on the parameters to be considered, when choosing a position, where to place the vehicle.

Parameters Relevant to the Location of a Police Vehicle

The material presented below is taken essentially from García, Hernández and Hernández (2014).

The parameters to locate any kind of vehicles for emergencies, are often very similar, in the particular case of locating police vehicles, García, Hernández & Hernández (2014) used: Conditions of the way (Cvia), Average velocity that can develop the vehicles (VmPa), Traffic volume (VoTr), Average distance to the main ways (DiPr), Population (Pobl) (takes the entire population, without discriminating between floating and fixed), Space for parking (EsAp), Greater crimes (DeMa) and Minors crimes (DeMe).

Among other aspects, the conditions of the candidate sites must be known, with respect to each of the parameters. The candidates will be represented as LDi, although in the original work 15 places were evaluated, here only 10 will be used, so i will vary from 01 to 10, as can be seen in Table 4, where the characterization of each of these places will be presented, for which it is used: Excellent (EXE), Very good (MBU), More than good (MQB), Good (BUE), More than regular (MQR), Regular (REG), Below regular (DDR), Better than bad (MQM), Bad (MAL) and Very bad (MMA).

For the evaluation of each of these parameters, rules must be established, by way of illustration the case is shown for DeMa. In the Table 5 a percentage range is defined according to the characteristics of the parameter to be measured.

Similar evaluations must be performed for the remaining parameters. Recalling that, since these valuations are represented in percentages, they must be translated into the valuation range of each of the criteria. These ranges can be seen in Table 6, where it is also observed that the parameters of major importance are the DeMa (1-50) and the DeMe (1-40). Here a second simplification has been made and only the first five places have been evaluated.

The MDPcFm-MC for the Location of Police Vehicles

To convert the original matrix in a Multilayer Matrix Of Weighing with multiplicative factors (ML-MOWwMf [MDPcFm-MC]), it worked with a multiplicative factor, Availability of the place (DL), which was not reflected in the table, since for the five localities evaluated was equal to 1 and would not contribute with information to the analysis. And like what was done in the previous case, in Table 6, at the end were added a pair of rows, Points contributed and % of contribution, which refer to the criteria.

Although all the parameters made relatively high percentage contributions, equal or superior to the 60%. As expected, the parameter that contributed the most points were the DeMa, with 200, but surprisingly, the parameter, of greater weight, percentage, in this hierarchy, was Cvia, with a 94%. Again, with this illustration, we see the importance of the MDPcFm-MC, since they, besides making it possible to

Table 4. Characterization of the ten available places

		Parameters to consider							
		Cvia	VmPr	VoTr	DiPr	Pobl	EsAp	DeMa	DeMe
Alternatives (A$_k$)	LD$_{01}$	EXC	MBU	EXC	EXC	EXC	EXC	EXC	EXC
	LD$_{02}$	EXC	MBU	MBU	EXC	EXC	MQB	MQB	MBU
	LD$_{03}$	MBU	MBU	EXC	REG	MBU	MQR	MQB	MQB
	LD$_{04}$	MBU	MQB	MQR	DDR	MQB	REG	BUE	BUE
	LD$_{05}$	MBU	MQB	EXC	DDR	BUE	MMA	BUE	MQB
	LD$_{06}$	MQB	MBU	MBU	REG	MQB	MQM	MQR	MQR
	LD$_{07}$	MQB	BUE	EXC	MQM	DDR	DDR	MQR	MQB
	LD$_{08}$	MQB	BUE	EXC	MQM	MQM	MBU	DDR	DDR
	LD$_{09}$	MQB	MBU	EXC	EXC	EXC	MBU	MBU	MAL
	LD$_{10}$	BUE	MQB	MBU	DDR	MAL	MQR	DDR	MQM

Source: Modified from García, Hernández & Hernández (2014).

Table 5. Assessment of Greater crimes (DeMa)

DeMa range, above, to criminal mean	Points. % of the total	Range of DeMa, below, to average crime	Points. % of the total
DeMa > 20%	91 to 100 (EXE)	0% < DeMa ≤ 5%	41 to 50 (REG)
15% < DeMa ≤ 20%	81 to 90 (MBU)	5% < DeMa ≤ 10%	31 to 40 (DDR)
10% < DeMa ≤ 15%	71 to 80 (MQB)	10% < DeMa ≤ 15%	21 to 30 (MQM)
5% < DeMa ≤ 10%	61 to 70 (BUE)	15% < DeMa ≤ 20%	11 to 20 (MAL)
0% < DeMa ≤ 5%	51 to 60 (MQR)	DeMa > 20%	1 to 10 (MMA)

Source: García, Hernández & Hernández (2014).

Table 6. Valuations through a MDPcFm-MC

		Parameters to consider							
		Cvia	VmPr	VoTr	DiPr	Pobl	EsAp	DeMa	DeMe
	Weight	1 - 10	1 - 20	1 - 25	1 - 10	1 - 40	1 - 30	1 - 50	1 - 40
Alternatives (A_k)	LD_{01}	10	18	25	10	40	30	50	40
	LD_{02}	10	17	22	10	39	24	40	36
	LD_{03}	9	17	24	05	36	18	40	32
	LD_{04}	9	16	15	04	32	15	35	26
	LD_{05}	9	15	25	04	28	03	35	30
Points contributed	- - -	47	83	111	33	175	90	**200**	164
% of contribution	- - -	**94.0**	83.0	88.8	66.0	87.5	60.0	80.0	82.0

Source: Modified from García, Hernández & Hernández (2014).

rank the alternatives, allow us to see the true importance of the criteria, at the moment of making an assessment.

Presented the MDPcFm-MC, in the (UVAE), will then go on to illustrate the latter case, its use in inventory control.

A MDPcFm-MC to Help Visualize the Alternatives to Be Used to Face State Measures That Affect Inventory Control

This case, although its fundamental aspects correspond to the business sphere, it continues the same as the previous two, being a case of social interest, since to affect the control of inventories (CI) of the companies, the supply system is affected and with this globally to the society.

The problem itself was first treated by Schwarz et al. (2016), but the use of Multilayer Matrix Of Weighing with multiplicative factors (ML-MOWwMf [MDPcFm-MC]) was introduced by García et al. (2017). And it will be the work of García et al. (2017) from which most of the information to be presented below will be taken.

As in the two previous practical applications, it is necessary to establish the problem, before presenting the MDPcFm-MC, so afterwards some comments will be made on the intervention of the state and the CI.

Analysis of the Consequences of State Intervention in the CI

The work of Schwarz et al. (2016), was devoted to studying the harmful consequences, which for society could have restrictions imposed by the state, that affect the control of inventories (CI), their findings were reflected in a table that expressed the social impact of government measures that affecting inventories. The information reflected in this table served to García et al. (2017), to carry out a quantitative study of the situation, based on a multicriteria model, particularly using Multilayer Matrix Of Weighing with multiplicative factors (MDPcFm-MC).

Given the importance of the IC, for logistics, companies and society, as reflected Schwarz et al. (2016) and García et al. (2017), by making references to multiple authors who treat the subject from different perspectives (Costantino et al., 2014; Disney et al., 2015; Mousavi et al., 2014; Schwarz & Schwarz, 2015), García et al. (2017), focused their study on the Inventory Manager (IM) of the Logistics Model Based on Positions (LoMoBaP [MoLoBaC]) and determined almost 100 functions that this manager performs.

Of the 98 functions found by García et al. (2017), 40 were taken, which in one way or another had greater influence on the IC and these functions became the alternatives of the MDPcFm-MC.

From the information provided by Schwarz et al. (2016) it is extracted those who come to be the criteria of MDPcFm-MC: A: Stop producing, which leads to the almost immediate closure of the company. B: Keep the company operational, but dedicated to eliminate inventories, understanding that, when exhausting all possible inventories, the company closes. Try to stop producing temporarily, which would translate into two different criteria: C: Temporary closure of the company, for a certain time, with possibilities to extend it upon expiration, and may even become a definitive closure and D: Decrease the time of work, whether working fewer hours per day or fewer days per period or even a combination of both, in any case, also, can become a definitive closure. E: Maintain a production of products equivalent to the current ones, but with substitute inputs. F: Start producing new products, similar to the current ones and targeting the same markets. G: Start producing new products different from current ones and even targeting other markets. H: Keep producing while maintaining current conditions as long as possible. The criteria A, B, C, D and H, in general will lead to the definitive closure of the organization in a short time. Hence, the criteria, which the organization must pursue are E, F and G, since they probably offer a little more useful life for the company. To have more details on these criteria, it is recommended to review the works of Schwarz et al. (2016) and of García et al. (2017).

Additionally (García et al., 2017), although they do not detail them, they propose the use of scenarios and in a simplified way mention as scenarios the flexibility, on the one hand, of resources, in this case: economic (ECO), labor (LAB) and technological (TEC) and also consider the flexibility of the market (MAR). And comment (García et al., 2017), that, although different ranges can be handled, even for each of the different scenarios, it will be assumed that each of these four scenarios will move in three strata: low (l), medium (m) and high (h). But by greater simplification and, hypothetically, assume that all four scenarios are low.

Considering the scenario, alternatives and criteria previously mentioned, is going to construct the MDPcFm-MC, to help make decisions in the case of interference, the state, on the CI.

The MDPcFm-MC to Face State Intervention in the CI

For the forty selected functions of the Inventory Manager (IM), will consider its possible impact on the situation that is presented, that is to say, on the loss of the IC, given the intervention of the state. This impact measurement should be viewed very carefully, since in general, in a normal study on IM, one would be measuring, for each function, how the IM works in the same.

The MDPcFm-MC is shown in Table 7. The chosen functions of the IM will only be represented by their respective number, which is recommended to review the work of García et al. (2017), to know what function each number refers to. It should be emphasized that what is measured is the impact that these functions may have. Regarding the variant of the MC-MDPcFm used, although there are criteria that could be more interesting than others, will type three (see Hernández, García & Hernández, 2011), that is, all the ranges of the weights of the criteria equals (0 to 10) and with multiplicative values (vj).

Although no details of these multiplicative values are given, in this case, there will be two functions to guarantee a higher valuation to the most desired criteria and the other give a greater strength to those functions that promote each of the criteria, is to say, the larger the vj, the greater contribution will offer the functions that support that criterion.

In the Table 7 this vj have been placed next to each letter that identifies each of the criteria. Likewise, under each criterion has been placed the rating range. It has also been considered a multiplicative factor Possibility to implement (POI), which, for simplicity, has been taken as 1 for all possible actions. On the other hand, in this Table 7, in the columns of the criteria (possible actions) and in Total, the first number is without multiplication by the vj and the number in parentheses is with the use of them.

Among other aspects, it is interesting to note, in Table 7, that function 01, independent of a very pessimistic scenario being handled in all areas (ECO (l), LAB (l), TEC (l) and MAR (l)) gets a very high score for all criteria. This is not a surprise, since this function is related to establishing all the policies to follow and their impact will be independent of the scenario and the criterion. This is ironic in some ways, since an alternative that is highly evaluated, however, could be discarded, since it impacts equally on all criteria and therefore does not help to discern.

In this regard, highlights García et al. (2017) that there are other situations that are more interesting, one is the function 88, which has a 91.25% (93.85%) of impact and has no equal influence on all the criteria. Or what happens with functions 19, 21, 45 and 90, where the first three have a direct impact of 90.00% and the last one of 87.50%, but when viewing the weighted impact function 19 is equal to that of function 21 of 90.77%, while the weighted impact of functions 90 and 45 are 89.74% and 90.00% respectively. Which also it should be noted that for the function 45, match the direct impact and weighted impact.

From the point of view of this work, the most important to point out, like the two previous cases, are the last rows, Total and Total %, because on them becomes more evident the importance of using the MDPcFm-MC.

In Total % it can see that the criteria (columns A to H), except what would be action A, which only gets 58%, all others exceed the 70%, what can be considered a high value. Although criterion H, with a percentage of 81.75%, is misleading, since this column only achieves 46.71% of the maximum attainable. So, the three most valued actions are E, F and G, which have percentages, with respect to the maximum attainable, of 81.75%, 79.75% and 78.00% respectively.

This discussion can be seen with a little more depth in García et al. (2017), but for the purposes of this work, with Table 7, it is demonstrated that the MDPcFm-MC can be very useful when handling problems related to CI.

Table 7. MDPcFm-MC which measures the impact of IM functions on actions to be taken in response to state interventions that affect the CI

Function	Scenario: ECO (l), LAB (l), TEC (l) and MAR (l)								Total
	Criteria								
	A (2) (0 to 10)	B (3) (0 to 10)	C (4) (0 to 10)	D (5) (0 to 10)	E (7) (0 to 10)	F (7) (0 to 10)	G (7) (0 to 10)	H (4) (0 to 10)	
01	10 (20)	10 (30)	10 (40)	10 (50)	10 (70)	10 (70)	10 (70)	10 (40)	80 (390)
04	2 (4)	9 (27)	8 (32)	8 (40)	9 (63)	8 (56)	8 (56)	9 (36)	61 (314)
05	1 (2)	2 (6)	5 (20)	5 (25)	8 (56)	7 (49)	7 (49)	8 (32)	43 (239)
07	8 (16)	8 (24)	6 (24)	7 (35)	9 (63)	8 (56)	8 (56)	9 (36)	63 (310)
11	3 (6)	7 (21)	7 (28)	8 (40)	9 (63)	8 (56)	7 (49)	8 (32)	57 (295)
15	7 (14)	7 (21)	6 (24)	7 (35)	8 (56)	7 (49)	7 (49)	8 (32)	57 (280)
16	6 (12)	8 (24)	7 (28)	7 (35)	7 (49)	6 (42)	5 (35)	7 (28)	53 (253)
18	5 (10)	8 (24)	9 (36)	9 (45)	8 (56)	8 (56)	8 (56)	9 (36)	64 (319)
19	5 (10)	9 (27)	9 (36)	9 (45)	10 (70)	9 (63)	9 (63)	10 (40)	70 (354)
21	7 (14)	10 (30)	9 (36)	9 (45)	9 (63)	9 (63)	9 (63)	10 (40)	72 (354)
25	7 (14)	7 (21)	8 (32)	8 (40)	8 (56)	8 (56)	8 (56)	9 (36)	63 (311)
26	8 (16)	8 (24)	6 (24)	7 (35)	8 (56)	6 (42)	7 (49)	8 (32)	58 (278)
28	6 (12)	7 (21)	8 (32)	8 (40)	8 (56)	8 (56)	7 (49)	9 (36)	61 (302)
29	5 (10)	6 (18)	7 (28)	7 (35)	10 (70)	9 (63)	8 (56)	7 (28)	59 (308)
32	9 (18)	9 (27)	9 (36)	9 (45)	8 (56)	9 (63)	8 (56)	9 (36)	70 (337)
34	7 (14)	8 (24)	8 (32)	9 (45)	8 (56)	8 (56)	7 (49)	10 (40)	65 (316)
37	8 (16)	7 (21)	6 (24)	6 (30)	6 (42)	6 (42)	6 (42)	7 (28)	52 (245)
39	7 (14)	10 (30)	8 (32)	8 (40)	10 (70)	9 (63)	8 (56)	9 (36)	69 (341)
43	3 (6)	4 (12)	5 (20)	5 (25)	6 (42)	9 (63)	8 (56)	7 (28)	47 (252)
45	9 (18)	9 (27)	9 (36)	9 (45)	9 (63)	9 (63)	9 (63)	9 (36)	72 (351)
46	6 (12)	8 (24)	7 (28)	7 (35)	8 (56)	8 (56)	8 (56)	7 (28)	59 (295)
48	7 (14)	8 (24)	7 (28)	7 (35)	8 (56)	8 (56)	8 (56)	8 (32)	61 (301)
50	3 (6)	6 (18)	7 (28)	7 (35)	8 (56)	7 (49)	7 (49)	5 (20)	50 (261)
52	9 (18)	6 (18)	7 (28)	8 (40)	7 (49)	6 (42)	6 (42)	9 (36)	58 (273)
61	4 (8)	4 (12)	6 (24)	8 (40)	8 (56)	8 (56)	7 (49)	8 (32)	53 (277)
66	5 (10)	9 (27)	8 (32)	8 (40)	9 (63)	8 (56)	8 (56)	9 (36)	64 (320)
67	7 (14)	8 (24)	8 (32)	9 (45)	9 (63)	9 (63)	9 (63)	9 (36)	68 (340)
75	2 (4)	4 (12)	6 (24)	6 (30)	7 (49)	7 (49)	8 (56)	4 (16)	44 (240)
79	3 (6)	4 (12)	6 (24)	7 (35)	7 (49)	6 (42)	5 (35)	5 (20)	43 (223)
80	5 (10)	7 (21)	7 (28)	7 (35)	8 (56)	7 (49)	6 (42)	8 (32)	55 (273)
81	3 (6)	8 (24)	8 (32)	8 (40)	8 (56)	8 (56)	8 (56)	8 (32)	59 (302)
83	4 (8)	8 (24)	7 (28)	8 (40)	8 (56)	8 (56)	8 (56)	8 (32)	59 (300)
86	6 (12)	7 (21)	8 (32)	8 (40)	7 (49)	7 (49)	7 (49)	8 (32)	58 (284)

continued on following page

Table 7. Continued

	Scenario: ECO (I), LAB (I), TEC (I) and MAR (I)								
Function	**Criteria**								**Total**
	A (2) **(0 to 10)**	**B (3)** **(0 to 10)**	**C (4)** **(0 to 10)**	**D (5)** **(0 to 10)**	**E (7)** **(0 to 10)**	**F (7)** **(0 to 10)**	**G (7)** **(0 to 10)**	**H (4)** **(0 to 10)**	
87	7 (14)	9 (27)	8 (32)	9 (45)	8 (56)	9 (63)	10 (70)	8 (32)	68 (339)
88	7 (14)	9 (27)	8 (32)	10 (50)	9 (63)	10 (70)	10 (70)	10 (40)	73 (366)
89	5 (10)	5 (15)	6 (24)	6 (30)	8 (56)	9 (63)	9 (63)	10 (40)	58 (301)
90	10 (20)	10 (30)	8 (32)	8 (40)	9 (63)	9 (63)	10 (70)	8 (32)	72 (350)
92	6 (12)	6 (18)	7 (28)	7 (35)	9 (63)	8 (56)	7 (49)	9 (36)	59 (297)
94	4 (8)	5 (15)	6 (24)	6 (30)	7 (49)	8 (56)	9 (63)	6 (24)	51 (269)
98	6 (12)	7 (21)	7 (28)	8 (40)	7 (49)	8 (56)	8 (56)	8 (32)	59 (294)
POI	1	1	1	1	1	1	1	1	---
Total	232 (464)	291 (873)	292 (1168)	307 (1535)	327 (2289)	319 (2233)	312 (2184)	327 (1308)	2407 (12054)
Total %	58.00	72.75	73.00	76.75	81.75	79.75	78.00	81.75	75.22 (77.27)

Source: García et al. (2017).

Showing the three cases where the MDPcFm-MC are used, we will present some lines of future research, and then close with some conclusions.

FUTURE RESEARCH DIRECTIONS

To the comment on the latest developments in the field of the Matrixes Of Weighing (MOW [MDP]), any future research to follow, will be oriented in this sense, to deepen the study of this simple, but very useful model for multicriteria decision making.

An interesting case would be to study, in more depth, those models that are very similar to an MDP, although they do not have their formal structure.

And there are two aspects that stand out, the first is to deepen the study and look for practical applications for the Vectors Of Weighing (VOW [VDP]) and the second, very similar, continue to deepen and increase the number of applications of the Multilayer Matrix Of Weighing with Multiplicative factors (ML-MOWwMf [MDPcFm-MC]), both in the business and in the social sphere, as have been the three applications, shown in this work.

CONCLUSION

In this paper, a brief update has been made, starting in 2011, on the Matrixes Of Weighing (MOW [MDP]), where it is possible to emphasize, the presence of models similar to the MDP, but that do not have its formal structure. Equally worthy of mention are the Vectors Of Weighing (VOW [VDP]), but the most important thing to note is the high possibility of application that have the Multilayer Matrix Of Weighing with Multiplicative factors (ML-MOWwMf [MDPcFm-MC].

With the presentation of three examples of application, in the social field, of the MDPcFm-MC, it is possible to affirm that the objectives of the work have been fulfilled, that is to say, not only current aspects of the MDP have been presented, but the application of one of its more complete variants, the MDPcFm-MC.

Although MDPcFm-MC is a more complete model and allows a greater field of application and the study of a greater number of parameters, it still retains the simplicity, ease of implementation and robustness of the original MDP.

This robustness of the MDPcFm-MC is given mainly because it will always allow to measure, expressed in percentages, the efficient or not, which is, for the problem under study, each of the evaluated parameters.

REFERENCES

Bonacin, D., Bonacin, D., & Bilić, Ž. (2015). Real position of law in well regulated sport market. *Acta Kinesiologica, 9*(Suppl. 1), 70–73.

Boukioudi, F., Ozguler, A., Chauvet, A., Despereaux, T., Loeb, T., Baer, M., & Descatha, A. (2016). Description of life-threatening events occurring in workplaces and requiring dispatch Advanced Life Support Ambulances in an urban area. *Resuscitation, 101,* e3–e4. doi:10.1016/j.resuscitation.2016.01.014 PMID:26829702

Chow, Y., Tamar, A., Mannor, S., & Pavone, M. (2015). Risk-sensitive and robust decision-making: a CVaR optimization approach. Advances in Neural Information Processing Systems, 1522-1530.

Chu, E. T. H., Chen, Y. L., Lin, J. Y., & Liu, J. W. (2012). Crowdsourcing support system for disaster surveillance and response. *Wireless Personal Multimedia Communications (WPMC), 2012 15th International Symposium on IEEE,* 21-25.

Costantino, F., Di Gravio, G., Shaban, A., & Tronci, M. (2014). The impact of information sharing and inventory control coordination on supply chain performances. *Computers & Industrial Engineering, 76,* 292–306. doi:10.1016/j.cie.2014.08.006

Disney, S. M., Gaalman, G. J., Hedenstierna, C. P. T., & Hosoda, T. (2015). Fill rate in a periodic review order-up-to policy under auto-correlated normally distributed, possibly negative, demand. *International Journal of Production Economics, 170,* 501–512. doi:10.1016/j.ijpe.2015.07.019

Ebrahimi, P., & Fadaei, M. (2016). The Impact of Relationship Marketing on Team Loyalty (The Case Study: Sport Team Fans of Azadeghan Football League of Iran). *International Journal of Medical Research & Health Sciences, 5*(5), 52–68.

Eide, A. W., Haugstveit, I. M., Halvorsrud, R., & Borén, M. (2013). Inter-organizational collaboration structures during emergency response: A case study. *Proceedings of the 10th International ISCRAM Conference*, 94-104.

García, G. M. J., Hernández, G. G. J., & Hernández, R. J. G. (2015). An approach to the ranking of projects to undertake [Una aproximación para la jerarquización de proyectos a emprender]. In Gobernanza empresarial de Tecnología de la Información. Universidad de Cantabria.

García, G. M. J., Schwarz, I. L. M., Schwarz, I. T. M., Hernández, G. G. J., & Hernández, R. J. G. (2017). Inventories control, the Inventory manager and Matrixes Of Weighing with multiplicative factors (MOWwMf). *Journal of Global Business and Technology*, *13*(1), 40–56.

García, M. J., Hernández, G., & Hernández, R. J. G. (2014). Ubicación de radiopatrullas policiales para la vigilancia pública con dos modelos multicriterios. *Revista de Matemática: Teoría y Aplicaciones*, *21*(1), 145–158.

Garg, R. H. (2012). Who killed Rambhor? The state of emergency medical services in India. *Journal of Emergencies, Trauma and Shock*, *5*(1), 49–54. doi:10.4103/0974-2700.93113 PMID:22416155

Gaspars-Wieloch, H. (2017). A decision rule based on goal programming and one-stage models for uncertain multi-criteria mixed decision making and games against nature. *Croatian Operational Research Review*, *8*(1), 63–78. doi:10.17535/crorr.2017.0004

Hernández, G. J. J., García, G. M. J., Hernández, G. G. J., & Hernández, R. J. G. (2014). Fantastic Sport Leagues and Matrixes Of Weighing. Document presented in Optimization 2014 Conference, Guimaraes, Portugal.

Hernández, G. J. J., García, G. M. J., & Hernández, R. J. G. (2014). Fantasy Leagues and Decision making under uncertainty. An approach. Proceedings, 15th Applied Stochastic Models and Data Analysis (ASMDA2013), 415-427.

Hernández, J. G., García, M. J., & Hernández, G. J. (2012). Dynamic knowledge: Diagnosis and Customer Service. In Service Science Research, Strategy, and Innovation: Dynamic Knowledge Management Methods. IGI Global.

Hernández, R. J. G., García, G. M. J., & Hernández, G. G. J. (2011). Matrixes Of Weighing and catastrophes. *International Journal of Distributed Systems and Technologies*, *2*(1), 14–28. doi:10.4018/jdst.2011010102

Hyatt, C. G., Sutton, W. A., Foster, W. M., & McConnell, D. (2013). Fan involvement in a professional sport team's decision making. *Sport, Business and Management. International Journal (Toronto, Ont.)*, *3*(3), 189–204.

Jassbi, J. J., Ribeiro, R. A., & Dargam, F. (2014). Dynamic MCDM for Multi Group Decision Making. In *Joint International Conference on Group Decision and Negotiation*. Springer. 10.1007/978-3-319-07179-4_10

Jeney, A. (2014). *Impacto del Gerente de Sistemas de Información y Redes del Modelo Logístico Basado en Cargos en la gestión del conocimiento de una organización, medido a través de una Matriz De Ponderación. Disertación Maestría en Gerencia de sistemas*. Caracas, Venezuela: Universidad Metropolitana.

Li, G., Kou, G., & Peng, Y. (2016). A Group Decision Making Model for Integrating Heterogeneous Information. *IEEE Transactions on Systems, Man, and Cybernetics. Systems*, 1–11. doi:10.1109/TSMC.2015.2422267

Mousavi, S. M., Hajipour, V., Niaki, S. T. A., & Aalikar, N. (2014). A multi-product multi-period inventory control problem under inflation and discount: A parameter-tuned particle swarm optimization algorithm. *International Journal of Advanced Manufacturing Technology*, 70(9-12), 1739–1756. doi:10.100700170-013-5378-y

Schwarz, I. L. M., Schwarz, I. T. M., García, G. M. J., Hernández, G. G. J., & Hernández, R. J. G. (2016). Social Impact of Restrictions on Inventory Management. In *Proceedings ICIL2016*. AGH University of Science and Technology in Krakow.

Schwarz, L. M., & Schwarz, T. M. (2015). *Propuesta de modelo de toma de decisiones en la planificación de ventas y operaciones de empresas Venezolanas de consumo masivo*. Caracas, Venezuela: Disertación en Ingeniería de Producción, Universidad Metropolitana.

Wu, Z., Xu, J., & Xu, Z. (2016). A multiple attribute group decision making framework for the evaluation of lean practices at logistics distribution centers. *Annals of Operations Research*, 247(2), 735–757. doi:10.100710479-015-1788-6

Xu, J., Wu, Z., & Zhang, Y. (2014). A consensus based method for multi-criteria group decision making under uncertain linguistic setting. *Group Decision and Negotiation*, 1–22.

ADDITIONAL READING

Acevedo-Ojeda, A., Contreras, I., & Chen, M. (2015). Two-Level Lot-Sizing with Raw-Material Perishability and Deterioration. *International Journal of Production Research*, 1–16.

Barreto, O. E. A., Hernández, G. G. J., García, G. M. J., & Hernández, R. J. G. (2016). Security & Safety (S&S) and the Logistics Business. In *Proceedings ICIL2016*, AGH University of Science and Technology in Krakow, Krakow, Poland, 12-23.

Belavina, E. (2016). The Structure of Grocery Retail Markets and Food Waste. Working paper 16-23. University of Chicago Booth School of Business, USA, 1-49.

Chen, P. Y. (2017). Economic Order Quality Model for Determining the Sales Prices of Fresh Goods at Various Points in Time. *Journal of Food Quality*, 1–12.

Coelho, L. C., & Laporte, G. (2014). Optimal joint replenishment, delivery and inventory management policies for perishable products. *Computers & Operations Research*, 47, 42–52. doi:10.1016/j.cor.2014.01.013

Eagleman, A. N., & Krohn, B. D. (2012). Sponsorship awareness, attitudes, and purchase intentions of road race series participants. *Sport Marketing Quarterly*, *21*(4), 210–220.

Galal, N. M., & El-Kilany, K. S. (2016). Sustainable Agri-Food Supply Chain with uncertain demand and lead time. *International Journal of Simulation Modelling*, *15*(3), 485–496. doi:10.2507/IJSIMM15(3)8.350

García, G. M. J., Hernández, G. G. J., & Hernández, R. J. G. (2014). A Methodology of The Decision Support Systems applied to other projects of Investigation. In Mehdi K. (Ed.), Encyclopedia of Information Science and Technology, Third Edition: Hershey, PA: IGI Global, V3, 1978-1990.

García, G. M. J., Hernández, G. G. J., & Hernández, R. J. G. (2017). The Primes numbers in the kitchen. In *GBATA Reading Book 2017* (pp. 178–186). USA: GBATA.

Gaukler, G., Ketzenberg, M., & Salin, V. (2017). Establishing dynamic expiration dates for perishables: An application of RFID and sensor technology. *International Journal of Production Economics*, *193*, 617–632. doi:10.1016/j.ijpe.2017.07.019

Hernández, J. J., García, M. J., Hernández, G. J., & Hernández, J. G. (2013). Multiatribute Models with Multiplicative factors in the Fantasy Sports. In *GBATA Reading Book 2013* (pp. 406–413). USA: GBATA.

Hernández, R. J., García, G. M., & Hernández, G. G. (2013). Enterprise logistics, indicators and Physical distribution manager. *Research in Logistics & Production*, *3*(1), 5–20.

Hernández, R. J. G., García, G. M. J., & Hernández, G. G. J. (2016). Enterprise diagnosis and the Environmental manager of LoMoBaP. *Journal of Global Business and Technology*, *12*(1), 60–76.

Janssen, L., Claus, T., & Sauer, J. (2016). Literature review of deteriorating inventory models by key topics from 2012 to 2015. *International Journal of Production Economics*, *182*, 86–112. doi:10.1016/j.ijpe.2016.08.019

Jeney, A., Hernández, J. G., García, M. J., & Hernández, G. J. (2015). Generation and Knowledge Management System Through the information and networks manager. In Seventeenth annual International Conference Global Business And Technology Association, Reading Book: USA, GBATA, 244- 251.

Kumar, S., Chakraborty, D., & Malik, A. K. (2017). A Two Warehouse Inventory Model with Stock-Dependent Demand and variable deterioration rate. *International Journal on Future Revolution in Computer Science & Communication Engineering*, *3*(9), 20–24.

Lee, Ph. (2013). *The Philip Lee Sport Report* (pp. 1–48). Dublin, Ireland.

McKelvey, S., Carter, B., & Martin, W. (2012). Industry Insider: Action Sports Execs. *Sport Marketing Quarterly*, *21*(4), 206–209.

Parris, D. L., Drayer, J., & Shapiro, S. L. (2012). Developing a pricing strategy for the Los Angeles Dodgers. *Sport Marketing Quarterly*, *21*(4), 256–264.

Pronschinske, M., Groza, M. D., & Walker, M. (2012). Attracting Facebook 'Fans': The Importance of authenticity and engagement as a Social networking strategy for professional sport teams. *Sport Marketing Quarterly*, *21*(4), 221–231.

Song, D. P., Dong, J. X., & Xu, J. J. (2014). Integrated inventory management and supplier base reduction in a supply chain with multiple uncertainties. *European Journal of Operational Research, 232*(3), 522–536. doi:10.1016/j.ejor.2013.07.044

Soysal, M., Bloemhof-Ruwaard, J. M., Haijema, R., & van der Vorst, J. G. (2015). Modeling an Inventory Routing Problem for perishable products with environmental considerations and demand uncertainty. *International Journal of Production Economics, 164*, 118–133. doi:10.1016/j.ijpe.2015.03.008

KEY TERMS AND DEFINITIONS

Inventories Control (IC [CI]): It is one of the most relevant and delicate tasks of logistics and by extension of the organization. It is related to the final product and all the components that are needed in its production process, whether they are a direct part of it or are necessary for the proper operability of the organization. Through the control of inventories, it must be ensured that each of these components must be available at the time, conditions and quantities required, so that production does not stop.

Location of Vehicles to Handle Emergencies (LVHE [UVAE]): It is a necessity that arises in very large cities, which generally tend to have strong traffic problems, as an appropriate vehicle location to handle emergencies, in specific locations, it can guarantee that these come more quickly where they are needed. Of these vehicles for emergencies, mainly include ambulances, fire trucks and police vehicles.

Matrices of Weighing (MOW [MDP]): They are simply a numerical arrangement of rows and columns, which allow hierarchy and even facilitate the selection of alternatives, in accordance with a set of established criteria. The MDP are one of the simplest multicriteria models to construct and implement. However, their simplicity, they can offer very robust solutions when it comes to hierarchizing and, specially, selecting alternatives.

Matrices of Weighing With Multiplicative Factors (MOWwMf [MDPcFm]): They are MDP, which manage a concept taken from the Multiattribute Models (MM), the multiplicative factors, which give them a greater diversity and field of application.

Multilayer Matrix of Weighing With Multiplicative Factors (ML-MOWwMf [MDPcFm-MC]): They are MDPcFm, which in addition to hierarchizing and facilitating the selection of alternatives, in turn allow assessment and knowledge of the real influence of each of the criteria, through which these alternatives are being evaluated. Additionally, they facilitate valuations under multiple scenarios.

Sport Fantastic Leagues (SFL [LFD]): They are a new way of living sports, where participants, in groups of approximately twelve people, enjoy the experiences of their favorite sports, compete, following established rules and without necessarily being close to each other, and almost always away from sports arenas. These participants, accumulate points, according to the performance of the athletes, who compete in the real world and that they have selected for their respective squads.

Chapter 23
Segmenting Low-Carbon Tourists by Low-Carbon Travel Scale

You-Yu Dai
Shandong Jiaotong University, China

ABSTRACT

This chapter expands research on low-carbon tourism by using the low-carbon travel scale (LCTS) to profile low-carbon tourists. The results demonstrate the LCTS's ability to effectively identify different levels of low-carbon tourists. A priori segmentation was conducted using the respondents' overall LCTS score as the segmenting criterion. The resulting four segments were labeled "not a low-carbon tourist," "minimal low-carbon tourists," "moderate low-carbon tourists," and "strong low-carbon tourists." This study (1) confirms the usefulness of the LCTS for identifying and segmenting travelers and (2) provides the sustainable tourism field with a more holistic tool for measuring sustainable travelers. Destination managers interested in marketing to low-carbon tourists can use this tool to identify how many low-carbon tourists come to their area, level of low-carbon tourists' tendencies, and what the destination can focus on to attract more of this travel segment.

1. INTRODUCTION

Tourism industry and tourist activity emission carbon dioxide account for about 5-14 percent of the global total (World Tourism Organization, WTO & United Nations Environment Programme, UNEP, 2008), and annual rate about 3.2% continued to increase (Peeters & Dubois, 2011). Among them, tourists vehicles (aircraft, cars, ships, etc.), and accommodations, as well as tourism activities caused by the energy consumption and carbon emissions of the most significant (Simpson, Gössling, Scott, Hall, & Gladin, 2008; Horng, Hu, Teng, & Lin, 2014a). Sustrans (2007) and Simpson, et al. (2008) have said that if visitors can alter energy consumption and high carbon travel behavior, you can slow down carbon emissions to increase. Therefore, how to engage in low-carbon tourism industry and academia in recent years has become a topic of concern.

DOI: 10.4018/978-1-5225-7214-5.ch023

Tourism is one of the important economic sectors in the world. The ultimate goal of low-carbon tourism is to alleviate climate change and realize the sustainable development of the society (Hsiao, Sung, & Lu, 2017). To improve travel environment, creating comfortable low carbon travel conditions and advocating green low-carbon travel have been an important measure for the government to construct low-carbon city (Qian, Zhou, & Chen, 2017). Zhu, Zhang, Liao, and Jin (2017) suggested There are many synergies between the low carbon transition and the pursuit of environmental goals, such as reducing water pollution and conserving biodiversity.

Although the study has been aimed at low-carbon tourism involved in the planning, transportation, accommodation, catering, shopping and other aspects of the discussion, however, many people interested in low-carbon tourism is still unable to arrange from the integration point of view to arrange low-carbon tourism. Therefore, it is the subject of this study which tourists can engage in low-carbon tourism activities. Compared to group visitors, since independent travelers can plan and arrange the characteristics of the run, so that it has the opportunity to practice low-carbon travel behavior in the run. Therefore, if you can guide independent travelers engaged in low-carbon tourism will be able to achieve the initiative to promote low-carbon tourism. The aim of this study is to apply a low-carbon travel scale (LCTS) to guide independent travelers to understand the orientation and content of the low-carbon travel behavior.

2. LITERATURE REVIEW

2.1. Low-Carbon Travel and Sustainable Tourism

Since tourists' travel behavior produce large amounts of carbon dioxide emissions, so that visitors aware of environmental threats caused by carbon emissions issues (McKercher et al, 2010; Peeters & Dubois, 2011), also contributed to the visitors to focus on reducing the carbon footprint on various holiday specific actions (Dickinson & Lumsdon, 2010, p 85; Dickinson et al, 2011.). Hu, Horng, Teng and Chou (2012) believed that visitors to have a sustainable environment has generally reduce greenhouse gases, carbon emission reductions and other self-concept, which focuses on the practice of saving energy and reducing carbon. Visitors will not only meet the low-carbon travel preferences carbon reduction recreational needs, change some tourists high carbon emissions recreation behavior (Dickinson et al., 2011), and tourists through carbon reduction behavior contribute to environmental protection. Therefore, low-carbon tourism in the tourism process focus on reducing carbon emissions, reduce carbon footprint, encouraging visitors to use less energy while traveling and stay in order to reduce the environmental impact (Lumsdon & McGrath, 2011). In summary, today's tourists have gradually awareness of the importance of low-carbon tourism sustainable tourism environment.

Compared with the general tourism, low-carbon tourism focuses on reducing carbon emissions in the tourism process, reduce carbon footprint. Simpson et al. (2008) argued that low-carbon tourism is a low-carbon transport in the run-in to the nearby tourist destinations do stay long way to travel. Kuo and Dai (2012) further pointed out, visitors can choose a tourist destination by environmental friendliness of transport equipment, accommodation with environmental certification, and local or organic food diet dining options and other means, to achieve low levels of carbon dioxide emissions purposes. Therefore, low-carbon tourism tourist stressed individuals to change travel behavior and reduce energy consumption of tourism activities, taking into account the lowering carbon dioxide emissions (Sustrans, 2007). In Taiwan, the existing low-carbon tourism activities in the industry and local governments to design tour packages based, such as "low-carbon travel in Pinglin", "low-carbon travel in Shungxi by bike and train", " low-carbon travel to visit Green Island by bike", and" low-carbon travel in Hualien", etc.

Overall, low-carbon tourism on the tourism environment with low energy consumption and low pollution features, is the depth of environmental tourism concept (Zhang & Liu, 2011). Low-carbon tourism may not apply to every situation sightseeing, but a low-carbon travel in most of the world's domestic or short holiday considerable development potential. For example, Ceron and Dubois (2007) pointed out that France's future, even if the 2050 reduction in carbon dioxide emissions is currently a quarter of tourism, many tourisms is clearly feasible. Gössling, Peeters and Scott's (2008) survey about poverty and tourism-dependent countries revealed a low-carbon tourism market of environmental conservation as a precondition transition, the number of visitors would still show growth. Dickinson et al. (2010) considered the future of low-carbon tourism slow travel is a viable strategy, and tourists will travel in the slow tourism more sustainable development.

Researchers in the past have started to discuss the relationship between the development of low-carbon tourism and sightseeing sustainable environmental, economic, and social-oriented. On the environment, due to non-low-carbon tourism environment bring negative effects, it is necessary to low-carbon tourism as one of the guidelines of sustainable tourism. Becken and Patterson (2009) and Juvan and Dolnicar (2014) agreed that the tourism organization shall provide easy and reliable tool that enables visitors to be calculated and compared to quantify the impact of tourism activities on the environment and society. Becken and Patterson (2009) also believed that the underlying causes of the different roles to be exploring ways to qualitative changes in behavior of tourists, as well as sightseeing in the public sector and the private sector take forward a more sustainable form of tourism plays. In this way, we will be able nature of low-carbon tourism, tourists' behavior, and comparison of low-carbon tourism and general tourism carbon emissions to a complete understanding of the impact of low-carbon tourism environment.

On the economic front, low-carbon tourism is based on a low-carbon economy to achieve sustainable development (Teng, Shi, & Liu, 2011). Core concept of low-carbon economy means tourism industry with fewer carbon emissions to get more economic, environmental and social benefits (Zhang & Liu, 2011). Thus, the tourism industry through technological and institutional innovations, industrial restructuring and other methods, saving energy and reducing carbon as possible in order to achieve sustainable social and economic and environmental tourism of win. On the social level, because the tourism industry is a mixture of industry from private enterprises, public authorities and non-profit organizations, and sustainable tourism development requires the parties to participate in planning (Liu, Tzeng, & Lee, 2012). Therefore, the government's low-carbon tourism policy needs of tourists and individual community coordination, cooperation, participation and management in order to increase public interest in sustainable development and conservation. As a result, tourism communities and visitors will be able to bring people in coexistence between the two sides through the development of low-carbon travel. These results show the development of low-carbon tourism, improve low-carbon travel behavior of tourists for the promotion of sustainable tourism development has played an important role.

Given the international pressure to reduce carbon footprint more and more sustainable outcomes is likely to be an important stimulating low-carbon tourism, not only help to alleviate the impact of climate change, while the tourism industry in terms of avoided because climate Change mitigation policies and pay more of the cost (Dickinson et al., 2011). Low-carbon tourism visitors understand the motivation, reduce obstacles to low-carbon tourism tourist perception, will enable the industry to more effectively plan the best way to low-carbon tourism activities in the future, to promote and change the behavior of tourists, urging visitors to engage low-carbon tourism behavior, and reduce pressure on the environment (Horng, Hu, Teng, Hsiao, Tsai, & Liu, 2014b).

2.2. Low-Carbon Travel Behavior

Kuo and Dai (2012) refer to the past to focus on how to plan and design low-carbon tourism activities and run, but little attention to the behavior of tourists. Kuo and Chen (2009) from the perspective of tourism analysis of energy consumption and waste manufacturing need to consider the transport, tourism, accommodation, diet and other factors. These components interact with each other (Horng et al., 2014). At present, Simo et al. (2008) proposed suggestions for both planning and selection of transport, and Horng et al. (2014) proposed visitors based on industry policies in hotels, restaurants, as well as tourism to practice the energy saving and carbon reduction behavior. Although Kuo and Dai (2012) mentioned the importance of tourists engaged in low-carbon behavior throughout the run, but not in-depth discussion. Therefore, this study suggests that to analyze the low-carbon tourism behavior of tourists, from the various aspects of the runners to discuss, including travel planning, transportation, accommodation, catering, consumption, and behavioral orientation and so on.

2.2.1. Low-Carbon Journey Planning

In low-carbon tourism context, the choice of tourist mode is a key factor (Dickinson, Robbins, & Lumsdon, 2010). The World Tourism Organization (WTO), the United Nations Environment Program (UNEP) and the World Meteorological Organization (WMO) (2008) recommend that visitors choose pro-friendly travel trips and engage in environmentally friendly activities at the tourist destination to reduce carbon footprint. Horng, Hu, Teng, Hsiao and Liu (2013) point out that it is helpful to reduce the carbon emissions by selecting a simple package run and changing holiday habits. Sustrans (2007) and Simpson et al. (2008) suggest that visitors can reduce the itinerary, travel around, and stay in the tourist area for a long time. To sum up, visitors' low-carbon travel planning focuses on simplifying itinerary to achieve the goal of reducing carbon emissions.

2.2.2. Low-Carbon Transport

Low-carbon transport can be seen as the core concept of low-carbon tourism. Many studies suggest that visitors should avoid using airplanes and cars to travel and explore other ways to develop low-carbon tourism markets (Gössling, Peeters, & Scott, 2008; Scott, Peeters, & Gössling, 2010). Trains, buses, bicycles, and walking are even lower than cruise ships, airplanes and self-driving carbon footprints (Dickinson et al., 2011). Schwarz (2006) suggested that people try to take the train to replace the plane to the destination, carbon dioxide emissions will be reduced (Miller, Rathouse, Scarles, Holmes, & Tribe, 2010). (Simpson et al., 2008; Kuo & Dai, 2012), including: walking, cycling (Dickinson et al., 2011), and by public transport (see) Such as MRT, trains, highways or passenger) (Horng et al., 2014).

2.2.3. Low-Carbon Accommodation

The food industry is seen as one of the main sources of greenhouse gas emissions (Vaze, 2009), while energy savings can lead to a significant reduction in greenhouse carbon emissions (Filimonau, Dickinson, Robbins, & Huijbregts, 2011). (Kuo & Dai, 2012), towels are reused in the hotel room and are not changed daily (Mckercher et al., 2010), with personal toiletries (e.g. shampoo, bathing) Milk, toothbrush, toothpaste), saving energy and water (Horng et al., 2014) can help the hotel to reduce resource consumption. It can be said that visitors follow these instructions to reduce carbon emissions, and thus achieve low-carbon accommodation.

2.2.4. Low-Carbon Diet

Low-carbon diet reduces greenhouse gas emissions from energy use (Nerlich, Evans, & Koteyko, 2011). The main principles of low-carbon dining include eating and eating locally grown and seasonal foods in the local restaurant, eating and processing food and eating, and reducing the waste of food (Salt Spring Island Climate Action Council, 2011). For example, Schwarz (2006) advises travelers not to go to the mountains for seafood. Visitors eat more vegetables, carry reusable cutlery, choose local and seasonal food or organic food (Kuo & Dai, 2012; Horng et al., 2014) can also reduce food and beverage activity of carbon dioxide emissions.

2.2.5. Low-Carbon Consumption

Shopping is a common and preferred behavior for tourists in the tour (Timothy & Butler, 1995). However, many shopping activities will produce higher carbon dioxide emissions. If visitors buy non-local production of souvenirs, will produce a higher carbon footprint. Visitors' purchase commercially available beverage packaging for the environment is a load (Kuo & Chen, 2009). In addition, visitors may often buy products inadvertently discard layers of wrapping paper or gift boxes, but not only a waste of resources also caused high-carbon emissions of the real environment. Therefore, visitors carry reusable shopping bags (Horng et al., 2014), which are engaged in green consumption (e.g., products that buy energy-saving, locally produced, or environmentally friendly) (Teng et al., 2014) can reduce the consumption of carbon dioxide emissions in order to achieve energy saving and carbon reduction.

2.2.6. Low-Carbon Tendencies

McKercher et al. (2010) pointed out that most visitors are willing to contribute to carbon reduction during the holidays, for example, visitors are willing to spend more time to engage in low-carbon activities, voluntarily buy carbon taxes, and choose low carbon footprints, tourism. Kuo and Dai (2012) pointed out that visitors are willing to engage in low-carbon tourism in the future, and recommend friends and family engaged in low-carbon tourism. Horng et al. (2014) investigated the willingness of visitors to engage in low-carbon tourism. Hsiao, et al. (2017) believed consumers' uncertainty about products influenced their purchase intention, and consumers who possessed knowledge about sustainable consumption and showed purchase intention did not necessarily demonstrate actual purchase behavior. Therefore, this study suggests that low-carbon tourism is not only willing to start from the tourists themselves, so that the holiday travel activities to reduce carbon emissions, but also called on others to participate.

The above-mentioned literature provides a lot of direction and content for this study to guide visitors in low-carbon tourism. Therefore, the researchers review these documents, search for low-carbon tourism can be clearly defined its definition of important components, to capture the low-carbon tourism scale for the content and content. It can be said that the researchers confirm that these orientation and content-based development of the scale of the collection of topics to lay a solid foundation.

3. METHODOLOGY

The Low-Carbon Travel Scale (LCTS) (Tsaur & Dai, 2016) was used to collect data from travelers at low-carbon tourism destinations designated on Pinglin and Penghu in Taiwan during the spring and summer of 2015. Low-carbon tourism destination refers to the destinations travel planning and business services with low-carbon tourism concepts and low carbon footprint (Gössling & Scott, 2012). Pinglin is not only Taiwan's first low-carbon tourism destination, the Pinglin low-carbon tourism has also become a trend. Currently New Taipei City Government Environmental Protection Agency (2014) promotes low-carbon, energy-saving, and environmentally friendly travel patterns by green transportation, renewable energy, low-carbon behavior, and carbon sinks coupons, waste reduction and green-oriented shops in Pinglin. These would guide people travel and environmental protection at the same time. In addition, Penghu National Scenic Area Administration (2011) established Penghu as low-carbon Island and cooperate with the industry to promote high-quality journey such as "Penghu fresh play", the main focus is low-carbon and eco-tourism. Local industry in Penghu must comply with: (1) lodging industry does not take the initiative to provide disposable toiletries; (2) the restaurant industry does not provide disposable tableware in favor of reuse can wash dishes and encourage people to bring their own tableware; (3) Travel remind visitors with the living area to create a low-carbon island project.

The LCTS was administered on-site to tourists traveled more than one time in the past one year. Compared to the group package tourists, independent tourists have characteristics of plan and schedule journey by themselves, and they have rich knowledge of tourism product purchase and use. Independent tourists would pay more desire to meet their personal internal psycho-social needs, and easier to be attracted by tourism property than group package tourists. Therefore, independent tourists need a lot of time and effort to make whether to start or continue a low-carbon tourism decision. So, researchers studied Pinglin and Penghu as low-carbon tourism destination survey locations. The survey population are independent tourists who visited Pinglin and Penghu. In order to control the characteristics of sample representative of the population, in this study we take a random sampling method.

Each eligible traveler in a group was asked to participate since individual behaviors may differ within the group. In total, 556 individuals were intercepted, with 533 participating in the study resulting in a 95.9% response rate. Of the 533 surveys collected, 10 were deleted because of missing data within the LCTS questions and an extra 26 were deleted due to the failure to include one or more demographic variables resulting in 497 usable responses and a usable response rate of 89.4%.

The sample had an even gender distribution (46.9% male/53.11% female). Respondents were highly educated and very affluent, with 82.3% holding a bachelor's degree or higher and 79.3% with monthly household incomes of less than NTD 40,000. The most age was 21 to 30 years old and average length of stay was two to three days in the region.

The overall LCTS was calculated by taking the mean score of the six summated dimensions within the LCTS. The LCTS consists of 27 items (Tsaur & Dai, 2016). The LCTS includes low-carbon tourism's definition in order to provide a more accurate representation of one's predisposition to low-carbon travel behaviors. The definition of low-carbon tourism is multidimensional, meaning that all dimensions of low-carbon tourism must be considered when determining if someone is a low-carbon tourist.

Since all dimensions in the LCTS were measured on a Likert scale ranging from 1 to 5, the LCTS has a range of 1–5 with one representing a non-low-carbon tourist and five representing a perfect low-carbon tourist based upon the definition of low-carbon tourism. In the motivation and constraint dimensions, one equals "strongly disagree" and five represents "strongly agree". It was possible to create an overall LCTS since the motivation and constraint dimensions, were both measured with this 1–5 range. The LCTS is believed to be an acceptable indicator of whether one could be considered a low-carbon tourist or not (Dai, 2015).

4. RESULTS

A detailed analysis of the LCTS's reliability and validity through a CFA is provided by Tsaur & Dai (2016). This study builds upon his work by empirically testing the LCTS within Pinglin and Penghu in Taiwan to see if it is capable of profiling low-carbon tourists at different levels of low-carbon travel motivations.

4.1. A Priori Segmentation Using the LCTS

This study focused on the differences in characteristics among varying levels of low-carbon tourists. The LCTS revealed that visitors to Pinglin and Penghu sample (n = 497) were low-carbon tourists with an average LCTS of 3.89 (S.D. = 0.64) and LCS of 3.89 (S.D. = 0.64). The criteria used to determine one's degree of low-carbon travel motivations and constraint was based upon the magnitude of their LCTS and LCS. Since the purpose of this study was to identify unique low-carbon tourist segments, respondents were segmented into a "minimal low-carbon tourist" group (scores lower than 3.39), "moderate low-carbon tourist" group (scores from 3.39 to 4.39) and "strong low-carbon tourist" group (scores greater than 4.39) by their overall LCTS. This segmentation of low-carbon tourists into low, medium and high segments is similar to the growing trend to view low-carbon tourists along a hard to soft spectrum where "hard low-carbon tourists" are characterized as active and deep while "soft low-carbon tourists" are labeled as passive and shallow (Dai, 2015).

Demographic differences between the three groups were tested using crosstab analysis and the Pearson Chi-Square statistic. The Chi-square tests revealed significant differences between "minimal low-carbon tourists", "moderate low-carbon tourists" and "strong low-carbon tourists" on the variables of gender, age, education and monthly income (Table 1). Significant differences on the variables of level of gender, education and age, monthly income was not found to be significantly different between the three groups.

4.2. Minimal Low-Carbon Tourists (Segment 1, n = 230)

Members of this first segment entitled "minimal low-carbon tourists" were identified based upon their low-carbon travel score being below 3.39. This is the largest segment with 230 members representing 46.3% of the sample. As segmented, "minimal low-carbon tourists" are the least likely to protect environment, seek low-carbon travel experience, escape daily life or get social bounding by low-carbon travel (Table 2). Their behaviors toward the industry, product and transportation of low-carbon travel are also significantly lower than "moderate low-carbon tourists" and "strong low-carbon tourists". "Minimal low-carbon tourists" have an overall LCTS of 3.37. They differed from "moderate low-carbon tourists"

Table 1. Demographic characteristics by low-carbon tourist segment

Variables	Total sample	Minimal low-carbon tourist (n = 230)	Moderate low-carbon tourist (n = 165)	Strong low-carbon tourist (n = 102)	t-Test value	df	p*
Gender	%	%	%	%			
Male	46.9	53.5	44.8	35.3	6.71	2	0.03
Female	53.1	46.5	55.2	64.7			
Age							
Less than 21 years old	17.3	14.3	15.8	26.5	8.76	10	0
21 – 30 years old	45.1	44.8	49.1	39.2			
31 – 40 years old	15.1	15.2	13.9	16.7			
41 – 50 years old	11.5	13.5	11.5	6.9			
51 – 60 years old	7.6	8.7	6.1	7.8			
Above 60 years old	3.4	3.5	3.6	2.9			
Education							
Less than high school	3.4	2.2	6.1	2.0	13.08	6	0.04
High school diploma or the equivalent (GED)	14.3	16.1	13.3	11.8			
Bachelor's degree	65.0	58.7	66.1	77.5			
Masters and Doctors degree	17.3	23.0	14.5	8.8			
Monthly income (NTD)							
Less than 20,001	49.7	48.3	51.5	50.0	5.42	8	0.71
20,001-40,000	29.6	28.7	27.3	35.3			
40,001-60,000	11.5	11.7	13.9	6.9			
60,001-80,000	5.8	6.5	4.8	5.9			
More than 80,000	3.4	4.8	2.4	2.0			
Length of stay							
1 day	23.7	26.1	21.8	21.6	5.42	6	0.49
2 days	25.6	27.0	25.5	22.5			
3 days	29.8	31.7	25.5	32.4			
More than 3 days	20.9	15.2	27.3	23.5			

*Bold type indicates a statistical difference at the 0.05 level.

and "strong low-carbon tourists" by gender, age, and education. Most "minimal low-carbon tourists" are male (53.5%), 21 to 30 years old (44.8%), more than half (58.7%) have bachelor's degree and 48.3% having a monthly income less than NTD 20,000 (Table 1). The "minimal low-carbon tourist" segment represents the majority of travelers to Pinglin and Penghu. This is important because it shows that many visitors to low-carbon tourism destinations have minimal low-carbon travel behaviors. Although they are lower segment, this is still an attractive market segment for destinations interested in low-carbon tourism as a sustainable management and marketing strategy.

4.3. Moderate Low-Carbon Tourists (Segment 2, n = 165)

Members of the "moderate low-carbon tourists" segment were identified based upon having low-carbon tourism scores ranging from 3.39 to 4.39. Overall low-carbon travel behavior scores between 3.39 and 4.39 indicate general agreement with the likelihood of participating in low-carbon travel behavior. This segment has 165 members and accounts for 33.2% of the sample. "Moderate low-carbon tourists" were likely to participate in low-carbon travel behavior, but not to be "strong low-carbon tourists". They were likely to participate in low-carbon travel behavior such as buy local products (3.99), eat local foods (4.23), and buy environmentally friendly products (3.74). Their behavioral intention toward the industry, product and transportation of low-carbon travel generally aligned with the principles of low-carbon tourism, but because of the a priori segmentation, were also significantly lower than "strong low-carbon tourists" and significantly higher than "minimal low-carbon tourists" on these dimensions. Their mean low-carbon travel score was 4.12 (Table 2). "Moderate low-carbon tourists" were evenly more female, most age range was 21 to 30 years old, highest educated segment with 66.1% having a bachelor's degree and 51.5% having a monthly household income less than NTD 20,000 (Table 1).

4.4. Strong Low-Carbon Tourists (Segment 3, n = 102)

Lastly, respondents with scores above 4.39 were indicated as "strong low-carbon tourists" because their answers to the LCTS showed most strong agreement with the low-carbon travel questions and a highest behavioral intention to act like a low-carbon tourist. This segment of participants has 102 members, represents 20.5% of the sample. Their average of low-carbon travel score was 4.66. "Strong low-carbon tourists" were found to be predominantly female (64.7%), have a most age range of 21 to 30 years old, have a high level of education and also low monthly household incomes (Table 1).

4.5. LCTS Differences

The next step was to statistically examine the six dimensions of low-carbon travel between the three segments. Table 2 provides average scores for the entire sample as well as for each segment based upon the 24 items within the LCTS and across the six dimensions. Since the priori segmentation of the groups based upon their overall LCTS, it would be expected that the differences between each group would be significant. Multiple analysis of variance (MANOVA) was adopted to verify the differences between "minimal low-carbon tourist", "moderate low-carbon tourist" and "strong low-carbon tourist" segments. The results of MANOVA show that there are statistically significant differences between the categories on each item at the 0.05 level of p-value (Table 2).

A post hoc Sheffe test also shows the significant statistical differences at the 0.05 level. The significant differences between the three groups were found between their answers on the six dimensions of environmental protection, experience seeking, escape/social bounding, the industry's demands and measures for environmental protection, local products, and green transportation. The "strong low-carbon tourists" answered higher on these dimensions than the "minimal low-carbon tourists". The results indicate that there is significant heterogeneity between the segments on the individual items of the LCTS as well as on the overall LCTS.

All items were tested for statistical significance using MANOVA and a Scheffe post hoc test. Significant differences were found between the segments at the 0.000 level.

Table 2. Responses to the Low-Carbon Travel Motivation and Constraints Scale by segment

Dimensions and items description		Minimal low-carbon tourist (n = 230)	Moderate low-carbon tourist (n = 165)	Strong low-carbon tourist (n = 102)	*MANOVA significant
Low-carbon journey planning	Compared with foreign travel, I prefer engaging in domestic tourism nearly.	3.55	4.31	4.78	0.000
	I would stay long in destination.	3.71	4.45	4.89	0.000
	I would follow the established journey planning and reduce unnecessary trips.	3.60	4.31	4.79	0.000
	I would visit green-labeled places or a low-carbon footprint destination.	3.76	4.56	4.90	0.000
Low-carbon transport	I would try to take public transportation, such as buses, trains, and high-speed rail.	3.47	4.29	4.84	0.000
	Between tourism attractions, I would bike or walk as mobile tools.	3.17	3.90	4.42	0.000
	I would reduce taking high-carbon emissions transportation, such as aircraft and cruise.	3.58	4.36	4.82	0.000
	I would try to reduce the weight of baggage.	3.42	4.19	4.69	0.000
low-carbon accommodation	I would use my own toiletries during my stay.	3.46	4.25	4.66	0.000
	I would not require changing towels and bed linen daily during my stay.	3.45	4.28	4.74	0.000
	I would choose environmental or ecological oriented accommodation.	3.41	4.10	4.69	0.000
	I would save water and electricity during my stay.	3.29	4.12	4.59	0.000
	I would choose accommodation providing fixed connection.	3.47	4.22	4.80	0.000
Low-carbon diet	I would choose green-labeled restaurants.	3.28	4.04	4.55	0.000
	I do not waste food.	3.34	4.16	4.62	0.000
	I would choose restaurant using low food miles (local food ingredients).	3.22	3.99	4.42	0.000
	I would buy local and on seasonal food.	3.19	3.84	4.40	0.000
	I would eat more plant-based diet, reducing meat intake.	3.47	4.25	4.78	0.000
	I would reduce the consumption of bottled beverages/water.	3.17	3.96	4.50	0.000
Low-carbon consumption	I would buy local products.	3.19	3.90	4.60	0.000
	I would buy environmentally-friendly or environmentally-labeled products.	3.14	3.76	4.54	0.000
	I would reduce consuming excessive packaging and processing products.	3.24	3.96	4.60	0.000
	I would bring my own environmental equipment (such as shopping bags, reusable chopsticks, etc.).	3.18	3.99	4.66	0.000
Low-carbon tendency	I consciously have a responsibility to protect the tourism environment willing to reduce my carbon footprint.	3.33	3.99	4.70	0.000
	I am happy to get low-carbon knowledge learning.	3.32	3.99	4.71	0.000
	I would engage in low-carbon travel activities in the future.	3.50	4.23	4.76	0.000
	I would recommend family and friends engaging in low-carbon travel.	3.17	3.74	4.63	0.000

5. DISCUSSION

This paper used the overall LCTS to segment low-carbon destination sample based upon their degree of low-carbon travel behaviors. According results, low-carbon tourists can be distinguished by "minimal", "moderate" and "strong" low-carbon tourists based on their response to the LCTS. Low-carbon tourists are an important travel segment for destinations to target because they tend to use local businesses. Further, Kuo and Dai (2012) found low-carbon tourists spend more behavioral intention while on vacation. Lastly, the results from this study confirm sizes of the low-carbon tourist market segment. Based upon the overall LCTS, 53.4% visitors of Pinglin and Penghu have low-carbon travel behavior scores of 3.39 or higher out of 5 possible points.

Significant differences between the three segments were found on the variables of gender, age and education. This suggests that some personal characteristics are good predictors of variances in low-carbon travel behaviors. Furthermore, a mixture of psychographic and demographic variables may be a better strategy for understanding these market segments. The findings that "strong low-carbon tourists" were more likely to be female than male and higher education is consistent with findings from Boley and Nickerson (2013). Boley and Nickerson's (2013) study on geotourism found women have much more geotravel tendencies than men, and responses have higher education level.

Finding no significant statistical differences between low-carbon travel market segments on monthly income was not anticipated based on the previous research on low-carbon tourism (Kuo & Dai, 2012), but at the same time, it is not uncommon within the sustainable tourism literature to have contradictory findings about socio-demographic variables. This is exemplified by this study and Boley and Nickerson's (2002) study which found significant differences on gender, age and education, but not in monthly income. Based upon the lack of findings and the contradictory nature of the findings, Dolnicar and Long (2009) suggested that difference in socio-demographic characteristics still need to be researched more before conclusions can be made.

These mixed results also support the use of psychographic variables such as motivations found within the LCTS to effectively segment sustainable tourists from non-sustainable tourists. The study results reflect tourists' low-carbon travel behaviors in other relative literature. For example, the low-carbon tendency was also mentioned by Kuo and Dai (2012) and Horng et al. (2014).

6. CONCLISION AND IMPLICATION

6.1. Conclusion

More and more attention of scholars engaged in low-carbon travel behaviors (e.g., Kuo & Dai, 2012; Horng, Hu, Teng et al, 2014a.). This study provides travel behaviors concept can be measured. Therefore, this study aims to understand the behaviors of tourists in the low-carbon travel and confirmed that LCTS. Low-carbon tourism is quite broad concept, and individual travelers in the low-carbon travel decisions will vary according to different behaves. Existing literature has emphasized the development of low-carbon tourism contributes sustainable tourism (Kuo & Dai, 2012; Horng et al, 2014.). We believe that deeply understanding individual travelers in the behavioral factors contribute to travelers engaged in low-carbon tourism. So, whether tourists or tourism purposes modes why, empirical findings buffet key low-carbon travelers have behaviors. In this study, LCTS lay sound theoretical basis. Further, it was confirmed not only the continuation of LCTS studies in the past, but also to provide a practical assessment tools and guidance for tourists and scholars.

This study based on independent tourism perspective to prove LCTS. The contribution is that confirm the usefulness of LCTS and sightseeing in the field of low-carbon tourism market segments appropriate guidelines. The results confirmed stability, reliability and validity of LCTS. Therefore, LCTS does provide low-carbon tourism industry and tourist confirmed that low-carbon tourism in the grounds, and thus tourists on a trip to practice low-carbon travel. From a theoretical development point, LCTS was used to measure low-carbon travel motivation to do when making decisions. If it can do to further explore the low-carbon tourist hinder decision-making consultations and connecting low-carbon travel behavior and travel intentions, will further construct a causal model to interpret the behavior of low carbon tourists. The scale of this study can be used to investigate the effects of different fitness-oriented tourism in the low-carbon travel behaviors.

6.2. Theoretical Implication

For low-carbon destinations, the competent authority must strive to maintain recreational resources and plan low-carbon trips for food, accommodation, tourism, and shopping in order to attract independent tourists and make long stays. It is necessary for the competent authority to implement a low-carbon certification system for recreational sites and provide visitors with a carbon footprint calculation method that will allow visitors to know how to select low-carbon sites.

For low-carbon transportation, it appeals that independent passengers to travel by mass transit, they should cooperate with traffic units to build seamless interchanges to facilitate independent travelers to reduce the use of personal vehicle equipment. In addition, the tourism park can be planned with comprehensive hardware facilities for bicycle paths and landscape trails to attract tourists to choose low-carbon emission and healthier methods while moving between attractions. Tourist destinations can also call on tourists to reduce their luggage load. They can easily enjoy the openness and convenience of mass transit through simple and easy installation. Sustainable transport policy encompasses many related but distinct aspects, such as air quality, health, social justice and welfare (Geng, Long, Chen, & Li, 2018).

With respect to low-carbon accommodation, the competent authorities should cooperate with the lodging industry. In addition to advocating the promotion of water conservation and electricity consumption, independent travelers can be rewarded for using their own toiletries during the stay, and not to change towels or bed linen daily. Secondly, hotel operators located outside the public transport network can be encouraged to provide fixed-point connection services for residents to reduce carbon emissions by way of guest sharing. In addition, tourism destinations may encourage local accommodation operators to apply for different levels of green hotel badges based on their own status or ability to facilitate independent travelers to choose environmentally friendly or ecologically oriented accommodation.

For low-carbon diet, restaurant operators in tourism destinations should be encouraged to create low-carbon health restaurants or environmentally-friendly restaurants so that independent travelers can find out which restaurants use low-food (local ingredients) and seasonal foods. In addition, the competent authority should work with catering companies and agricultural units to promote natural and healthy food and vegetables and reduce the intake of meat by independent tourists. The industry can also appeal to independent travelers not to waste food and encourage consumption of bottled beverages or self-contained drinking water. As a result, the independent tourists' catering activities at the tourism destination will reduce the negative impact of many carbon emissions on the environment.

With respect to low-carbon consumption, the competent authorities can work with local businesses to promote independent travelers' products that reduce over-packaging and processing and provide consumers with discounted discounts to bring their own green appliances. Secondly, we can conduct production resume certification for local products and promote the implementation of environmentally friendly products or products' eco-labelling system to facilitate independent tourists to purchase low-carbon products with local characteristics at tourist destinations.

As regards the low-carbon tendency, relevant departments should provide education information on independent tourists and low-carbon tourism to increase independent tourists' awareness of low-carbon tourism so that they consciously have the responsibility to protect the tourism environment and are willing to reduce their carbon footprint. For example, the competent authority may assist the independent travelers to obtain specific and practical low-carbon tourism information through the media. At the same time, the competent authority can provide independent passengers with opportunities to learn about low-carbon information during trips, such as event-related activities, in order to motivate independent travelers to enjoy low-carbon knowledge learning. The competent authorities should appeal to independent tourists for the benefits of low-carbon tourism, such as promoting health, protecting the environment, and maintaining recreational resources for the next generation in order to stimulate independent tourists to engage in or promote low-carbon tourism activities.

6.3. Managerial Implication

Simpson et al. (2008) believed that the current social trends are ready to create a new market for low carbon tourism products. According to the results of the study, tourism operators should not regard homogenous groups as those with low-carbon tourism experience and those without low-carbon tourism experience. Instead, they should regard the low-carbon tourism experience of independent travelers as a spectrum concept and be divided into highly low-carbon tourism experiences. As a result, tourism operators can provide different marketing programs for different groups to retain existing low-carbon tourists and attract new low-carbon tourists.

Visitors will draw a lot of information from the media. For tourism operators and authorities, they can effectively use the resources and capabilities they possess, so that independent travelers can continue to maintain a high level of environmental protection, green transport, and environmental protection. With measures and other motivations, further strengthening of low-carbon tourism can provide a travel experience for independent travelers, so that independent travelers, regardless of their experience in low-carbon tourism, can increase their motivation for low-carbon tourism. On the other hand, tourism operators and authorities should strive to reduce the barriers of independent tourists engaging in low-carbon tourism, especially those without low-carbon tourism experience, so that low-carbon tourism barriers are not due to differences in the experience of low-carbon tourism.

According to Jackson and Dunn's (1988) narrative on the correlation between tourism participants-non-participants and effective demand and significant demand, researchers who are interested in low-carbon tourism and do not have low-carbon tourism experience can summarize it. For potential tourists. Once they participate in low-carbon tourism, many obstacles to tourism will be overcome. In short, the tourism agencies and tourism authorities should continue their efforts to attract people with low carbon tourism experience to engage in low-carbon tourism.

Finally, some current travel agencies advocate low-carbon tourism. Low-carbon tourism motivation and hindrance scales and low-carbon tourism behavior scales can be used to provide travel agencies that specialize in low-carbon tourism so that they can participate in the analysis of potential low-carbon tourist groups and plan their journeys. The content of the LCTS can be used to remind travelers to save energy while traveling. Carbon reduction behavior. In conclusion, the LCTS clearly points out the content and content of low-carbon tourism. This study not only provides management implications for low-carbon tourism destinations, but also provides relevant businesses as a reference for low-carbon operations.

6.4. Limitations and Suggestions

Future research is needed to better understand this niche travel market as well as understand low-carbon tourism's attractiveness as a management strategy for destinations trying to balance the positive and negative impacts of tourism. This study provides the first empirical test of the LCTS to see if it can identify low-carbon tourist segments within a destination. While already proven as a reliable and valid scale in low-carbon travel destinations and non-low-carbon destinations (Tsaur & Dai, 2016), more tests are needed to see the usefulness of the LCTS as a low-carbon tourist identification and segmentation tool.

There also needs to be more research on low-carbon tourism from the demand side. Another scale similar to Low-Carbon Travel Motivation and Constraint Scale, a scale designed to understand tourists' low-carbon travel psychology (Dai, 2015), should be created to assess the demand side of low-carbon tourism. This would provide a gauge for assessing tourists' low-carbon travel tendencies which could then be compared to visitor low-carbon travel intentions. A significant difference between the tourists' motivations and behavioral tendencies could alert the destination managers of incompatibility with those visiting, thus suggesting a new marketing direction.

Another research area needed on the supply side of low-carbon tourism is to see how successful the industries with low-carbon tourism destinations have been in increasing spending within the local economy and protecting the environmental and local resources that make the destination unique and competitive. Additionally, the low-carbon destinations were established from 2006, but there has been little research on residents' attitudes, motivations, or behaviors toward low-carbon tourism or how it has positively or negatively affected the region.

ACKNOWLEDGMENT

This research was supported by National Science Council of Taiwan (Program No.: NSC 102-2420-H-415-003-DR), and Doctoral Scientific Research Starting up Fund of Shandong Jiaotong University in China.

REFERENCES

Becken, S., & Patterson, M. (2009). Measuring national carbon dioxide emissions from tourism as a key step towards achieving sustainable tourism. *Journal of Sustainable Tourism*, *14*(4), 323–338. doi:10.2167/jost547.0

Ceron, J. P., & Dubois, G. (2007). Limits to Tourism? A back-casting scenario for sustainable tourism mobility in 2050. *Tourism and Hospitality Planning & Development*, *4*(3), 191–209. doi:10.1080/14790530701736598

Chan, J. K. L., & Baum, T. (2007). Motivation factors of ecotourists in ecolodge accommodation: The push and pull factors. *Asia Pacific Journal of Tourism Research, 12*(4), 349–364. doi:10.1080/10941660701761027

Crandall, R. (1980). *Motivations for leisure*. New York: Wiley.

Crompton, J. (1979). Motivations of pleasure vacations. *Annals of Tourism Research, 6*(4), 408–424. doi:10.1016/0160-7383(79)90004-5

Dai, Y.-Y. (2015). *Do low-carbon travel: Motivations, constraints and behaviors* (Unpublished doctoral thesis). Graduate Institute of Recreation, Tourism, and Hospitality Management, National Chiayi University, Chiayi, Taiwan.

Davies, N. J., Lumsdon, L. M., & Weston, R. (2012). Developing recreational trails: Motivations for recreational walking. *Tourism Planning & Development, 9*(1), 77–88. doi:10.1080/21568316.2012.653480

Dickinson, J. E., & Lumsdon, L. (2010). *Slow travel and tourism*. London: Earthscan.

Dickinson, J. E., Lumsdon, L., & Robbins, D. (2011). Slow travel: Issues for tourism and climate change. *Journal of Sustainable Tourism, 19*(3), 281–300. doi:10.1080/09669582.2010.524704

Dolnicar, S. (2004). Insights into sustainable tourists in Austria: A data-based a priori segmentation approach. *Journal of Sustainable Tourism, 12*(3), 209–218. doi:10.1080/09669580408667234

Dolnicar, S., & Long, P. (2009). Beyond ecotourism: The environmentally responsible tourist in the general travel experience. *Tourism Analysis, 14*(4), 503–513. doi:10.3727/108354209X12596287114291

Dwyer, L. (2005). Relevance of triple bottom line reporting to achievement of sustainable tourism: A scoping study. *Tourism Review International, 9*(1), 79–938. doi:10.3727/154427205774791726

Geng, J., Long, R., Chen, H., & Li, Q. (2018). Urban residents' response to and evaluation of low-carbon travel policies: Evidence from a survey of five eastern cities in China. *Journal of Environmental Management, 217*, 47–55. doi:10.1016/j.jenvman.2018.03.091 PMID:29587200

Goeldner, C. R., & Ritchie, J. R. B. (2006). *Tourism: Principles, Practices, Philosophies* (10th ed.). John Wiley & Sons, Inc.

Gössling, S., Peeters, P., & Scott, D. (2008). Consequences of climate policy for international tourist arrivals in developing countries. *Third World Quarterly, 29*(5), 873–901. doi:10.1080/01436590802106007

Gössling, S., & Scott, D. (2012). Scenario planning for sustainable tourism: An introduction. *Journal of Sustainable Tourism, 20*(6), 773–778. doi:10.1080/09669582.2012.699064

Han, H., Hsu, L. J., Lee, J. S., & Sheu, C. (2011). Are lodging customers ready to go green? An examination of attitude, demographics, and eco-friendly intentions. *International Journal of Hospitality Management, 30*(2), 345–355. doi:10.1016/j.ijhm.2010.07.008

Horng, J. S., Hu, M. L., Teng, C. C., Hsiao, H. L., & Liu, C. H. (2013). Development and validation of the low-carbon literacy scale among practitioners in the Taiwanese tourism industry. *Tourism Management, 35*, 255–262. doi:10.1016/j.tourman.2012.08.001

Horng, J. S., Hu, M. L., Teng, C. C., Hsiao, H. L., Tsai, C. Y., & Liu, C. H. (2014b). How the introduction of concepts of energy saving and carbon reduction (ESCR) can affect festival visitors' behavioural intentions: An investigation using a structural model. *Journal of Sustainable Tourism, 22*(8), 1216–1235. doi:10.1080/09669582.2014.884100

Horng, J. S., Hu, M. L., Teng, C. C., & Lin, L. (2012). Energy saving and carbon reduction management indicators for natural attractions: A case study in Taiwan. *Journal of Sustainable Tourism, 20*(8), 1125–1149. doi:10.1080/09669582.2012.663380

Horng, J. S., Hu, M. L., Teng, C. C., & Lin, L. (2014a). Energy saving and carbon reduction behaviors in tourism - A perception study of Asian visitors from a Protection Motivation Theory perspective. *Asia Pacific Journal of Tourism Research, 19*(6), 721–735. doi:10.1080/10941665.2013.797002

Hsiao, T.-Y., Sung, P.-L., & Lu, C.-Y. (2017). International tourists purchase intention towards low-carbon tour packages. *Journal of Tourism. Hospitality & Culinary Arts, 9*(3), 1–13.

Hu, M. L., Horng, J. S., Teng, C. C., & Chou, S. F. (2012). Exploring the energy-saving and carbon reduction literacy of restaurant employees. In M. Kasimoglu & H. Aydin (Eds.), *Strategies for Tourism Industry - Micro and Macro Perspectives* (pp. 313–326). InTech. doi:10.5772/38271

Huang, H. C., Lin, T. H., Lai, M. C., & Lin, T. L. (2014). Environmental consciousness and green customer behavior: An examination of motivation crowding effect. *International Journal of Hospitality Management, 40*, 139–149. doi:10.1016/j.ijhm.2014.04.006

Hung, K., & Petrick, J. F. (2012). Comparing constraints to cruising between cruisers and non-cruisers: A test of the constraint-effects-mitigation model. *Journal of Travel & Tourism Marketing, 29*(3), 242–262. doi:10.1080/10548408.2012.666171

Jackson, E. L., & Dunn, E. (1988). Integrating ceasing participation with other aspects of leisure behavior. *Journal of Leisure Research, 20*(1), 31–45. doi:10.1080/00222216.1988.11969755

Jang, S., & Wu, C. M. (2006). Seniors' travel motivation and the influential factors: An examination of Taiwanese seniors. *Tourism Management, 27*(2), 306–316. doi:10.1016/j.tourman.2004.11.006

Juvan, E., & Dolnicar, S. (2014). Can tourists easily choose a low carbon footprint vacation? *Journal of Sustainable Tourism, 22*(2), 175–194. doi:10.1080/09669582.2013.826230

Kuo, N. W., & Dai, Y. Y. (2012). Applying the Theory of Planned Behavior to predict low-carbon tourism behavior: A modified model from Taiwan. *International Journal of Technology and Human Interaction, 8*(4), 44–61. doi:10.4018/jthi.2012100103

Kuo, N. W., & Dai, Y. Y. (2015). Predicting low-carbon travel behavior: A modified Theory of Planned Behavior model from Taiwan. In A. M. DeMarco (Ed.), *Strategic E-Commerce Systems and Tools for Competing in the Digital Marketplace*. IGI Global. doi:10.4018/978-1-4666-8133-0.ch005

Liu, C. H., Tzeng, G. H., & Lee, M. H. (2012). Improving tourism policy implementation - The use of hybrid MCDM models. *Tourism Management, 33*(2), 413–426. doi:10.1016/j.tourman.2011.05.002

Lumsdon, L. M., & McGrath, P. (2011). Developing a conceptual framework for slow travel: A grounded theory approach. *Journal of Sustainable Tourism, 19*(3), 265–279. doi:10.1080/09669582.2010.519438

Luo, Y., & Deng, J. (2008). The new environmental paradigm and nature-based tourism motivation. *Journal of Travel Research, 46*(4), 392–402. doi:10.1177/0047287507308331

McIntosh, R., & Gupta, W. S. (1977). *Tourism: Principles, practices, philosophies* (3rd ed.). Grid Inc.

McIntosh, R. W., & Goeldner, C. R. (1986). *Tourism: Principles, Practices, Philosophies* (5th ed.). John Wiley.

McKercher, B., Prideaux, B., Cheung, C., & Law, R. (2010). Achieving voluntary reductions in the carbon footprint of tourism and climate change. *Journal of Sustainable Tourism, 18*(3), 297–317. doi:10.1080/09669580903395022

Millar, M., & Baliglu, S. (2011). Hotel guests' preferences for green guest room attributes. *Cornell Hospitality Quarterly, 52*(3), 302–311. doi:10.1177/1938965511409031

Nowaczek, A., & Smail, B. (2010). Exploring the predisposition of travellers to qualify as ecotourists: The Ecotourist Predisposition Scale. *Journal of Ecotourism, 9*(1), 45–61. doi:10.1080/14724040902883521

Oh, H., Assaf, A. G., & Baloglu, S. (2014). Motivations and goals of slow tourism. *Journal of Travel Research.*

Park, D. B., & Yoon, Y. S. (2009). Segmentation by motivation in rural tourism: A Korean case study. *Tourism Management, 30*(1), 99–108. doi:10.1016/j.tourman.2008.03.011

Pearce, P. L., Morrison, A. M., & Rutledge, J. L. (1998). *Tourism: Bridges across Continents.* Sydney, Australia: McGraw-Hill.

Qian, C., Zhou, Y., & Chen, J. (2017). The coupling strategy research of urban public space and traffic for improving the residents' low-carbon travel accessibility: A case study of Hexi New City Central Area in Nanjing. *Sustainability, 9*, 1–23.

Simpson, M. C., Gössling, S., Scott, D., Hall, C. M., & Gladin, E. (2008). Climate change adaptation and mitigation in the tourism sector: Frameworks, tools and practices. UNEP, University of Oxford, UNWTO, WMO.

Sustrans. (2007). *Low carbon travel information sheet.* Retrieved from http://www.climatlantic.co.uk/resource_files/KS3_4__travel_infosheet.pdf

Teng, C. C., Horng, J. S., Hu, M. L., & Chen, P. C. (2014). Exploring energy and carbon literacy structure for hospitality and tourism practitioners: Evidence from hotel employees in Taiwan. *Asia Pacific Journal of Tourism Research, 19*(4), 451–468. doi:10.1080/10941665.2013.764336

Teng, Z., Shi, C. B., & Liu, Z. (2011). Sustainable development of tourism industry in china under the low-carbon economy. *Energy Procedia, 5*, 1303–1307. doi:10.1016/j.egypro.2011.03.226

Tsaur, S. H., & Dai, Y. Y. (2016). How to do a low-carbon travel? Developing and validating low-carbon travel scale. *Journal of Outdoor Recreation Study, 29*(2), 27–53.

World Tourism Organization and United Nations Environment Programme. (2008). *Climate change and tourism: Responding to global challenges.* Madrid, Spain: World Tourism Organization.

Yoon, Y., & Uysal, M. (2005). An examination of the effects of motivation and satisfaction on destination loyalty: A structural model. *Tourism Management*, 26(5), 45–56. doi:10.1016/j.tourman.2003.08.016

Zhang, Q., & Liu, H. (2011). Study on design and research of tourist souvenirs on the background of low-carbon economy. *Energy Procedia*, 5, 2416–2420. doi:10.1016/j.egypro.2011.03.415

Zhu, H., Zhang, J., Liao, L., & Jin, S. (2017). Low carbon transition and sustainable development path of tourism industry. *IOP Conf. Series: Earth and Environmental Science*, 64(012053), 1-4. 10.1088/1755-1315/64/1/012053

KEY TERMS AND DEFINITIONS

Low-Carbon: Low-carbon refers to reduce energy consumption in lifestyles, thereby reducing the related carbon emissions, particularly CO2.

Low-Carbon Accommodation: Energy savings can lead to a significant reduction in greenhouse carbon emissions.

Low-Carbon Consumption: Visitors carry reusable shopping bags, which are engaged in green consumption (e.g., products that buy energy-saving, locally produced, or environmentally friendly). Can reduce the consumption of carbon dioxide emissions in order to achieve energy saving and carbon reduction.

Low-Carbon Diet: Low-carbon diet reduces greenhouse gas emissions from energy use.

Low-Carbon Journey Planning: Visitors' low-carbon travel planning focuses on simplifying itinerary to achieve the goal of reducing carbon emissions.

Low-Carbon Tendency: Low-carbon tendency refers low-carbon tourism is not only willing to start from the tourists themselves, so that the holiday travel activities to reduce carbon emissions, but also called on others to participate.

Low-Carbon Transport: Low-carbon transport can be seen as the core concept of low-carbon tourism.

Low-Carbon Travel Behaviors: Low-carbon travel behaviors refers to tourists may reduce CO2 emission while they choose destinations, environmental friendly transport, and environmentally certified hotels, as well as eating in restaurants providing local, on season, and/or organic food.

Compilation of References

AABB Education. (n.d.). Retrieved August 15, 2017, from http://www.aabb.org/development/education/Pages/default.aspx

Abdelaziz, K. G. (2008). *Knowledge Gap Survey (internal report)*. Khartoum, Sudan: Practical Action.

Abdella, E.Y., Hajjeh, R., & Smit Sibinga, C. T. (2018). Availability and safety of blood transfusion during humanitarian emergencies. *EMHJ,24 (3),* (in press)

Abdi, S., Awan, H., & Bhatti, M. (2008). Is quality management a prime requisite for globalization? Some facts from the sports industry. *Quality & Quantity, 42*(6), 821–833. doi:10.100711135-007-9135-x

Action, P. (2009). The Knowledge Gap Survey – Blue Nile State, Rosaris and Bau Localities (internal report).

Adams, D. A., Nelson, R. R., & Todd, P. A. (1992). Perceived usefulness, ease of use, and usage of information technology: A replication. *Management Information Systems Quarterly, 16*(2), 227–247. doi:10.2307/249577

Agarwal, R., & Karahanna, E. (2000). Time flies when you're having fun: Cognitive absorption and beliefs about information technology use. *Management Information Systems Quarterly, 24*(4), 665–694. doi:10.2307/3250951

Agnes, M. (2017). 3 Important Crisis Management Trend Projections For 2017. *Forbes*. Retrieved 4 25, 2018, from https://www.forbes.com

Agourram, H., Robson, B., & Amine, N. T. (2007). Defining Information System Success in France. *International Journal of Enterprise Information Systems, 3*(3), 66–69, 71–80. doi:10.4018/jeis.2007070105

Aide Memoire for eHealth for Health-care Delivery. (2006). Retrieved August 15, 2017, from http://www.who.int/eht/areas/eHealthFlyerAideMemoire.pdf

Aide Mémoire for National Health Authorities and Hospital Management, Clinical Transfusion Process and Patient Safety. (2010). WHO/EHT/10.05. World Health Organization.

Aide Mémoire for National Health Programmes. (2003). The Clinical Use of Blood. WHO/EHT/04.07. World Health Organization.

Aiken, M., & Hage, J. (1971). The Organic Organization and Innovation. *Sociology, 5*(1), 63-82.

Ainuddin, R. A., Beamish, P. W., Hulland, J. S., & Rouse, M. J. (2007). Resource attributes and firm performance in international joint ventures. *Journal of World Business, 42*(1), 47–60. doi:10.1016/j.jwb.2006.11.001

Ajmal, M., Helo, P., & Kekäle, T. (2010). Critical factors for knowledge management in project business. *Journal of Knowledge Management, 14*(1), 156–168. doi:10.1108/13673271011015633

Ajzen, I. (1991). The theory of planned behavior. *Organizational Behavior and Human Decision Processes, 50*(2), 179–211. doi:10.1016/0749-5978(91)90020-T

Ajzen, I., & Fishbein, M. (1980). *Understanding attitudes and predicting social behavior.* Englewood Cliffs, NJ: Prentice-Hall.

Ajzen, I., & Fishbein, M. (1980). *Understanding Attitudes and Predicting Social.* Englewood Cliffs, NJ: Prentice-Hall.

AlBayan newspaper. (2016). Experts: Emirates has provided professional lessons in crisis management. Retrieved from https://www.albayan.ae/economy/local-market/2016-08-08-1.2692476

Albrecht, K. (2005). *Spychips: How major corporations and government plan to track your every move with RFID.* Thomas Nelson.

Ale, M. A., Toledo, C. M., Chiotti, O., & Galli, M. R. (2014). A conceptual model and technological support for organizational knowledge management. *Science of Computer Programming, 95*(1), 73–92. doi:10.1016/j.scico.2013.12.012

Alexander, K. M. (2014). *Generation Y knowledge workers' experience of work motivation: A grounded theory study* [Doctoral dissertation]. Retrieved from https://pqdtopen.proquest.com/doc/1658144350.html?FMT=AI

Alijani, G. S., Mancuso, L. C., Kwun, O., & Omar, A. (2010). Effectiveness of online advertisement factors in recalling a product. *Academy of Marketing Studies Journal, 14*(1), 1–11.

Ali, K. A. M., & Alolayyan, M. N. (2013). The impact of total quality management (TQM) on the hospital's performance: An empirical research. *International Journal of Services and Operations Management, 15*(4), 482–506. doi:10.1504/IJSOM.2013.054904

Al-Jenaibi, B. (2011). The Changing Representation of the Arab Woman in Middle East Advertising and Media, Global Media Journal--Arabian Edition, 1(2).

Al-Jenaibi, B. (2008). The effects of media campaigns on different cultures. *World Academy of Science. Engineering and Technology International Journal of Humanities and Social Sciences, 2*(10), 1067–1070.

Al-Jenaibi, B. (2015). E-Collaboration, Public Relations and Crises Management in UAE Organizations. *International Journal of e-Collaboration, 11*(3), 10–28. doi:10.4018/ijec.2015070102

Alkureishi, M. A., Lee, W. W., Lyons, M., Press, V. G., Imam, S., Nkansah-Amankra, A., … Arora, V. M. (2016). Impact of Electronic Medical Record Use on the Patient–Doctor Relationship and Communication: A Systematic Review. *Journal of General Internal Medicine, 31*(5), 548-560.

Allérès, D. (1995). *Luxe: un management spécifique.* Paris: Economica.

Aloini, D., Dulmin, R., & Mininno, V. (2007). Risk management in ERP project introduction: Review of the literature. *Information & Management, 44*(6), 547–567. doi:10.1016/j.im.2007.05.004

Al-Smadi, M. O. (2012). Factors affecting the adoption of electronic banking: An analysis of the perspectives of bank's customers. *International Journal of Business and Social Science, 3*(17), 294–309.

Alt, F., Balz, M., Kristes, S., Shirazi, A. S., Mennenöh, J., Schmidt, A., & Goedicke, M. (2009). *Adaptive user profiles in pervasive advertising environments. In Ambient Intelligence* (pp. 276–286). Berlin, Germany: Springer.

Alwi, S. F. S., & Da Silva, R. V. (2007). Online and offline corporate brand images: Do they differ? *Corporate Reputation Review, 10*(4), 217–244. doi:10.1057/palgrave.crr.1550056

Ambulkar, S., Blackhurst, J. V., & Cantor, D. E. (2016). Supply chain risk mitigation competency: An individual-level knowledge-based perspective. *International Journal of Production Research, 54*(5), 1398–1411. doi:10.1080/0020754 3.2015.1070972

Amine, A. (1998). Consumers' true brand loyalty: The central role of commitment. *Journal of Strategic Marketing, 6*(4), 305–319. doi:10.1080/096525498346577

Andersen, S. T., & Aanestad, M. (2008). Possibilities and challenges of transition to ambulant health service delivery with ICT support in psychiatry. *IFIP TC8 WG8.2 International Working Conference.* 10.1007/978-0-387-09768-8_9

Andersen, S. T., & Jansen, A. (2012). Installed base as a facilitator for user-driven innovation? How user innovation can challenge existing institutional barriers. *International Journal of Telemedicine and Applications.* doi: 10.1155/2012/673731

Andersen, S. T., & Van der Velden, M. (2010). Mobile phone-based healthcare delivery in a Sami area: Reflections on technology and culture. *CATAc International Conference.*

Andersen, S. T. (2013). *User-centered innovation in psychiatric healthcare by using mobile technology (PhD-thesis).* Oslo: University of Oslo.

Andersen, S. T., & Jansen, A. (2011). Innovation in ICT-Based Health Care Provision. *International Journal of Healthcare Information Systems and Informatics, 6*(2). doi:10.4018/jhisi.2011040102

Anderson, J. C., & Gerbing, D. W. (1988). Structural Equation Modeling in Practice: A Review and Recommended Two-step Approach. *Psychological Bulletin, 103*(3), 411–423. doi:10.1037/0033-2909.103.3.411

Andrews, L., Cacho-Elizondo, S., Drenna, J., & Tossan, V. (2013). Consumer Acceptance of an SMS-assisted Smoking Cessation Intervention: A Multi Country Study. *Journal of Health Marketing Quarterly, 30*(1), 47–62. doi:10.1080/07 359683.2013.758015 PMID:23458481

Angeles, R. (2005). RFID technologies: Supply-chain applications and implementation issues. *Information Systems Management, 22*(1), 51–65. doi:10.1201/1078/44912.22.1.20051201/85739.7

Ang, L. (2010). Community Relationship Management and Social Media. *Database Marketing & Customer Strategy Management, 18*(1), 31–38. doi:10.1057/dbm.2011.3

Angst, C. M., Agarwal, R., Sambamurthy, V., & Kelley, K. (2010). Social Contagion and Information Technology Diffusion: The Adoption of Electronic Medical Records in Us Hospitals. *Management Science, 56*(8), 1219-1241.

Ankeny, J. (2011). Face lift. *Entrepreneur, 39*(1), 56–59.

An, L. C., Klatt, C., Perry, C. L., Lein, E. B., Hennrikus, D. J., Pallonen, U. E., & Ehlinger, E. P. (2008). The RealU online cessation intervention for college smokers: A randomized controlled trial. *Preventive Medicine, 47*(2), 194–199. doi:10.1016/j.ypmed.2008.04.011 PMID:18565577

Annie Jin, S. A. (2012). The potential of social media for luxury brand management. *Marketing Intelligence & Planning, 30*(7), 687–699. doi:10.1108/02634501211273805

Anton, J., & Petouhoff, N. (2002). *Customer Relations Management: The Bottom Line to Optimizing Your ROI.* Prentice Hall.

Antonsen, T. (1988). *Telemedisin i Nord-Norge: forprosjekt* [Telemedicine in North Norway: a pilot study]. Tromsø: FORUT.

Applegate, L. M., Austin, R. D., & McFarlan, F. W. (2007). *Corporate Information Strategy and Management: Text and Cases* (7th ed.). McGraw-Hill Irwin Publishers.

Arab Knowledge Report. (2009). *Towards productive intercommunication for knowledge.* Dubai: Mohammed bin Rashid Al-Maktoum Foundation and United Nations Development Programme.

Argote, L., McEvily, B., & Reagans, R. (2003). Managing Knowledge in Organizations: An Integrative Framework and Review of Emerging Themes. *Management Science*, *49*(4), 571–582. doi:10.1287/mnsc.49.4.571.14424

Argyropoulou, M., Ioannou, G., Koufopoulos, D. N., & Motwani, J. (2009). Measuring the impact of an ERP project at SMEs: A framework and empirical investigation. *International Journal of Enterprise Information Systems*, *5*(3), 1–13. doi:10.4018/jeis.2009070101

Arinze, B. (2012). E-research collaboration in academia and industry. *International Journal of e-Collaboration*, *8*(2), 1–13. doi:10.4018/jec.2012040101

Armes, D. (2006). Online auctions prove their staying power. *Strategic Direction*, *22*(7), 6–7. doi:10.1108/02580540610669008

Armstrong, J. S., & Overton, T. S. (1977). Estimating nonresponse bias in mail surveys. *JMR, Journal of Marketing Research*, *14*(3), 396–492. doi:10.2307/3150783

Arrigo, E. (2018). Social media marketing in luxury brands: A systematic literature review and implications for management research. *Management Research Review*. doi:10.1108/MRR-04-2017-0134

Arthur, R. (2016). *The Risk Of Generation Z: Let's Talk About Luxury's Obsession With Teen-Endorsed Snapchat Campaigns.* Retrieved October 4th, 2017, from https://www.forbes.com/sites/rachelarthur/2016/02/03/the-risk-of-generation-z-lets-talk-about-fashions-obsession-with-teen-endorsed-snapchat-campaigns/#7b0b1772633b

Arthur, W. B. (1989). Competing Technologies: Increasing Returns, and Lock-In by Historical Events. *Economic Journal (London)*, *99*(394), 116–131. doi:10.2307/2234208

Arthur, W. B. (1996). Increasing Returns. *Harvard Business Review*, *74*(4), 100–109. PMID:10158472

Arya, D. P. (2010). Advertisement effectiveness: Role of 'word-of mouth' in success of educational institutes in non-metro cities. *IUP Journal of Management Research*, *9*(1), 1–20.

Ascari, A., Bakshi, A. & Grijpink, F. (2010). *mHealth: A New Vision for Healthcare*. McKinsey & Company, Inc.

Ashcroft, L. S. (1997). Crisis management - public relations. *Journal of Managerial Psychology*, *12*(5), 325–332. doi:10.1108/02683949710183522

Attewell, P. (1992, February). Technology diffusion and organizational learning: The case of business computing. *Organization Science*, *3*(1), 1–19. doi:10.1287/orsc.3.1.1

AuBuchon, J. P., Puca, K., Saxena, S., Shulman, I. A., & Waters, J. H. (2011). *Getting started in Patient Blood Management*. Bethesda, MD: AABB Press.

Aula, P. (2010). Social media, reputation risk and ambient publicity management. *Strategy and Leadership*, *38*(6), 43–49. doi:10.1108/10878571011088069

Bagozzi, R. P., Davis, F. D., & Warshaw, P. R. (1992). development and test of a theory of technological learning and usage. *Human Relations*, *45*(7), 660–686. doi:10.1177/001872679204500702

Bagozzi, R. P., & Yi, Y. (1991). Multitrait-Multimethod Matrices in Consumer Research. *JMR, Journal of Marketing Research*, *17*, 426–439.

Baier, A. (1986). Trust and Antitrust. *Ethics*, *96*(2), 231-260.

Bain & Company. (2014). *Luxury Goods Worldwide Market Study, Fall-Winter 2014: The rise of the borderless consumer*. Bain & Company for Fondazione Altagamma. Retrieved September 20th, 2017, from http://www.bain.com/publications/articles/luxury-goods-worldwide-market-study-december-2014.aspx

Bain & Company. (2015). *Génération #hashtag 2015: l'ère du numérique natif.* Bain & Company. Retrieved September 20th, 2017, from http://www.bain.fr/Images/2015_Etude%20Generation_Hashtag.pdf

Bain & Company. (2016). *Luxury Goods Worldwide Market Study, Fall-Winter 2016: As Luxury Resets to a New Normal, Strategy Becomes.* Bain & Company for Fondazione Altagamma. Retrieved September 20th, 2017, from http://www.bain.com/publications/articles/luxury-goods-worldwide-market-study-fall-winter-2016.aspx

Bain & Company. (2017). *Bain Luxury Study 2017 Spring Update.* Retrieved September 20th, 2017, from http://www.bain.com/about/press/press-releases/global-personal-luxury-goods-market-expected-to-grow-by-2-4-percent.aspx

Baker, J. (2012). The Technology–Organization–Environment Framework. In *Information Systems Theory* (pp. 231–245). Springer. doi:10.1007/978-1-4419-6108-2_12

Baldwin, C. Y., & Clark, K. B. (2000). *Design Rules - The Power of Modularity.* Cambridge, MA: MIT Press.

Ball, M. J., & Lillis, J. (2001). E-health: Transforming the physician/patient relationship. *International Journal of Medical Informatics, 61*(1), 1–10. doi:10.1016/S1386-5056(00)00130-1 PMID:11248599

Bandura, A. (1977). Self-efficacy: Toward a unifying theory of behavioral change. *Psychological Review, 84*(2), 191–215. doi:10.1037/0033-295X.84.2.191 PMID:847061

Banks, K. F. (2001). *Crisis communications: A casebook approach 2nd Edi.* Mahwah, NJ: Lawrence Erlbaum.

Barkhordari, M., & Niamanesh, M. (2014, August). ScadiBino: An effective MapReduce-based association rule mining method. In *Proceedings of the Sixteenth International Conference on Electronic Commerce* (p. 1). ACM. 10.1145/2617848.2617853

Barkhordari, M., & Niamanesh, M. (2015). ScaDiPaSi: An effective scalable and distributable MapReduce-based method to find patient similarity on huge healthcare networks. *Big Data Research, 2*(1), 19–27. doi:10.1016/j.bdr.2015.02.004

Barkhordari, M., & Niamanesh, M. (2017). Aras: A Method with Uniform Distributed Dataset to Solve Data Warehouse Problems for Big Data. *International Journal of Distributed Systems and Technologies, 8*(2), 47–60. doi:10.4018/IJDST.2017040104

Barkhordari, M., & Niamanesh, M. (2017). Atrak: A MapReduce based warehouse for big data. *The Journal of Supercomputing, 73*(10), 4596–4610. doi:10.100711227-017-2037-3

Barkhordari, M., & Niamanesh, M. (2017). ScaDiGraph: A MapReduce-based Method for Solving Graph Problems. *Journal of Information Science and Engineering, 33*(1).

Barkhordari, M., & Niamanesh, M. (2018). Arvand: A Method to Integrate Multidimensional Data Sources Into Big Data Analytic Structures. *Journal of Information Science and Engineering, 34*(2), 505–518.

Barton, L. (2011). *Crisis in organizations II* (2nd ed.). Cincinnati, OH: College Divisions South-Western.

Ba, S., & Pavlou, P. A. (2002). Evidence of the effect of trust building technology in electronic markets: Price premiums and buyer behavior. *Management Information Systems Quarterly, 26*(3), 243–268. doi:10.2307/4132332

Basecamp. (2015). Basecamp is free for teachers! Retrieved from https://basecamp.com/teachers

Bassellier, G., Reich, B. H., & Benbasat, I. (2001). Information technology competence of business managers: A definition and research model. *Journal of Management Information Systems, 17*(4), 159–182. doi:10.1080/07421222.2001.11045660

Basu, B., & Sengupta, K. (2007). Assessing success factors of knowledge management initiatives of academic institutions– a case of an Indian business school. *Electronic Journal of Knowledge Management, 5*(3), 273–282.

Bateman, P. J., Pike, J. C., & Butler, B. S. (2010). To disclose or not: Publicness in social networking sites. *Information Technology & People*, *24*(1), 78–100. doi:10.1108/09593841111109431

Battenhall. (2017). *FTSE100 Social Media Report. An analysis of the use of social media for brand and corporate communications by the FTSE 100 companies*. Academic Press.

Baxter, K. (2017). Diversity, talent on the rise in U.S. women's soccer. *Los Angeles Times*. Retrieved September 18, 2017 from http://www.latimes.com/sports/soccer/la-sp-soccer-baxter-20170121-story.html

BBC News. (2011). Microsoft confirms takeover of Skype. Retrieved from http://www.bbc.com/news/business-13343600

Bearden, W. O., Money, R. B., & Nevins, J. L. (2006). A Measure of Long-term Orientation: Development and Validation. *Journal of the Academy of Marketing Science*, *34*(3), 456–467. doi:10.1177/0092070306286706

Becken, S., & Patterson, M. (2009). Measuring national carbon dioxide emissions from tourism as a key step towards achieving sustainable tourism. *Journal of Sustainable Tourism*, *14*(4), 323–338. doi:10.2167/jost547.0

Becker, J. (2011). *La galaxy announce $55 million TV contract*. Retrieved March 1, 2018 from http://losangeles.sbnation.com/los-angeles-galaxy/2011/11/15/2565118/la-galaxy-55-million-TV-contract-time-warner

Bélanger, F., & Crossler, R. E. (2011). Privacy in the digital age: A review of information privacy research in information systems. *Management Information Systems Quarterly*, *35*(4), 1017–1042. doi:10.2307/41409971

Beldona, S., & Tsatsoulis, C. (2010). Identifying buyers with similar seller rating models and using their opinions to choose sellers in electronic markets. *International Journal of Information and Decision Sciences*, *2*(1), 1–16. doi:10.1504/IJIDS.2010.029901

Bellman, L. M., Teich, I., & Clark, S. D. (2009). Fashion accessory buying intentions among female millennials. *Review of Business*, *30*(1), 46–57.

Benbast, I., & Zmud, R. W. (1999, March). Empirical research in information systems: The practice of relevance. *Management Information Systems Quarterly*, *23*(1), 3–16. doi:10.2307/249403

Bennett, S. (2014). Pinterest, Twitter, Facebook, Instagram, Google+, LinkedIn – Social Media Stats 2014 [INFOGRAPHIC]. *AllTwitter*. Retrieved July 8, 2017 from http://www.mediabistro.com/alltwitter/social-media-stats-2014_b5424.3

Ben-Shabat, H. (2017). *Gen Z and the Paradox of Luxury*. Retrieved October 4th, 2017, from http://www.therobinreport.com/gen-z-and-the-paradox-of-luxury

Benson, E. P. (2004). Online learning: A means to enhance professional development. *Critical Care Nurse*, *24*(1), 60–63. PMID:15007894

Benson, J. K. (1977). Organizations: A Dialectical View. *Administrative Science Quarterly*, *22*(1), 1–21. doi:10.2307/2391741

Bernhardt, J. M., Runyan, C. W., Bou-Saada, I., & Felter, E. M. (2003). Implementation and evaluation of a Web-based continuing education course in injury prevention and control. *Health Promotion Practice*, *4*(2), 120–128. doi:10.1177/1524839902250758 PMID:14610981

Bernstein, D. A., Penner, L. A., Clarke-Stewart, A., & Roy, E. J. (2017). [*th ed.*). Cengage Inc. Retrieved from http://college.cengage.com/psychology/bernstein/psychology/6e/students/index.html]. *Psychology (Irvine, Calif.)*, *6*.

Berry, G. R. (2006). Can computer-mediated asynchronous communication improve team processes and decision-making?: Learning from the management literature. *Journal of Business Communication*, *43*(1), 344–366. doi:10.1177/0021943606292352

Berry, G. R. (2011). Enhancing effectiveness on virtual teams. *Journal of Business Communication, 48*(2), 186–206. doi:10.1177/0021943610397270

Best, S. G. (Ed.). (2006). *Introduction to peace and conflict studies in West Africa: A reader.* Spectrum Books.

Bhamu, J., Khandelwal, A., & Sangwan, K. S. (2013). Lean manufacturing implementation in an automated production line: A case study. *International Journal of Services and Operations Management, 15*(4), 411–429. doi:10.1504/IJSOM.2013.054883

Bhattacherjee, A., & Hikmet, N. (2007). Physicians' Resistance toward Healthcare Information Technology: A Theoretical Model and Empirical Test. *European Journal of Information Systems, 16*(6), 725-737.

Bhurjee, A. K., Kumar, P., & Padhan, S. K. (2018). Solid transportation problem with budget constraints under interval uncertain environments. *International Journal of Process Management and Benchmarking, 7*(2), 172–182. doi:10.1504/IJPMB.2017.083104

Binney, W., Oppenheim, P., & Hall, J. (2006). Towards the confirmation of the MOA model: an applied approach. In *Proceedings of the 2006 Australian and New Zealand Academy of Marketing conference.* Brisbane, AU: ANZMAC.

Bishop, C. M. (1995). *Neural Networks for Pattern Recognition.* Oxford, UK: Oxford University Press.

Blackden, E. (2016). *6 Key Luxury Trends That Will Make Or Break Brands In 2016.* Retrieved September 20th, 2017, from https://luxurysociety.com/en/articles/2016/01/6-key-luxury-trends-that-will-make-or-break-brands-in-2016

Black, S. (1989). *Introduction to Public Relations.* West African Book Publishers Ltd.

Blackshaw, P., & Nazzaro, M. (2004). *Consumer-Generated Media (CGM) 101: Word-of-mouth in the age of the Web-fortified consumer.* Nielsen BuzzMetrics White paper.

Bland, E., & Barrett, R. T. (2006). A measure of the factors impacting the effectiveness and efficiency of eBay in the supply chain of online firms. *The Costal Business Journal, 18*(2), 1–15.

Blili, S., & Raymond, L. (1993, December). Information technology: Threats and opportunities for small and medium-sized enterprises. *International Journal of Information Management, 13*(6), 439–448. doi:10.1016/0268-4012(93)90060-H

Bloch, P. H. (1982). Involvement beyond the Purchase Process: Conceptual Issues and Empirical Investigation. *Advances in Consumer Research. Association for Consumer Research (U. S.), 9*(1), 413–417.

Blood Safety and Availability, fact sheet reviewed June 2017. (n.d.). Retrieved August 15, 2017, from http://www.who.int/mediacentre/factsheets/fs279/en/

Blood Safety and Clinical Technology. Strategy 2000-2003. (2001). WHO/BCT/01.01.

BloodSafe elearning Australia. (n.d.). Retrieved August 15, 2017, from https://bloodsafelearning.org.au/our-courses/

Bloxsome, E. L., Voges, K. E., & Pope, N. K. (2011). Sport sponsorship: Appeal and risks. *The International Journal's Research Journal of Social Science and Management, 1*(8), 133–145.

Blumenthal, D. (2009). Stimulating the Adoption of Health Information Technology. *New England Journal of Medicine, 360*(15), 1477-1479.

Bobrow, D. G., Cheslow, R., & Whalen, J. (2000). *Community Knowledge Sharing in Practice Systems and Practices Laboratory. Xerox Palo Alto Research Center.*

Bock, G. M., & Kim, Y. G. (2002). Breaking the Myths of Rewards: An Exploratory Study of Attitudes about Knowledge Sharing. *Information Resources Management Journal, 15*(2), 14–21. doi:10.4018/irmj.2002040102

Bock, G. W., Zmud, R. W., Kim, Y. G., & Lee. (2005). Behavioral Intention Formation in Knowledge Sharing: Examining the Roles of Extrinsic Motivators, Social-Psychological Forces, and Organizational Climate. *Management Information Systems Quarterly, 29*(10), 87–111. doi:10.2307/25148669

Boland, R. J. Jr, Lyytinen, K., & Yoo, Y. (2007). Wakes of innovation in project networks: The case of digital 3- D representations in architecture, engineering, and construction. *Organization Science, 18*(4), 631–647. doi:10.1287/orsc.1070.0304

Bolton, G. E., Katok, E., & Ockenfels, A. (2004). Trust among Internet traders: A behavioral economics approach. *Analyse & Kritik, 26*(1), 185–202. doi:10.1515/auk-2004-0110

Bonacin, D., Bonacin, D., & Bilić, Ž. (2015). Real position of law in well regulated sport market. *Acta Kinesiologica, 9*(Suppl. 1), 70–73.

Bonson, E., & Flores, F. (2010). Social media and corporate dialogue: The Response of global financial institutions. *Online Information Review, 35*(1), 34–49. doi:10.1108/14684521111113579

Booth, N., & Matic, J. A. (2011). Mapping and leveraging influences in social media to shape corporate brand perceptions. *Corporate Communications, 16*(3), 184–191. doi:10.1108/13563281111156853

Borelli, B., Bartlet, Y. K., Tootley, E., Armitage, C. J., & Wearden, A. (2015). Prevalence and frequency of mHealth and eHealth use among US and UK smokers and differences by motivation to quit. *Journal of Medical Internet Research, 17*(7). PMID:26149323

Borgatti, S. P., Everett, M. G., & Freeman, L. C. (2002). *Ucinet for Windows: Software for Social Network Analysis.* Harvard, MA: Analytic Technologies.

Borman, W. C., & Motowidlo, S. J. (1997). Task performance and contextual performance: The meaning for personnel selection research. *Human Performance, 10*(2), 99–109. doi:10.120715327043hup1002_3

Bosch-Sijtsema, P. M., Fruchter, R., Vartiainen, M., & Ruohomäki, V. (2011). A framework to analyze knowledge work in distributed teams. *Group & Organization Management, 36*(3), 275–307. doi:10.1177/1059601111403625

Bosch-Sijtsema, P. M., & Sivunen, A. (2013). Professional virtual worlds supporting computer-mediated communication, collaboration, and learning in geographically distributed contexts. *IEEE Transactions on Professional Communication, 56*(2), 1112–1124. doi:10.1109/TPC.2012.2237256

Boukioudi, F., Ozguler, A., Chauvet, A., Despereaux, T., Loeb, T., Baer, M., & Descatha, A. (2016). Description of life-threatening events occurring in workplaces and requiring dispatch Advanced Life Support Ambulances in an urban area. *Resuscitation, 101*, e3–e4. doi:10.1016/j.resuscitation.2016.01.014 PMID:26829702

Boulon, J., Konwinski, A., Qi, R., Rabkin, A., Yang, E., & Yang, M. (2008, October). Chukwa, a large-scale monitoring system. *Proceedings of CCA, 8*, 1-5.

Bourdieu, P. (1984). *Distinction: A Social Critique of the Judgement of Taste.* Harvard University Press.

Boyd, J. (2002). In community we trust: Online security communication at eBay. *Purdue University, 25*(1), 1-25.

Brazil. (2014). *General Strategy of Information Technology and Communications 2014-1015.* Ministry of Planning, Budget and Management – Brasília.

Breen, H. (2013). Virtual collaboration in the online educational setting. *Nursing Forum, 48*(4), 284–299. doi:10.1111/nuf.12034 PMID:24188438

Brennan, P., & Safran, C. (2003). Report of conference track 3: Patient empowerment. *International Journal of Medical Informatics*, *69*(2-3), 301–304. doi:10.1016/S1386-5056(03)00002-9 PMID:12810134

Briguglio, P. (2004). Crisis Management: A White Paper. *MMI Public Relations*. Retrieved 8 31, 2013, from http://www.mmipublicrelations.com/white/paper/crisis-management-a-white-paper/

Brinkley, I., Fauth, R., Mahdon, M., & Theodoropoulou, S. (2009). *Knowledge Workers and Knowledge Work: A Knowledge Economy Programme Report*. London, UK: The Work Foundation.

Broadcast Ethics and Program Improvement Organization. (2013). *Broadcast Ethics and Program Improvement Organization Agreement*. Retrieved from http://www.bpo.gr.jp/wp/wp-content/themes/codex/pdf/bpo/20130529BPOkiyaku.pdf (in Japanese)

Bronfenbrenner, U. (1979). *The ecology of human development: experiments by nature and design*. Cambridge, MA: Harvard University Press.

Brown, D. H., & He, S. (2007). Patterns of ERP adoption and implementation in China and some implications. *Electronic Markets*, *17*(2), 132–141. doi:10.1080/10196780701296287

Brown, H. G., Poole, M. S., & Rodgers, T. L. (2004). Interpersonal traits, complementarity, and trust in virtual collaboration. *Journal of Management Information Systems*, *20*(4), 115–138. doi:10.1080/07421222.2004.11045785

Brown, J. S., & Duguid, P. (2017). *The Social Life of Information: Updated, with a New Preface*. Harvard Business Review Press.

Brown, J., Broderick, A., & Lee, N. J. (2007). Word of mouth communication within online communities: Conceptualizing the online social network. *Interactive Marketing*, *21*(3), 2–20. doi:10.1002/dir.20082

Brown, N. R. (2002). "Community" metaphors online: A critical and rhetorical study concerning online groups. *Business Communication Quarterly*, *65*(2), 92–100. doi:10.1177/108056990206500210

Brown, N., Billings, A. C., & Ruihley, B. (2012). Exploring the change in motivations for fantasy sport participation during the life cycle of a sports fan. *Communication Research Reports*, *29*(4), 333–342. doi:10.1080/08824096.2012.723646

Bruner, G. C. II, & Kumar, A. (2005). Explaining consumer acceptance of handheld internet devices. *Journal of Business Research*, *58*(5), 553–558. doi:10.1016/j.jbusres.2003.08.002

Buhr, S. (2014). *An e-commerce site where you can haggle down the price*. Retrieved October 7, 2017 from https://techcrunch.com/2014/07/04/an-ecommerce-site-where-you-can-negotiate-the-price-you-want-to-pay/

Bundy, J., Pfarrer, M. D., Short, C. E., & Coombs, W. T. (2017). Crises and crisis management: Integration, interpretation, and research development. *Journal of Management*, *43*(6), 1661–1692. doi:10.1177/0149206316680030

Burkhardt, M. E., & Brass, D. J. (1990). Changing patterns or patterns of change: The effects of a change in technology on social network structure and power. *Administrative Science Quarterly*, *35*(1), 104–121. doi:10.2307/2393552

Burn, J. M., & Szeto, C. (2000). A comparison of the views of business and IT management on success factors for strategic alignment. *Information & Management*, *37*(4), 197–216. doi:10.1016/S0378-7206(99)00048-8

Burrus, D. (2014). *The Internet of Things Is Far Bigger Than Anyone Realizes*. Academic Press.

Burton-Jones, A., & Hubona, G. S. (2005). Individual differences and usage behavior: Revisiting a technology acceptance model assumption. *The Data Base for Advances in Information Systems*, *36*(2), 58–77. doi:10.1145/1066149.1066155

Butson, R., & Thomson, C. (2014). Challenges of effective collaboration in a virtual learning environment among undergraduate students. *Creative Education*, *5*(1), 1449–1459. doi:10.4236/ce.2014.516162

Bu, Y., Howe, B., Balazinska, M., & Ernst, M. D. (2010). HaLoop: Efficient iterative data processing on large clusters. *Proceedings of the VLDB Endowment International Conference on Very Large Data Bases*, *3*(1-2), 285–296. doi:10.14778/1920841.1920881

Cabinet Office. (2006). *5th Annual Survey Report on Information Society and Young People*. Retrieved from http://www8.cao.go.jp/youth/kenkyu/jouhou5/index.html (in Japanese)

Cacho-Elizondo S., Shahidi N. & Tossan V. (2013). Intention to adopt a text message-based mobile coaching service to help stop smoking: which explanatory variables? *International Journal of Technology and Human Interaction*, (4).

Cadogan, J. W., & Foster, B. D. (2000). Relationship Selling and Customer Loyalty: An Empirical Investigation. *Marketing Intelligence & Planning*, *18*(4), 185–199. doi:10.1108/02634500010333316

Cafferky, M. E. (1995). *Let your customers do the talking: 301 + WOM Marketing Tactics Guaranteed to Boost Profits*. Chicago, IL: Upstart Publishing Co.

Callaway, S. K. (2011). Internet banking and performance. *American Journal of Business*, *26*(1), 12–25. doi:10.1108/19355181111124070

Campbell, R. R. (2013). Becoming a Techno-Industrial Power: Chinese Science and Technology Policy. *Issues in Technology Innovation*, *23*, 1-15. Retrieved from https://www.brookings.edu/wpcontent/uploads/2016/06/29-science-technology-policy-china-campbell.pdf

Carleton, K. (2011). How to motivate and retain knowledge workers in organizations: A review of the literature. *International Journal of Management*, *28*(2), 459.

Carlile, P. R. (2002). A pragmatic view of knowledge and boundaries: Boundary objects in new product development. *Organization Science*, *13*(4), 442–455. doi:10.1287/orsc.13.4.442.2953

Carmeli, A., Gelbard, R., & Reiter-Palmon, R. (2013). Leadership, Creative Problem-Solving Capacity, and Creative Performance: The Importance of Knowledge Sharing. *Human Resource Management*, *52*(1), 95–121. doi:10.1002/hrm.21514

Carney, A., & Jorden, A. (1993). Prepare for business-related crises. *The Public Relations Journal*, *49*(8), 34–35.

Carraher Wolverton, C., & Thomas, D. (2018). The Development of an Integrated Model of Emr Adoption: Incorporating the Organization Artifact. *Journal of Information Technology Theory and Application*. (in press)

Cartman, C., & Salazar, A. (2011). The influence of organizational size, internal IT capabilities, and competitive and vendor pressures on ERP adoption in SMEs. *International Journal of Enterprise Information Systems*, *7*(3), 68–92. doi:10.4018/jeis.2011070104

Cartner-Morley, J. (2016). *Brooklyn Beckham, Burberry and the new celebrity aristocracy*. Retrieved October 4th, 2017, from https://www.theguardian.com/fashion/2016/feb/01/brooklyn-beckham-burberry-celebrity-artistocracy-16-photography-snobbery-instagram-followers

Cassivi, L., Hadaya, P., Lefebvre, E., & Lefebvre, L. A. (2008). The role of collaboration on process, relational, and product innovations in a supply chain. *International Journal of e-Collaboration*, *4*(4), 11–32. doi:10.4018/jec.2008100102

Cassivi, L., Lefebvre, L., Lefebvre, L. A., & Leger, P. (2004). The impact of e-collaboration tools on firms' performance. *International Journal of e-Collaboration*, *15*(1), 91–110.

Castarède, J. (1992). *Le luxe*. Presses universitaires de France.

Castellano, S., Khelladi, I., Chipaux, A., & Kupferminc, C. (2014). The Influence of Social Networks on E-Reputation: How Sportspersons Manage the Relationship with Their Online Community. *International Journal of Technology and Human Interaction, 10*(4), 65–79. doi:10.4018/ijthi.2014100105

Cegielski, C. G., Allison Jones-Farmer, L., Wu, Y., & Hazen, B. T. (2012). Adoption of cloud computing technologies in supply chains: An organizational information processing theory approach. *International Journal of Logistics Management, 23*(2), 184–211. doi:10.1108/09574091211265350

Central Agency for Public Mobilization and Statistics. (2018). *Population in Egypt*. Cairo: CAPMAS publications.

Ceron, J. P., & Dubois, G. (2007). Limits to Tourism? A back-casting scenario for sustainable tourism mobility in 2050. *Tourism and Hospitality Planning & Development, 4*(3), 191–209. doi:10.1080/14790530701736598

Certify. (2017). Understanding the average cost of business travel. Retrieved from https://www.certify.com/Infographic-TheAverageCostOfBusinessTravel.aspx

Cestre, G. (1996). Diffusion et Innovativité: Définition, Modélisation et Mesure. *Recherche et Applications en Marketing, 11*(1), 69–88. doi:10.1177/076737019601100105

Chadburn, A., Smith, J., & Milan, J. (2017). Productivity drivers of knowledge workers in the central London office environment. *Journal of Corporate Real Estate, 19*(2), 66–79. doi:10.1108/JCRE-12-2015-0047

Chan, C. (2010). Using online advertising to increase the impact of a library Facebook page. *Library Management, 32*(4/5), 361–370. doi:10.1108/01435121111132347

Chang, A., Hsieh, S., & Tseng, T. H. (2013). Online brand community response to negative brand events: The role of group eWOM. *Internet Research, 23*(4), 486–506. doi:10.1108/IntR-06-2012-0107

Chang, F., Dean, J., Ghemawat, S., Hsieh, W. C., Wallach, D. A., Burrows, M., ... Gruber, R. E. (2008). Bigtable: A distributed storage system for structured data. *ACM Transactions on Computer Systems, 26*(2), 4. doi:10.1145/1365815.1365816

Chang, H.-T., & Liou, S.-N. (2002). Exploring Employee's Knowledge Sharing: The Social Network Approach. *Human Resource Management Review, 2*(3), 101–113.

Chang, L. (2011). A comparison of Taiwan and Malaysia in negotiation style. *Journal of International Business Management, 6*(1), 9–17.

Chang, L., Furner, C. P., & Zinko, R. (2010). A study of negotiation within the ethnic Chinese community between Taiwan and Hong Kong. *Management Research and Practice, 2*(4), 329–343.

Chang, Y. Y., Gong, Y., & Peng, M. W. (2012). Expatriate knowledge transfer, subsidiary absorptive capacity, and subsidiary performance. *Academy of Management Journal, 55*(4), 927–948. doi:10.5465/amj.2010.0985

Chan, H. K., & Chan, F. T. S. (2010). Comparative study of adaptability and flexibility in distributed manufacturing supply chains. *Decision Support Systems, 48*(2), 331–341. doi:10.1016/j.dss.2009.09.001

Chan, H., Huang, W., Lynch, J., Pan, J., & Yu, J. (2016). *China Internet and Software: All eyes on cloud and internet finance*. Macquarie Capital Limited.

Chan, J. K. L., & Baum, T. (2007). Motivation factors of ecotourists in ecolodge accommodation: The push and pull factors. *Asia Pacific Journal of Tourism Research, 12*(4), 349–364. doi:10.1080/10941660701761027

Chan, J. O. (2005). Enterprise Information Systems Strategy and Planning. *The Journal of American Academy of Business, Cambridge, 6*(2), 148–153.

536

Chan, S., & Lu, M. (2004). Understanding Internet banking adoption and use: A Hong Kong perspective. *Journal of Global Information Management, 12*(3), 21–42. doi:10.4018/jgim.2004070102

Chaturvedi, S., & Chakrabarti, D. (2018). Operational efficiency in manufacturing process using design of experiments. *International Journal of Process Management and Benchmarking, 7*(2), 249–261. doi:10.1504/IJPMB.2017.083111

Chau, P. Y. K., & Tam, K. Y. (1997). Factors Affecting the Adoption of Open Systems: An Exploratory Study. *MIS Quarterly, 21*(1), 1-24.

Chaudhuri, S. (2015). Urban poor, economic opportunities and sustainable development through traditional knowledge and practices. *Global Bioethics, 26*(2), 86–93. doi:10.1080/11287462.2015.1037141

Chaudhury, A., Mallick, D. N., & Rao, H. R. (2001). Web channels in e-commerce. *Communications of the ACM, 44*(1), 99–104. doi:10.1145/357489.357515

Chau, P. Y. K. (1996). An empirical assessment of a modified technology acceptance model. *Journal of Management Information Systems, 13*(2), 185–204. doi:10.1080/07421222.1996.11518128

Chen, D. Q., Preston, D. S., & Swink, M. (2015). How the use of big data analytics affects value creation in supply chain management. *Journal of Management Information Systems, 32*(4), 4–39. doi:10.1080/07421222.2015.1138364

Chen, L., Zhao, Z., Tang, O., Price, L., Zhang, S., & Zhu, W. (2017). Supply chain collaboration for sustainability: A Literature review and future research agenda. *International Journal of Production Economics, 194*, 73–87. doi:10.1016/j.ijpe.2017.04.005

Chennamaneni, A., Teng, J. T., & Raja, M. K. (2012). A unified model of knowledge sharing behaviors: Theoretical development and empirical test. *Behaviour & Information Technology, 31*(11), 1097–1115. doi:10.1080/0144929X.2011.624637

Chen, S., Chen, H., & Chen, M. (2009). Determinants of satisfaction and continuace intention toward self-service technologies. *Industrial Management & Data Systems, 109*(9), 1248–1263. doi:10.1108/02635570911002306

Cheong, G. (2016). *How Luxury Brands are Using Social Media to Woo A New Generation of Customers*. Retrieved October 4th, 2017, from http://thepeakmagazine.com.sg/fashion-watches/how-luxury-brands-are-using-social-media-to-woo-a-new-generation-of-customers

Cheong, R. K., & Tsui, E. (2011). From Skills and Competencies to Outcome-based Collaborative Work: Tracking a Decade's Development of Personal Knowledge Management (PKM) Models. *Knowledge and Process Management, 18*(3), 175–193. doi:10.1002/kpm.380

Chevalier, M., & Mazzalovo, G. (2008). *Luxury brand management: a world of privilege*. John Wiley & Sons.

Chiarini, A., Vagnoni, E., & Chiarini, L. (2018). ERP implementation in public healthcare, achievable benefits and encountered criticalities - an investigation from Italy. *International Journal of Services and Operations Management, 29*(1), 1–17. doi:10.1504/IJSOM.2018.088460

Chi, H., Yeh, H. R., & Yang, Y. (2011). Applying theory of reasoned action and technology acceptance model to investigate purchase behavior on smartphone. *Journal of International Management Studies, 6*(3), 1–11.

Chinese Culture Connection. (1987). Chinese values and the search for culture-free dimensions of culture. *Journal of Cross-Cultural Psychology, 18*(2), 143–164. doi:10.1177/0022002187018002002

Chow, Y., Tamar, A., Mannor, S., & Pavone, M. (2015). Risk-sensitive and robust decision-making: a CVaR optimization approach. Advances in Neural Information Processing Systems, 1522-1530.

Chowdhury, H. K., Parvin, N., Weitenberner, C., & Becker, M. (2006). Consumer Attitude toward Mobile Advertising in an Emerging Market: An Empirical Study. *International Journal of Mobile Marketing, 1*(2).

Chu, C. T., Kim, S. K., Lin, Y. A., Yu, Y., Bradski, G., Olukotun, K., & Ng, A. Y. (2007). Map-reduce for machine learning on multicore. In Advances in neural information processing systems (pp. 281-288). Academic Press.

Chu, E. T. H., Chen, Y. L., Lin, J. Y., & Liu, J. W. (2012). Crowdsourcing support system for disaster surveillance and response. *Wireless Personal Multimedia Communications (WPMC), 2012 15th International Symposium on IEEE*, 21-25.

Chuang, C. C., & Hu, F. (2012). Customer adoption of Internet banking: An empirical investigation in Taiwanese banking context. *Information Management and Business Review, 4*(11), 570–582.

Chun, R., & Davies, G. (2001). E-reputation: The role of mission and vision statements in positioning Strategy. *Journal of Brand Management, 8*(4), 315–333. doi:10.1057/palgrave.bm.2540031

Clemmitt, M. (2006). Cyber socializing. *CQ Researcher, 16*(27), 625–648.

Clemmitt, M. (2010). Social networking. *CQ Researcher, 20*(32), 749–772.

Cleveland, S., & Ellis, T. J. (2015). Rethinking knowledge sharing barriers: A content analysis of 103 studies. *International Journal of Knowledge Management, 11*(1), 28–51. doi:10.4018/IJKM.2015010102

Coates, D., & Humphreys, B. R. (2010). Week to week attendance and competitive balance in the national football league. *International Journal of Sport Finance, 5*(4), 239–252.

Coche, R. (2016). Promoting women's soccer through social media: How the US federation used Twitter for the 2011 World Cup. *Soccer and Society, 17*(1), 90–101. doi:10.1080/14660970.2014.919279

Cogburn, D. L., & Levinson, N. S. (2003). US–Africa virtual collaboration in globalization studies: Success factors for complex, cross-national learning teams. *International Studies Perspectives, 4*(1), 34–51. doi:10.1111/1528-3577.04103

Cohen, B. C. (1963). *The Press and Foreign Policy*. Princeton, NJ: Princeton University.

Cohen, J. R. (1999). Advising clients to apologize. *California Law Review, 72*, 1009–1131.

Cohen, S. G., & Gibson, C. B. (2003). *In the beginning: Introduction and framework*.

Coin Market Cap. (2017). *Cryptocurrency Market Capatilization – Bitcoin*. Retrieved from https://coinmarketcap.com/currencies/bitcoin/

Collins, L. (2009). Check Mate. Burberry's working-class hero. *The New Yorker*. Retrieved October 4th, 2017, from https://www.newyorker.com/magazine/2009/09/14/check-mate

Collins, C., & Kehoe, R. (2017). Examining strategic fit and misfit in the management of knowledge workers. *Industrial & Labor Relations Review, 70*(2), 308–335. doi:10.1177/0019793916654481

Collins, D. (1997). Knowledge work or working knowledge? Ambiguity and confusion in the analysis of the "knowledge age". *Employee Relations, 19*(1), 38–50. doi:10.1108/01425459710163570

Colvin, G. (1997). The changing art of becoming unbeatable. *Fortune, 136*(10), 299–300.

Comming, J. N. (2004). Work group structure diversity and knowledge sharing in a global organization. *Management Science, 50*(3), 352–364. doi:10.1287/mnsc.1030.0134

Compeau, D. R., & Higgins, C. A. (1995). Computer self-efficacy: Development of a measure and initial test. *Management Information Systems Quarterly, 19*(2), 189–211. doi:10.2307/249688

Complinet. (2010). *DFSA Takes Action Over Damas Failures.* USA: Thomson Reuters.

Connelly, C., & Kelloway, E. (2004). Predictors of employees' perceptions of knowledge sharing cultures. *Leadership and Organization Development Journal, 24*(5/6), 294–301.

Conway, J. M. (1999). Distinguishing contextual performance from task performance for managerial jobs. *The Journal of Applied Psychology, 84*(1), 3–13. doi:10.1037/0021-9010.84.1.3

Coombs, W. T. (2004). Structuring crisis discourse knowledge: The West Pharmaceutics case. *Public Relations Review, 30*(4), 467–473. doi:10.1016/j.pubrev.2004.08.007

Coombs, W. T. (2007). *Crisis Management and Communications. UAE*: Institute of PR.

Coombs, W. T. (2007). *Ongoing Crisis Communication: Planning,* Managing, and Responding.

Coombs, W. T. (2007). Protecting organization reputations during a crisis: The development and application of situational crisis communication theory. *Corporate Reputation Review,* 10(3), 163-176.

Cooper, R. B., & Zmud, R. W. (1990). Information Technology Implementation research: A technological Diffusion Perspective. *Management Science, 3*(1), 60–95.

Costantino, F., Di Gravio, G., Shaban, A., & Tronci, M. (2014). The impact of information sharing and inventory control coordination on supply chain performances. *Computers & Industrial Engineering, 76,* 292–306. doi:10.1016/j.cie.2014.08.006

Council, C. L. (2003). *Crisis management strategies.*

Crandall, R. (1980). *Motivations for leisure.* New York: Wiley.

Crompton, J. (1979). Motivations of pleasure vacations. *Annals of Tourism Research, 6*(4), 408–424. doi:10.1016/0160-7383(79)90004-5

Cross, R., & Cummings, J. N. (2004). Tie and Network Correlates of Individual Performance in Knowledge Intensive Work. *Academy of Management Journal, 47*(6), 928–937.

Cruz-Cunha, M. M., Miranda, I. M., & Goncalves, P. (2013). *Handbook of research on ICTs for human-centered health-care and social care services.* Hershey, PA: IGI Global. doi:10.4018/978-1-4666-3986-7

Cruz, N. M., Pérez, V. M., & Cantero, C. T. (2009). The influence of employee motivation on knowledge transfer. *Journal of Knowledge Management, 13*(6), 478–490. doi:10.1108/13673270910997132

Cumming, S. (1993). Neural networks for monitoring of engine condition data. *Neural Computing & Applications, 1*(1), 96–102. doi:10.1007/BF01411378

d'Hauteville, F. (1994). *Un Modèle d'Acceptation du Nouveau Produit par le Consommateur: Cas du Vin allégé en Alcool* (Unpublished Doctoral Dissertation). Université Montpellier II, France.

Da Silva Cruz, C. (2009). *Elaboration The Information Technology Strategic Plan - ITSP.* Brasília, Brazil: ENAP.

Dai, Y.-Y. (2015). *Do low-carbon travel: Motivations, constraints and behaviors* (Unpublished doctoral thesis). Graduate Institute of Recreation, Tourism, and Hospitality Management, National Chiayi University, Chiayi, Taiwan.

Damanpour, F. (1992). Organizational Size and Innovation. *Organization Studies, 13*(3), 375-402.

Damas. (2013). *About Damas.* Retrieved 8 31, 2013, from http://www.damasjewel.com/articledisplay.aspx?mid=33&id=25

Damsgaard, J., Rogaczewski, A., & Lyytinen, K. (1994). How Information Technologies Penetrate Organisations. An Analysis of Four Alternative Models. In I. Levine (Ed.), Diffusion, transfer and Implementation of Information Technology. North Holland.

Davenport, T. H. (2015). Process management for knowledge work. In J. vom Brocke & M. Rosemann (Eds.), *Handbook on Business Process Management 1* (2nd ed., pp. 17–35). New York, NY: Springer.

Davenport, T. H., & Prusak, L. (1998). *Working Knowledge: How Organizations Manage What They Know*. Boston: Harvard Business School Press.

David, P. (1985). Clio and the Economics of QWERTY. *Economy and History, 75*, 227–332.

Davies, N. J., Lumsdon, L. M., & Weston, R. (2012). Developing recreational trails: Motivations for recreational walking. *Tourism Planning & Development, 9*(1), 77–88. doi:10.1080/21568316.2012.653480

Davis, F. D. (1989). Perceived usefulness, perceived ease of use, and user acceptance of information technology. *Management Information Systems Quarterly, 13*(3), 319–340. doi:10.2307/249008

Davis, F. D. (1993). User acceptance of information technology: System characteristics, user perceptions and behavioral impacts. *International Journal of Man-Machine Studies, 38*(3), 475–487. doi:10.1006/imms.1993.1022

Davis, F. D. (1993). *User Acceptance of Information Technology: System Characteristics*. User Perceptions and Behavioral Impacts.

Davis, F. D., Bagozzi, R. P., & Warshaw, P. R. (1989). User acceptance of computer technology: A comparison of two theoretical models. *Management Science, 35*(8), 982–1003. doi:10.1287/mnsc.35.8.982

Davis, G. B. (2002). Anytime/anyplace computing and the future of knowledge work. *Communications of the ACM, 45*(12), 67–73. doi:10.1145/585597.585617

Davis, N. W., & Duncan, M. C. (2006). Sports knowledge is power: Reinforcing masculine privilege through fantasy sport league participation. *Journal of Sport and Social Issues, 30*(3), 244–253. doi:10.1177/0193723506290324

Davison, R. M., Ou, C. X. J., & Martinsons, M. G. (2012). Information technology to support informal knowledge sharing. *Information Systems Journal, 23*(1), 89–109. doi:10.1111/j.1365-2575.2012.00400.x

Davis, T. (1993). Effective supply chain management. *Sloan Management Review, 35*(4), 35–16.

Dawson, R., & Clements, K. (2004). Virtual collaboration with clients. *Consulting to Management, 15*(4), 50–53.

Daye, D. (2006). Brand quote. *Branding Strategy Insider*. Retrieved September 6, 2015 from http://www.brandingstrategyinsider.com/2006/09

De Mattos, C. A., & Laurindo, F. J. B. (2017). Information technology adoption and assimilation: Focus on the suppliers portal. *Computers in Industry, 85*, 48–57. doi:10.1016/j.compind.2016.12.009

De Palma, A., Myers, G. M., & Papageorgiou, Y. Y. (1994). Rational Choice under an Imperfect Ability to Choose. *The American Economic Review*, 419–440.

De Vreede, G.-J., & Briggs, R. O. (2005, January) Collaboration engineering: Designing repeatable processes for high-value collaborative tasks. *Paper presented at the annual Hawaii International Conference on Systems Science*, Maui, HI. 10.1109/HICSS.2005.144

Dean, D. H. (2004). Consumer reaction to negative publicity: Effects of corporate reputation, response, and responsibility for a crisis event. *Journal of Business Communication, 41*(2), 192–211. doi:10.1177/0021943603261748

Dean, J., & Ghemawat, S. (2008). MapReduce: Simplified data processing on large clusters. *Communications of the ACM, 51*(1), 107–113. doi:10.1145/1327452.1327492

Deephouse, D. L. (2000). Media reputation as a strategic resource: An integration of mass communication and resource-based theories. *Journal of Management, 26*(6), 1091–1112. doi:10.1177/014920630002600602

Dees, W. (2011). New media and technology use in corporate sport sponsorship: Performing activational leverage from an exchange perspective. *International Journal of Sport Management and Marketing, 10*(3/4), 272–285. doi:10.1504/IJSMM.2011.044795

DeLone, W. H., & McLean, E. R. (1992). Information Systems Success: The Quest for the Dependent Variable. *Information Systems Research, 3*(1), 60-95.

DeLone, W. H., & McLean, E. R. (1992). Information systems success: The quest for the dependent variable. *Information Systems Research, 3*(1), 60–95. doi:10.1287/isre.3.1.60

DesRoches, C. M., Campbell, E. G., Rao, S. R., Donelan, K., Ferris, T. G., Jha, A., … Shields, A. E. (2008). Electronic Health Records in Ambulatory Care—a National Survey of Physicians. *New England Journal of Medicine, 359*(1), 50-60.

Dharamdass, S., & Fernando, Y. (2018). Contact centre service excellence: A proposed conceptual framework. *International Journal of Services and Operations Management, 29*(1), 18–41. doi:10.1504/IJSOM.2018.088470

Dholakia, U. M. (2004). The usefulness of bidders' reputation ratings to sellers in online auctions. *Journal of Interactive Marketing, 19*(1), 31–40. doi:10.1002/dir.20029

Dholakia, U. M., & Simonson, I. (2005). The effect of explicit reference points on consumer choice and online bidding behavior. *Marketing Science, 24*(2), 206–217. doi:10.1287/mksc.1040.0099

Dickinson, J. E., & Lumsdon, L. (2010). *Slow travel and tourism*. London: Earthscan.

Dickinson, J. E., Lumsdon, L., & Robbins, D. (2011). Slow travel: Issues for tourism and climate change. *Journal of Sustainable Tourism, 19*(3), 281–300. doi:10.1080/09669582.2010.524704

Dilenschneider, R. L. (2000). *The corporate communications bible: Everything you need to know to become a public relations expert*. Beverly Hills: New Millennium.

DiMaggio, P. J., & Powell, W. W. (1983). The Iron Cage Revisited: Institutional Isomorphism and Collective Rationality in Organizational Fields. *American Sociological Review, 48*(2), 147–160. doi:10.2307/2095101

Dirks, S., Keeling, M., & Lyons, R. (2008). Lessons from global e-readiness trends of national economies. *Proceedings of the VI Globelics Conference*.

Disney, S. M., Gaalman, G. J., Hedenstierna, C. P. T., & Hosoda, T. (2015). Fill rate in a periodic review order-up-to policy under auto-correlated normally distributed, possibly negative, demand. *International Journal of Production Economics, 170*, 501–512. doi:10.1016/j.ijpe.2015.07.019

Dittman, D. R., Hawkins, M., Deokar, A. V., & Sarnikar, S. (2010). Improving virtual collaboration outcomes through collaboration process structuring. *The Quarterly Review of Distance Education, 11*(4), 195–209.

Dodds, W. B., Monroe, K. B., & Grewal, D. (1991). Effects of Price, Brand, and Store Information on Buyers' Product Evaluations. *JMR, Journal of Marketing Research, 28*(3), 307–319. doi:10.2307/3172866

Doherty, N. F., Marples, C. G., & Suhaimi, A. (1999). The relative success of alternative approaches to strategic information systems planning: An empirical analysis. *The Journal of Strategic Information Systems, 8*(3), 263–283. doi:10.1016/S0963-8687(99)00024-4

Doing Business. (2018). *Reforming to create jobs*. Washington, DC: A World Bank Group Report.

Dolnicar, S. (2004). Insights into sustainable tourists in Austria: A data-based a priori segmentation approach. *Journal of Sustainable Tourism, 12*(3), 209–218. doi:10.1080/09669580408667234

Dolnicar, S., & Long, P. (2009). Beyond ecotourism: The environmentally responsible tourist in the general travel experience. *Tourism Analysis, 14*(4), 503–513. doi:10.3727/108354209X12596287114291

Dong, Y., Bartol, K. M., Zhang, Z.-X., & Li, C. (2017). Enhancing employee creativity via individual skill development and team knowledge sharing: Influences of dual-focused transformational leadership. *Journal of Organizational Behavior, 38*(3), 439–458. doi:10.1002/job.2134

DOU 254. (2008). Brazilian Federal Official Gazette, No. 254 of Dec 31st, 2008.

Downing, J. R. (2003). American Airlines' use of mediated employee channels after the 9/11 attacks. *Public Relations Review*, 30(1), 37–48.

Drucker, P. F. (1998, Oct 5). Management's New Paradigms. *Forbes*. Retrieved from https://www.forbes.com/forbes/1998/1005/6207152a.html#5abe555931ee

Drucker, P. F. (2006). *The effective executive: The definitive guide to getting the right things done* (5th ed.). New York, NY: HarperCollins.

Dubois, D. (2013). *Why Social Media Is Luxury's Best Friend*. Retrieved October 4th, 2017, from https://knowledge.insead.edu/strategy/why-social-media-is-luxurys-best-friend-2951

Dubois, D. (2014). *"Social Media New Deal" for Luxury Brands*. Retrieved October 4th, 2017, from https://knowledge.insead.edu/marketing-advertising/the-social-media-new-deal-for-luxury-brands-3649

DuBois, S. (2013). How IKEA can get back on the horse after a meat scandal. *CNN*. Retrieved 09 01, 2013, from http://management.fortune.cnn.com/2013/02/26/ikea-horsemeat/

Duong, L. N. K., Wood, L. C., & Wang, X. (2016). Review of RFID applications in perishable inventory management. In B. Christiansen (Ed.), *Handbook of Research on Global Supply Chain Management* (pp. 139–146). Hershey, PA: IGI Global. doi:10.4018/978-1-4666-9639-6.ch008

Durán, G., Guajardo, M., & Wolf-Yadlin, R. (2012). Operations research techniques for scheduling Chile's second division soccer league. *Interfaces, 42*(3), 273–285, 326, 328. doi:10.1287/inte.1110.0608

Dure, B. (2011). Getting bigger, major league soccer seeks better TV ratings: New clubs add buzz, but getting more viewers to tune in is trick. *USA Today*. Retrieved March 1, 2017 from http://www.usatoday.com/SPORTS/usaedition/2011-03-14-mls14_st_U.htm

Dutot, V., & Castellano, S. (2015). Designing a measurement scale for e-reputation. *Corporate Reputation Review, 18*(4), 294–313. doi:10.1057/crr.2015.15

Dwyer, L. (2005). Relevance of triple bottom line reporting to achievement of sustainable tourism: A scoping study. *Tourism Review International, 9*(1), 79–938. doi:10.3727/154427205774791726

eBay's bid to win back buyers. (2007). *BusinessWeek*. Retrieved October 7, 2017 from http://www.businessweek.com/print/technology/content/sep2007/tc20070917_75070.htm

Ebersole, G. (2013). The Importance of Public Relations and Crisis Management Planning To Your Business. *Crisistraining.net*. Retrieved 9 1, 2013 from http://www.crisistraining.net/crisis-media-training_workshops_The-Importance-of-Public-Relations-and-Crisis-Management-Planning-To-Your-Business.htm

Ebrahimi, P., & Fadaei, M. (2016). The Impact of Relationship Marketing on Team Loyalty (The Case Study: Sport Team Fans of Azadeghan Football League of Iran). *International Journal of Medical Research & Health Sciences*, 5(5), 52–68.

Ebru, E., Duyguy, T., & Ceren, A. (2015). An Analysis of Interdepartmental Relations in Enterprise Resource Planning Implementation: A Social Capital Perspective. *International Journal of Enterprise Information Systems*, 11(3), 68–93.

Economic and Social Commission for Western Asia. (2005). *Measuring the information society.* ESCWA.

Economic and Social Commission for Western Asia. (2007). *The Information Society from declaration to implementation.* ESCWA.

Efimova, L. (2004). Discovering the iceberg of knowledge work: A weblog case. *Paper presented at the Fifth European Conference on Organization, Knowledge, Learning and Capabilities*, Innsbruck, Austria. Retrieved from http://citeseerx.ist.psu.edu/viewdoc/summary?doi=10.1.1.128.9265

Eichbaum, Q., Murphy, M., Liu, Y., Kajja, I., Abrahao, H. L., & Smit Sibinga, C. (2016). Patient blood management: An international perspective. *Anesthesia and Analgesia*, 123(6), 1574–1581. doi:10.1213/ANE.0000000000001597 PMID:27870740

Eide, A. W., Haugstveit, I. M., Halvorsrud, R., & Borén, M. (2013). Inter-organizational collaboration structures during emergency response: A case study. *Proceedings of the 10th International ISCRAM Conference*, 94-104.

Ekanayake, J., Li, H., Zhang, B., Gunarathne, T., Bae, S. H., Qiu, J., & Fox, G. (2010, June). Twister: a runtime for iterative mapreduce. In *Proceedings of the 19th ACM international symposium on high performance distributed computing* (pp. 810-818). ACM.

El-Farr, H. (2009). Knowledge work and workers: A critical literature review. *Leeds University Business School Working Paper Series*, 1(1).

El-Gayar, O. F., & Fritz, B. D. (2010). A web-based multi-perspective decision support system for information security planning. *Decision Support Systems*, 50(1), 43–54. doi:10.1016/j.dss.2010.07.001

El-Mikawy, N., & Ghoneim, A. (2005). *The information base, knowledge creation and knowledge dissemination in Egypt.* Bonn: Center for Development Research, University of Bonn.

Emiliani, M. L. (2000). Business-to-business online auctions: Key issues for purchasing process improvement. *Supply Chain Management*, 5(4), 176–193. doi:10.1108/13598540010347299

Emirates247. (2013). Global Village rides closed after visitor's death; 3 arrestedError! Hyperlink reference not valid.. Retrieved 09 1, 2013 from http://www.emirates247.com/news/emirates/global-village-rides-closed-after-visitor-s-death-3-arrested-2013-01-26-1.492484

Entman, R. M. (2007). Framing bias media in the distribution of power. *Journal of Communication*, 57(1), 163–173. doi:10.1111/j.1460-2466.2006.00336.x

Erkan, I. (2015). Electronic word of mouth on Instagram: Customers' engagements with brands in different sectors. *International Journal of Management, Accounting and Economics*, 2(12), 1435–1444.

EuBis. (n.d.). Retrieved August 15, 2017, from www.eubis-europe.eu/objectives.ph

Evans, S. (2012). *Soccer-television ratings missing link for growing major league soccer.* Retrieved July 9, 2017 from http://www.reuters.com/article/2012/03/09/soccer-mls-television-idUSB67913220120309

Evans, D. M., & Smith, A. C. T. (2004). The Internet and competitive advantage: A study of Australia's four premier professional sporting leagues. *Sport Management Review*, 7(1), 27–56. doi:10.1016/S1441-3523(04)70044-3

Exencia Pharma Academy Ltd. (n.d.). Retrieved August 15, 2017, from http://www.volgopleidingen.nl/almere/exencia-pharma-academy

Expression of Interest Integrated Project. (2003). *E-Learning- the cultural and societal impacts on the design and perception of e-learning solutions.* Call for Expression of Interest. Retrieved August 15, 2017, from http://kmr.nada.kth.se/papers/SemanticWeb/EOI_PAeLLA_fainal.pdf

Ey-Ling, S. (2011). 2010 Practice Analysis: Professional competencies and work categories in public relations today. *Public Relations Review, 37(3),* 187–196.

Fagundes, V. (2011). *PDGovTI – A Model of The Information Technology Strategic Plan: Based on Enterprise Architecture and IT Governance the Government.* Federal University of Rio de Janeiro.

Fang, T. (2003). A critique of Hofstede's fifth dimension. *International Journal of Cross Cultural Management, 3*(3), 347–368. doi:10.1177/1470595803003003006

Feagin, J., Orum, A., & Sjoberg, G. (Eds.). (1991). *A case for case study.* Chapel Hill, NC: University of North Carolina Press.

Fedorowicz, J., Laso-Ballesteros, I., & Padilla-Melendez, A. (2008). Creativity, innovation, and E-collaboration. *International Journal of e-Collaboration, 4*(4), 1–10. doi:10.4018/jec.2008100101

Fernandez, P. (2009). Balancing outreach and privacy in Facebook: Five guiding decisions points. *Library Hi Tech News, 26*(3/4), 10–12. doi:10.1108/07419050910979946

Fernie, J., & Azuma, N. (2004). The changing nature of Japanese fashion – Can quick response improve supply chain efficiency? *European Journal of Marketing, 38*(7), 790–808. doi:10.1108/03090560410539258

Ferraro, G. P. (2002). *The cultural dimension of international business.* Upper Saddle River, NJ: Pearson.

Figuères, C. (2011). *Innovation and Technology for Poverty Eradication, report, International institute for Communication and Development.* IICD.

Fink, L. (2007). Coordination, learning, and innovation: The organizational roles of e-collaboration and their impacts. *International Journal of e-Collaboration, 3*(3), 53–70. doi:10.4018/jec.2007070104

Finn, G. (2014). Still the One: Facebook gains ground as the leader in social logins. *Marketing Land.* Retrieved July 9, 2017 from http://marketingland.com/still-one-facebook-gains-ground-leader-social-logins-81115

Flor, A. G. (2005). Participation and Partnerships in Rural Information Networks: Lessons Learned from five Asian Countries. In FAO Experts' Meeting on Rural Information Networks in Asia-Pacific: Innovative Practices and Future Directions, Bangkok, Thailand, December 14-16.

Fombrun, C. (1996). *Reputation.* John Wiley & Sons, Ltd.

Forman, J., & Argenti, P. A. (2005). How Corporate Communication Influences Strategy Implementation, Reputation and the Corporate Brand: An Exploratory Qualitative Study. *Corporate Reputation Review, 8*(3), 245–264. doi:10.1057/palgrave.crr.1540253

Fornell, C., & Larcker, D. F. (1981). Evaluating structural equation models with unobservable variables and measurement error. *JMR, Journal of Marketing Research, 1*(1), 39–50. doi:10.2307/3151312

Fornell, C., & Larcker, D. F. (1981). Structural equation models with unobservable variables and measurement error: Algebra and statistics. *JMR, Journal of Marketing Research, 18*(3), 382–388. doi:10.2307/3150980

Fortunato, J. (2011). The relationship of fantasy football participation with NFL television ratings. *Journal of Sport Administration and Supervision, 3*(1), 74–90.

Foundation, R. J. W. (2012). *Health Information Technology in the United States: Driving toward Delivery System Change, 2012*. Retrieved from http://www.rwjf.org/content/dam/farm/reports/reports/2012/rwjf72707

Foxall, G., & Haskins, C. G. (1986). Cognitive Style and Consumer Innovativeness: An Empirical Test of Kirton's Adaptation-Innovation Theory in the Context of Food Purchasing. *European Journal of Marketing, 20*(3/4), 63–80. doi:10.1108/EUM0000000004755

Franceschini, F., & Mastrogiacomo, L. (2018). Service gap deployment: A framework to link quality gaps to service activities. *International Journal of Services and Operations Management, 29*(1), 85–99. doi:10.1504/IJSOM.2018.088474

Frank, S. M., & Waters, J. H. (2016). *Patient Blood Management: Multidisciplinary Approaches to Optimize Care*. AABB Press.

French, J. R. P. Jr., & Raven, B. (1968). The bases of social power. In D. Cartwright (Ed.), Studies in Social Power (pp. 150-167).

Fried, J. (2004). Basecamp launches. *Signal vs. Noise*. Retrieved from https://signalvnoise.com/archives/000542.php

Frisby, W. (2005). The good, the bad, and the ugly: Critical sport management research. *Journal of Sport Management, 19*(1), 1–12. doi:10.1123/jsm.19.1.1

Fry, R. (2013). *A rising share of young adults live in their parents' home*. Pew Research Center. Retrieved from http://www.pewsocialtrends.org/files/2013/07/SDT-millennials-living-with- parents-07-2013.pdf

FSOhio and Columbus crew announce television agreement. (2012). Retrieved March 1, 2018 from http://www.foxsportsohio.com/02/22/12/FSOhio-and-Columbus-Crew-announce-televi/landing_crew.html?blockID=671512

Gans, H. (2009). Public ethnography: Ethnography as public sociology. *Qualitative Sociology, 33*(2010), 97-104. Retrieved August 4, 2017 from http://herbertgans.org/wp-content/uploads/2013/11/Public-Ethnography.pdf

Ganzach, Y., Saporta, I., & Weber, Y. (2000). Interaction in linear versus logistic models: A substantive illustration using the relationship between motivation, ability, and performance. *Organizational Research Methods, 3*(3), 237–253. doi:10.1177/109442810033002

García, G. M. J., Hernández, G. G. J., & Hernández, R. J. G. (2015). An approach to the ranking of projects to undertake [Una aproximación para la jerarquización de proyectos a emprender]. In Gobernanza empresarial de Tecnología de la Información. Universidad de Cantabria.

García, G. M. J., Schwarz, I. L. M., Schwarz, I. T. M., Hernández, G. G. J., & Hernández, R. J. G. (2017). Inventories control, the Inventory manager and Matrixes Of Weighing with multiplicative factors (MOWwMf). *Journal of Global Business and Technology, 13*(1), 40–56.

García, M. J., Hernández, G., & Hernández, R. J. G. (2014). Ubicación de radiopatrullas policiales para la vigilancia pública con dos modelos multicriterios. *Revista de Matemática: Teoría y Aplicaciones, 21*(1), 145–158.

Garfinkel, H. (1963). A Conception of and Experiments with" Trust" as a Condition of Concerted Stable Actions. The production of reality: Essays and readings on social interaction, 381-392.

Garfinkel, S. L., Juels, A., & Pappu, R. (2005). RFID privacy: An overview of problems and proposed solutions. *Security & Privacy, IEEE, 3*(3), 34–43. doi:10.1109/MSP.2005.78

Garg, R. H. (2012). Who killed Rambhor? The state of emergency medical services in India. *Journal of Emergencies, Trauma and Shock, 5*(1), 49–54. doi:10.4103/0974-2700.93113 PMID:22416155

Garrett, L. E., Spreitzer, G. M., & Bacevice, P. A. (2017). Co-constructing a sense of community at work: The emergence of community in coworking spaces. *Organization Studies, 38*(6), 821–842. doi:10.1177/0170840616685354

Garson, G. D. (2008). *Path analysis*. From Statnotes: topics in multivariate analysis. Retrieved from http://ondrej.vostal.net/pub/skola/statnote.htm

Garud, R., & Karnøe, P. (2001). Path Creation as a Process of Mindful Deviation. In Path Dependence and Creation. Lawrence Erlbaum Associates.

Garud, R., & Karnøe, P. (2003). Bricolage versus Breakthrough: Distributed and Embedded Agency in Technology Entrepreneurship. *Research Policy, 32*(2), 277–300. doi:10.1016/S0048-7333(02)00100-2

Garud, R., Kumaraswamy, A., & Karnøe, P. (2010). Path dependence or path creation? *Journal of Management Studies, 47*(4), 760–774. doi:10.1111/j.1467-6486.2009.00914.x

Gaspars-Wieloch, H. (2017). A decision rule based on goal programming and one-stage models for uncertain multi-criteria mixed decision making and games against nature. *Croatian Operational Research Review, 8*(1), 63–78. doi:10.17535/crorr.2017.0004

Gatignon, H., & Robertson, T. S. (1985). A propositional Inventory for New Diffusion Research. *The Journal of Consumer Research, 11*(4), 849–867. doi:10.1086/209021

Gaylord, C. (2007). Why we do what we do on eBay. *The Christian Science Monitor,* 13-14. Retrieved October 7, 2017 from http://www.csmonitor.com/2007/0716/p13s02-wmgn.html

Geldof, M., Grimshaw, D.J., Kleine, D., & Unwin T. (2011). What are the key lessons of ICT4D partnerships for poverty reduction? policy brief. DFID.

Geng, J., Long, R., Chen, H., & Li, Q. (2018). Urban residents' response to and evaluation of low-carbon travel policies: Evidence from a survey of five eastern cities in China. *Journal of Environmental Management, 217,* 47–55. doi:10.1016/j.jenvman.2018.03.091 PMID:29587200

Gergle, D., Kraut, R. E., & Fussell, S. R. (2013). Using visual information for grounding and awareness in collaborative tasks. *Human-Computer Interaction, 28*(1), 1–39.

Gerkin, K. L., Taylor, T. H., & Weatherby, F. M. (2009). The Perception of Learning and Satisfaction of Nurses in the Online Environment. *Journal for Nurses in Staff Development, 25*(1), E8–E13. doi:10.1097/NND.0b013e318194b6a4 PMID:19182548

Gibson, C. B., & Cohen, S. G. (Eds.), *Virtual teams that work: Creating conditions for virtual team effectiveness* (pp. 1–14). San Francisco, CA: Jossey-Bass.

Global Database on Blood Safety (GDBS). (2008). Report 2004-2005. Retrieved August 15, 2017, from http://www.who.int/bloodsafety/global_database/GDBSReport2004-2005.pdf?ua=1

GlobalWebIndex. (2017). *Social summary. Quarterly report on the latest trends in social networking*. Author.

Gniazdowski, A., & Chafetz, R. (2005). Knowledge Management for Mountain Development - Managing Knowledge with Context. *ICIMOD Newsletter, 47*(Winter), 15–18.

Goeldner, C. R., & Ritchie, J. R. B. (2006). *Tourism: Principles, Practices, Philosophies* (10th ed.). John Wiley & Sons, Inc.

Goldie, L. (2007). Social networks build up brand opportunities. *News Analysis, 16.*

Goldsmith, R. E., d'Hauteville, F., & Flynn, L. R. (1998). Theory and Measurement of Consumer Innovativeness. *European Journal of Marketing, 32*(3/4), 340–353. doi:10.1108/03090569810204634

Goldsmith, R. E., & Hofacker, C. H. (1991). Measuring Consumer Innovativeness. *Journal of the Academy of Marketing Science, 19*(3), 209–221. doi:10.1007/BF02726497

Goodhue, D. L., Quillard, J. A., & Rockart, J. F. (1988). Managing the Data Resource: A Contingency Perspective. *Management Information Systems Quarterly, 12*(3), 373–392. doi:10.2307/249204

Goodhue, D. L., & Thompson, R. L. (1995). Task-Technology Fit and Individual Performance. *Management Information Systems Quarterly, 19*(2), 213–236. doi:10.2307/249689

Goodhue, D. L., Wybo, M. D., & Kirsch, L. J. (1992). The Impact of Data Integration on the Costs and Benefits of Information Systems. *Management Information Systems Quarterly, 16*(3), 293–311. doi:10.2307/249530

Gössling, S., Peeters, P., & Scott, D. (2008). Consequences of climate policy for international tourist arrivals in developing countries. *Third World Quarterly, 29*(5), 873–901. doi:10.1080/01436590802106007

Gössling, S., & Scott, D. (2012). Scenario planning for sustainable tourism: An introduction. *Journal of Sustainable Tourism, 20*(6), 773–778. doi:10.1080/09669582.2012.699064

Gothwal, S., & Raj, T. (2018). Prioritising the performance measures of FMS using multi-criteria decision making approaches. *International Journal of Process Management and Benchmarking, 8*(1), 59–78. doi:10.1504/IJPMB.2018.088657

Gottschalk, P. (1999). Strategic information systems planning: The IT strategy implementation matrix. *European Journal of Information Systems, 8*(8), 107–118. doi:10.1057/palgrave.ejis.3000324

Granados, N. (2017). *Gen Z Media Consumption: It's A Lifestyle, Not Just Entertainment.* Retrieved October 4th, 2017, from https://www.forbes.com/sites/nelsongranados/2017/06/20/gen-z-media-consumption-its-a-lifestyle-not-just-entertainment/#15f4a2da18c9

Granovetter, M. D. (2004). The impact of social structures on economic development. *The Journal of Economic Perspectives, 19*(1), 33–50. doi:10.1257/0895330053147958

Granovetter, M. S. (1973). The Strength of Weak Ties. *American Journal of Sociology, 78*(6), 1360–1380. doi:10.1086/225469

Granville, K. (2018). Facebook and Cambridge Analytica: What you need to know as fallout widens. *The New York Times.* Retrieved April 12, 2018 from https://www.nytimes.com/2018/03/19/technology/facebook-cambridge-analytica-explained.html

Great tools to help eBay sellers; expert recommends five tools to determine what items to sell on eBay. (2007). *PS Newswire.* Retrieved October 7, 2017 from http://reddog.rmu.edu:2079/pqdweb?index=1&did=1195547291&SrchMode=1&sid=6&Fmt=3&VInst=PROD&VType=PQD&RQT=309&VName=PQD&TS=1193760199&clientId=2138

Green, B. C., Murray, N., & Warner, S. (2011). Understanding website useability: An eye-tracking study of the Vancouver 2010 Olympic Games website. *International Journal of Sport Management and Marketing, 10*(3/4), 257–271. doi:10.1504/IJSMM.2011.044793

Greenhow, C. (2011). Online social networks and learning. *On the Horizon, 19*(1), 4–12. doi:10.1108/10748121111107663

Grembergen, W. V. (2004). Strategies for Information Technology Governance. Idea Group Publishing. doi:10.4018/978-1-59140-140-7

Greve, H. R. (2003). A Behavioral Theory of R&D Expenditures and Innovations: Evidence from Shipbuilding. *Academy of Management Journal, 46*(6), 685-702.

Griffith, T. L., & Neale, M. A. (2001). Information processing in traditional, hybrid, and virtual teams: From nascent knowledge to transactive memory. *Research in Organizational Behavior, 23*(4), 379–421. doi:10.1016/S0191-3085(01)23009-3

Grunfeld, H. (2011). The Contribution of Information and Communication Technologies for Development (ICT4D) Projects to Capabilities, Empowerment and Sustainability: A Case Study of iREACH in Cambodia [PhD Thesis]. Centre for Strategic Economic Studies, Faculty of Business and Law Victoria University, Melbourne, Australia

GSMS. (n.d.). Retrieved August 15, 2017, from http://www.rug.nl/research/gradschool-medical-sciences/master-programme/

Guha, S., & Daswani, N. (2005, December 16). An experimental study of the Skype Peer-to-Peer VoIP System. Retrieved from http://techreports.library.cornell.edu:8081/Dienst/UI/1.0/Display/cul.cis/TR2005-2011

Gumusluoglu, L., & Karakitapoglu-Aygün, Z. (2010). Bilgi Çalisanlarinin Adalet ve Güçlendirme Algilarinin Örgüte, Lidere ve Ise Baglilik Üzerindeki Etkileri. *Türk Psikoloji Dergisi, 25*(66), 21–36.

Gurau, C. (2012). A life-stage analysis of consumer loyalty profile: Comparing Generation X and Millennial consumers. *Journal of Consumer Marketing, 29*(2), 103–113. doi:10.1108/07363761211206357

Haapaniemi, T., & Mäkinen, S. (2009). Moderating effect of national attributes on the role of cultural dimensions in technology adoption takeoff. *Management Research News, 32*(1), 56–63.

Hadaya, P., & Pellerin, R. (2008). Determinants of manufacturing firms' intent to use web-based systems to share inventory information with their key suppliers. *International Journal of e-Collaboration, 4*(2), 29–54. doi:10.4018/jec.2008040102

Hage, J. (1980). *Theories of Organizations: Form, Process, and Transformation*. Wiley New York.

Hair, J. F. Jr, Hult, G. T. M., Ringle, C., & Sarstedt, M. (2013). *A primer on partial least squares structural equation modeling (PLS-SEM)*. Thousand Oaks, CA: SAGE.

Hallahan, K. (2001). Enhancing motivation, ability, and opportunity to process public relations messages. *Public Relations Review, 26*(4), 463–480. doi:10.1016/S0363-8111(00)00059-X

Hall, E. T. (1976). *Beyond Culture*. Anchor Doubleday Press.

Ham, L. (2011). Chasing a bargain: Who pays? *Media Watch,* 7-8.

Handbook. (2002). *The Clinical Use of Blood*. WHO.

Han, H., Hsu, L. J., Lee, J. S., & Sheu, C. (2011). Are lodging customers ready to go green? An examination of attitude, demographics, and eco-friendly intentions. *International Journal of Hospitality Management, 30*(2), 345–355. doi:10.1016/j.ijhm.2010.07.008

Han, J. H., Wang, Y., & Naim, M. (2017). Reconceptualization of information technology flexibility for supply chain management: An empirical study. *International Journal of Production Economics, 187,* 196–215. doi:10.1016/j.ijpe.2017.02.018

Hansen, R. (2011). How Fashion Brands Learned to Click–A Longitudinal Study of the Adoption of Online Interactive and Social Media by Luxury Fashion Brands. In IRIS (No. 34). Akademika forlag.

Hansen, J. M., & Levin, M. A. (2010). Retail e-learning assessment: Motivation, location, and prior experience. *International Journal of Retail & Distribution Management, 38*(10), 789–805. doi:10.1108/09590551011076551

Hansen, M. T. (1999). The search transfer Problem: The role of weak ties in sharing knowledge across organization subunits. *Administrative Science Quarterly*, *44*(1), 82–112. doi:10.2307/2667032

Hansen, M. T., Nohria, N., & Tierney, T. (1999). What's Your Strategy for Managing Knowledge? *Harvard Business Review*, *77*(2), 106–116. PMID:10387767

Hanseth, O. (2000). The Economics of Standards. In From Control to Drift - The Dynamics of Corporate Information Infrastructures. Oxford University Press.

Hara, N., Solomon, P., Kim, S. L., & Sonnenwald, D. H. (2003). An emerging view of scientific collaboration: Scientists' perspectives on collaboration and factors that impact collaboration. *Journal of the Association for Information Science and Technology*, *54*(10), 952–965.

Harbi, R., Abdelaziz, I., Kalnis, P., Mamoulis, N., Ebrahim, Y., & Sahli, M. (2016). Accelerating SPARQL queries by exploiting hash-based locality and adaptive partitioning. *The VLDB Journal*, *25*(3), 355–380. doi:10.100700778-016-0420-y

Hargittai, E. (2010). Digital na (t) ives? Variation in internet skills and uses among members of the "net generation". *Sociological Inquiry*, *80*(1), 92–113. doi:10.1111/j.1475-682X.2009.00317.x

Hartvigsen, G., & Pedersen, S. (2015). Lessons learned from 25 years with telemedicine in Northern Norway. University Hospital of North Norway Norwegian Centre for Integrated Care and Telemedicine.

Hau, Y. S., Kim, B., Lee, H., & Kim, Y. (2013). The effects of individual motivations and social capital on employees' tacit and explicit knowledge sharing intentions. *International Journal of Information Management*, *33*(2), 356–366. doi:10.1016/j.ijinfomgt.2012.10.009

Hazan, C. (2010). Definition of a Methodology for Development the ITSP based on Zach Framework. *WCGE*.

Hearit, K. M. (2006). *Crisis management by apology: Corporate response to allegations of wrongdoing*. New Jersey: Lawrence Erlbaum Associates.

Hearn, S., & White, N. (2009). *Communities of practice: linking knowledge, policy and practice*. UK: Overseas Development Institute.

Hebden, L., Cook, A., van der Ploeg, H. P., King, L., Bauman, A., & Allman-Farinelli, M. (2013). A mobile health intervention for weight management among young adults: A pilot randomised controlled trial. *Journal of Human Nutrition and Dietetics*, *27*(4), 322–332. doi:10.1111/jhn.12155 PMID:23992038

Heeks, R. (2006). *Implementing and Managing eGovernment: An international text*. London: SAGE Publications.

Heiner, R. A. (1983). The Origin of Predictable Behavior. *The American Economic Review*, *73*(4), 560-595.

Heiskanen, E., Lovio, R., & Jalas, M. (2011). Path creation for sustainable consumption: Promoting alternative heating systems in Finland. *Journal of Cleaner Production*, *19*(16), 1892–1900. doi:10.1016/j.jclepro.2011.02.005

Helland, K. (2007). Changing sports, changing media: Mass appeal, the sports/media complex and TV sports rights. *Nordicom Review*, *28*(2), 105–119.

Helsper, E. J. (2008). *Digital Inclusion: An Analysis of Social Disadvantage and the Information Society*. Queen's Printer and Controller of Her Majesty's Stationery Office.

Heltai, G. (2016). *What Millennials' YouTube Usage Tells Us about the Future of Video Viewership*. Retrieved October 4th, 2017, from https://www.comscore.com/ita/Insights/Blog/What-Millennials-YouTube-Usage-Tells-Us-about-the-Future-of-Video-Viewership

Hemsley, J., & Mason, R. M. (2012, January). The Nature of Knowledge in the Social Media Age: Implications for Knowledge Management Models. In *2012 45ᵗʰ Hawaii International Conference on System Science (HICSS)* (pp. 3928-3937). IEEE.

Hendriks, P. (1999). Why share knowledge? The influence of ICT on the motivation for knowledge sharing. *Knowledge and Process Management, 6*(2), 91–100. doi:10.1002/(SICI)1099-1441(199906)6:2<91::AID-KPM54>3.0.CO;2-M

Henfridsson, O., Yoo, Y., & Svahn, F. (2009). *Path Creation in Digital Innovation: A Multi-Layered Dialectics Perspective.* Sprout Working papers on Information Systems. Retrieved from http://sprouts.aisnet.org/9-20

Henfridsson, O., & Bygstad, B. (2013). The generative mechanisms of digital infrastructure evolution. *Management Information Systems Quarterly, 37*(3), 907–931. doi:10.25300/MISQ/2013/37.3.11

Hennigs, N., Wiedmann, K. P., & Klarmann, D. O. C. (2012). Luxury brands in the digital age–exclusivity versus ubiquity. *Marketing Review St. Gallen, 29*(1), 30–35. doi:10.100711621-012-0108-7

Henseler, J., Ringle, C. M., & Sinkovics, R. R. (2009). The use of partial least squares path modeling in international marketing. *Advances in International Marketing, 20*, 277-319.

Hernández, G. J. J., García, G. M. J., & Hernández, R. J. G. (2014). Fantasy Leagues and Decision making under uncertainty. An approach. Proceedings, 15th Applied Stochastic Models and Data Analysis (ASMDA2013), 415-427.

Hernández, G. J. J., García, G. M. J., Hernández, G. G. J., & Hernández, R. J. G. (2014). Fantastic Sport Leagues and Matrixes Of Weighing. Document presented in Optimization 2014 Conference, Guimaraes, Portugal.

Hernández, J. G., García, M. J., & Hernández, G. J. (2012). Dynamic knowledge: Diagnosis and Customer Service. In Service Science Research, Strategy, and Innovation: Dynamic Knowledge Management Methods. IGI Global.

Hernández, R. J. G., García, G. M. J., & Hernández, G. G. J. (2011). Matrixes Of Weighing and catastrophes. *International Journal of Distributed Systems and Technologies, 2*(1), 14–28. doi:10.4018/jdst.2011010102

Herodotou, H., Lim, H., Luo, G., Borisov, N., Dong, L., Cetin, F. B., & Babu, S. (2011, January). Starfish: A Self-tuning System for Big Data Analytics. CIDR, 11, 261-272.

Herodotou, H., Dong, F., & Babu, S. (2011). Mapreduce programming and cost-based optimization? crossing this chasm with starfish. *Proceedings of the VLDB Endowment International Conference on Very Large Data Bases, 4*(12), 1446–1449.

Higgins, J. M. (1995). Innovation: The core competence. *Strategy and Leadership, 23*(6), 32–36.

Higuchi, S. (2013). *Net Dependency.* PHP Laboratory. (in Japanese)

Hiltz, S. R., & Wellman, B. (1997). Asynchronous learning networks as a virtual classroom. *Communications of the ACM, 40*(9), 44–49. doi:10.1145/260750.260764

Hinds, P. J., & Weisband, S. P. (2003). Knowledge sharing and shared understanding in virtual teams. In C. B. Gibson & S. G. Cohen (Eds.), *Virtual teams that work: Creating conditions for virtual team effectiveness* (pp. 21–36). San Francisco, CA: Jossey-Bass.

Hislop, D. (2008). Conceptualizing Knowledge Work Utilizing Skill and Knowledge-based Concepts the Case of Some Consultants and Service Engineers. *Management Learning, 35*(5), 579–596. doi:10.1177/1350507608098116

Hofstede, G., & Hofstede, G. J. (2005). Cultures and organizations. Software of the mind (2nd ed.). New York, NY: McGraw-Hill.

Hofstede, G. (1984). *Culture's Consequences: International Differences in Work-related Values.* Sage Publications.

Hofstede, G. (1991). *Culture and organization: Software of mind*. London, UK: McGraw-Hill.

Hofstede, G. (1994). *Values survey module 1994 manual*. Maastricht, The Netherlands: Institute of Research On Intercultural Cooperation.

Hofstede, G. (2001). *Culture's consequences: Comparing values, behaviors, institutions, and organizations across nations*. Thousand Oaks, CA: Sage.

Hofstede, G., & Bond, M. H. (1988). The Confucius connection: From cultural roots to economic growth. *Organizational Dynamics, 16*(4), 4–21. doi:10.1016/0090-2616(88)90009-5

Hofstede, G., Hofstede, G. J., & Minkov, M. (2010). *Cultures and organizations: Software of the mind* (3rd ed.). New York, NY: McGraw-Hill.

Hollenbeck, J. R., & Jamieson, B. B. (2015). Human Capital, Social Capital, and Social Network Analysis: Implications for Strategic Human Resource Management. *The Academy of Management Perspectives, 29*(3), 370–385. doi:10.5465/amp.2014.0140

Hong E. K. (2009). Information Technology Strategic Planning. *IT Professional, 11*(6).

Hong, S., & Tam, K. Y. (2006). Understanding the Adoption of Multipurpose Information Appliances: The Case of Mobile Data Services. *Information Systems Research, 17*(2), 162–179. doi:10.1287/isre.1060.0088

Hongwei, W., Yuan, M., & Wei, W. (2013). The role of perceived interactivity in virtual communities: Building trust and increasing stickiness. *Connection Science, 25*(1), 55–73. doi:10.1080/09540091.2013.824407

Hootsuite. (2017). *Digital in 2017 Global Overview. A Collection of Internet, Social Medial, and Mobile Data from around the World*. Retrieved September 20th, 2017, from https://hootsuite.com/fr/newsroom/press-releases/digital-in-2017-report

Hope, T. G. (2009, December 16). Damas says it must restructure, delay debt payments to survive. *The National*. Retrieved from http://www.thenational.ae/business/banking/damas-says-it-must-restructure-delay-debt-payments-to-survive

Hopp, W. J., & Spearman, M. L. (2008). *Factory physics*. New York: McGraw Hill.

Hoq, K. M. G., & Akter, R. (2012). Knowledge management in universities: Role of knowledge workers. *Bangladesh Journal of Library and Information Science, 2*(1), 92–102. doi:10.3329/bjlis.v2i1.12925

Horng, J. S., Hu, M. L., Teng, C. C., Hsiao, H. L., & Liu, C. H. (2013). Development and validation of the low-carbon literacy scale among practitioners in the Taiwanese tourism industry. *Tourism Management, 35*, 255–262. doi:10.1016/j.tourman.2012.08.001

Horng, J. S., Hu, M. L., Teng, C. C., Hsiao, H. L., Tsai, C. Y., & Liu, C. H. (2014b). How the introduction of concepts of energy saving and carbon reduction (ESCR) can affect festival visitors' behavioural intentions: An investigation using a structural model. *Journal of Sustainable Tourism, 22*(8), 1216–1235. doi:10.1080/09669582.2014.884100

Horng, J. S., Hu, M. L., Teng, C. C., & Lin, L. (2012). Energy saving and carbon reduction management indicators for natural attractions: A case study in Taiwan. *Journal of Sustainable Tourism, 20*(8), 1125–1149. doi:10.1080/0966958 2.2012.663380

Horng, J. S., Hu, M. L., Teng, C. C., & Lin, L. (2014a). Energy saving and carbon reduction behaviors in tourism - A perception study of Asian visitors from a Protection Motivation Theory perspective. *Asia Pacific Journal of Tourism Research, 19*(6), 721–735. doi:10.1080/10941665.2013.797002

Horrigan, J. B. (2001). *Online communities: Networks that nurture long-distance relationships and local ties*. Pew Internet & American Life Project.

Hossain, L., & Wigand, R. T. (2004). ICT enabled virtual collaboration through trust. *Journal of Computer-Mediated Communication, 10*(1).

Hossain, M. M., & Prybutok, V. R. (2008). Consumer acceptance of RFID technology: An exploratory study. *Engineering Management. IEEE Transactions on, 55*(2), 316–328.

Hossain, M. S., & Hossain, M. M. (2018). Application of interactive fuzzy goal programming for multi-objective integrated production and distribution planning. *International Journal of Process Management and Benchmarking, 8*(1), 35–58. doi:10.1504/IJPMB.2018.088656

Howell, N. (2009). If click-through isn't a measure, what's engagement? *New Media Age, 2.*

Hsiao, T.-Y., Sung, P.-L., & Lu, C.-Y. (2017). International tourists purchase intention towards low-carbon tour packages. *Journal of Tourism. Hospitality & Culinary Arts, 9*(3), 1–13.

Hsu, P. F., Yen, H. R., & Chung, J. C. (2015). ERP system quality, information quality, and service quality, user satisfaction, users' individual benefits. *Information & Management, 52*(8), 925–942. doi:10.1016/j.im.2015.06.009

Huang, H. C., Lin, T. H., Lai, M. C., & Lin, T. L. (2014). Environmental consciousness and green customer behavior: An examination of motivation crowding effect. *International Journal of Hospitality Management, 40*, 139–149. doi:10.1016/j.ijhm.2014.04.006

Huang, M. C., Chiu, Y. P., & Lu, T. C. (2013). Knowledge governance mechanisms and repatriate's knowledge sharing: The mediating roles of motivation and opportunity. *Journal of Knowledge Management, 17*(5), 677–694. doi:10.1108/JKM-01-2013-0048

Huang, X., Radkowski, P., & Roman, P. (2007). Computer crimes. *The American Criminal Law Review, 44*(2), 285–335.

Huang, Z. M., & Cai, S. (2005). Developing Medium and Small Technological Enterprises in China: Informatization Issues and Counter-Measures. *International Journal of Enterprise Information Systems, 1*(4), 20–38. doi:10.4018/jeis.2005100102

Hu, B., Meng, C., Xu, D., & Son, Y.-J. (2016). Three-echelon supply chain coordination with a loss-averse retailer and revenue sharing contracts. *International Journal of Production Economics, 179*, 192–202. doi:10.1016/j.ijpe.2016.06.001

Hu, G., Wang, L., Fetch, S., & Bidanda, B. (2008). A multi-objective model for project portfolio selection to implement lean and Six Sigma concepts. *International Journal of Production Research, 46*(23), 6611–6648. doi:10.1080/00207540802230363

Hu, M. L., Horng, J. S., Teng, C. C., & Chou, S. F. (2012). Exploring the energy-saving and carbon reduction literacy of restaurant employees. In M. Kasimoglu & H. Aydin (Eds.), *Strategies for Tourism Industry - Micro and Macro Perspectives* (pp. 313–326). InTech. doi:10.5772/38271

Humphrey, W. S. (1988). Characterizing the software process: A maturity framework. *IEEE Software, 56*(2), 73–79. doi:10.1109/52.2014

Hung, K., & Petrick, J. F. (2012). Comparing constraints to cruising between cruisers and non-cruisers: A test of the constraint-effects-mitigation model. *Journal of Travel & Tourism Marketing, 29*(3), 242–262. doi:10.1080/10548408.2012.666171

Hurt, H. T., Joseph, K., & Cook, C. D. (1977). Scales for the Measurement of Innovativeness. *Human Communication Research, 4*(1), 58–65. doi:10.1111/j.1468-2958.1977.tb00597.x

Hussain, I., Ahmed, S., & Si, S. (2010). Personal knowledge abilities and knowledge management success. *Journal of Information and Knowledge Management, 9*(4), 319–327. doi:10.1142/S021964921000270X

Hutchins, B. (2011). The acceleration of media sport culture. *Information Communication and Society, 14*(2), 237–257. doi:10.1080/1369118X.2010.508534

Hutchinson, S. (2013). *Performance management theory and practice.* London, UK: Chartered Institute of Personnel and Development.

Huysman, M., & Wulf, V. (2006). IT to support knowledge sharing in communities, towards a social capital analysis. *Journal of Information Technology, 21*(1), 40–51. doi:10.1057/palgrave.jit.2000053

Hwang, K. M., & Lee, S. J. (2016). How does electronic data interchange (EDI) affect the competitiveness of a firm's supply chain management? *Journal of Marketing Thought, 3*(2), 13–18.

Hwang, Y. (2005). Investigating enterprising systems adoption: Uncertainty avoidance, intrinsic motivation, and the technology acceptance model. *European Journal of Information Systems, 14*(2), 150–161. doi:10.1057/palgrave.ejis.3000532

Hyatt, C. G., Sutton, W. A., Foster, W. M., & McConnell, D. (2013). Fan involvement in a professional sport team's decision making. *Sport, Business and Management. International Journal (Toronto, Ont.), 3*(3), 189–204.

Iacono, C. S., & Weisband, S. (1997, January). Developing trust in virtual teams. *Paper presented at the annual Hawaii International Conference on Systems Science*, Maui, HI.

Ibarra, H., & Andrews, S. B. (1993). Power, social influence, and sense making: Effects of network centrality and proximity on employee perceptions. *Administrative Science Quarterly, 38*(2), 277–303. doi:10.2307/2393414

Iconosquare Index Brand. (2017). *Top Brands.* Retrieved September 20th, 2017, from https://index.iconosquare.com/category/luxury

INPES (French National Health Prevention and Education Institute). (2007). Le tabac tue un fumeur sur deux. L'industrie du tabac compte sur vous pour les remplacer. *Espace Presse.* Retrieved April 4, 2015 from: www.inpes.sante.fr/70000/cp/07/cp070820.asp

Internet World Stats. (2017). *Top 20 Countries with the Highest Number of Internet Users.* Retrieved September 20th, 2017, from http://www.internetworldstats.com/top20.htm

IPSOS. (2017). *Génération Z, les nouveaux partenaires de consommation.* Retrieved September 20th, 2017, from https://www.ipsos.com/fr-fr/generation-z-les-nouveaux-partenaires-de-consommation

ISACA. (2012). *COBIT 5. Corporate Model for IT Governance and Management of the Organization.* ISACA.

ITSP BH. (2010). *Information Technology Strategic Plan.* Available at: http://itsp.pph.com.br

Jackson, E. L., & Dunn, E. (1988). Integrating ceasing participation with other aspects of leisure behavior. *Journal of Leisure Research, 20*(1), 31–45. doi:10.1080/00222216.1988.11969755

Jacobs, R. L. (2017). Knowledge work and human resource development. *Human Resource Development Review, 16*(2), 176–202. doi:10.1177/1534484317704293

Jaffie, B. (2009). Getting more bang for your marketing buck – leveraging technology to help your effectiveness. *Proofs*, 62-63.

Jain, N., & D'lima, C. (2018). Organisational culture preference for gen Y's prospective job aspirants: A personality-culture fit perspective. *International Journal of Process Management and Benchmarking, 7*(2), 262–275. doi:10.1504/IJPMB.2017.083122

Jain, V., Benyoucef, L., & Deshmukh, S. G. (2008). What's the buzz about moving from 'lean' to 'agile' integrated supply chains? A fuzzy intelligent agent-based approach. *International Journal of Production Research*, *46*(23), 6649–6678. doi:10.1080/00207540802230462

Jang, S., & Wu, C. M. (2006). Seniors' travel motivation and the influential factors: An examination of Taiwanese seniors. *Tourism Management*, *27*(2), 306–316. doi:10.1016/j.tourman.2004.11.006

Japan Internet Safety Promotion Association. (2010). *Mobile family Mobami*. Press release. Retrieved from http://good-net.jp/modules/news/uploadFile/2010020334.pdf (in Japanese)

Japan Internet Safety Promotion Association. (2015). *ILAS2015 Final Report*. Japan Internet Safety Promotion Association. (in Japanese)

Jarvenpaa, S. L., Knoll, K., & Leidner, D. E. (1998). Is anybody out there? Antecedents of trust in global virtual teams. *Journal of Management Information Systems*, *14*(4), 29–64. doi:10.1080/07421222.1998.11518185

Jassbi, J. J., Ribeiro, R. A., & Dargam, F. (2014). Dynamic MCDM for Multi Group Decision Making. In *Joint International Conference on Group Decision and Negotiation*. Springer. 10.1007/978-3-319-07179-4_10

Jemielniak, D. (2012). *The new knowledge workers*. Cheltenham, UK: Edward Elgar Publishing. doi:10.4337/9780857933119

Jeney, A. (2014). *Impacto del Gerente de Sistemas de Información y Redes del Modelo Logístico Basado en Cargos en la gestión del conocimiento de una organización, medido a través de una Matriz De Ponderación. Disertación Maestría en Gerencia de sistemas*. Caracas, Venezuela: Universidad Metropolitana.

Jenkins, J. J. (2014). The diversity paradox: Seeking community in an intercultural church. New York: Lexington.

Jenkins, J. J. (2012). Engaging the internet generation: An experiential analysis of the world's wealthiest nonprofit organizations. *Florida Communication Journal*, *40*(1), 17–28.

Jenkins, M., & Hanson, J. (2003). *E-learning Series: A Guide for Senior Managers, Learning and Teaching Support Network (LSTN)*. Generic Centre.

Jennex, M. E., Smolnik, S., & Croasdell, D. (2016). The search for knowledge management success. *Paper presented at the 49th Hawaii International Conference on System Sciences*, Koloa, HI. doi:10.1109/HICSS.2016.521

Jennex, M. E., Smolnik, S., & Croasdell, D. T. (2009). Towards a consensus knowledge management success definition. *Vine*, *39*(2), 174–188. doi:10.1108/03055720910988878

Jennex, M., & Olfman, L. (2005). Assessing knowledge management success. *International Journal of Knowledge Management*, *1*(2), 33–49. doi:10.4018/jkm.2005040104

Jenning, J. (2017). Generation Z: Two billion people coming of age. *Business Today*. Retrieved September 20th, 2017, from http://www.businesstoday.co.om/Issues/Top-companies-on-MSM/Generation-Z-Two-billion-people-coming-of-age

Jiang, K., Lepak, D. P., Hu, J., & Baer, J. C. (2012). How does human resource management influence organizational outcomes? A meta-analytic investigation of mediating mechanisms. *Academy of Management Journal*, *55*(6), 1264–1294. doi:10.5465/amj.2011.0088

Jia, Q., Guo, Y., & Barnes, S. (2017). Enterprise 2.0 post-adoption: Extending the information system continuance model based on the technology-Organization-environment framework. *Computers in Human Behavior*, *67*, 95–105. doi:10.1016/j.chb.2016.10.022

Johansson, B., & Newman, M. (2010). Competitive advantage in the ERP system's value-chain and its influence on future development. *Enterprise Information Systems*, *4*(1), 79–93. doi:10.1080/17517570903040196

Jones, C. M., McCarthy, R. V., & Halawi, L. (2010). Utilizing technology acceptance model to assess the employee adoption of information systems security measures. *Journal of International Technology and Information Management, 19*(2), 43.

Jones, E. C., & Chung, C. A. (2006). A methodology for measuring engineering knowledge worker productivity. *Engineering Management Journal, 18*(1), 32–38. doi:10.1080/10429247.2006.11431682

Jones, P., Clarke-Hill, C., Hillier, D., & Comfort, D. (2005). The benefits, challenges and impacts of radio frequency identification technology (RFID) for retailers in the UK. *Marketing Intelligence & Planning, 23*(4), 395–402. doi:10.1108/02634500510603492

Juels, A., Rivest, R. L., & Szydlo, M. (2003). The blocker tag: Selective blocking of RFID tags for consumer privacy. *Proceedings of the 10th ACM conference on Computer and communications security.* 10.1145/948109.948126

Juvan, E., & Dolnicar, S. (2014). Can tourists easily choose a low carbon footprint vacation? *Journal of Sustainable Tourism, 22*(2), 175–194. doi:10.1080/09669582.2013.826230

Jyoti, J., & Rani, A. (2017). High performance work system and organisational performance: Role of knowledge management. *Personnel Review, 46*(8), 1770–1795. doi:10.1108/PR-10-2015-0262

Kalakota, R., & Robinsion, M. (2001). e-Business: Road map for Success (2nd ed.). Boston: Addison Wesley.

Kalman, M. E., Monge, P., Fulk, J., & Heino, R. (2002). Motivations to resolve communication dilemmas in database-mediated collaboration. *Communication Research, 29*(2), 125–155. doi:10.1177/0093650202029002002

Kamel, S & Abouseif, M. (2015). *A study of the role and impact of cloud computing on small and medium size enterprises (SMEs) in Egypt.* Microsoft Corporation.

Kamel, S & Tooma, E. (2005). *Exchanging debt for development: lessons from the Egyptian debt-for-development swap experience.* Cairo: Economic Research Forum and Ministry of Communications and Information Technology, September.

Kamel, S. (2014b). Egypt's ongoing uprising and the role of social media: is there development? *Journal of Information Technology for Development, 20*, 78-91.

Kamel, S. (1998a). Building the African information infrastructure. In P. Banerjee, R. Hackney, G. Dhillon, & R. Jain (Eds.), *Business Information Technology Management: Closing the International Divide* (pp. 118–144). New Delhi: Har-Anand Publications.

Kamel, S. (1998b). Building an information highway. *Proceedings of the 31st Hawaii International Conference on System Sciences,* 31-41.

Kamel, S. (2005a). Assessing the impacts of establishing an internet café in the context of a developing nation. *Proceedings of the 16th International Information Resources Management Association conference on managing modern organizations with information technology,* 176-181.

Kamel, S. (2005b). *The evolution of information and communication technology infrastructure in Egypt.* In G. Hunter & A. Wenn (Eds.), *Information Systems in an e-World* (pp. 117–135). The Information Institute.

Kamel, S. (2007). *The evolution of the ICT industry in Egypt.* In A. Ahmed (Ed.), *Science, Technology and Sustainability in the Middle East and North Africa* (pp. 65–79). Brighton, UK: Interscience Enterprises Limited.

Kamel, S. (2014a). The value of social media in Egypt's uprising and beyond. *The Electronic Journal on Information Systems in Developing Countries, 60*(5), 1–7. doi:10.1002/j.1681-4835.2014.tb00426.x

Kamel, S. (2016). Startup, *Global Focus. The European Foundation for Management Development Business Magazine, 10*(3), 52–55.

Kandampully, J. (2002). Innovation as the core competence of a service organisation: The role of technology, knowledge and networks. *European Journal of Innovation Management, 5*(1), 18–26. doi:10.1108/14601060210415144

Kang, S. C., Morris, S. S., & Snell, S. A. (2003). Extending the Human Resource Architecture: Relational Archetypes and Value Creation (working paper). CAHRS'.

Kankanhalli, A., Tan, B. C., & Wei, K. K. (2005). Contributing knowledge to electronic knowledge repositories: An empirical investigation. *Management Information Systems Quarterly, 29*(1), 113–143. doi:10.2307/25148670

Kapferer, J. N. (2012). *The luxury strategy: Break the rules of marketing to build luxury brands.* Kogan Page Publishers.

Kapferer, J. N., & Bastien, V. (2009). The specificity of luxury management: Turning marketing upside down. *Journal of Brand Management, 16*(5), 311–322. doi:10.1057/bm.2008.51

Kaplan, B. (1998). *Social Interactionist Framework for Information Systems Studies: The 4Cs IFIPWG8.2&WG8.6 Joint Working Conference on Information Systems: Current Issues and Future Changes.* International Federation for Information Processing.

Kaplan, A. M., & Haenlein, M. (2010). Users of the world, unite! The challenges and opportunities of social media. *Business Horizons, 53*(1), 59–68. doi:10.1016/j.bushor.2009.09.003

Karp, A. (2012). *Final ratings: Major League Soccer on pace for best season on ESPN; Strong first year on NBCSN.* Retrieved March 1, 2018 from http://m.sportsbusinessdaily.com/Daily/Issues/2012/07/20/Media/Final-Ratings.aspx

Karpova, E., Correia, A., & Baran, E. (2008). Learn to use and use to learn: Technology in a virtual collaboration experience. *The Internet and Higher Education, 12*(4), 45–52.

Katz v. United States - 389 U.S. 347; 347 - 373 (1967).

Kaur, K. (2015). Teacher motivation: A theoretical perspective. *Indian Streams Research Journal, 5*(2), 1–4.

Kavoussi, B. (2013). *Ikea Horse Meat Controversy Hurts Company's Reputation: Analysis. The Huffington Post.*

Ke, J., Sun, J., Shi, J., & Gu, Q. (2007). The Empirical Research on the Relation between Social Capital and Team Performance in the R&D Department: The Mediating Role of Knowledge Sharing and Knowledge Integration. *Management World, 3*, 89–102.

Kellerman, B. (2006). When should a leader apologize and when not? *Harvard Business Review, 84*(4), 73–81. PMID:16579415

Kelloway, E. K., & Barling, J. (2000). Knowledge work as organizational behavior. *International Journal of Management Reviews, 2*(3), 287–304. doi:10.1111/1468-2370.00042

Kennedy, F. A., & Widener, S. K. (2008). A control framework: Insights from evidence on lean accounting. *Management Accounting Research, 19*(4), 301–319. doi:10.1016/j.mar.2008.01.001

Kennedy, G. E., Judd, T. S., Churchward, A., Gray, K., & Krause, K. L. (2008). First year students' experiences with technology: Are they really digital natives? *Australasian Journal of Educational Technology, 24*(1). doi:10.14742/ajet.1233

Kent, M. T. (2007). Taxonomy of mediated crisis responses. *Public Relations Review, 33*(2), 140–146.

Khetrapal, A., & Ganesh, V. (2006). *HBase and Hypertable for large scale distributed storage systems.* Dept. of Computer Science, Purdue University; doi:10.1145/1376616.1376726

Kietzmann, J. H., Hermkens, K., McCarthy, I. P., & Silvestre, B. S. (2011). Social media? Get serious! Understanding the functional building blocks of social media. *Business Horizons, 54*(3), 241–251. doi:10.1016/j.bushor.2011.01.005

Kihyun, K., Gyenung-Min, K., & Eun Sook, K. (2009). Measuring the Compatibility Factors in Mobile Entertainment Service Adoption. *Journal of Computer Information Systems*, (Fall): 141–148.

Kim, A. J. (2000). *Community building on the web: Secret strategies for successful online communities*. Berkeley, CA: Peachpit Press.

Kim, A. J., & Ko, E. (2012). Do social media marketing activities enhance customer equity? An empirical study of luxury fashion brand. *Journal of Business Research*, *65*(10), 1480–1486. doi:10.1016/j.jbusres.2011.10.014

Kimberly, J. R., & Evanisko, M. J. (1981). Organizational Innovation: The Influence of Individual, Organizational, and Contextual Factors on Hospital Adoption of Technological and Administrative Innovations. *Academy of Management Journal*, *24*(4), 689-713.

King, W. R., & He, J. (2006). A meta-analysis of the technology acceptance model. *Information & Management*, *43*(6), 740–755. doi:10.1016/j.im.2006.05.003

Kirat, M. (2007). Promoting Online Media Relations: Public Relations Departments' Use of Internet in the UAE. *Public Relations Review*, *33*(2), 166–174. doi:10.1016/j.pubrev.2007.02.003

Kirat, M. (2012). *Crisis Management Strategies*. Sharjah: University of Sharjah.

Kirat, M. (2012). *Dubai Police PR Management: Strategy of Almabhouh Assassination Crisis*. University of Sharjah.

Kirkham, B. L., Rosen, B. M., Gibson, C. B., Tesluk, P. E., & McPherson, S. O. (2002). Five challenges to virtual team success: Lessons from Sabre Inc. *The Academy of Management Executive*, *16*(3), 67–79.

Klein, J., & Barrett, B. (2001). One foot in a global team, one foot at the local site: Making sense out of living in two worlds simultaneously. In M. Beyerlein (Ed.), *Advances in interdisciplinary studies of work teams: Virtual teams* (Vol. 8, pp. 107–125). Stamford, CT: JAI. doi:10.1016/S1572-0977(01)08021-9

Klein, R. (2005). Customization and real time information access in integrated eBusiness supply chain relationships. *Journal of Operations Management*, *25*(6), 1366–1381. doi:10.1016/j.jom.2007.03.001

Klein, R., & Rai, A. (2009). Inter-firm strategic information flows in logistics supply chain relationships. *Management Information Systems Quarterly*, *33*(4), 735–762. doi:10.2307/20650325

Kobayashi, N. (2011). *Cases of Social Media Flame Incidents*. Nikkei Digital Marketing. (in Japanese)

Kock, N. (2000). Benefits for virtual organizations from distributed groups. *Communications of the ACM*, *43*(11), 107–112. doi:10.1145/353360.353372

Kock, N. (2005). Using action research to study e-collaboration. *International Journal of e-Collaboration*, *1*(4), i–vii.

Kock, N. (2008). E-collaboration and e-commerce in virtual worlds: The potential of Second Life and World of Warcraft. *International Journal of e-Collaboration*, *4*(3), 1–13. doi:10.4018/jec.2008070101

Kock, N. (2010). Using WarpPLS in e-collaboration studies: An overview of five main analysis steps. *International Journal of e-Collaboration*, *6*(4), 1–11. doi:10.4018/jec.2010100101

Kock, N. (2013). Using WarpPLS in e-collaboration studies: What if I have only one group and one condition? *International Journal of e-Collaboration*, *9*(3), 1–12. doi:10.4018/jec.2013070101

Koenigstorfer, J., & Groeppel-Klein, A. (2012). Consumer Acceptance of the Mobile Internet. *Marketing Letters*, *23*(4), 917–928. doi:10.100711002-012-9206-1

Kompaso, S. M., & Sridevi, M. S. (2010). Employee engagement: The key to improving performance. *International Journal of Business and Management, 5*(12). doi:10.5539/ijbm.v5n12p89

Konradt, U., & Hoch, J. E. (2007). A work roles and leadership functions of managers in virtual teams. *International Journal of e-Collaboration, 3*(2), 16–35. doi:10.4018/jec.2007040102

Konstantinou, E., & Fincham, R. (2010). Not sharing but trading: Applying a Maussian exchange framework to knowledge management. *Human Relations, 64*(6), 823–842. doi:10.1177/0018726710388676

Kooper, M. N., Maes, R., & Roos Lindgreen, E. E. O. (2011). On the governance of information: Introducing a new concept of governance to support the management of information. *International Journal of Information Management, 31*(3), 195–200. doi:10.1016/j.ijinfomgt.2010.05.009

Kosoff, M. (2016). *Dozens of teenagers told us what's cool in 2016 — these are their favorite (and least favorite) apps.* Retrieved October 4th, 2017, from:www.businessinsider.com/teens-favorite-apps-in-2016-2016-1+&cd=1&hl=fr&ct=clnk&gl=fr&client=firefox-b

Kosonen, M., Gan, C., Vanhala, M., & Blomqvist, K. (2014). User Motivation and Knowledge sharing in Idea Crowdsource. *International Journal of Innovation Management, 18.*

Kothari, R. (1979). *The North-South Issue.* Mazingria.

Kothe, E. J., & Mullan, B. A. (2014). A randomised controlled trial of a theory of planned behavior to increase fruit and vegetable consumption. *Fresh Facts Appetite, 78*, 68–75. doi:10.1016/j.appet.2014.03.006 PMID:24656949

Kotler, P., & Armstrong, G. (2006). *Principles of Marketing* (11th ed.). Pearson Prentice-hall.

Kotz, D., Brown, J., & West, R. (2014, March). "Real-world" effectiveness of smoking cessation treatments: A population study. *Addiction (Abingdon, England), 109*(3), 491–499. doi:10.1111/add.12429 PMID:24372901

Krebs, P., & Duncan, D. T. (2015, November). Health app use among US mobile phone owners: A national survey. *JMIR mHealth and uHealth, 3*(4), e101. doi:10.2196/mhealth.4924 PMID:26537656

Krishnan, S., Teo, T. S. H., & Lymm, J. (2017). Determinants of electronic participation and electronic government maturity: Insights from cross-country data. *International Journal of Information Management, 37*(4), 297–312. doi:10.1016/j.ijinfomgt.2017.03.002

Kristianto, Y., Gunasekaran, A., Helo, P., & Sandhu, M. (2012). A decision support system for integrating manufacturing and product design into the reconfiguration of the supply chain networks. *Decision Support Systems, 52*(4), 790–801. doi:10.1016/j.dss.2011.11.014

Krivak, T. (2008). Facebook 101: Ten things you need to know about Facebook. *Information Today, 25*(3), 42-44.

Krolikowski, M., & Yuan, X. (2017). Friend or foe: Customer-supplier relationships and innovation. *Journal of Business Research, 78*, 53–68. doi:10.1016/j.jbusres.2017.04.023

Kuan, K. K. Y., & Chau, P. Y. K. (2001). A Perception-Based Model for Edi Adoption in Small Businesses Using a Technology-Organization-Environment Framework. *Information & Management, 38*(8), 507-521.

Kukard, W. A. (2015). *Consumers' Perception of Item-level RFID Use in FMCG: A Balanced Perspective of Benefits and Risks* (PhD dissertation). Auckland University of Technology.

Kukard, W. A., & Wood, L. C. (2017). Consumer's perceptions of item-level RIFD use in FMCG: A balanced perspective of benefits and risks. *Journal of Global Information Management, 27*(1), 21–42. doi:10.4018/JGIM.2017010102

Kuo, N. W., & Dai, Y. Y. (2012). Applying the Theory of Planned Behavior to predict low-carbon tourism behavior: A modified model from Taiwan. *International Journal of Technology and Human Interaction, 8*(4), 44–61. doi:10.4018/jthi.2012100103

Kuo, N. W., & Dai, Y. Y. (2015). Predicting low-carbon travel behavior: A modified Theory of Planned Behavior model from Taiwan. In A. M. DeMarco (Ed.), *Strategic E-Commerce Systems and Tools for Competing in the Digital Marketplace*. IGI Global. doi:10.4018/978-1-4666-8133-0.ch005

Kuo, T. H. (2011). How to improve organizational performance through learning and knowledge? *International Journal of Manpower, 32*(5/6), 581–603. doi:10.1108/01437721111158215

L2 Digital IQ Index. (2016). *Digital IQ Index Fashion 2016.* Author.

Lai, I. K. W. (2006). The critical success factors across ERP implementation models: An empirical study in China. *International Journal of Enterprise Information Systems, 2*(3), 24–42. doi:10.4018/jeis.2006070103

Lair, D. J., Sullivan, K., & Cheney, G. (2005). Marketization and the recasting of the professional self: The rhetoric and ethics of personal branding. *Management Communication Quarterly, 18*(3), 307–343. doi:10.1177/0893318904270744

Lakon, C. M., Pechmann, C., Cheng, W., Li, P., Delucchi, K., & Prochaska, J. J. (2016). Mapping Engagement in Twitter-Based Support Networks for Adult Smoking Cessation. *American Journal of Public Health, 106*(8), 1374–1380. doi:10.2105/AJPH.2016.303256 PMID:27310342

Lakshman, A., & Malik, P. (2009). Cassandra: A structured storage system on a p2p network. In *Proceedings of the twenty-first annual symposium on Parallelism in algorithms and architectures* (pp. 47–47). ACM. 10.1145/1583991.1584009

Landsteiner, K. (1901). Uber Agglutinationsverscheinungen normalen menschlichen Blutes. *Wiener Klinische Wochenschrift, 14*, 1132.

Lanfranchi, M., Giannetto, C., & De Pascale, A. (2016). Information asymmetry on RFID system in the agrifood sector: A study of consumer behaviour. *Calitatea: Acces La Success, 17*(151), 73–77.

Lansing, P., & Hubbard, J. (2002). Online auctions: The need for alternative dispute resolution. *American Business Review, 20*(1), 108–115.

Lapointe, L., & Rivard, S. (2005). A Multilevel Model of Resistance to Information Technology Implementation. *MIS Quarterly, 29*(3), 461-492.

Larkin, B., & Fink, J. (2016). Fantasy Sport, FoMO, and Traditional Fandom: How second-screen use of social media allows fans to accommodate multiple identities. *Journal of Sport Management, 30*(6), 643–655. doi:10.1123/jsm.2015-0344

Larkin, J. (2003). *Strategic reputation risk management.* Palgrave McMillian.

Lavastre, O., Gunasekaran, A., & Spalanzani, A. (2012). Supply chain risk management in French companies. *Decision Support Systems, 52*(4), 828–838. doi:10.1016/j.dss.2011.11.017

Law, F. (2017). Breaking the outsourcing path: Backsourcing process and outsourcing lock-in. *European Management Journal.*

Le Louarn, P. (1997). La Tendance à Innover des Consommateurs: Analyse Conceptuelle et Proposition d'une Échelle de Mesure. *Recherche et Applications en Marketing, 12*(1), 3–19. doi:10.1177/076737019701200101

Le Nagard-Assayag, E., & Manceau, D. (2011). *Le Marketing de l'Innovation, de la Création au Lancement de Nouveaux Produits* (2nd ed.). Paris: Dunod.

Ledinghan, J. A., & Bruning, S. D. (1998). Relationship management in public relations: Dimensions of an organization-public relationship. *Public Relations Review, 24*(1), 55–65. doi:10.1016/S0363-8111(98)80020-9

Lee, O.-K., Wang, M., Lim, K. H., & Peng, Z. (2009). Knowledge Management Systems Diffusion in Chinese Enterprises: A Multistage Approach Using the Technology-Organization-Environment Framework. *Journal of Global Information Management, 17*(1), 70-84.

Lee, J. N. (2001). The impact of knowledge sharing, organizational capability and partnership quality on IS outsourcing success. *Information & Management, 38*(5), 323–335. doi:10.1016/S0378-7206(00)00074-4

Lee, K. C., Lee, S., & Kang, I. W. (2005). KMPI: Measuring knowledge management performance. *Information & Management, 42*(3), 469–482. doi:10.1016/j.im.2004.02.003

Lee, L. S., Fiedler, K. D., & Smith, J. S. (2008). Radio frequency identification (RFID) implementation in the service sector: A customer-facing diffusion model. *International Journal of Production Economics, 112*(2), 587–600. doi:10.1016/j.ijpe.2007.05.008

Lee, M. (2009). Factors influencing the adoption of Internet banking: An integration of TAM and TPB with perceived risk and perceived benefits. *Electronic Commerce Research and Applications, 8*(3), 130–141. doi:10.1016/j.elerap.2008.11.006

Lee, S., Xiang, J. Y., & Kim, J. K. (2011). Information technology and productivity: Empirical evidence from the Chinese electronics industry. *Information & Management, 48*(2-3), 79–87. doi:10.1016/j.im.2011.01.003

Lee, W.-Y., Kwak, D. H., Lim, C., Pedersen, P. M., & Miloch, K. S. (2011). Effects of personality and gender on fantasy sports game participation: The moderating role of perceived knowledge. *Journal of Gambling Studies, 27*(3), 427–441. doi:10.100710899-010-9218-9 PMID:20865303

Lee, Y. (2006). An empirical investigation into factors of influencing the adoption of an e-learning systems. *Online Information Review, 30*(5), 517–541. doi:10.1108/14684520610706406

Lee, Y., Kozar, K. A., & Larsen, K. R. T. (2003). The technology acceptance model: Past, present, and future. *Communications of the AIS, 12*(50), 752–780.

Lerbinger, O. (1997). *The crisis manager: Facing risk and responsibility.* New Jersey: Lawrence Erlbaum.

Lester, D. H., Forman, A. M., & Loyd, D. (2005). Internet shopping behavior of college students. *Services Marketing Quarterly, 27*(2), 123–138.

Leung, X. Y., & Bai, B. (2013). How motivation, opportunity, and ability impact travelers' social media involvement and revisit intention. *Journal of Travel & Tourism Marketing, 30*(1-2), 58–77. doi:10.1080/10548408.2013.751211

Levin, D. Z., & Cross, R. (2004). The Strength of Weak Ties You Can Trust: The Mediating Role of Trust in Effective Knowledge Transfer. *Management Science, 50*(11), 1477–1490. doi:10.1287/mnsc.1030.0136

Lewis, J. D., & Weigert, A. (1985). Trust as a Social Reality. *Social Forces, 63*(4), 967-985.

Li, H., Ward, R., & Zhang, H. (2007). Risk, convenience, cost and online payment choice: a study of eBay transactions. *Commerce Center od DuPree College of Management, 8*(4), 1-36.

Li, G., Kou, G., & Peng, Y. (2016). A Group Decision Making Model for Integrating Heterogeneous Information. *IEEE Transactions on Systems, Man, and Cybernetics. Systems*, 1–11. doi:10.1109/TSMC.2015.2422267

Lilleoere, A. M., & Hansen, E. H. (2011). Knowledge sharing enablers and barriers in pharmaceutical research and development. *Journal of Knowledge Management, 15*(1), 53–70. doi:10.1108/13673271111108693

Lin, H.-F., & Lin, S.-M. (2008). Determinants of E-Business Diffusion: A Test of the Technology Diffusion Perspective. *Technovation*, *28*(3), 135-145.

Lindlof, T. R., & Taylor, B. C. (2011). *Qualitative communication research methods*. Thousand Oaks, CA: Sage.

Lin, H. F. (2007). Effects of extrinsic and intrinsic motivation on employee knowledge sharing intentions. *Journal of Information Science*, *33*(2), 135–149. doi:10.1177/0165551506068174145

Lin, H. F. (2007). Knowledge sharing and firm innovation capability: An empirical study. *International Journal of Manpower*, *28*(3/4), 315–332. doi:10.1108/01437720710755272

Lin, H. F. (2014). Contextual factors affecting knowledge management diffusion in SMEs. *Industrial Management & Data Systems*, *114*(9), 1415–1437. doi:10.1108/IMDS-08-2014-0232

Lin, L., & Daim, T. U. (2005). Platform strategy framework for Internet-based service development: Case of eBay. *International Journal of Services Technology and Management*, *11*(4), 334–354. doi:10.1504/IJSTM.2009.024565

Lipnack, J. S., & Stamps, J. (2000). *Virtual teams: People working across boundaries with technology*. New York, NY: John Wiley.

Li, S., Visich, J. K., Khumawala, B. M., & Zhang, C. (2006). Radio frequency identification technology: Applications, technical challenges and strategies. *Sensor Review*, *26*(3), 193–202. doi:10.1108/02602280610675474

Lister, C., West, J. H., Cannon, B., Sax, T., & Brodegard, D. (2014, August 4). Just a fad? Gamification in health and fitness apps. *JMIR Serious Games*, *2*(2), e9. doi:10.2196/games.3413 PMID:25654660

Liu, M. (2008). Determinants of E-Commerce Development: An Empirical Study by Firms in Shaanxi, China. In *Wireless Communications, Networking and Mobile Computing, 2008. WiCOM'08. 4th International Conference on*. IEEE. 10.1109/WiCom.2008.2143

Liu, C. H., Tzeng, G. H., & Lee, M. H. (2012). Improving tourism policy implementation - The use of hybrid MCDM models. *Tourism Management*, *33*(2), 413–426. doi:10.1016/j.tourman.2011.05.002

Liu, M. S. (2012). Impact of knowledge incentive mechanisms on individual knowledge creation behavior – an empirical study for Taiwanese R&D professionals. *International Journal of Information Management*, *32*(5), 442–450. doi:10.1016/j.ijinfomgt.2012.02.002

Lockton, V., & Rosenberg, R. S. (2005). RFID: The next serious threat to privacy. *Ethics and Information Technology*, *7*(4), 221–231. doi:10.100710676-006-0014-2

Lone, J. A. (2016). Exploring knowledge work: Organizational practices and work characteristics in three knowledge work settings [Doctoral dissertation]. Retrieved from https://www.duo.uio.no/handle/10852/55141

Long, J. (2010). Do what yourself: Reevaluation of the value created by online and traditional intermediary. *International Journal of Information and Decision Sciences*, *2*(3), 304–317. doi:10.1504/IJIDS.2010.033453

Looyestyn, J., Kernot, J., Boshoff, K., Ryan, J., Edney, S., & Maher, C. (2017). Does gamification increase engagement with online programs? A systematic review. *PLoS One*, *12*(3), 1–19. doi:10.1371/journal.pone.0173403 PMID:28362821

Lumsdon, L. M., & McGrath, P. (2011). Developing a conceptual framework for slow travel: A grounded theory approach. *Journal of Sustainable Tourism*, *19*(3), 265–279. doi:10.1080/09669582.2010.519438

Lundvall, B.-Å., & Borras, S. (1999) The Globalising Learning Economy: Implications for Innovation Policy. Academic Press.

Luo, J. D. (2010). *Social Network Analysis*. Beijing, China: Society and Science Publication.

Luo, Y., & Deng, J. (2008). The new environmental paradigm and nature-based tourism motivation. *Journal of Travel Research*, *46*(4), 392–402. doi:10.1177/0047287507308331

Lutchen, M. D. (2004). *Managing IT as a business: a survival guide for CEOs*. John Wiley & Sons, Inc.

LVMH. (2017). *LVMH Résultats 2016 records*. Retrieved September 20th, 2017, from https://www.lvmh.fr/actualites-documents/communiques/resultats-2016-records

Madlberger, M. (2009). What drives firms to engage in interorganizational information sharing in supply chain management? *International Journal of e-Collaboration*, *5*(2), 18–42. doi:10.4018/jec.2009040102

Mafabi, S., Nasiima, S., Muhimbise, E. M., Kaekende, F., & Nakiyonga, C. (2017). The mediation role of intention in knowledge sharing behavior. *VINE Journal of Information and Knowledge Management Systems*, *47*(2), 172–193. doi:10.1108/VJIKMS-02-2016-0008

Majchrzak, A., Rice, R. E., King, N., Malhotra, A., & Ba, S. (2000). Computer-Mediated Inter-Organizational Knowledge-Sharing: Insights From a Virtual Team Innovating Using a Collaborative Tool. *Information Resources Management Journal*, *13*(1), 44–53. doi:10.4018/irmj.2000010104

Makela, K., Kalla, H. K., & Piekkari, R. (2007). Interpersonal similarity as a driver of knowledge sharing with in multinational corporations. *International Business Review*, *16*(1), 1–22. doi:10.1016/j.ibusrev.2006.11.002

Malaurent, J., & Avison, D. (2015). From an apparent failure to a success story: ERP in China - Post implementation. *International Journal of Information Management*, *35*(5), 643–646. doi:10.1016/j.ijinfomgt.2015.06.004

Maldonado, M., & Sierra, V. (2013). User satisfaction as the foundation of the success following an ERP adoption: An empirical study from Latin America. *International Journal of Enterprise Information Systems*, *9*(3), 77–99. doi:10.4018/jeis.2013070104

Maloni, M. J., & Benton, W. C. (1997). Supply chain partnerships: Opportunities for operations research. *European Journal of Operational Research*, *101*(3), 419–429. doi:10.1016/S0377-2217(97)00118-5

March, J. G. (1978). Rationality, Ambiguity, and the Engineering of Choice. *The Bell Journal of Economics*, *9*(9), 587–608. doi:10.2307/3003600

Margulis, A., Boeck, H., Bendavid, Y., & Durif, F. (2016). Building theory from consumer reactions to RFID: Discovering Connective Proximity. *Ethics and Information Technology*, *18*(2), 81–101. doi:10.100710676-016-9388-y

Markus, M. L. (2005). Technology-shaping effects of e-collaboration technologies: Bugs and features. *International Journal of e-Collaboration*, *1*(1), 1–23. doi:10.4018/jec.2005010101

Markus, M. L., & Tanis, C. (2000). The Enterprise System Experience – From Adoption to Success. In R. W. Zmud (Ed.), *Framing the Domains of IT Research: Glimpsing the Future Through the Past* (pp. 173–207). Cincinnati, OH: Pinnaflex Educational Resources.

Martin, C. (2015). Social networking usage and grades among college students: A study to determine the correlation of social media usage and grades. Retrieved August 4, 2016 from http://www.unh.edu/news/docs/UNHsocialmedia.pdf

Martinez-Caro, E., & Cegarra-Navarro, J. G. (2009). The impact of e-business on capital productivity. *International Journal of Operations & Production Management*, *30*(5), 488–507. doi:10.1108/01443571011039597

Mason, M., Benotsch, E. G., Way, T., Kim, H., & Snipes, D. (2014). Text messaging to increase readiness to change alcohol use in college students. *The Journal of Primary Prevention*, *35*(1), 47–52. doi:10.100710935-013-0329-9 PMID:24114551

Masson, J. (2010). *Effets de la Modification d'un Attribut Constitutif d'un Produit Alimentaire sur son Adoption par les Consommateurs: Le cas du Vin à teneur réduite en Alcoo.* (Unpublished Doctoral Dissertation). Montpellier Supagro, Centre International d'Etudes Supérieures en Sciences Agronomiques, France.

Masudi, F. (2013, 03 01). *Meatballs on menu are halal.* Retrieved 09 01, 2013, from Gulf News: http://gulfnews.com/news/gulf/uae/general/meatballs-on-menu-are-halal-ikea-says-1.1152651

Matchett, K. (2012). *ESPN TV ratings for Euro 2012: New record viewings in US for soccer final.* Retrieved March 1, 2018 from http://bleacherreport.com/articles/1244834-espn-TV-ratings-for-euro-2012-new-record-viewings-in-us-for-soccer-final

Mateen, A., & More, D. (2013). Applying TOC thinking process tools in managing challenges of supply chain finance: A case study. *International Journal of Services and Operations Management, 15*(4), 389–410. doi:10.1504/IJSOM.2013.054882

Mathieson, K. (1991). Predicting User Intentions: Comparing the Technology Acceptance Model with the Theory of Planned Behavior. *Information Systems Research, 2*(3), 173–191. doi:10.1287/isre.2.3.173

Mauss, M. (2002). *The Gift: The Form and Reason for Exchange in Archaic Societies.* London: Routledge.

Maznevski, M. L., & Chudoba, K. (2000). Building space over time: Global virtual team dynamics and effectiveness. *Organization Science, 11*(1), 473–492. doi:10.1287/orsc.11.5.473.15200

McCormick, A. (2006). Everyone needs to keep an eye on the ball. *News Analysis,* 16.

McCoy, S., Everard, A., & Jones, B. M. (2005). An examination of technology acceptance model in Uruguay and the US: A focus on culture. *Journal of Global Information Technology Management, 8*(2), 27–45. doi:10.1080/1097198X.2005.10856395

McCullagh, D. (2003). *RFID tags: Big Brother in small packages.* Retrieved from https://www.student.cs.uwaterloo.ca/~cs492/11public_html/papers/rfid.pdf

McGaughey, R. E., & Gunasekaran, A. (2007). Enterprise Resource Planning (ERP): Past, Present and Future. *International Journal of Enterprise Information Systems, 3*(3), 23–35. doi:10.4018/jeis.2007070102

McHugh, J. (2004). Attention, shoppers: You can now speed straight through checkout lines. *Wired Magazine, 12,* 135–139. Retrieved from http://www.wired.com/wired/archive/12.07/shoppers.html

McIntosh, R., & Gupta, W. S. (1977). *Tourism: Principles, practices, philosophies* (3rd ed.). Grid Inc.

McKercher, B., Prideaux, B., Cheung, C., & Law, R. (2010). Achieving voluntary reductions in the carbon footprint of tourism and climate change. *Journal of Sustainable Tourism, 18*(3), 297–317. doi:10.1080/09669580903395022

McKinsey & Company. (2014). *The Future Role of US Retailing Banking Distribution.* Author.

McKnight, D. H., Choudhury, V., & Kacmar, C. (2002). Developing and Validating Trust Measures for E-Commerce: An Integrative Typology. *Information Systems Research, 13*(3), 334-359.

McKnight, D., & Chervany, N. (2000). *The meanings of trust.* Minneapolis, MN: Carlson School of Management.

Mcnurlin, B. C., & Sprague, R. H. (2003). *Information Systems Management in Practice (6th ed.).* Prentice Hall.

McPherson, K. (2007). Using eBay as a collection development tool. *Teacher Librarian, 34*(5), 71–73.

Melnik, M. (2005). *Seller reputation, information signals, and prices for heterogeneous coins on eBay.* Retrieved October 7, 2017 from http://reddog.rmu.edu:2079/pqdweb?index=34&did=911359041&SrchMode=1&sid=2&Fmt=3&VInst=PROD&VType=PQD&RQT=309&VName=PQD&TS=1193075203&clientId=2138

Melnik, M. I., & Alm, J. (2005). Seller reputation, information signals, and prices for heterogeneous coins on eBay. *Southern Economic Journal, 72*(2), 305–315. doi:10.2307/20062113

Melnyk, S. A., Davis, E. W., Spekman, R. E., & Sandor, J. (2010). Outcome-driven supply chains. *MIT Sloan Management Review, 51*(2), 3833–3851.

Merrill, M. (2011a). HHS mHealth initiatives target smoking cessation. *Healthcare IT News*. Retrieved April 4, 2015 from www.healthcareitnews.com/news/hhs-mhealth-initiatives-target-smoking-cessation

Merrill, M. (2011b). Study finds potential in social media tools for smoking cessation. *Healthcare IT News*. Retrieved April 4, 2015 from www.healthcareitnews.com/news/study-find-potential-social-media-health-tools-smoking-cessation

Microsoft. (2011). *Governance Manual*. Available at http://www.microsoft/brasil/setorpublico/governanca/pdti

Midgley, D. F., & Dowling, G. R. (1993). A Longitudinal Study of Product Form Innovation: The Interaction between Predispositions and Social Messages. *The Journal of Consumer Research, 19*(4), 611–625. doi:10.1086/209326

Mikolajuk, Z., Cartridge, R., & Noble, N. (2008), Practical Answers: A platform for knowledge sharing. *Waterlines- an International Journal of Water, Sanitation and Waste, 27*(2).

Mikolajuk, Z. (2004). Linking Knowledge Providers and Knowledge Users. In *Proceedings of the 21st Anniversary Symposium: "Securing Sustainable Livelihoods in the Hindu-Kush Himalayas: Directions for Future Research, Development and Cooperation", Working Session IV: ICIMOD*, Kathmandu, Nepal, December 5-6.

Mikolajuk, Z. (2005), Mountain Knowledge Partnership: A System for Knowledge Delivery in the Hindu Kush – Himalayan Region. In *Proceedings of the International Conference on Knowledge Management (ICKM)*, Malaysia, July 7-9.

Mikolajuk, Z. (2005). Basics of Information and Knowledge Management. *ICIMOD Newsletter, 47*(Winter), 4–6.

Mikolajuk, Z. (2005). Information and Knowledge Management at ICIMOD – A Strategy Framework. *ICIMOD Newsletter, 47*(Winter), 7–10.

Mikolajuk, Z. (2006), A Computer-based Knowledge Delivery System for Rural Communities – A Case Study using Beekeeping. In *Proceedings of the Knowledge Management International Conference and Exhibition, KMICE06*, Kuala Lumpur, Malaysia.

Millar, M., & Baliglu, S. (2011). Hotel guests' preferences for green guest room attributes. *Cornell Hospitality Quarterly, 52*(3), 302–311. doi:10.1177/1938965511409031

Miller, C. (2003). Hidden in Plain Sight: Understanding Nonprofit Capital Structure. *The Nonprofit Quarterly, 10*(1), 1-7.

Miller, D., & Friesen, P. H. (1982). Innovation in Conservative and Entrepreneurial Firms: Two Models of Strategic Momentum. *Strategic Management Journal, 3*(1), 1-25.

Miller, R. K. (2011). *Healthcare Business Market Research Handbook*. Loganville, GA: Richard K. Miller and Associates.

Miller, W. L., & Morris, L. (1999). *Fourth Generation R & D: Managing Knowledge, Technology and Innovation*. John Wiley & Sons, Inc.

Milner, H. (2010). *The internet generation*. Medford, MA: Tufts University Press.

Minbaeva, D. B. (2013). Strategic HRM in building micro-foundations of organizational knowledge-based performance. *Human Resource Management Review, 23*(4), 378–390. doi:10.1016/j.hrmr.2012.10.001

Ministry of Communications and Information Technology. (2005a). *Egypt information society initiative* (4th ed.). Cairo: MCIT Publications.

Ministry of Communications and Information Technology. (2005b). *Building digital bridges: Egypt's vision of the information society.* Cairo: MCIT Publications.

Ministry of Communications and Information Technology. (2011a). *ICT Indicators in Brief September Issue.* Retrieved from http://www.mcit.gov.eg/Publications

Ministry of Communications and Information Technology. (2011b). *Information and Communications Technology Indicators Bulletin June Issue.* Retrieved from http://www.mcit.gov.eg/Publications

Ministry of Communications and Information Technology. (2015). *ICT Indicators in Brief December Issue.* Retrieved from http://www.mcit.gov.eg/Publications

Ministry of Communications and Information Technology. (2017). *ICT Indicators in Brief September Issue.* Retrieved from http://www.mcit.gov.eg/Publications

Ministry of Education, Culture, Sports, Science and Technology. (2008). *Survey Report on Unofficial School Informal Sites Used by Students.* Retrieved from http://www.mext.go.jp/a_menu/sports/ikusei/taisaku/1262855.htm (in Japanese)

Ministry of Education, Culture, Sports, Science and Technology. (2012a). *The Kei-tai Moral Caravan course.* Retrieved from http://www.mext.go.jp/a_menu/seisyounen/moral/1313273.htm (in Japanese)

Ministry of Education, Culture, Sports, Science and Technology. (2012b). *Research Report of the Promoting Measures to Harmful Informations to Face the Youth.* Retrieved from http://www.mext.go.jp/a_menu/seisyounen/moral/1328093.htm (in Japanese)

Ministry of Education, Culture, Sports, Science and Technology. (2016). *Survey on Problems Related to Student Guidance to Problematic Behavior of Students in FY2008.* Retrieved from http://www.mext.go.jp/b_menu/houdou/29/10/__icsFiles/afieldfile/2017/10/26/1397646_001.pdf (in Japanese)

Ministry of Internal Affairs and Communications. (2009a). *Survey Research on Trouble Cases in the Internet Usage - Internet Troubles Case Study* (Vol. 3). Retrieved from http://www.soumu.go.jp/main_content/000173733.pdf (in Japanese)

Ministry of Internal Affairs and Communications. (2009b). *Program for the Development of Safe and Secure Internet Environment - Safety Network Promotion Program.* Retrieved from http://www.soumu.go.jp/menu_news/s-news/2009/pdf/090116_2_bs.pdf (in Japanese)

Ministry of Internal Affairs and Communications. (2009c). *Final report of Study Group on Measures to Illegal and Harmful Information on the Internet: Internet Safety Promotion Program.* Tokyo: Ministry of Internal Affairs and Communications. (in Japanese)

Minkov, M. (2007). *What makes us different and similar: A new interpretation of the World Values Survey and other cross-cultural data.* Sofia, Bulgaria: Klasika y Stil Publishing House.

Mishina, Y., Pollock, T. G., & Porac, J. F. (2004). Are More Resources Always Better for Growth? Resource Stickiness in Market and Product Expansion. *Strategic Management Journal, 25*(12), 1179-1197.

Mládková, L. (2015). Knowledge workers and the principle of 3S (self-management, self-organization, self-control). *Procedia: Social and Behavioral Sciences, 181,* 178–184. doi:10.1016/j.sbspro.2015.04.879

Module, D. L. (2002). *The Clinical Use of Blood in Medicine, Obstetrics, Paediatrics, Surgery & Anaesthesia, Trauma & Burns.* WHO.

Moore, G. C., & Benbasat, I. (1991). Development of an Instrument to Measure the Perceptions of Adopting an Information Technology Innovation. *Information Systems Research, 2*(3), 192-222.

Morgan, J. (2015). *A simple explanation of 'the Internet of Things'*. Retrieved from https://www.forbes.com/sites/jacobmorgan/2014/05/13/simple-explanation-internet-things-that-anyone-can-understand/#16567b691d09

Morgan, W. J. (Ed.). (1979). *Sport and the humanities: A collection of original essays*. Knoxville, TN: University of Tennessee.

Morimoto, M., & Chang, S. (2009). Psychological factors affecting perceptions of unsolicited commercial email. *Journal of Current Issues and Research in Advertising, 31*(1), 63–73. doi:10.1080/10641734.2009.10505257

Morse, J. M. (1994). "Emerging from the data": The cognitive processes of analysis in qualitative inquiry. In J. M. Morse (Ed.), *Critical issues in qualitative research methods* (pp. 23–43). Thousand Oaks, CA: Sage.

Moth, D. (2013). *How Burberry uses Facebook, Twitter, Pinterest and Google+*. Retrieved October 4th, 2017, from https://econsultancy.com/blog/62897-how-burberry-uses-facebook-twitter-pinterest-and-google

Motowidlo, S. J., & Van Scotter, J. R. (1994). Evidence that task performance should be distinguished from contextual performance. *The Journal of Applied Psychology, 79*(4), 475–480. doi:10.1037/0021-9010.79.4.475

Mousavi, S. M., Hajipour, V., Niaki, S. T. A., & Aalikar, N. (2014). A multi-product multi-period inventory control problem under inflation and discount: A parameter-tuned particle swarm optimization algorithm. *International Journal of Advanced Manufacturing Technology, 70*(9-12), 1739–1756. doi:10.100700170-013-5378-y

Mowshowitz, A. (1997). Virtual organization. *Communications of the ACM, 40*(9), 30–37. doi:10.1145/260750.260759

Muhammed, S., Doll, W. J., & Deng, X. (2009). A model of interrelationships among individual level knowledge management success measures. *International Journal of Knowledge Management, 5*(1), 1–16. doi:10.4018/jkm.2009010101

Mukoda, K. (2003). *TV and cognitive abilities. In Media and Human Development - Psychological Impact of TV, TV Game, Internet, and Robots* (pp. 23–40). Gakubunsha. (in Japanese)

Müller-Seitz, G., Dautzenberg, K., Creusen, U., & Stromereder, C. (2009). Customer acceptance of RFID technology: Evidence from the German electronic retail sector. *Journal of Retailing and Consumer Services, 16*(1), 31–39. doi:10.1016/j.jretconser.2008.08.002

Mulvihill, A. (2011). Measuring the value of a 'like.'. *EContent (Wilton, Conn.), 34*(6), 8–12.

Munkvold, B. E., & Zigurs, I. (2007). Process and technology challenges in swift-starting virtual teams. *Information & Management, 44*(3), 287–299. doi:10.1016/j.im.2007.01.002

Murphy, M. F., Saxena, S., & Smit Sibinga, C. T. (2013). Patient Safety and Quality Management at the Clinical Interface. In Quality Management in Transfusion Medicine (pp. 283-314). Nova Science Publ. Inc.

Murphy, P. (2010). The intractability of reputation: Media coverage as a complex system in the case of Martha Stewart. *Journal of Public Relations Research, 22*(2), 209–237. doi:10.1080/10627261003601648

Muscatello, J. R., & Chen, I. J. (2008). Enterprise Resource Planning (ERP) Implementations: Theory and Practice. *International Journal of Enterprise Information Systems, 4*(1), 63–77. doi:10.4018/jeis.2008010105

Myers, M. (1997). Qualitative Research in Information Systems. *MISQ Discovery, 2*.

Myers, M., & Avison, D. (Eds.). (2002). Qualitative Research in Information Systems. London: Sage. doi:10.4135/9781849209687

Nambisian, S., Lyytinen, K., Majchrzak, A., & Song, M. (2017). Digital innovation Management: Reinventing innovation management research in a digital world. *MIS Quarterly, 41*(1), 223-238.

Nan, N., & Lu, Y. (2014). Harnessing the power of self-organization in an online community during organizational crisis. *Management Information Systems Quarterly, 38*(4), 1135–1158. doi:10.25300/MISQ/2014/38.4.09

Napolitano, M. A., Hayes, S., Bennett, G. G., Ives, A. K., & Foster, G. D. (2013). Using facebook and text messaging to deliver a weight loss program to college students. *Obesity (Silver Spring, Md.), 21*(1), 25–31. doi:10.1002/oby.20232 PMID:23505165

Narayanan, R. P., Kirk, P., & Lewis, S. (2008). Uptake and perceptions of an e-learning package on blood transfusion by trainees in Wales. *Journal of the Royal College Physicians Edinburgh, 38*, 298–301.

Nathan, M., James, X., & Jason, J. (2012). *Storm: Distributed real-time computation system.* Academic Press.

National Intelligence Council. (2008). *Disruptive civil technologies: Six technologies with potential impacts on US interests out to 2025.* Conference Report CR 2008-07. Retrieved from https://www.fas.org/irp/nic/disruptive.pdf

National Police Agency. (2017). *Current Situation and Countermeasures of Offenses Arising from Community Sites etc. in the First Half of FY2017.* Retrieved from https://www.npa.go.jp/cyber/statics/h29/H29_siryou.pdf (in Japanese)

Nelson, R. R., Todd, P. A., & Wixom, B. H. (2005). Antecedents of Information and System Quality: An Empirical Examination within the Context of Data Warehousing. *Journal of Management Information Systems, 21*(4), 199-235.

Nesbit, T. M., & King, K. A. (2010). The impact of fantasy sports on television viewership. *Journal of Media Economics, 23*(1), 24–41. doi:10.1080/08997761003590721

Netflix just became cable's biggest TV network. (2012). Retrieved March 1, 2018 from http://www.textually.org/TV/archives/2012/07/030853.htm

Neumeyer, L., Robbins, B., Nair, A., & Kesari, A. (2010, December). S4: Distributed stream computing platform. In *Data Mining Workshops (ICDMW), 2010 IEEE International Conference on* (pp. 170-177). IEEE.

Newman, J. (2014). Dropbox and you: A future where apps drive cloud storage. *PC World, 32*(7), 40–43.

News, C. (2013, 02 25). *Horsemeat found in Ikea meatballs in Europe.* Retrieved 09 1, 2013, from CBC NEWS World: http://www.cbc.ca/news/world/story/2013/02/25/horse-meat-ikea-meat-balls.html

Nobari, A., Khierkhah, A. S., & Hajipour, V. (2018). A Pareto-based approach to optimise aggregate production planning problem considering reliable supplier selection. *International Journal of Services and Operations Management, 29*(1), 59–84. doi:10.1504/IJSOM.2018.088473

Normative Instruction 04. (2008). MPOG (Ministry of Planning and Budget) – SLTI (Department of Logistics and Information Technology).

North, K., & Gueldenberg, S. (Eds.). (2011). *Effective knowledge work: answers to the management challenge of the 21st century.* Bingley, UK: Emerald.

Novak, T. P., Hoffman, D. L., & Yung, Y. F. (2000). Measuring the customer experience in on-line environment: A structural modeling approach. *Marketing Science, 19*(1), 22–42. doi:10.1287/mksc.19.1.22.15184

Nowaczek, A., & Smail, B. (2010). Exploring the predisposition of travellers to qualify as ecotourists: The Ecotourist Predisposition Scale. *Journal of Ecotourism, 9*(1), 45–61. doi:10.1080/14724040902883521

Nunnally, J. C. (1978). *Psychometric theory.* New York, NY: McGraw-Hill.

Nwosu, I. E. (1996). *Mass Media and African War.* Star Printing and Publishing Corporation Limited.

ODI, Overseas Development Institute, UK. (2006). R0093 Concept Note. Retrieved from http://www.odi.org.uk/RAPID/projects/R0093/Concept.html

Oey, E., & Nofrimurti, M. (2018). Lean implementation in traditional distributor warehouse - a case study in an FMCG company in Indonesia. *International Journal of Process Management and Benchmarking*, *8*(1), 1–15. doi:10.1504/IJPMB.2018.088654

Oh, H., Assaf, A. G., & Baloglu, S. (2014). Motivations and goals of slow tourism. *Journal of Travel Research*.

Ohkubo, M., Suzuki, K., & Kinoshita, S. (2005). RFID privacy issues and technical challenges. *Communications of the ACM*, *48*(9), 66–71. doi:10.1145/1081992.1082022

Oja, E. (1989). Neural networks, principal components, and subspaces. *International Journal of Neural Systems*, *1*(1), 61–68. doi:10.1142/S0129065789000475

Ojha, A., Sahu, G. P., & Gupta, M. P. (2009). Antecedents of paperless income tax filing by young professionals in India: An exploratory study. *Transforming Government: People. Process and Policy*, *3*(1), 65–90.

Okonkwo, U. (2009). Sustaining the luxury brand on the Internet. *Journal of Brand Management*, *16*(5-6), 302–310. doi:10.1057/bm.2009.2

Okorogu, C. I. (2015). *First generation meta-analytic review of the influence of human resource management single practices on organizational outcomes*: 1985-2015 [Doctoral dissertation]. Retrieved from http://aut.researchgateway.ac.nz/handle/10292/9829

Oliveira, T., & Martins, M. F. (2010). Firms Patterns of E-Business Adoption: Evidence for the European Union- 27. *The Electronic Journal Information Systems Evaluation Volume*, *13*(1), 47-56.

Oliveira, T., & Martins, M. F. (2009). *Determinants of Information Technology Adoption in Portugal*. ICE-B.

Oliveira, T., Thomas, M., & Espadanal, M. (2014). Assessing the determinants of cloud computing adoption: An analysis of the manufacturing and services sectors. *Information & Management*, *51*(5), 497–510. doi:10.1016/j.im.2014.03.006

Oliver, R. K., & Webber, M. D. (1982). Supply-chain management: logistics catches up with strategy. In M. G. Christopher (Ed.), *Logistics, The Strategic Issue*. London: Chapman & Hall.

Olsen, K. M. (2016). The power of workers: Knowledge work and the power balance in Scandinavian countries. *Employee Relations*, *38*(3), 390–405. doi:10.1108/ER-10-2014-0121

Olston, C., Chiou, G., Chitnis, L., Liu, F., Han, Y., Larsson, M., ... Tian, C. (2011, June). Nova: continuous pig/hadoop workflows. In *Proceedings of the 2011 ACM SIGMOD International Conference on Management of data* (pp. 1081-1090). ACM. 10.1145/1989323.1989439

Olston, C., Reed, B., Srivastava, U., Kumar, R., & Tomkins, A. (2008, June). Pig latin: a not-so-foreign language for data processing. In *Proceedings of the 2008 ACM SIGMOD international conference on Management of data* (pp. 1099-1110). ACM.

One month without tobacco event. (n.d.). Retrieved from http://mois-sans-tabac.tabac-info-service.fr/

Online price negotiation: How Automation is driving conversion. (2017). Retrieved October 7, 2017 from https://www.pricewaiter.com/2017/03/online-price-negotiation-automation-driving-conversion/

Oosterveen, E., Tzelepis, F., Ashton, L., & Hutchesson, M. (2017). A systematic review of eHealth behavioral interventions targeting smoking, nutrition, alcohol, physical activity and/or obesity for young adults. *Preventive Medicine*, *99*, 197–206. doi:10.1016/j.ypmed.2017.01.009 PMID:28130046

Ornes, L., & Ransdell, L. B. (2007). Web-based physical activity intervention for college-aged women. *International Electronic Journal of Health Education, 10*, 126–137.

Osman, A., El-Refaey, M., & Elnaggar, A. (2013, June). Towards real-time analytics in the cloud. In *Services (SERVICES), 203 IEEE Ninth World Congress on* (pp. 428-435). IEEE. 10.1109/SERVICES.2013.36

Ostlund, L. E. (1974). Perceived innovation attributes as predictors of innovativeness. *The Journal of Consumer Research, 1*(2), 23–29. doi:10.1086/208587

Östman, H. (2013). Grocery industry operations are facing a real paradigm shift. *RFID Areana*. Retrieved from http://www.rfidarena.com/2013/4/11/grocery-industry-operations-are-facing-a-real-paradigm-shift.aspx

Øvretveit, J., Scott, T., Rundall, T. G., Shortell, S. M., & Brommels, M. (2007). Improving Quality through Effective Implementation of Information Technology in Healthcare. *International Journal for Quality in Health Care, 19*(5), 259-266.

Owunwanne, D., & Goel, R. (2016). Radio frequency identification (RFID) technology: Gaining a competitive value through cloud computing. *International Journal of Management & Information Systems, 20*(2), 37–44.

Oyekola, O. (1995). *Foundations of public relations.* Western Africa: Ibadan Bombshell Publication.

Packirisamy, P., Meenakshy, M., & Jagannathan, S. (2017). Burnout during early career: Lived experiences of the knowledge workers in India. *Journal of Enterprise Information Management, 30*(1), 96–121. doi:10.1108/JEIM-01-2016-0041

Pagani, M. (2007). A Vicarious Innovativeness Scale for 3G Mobile Services: Integrating the Domain Specific Innovativeness Scale with Psychological and Rational Indicators. *Technology Analysis and Strategic Management, 19*(6), 709–728. doi:10.1080/09537320701711207

Pallot, M., Martinez-Carreras, M. A., & Prinz, W. (2010). Collaborative Distance. *International Journal of e-Collaboration, 6*(2), 1–32. doi:10.4018/jec.2010040101

Palvalin, M. (2017). How to measure impacts of work environment changes on knowledge work productivity –validation and improvement of the SmartWoW tool. *Measuring Business Excellence, 21*(2), 175–190. doi:10.1108/MBE-05-2016-0025

Palvalin, M., Vuolle, M., Jääskeläinen, A., Laihonen, H., & Lönnqvist, A. (2015). SmartWoW–constructing a tool for knowledge work performance analysis. *International Journal of Productivity and Performance Management, 64*(4), 479–498. doi:10.1108/IJPPM-06-2013-0122

Park, B.-N., & Min, H. (2013). Global supply chain barriers of foreign subsidiaries: The case of Korean expatriate manufacturers in China. *International Journal of Services and Operations Management, 15*(1), 67–78. doi:10.1504/IJSOM.2013.050562

Park, D. B., & Yoon, Y. S. (2009). Segmentation by motivation in rural tourism: A Korean case study. *Tourism Management, 30*(1), 99–108. doi:10.1016/j.tourman.2008.03.011

Park, J. Y., Im, K. S., & Kim, J. S. (2011). The role of IT human capability in the knowledge transfer process in IT outsourcing context. *Information & Management, 48*(1), 53–61. doi:10.1016/j.im.2011.01.001

Patalas-Maliszewska, J. (2013). *Managing knowledge workers: Value assessment, methods, and application tools.* New York, NY: Springer. doi:10.1007/978-3-642-36600-0

Patel, D. (2017). 10 Tips For Marketing To Gen Z On Social Media. *Forbes*. Retrieved September 20th, 2017, from https://www.forbes.com/sites/deeppatel/2017/08/08/10-tips-for-marketing-to-gen-z-on-social-media/#54651b422718

Pathak, J. (2003). Assurance and e-auctions: Are the existing business models still relevant? *Managerial Auditing Journal, 18*(4), 292–294. doi:10.1108/02686900310474307

Pearce, P. L., Morrison, A. M., & Rutledge, J. L. (1998). *Tourism: Bridges across Continents*. Sydney, Australia: McGraw-Hill.

Pedersen, P. M. (2013). Reflections on communication and sport: On strategic communication and management. *Communication and Sport*, *1*(1/2), 55–67. doi:10.1177/2167479512466655

Peng, J., Zhang, G., Chen, R., & Tan, Y. (2011). Impacts of Essential Elements of Management on IT Application Maturity—A Perspective from Firms in China. *Decision Support Systems*, *51*(1), 88–98. doi:10.1016/j.dss.2010.11.031

Pentina, I., Guilloux, V., & Micu, A. C. (2018). Exploring Social Media Engagement Behaviors in the Context of Luxury Brands. *Journal of Advertising*, *47*(1), 55–69. doi:10.1080/00913367.2017.1405756

Perez, S. (2012, December). LogMeIn's Dropbox competitor Chubby reveals pricing. *Tech Crunch*. Retrieved from http://techcrunch.com/2012/12/17/logmeins- dropbox-competitor-cubby-reveals-pricing-stays-competitive-at-7-per-month-for- 100-gb/

Peters, L. M., & Manz, C. C. (2007). Identifying antecedents of virtual team collaboration. *Team Performance Management: An International Journal*, *13*(3), 1–14.

Peterson, D., Robinson, K., Verall, T., Quested, B., & Saxon, B. (2007). E-learning and Transfusion Medicine. *ISBT Science Series*, *2*(2), 27-32.

Petrazzini, B. H. G. (1996). Information infrastructure initiatives in emerging economies: the case of India. In The National Information Infrastructure Initiatives. Cambridge, MA: Massachusetts Institute of Technology Press.

Petrescu, M. (2013). Marketing Research Using Single-Item Indicators in Structural Equation Models. *Journal of Marketing Analytics*, *1*(2), 99-117.

Petter, S., Straub, D., & Rai, A. (2007). Specifying formative constructs in information systems research. *Management Information Systems Quarterly*, *31*(4), 623–656. doi:10.2307/25148814

Phang, M. S., & Foong, S. Y. (2006). Enhancing knowledge sharing with information and communication technology. In *Proceedings of 3rd International Business Research Conference 2006*, World Business Institute, Melbourne, Vic.

Phan, M. (2011). Do social media enhance consumer's perception and purchase intentions of luxury fashion brands. *The Journal for Decision Makers*, *36*(1), 81–84.

Phan, M., Thomas, R., & Heine, K. (2011). Social media and luxury brand management: The case of Burberry. *Journal of Global Fashion Marketing*, *2*(4), 213–222. doi:10.1080/20932685.2011.10593099

Pick, B. J., Romano, N. C. Jr, & Roztocki, N. (2009). Synthesizing the research advances in electronic collaboration: Theoretical frameworks. *International Journal of e-Collaboration*, *5*(1), 1–12. doi:10.4018/jec.2009010101

Pikkarainen, T., Pikkarainen, K., Karjaluoto, H., & Pahnila, S. (2004). Customer acceptance of online banking: An extension of technology acceptance model. *Internet Research*, *14*(3), 224–235. doi:10.1108/10662240410542652

Plant, R. (2004). Online communities. *Technology in Society*, *26*(1), 51–65. doi:10.1016/j.techsoc.2003.10.005

Polo, J., Carrera, D., Becerra, Y., Torres, J., Ayguadé, E., Steinder, M., & Whalley, I. (2009). *Performance management of mapreduce applications*. Academic Press.

Ponomarov, S. Y., & Holcomb, M. C. (2009). Understanding the concept of supply chain resilience. *International Journal of Logistics Management*, *20*(1), 124–143. doi:10.1108/09574090910954873

Pookulangara, S., & Koesler, K. (2011). Cultural influence on consumers' usage of social networks and its impact on online purchase intentions. *Journal of Retailing and Consumer Services*, *18*(4), 348–354. doi:10.1016/j.jretconser.2011.03.003

Potter, J. A., & Smith, A. D. (2010). Performance appraisals and the strategic development of the professional intellect within non-profits. *International Journal of Management Education*, *3*(2), 188–203.

Practical Action Dhaka. (2007). Knowledge Management of Rural Poor Communities - Bangladesh (final internal technical report).

Prakash, R. (2016). *Burberry partners with Pinterest to create a customized beauty experience*. Retrieved October 4th, 2017, from https://business.pinterest.com/en/blog/burberry-partners-with-pinterest-to-create-a-customized-beauty-experience

Prasad, N., Bryan, D., & Reeves, D. (2007). Pennies from eBay: The determinants of price in online auctions. *The Journal of Industrial Economics*, *25*(2), 223–233.

Proenca, J. F., & Silva, M. M. (2005). Banking relationships and Internet banking. *IADIS International Journal on WWW/Internet*, *5*(2), 181-192.

Proenca, J. F., Silva, M. M., & Fernandes, T. (2010). The impact of Internet on bank marketing. *Journal of Financial Services Marketing*, *15*(2), 160–175. doi:10.1057/fsm.2010.12

Protalinski, E. (2014). Google announces 10% prices cut for all compute engine instances. *TNW News*. Retrieved August 1, 2015 from http://thenextweb.com/google/2014/10/01/google-announces-10-price-cut-compute-engine-instances-google-drive-passed-240m-active-users/

PwC (PricewaterhouseCooper). (2013). *Socio-economic impact of m-health, An assessment report for the European Union*. Retrieved November 2014, from http://www.pwc.fr/socio-economic-impact-of-mhealth-an-assessment-report-for-the-european-union.html

Qian, C., Zhou, Y., & Chen, J. (2017). The coupling strategy research of urban public space and traffic for improving the residents' low-carbon travel accessibility: A case study of Hexi New City Central Area in Nanjing. *Sustainability*, *9*, 1–23.

Quigley, N. R., Tesluk, P. E., Locke, E. A., & Bartol, K. M. (2007). A Multilevel Investigation of the Motivational Mechanisms Underlying Knowledge Sharing and Performance. *Organization Science*, *18*(1), 71–88. doi:10.1287/orsc.1060.0223

Raice, S., & Ante, S. (2012). Insta-Rich: $1 Billion for Instagram. *The Wall Street Journal*. Retrieved July 9, 2017 from http://online.wsj.com/news/articles/SB10001424405270230381540

Rajapakshe, T., Dawande, M., & Sriskandarajah, C. (2013). On the trade-off between remanufacturing and recycling. *International Journal of Services and Operations Management*, *15*(1), 1–53. doi:10.1504/IJSOM.2013.050560

Rajeev, V. (2013). Impact of service co-creation on performance of firms: The mediating role of market oriented strategies. *International Journal of Services and Operations Management*, *15*(4), 449–466. doi:10.1504/IJSOM.2013.054885

Ravasan, A. Z., & Rouhani, S. (2014). An Expert System for Predicting ERP Post-Implementation Benefits Using Artificial Neural Network. *International Journal of Enterprise Information Systems*, *10*(3), 24–45. doi:10.4018/ijeis.2014070103

Reardon, J. L., & Davidson, E. (2007). An Organizational Learning Perspective on the Assimilation of Electronic Medical Records among Small Physician Practices. *European Journal of Information Systems*, *16*(6), 681-694.

Rechberg, I. D. W., & Syed, J. (2014). Appropriation or participation of the individual in knowledge management. *Management Decision*, *52*(3), 426–445. doi:10.1108/MD-04-2013-0223

Rechberg, I., & Syed, J. (2014). Knowledge management practices and the focus on the individual. *International Journal of Knowledge Management*, *10*(1), 26–42. doi:10.4018/ijkm.2014010102

Rego, S., Kumar, N., & Mukherjee, P. N. (2018). Impact of policy implementation on telecommunication diffusion in India. *International Journal of Process Management and Benchmarking, 8*(1), 16–34. doi:10.1504/IJPMB.2018.088655

Rein, G. (2017). *How luxury brands should engage on Instagram and Snapchat.* Retrieved October 4th, 2017, from http://www.retaildive.com/ex/mobilecommercedaily/how-luxury-brands-should-engage-on-instagram-and-snapchat

Reinhardt, W., Schmidt, B., Sloep, P., & Drachsler, H. (2011). Knowledge worker roles and actions—results of two empirical studies. *Knowledge and Process Management, 18*(3), 150–174. doi:10.1002/kpm.378

Ressler, C., & Thompson, J. (2010). *Why work sucks and how to fix it: The results-only revolution.* New York, NY: Portfolio Publishing.

Rezende, D. A. (2003). Computing and Information Systems Planning. Atlas.

Rheingold, H. (2001). *The virtual community: Homestead on the electronic frontier.* New York: HarperPerennial.

Richard, P. J., & Devinney, T. M. (2005). Modular strategies: B2B technology and architectural knowledge. *California Management Review, 47*(4), 86–113. doi:10.2307/41166318

Ridinger, L. L., & Funk, D. C. (2006). Looking at gender differences through the lens of sport spectators. *Sport Marketing Quarterly, 5*(3), 155–166.

Riffai, M. M. M. A., Grant, K., & Edgar, D. (2012). Big TAM in Oman: Exploring the promise of on-line banking, its adoption by customers and the challenges of banking in Oman. *International Journal of Information Management, 32*(3), 239–250. doi:10.1016/j.ijinfomgt.2011.11.007

RIN and JISC. (2009). Communicating knowledge: How and why UK researchers publish and disseminate their findings. A Research Information Network. Retrieved from www.rin.ac.uk/communicating-knowledge/JISC

Ringard, Å., Sagan, A., Sperre, S. I., & Lindahl, A. K. (2013). Norway: Health system review. *Health Systems in Transition, 15*(8), 1–162. PMID:24434287

Rivero, O. (2014). *Importance of Public Relations in Corporate Sustainability.* Retrieved from https://globaljournals.org/GJMBR_Volume14/4-The-Importance-of-Public-Relations.pdf

Rizk, N., & Kamel, S. (2013). ICT and building a knowledge society in Egypt. *International Journal of Knowledge Management, 9*(1), 1–20. doi:10.4018/jkm.2013010101

Robey, D., & Boudreau, M. C. (1999). Accounting for the Contradictory Organizational Consequences of Information Technology: Theoretical Directions and Methodological Implications. *Information Systems Research, 10*(10), 167–185. doi:10.1287/isre.10.2.167

Robinson, M. J., & Trail, G. T. (2005). Relationships among spectator gender, motives, points of attachment, and sport preference. *Journal of Sport Management, 19*(1), 58–80. doi:10.1123/jsm.19.1.58

Rodriguez, W., Zalewski, J., & Kirche, E. (2007). Beyond intelligent agents: E-sensors for supporting supply chain collaboration and preventing the bullwhip effect. *International Journal of e-Collaboration, 3*(2), 1–15. doi:10.4018/jec.2007040101

Roehrich, G. (1994). Innovativités Hédoniste et Sociale: Proposition d'une Échelle de Mesure. *Recherche et Applications en Marketing, 9*(2), 19–42. doi:10.1177/076737019400900202

Rogers, E. M. (1995). *Diffusion of innovations* (4th ed.). New York: Free Press.

Rogers, E. M. (Ed.). (1962). *Diffusion of Innovations.* New York: The Free Press.

Rokeach, M. (1973). *The Nature of Human Values*. New York: The Free Press.

Roman, S. (2007). The ethics of online retailing: A scale development and validation from the consumers' perspective. *Journal of Business Ethics*, *72*(2), 131–148. doi:10.100710551-006-9161-y

Rosenberg, M. J. (2001). *E-learning: Strategies for building online learning in the digital age*. New York: McGraw-Hill.

Rotter, P. (2008). A framework for assessing RFID system security and privacy risks. *IEEE Pervasive Computing*, *7*(2), 70–77. doi:10.1109/MPRV.2008.22

Rouse, M. (2016). *IT strategic plan (information technology strategic plan)*. Available at https://searchcio.techtarget.com/definition/IT-strategic-plan-information-technology-strategic-plan

Roy, S. K., Kesharwani, A., & Singh Bisht, S. (2012). The impact of trust and perceived risk on internet banking adoption in India: An extension of technology acceptance model. *International Journal of Bank Marketing*, *30*(4), 303–322. doi:10.1108/02652321211236923

Ruane, L., & Wallace, E. (2015). Brand tribalism and self-expressive brands: Social influences and brand outcomes. *Journal of Product and Brand Management*, *24*(4), 333–348. doi:10.1108/JPBM-07-2014-0656

Rupprecht, L., Zhang, R., Owen, B., Pietzuch, P., & Hildebrand, D. (2017, April). SwiftAnalytics: Optimizing Object Storage for Big Data Analytics. In *Cloud Engineering (IC2E), 2017 IEEE International Conference on* (pp. 245-251). IEEE.

Ryan, R. M., & Deci, E. L. (2000). Intrinsic and extrinsic motivations: Classic definitions and new directions. *Contemporary Educational Psychology*, *25*(1), 54–67. doi:10.1006/ceps.1999.1020 PubMed

Rymaszewska, A., Helo, P., & Gunasekaran, A. (2017). IoT powered servitization of manufacturing – an exploratory case study. *International Journal of Production Economics*, *192*, 92–105. doi:10.1016/j.ijpe.2017.02.016

Ryu, S., & Kim, E. (2010). The moderating effect of long-term orientation on the relationship between inter firm power asymmetry and inter firm contracts: The case of Korea and USA. *Journal of Applied Marketing Research*, *26*(6), 135–146.

Ryu, S., & Moon, C. W. (2009). Long-term orientation as a determinant of relationship quality between channel members. *International Business and Economics Research Journal*, *8*(11), 1–9.

Ryu, S., Park, J. E., & Min, S. (2007). Factors determining long-term orientation in inter-firm relationships. *Journal of Business Research*, *60*(12), 1225–1233. doi:10.1016/j.jbusres.2006.09.031

Saade, R. G., & Nijher, H. (2016). Critical Success Factors in Enterprise Resource Planning Implementation: A Review of Case Studies. *Journal of Enterprise Information Management*, *29*(1), 72–96. doi:10.1108/JEIM-03-2014-0028

Saeed, K. A., & Abdinnour-Helm, S. (2008). Examining the Effects of Information System Characteristics and Perceived Usefulness on Post Adoption Usage of Information Systems. *Information & Management*, *45*(6), 376-386.

Safe Blood and Blood Products : Establishing a distance learning programme in blood safety: a guide for programme coordinators. (2009). WHO/BCT.

Safety, B. (2002). Aide Mémoire for National Blood Programmes. WHO/BCT/02.03.

Saito, N., & Yoshida, T. (2013). The Policy Issues for the Environmental Improvement of Smartphone Usage for Youth: Examination of Policy Issues by Analysis of Empirical Data. *Information and Communications Policy Review*, *6*, 1–21.

Salam, M. A. (2011). Supply chain commitment and business process integration: The implications of Confucian dynamism. *European Journal of Marketing*, *45*(3), 358–382. doi:10.1108/03090561111107230

Sandomir, R. (2010). For ESPN and Univision, the US is a soccer country. *The New York Times*. Retrieved March 1, 2018 from http://www.nytimes.com/2010/06/08/sports/soccer/08sandomir.html

Scherrer-Rathje, M., Boyle, T. A., & Deflorin, P. (2009). Lean, take two! Reflections from the second attempt at lean implementation. *Business Horizons*, *52*(1), 79–85. doi:10.1016/j.bushor.2008.08.004

Schienstock, G. (2007). From path dependency to path creation: Finland on its way to the knowledge-based economy. *Current Sociology*, *55*(1), 92–109. doi:10.1177/0011392107070136

Schirato, T. (2012). Fantasy sport and media interactivity. *Sport in Society: Cultures, Commerce, Media. Politics*, *15*(1), 78–87.

Schroeder, C. (2004). Online ads. *Campaigns and Elections*, *25*(1), 38–39.

Schwab, K. (2016). *The fourth industrial revolution*. London: Penguin Random House.

Schwarz, A., Schwarz, C., & Cenfetelli, R. T. (2012). A Profile of Rejecters of Electronic Medical Record Technology. AMCIS 2012 Proceedings.

Schwarz, C., & Schwarz, A. (2014). To Adopt or Not to Adopt: A Perception-Based Model of the Emr Technology Adoption Decision Utilizing the Technology-Organization-Environment Framework. *Journal of Organizational and End User Computing*, *26*(4), 57-79.

Schwarz, A., Chin, W., Hirschheim, R., & Schwarz, C. (2014). Toward a Process-Based View of Information Technology Acceptance. *Journal of Information Technology*, *29*(1), 73–96. doi:10.1057/jit.2013.31

Schwarz, I. L. M., Schwarz, I. T. M., García, G. M. J., Hernández, G. G. J., & Hernández, R. J. G. (2016). Social Impact of Restrictions on Inventory Management. In *Proceedings ICIL2016*. AGH University of Science and Technology in Krakow.

Schwarz, L. M., & Schwarz, T. M. (2015). *Propuesta de modelo de toma de decisiones en la planificación de ventas y operaciones de empresas Venezolanas de consumo masivo*. Caracas, Venezuela: Disertación en Ingeniería de Producción, Universidad Metropolitana.

Schwerdtfeger, A. R., Schmitz, C., & Warken, M. (2012). Using text messages to bridge the intention- behavior gap? A pilot study on the use of text message reminders to increase objectively assessed physical activity in daily life. *Frontiers in Psychology*, 3. PMID:22876237

Scott, W. R. (1987). The Adolescence of Institutional Theory. *Administrative Science Quarterly*, *32*(4), 493–511. doi:10.2307/2392880

Scott, W. R. (2003). *Organizations: Rational, Natural & Open Systems*. Prentice Hall.

Seddon, P. B., Calvert, C., & Yang, S. (2010). A multi-project model of key factors affecting Organizational benefits from enterprise systems. *Management Information Systems Quarterly*, *34*(2), 305–328. doi:10.2307/20721429

Sedighi, M., van Splunter, S., Zand, F., & Brazier, F. (2015). Evaluating Critical Success Factors Model of Knowledge Management: An analytic hierarchy process (AHP) approach. *International Journal of Knowledge Management*, *11*(3), 17–36. doi:10.4018/IJKM.2015070102

Seguin, B., Richelieu, A., & O'Reilly, N. (2008). Leveraging the Olympic brand through the reconciliation of corporate and consumers' brand perceptions. *International Journal of Sport Management and Marketing*, *3*(1/2), 3–22. doi:10.1504/IJSMM.2008.015958

Seidman, R. (2010). *World cup ratings: Out of home viewing adds 14%, non-TV platforms add 32%.* Retrieved March 1, 2018 from http://TVbythenumbers.zap2it.com/2010/07/18/world-cup-ratings-out-of-home-viewing-adds-14-non-TV-platforms-add-32/57429/

Senge, P. (1997). Sharing knowledge. *Executive Excellence, 14*(11), 17–18.

Senthilmurugan, P. R., Jegadheesan, C., & Devadasan, S. R. (2018). Improving the quality and yield in the casting of compressor pulley through the application of total failure mode and effects analysis. *International Journal of Services and Operations Management, 29*(1), 42–58. doi:10.1504/IJSOM.2018.088472

Seo, M.-G., & Creed, W. E. D. (2002). Institutional Contradictions, Praxis, and Institutional Change: A Dialectical Perspective. *Academy of Management Review, 27*(2), 222–247. doi:10.5465/amr.2002.6588004

Serrat, O. (2017). *Knowledge solutions: Tools, methods, and approaches to drive organizational performance.* Springer Open. doi:10.1007/978-981-10-0983-9

Seyal, A. H., & Rahman, M. N. A. (2014). Evaluating the Internal and External Factors Toward ERP Success: Examples from Bruneian Businesses. *International Journal of Enterprise Information Systems, 10*(4), 73–95. doi:10.4018/ijeis.2014100105

Shah, R., Chandrasekaran, A., & Linderman, K. (2008). In pursuit of implementation patterns: The context of Lean and Six Sigma. *International Journal of Production Research, 46*(23), 6679–6698. doi:10.1080/00207540802230504

Sharma, A., & Sharma, R. K. (2018). Modelling and analysis of enablers for successful implementation of cellular manufacturing system. *International Journal of Process Management and Benchmarking, 8*(1), 103–123. doi:10.1504/IJPMB.2018.088659

Shaw, G. L., & Harrald, J. (2006). The Core Competencies Required of Executive Level Business Crisis and Continuity Managers. In 11th Annual 2006/2007 Disaster Resource Guide (pp. 66-69).

Sheehy, K. (2014, August 24). 5 must-download apps for college students. *U.S. News & World Report.* Retrieved from http://www.usnews.com/education/best-colleges/articles/2014/08/21/5-must-download-apps-for-college-students

Shekelle, P., Morton, S. C., & Keeler, E. B. (2006). *Costs and Benefits of Health Information Technology.* Academic Press.

Sherer, S. A., Meyerhoefer, C. D., & Peng, L. (2016). Applying Institutional Theory to the Adoption of Electronic Health Records in the U.S. *Information & Management, 53*(5), 570–580. doi:10.1016/j.im.2016.01.002

Shi, W., Shambare, N., & Wang, J. (2008). The Adoption of Internet Banking: An Institutional Theory Perspective. *Journal of Financial Services Marketing, 12*(4), 272-286.

Shields, M. (2009). Facebook friends' brands. *Media Week, 18*(30), 8.

Shimoda, H. (2008). *School Back Site.* Toyo Keizai Inc. (in Japanese)

Shore, B. (2001). Information sharing in global supply chain systems. *Journal of Global Information Technology Management, 4*(3), 27–50. doi:10.1080/1097198X.2001.10856306

Shujahat, M., Sousa, M. J., Hussain, S., Nawaz, F., Wang, M., & Umer, M. (2017). Translating the impact of knowledge management processes into knowledge-based innovation: The neglected and mediating role of knowledge-worker productivity. *Journal of Business Research.* doi:10.1016/j.jbusres.2017.11.001

Shu, W., & Chuang, Y. (2011). Why people share knowledge in virtual communities. *Society for Personality Research, 39*(5), 671–690.

Sicard, M.-C. (2003). *Luxe, mensonge et marketing, Mais que font les marques de luxe.* Paris: Village Mondial.

Siemsen, E., Roth, A. V., & Balasubramanian, S. (2008). How motivation, opportunity, and ability drive knowledge sharing: The constraining-factor model. *Journal of Operations Management, 26*(3), 426–445. doi:10.1016/j.jom.2007.09.001

Silva, W. N., Vaz, M. A., & Souza, J. M. (2012). A Collaborative Model of Information Technology Strategic Plan for the Government Sector. IADIS Collaborative Technologies.

Simatupang, T., & Sridharan, R. (2005). An integrative framework for supply chain collaboration. *International Journal of Logistics Management, 16*(2), 257–274. doi:10.1108/09574090510634548

Simmons, V. N., Heckman, B. W., Fink, A. C., Small, B. J., & Brandon, T. H. (2013). Efficacy of an experiential, dissonance-based smoking intervention for college students delivered via the internet. *Journal of Consulting and Clinical Psychology, 81*(5), 810–820. doi:10.1037/a0032952 PMID:23668667

Simon, H. A. (1955). A Behavioral Model of Rational Choice. *The Quarterly Journal of Economics, 69*(1), 99-118.

Simpson, M. C., Gössling, S., Scott, D., Hall, C. M., & Gladin, E. (2008). Climate change adaptation and mitigation in the tourism sector: Frameworks, tools and practices. UNEP, University of Oxford, UNWTO, WMO.

SISP. (2012). *Guide for Preparation of Information Technology Strategic Plan. System Administration Resources Information Technology.* SISP.

Smit Sibinga, C. Th. (2010). Post-academic Masters in Management of Transfusion Medicine (MMTM): An evaluation of the e-learning part of the course. In *Proceedings of the 9th European Conference on e-Learning* (pp. 826-828). Academic Publ. Ltd.

Smit Sibinga, C. Th., & de Gunst, R. (2008). E-academy for international development of transfusion medicine – a unique institution. In *Proceedings of the 7ᵗʰ European Conference on e-Learning* (pp. 479-484). Academic Publ. Ltd.

Smit Sibinga, C. Th., & Dodd, R. Y. (2002). Transmissible Diseases and Blood Transfusion. Kluwer Academic Publ.

Smit Sibinga, C. Th., & Pitman, J.P. (2011). Transmission of HIV Through Blood – How To Bridge the Knowledge Gap. In HIV and AIDS – Updates on Biology, Immunology, Epidemiology and Treatment Strategies (pp. 583-618). InTech.

Smit Sibinga, C. (2013). Bridging the Knowledge Gap in Management and Operations of Transfusion Medicine: Planning, Policy and Leadership Issues. *Journal of Cases on Information Technology, 15*(1), 69–82. doi:10.4018/jcit.2013010105

Smit Sibinga, C. Th. (2009). Filling a gap in transfusion medicine education and research. *Transfusion Medicine Reviews, 23*(4), 284–291. doi:10.1016/j.tmrv.2009.06.003 PMID:19765517

Smit Sibinga, C. Th., Oladejo, M.A., Adejumo, O.H., Midori, K., Shuichi, K., Zolfaghari, S., ... Satti, M.M.H. (2017). Clinicians' Awareness, Accessibility, Utilization of E-Learning and Continous Education Programs; A Global Survey. Quality and efficacy of clinical use of blood: Policy considerations. *International Journal of Clinical Transfusion Medicine., 5*, 69–82. doi:10.2147/IJCTM.S136047

Smith, A. A., Synowka, D. P., & Smith, A. D. (2010). Exploring fantasy sports and its fan base from a CRM perspective. *International Journal of Business Innovation and Research, 4*(1-2), 103–142. doi:10.1504/IJBIR.2010.029543

Smith, A. A., Synowka, D. P., & Smith, A. D. (2014). E-commerce quality and adoptive elements of e-ticketing for entertainment and sporting. *International Journal of Business Information Systems, 15*(4), 450–487. doi:10.1504/IJBIS.2014.060397

Smith, A. D. (2002). Loyalty and e-marketing issues: Customer retention on the Web. *Quarterly Journal of E-commerce, 3*(2), 149–161.

Smith, A. D. (2005). Accountability in EDI systems to prevent employee fraud. *Information Systems Management, 22*(2), 30–38. doi:10.1201/1078/45099.22.2.20050301/87275.4

Smith, A. D. (2005). Exploring the inherent benefits of RFID and automated self-serve checkouts in a B2C environment. *International Journal of Business Information Systems, 1*(1), 149–181. doi:10.1504/IJBIS.2005.007405

Smith, A. D. (2006). Supply chain management using electronic reverse auction: A multi-firm case study. *International Journal of Services and Standards, 2*(2), 176–189. doi:10.1504/IJSS.2006.008731

Smith, A. D. (2009a). The impact of e-procurement systems on customer relationship management: A multiple case study. *International Journal of Procurement Management, 2*(3), 314–338. doi:10.1504/IJPM.2009.024814

Smith, A. D. (2009b). Leveraging concepts of knowledge management with total quality management: Case studies in the service sector. *International Journal of Logistics Systems and Supply Management, 5*(6), 631–653. doi:10.1504/IJLSM.2009.024795

Smith, A. D. (2010). Retail-based loyalty card programs and CRM concepts: An empirical study. *International Journal of Innovation and Learning, 7*(3), 303–330. doi:10.1504/IJIL.2010.031949

Smith, A. D. (2012). Social media and online dating service providers: Re-examining the new face of romance in the current global economic recession. *International Journal of Business Information Systems, 9*(2), 127–148. doi:10.1504/IJBIS.2012.045166

Smith, A. D. (2013). Online social networking and office environmental factors that affect worker productivity. *International Journal of Procurement Management, 6*(5), 578–608. doi:10.1504/IJPM.2013.056173

Smith, A. D., & Lias, A. R. (2005). Identity theft and e-fraud as critical CRM concerns. *International Journal of Enterprise Information Systems, 1*(2), 17–36. doi:10.4018/jeis.2005040102

Smith, A. D., & Potter, J. A. (2010). Loyalty card programs, customer relationships, and information technology: An exploratory approach. *International Journal of Business Innovation and Research, 4*(1-2), 65–92. doi:10.1504/IJBIR.2010.029541

Smith, A. D., & Rupp, W. T. (2013). Data quality and knowledge/information management in service operations management: Regional supermarket case study. *International Journal of Knowledge-Based Organizations, 3*(3), 35–52. doi:10.4018/ijkbo.2013070103

Smith, J. K. (1983). Quantitative versus qualitative research: An attempt to clarify the issue. *Educational Researcher, 12*(3), 6–13. doi:10.3102/0013189X012003006

Smith, J. S., Gleim, M. R., Robinson, S. G., & Kettinger, W. J. (2013). Using an old dog for new tricks: A regulatory focus perspective on consumer acceptance of RFID applications. *Journal of Service Research.*

Smock, A. D., Ellison, N. B., Lampe, C., & Wohn, D. Y. (2011). Facebook as a toolkit: A uses and gratification approach to unbundling feature use. *Computers in Human Behavior, 27*(6), 2322–2329. doi:10.1016/j.chb.2011.07.011

Smuts, H., van der Merwe, A., & Loock, M. (2009). Key Characteristics in Selecting Software Tools for Knowledge Management, UNISA report, South Africa

Snijders, C., & Zijdeman, R. (2004). Reputation and Internet auctions: eBay and beyond. *Analyse & Kritik, 26*(1), 158–184. doi:10.1515/auk-2004-0109

Snowden, D. (2004). Notes from the workshop – Social network simulation: Creating knowledge flow, not knowledge content. In *Conference: Knowledge Management Asia 2004*, Suntec Singapore International Convention and Exhibition Centre, November 2-4.

Sobel, M. E. (1982). Asymptotic intervals for indirect effects in structural equations models. In S. Leinhart (Ed.), *Sociological methodology* (pp. 290–312). San Francisco: Jossey-Bass. doi:10.2307/270723

Soetanto, R., Childs, M., Poh, P., Austin, S., & Hao, J. (2012). Global multidisciplinary learning in construction education: Lessons from virtual collaboration of building design teams. *Civil Engineering Dimension*, *14*(3), 173–181.

Solomon, C. M. (2001). Managing virtual teams. *Workforce*, *80*(1), 60–64.

Son, J.-Y., & Benbasat, I. (2007). Organizational Buyers' Adoption and Use of B2b Electronic Marketplaces: Efficiency- and Legitimacy-Oriented Perspectives. *Journal of Management Information Systems*, *24*(1), 55-99.

Soosay, C. A., Hyland, P. W., & Ferrer, M. (2008). Supply chain collaboration: Capabilities for continuous innovation. *Supply Chain Management*, *13*(2), 160–169. doi:10.1108/13598540810860994

Spencer, J. W. (2003). Firms' knowledge-sharing strategies in the global innovation system: Empirical evidence from the flat panel display industry. *Strategic Management Journal*, *24*(3), 217–233. doi:10.1002mj.290

Spiekermann, S., & Evdokimov, S. (2009). Critical RFID privacy-enhancing technologies. *Security & Privacy, IEEE*, *7*(2), 56–62. doi:10.1109/MSP.2009.31

Sprovieri, J. (2008). A Modest Increase. *Assembly*, *51*(13), 22–41.

Sriramatr, S., Berry, T. R., & Spence, J. C. (2014). An Internet-based intervention for promoting and maintaining physical activity: A randomized controlled trial. *American Journal of Health Behavior*, *38*(3), 430–439. doi:10.5993/AJHB.38.3.12 PMID:25181763

Stair, R., & Reynolds, G. (2005). *Principles of Information Systems* (7th ed.). Boston: Course Technology, Cengage Learning.

Stake, R. E. (2006). *Multiple Case Study Analysis*. New York: Guilford Press.

Statista. (2017a). *Number of social media users worldwide from 2010 to 2021 (in billions)*. Retrieved September 20th, 2017, from https://www.statista.com/statistics/278414/number-of-worldwide-social-network-users

Statista. (2017b). *Market value of luxury goods in France from 2012 to 2017 (in million euros)*. Retrieved September 20th, 2017, from https://www.statista.com/statistics/494154/luxury-goods-france-market-value

Statista. (2017c). *Number of monthly active Instagram users from January 2013 to September 2017 (in millions)*. Retrieved October 4th, 2017, from https://www.statista.com/statistics/253577/number-of-monthly-active-instagram-users

Steenkamp, J.-B. E. M., & Gielens, K. (2003). Consumer and Market Drivers of the Trial Probability of New Consumer Packaged Goods. *The Journal of Consumer Research*, *29*(December), 368–384. doi:10.1086/378615

Steinberg, L. (2001). The consequences of pairing questions: Context effects in personality measurement. *Journal of Personality and Social Psychology*, *81*(2), 332–342. doi:10.1037/0022-3514.81.2.332 PMID:11519936

Steinfield, C., DiMicco, J. M., Ellison, N. B., & Lampe, C. (2009, June). Bowling online: social networking and social capital within the organization. In *Proceedings of the fourth international conference on Communities and technologies* (pp. 245-254). ACM. 10.1145/1556460.1556496

Stevenson, M. A. (1997). The Antecedents and consequences of interpersonal trust in mixed-motive dyadic negotiation [Doctoral dissertation]. The Ohio State University.

Stiglitz, J. (2002). *Transparency in government. In The right to tell: the role of mass media in economic development* (pp. 27–44). Washington, DC: World Bank Publications.

Strader, T. J., Lin, F. R., & Shaw, M. J. (1999). The impact of information sharing on order fulfillment in divergent differentiation supply chains. *Journal of Global Information Management, 7*(1), 16–25. doi:10.4018/jgim.1999010102

Subaihi, T. A. (2013, 1 26). Operator warned before Global Village Ferris wheel death. *The National.* Retrieved 09 01, 2013, from http://www.thenational.ae/news/uae-news/operator-warned-before-global-village-ferris-wheel-death-says-family

Subin, I., Mason, C. H., & Houston, M. B. (2007). Does Innate Consumer Innovativeness relate to New Product/ Service Adoption Behavior? The Intervening Role of Social Learning via Vicarious Innovativeness? *Journal of the Academy of Marketing Science, 35*(1), 63–75. doi:10.100711747-006-0007-z

Suffoletto, B., Kristan, J., Callaway, C., Kim, K. H., Chung, T., Monti, P. M., & Clark, D. B. (2014). A text message alcohol intervention for young adult emergency department patients: A randomized clinical trial. *Annals of Emergency Medicine, 64*(6), 664–672. doi:10.1016/j.annemergmed.2014.06.010 PMID:25017822

Summers, G. J., & Scherpereel, C. M. (2008). Decision making in product development: Are you outside-in or inside-out? *Management Decision, 46*(9), 1299–1314. doi:10.1108/00251740810911957

Sustrans. (2007). *Low carbon travel information sheet.* Retrieved from http://www.climatlantic.co.uk/resource_files/KS3_4__travel_infosheet.pdf

Swan, K. (2001). Virtual interaction: Design factors affecting student satisfaction and perceived learning in asynchronous online courses. *Distance Education, 22*(2), 306–331. doi:10.1080/0158791010220208

Swanson, E. B. (1994). Information systems innovation among organizations. *Management Science, 40*(9), 1069–1092. doi:10.1287/mnsc.40.9.1069

Swart, J., Kinnie, N., Rossenberg, Y., & Yalabik, Z. Y. (2014). Why should I share my knowledge? A multiple foci of commitment perspective. *Human Resource Management Journal, 24*(3), 269–289. doi:10.1111/1748-8583.12037

Swayne, M. (2013). Bonding with your virtual self may alter your actual perceptions. *Penn State News.* Retrieved September 1, 2015 from http://news.psu.edu/story/275626/2013/05/02/research/bonding-your-virtual-self-may-alter-your-actual-perceptions

Sweeney, R. (2006). Millennial behaviors and demographics. Newark, NJ: New Jersey Institute of Technology.

Sydow, J., Schrey, G., & Koch, J. (2009). Organizational Path Dependence: Opening the Black Box. *Academy of Management Review, 34*(4), 689–709.

Sydow, J., Windeler, A., Schubert, C., & Möllering, G. (2012). Organizing R&D consortia for path creation and extension: The case of semiconductor manufacturing technologies. *Organization Studies, 33*(7), 907–936. doi:10.1177/0170840612448029

Syed, S. F., & Nurullah, A. S. (2011). Use of Mobile Phones and the Social Lives of Urban Adolescents: A Review of Literature. *Trends in Information Management, 7*(1), 1–18.

Sykes, T. A., & Venkatesh, V. (2017). Explaining Post-Implementation Employee System Use and Job Performance: Impacts of the Content and Source of Social Network ties. *Management Information Systems Quarterly, 41*(3), 917–936. doi:10.25300/MISQ/2017/41.3.11

Systems, B. (n.d.). Retrieved August 15, 2017, from http://www.bloodsystemseducation.org/

Szymanski, S. (2006). The economic evolution of sport and broadcasting. *The Australian Economic Review, 39*(4), 428–434. doi:10.1111/j.1467-8462.2006.00432.x

Taghaboni-Dutta, F., & Velthouse, B. (2006). RFID technology is revolutionary: Who should be involved in this game of tag? *The Academy of Management Perspectives, 20*(4), 65–78. doi:10.5465/amp.2006.23270307

Tagliaventi, M. R., & Mattarelli, E. (2006). The role of networks of practice, value sharing and operational proximity in knowledge flows between professional groups. *Human Relations, 59*(3), 291–319. doi:10.1177/0018726706064175

Tainsky, S., & McEvoy, C. D. (2011). Television broadcast demand in markets without local teams. *Journal of Sports Economics, 13*(3), 250–265. doi:10.1177/1527002511406129

Talyarkhana, S., Grimshaw, D. J., & Lowe, L. (2003). *Reaching the last mile: knowledge sharing for development. Knowledge and Information Services Unit, Intermediate Technology Development Group*, UK.

Tang, Z., Liu, M., Ammar, A., Li, K., & Li, K. (2016). An optimized MapReduce workflow scheduling algorithm for heterogeneous computing. *The Journal of Supercomputing, 72*(6), 2059–2079. doi:10.100711227-014-1335-2

Tan, P. S., Lee, S. S. G., & Goh, A. E. S. (2012). Multi-criteria decision techniques for context-aware B2B collaboration in supply chains. *Decision Support Systems, 52*(4), 779–789. doi:10.1016/j.dss.2011.11.013

Tate, A., Hansberger, J. T., Potter, S., & Wickler, G. (2014). Virtual collaboration spaces: Bringing presence to distributed collaboration. *Journal of Virtual Worlds Research, 7*(2), 111–122.

Taylor, D. G., Lewin, J. E., & Strutton, D. (2011). Friends, fans, and followers: Do ads work on social networks? *Journal of Advertising Research, 51*(1), 258–275. doi:10.2501/JAR-51-1-258-275

Tea, B. (2016). Case Study: Is Burberry's Social Media Use the Best Amongst Luxury Brands? *Socialwall.me*. Retrieved October 4th, 2017, from https://socialwall.me/en/burberry-social-media-use-luxury-brands

Teng, C. C., Horng, J. S., Hu, M. L., & Chen, P. C. (2014). Exploring energy and carbon literacy structure for hospitality and tourism practitioners: Evidence from hotel employees in Taiwan. *Asia Pacific Journal of Tourism Research, 19*(4), 451–468. doi:10.1080/10941665.2013.764336

Teng, Z., Shi, C. B., & Liu, Z. (2011). Sustainable development of tourism industry in china under the low-carbon economy. *Energy Procedia, 5*, 1303–1307. doi:10.1016/j.egypro.2011.03.226

Teo, T. S., Ranganathan, C., & Dhaliwal, J. (2006). Key Dimensions of Inhibitors for the Deployment of Web-Based Business-to-Business Electronic Commerce. *Engineering Management, IEEE Transactions on, 53*(3), 395-411.

Teo, H. H., Wei, K. K., & Benbasat, I. (2003). Predicting Intention to Adopt Interorganizational Linkages: An Institutional Perspective. *Management Information Systems Quarterly, 27*(1), 19–49. doi:10.2307/30036518

The World Bank. (2011). *The State of World Bank Knowledge Services - Knowledge for Development*. International Bank for Reconstruction and Development/The World Bank.

Thiesse, F. (2007). RFID, privacy and the perception of risk: A strategic framework. *The Journal of Strategic Information Systems, 16*(2), 214–232. doi:10.1016/j.jsis.2007.05.006

Thiesse, F., Al-Kassab, J., & Fleisch, E. (2009). Understanding the value of integrated RFID systems: A case study from apparel retail. *European Journal of Information Systems, 18*(6), 592–614. doi:10.1057/ejis.2009.33

Thirumalai, S., & Sinha, K. K. (2011). Customization of the online purchase process in electronic retailing and customer satisfaction: An online field study. *Journal of Operations Management, 29*(5), 477–487. doi:10.1016/j.jom.2010.11.009

Thite, M. (2004). Strategic positioning of HRM in knowledge-based organizations. *The Learning Organization*, *11*(1), 28–44. doi:10.1108/09696470410515715

Thompson, C., & Wembridge, M. (2012, August 12). Big Tobacco Push for Cigarette Alternatives. *Financial Times*.

Thompson, R. L., Higgins, C., & Howell, J. M. (1991). Personal computing: Toward a conceptual model of utilization. *Management Information Systems Quarterly*, *15*(1), 125–143. doi:10.2307/249443

Thusoo, A., Sarma, J. S., Jain, N., Shao, Z., Chakka, P., Zhang, N., . . . Murthy, R. (2010, March). Hive-a petabyte scale data warehouse using hadoop. In *Data Engineering (ICDE), 2010 IEEE 26th International Conference on* (pp. 996-1005). IEEE. 10.1109/ICDE.2010.5447738

Tian, F., & Xu, S. X. (2015). How Do Enterprise Resource Planning Systems Affect Firm Risk? Post-Implementation Impact. *Management Information Systems Quarterly*, *39*(1), 39–60. doi:10.25300/MISQ/2015/39.1.03

Tidey, W. (2012). *ESPN ratings for Euro 2012 demonstrate soccer's growing reach in America*. Retrieved July 9, 2014 from http://bleacherreport.com/articles/1245475-us-audience-for-euro-2012-demonstrates-soccers-growing-reach-in-america

Timmerman, T. A. (2000). Racial diversity, age diversity, interdependence, and team performance. *Small Group Research*, *31*(1), 592–606. doi:10.1177/104649640003100505

Timonen, H., & Paloheimo, K. S. (2008). The emergence and diffusion of the concept of knowledge work. *Electronic Journal of Knowledge Management*, *6*(2), 177–190.

Todericiu, R., Şerban, A., & Dumitraşcu, O. (2013). Particularities of knowledge worker's motivation strategies in Romanian organizations. *Procedia Economics and Finance*, *6*, 405–413. doi:10.1016/S2212-5671(13)00155-X

Todor, R. D. (2016). Blending traditional and digital marketing. *Bulletin of the Transilvania University of Brasov. Series V, Economic Sciences*, *9*(1), 51–56.

Tonelli, A. O., Bermejo, P. H. S., Santos, P. A., Zuppo, L., & Zambalde, A. L. (2015). IT governance in the public sector: A conceptual model. *Information Systems Frontiers*.

Toomey, L., & Adams, L. (2000). *U.S. Patent No. 6,119,147*. Washington, DC: U.S. Patent and Trademark Office.

Tornatzky, L. G., & Fleischer, M. (1990). *The processes of technological innovation*. Lexington, MA: Lexington Books.

Tornatzky, L. G., & Fleischer, M. (1990). *The Processes of Technological Innovation*. Lexington, MA: Lexington Books.

Touzani, M., Charfi, A. A., Boistel, P., & Niort, M.-C. (2017). *Connecto ergo sum!* An Exploratory Study of Motivations behind the Usage of Connected Objects. *Information & Management*.

Townsend, S. (2017). UAE economy on the up in 2017, but late payments still an issue. *Arabianbusiness.com*. Retrieved from http://www.arabianbusiness.com/uae-economy-on-up-in-2017-but-late-payments-still-issue-662176.html

Trkman, P., McCormack, K., Valandares de Oliveria, M. P., & Ladeira, M. B. (2010). The impact of business analytics on supply chain performance. *Decision Support Systems*, *49*(3), 318–327. doi:10.1016/j.dss.2010.03.007

Trocchia, P. J., & Ainscough, T. L. (2012). Consumer attitudes toward RFID tracking in the retail environment. *Review of Business Information Systems*, *16*(2), 67–72. doi:10.19030/rbis.v16i2.6893

Tsaur, S. H., & Dai, Y. Y. (2016). How to do a low-carbon travel? Developing and validating low-carbon travel scale. *Journal of Outdoor Recreation Study*, *29*(2), 27–53.

Tse, E. (2016). *The Rise of Entrepreneurship in China*. Retrieved from https://www.forbes.com/sites/tseedward/2016/04/05/the-rise-of-entrepreneurship-in-china/#51f8b4403efc

Tsotsis, A. (2011, October 18). AngelPad's third demo day: Fifteen startups take flight. *TechCrunch*. Retrieved from http://techcrunch.com/2011/10/18/angelpads-third-demo-day-fifteen-startups-take-flight/

Tuomi, I. (2002). *Networks of innovation*. Oxford University Press Oxford.

Turri, A. M., Smith, R. J., & Kopp, S. W. (2017). Privacy and RFID technology: A review of regulatory efforts. *The Journal of Consumer Affairs, 51*(2), 329–354. doi:10.1111/joca.12133

Turriago-Hoyos, A., Thoene, U., & Arjoon, S. (2016). Knowledge workers and virtues in Peter Drucker's management theory. *SAGE Open, 6*(1). doi:10.1177/2158244016639631

Tutton, M. (2009). Going to the virtual office in Second Life. *CNN News*. Retrieved September 10, 2015 from http://www.cnn.com/2009/BUSINESS/11/05/second.life.virtual.collaboration/

Tuuli, M. M. (2012). Competing models of how motivation, opportunity and ability drive performance behaviors. In S. Laryea, S. A. Agyepong, R. Leiringer, & W. Hughes (Eds). In *Proceedings of the 4th West Africa Built Environment Research Conference*. Abuja, Nigeria: *WABER*.

Tyler, L. (1997). Liability means never being able to say you're sorry: Corporate guilt, legal constraints, and defensiveness in corporate communication. *Management Communication Quarterly, 11*(1), 51–73. doi:10.1177/0893318997111003

Ubhi, H. K., Kotz, D., Michie, S., Van Schayck, O. C. P., Sheard, D., Selladurai, A., & West, R. (2016). Comparative analysis of smoking cessation smartphone applications available in 2012 versus 2014. *Addictive Behaviors, 58*, 175–181. doi:10.1016/j.addbeh.2016.02.026 PMID:26950256

Ueki, Y. (2016). Customer pressure, customer-manufacturer-supplier relationships, and quality control performance. *Journal of Business Research, 69*(6), 2233–2238. doi:10.1016/j.jbusres.2015.12.035

Ulmer, R. R. T. L. (2006). Effective Crisis Communication: Moving from crisis to opportunity. Thousand Oaks, CA: Sage.

UNDP Human Development Index. (n.d.). Retrieved August 15, 2017, from http://hdr.undp.org/en/content/human-development-index-hdi

UNESCO. (2005). *Towards knowledge societies*. Paris: United Nations Educational, Scientific and Cultural Organization.

United Nations Universal Declaration of Human Rights. (1948). Retrieved August 15, 2017, from www.un.org/en/documents/udhr/nde.shtml

United Nations. (2012). Resolution 67/81 Global Health and Foreign Policy.

Urgin, J. C. (2009). The Effect of System Characteristics, Stage of Adoption, and Experience on Institutional Explanations for Erp Systems Choice. *Accounting Horizons, 23*(4), 365-389.

US Census Bureau. (2012). *2011 Household income distribution*. Retrieved from http://www.census.gov/hhes/www/cpstables/032012/hhinc/toc.htm

Vaiman, V. (Ed.). (2010). *Talent management of knowledge workers: Embracing the non-traditional workforce*. New York, NY: Springer. doi:10.1057/9780230277526

Valette-Florence, P. (1989). Conceptualisation et Mesure de l'Implication. *Recherche et Applications en Marketing, 4*(1), 57–78. doi:10.1177/076737018900400104

Van de Ven, A. H. (2005). Running in Packs to Develop Knowledge-Intensive Technologies. *Management Information Systems Quarterly, 29*(2), 365–377. doi:10.2307/25148683

Van de Ven, A. H., Polley, D., & Garud, R. (2008). *The innovation journey*. Oxford University Press.

Van Iddekinge, C. H., Aguinis, H., Mackey, J. D., & DeOrtentiis, P. S. (2017). A meta-analysis of the interactive, additive, and relative effects of cognitive ability and motivation on performance. *Journal of Management, 31*(1), 249–279.

Van Scotter, J. R., & Motowidlo, S. J. (1996). Interpersonal facilitation and job dedication as separate facets of contextual performance. *The Journal of Applied Psychology, 81*(5), 525–531. doi:10.1037/0021-9010.81.5.525

van Velsen, L., Huijs, C., & van der Geest, T. (2008). Eliciting User Input for Requirements on Personalization: The Case of a Dutch ERP System. *International Journal of Enterprise Information Systems, 4*(4), 34–46. doi:10.4018/jeis.2008100103

Van Weele, A., & van Raaij, E. (2005). The future of purchasing and supply management research: About relevance and rigor. *The Journal of Supply Chain Management, 50*(1), 56–72. doi:10.1111/jscm.12042

Velcu, O. (2010). Strategic alignment of ERP implementation stages: An empirical investigation. *Information & Management, 47*(3), 158–166. doi:10.1016/j.im.2010.01.005

Venkataraman, S., Roy, I., Schreiber, R. S., & AuYoung, A. (2011). *Presto: Complex and continuous analytics with distributed arrays.* Academic Press.

Venkatesh, V., Thong, J. Y. L., & Xu, X. (2012). Consumer Acceptance and Use of Information Technology: Extending the Unified Theory of Acceptance and Use of Technology. *MIS Q., 36*(1), 157-178.

Venkatesh, V., & Bala, H. (2008). Technology Acceptance model 3 and a research agenda on interventions. *Decision Sciences, 39*(2), 273–315. doi:10.1111/j.1540-5915.2008.00192.x

Venkatesh, V., & Brown, S. (2001). A Longitudinal Investigation of Personal Computers in Homes: Adoption Determinants and Emerging Challenges. *Management Information Systems Quarterly, 25*(1), 71–102. doi:10.2307/3250959

Venkatesh, V., & Davis, D. F. (2000). A theoretical extension of the technology acceptance model: Four longitudinal field studies. *Management Science, 46*(2), 186–204. doi:10.1287/mnsc.46.2.186.11926

Venkatesh, V., & Morris, M. G. (2000). Why don't men ever stop to ask for directions? Gender, social influence, and their role in technology acceptance and usage behavior. *Management Information Systems Quarterly, 24*(1), 115–139. doi:10.2307/3250981

Venkatesh, V., Morris, M., Davis, G., & Davis, F. (2003). User acceptance of information technology: Toward a unified view. *Management Information Systems Quarterly, 27*(3), 425–478. doi:10.2307/30036540

Venkatesh, V., Speier, C., & Morris, M. G. (2002). User acceptance enablers in individual decision making about technology: Toward an integrated model. *Decision Sciences, 33*(2), 297–316. doi:10.1111/j.1540-5915.2002.tb01646.x

Venkatraman, M. P., & Price, L. (1990). Differentiating between Cognitive and Sensory Innovativeness: Concepts, Measurement, and Implications. *Journal of Business Research, 20*(4), 293–315. doi:10.1016/0148-2963(90)90008-2

Ventakatesh, V., & Davis, D. F. (1996). A model of perceived ease of use: Development and test. *Decision Sciences, 27*(3), 451–483. doi:10.1111/j.1540-5915.1996.tb01822.x

Verma, P., Sharma, R. R. K., & Kumar, V. (2018). The sustainability issues of diversified firms in emerging economies context: A theoretical model and propositions. *International Journal of Process Management and Benchmarking, 7*(2), 224–248. doi:10.1504/IJPMB.2017.083107

Vicente, C. (2005). *ITCSP – Information Technology and Communication Strategic Plan.* Available at http://www.macmt.com.br/Arquivos/Livro%20PDTIC%20Registrado%20na%20Biblioteca%20Nacional.pdf

Viner, S. (2014). Social media statistics: How college students are using social networking. *Study Breaks Magazine*. Retrieved September 8, 2015 from http://studybreakscollegemedia.com/2014/social-media-statistics-how-college-students-are-using-social-networking/

Vinodh, S., Sundararaj, G., Devadasan, S. R., Maharaja, R., Rajanayagam, D., & Goyal, S. K. (2008). DESSAC: A decision support system for quantifying and analyzing agility. *International Journal of Production Research*, *46*(23), 6759–6678. doi:10.1080/00207540802230439

Von Hippel, E. (1988). *Sources of Innovation*. Oxford, UK: Oxford University Press.

Von Hippel, E. (1994). Sticky Information and the Locus of Problem Solving: Implications for Innovation. *Management Science*, *40*(4), 429–439. doi:10.1287/mnsc.40.4.429

Von Hippel, E. (2005). *Democratizing innovation*. Cambridge, MA: MIT Press.

Von Hippel, E., & Tyre, M. J. (1995). How learning by doing is done: Problem identification in novel process equipment. *Research Policy*, *24*(1), 1–12. doi:10.1016/0048-7333(93)00747-H

Von Hippell, E. (2005). *Democratizing Innovation*. Retrieved from http://web.mit.edu/evhippel/www/books.htm

Walsham, G. (1993). *Interpreting Information Systems in Organizations*. Chichester, UK: Wiley.

Walsham, G. (2006). Doing Interpretive Research. *European Journal of Information Systems*, *15*(3), 320–330. doi:10.1057/palgrave.ejis.3000589

Walsham, G. (2017). ICT4D research: Reflections on history and future agenda. *Journal Information Technology for Development*, *23*(1).

Wang, S., Zhou, X., Zhang, L., & Jiang, C. (2017, July). Network-Adaptive Scheduling of Data-Intensive Parallel Jobs with Dependencies in Clusters. In *Autonomic Computing (ICAC), 2017 IEEE International Conference on* (pp. 155-160). IEEE. 10.1109/ICAC.2017.13

Wang, T., Wang, J., Nguyen, S. N., Yang, Z., Mi, N., & Sheng, B. (2017, July). EA2S2: An Efficient Application-Aware Storage System for Big Data Processing in Heterogeneous Clusters. In *Computer Communication and Networks (ICCCN), 2017 26th International Conference on* (pp. 1-9). IEEE.

Wang, D., Guo, W., & Liu, X. (2009). Study on the Impact of Group Internal Social Network on Group Creativity. *Management Science*, (9): 25–28.

Wang, J., Hedman, J., & Tuunainen, V. K. (2016). Path creation, path dependence and breaking away from the path: Re-examining the case of Nokia. *Journal of Theoretical and Applied Electronic Commerce Research*, *11*(2), 16–27. doi:10.4067/S0718-18762016000200003

Wang, S., & Noe, R. A. (2010). Knowledge sharing: A review and directions for future research. *Human Resource Management Review*, *20*(2), 115–131. doi:10.1016/j.hrmr.2009.10.001

Wang, S., Noe, R. A., & Wang, Z. M. (2011). Motivating Knowledge Sharing in Knowledge Management Systems. *Journal of Management*, *40*(4), 978–1009. doi:10.1177/0149206311412192

Wang, W., Zhu, K., Ying, L., Tan, J., & Zhang, L. (2016). Maptask scheduling in mapreduce with data locality: Throughput and heavy-traffic optimality. *IEEE/ACM Transactions on Networking*, *24*(1), 190–203. doi:10.1109/TNET.2014.2362745

Wang, X., Zhang, X., Xu, X., & Gao, Y. (2018). Electronic cigarette use and smoking cessation behavior among adolescents in China. *Addictive Behaviors*, *82*, 129–134. doi:10.1016/j.addbeh.2018.02.029 PMID:29522934

Warkentin, M., & Beranek, P. M. (1999). Training to improve virtual team communication. *Information Systems, 9*(4), 271–289. doi:10.1046/j.1365-2575.1999.00065.x

Warnock, K., & Wickremasinghe, R. (2005). *Information and Communication Technologies and large-scale poverty reduction Lessons from Asia, Africa, Latin America and the Caribbean* (K. Warnock & R. Wickremasinghe, Eds.). London, UK: Panos London.

Wasko, M. M., & Faraj, S. (2005). Why should I share? Examining social capital and knowledge contribution in electronic networks of practice. *Management Information Systems Quarterly, 29*(1), 35–57. doi:10.2307/25148667

Weeks, C. S., Cornwell, T. B., & Drennan, J. C. (2008). Leveraging sponsorships on the Internet: Activation, congruence, and articulation. *Psychology and Marketing, 25*(7), 637–654. doi:10.1002/mar.20229

Weill, P., Ross, J. W., & Robertson, D. C. (2006). *Enterprise Architecture as Strategy: Creating a Foundation for Business Execution.* Harvard Business School Press.

Welschen, J., Todorova, N., & Mills, A. M. (2012). An investigation of the impact of intrinsic motivation on organizational knowledge sharing. *International Journal of Knowledge Management, 8*(2), 23–42. doi:10.4018/jkm.2012040102

Wembridge, M., & Thompson, C. (2012). Big Tobacco bets on e-cigarette future. *Financial Times.* Retrieved November, 2014, from http://www.ft.com/cms/s/0/cb76997ee0a511e1b46500144feab49a.html#ixzz23RJXFAJZ

West, R., Walia, A., Hyder, N., Shahab, L., & Michie, S. (2010). Behavior change techniques used by the English stop smoking services and their associations with short-term quit outcomes. *Nicotine & Tobacco Research, 12*(7), 742–747. doi:10.1093/ntr/ntq074 PMID:20478957

WHA63. (2010). *12 – Availability, safety and quality of blood products.* Geneva: WHA Resolution.

Whittaker, R., Maddison, R., McRobbie, H., Bullen, C., Denny, S., Dorey, E., & Rodgers, A. (2008). A Multimedia Mobile Phone-Based Youth Smoking Cessation Intervention: Findings from Content Development and Piloting Studies. *Journal of Medical Internet Research, 10*(5), e49. doi:10.2196/jmir.1007 PMID:19033148

WHO Global Status Report on Blood Safety and Availability 2016. (2017). Geneva: WHO.

WHO Universal Health Coverage. (n.d.). Accessed on April 08, 2018 from http://www.who.int/universal_health_coverage/en/

WHO. (2013). *Global Database on Blood Safety, Summary Report 2013.* Retrieved April 08, 2017, from http://www.who.int/bloodsafety/global_database/GDBS_Summary_Report_2013.pdf?ua=1

WHO. (2017). *Technical Report Series no. 1004:67, 2017 – Annex 3. Guidelines on management of blood and blood components as essential medicines.* WHO.

WHO. (n.d.). *Distance Learning Material, accessible through Education and training in blood transfusion safety.* Retrieved August 15, 2017, from www.who.int/bloodsafety/publications/en/index.html

WHO/BTC/BTS/01.3. (2001). *Developing a National Policy and Guidelines on the Clinical Use of Blood. Recommendations.* World Health Organization.

Widmann, B. S. (2013). *Influence of leadership style on work engagement of knowledge workers in an engineering organization* [Doctoral dissertation]. Retrieved from https://pqdtopen.proquest.com/doc/1428738809.html?FMT=ABS

Wilson, W., & Duffy, K. P. (2010). Improved information connectivity and visibility throughout the global supply base. *International Journal of e-Collaboration, 6*(4), 54–68. doi:10.4018/jec.2010100104

Wimbush, J. C., Shepard, J. M., & Markham, S. E. (1997). An empirical examination of the relationship between ethical climate and ethical behavior from multiple levels of analysis. *Journal of Business Ethics*, *16*(16), 1705–1716. doi:10.1023/A:1017952221572

Winkler, T. J. (2013). IT Governance Mechanisms and Administration/IT Alignment in the Public Sector: A Conceptual Model and Case Validation. *Wirtschaftsinformatik Proceedings*. Retrieved from http://aisel.aisnet.org/wi2013/53

Wolinski, C. (2016). They're Post-Millennial, Pre-Myopic Digital Natives...How Will You Connect With Gen Z? *Vision Monday*. Retrieved September 20th, 2017, from http://www.visionmonday.com/eyecare/optometry/article/theyre-postmillennial-premyopic-digital-natives

Wong, L. (2005). Chinese management as discourse: Chinese as a technology of self and control. *Asian Business & Management*, *4*(4), 431–453. doi:10.1057/palgrave.abm.9200142

Wood, C., Reiners, T., & Srivastava, H. S. (2016). Effective use of information can allow operational decisions to be made that minimise costs of the firm and position them to respond more quickly to market changes. *International Journal of Logistics Research and Applications*, *20*(5), 426–443. doi:10.1080/13675567.2016.1267126

World Bank. (2017). *Egypt's economic outlook*. Washington, DC: World Bank publications.

World Health Organization. (2011). Global Database on Blood Safety. In *Blood transfusions safety*. WHO. Retrieved August 15, 2017, from http://www.who.int/bloodsafety/global_database/en/

World Tourism Organization and United Nations Environment Programme. (2008). *Climate change and tourism: Responding to global challenges*. Madrid, Spain: World Tourism Organization.

Worldwide, D. E. I. (2008). *The impact of social media on purchasing behavior. Engaging Consumers Online. The impact of social media on purchasing behavior*. Retrieved September 20th, 2017, from https://themarketingguy.files.wordpress.com/2008/12/dei-study-engaging-consumers-online-summary.pdf

Wright, K. (2005). Personal knowledge management: Supporting individual knowledge worker performance. *Knowledge Management Research and Practice*, *3*(3), 156–165. doi:10.1057/palgrave.kmrp.8500061

Wu, I. L., & Chuang, C. H. (2010). Examining the diffusion of electronic supply chain management with external antecedents and firm performance: A multi-stage analysis. *Decision Support Systems*, *50*(1), 103–115. doi:10.1016/j.dss.2010.07.006

Wu, J. H., Wang, S. C., & Tsai, H. H. (2011). Falling in love with online games: The uses and gratifications perspective. *Computers in Human Behavior*, *26*(6), 1862–1871. doi:10.1016/j.chb.2010.07.033

Wu, J., Wu, Z., & Si, S. (2016). The influences of internet-based collaboration and intimate interactions in buyer-supplier relationship on product innovation. *Journal of Business Research*, *69*(9), 3780–3787. doi:10.1016/j.jbusres.2015.12.070

Wu, M. (2006). Hofstede's cultural dimensions 30years later: A study of Taiwan and the United States. *Intercultural Communication Studies*, *15*(1), 33–42.

Wüst, K., & Gervais, A. (2017). Do you need a blockchain? *IACR Cryptology ePrint Archive*, *2017*, 375-382.

Wu, Y., Cegielski, C. G., Hazen, B. T., & Hall, D. J. (2013). Cloud computing in support of supply chain information system infrastructure: Understanding when to go to the cloud. *The Journal of Supply Chain Management*, *49*(3), 25–41. doi:10.1111/j.1745-493x.2012.03287.x

Wu, Z., Xu, J., & Xu, Z. (2016). A multiple attribute group decision making framework for the evaluation of lean practices at logistics distribution centers. *Annals of Operations Research*, *247*(2), 735–757. doi:10.100710479-015-1788-6

Xu, J., Wu, Z., & Zhang, Y. (2014). A consensus based method for multi-criteria group decision making under uncertain linguistic setting. *Group Decision and Negotiation*, 1–22.

Xu, Y., Tiwari, A., Chen, H. C., & Turner, C. J. (2018). Development of a validation and qualification process for the manufacturing of medical devices: A case study based on cross-sector benchmarking. *International Journal of Process Management and Benchmarking*, 8(1), 79–102. doi:10.1504/IJPMB.2018.088658

Yamshon, L. (2014). Skitch is a multi-purpose editing tool for doodling on any document. *Tech Hive*. Retrieved from http://www.techhive.com/article/2450075/skitch-is-a-multi-purpose-editing-tool-for-doodling-on-any-document.html

Yang, H., & Zhou, L. (2011). Extending TPB and TAM to mobile viral marketing: An exploratory study of American young consumers' mobile viral marketing attitude, intent, and behaviour. *Journal of Targeting. Measurement and Analysis for Marketing*, 19(2), 85–98. doi:10.1057/jt.2011.11

Yao, Y., Wang, J., Sheng, B., Tan, C. C., & Mi, N. (2017). Self-adjusting slot configurations for homogeneous and heterogeneous hadoop clusters. *IEEE Transactions on Cloud Computing*, 5(2), 344–357. doi:10.1109/TCC.2015.2415802

Yazdi, A. K., & Esfeden, G. A. (2018). Designing robust model of Six Sigma implementation based on critical successful factors and MACBETH. *International Journal of Process Management and Benchmarking*, 7(2), 158–171. doi:10.1504/IJPMB.2017.083103

Ybarra, M. L., Holtrop, J. S., Prescott, T. L., Rahbar, M. H., & Strong, D. (2013). Pilot RCT results of stop my smoking USA: A text messaging-based smoking cessation program for young adults. *Nicotine & Tobacco Research*, 15(8), 1388–1399. doi:10.1093/ntr/nts339 PMID:23348969

Yee, W. F., & Sidek, Y. (2008). Influence of brand loyalty on consumer sportswear. *International Journal of Economics and Management*, 2(2), 221–236.

Yeung, I. Y. M., & Tung, R. L. (1996). Achieving business success in Confucian societies: The importance of Guanxi (connections). *Organizational Dynamics*, 25(2), 54–65. doi:10.1016/S0090-2616(96)90025-X

Yew Wong, K. (2005). Critical success factors for implementing knowledge management in small and medium enterprises. *Industrial Management & Data Systems*, 105(3), 261–279. doi:10.1108/02635570510590101

Yin, R. (1993). *Applications of case study research*. Newbury Park, CA: Sage Publishing.

Yin, R. (1994). *Case study research - design and methods*. Thousand Oaks, CA: Sage publishing.

Yin, R. K. (2005). Applied Social Research Methods Series (Vol. 5. *Case Study Research: Design & Methods, 3rd ed.*). Sage.

Yoon, C. (2009). The effects of national culture values on consumer acceptance of e-commerce: Online shoppers in China. *Information & Management*, 46(5), 294–301. doi:10.1016/j.im.2009.06.001

Yoon, K. S. (2012). Measuring the influence of expertise and epistemic engagement to the practice of knowledge management. *International Journal of Knowledge Management*, 8(1), 40–70. doi:10.4018/jkm.2012010103

Yoon, Y., & Uysal, M. (2005). An examination of the effects of motivation and satisfaction on destination loyalty: A structural model. *Tourism Management*, 26(5), 45–56. doi:10.1016/j.tourman.2003.08.016

Yoo, Y., Boland, R. J. Jr, & Lyytinen, K. (2006). From Organization Design to Organization Designing. *Organization Science*, 17(2), 215–229. doi:10.1287/orsc.1050.0168

Yoshimi, T., & Mizukoshi, S. (2004). *Media theories*. The Open University of Japan. (in Japanese)

Youssef, A. B., Martin, L., & Omrani, N. (2014). The complementarities between Information and Communication Technologies Use, New Organizational Practices and Employee's Contextual Performance: Evidence from Europe in 2005 and 2010. *Revue d Economie Politique Editions Dalloz, 124*(4), 493–504.

Yukawa, S. (2003). *TV and Violence. In Media and Human Development - Psychological Impact of TV, TV Game, Internet, and Robots* (pp. 41–57). Gakubunsha. (in Japanese)

Yun, E. K. (2013). Predictors of attitude and intention to use knowledge management system among Korean nurses. *Nurse Education Today, 33*(12), 1477–1481. doi:10.1016/j.nedt.2013.05.018 PMID:23806194

Yu, P., Li, H. C., & Gagnon, M. P. (2009). Health IT acceptance factors in long-term care facilities: A cross-sectional survey. *International Journal of Medical Informatics, 78*(4), 219–229. doi:10.1016/j.ijmedinf.2008.07.006 PMID:18768345

Zaczkiewicz, A. (2017). *Amazon, Wal-Mart and Apple top list of biggest e-commerce retailers.* Retrieved October 4, 2017 from http://wwd.com/business-news/business-features/amazon-wal-mart-apple-biggest-e-commerce-retailers-10862796/

Zaharia, M., Chowdhury, M., Das, T., Dave, A., Ma, J., McCauley, M., ... Stoica, I. (2012, April). Resilient distributed datasets: A fault-tolerant abstraction for in-memory cluster computing. In *Proceedings of the 9th USENIX conference on Networked Systems Design and Implementation* (pp. 2-2). USENIX Association

Zaney, K. (2004). Down with pop-ups. *Education Week, 21*(1), 41–42.

Zhang, B. (2015). *A Brief Introduction of Existing Big Data Tools.* Retrieved from scholarwiki.indiana.edu/Z604/slides/big%20data%20tools%20v2.pdf

Zhang, G., Li, C., Zhang, Y., Xing, C., & Yang, J. (2012). Mapreduce++: Efficient processing of mapreduce jobs in the cloud. *Journal of Computer Information Systems, 8*(14), 5757–5764.

Zhang, Q., & Cao, M. (2018). Exploring antecedents of supply chain collaboration: Effects of culture and interorganizational system appropriation. *International Journal of Production Economics, 195*, 146–157. doi:10.1016/j.ijpe.2017.10.014

Zhang, Q., & Liu, H. (2011). Study on design and research of tourist souvenirs on the background of low-carbon economy. *Energy Procedia, 5*, 2416–2420. doi:10.1016/j.egypro.2011.03.415

Zhang, Z., Lee, M. K. O., Huang, P., Zhang, L., & Huang, X. Y. (2005). A framework of ERP systems implementation success in China: An empirical study. *International Journal of Production Economics, 98*(1), 56–80. doi:10.1016/j.ijpe.2004.09.004

Zhou, T. (2011). Understanding online community user participation: A social influence perspective. *Internet Research, 21*(1), 67–81. doi:10.1108/10662241111104884

Zhu, H., Zhang, J., Liao, L., & Jin, S. (2017). Low carbon transition and sustainable development path of tourism industry. *IOP Conf. Series: Earth and Environmental Science, 64*(012053), 1-4. 10.1088/1755-1315/64/1/012053

Zhu, K., & Kraemer, K. L. (2005). Post-Adoption Variations in Usage and Value of E-Business by Organizations: Cross-Country Evidence from the Retail Industry. *Information Systems Research, 16*(1), 61-84.

Zhu, K., Kraemer, K. L., & Xu, S. (2006). The Process of Innovation Assimilation by Firms in Different Countries: A Technology Diffusion Perspective on E-Business. *Management Sciences, 52*(10), 1557-1576.

Zhu, K., Kraemer, K., & Xu, S. (2003). Electronic Business Adoption by European Firms: A Cross-Country Assessment of the Facilitators and Inhibitors. *European Journal of Information Systems, 12*(4), 251-268.

Zhu, Y., Li, Y., Wang, W., & Chen, J. (2010). What leads to post-implementation success of ERP? An empirical study of the Chinese retail industry. *International Journal of Information Management, 30*(3), 265–276. doi:10.1016/j.ijinfomgt.2009.09.007

Zimmerman, M. H., Clavio, G. E., & Lim, C. H. (2011). Set the agenda like Beckham: A professional sports league's use of YouTube to disseminate messages to its users. *International Journal of Sport Management and Marketing, 10*(3/4), 180–195. doi:10.1504/IJSMM.2011.044789

About the Contributors

Badreya Al-Jenaibi is Associate Professor in Mass Communication at the United Arab Emirates University. She has a Ph.D. in International Communication and Public Relations (August 2008) from the University of North Dakota in the USA. Her MA (2004) was in Mass Communication is from the University of Northern Iowa in the USA. Her BA (2001) was in Mass Communication from the University of the United Arab Emirates. Her research interests include International Communication, Public relations, organizational communication, the uses and effects of mass media, new media, particularly the international level, as well as public relations and communication. Her doctoral dissertation was bout Press freedom in the Arab world. She is the author of The Scope and Impact of Workplace Diversity in the United Arab Emirates – An Initial Study, The Role of the Public and Employee Relations Department in Increasing Social Support in the Diverse Workplaces of the United Arab Emirates, Gender Issues in the Diversity and Practice of Public Relations in the UAE-Case study of P.R. male managers and female P.R. practitioners, The Use of Social Media in the United Arab Emirates, The Changing Representation of the Arab Woman in Middle East Advertising and Media, Public Relation Practitioners, Independency, and Teamwork in the UAE Organizations, Book chapter accepted for publication in Handbook of Research on Business Social Networking: Organizational, Managerial, and Technological Dimensions 2011. Women in Public Relations and profit organizations: How Gender Influences Practice, Book chapter accepted for publication in Global Knowledge Work 2011.

Synnøve Thomassen Andersen, (PhD at UiT, The Arctic University in Alta), Her PhD is in informatics, and she holds a bachelor in child welfare. She lives and does research in the Arctic. Thomassen Andersen's scientific publications cover a number of areas, focusing on information infrastructures, user involvement, digitization, flexibility and studies of innovation and welfare technology.

Madoka Aragaki got her Ph.D degree in Graduate School of Medicine, University of Tokyo. After that, she has engaged in online education in several universities. She is interested in psychosocial aspects that internet affects on children and students.

Antonio Arredondo is a student of Communication at California State University Channel Islands.

Silvia Cacho-Elizondo is an Associate Professor of Marketing and Academic Director for In-Company Programs at IPADE Business School in México. She has been lecturer in several business schools in France, Spain and Mexico. She started her professional career as a Research & Commercial Engineer at an Electrical Research Institute, later on, she worked in Procter & Gamble. Also, she has collaborated with e-Medicis, a French start-up specialized in mobile health services. Furthermore, she has offered consultant services and strategic coaching to different companies in France and Mexico. Dr. Cacho-Elizondo earned her PhD in Management with a major in Marketing at HEC Paris. She holds a M.Sc. in Marketing & Strategy (Paris-IX Dauphine University, France), an MBA (IPADE Business School, México), a M.Sc. in Management of Technology (Sussex University, U.K.) and a bachelor degree in Electronic Systems Engineering (ITESM, Campus Monterrey). Her research interests include: Consumer-Brand Relationships, Consumer Behaviour, CRM, Innovation Adoption, Management of Technology, Online & Mobile Services, eHealth and CSR. She has published in: Journal of Retailing and Consumer Services, Journal of Health Marketing Quarterly, International Journal of Technology and Human Interaction, ISTMO, International Business Research Journal, International Journal of Hospitality Management, American Journal of Management, among others. She serves the local community as member of the Board of two rural schools and also donates her time by doing consulting projects in non-profit branding and entrepreneurship.

Colleen Carraher Wolverton is the Edith Winn Estate Endowed Assistant Professor at the University of Louisiana Lafayette. Her research interests include IT outsourcing, adoption of new technology, Distance Learning, and creativity with IT. She has won awards for her research, including the Outstanding Researcher of the Year Award from the BI Moody College of Business Administration and the Rising Star Award from the University of Louisiana Lafayette. Prior to her career in academia, Colleen was an IT professional, working as a project manager for an IT development firm, an IT analyst for a Fortune 50 oil and gas company, and organizational development in an IT department.

Sylvaine Castellano is an Associate Professor of Management at Paris School of Business. She graduated with a Doctoral degree in Management from the University of Luxembourg. She is the Research Dean at PSB, Paris School of Business. Her research interests mainly include institutional and competitive dynamics as well as entrepreneurship in the sport, wine and luxury industries. She particularly published articles related to the concepts of reputation, e-reputation, legitimacy, status, heritage and retro-industries.

Ping-Yu Chang is an Assistant Professor in the Department of Industrial Engineering and Management at Ming Chi University of Technology (MCUT), Taiwan. He received his master degree in Manufacturing Engineering at Syracuse University in 1996 and his Ph.D. degree in Industrial Engineering at Texas A&M University in 2002. His current research and teaching interests are in the Supply Chain and Production Management. In particular, he is interested in Supply Chain Management, Facility Location, Scheduling, and Simulation Modeling.

Steven R. Clinton received his Ph.D. degree (Major: Marketing; Minor: Logistics) from Michigan State University in 1998 and is currently a professor in the Department of Marketing at Robert Morris University. His research interests include international supply chain organization, customer service in logistics, logistics strategy, and selection processes involving international logistics service intermediaries. He has published in Journal of Business Logistics, Transportation Journal, International Journal of Physical Distribution and Logistics Management, Journal of Production and Inventory Management, and International Marketing Review as well as numerous conference proceedings.

You-Yu Dai is currently an associate professor of Department of Tourism Management, International Business School, Shandong Jiaotong University, China. He received Ph.D. from the Graduate Institute of Recreation, Tourism, and Hospitality Management, National Chiayi University, Taiwan. His research interests are in sustainable tourism management, human resource management in hospitality, and tourism and health sciences. Dr. Dai has published in journals such as Current Issues in Tourism (SSCI), International Journal of Contemporary Hospitality Management (SSCI), International Journal of Technology and Human Interaction (EI), and others. He also have review experiences for some SSCI journals, such as International Journal of Contemporary Hospitality Management, Tourism Management, Asia Pacific Journal of Tourism Research, and so on. He has got a "Outstnding Reviewer" award from Tourism Management, Elsevier. At the same time, Dr. Dai now is also a member of Phi Tau Phi Scholastic Honor Society of Taiwan, senior member of Hong Kong International Engeering and Technology Institute.

Alan J. Dubinsky (Ph.D., University of Minnesota) is Distinguished Visiting Professor of Marketing at Bloomsburg University of Pennsylvania (Bloomsburg, PA, USA) and Professor Emeritus at Purdue University (West Lafayette, IN, USA). He has published over 150 articles in such venues as Journal of Marketing, Journal of Marketing Research, Academy of Management Journal, Journal of Applied Psychology, Personnel Psychology, Journal of Retailing, Leadership Quarterly, Sloan Management Review, and Journal of the Academy of Marketing Sciences, among others. He is a former editor of Journal of Personal Selling and Sales Management and a co-author of three books.

Hadi El-Farr is a faculty member of Human Resources at the Human Resource Department, School of Management and Labor Relations, Rutgers University, United States of America. He completed his Ph.D. in Human Resource Management from the University of Leeds, United Kingdom. His current research interest is Knowledge Management and the impact of Human Resource Management practices on effective Knowledge Management activities.

María J. García G. is a Bachelor in Chemistry and has a master in Operations Research. Together others authors had increase their investigations, already above two hundred and forty, mainly in the areas of Evaluation and Management of Projects, Knowledge Management, Managerial and Social Decision making, Risk Management and Operations Research, especially in making decision under uncertainty and risk, and multi-criteria decision. They have been presented or published in different countries, having publications and offering their reports, chats or conferences in: Austria, Azerbaijan, Finland, Poland, Croatia, Switzerland, Greece, Germany, Italy, Czech Republic, Iceland, Lithuania, Spain, France, Portugal, United States, Panama, Uruguay, Brazil, Mexico, Argentina and Chile besides attending as guest speaker, in reiterated occasions, in lectures to relevant events in Colombia, Peru, Spain and Venezuela. Among other works she is coauthor of: "Inventories control, the Inventory manager and Matrixes Of Weighing with multiplicative factors (MOWwMf)"; "A Methodology of the Decision Support Systems Applied to Other Projects of Investigation"; "Matrixes Of Weighing and catastrophes"; "Multiattribute Model with Multiplicative Factors and Matrixes Of Weighing and the Problem of the Potable Water"; "Mathematical models generators of Decision Support Systems for help in case of catastrophes. An experience from Venezuela."

Gilberto Hernandez is a Bachelor in Chemistry and has a master in Technology of foods. Together others authors had increase their investigations, mainly in the areas of Food technologies, Playful, particularly in the fantastic sports leagues, Knowledge Management, Managerial and Social Decision making, Logistics, Risk Management and Operations research, especially in multi-criteria decision and making decision under uncertainty and risk. They have been presented or published in different countries, having publications and offering their reports, chats or conferences in: Austria, Azerbaijan, Finland, Poland, Croatia, Switzerland, Greece, Czech Republic, Spain, Portugal and United States besides attending as guest speaker, in lectures to relevant events in Costa Rica and Venezuela. Among other works he is co-author of: "Social Aspects of Reverse Logistics and Knowledge Management"; "Enterprise Logistics, Indicators and Physical Distribution Manager"; "Multiattribute Models with Multiplicative factors in the Fantasy Sports"; "The Industrial design manager of LoMoBaP and Knowledge Management"; "Dynamic knowledge: Diagnosis and Customer Service."

José G. Hernández R. is a Chemical Engineer and have a master in Operations Research. Together others authors had increase their investigations, already above two hundred and forty, mainly in the areas of Knowledge Management, Managerial and Social Decision making, Logistics, Risk Management and Operations research, especially in multi-criteria decision. They have been presented or published in different countries, having publications and offering their reports, chats or conferences in: Azerbaijan, Finland, Croatia, Switzerland, Greece, Germany, Italy, Czech Republic, Iceland, Lithuania, Spain, France, Portugal, United States, Panama, Paraguay, Uruguay, Brazil, Cuba, Mexico, Argentina and Chile besides attending as guest speaker, in reiterated occasions, in lectures to relevant events in Colombia, Peru, Costa Rica, Brazil, Spain and Venezuela. Among other works he is coauthor of: "Teaching Enterprise Logistics through Indicators: Dispatch Manager"; "Enterprise diagnosis and the Environmental manager of LoMoBaP"; "Logistics, Marketing and Knowledge Management in the Community of Consumer."

Rezvan Hosseingholizadeh, Ph.D., is Associate Professor of Educational Administration and Knowledge Management at the Department of Education at Ferdowsi University of Mashhad, Mashhad, Iran. She completed her Ph.D. degree in Educational Administration from University of Teharn, Teharan, Iran. Her current research interests include knowledge management and educational administration. Besides publishing several articles about knowledge management in Persian, she is teaching knowledge management courses in M.A. and Ph.D. at FUM.

Leelien Ken Huang is Associate Professor of Strategic Use of IT at Feng Chia University, Taiwan. His research interests include the IT business value, cross cultural research issues in IS, mobile technology, and e-learning. His recent study focuses on issues in the adoption of Fin-Tech based banking services, and issues in IT executives' education. Ken has ten years' experience in a banking managerial position. He is also the Founder Member and Managing Director of the Association for CIO Development Asia Pacific.

J. Jacob Jenkins received his PhD in Communication from the University of South Florida in 2012. He is currently a faculty member at California State University Channel Islands, where he also serves as Campus Coordinator for the Affordable Learning Solutions initiative. Jenkins has published more than 40 academic works and presented nearly 100 competitively selected presentations that explore the interconnection(s) between community, diversity, and faith-based organizations.

Megan Jones is a student of Communication at California State University Channel Islands.

Sherif Kamel is Professor of Management at the American University in Cairo. He is the founding dean of the School of Business. During his tenure as dean, the school was accredited by AACSB, AMBA, EQUIS and ACCET joining only 70 business school in the world that is known as triple-crowned accredited. In addition, he helped establish the Center for Entrepreneurship and Innovation and the university's Venture Lab becoming Egypt's primary university-based incubator. He was associate dean for executive education, director of the Management Center and director of the Institute of Management Development. Before joining AUC, he was director of the Regional IT Institute and helped establish and manage the training department of the Cabinet of Egypt Information and Decision Support Center. Kamel is an Eisenhower Fellow. His research and teaching interests include management of information technology, information technology transfer to developing nations, electronic business, decision support systems and entrepreneurship. His work is broadly published in IS and management journals.

Insaf Khelladi is an Assistant Professor at ICN Business School (Nancy). Her thesis is about the individual investor behavior. Her research interests include financial & mobile marketing, investor & consumer behavior, and generational analysis. Insaf holds an MBA in Global Finance, from IAE Nice, and a BA in financial economics from Algiers University. She has been working for ten years in managing development projects within several international organizations (ex: IFC, World Bank, UNDP).

Wesley Kukard is a current Doctor of Business Administration (DBA) with University of Otago (Dunedin, New Zealand). Previously gained a Master of Business Information Systems and Master of Professional Business Studies from the Auckland University of Technology (Auckland, New Zealand). His research interests are the internet of things (IoT), radio-frequency identification (RFID) and logistics in the fast-moving consumer goods (FMCG) industry.

Patricia Lanier is an Associate Professor of Management at the B.I. Moody III College of Business Administration, University of Louisiana at Lafayette. Dr. Lanier earned her B.S. M. in Accounting from the A.B. Freeman School of Business at Tulane University, her M.B.A. from the Hankamar School of Business at Baylor University and her D.B.A. in Management from Louisiana Tech University. She is a SPHR and SHRM – SCP certified HR Professional. Dr. Lanier holds the Van Eaton and Romero Professorship in Business. She also currently serves as a Board Member of the Southern Management Association. Dr. Lanier has published her work in notable academic journals including the Academy of Management Journal, Journal of Management History, Management Decision and Personality and Individual Differences.

Somayyeh Ebrahimi Koushk Mahdi is a Ph.D. candidate of educational administration at Ferdowsi University of Mashhad (FUM), Teacher assistant at FUM. Her current research interests span the topics of Genealogy of theorizing in educational administration/management/ leadership, critical theories and critical methodologies for studying educational administration/management/ leadership. Indeed she is interested in knowledge management, E-learning and besides publishing several articles about E-learning & Knowledge management. Somayyeh Ebrahimi Koushk Mahdi can be contacted at: ebrahimi.somayeh@mail.um.ac.ir

Zbigniew Mikolajuk, PhD, is a freelance consultant, ICT and Knowledge Management in Development Projects, Canada. He has over 40 years of experience in information technology and management of interdisciplinary projects in more than 30 countries. He worked as associate professor at Warsaw School of Economics in Poland (1974-1981) and adjunct professor at Carleton University in Canada (1996-1999). He held research positions in industry working for Shell-Nigeria, Philips, Gandalf, and Rockwood Informatics in Canada. His experience in development sector includes senior positions at IDRC, Canada (1993-2001); ICIMOD, Nepal (2003-2006); Practical Action, UK (2007-2011), and recently, consultant for the SESIP project, ADB-Bangladesh (2015-2017). His research interests include knowledge management, Web-based and multimedia applications, decision support systems, and project complexity assessment. He is author and co-author of 5 books and over 45 articles. He was involved in global initiatives in ICT sector for development - infoDev and Global Knowledge Partnership of the World Bank, Bellanet International Secretariat (KM4DEV), and ENRAP/IFAD (Electronic Networking for Rural Asia/Pacific Projects), ELLA (Experience and Learning from Latin America) Project, DFID.

Jano Moreira has graduated in Mechanical Engineering from Universidade Federal do Rio de Janeiro (1974), Master's in Computer Science from COPPE-Universidade Federal do Rio de Janeiro (1978) and Ph.D. in Information Systems from University of East Anglia (1986). Sabbatical at CERN from 1989 to 1993 (3 months a year). Researches and teaches in Computer Science, focusing on the following subjects: Databases, Knowledge Management, Social Networks, CSCW, Autonomic Computing and Negotiation Support Systems.

O. Felix Offodile is presently Professor of Management and Department Head of Management and Information Systems at Kent State University, located in Kent, OH. He received his PhD for Texas A&M in Operations Management and has numerous publications in practitioner and academic journals in management of manufacturing systems, cellular manufacturing, and process strategies and technologies.

Maruff Akinwale Oladejo is a Faculty member in the Department of Educational Management, University of Lagos, Akoka, Nigeria. He had his first, second and third degrees in Educational Management from the University of Ibadan, Ibadan, Nigeria. He is specialized in Educational Planning and Policy, with bias in the Efficiency of Open and Distance Learning System. He has written widely (both in local and international learned journals) in these areas. He has also presented papers and poster at several international Conferences such the European Conference on E-Learning (ECEL) 2011 and 2012 held at the University of Brighton, Brighton, UK and the University of Groningen, Groningen, the Netherlands respectively, and the European Conference on Research Methodology (ECRM 2012) at the University of Bolton, UK. He is a Mini Track Co-Chair at the 8th International Conference on E-Learning (ICEL 2013), South Africa. He was a visiting Research Fellow to the University of Malaya, Kuala Lumpur, Malaysia where he was involved in two international Research works with the Dean, Humanities and Ethics Research Cluster. He is a Reviewer to some international journals such as the Current Issue in Education (CIE) of the Mary Foulton College, Arizona State University, US.

Jianping Peng is an Associate Professor in the Department of Management Science in School Business, Sun Yat-sen University. He hold a Ph.D from Sun Yat-sen University. His research interests include enterprise management information systems, electronic commerce and process management, organizational behavior impact of employee social network. He has published in Information System Research,

Decision Support Systems, Management Information Systems (China), China Journal of Information System and Computer Engineering, International Journal of Information Management.

Jing Quan is an Associate Professor in the Department of Information and Decision Sciences in Perdue School of Business at Salisbury University. He holds a Ph.D. from the University of Florida. His research interests include organizational impact of information technology (IT), knowledge management, and IT professional and personnel issues. His work has appeared in such journals as Journal of Management Information Systems, Communications of the ACM, Information Technology & People, Electronic Commerce Research and Applications, Information Resources Management Journal, International Journal of Information Management Journal of Global Information Management, Journal of Computer Information Systems, International Journal of Project Management, and Communications of the AIS, and Journal of Organizational and End User Computing.

Nagla Rizk is professor of economics & founding director of the Access to Knowledge for Development Center (A2K4D), School of Business, AUC. Rizk is a faculty associate at Berkman Center for Internet and Society at Harvard University & an affiliated fellow of the Information Society Project at Yale Law School. Rizk is member of the Executive Committee of the International Economic Association, the steering committee of the Open Africa Innovation Research Project (Open A.I.R.) & a founding member of the Access to Knowledge Global Academy. She wrote the National Strategy for FOSS in Egypt. At AUC, Rizk served as associate dean for graduate studies and research, School of Business & chair of the economics department. She taught at Columbia University, Yale Law School & University of Toronto.

Nagayuki Saito is a former Policy Analyst of OECD, Directorate for Science, Technology and Industry, Special Appointment Senior Research Fellow of Ministry of Internal Affairs and Communications, Institution for Information and Communication Policy and visiting researcher of Aoyama-Gakuin University Human Innovation Research Center. He is instructor of Ochanomizu University Interdisciplinary liberal arts. He graduated from a Doctorate Program of Keio University Graduate School of Media Design and had a Master's degree of Economics at Chuo University Graduate School. He is a committee Member of the Committee for Information, Communications and Consumer Policy Division, Working Party on Information Security and Privacy in OECD. His research theme is making a safer Internet environment for the youth. It focuses on awareness of education, making collaborative e-learning system based on theory of social constructivism; information and communication policy.

Niousha Shahidi, PhD in Sciences in Applied Mathematics area (Université Paris Dauphine, France), is an associate professor in data analysis at EDC Paris Business School (Ecole des Dirigeants et Créateurs d'entreprise) and a member of OCRE (The Observatory and Centre for Research in Entrepreneurship). Her thesis dealt with optimization problems in insurance models (Ceremade). She worked at the Laboratory of Econometrics of Ecole Polytechique Paris. She has published in international journals and conferences on research themes which include theory of the decision, Information asymmetry models in insurance, Entrepreneurial intention and data analysis. She is a member of the AFM (Association Française de Marketing) and the AEI (Académie de l'Entrepreneuriat et de l'Innovation). She has published in: Economics Bulletin, International Journal of Technology and Human Interaction, Journal of Risk, Operations Research Letters, among others.

Wagner Silva obtained his master's degree in 2012 in Computer Systems Engineering Science by COPPE / UFRJ - Federal University of Rio de Janeiro. Since 2014 he has been a federal public servant at Oswaldo Cruz Foundation - Fiocruz, where he has been working in the area of information technology with emphasis on information systems and participating in research projects in Data Science. His main areas of activity, research and interest are: Data Science, Big Data, Data Mining, Machine Learning, Recommendation, Information Systems, Database.

Andrea M. Skinner is a graduate of Pepperdine University's MSHR program and holds a B.A. in Communication with a minor in Psychology from CSU Channel Islands.

Cees Th. Smit Sibinga is a clinical haematologist and Transfusion Medicine specialist. He is Emeritus professor of Interational Development of Transfusion Medicine at the University of Groningen, The Netherlands. Prof. Smit Sibinga has been and still is active in many international functions, teaching and training positions in Transfusion Medicine. He is still instrumental in numerous international development programmes, advising and guiding Governments in national blood safety and availability reform programmes. He is the organiser of 28 annual International Symposia on Blood Transfusion in Groningen, and the author/editor of over 350 scientific publications and 35 books on transfusion medicine aspects. Prof Smit Sibinga was the founding father of ESFH (1981) and a co-founder of WAA (1984). Lately (2012) he served as the President of the 11th European Congress on E-Learning (ECEL) in Groningen. Prof. Smit Sibinga is a Fellow in Transfusion Medicine of the Royal College of Physicians of Edinburgh and the Royal College of Pathologists in London, UK. Currently he serves WHO as an Member of the Expert Committee for Blood Transfusion and was the coordinator for the European Region of the WHO Quality Management Training courses.

Alan D. Smith is presently University Professor of Operations Management in the Department of Management and Marketing at Robert Morris University, Pittsburgh, PA. Previously he was Chair of the Department of Quantitative and Natural Sciences and Coordinator of Engineering Programs at the same institution, as well as Associate Professor of Business Administration and Director of Coal Mining Administration at Eastern Kentucky University. He holds concurrent PhDs in Engineering Systems/Education from The University of Akron and in Business.

Amber Smith-Ditizio has graduated from the doctoral program in the Department of Kinesiology from Texas Woman's University in Sports Administration, completed in May 2015. While acquiring strong analytical and professional skills after completing MS in Sport Management, BSBA and MBA from Robert Morris University, with BS from Kent State University in athletic training and related studies, she also holds various personal certifications in the sports performance and athletic areas. She is the author of several academic articles in the sports performance and athletic fields and plans to pursue an academic teaching/research career upon graduation.

Vesselina Tossan is associate professor at Le Cnam in Paris and also adjunct professor in EDC Paris Business School . She graduated from HEC in 1982, practiced marketing in renowned companies as Unilever, Mattel, Brossard and got a Phd in management science in 2003 in Centre de Gestion Scientifique, Ecole des Mines de Paris. She teaches marketing and her fields of research are consumer behavior, adoption models of innovation, management of innovation, branding. She published several articles in academic journals and pedagogic case studies.

Ashley Van Ostrand is a student of Communication at California State University Channel Islands.

Marco Vaz holds a Masters in Systems Engineering and Computing from COPEE - UFRJ. He is currently a professor of graduation at IBMEC Faculty (Rio de Janeiro). He has solid experience in software development and programming. He has worked as Software Development Manager in projects in partnership with COPPE-UFRJ for large public and private institutions. Has experience in the area of Computer Science, with emphasis on Database.

Ramon Visaiz is a student of Communication at California State University Channel Islands.

Wendy Wang is the associate professor, and Chair of Information Management Technology and Computer Science department at Trident University. She has a Ph.D. in Management Information System from the University of Mississippi with a minor in computer science. She has published in the proceedings of conferences and journals such as AMCIS, DSI, Journal of the American Society for Information Science and Technology, and International Journal of Enterprise Information Systems etc. Her research areas are: natural language processing, text abstraction and extraction, health care information systems, IT adoption, ERP implementation, telecommunication, and virtual organizations.

Spencer Wolfe is a student of Communication at California State University Channel Islands.

Lincoln C. Wood is a Senior Lecturer in operations and supply chain management in the Department of Management at the University of Otago (New Zealand) and an Adjunct Research Fellow at Curtin Business School (Australia). Dr Wood received the CSCMP's Young Researcher Award in 2009 in the USA and in 2010 he received the Outstanding Research Award at the International Higher Education Conference in Australia. His research focuses on the use of technology in supply chains and supply chain management to improve quality and productivity in construction. He is the Editor-in-Chief of the International Journal of Applied Logistics and sits on the Editorial Review Boards several logistics journals.

Yun Wu is an assistant professor in the Information & Decision Science Department at the Salisbury University. She graduated from Auburn University, August 2015, with a doctoral degree focused on MIS. Her research interests include IT business value in supply chain management, healthcare informatics, bigdata analytics and sharing economics. Her research has appeared in the proceedings of conferences and journals, such as the IEEE Transactions on Education, Journal of Educational Technology Systems, International Journal of Logistic Management, Journal of Supply Chain Management and others.

Guoying (Grace) Zhang received her PhD degree in Information Systems from Foster School of Business at the University of Washington Seattle. Her research and teaching interests include information resource management, social networks, data mining, and economics of information systems. Currently, she holds an associate professor position of Management Information Systems in Dillard College of Business Administration at Midwestern State University. She has published in two of the top three MIS journals: MIS Quarterly and Journal of Management Information Systems. Her works also appear in recognized journals such as Decision Support Systems, INFORMS Journal on Computing, Management Decision, Information Systems and e-Business Management, International Journal of Virtual Communities and Social Networking, International Journal of Networking and Virtual Organisations, Journal of International Technology and Information Management, International Journal of Information Management, among others.

Index

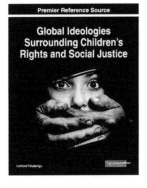

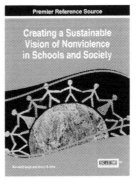

Ensure Quality Research is Introduced to the Academic Community

Become an IGI Global Reviewer for Authored Book Projects

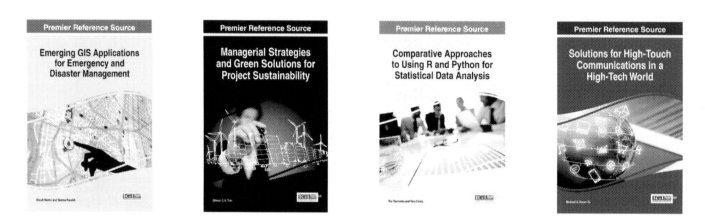

Premier Reference Source

Emerging GIS Applications for Emergency and Disaster Management

Premier Reference Source

Managerial Strategies and Green Solutions for Project Sustainability

Premier Reference Source

Comparative Approaches to Using R and Python for Statistical Data Analysis

Premier Reference Source

Solutions for High-Touch Communications in a High-Tech World

The overall success of an authored book project is dependent on quality and timely reviews.

In this competitive age of scholarly publishing, constructive and timely feedback significantly expedites the turnaround time of manuscripts from submission to acceptance, allowing the publication and discovery of forward-thinking research at a much more expeditious rate. Several IGI Global authored book projects are currently seeking highly qualified experts in the field to fill vacancies on their respective editorial review boards:

Applications may be sent to:
development@igi-global.com

Applicants must have a doctorate (or an equivalent degree) as well as publishing and reviewing experience. Reviewers are asked to write reviews in a timely, collegial, and constructive manner. All reviewers will begin their role on an ad-hoc basis for a period of one year, and upon successful completion of this term can be considered for full editorial review board status, with the potential for a subsequent promotion to Associate Editor.

If you have a colleague that may be interested in this opportunity, we encourage you to share this information with them.